Fahrenheit/Celsius

-40°F	=	-40°C	120°F	=	49°C	320°F	=	160°C
-30°F	=	-34°C	125°F	=	52°C	330°F	=	166°C
-20°F	=	-29°C	130°F	=	54°C	340°F	=	171°C
-10°F	=	-23°C	135°F	=	57°C	350°F	=	177°C
- 5°F	=	-21°C	140°F	=	60°C	360°F	=	182°C
0°F	=	-18°C	145°F	=	63°C	370°F	=	188°C
5°F	=	-15°C	150°F	=	66°C	380°F	=	193°C
10°F	=	-12°C	155°F	=	68°C	390°F	=	199°C
15°F	=	- 9°C	160°F	=	71°C	400°F	=	204°C
20°F	=	- 6°C	165°F	=	74°C	410°F	=	210°C
25°F	=	- 4°C	170°F	=	77°C	420°F	=	216°C
30°F	=	- 1°C	175°F	=	79°C	430°F	=	221°C
32°F	=	0°C	180°F	=	82°C	440°F	=	227°C
35°F	=	2°C	185°F	=	85°C	450°F	=	232°C
40°F	=	4°C	190°F	=	88°C	460°F	=	238°C
45°F	=	7°C	195°F	=	91°C	470°F	=	243°C
50°F	=	10°C	200°F	=	93°C	480°F	=	249°C
55°F	=	13°C	205°F	=	96°C	490°F	=	254°C
60°F	=	16°C	210°F	=	99°C	500°F	=	260°C
65°F	=	18°C	212°F	=	100°C	510°F	=	266°C
70°F	=	21°C	220°F	=	104°C	520°F	=	271°C
75°F	=	24°C	230°F	=	110°C	530°F	=	277°C
80°F	=	27°C	240°F	=	116°C	540°F	=	282°C
85°F	=	29°C	250°F	=	121°C	550°F	=	288°C
90°F	=	32°C	260°F	=	127°C	560°F	=	293°C
95°F	=	35°C	270°F	=	132°C	570°F	=	299°C
100°F	=	38°C	280°F	=	137°C	580°F	=	304°C
105°F	=	41°C	290°F	=	143°C	590°F	=	310°C
110°F	=	43°C	300°F	=	149°C	600°F	=	316°C
115°F	=	46°C	310°F	=	154°C			

Classical Cooking
the Modern Way

Classical Cooking
the Modern Way

Eugen Pauli

Second Edition

 Van Nostrand Reinhold
_____ **New York**

First published in Switzerland as Lehrbuch der Küche, 10, by Fachbuch-verlage, Schwiezer Wirteverband, Zurich; Union Helvetia, Lucerne; E. Pauli, Aarau; copyright © 1984 estate of E. Pauli, Aarau, represented by Philip Pauli.

I(T)P™ A division of International Thomson Publishing Inc.
      The ITP logo is a trademark under license

Printed in the United States of America
For more information, contact:

Van Nostrand Reinhold
115 Fifth Avenue
New York, NY 10003

International Thomson Publishing GmbH
Königswinterer Strasse 418
53227 Bonn
Germany

International Thomson Publishing Europe
Berkshire House 168–173
High Holborn
London WC1V 7AA
England

International Thomson Publishing Asia
221 Henderson Road #05 10
Henderson Building
Singapore 0315

Thomas Nelson Australia
102 Dodds Street
South Melbourne, 3205
Victoria, Australia

International Thomson Publishing Japan
Hirakawacho Kyowa Building, 3F
2-2-1 Hirakawacho
Chiyoda-ku, 102 Tokyo
Japan

Nelson Canada
1120 Birchmount Road
Scarborough, Ontario
Canada M1K 5G4

International Thomson Editores
Campos Eliseos 385, Piso 7
Col. Polanco
11560 Mexico D.F. Mexico

95 96 97 98 99 RRD HB 10 9 8 7 6

Library of Congress Cataloging-in-Publication Data

Pauli, Eugen
  Classical cooking the modern way.
  Previously published in French and German under the titles: Technologie cullinaire and Lehrbuch der Küche.
  Includes index.
  1. Cookery. 2. Food service. I. Title
TX652.P35   1989   641.5'7   88-20573
ISBN 0-442-27206-5

In memory of my father and to
all those entering the foodservice profession

Contents

Preface

Classical Cooking the Modern Way has become a standard text for foodservice professionals in many countries. The first German edition appeared in 1930; today, this book is also published in French, English, Dutch, Japanese, Italian, and Spanish. Why this success?

A great deal is due to the knowledge and dedication of the late Ernst Pauli and his son, the late Eugen Pauli. Their vast experience, love for their profession, and unusual expertise made them leaders in the foodservice profession. Their lives were dedicated to the advancement and education of the upcoming generation.

Unfortunately, Eugen Pauli passed away while preparing this new edition. He is remembered with gratitude and will never be forgotten.

As executor of the Pauli estate, Philip Pauli took over his father's work. With tireless effort and determination, he continued the preparation of this edition in his father's memory, managing and supervising its entire organization. He displayed a great talent for his new task, and in the future he will continue to share his father's and grandfather's knowledge with the foodservice profession.

Walter Schudel, who is associated with the Schweizerische Fachkommission für das Gastgewerbe in Zurich, Switzerland, has contributed his professional knowledge to this edition, filling the gap left by Eugen Pauli's death. Along with many distinguished professionals from all over Switzerland, he is responsible for the text of this edition.

This second edition, translated from the tenth German edition, is based on the principles of Auguste Escoffier's *Le Guide Culinaire*, just as the previous edition was. Above all, it is intended to aid in the education of chefs, graduates of hotel schools, and students of restaurant management. It is distinguished by an improved format, an attractive new cover, and many new color photographs. Many experts have undertaken the task of making the necessary corrections from the previous edition and revising text and recipes to accommodate today's dining and purchasing practices. It is anticipated that the new edition will appeal to a large audience—from service personnel to restaurateurs, hoteliers, butchers, and even architects and kitchen designers.

Without the contribution of many qualified experts, this book could not have been published. The following individuals reviewed the text and provided valuable references and advice:

Purchasing: E. Gall, Bern; G. Abfalter, Bern; A. Fuchs, Biel; H. Schmitz, Burgdorf; H. Weber, Solothurn.

Menus: F. Baggenstos, Zug; P. Casanova, Lucerne; Ad. Schmid, Rigi.

Cooking: H. Schmid, Zurich; R. Luginbühl, Zurich; F. Meier, Zurich; F. Mundrich, Würenlos; P. Schaffner, Zurich.

Cooking technique: Dr. H. R. Stoll, Bern.

Management: Ad. Kugler, St. Gall; K. Hanselmann, St. Gall; F. Prokora, St. Gall.

French: A. Sauthier, Sion.

Cataloging: W. Roellin, Kreuzlingen.

General: F. Ballmer, Baden-Rütihof; O. Jordak, Aarau.

Gratitude is also extended to the following consultants, institutions, and firms:

P. Blattner, Fachbuchverlag Schweizer Wirteverband, Zurich

K. Eugster, Union Helvetia, Lucerne

R. Frei, Schweizerische Fachkommission für Berufsbildung im Gastgewerbe, Zurich

Dr. X. Frei, Schweizer Wirteverband, Zurich

P. Schweizer, Orex-Treuhandgesellschaft, Winterthur

Eidgenössische Alkoholverwaltung, Abteilung Kartoffeln, Bern

Eidgenössisches Gesundheitsamt, Bern

Eidgenössisches Veterinäramt, Bern

Firma Buchdruckerei Stäfa AG, Stäfa

Firma Sais, Abteilung GK, Zurich

Firma Schwabenland und Co. AG, Zurich

Firma Therma, Zurich

Firma Walter Franke AG, Aarburg

Schweizerische Beratungsstelle für Unfallverhütung, Bern

Schweizerische Fachschule für den Detailhandel, Zurich

Schweizerische Fachschule für das Metzgereigewerbe, Spiez

Schweizerische Gemüseunion, Zurich

Schweizerische Kartoffelkommission, Düdingen

Schweizerische Käseunion AG, Bern

Schweizerische Kochfachlehrer-Vereinigung

Schweizerisches Tiefkühlinstitut, Zurich

Zentralverband Schweizerischer Milchproduzenten, Bern

Special acknowledgment for the many color photographs goes to Firma Knorr Nährmittel AG, Thayngen.

Philip Pauli
Walter Schudel

Preface to the First Edition

The first English language edition of *Classical Cooking the Modern Way* is based on the seventh German and the first French editions. It is designed to be used as a text by students preparing for careers in the foodservice industry and as a useful reference for persons actively engaged in the planning, production, and service of food.

This is no ordinary cookbook, but rather a manual that covers the *basic principles of kitchen management and cookery.* It is probably the only work in existence that deals both with kitchen management, that is, the organization that is prerequisite to cooking, and the whole field of cookery.

The fundamental principles of cooking contained in this volume are based on classical French cookery (Escoffier) and on the latest developments and trends in the foodservice industry. A unique feature is the description and illustration of all the basic forms of food preparation. The graphic presentation of these fundamental principles makes it possible for cooks, waiters, caterers, or hotel managers to grasp the essentials easily and quickly. The book should also be of considerable interest to persons in a wide range of related professions and industries, such as kitchen designers, architects, and personnel in the meat and food industries.

Special thanks are due to Peter C. March and Monroe S. Levine for undertaking the immense task of translating the work into English, and also to Mr. Willie Brand of George Brown College of Applied Arts and Technology for his fine reviewing assistance. My deepest thanks go to Marjorie S. Arkwright for the enormous work of adapting and editing the English version. I should also like to thank the publishers for their generous cooperation in preparing this English language edition for publication.

May every reader benefit from it and derive full satisfaction in the pursuit of his chosen profession.

Eugen Pauli
Aarau, Switzerland
March, 1978

Part I
General Theory

Chapter 1
Specialized Professional Knowledge

1.1 Professional Ethics

"At long last I have left school—life is finally beginning." You often hear young people say this when they leave school, but, once started on the long journey from beginner to expert in a profession, they find that school has started all over again.

The traditional method of training the inexperienced in the foodservice field has always been through some form of apprenticeship. A competent professional at the work place acts as a role model who, in ongoing activities, demonstrates the work to be done. The beginner observes and imitates the behavior, work style, and attitude being modeled.

Knowledge is power. It strengthens you and fills you with a feeling of satisfaction, while making you feel more secure in your relations with others. This means that everybody learns for his or her own good, not to please teachers or superiors. Unfortunately, this fact is not generally recognized. To gain knowledge and the strength that comes from it requires more than studying books. Your attitudes toward what you do and how you do it, at work or at home, play an important role in your ability to learn. To get the most out of every experience, you must try to:

- be productive
- work well with others
- get to know yourself and others
- adapt

- be creative
- recognize the beauty around you

Being Productive

You can see from figure 1-1 that the average person spends a great deal of his lifetime (while awake) doing work. Do not let this time go to waste through lack of interest, looking constantly at the clock, hoping the end of the working day will come. You should be conscious of the many good things your profession has to offer. Think of the satisfaction you derive from decorating an attractive plate, the special dish of the day, or a dish you have prepared at the special request of a devoted guest. When the guests walk into a room in which the chef has presented a beautiful cold buffet, they will exclaim: "Look at this fine display; the chef has gone out of his way!" Consider yourself lucky

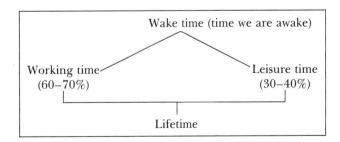

Figure 1-1. The average person spends 60 to 70 percent of his or her waking time engaged in work.

to have chosen a profession that offers so much opportunity to please other people. Nature provides you with countless colorful, delicious ingredients with the potential of becoming appealing and tasty foods. You can make even a simple breakfast of ham and eggs look like a "creation" by arranging nature's ingredients, in all their fine colors, in a special way. A few slices of tomato and some sprigs of fresh green parsley can turn an uninteresting plate into an attractive dish.

After doing a day's work with this attitude, there is time to enjoy and fill your leisure time in any useful way you choose. Persons who do not get much enjoyment out of their daily work usually are bored in their spare time as well.

Working Well with Others

We all tend to be selfish, some more than others. Selfishness is the enemy of cooperation. Conditions for teamwork include:

- *Tolerance:* Recognize others as personalities and individuals.
- *Objectivity:* Do not be biased; do not let first impressions or appearances form a basis for judging people.
- *Willingness:* To work with a team you must be willing and prepared to work with others.
- *Honesty:* Be yourself. Be fair and honest with your teammates. Be as good as your word, and you will soon be accepted by the others.
- *Understanding:* Keep selfishness at bay. Do not take yourself too seriously. Have some thought for your fellow worker.
- *Practice:* You must practice working with others as a team. Just a friendly "good morning" greeting is not enough.

If you apply these principles at and away from work, they will enrich your life.

Getting to Know Yourself and Others

Too many people do not know themselves. "Funny statement," you might say, but how many of us really look in the mirror from time to time and ask:

- Are the things I blame others for perhaps really my own fault?
- How would I feel in the other person's shoes?
- What steps should I take to improve my relationships with others?

If you think this way, you will better understand other people and be able to empathize with them. In so doing, you will be able to comply with the remaining three requisites discussed—being adaptive, being creative, and being conscious of the beauty around you.

Adapting

Adapting does not mean sacrificing your own personality. It does mean, however, that you must learn to respect other people's points of view and adjust your attitude accordingly.

Being Creative

Every person is inventive. Stimulate others to think up ideas and to talk about them—new ideas will further your profession and increase your pleasure in working in your profession.

Recognizing the Beauty around You

Look for the beauty in things around you; there is so much of it. Enjoying simple pleasures will help you endure the more difficult things in life and in your work. Seeing the beauty and bright sides of things makes you feel good, and others will respond positively to that good feeling.

1.2 Sanitation

1.2.1 *Basic Principles*

Good health is one of life's most precious gifts. High standards of sanitation are strategic to good physical and mental health. The National Sanitation Foundation, a nonprofit organization in Ann Arbor, Michigan, explains the importance of sanitation in these words:

> Sanitation is a way of life. It is the quality of living that is expressed in the clean home, the clean farm, the

clean business and industry, the clean neighborhood, the clean community. Being a way of life, it must come from within the people; it is nourished by knowledge and grows as an obligation and an ideal in human relations.

Particularly important are the thorough knowledge and the practice of high standards of sanitation in the foodservice industry. In any foodservice operation, the primary objective is to serve food that is safe, wholesome, attractive, and nutritious, in an environment that is safe and clean. This objective can be achieved only if everyone who works in foodservice assumes his or her individual responsibility. Each foodservice worker must know and practice high standards of sanitation to protect the consumer from health hazards and illness.

1.2.2 *Legal Background*

The laws pertaining to sanitation and safety in foodservice are established and enforced by national, state, and local government agencies.

The U.S. Department of Health and Human Services and the U.S. Department of Agriculture are two federal groups concerned with promoting a high level of health for every individual. These departments are also concerned with the sanitation aspects of food protection.

The U.S. Public Health Service and the Food and Drug Administration are also engaged in activities that promote high standards of sanitation in the foodservice industry. By providing educational and technical services to states and municipalities, the U.S. Public Health Service has encouraged adoption of uniform codes and ordinances that regulate foodservice operations. The provisions in these codes and ordinances have two primary goals: the protection of the consumer from contaminated foods and goods, and the protection of the consumer from fraud in the food industry (regulating inspections, providing for the sale of only unadulterated, wholesome, properly labeled foods).

The execution of the food controls is the responsibility of each state. Food analysts and inspectors are responsible for the application of the laws of sanitation. Foods, facilities, equipment, and utensils are covered by the sanitation controls. Dietitians and foodservice managers are responsible for developing and implementing educational programs for foodservice personnel that will promote high standards of sanitation in their respective establishments.

1.2.3 *Basic Principles of Microbiology*

Knowledge of the principles of microbiology is basic to an understanding of food sanitation. Microorganisms are living creatures so small that they can only be seen through a microscope. They consume food, give off waste, and multiply. Some are harmless, some are beneficial, and others are very dangerous.

Microorganisms can cause food spoilage and food-borne illnesses. Those that cause food spoilage are yeasts, bacteria, and molds. Most food-borne illnesses are caused by bacteria; however, viruses, parasites, and protozoa can also cause food-borne illnesses.

It is important for foodservice managers, dietitians, and all food handlers to understand the conditions that cause food spoilage and food-borne illnesses. They must also know how to prevent contamination of foods during processing, transporting, storing, preparing, and serving.

To prevent food-borne illnesses and food spoilage, it is the responsibility of management to develop and carry out educational programs for foodservice personnel emphasizing:

- Effective control of food temperatures during storage, cooking, and holding
- Protection of food from microorganisms, roaches, flies, rodents, and pests
- Protection of food from harmful substances, such as chemicals and poisonous materials
- Good health, personal hygiene, and safe food-handling practices

Microorganisms are classified as bacteria, molds, yeasts, and viruses.

Bacteria

Bacteria are round, rod-shaped, or spiral-shaped, as shown in figure 1-2. Most bacteria are harmless to human beings, and some can even be useful. Some types are important in the production of certain

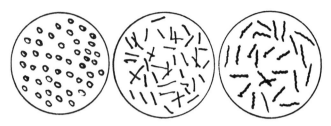

Figure 1-2. Bacteria: *left,* round bacteria, cocci; *center,* rod-shaped bacteria, rods without spores, and spore bacilli; *right,* spiral-shaped bacteria, spirilla.

foods, such as sour milk, yogurt, sauerkraut, and sourdough.

Bacteria reproduce by splitting into two parts (mitosis). The splitting of the cells proceeds very quickly (one to four divisions per hour) when there is adequate nourishment and when the temperature is between 90°F (32°C) and 105°F (41°C). Thus, assuming a doubling of numbers every fifteen minutes, approximately one million bacteria could be produced in five hours. Bacteria need moisture, food, and heat for growth. Some bacteria require oxygen; others thrive better without air.

The various kinds of bacteria differ in their food requirements. Dry foods, such as sugar, flour, rice, and dry pastries, do not have sufficient moisture for bacterial multiplication. Acid foods, such as citrus foods and items prepared with acid ingredients, are the foods least preferred by bacteria. Most bacteria prefer nonacidic, protein-rich foods, such as milk, milk products, eggs, meat, poultry, fish, glazes, and creams.

Bacterial contamination of foods can be retarded through constant and effective control of the temperature of food. Most bacteria develop best between 50° and 120°F (10° and 49°C). Bacteria practically stop growing and multiplying at temperatures above 165°F (74°C) and below 40°F (4°C). While all bacteria cannot be killed by cold temperatures, their growth can be arrested. The most suitable temperature for disease-producing organisms, pathogens, is body temperature, 98.6°F (37°C). Pathogenic agents can be transmitted by food and can be very dangerous to humans. The food can be contaminated by contact with dirty hands, soiled clothes and towels, dirty tables and utensils, dirty containers and machinery. Contamination of food may also result from contact with household pets, rats, mice, flies, cockroaches, insects, and polluted water. Diseases transmitted in this way include typhoid fever, salmonellosis, dysentery, cholera, jaundice, tuberculosis, and diphtheria.

Bacteria can be destroyed by:

- The use of high temperatures, boiling water—212°F (100°C); steam-cleaning tables, utensils, containers, and machines. Immersion in 180°F (82°C) water for ten seconds will destroy most pathogens.
- The application of heat when cooking (pasteurization) or the sterilization of foods.
- The use of chemical compounds, such as chlorine, iodine, or quaternary ammonium to clean and sanitize equipment and utensils. The following amounts in 10 gallons (45 liters) of water will kill bacteria: 4 ounces (113 grams) iodine-type disinfectant; 2¼ ounces (64 grams) of 5½ percent sodium hypochlorite.

Molds

Molds, a form of life called fungi, are made up of many cells that require air and moisture for growth. Different types of molds are different colors—white, blue, green, pink, and black. As molds develop, the growth resembles cobwebs or fine threads, and a powdery substance is easily visible. Some molds, like some bacteria, are helpful to mankind; others cause problems. Certain molds are used to make penicillin and tetracycline—well-known antibiotics.

Molds can grow on practically all foods—on sweet, sour, bitter, and even relatively dry foods. Some are intentionally introduced to foods to give a special flavor, as for blue, Roquefort, and Camembert cheeses. Molds, however, can cause food spoilage, which can be detected by the fuzzy growth, unpleasant odor, and musty flavor. Some molds produce wastes that can be classified among the most lethal poisons (aflatoxins) and can cause dangerous liver malfunctions. The formation of molds in foods can be prevented by controlling storage conditions and by avoiding long storage periods.

Most molds reproduce by the formation of spores, which are very lightweight and can be found almost anywhere, particularly in the soil. They are carried by air currents, insects, animals, and people. Mold and mold spores can be destroyed by the same methods used to eliminate bacteria.

Yeasts

Yeasts are one-celled organisms that absorb food and moisture and multiply by germinating. Yeast cells are important in fermentation and leavening processes. Whenever yeast cells are combined with warm temperatures, air, moisture, and sugar, they multiply and grow. Yeasts are important in making breads, wines, and alcoholic beverages and are also used as vitamin B_{12} supplements.

Yeast cells are very light and are often in the air. When these cells come in contact with food and start breaking down the starches and sugars, the food usually spoils. The spoilage can generally be identified by an alcoholic odor and the presence of bubbles. Although some types of yeast may cause skin infections, yeasts are usually considered harmless to humans and are destroyed by high temperatures.

Viruses

Viruses are not independent organisms and cannot reproduce in food. Viruses, however, can be transmitted by human beings to others through food. For example, the viruses responsible for jaundice and polio can be transmitted if the food has been infected with these viruses by people.

1.2.4 *Food Spoilage*

Food is very perishable, and because of its delicacy, it is susceptible to spoilage. The U.S. Public Health Food Service Ordinance and Code states:

> Food used in foodservice operations shall be from a source approved, or considered satisfactory by the health authority and which is in compliance with applicable state and local laws and regulations. Food from such sources shall have been protected from

contamination and spoilage during subsequent handling, packaging, and storage, and while in transit.

Causes of food spoilage include:

- Presence of bacteria and molds that produce toxins and break down sugars, proteins, and fats
- Contamination by insects and pests
- Chemical reactions that cause rancidity, when foods with high fat content have been overexposed to light or heat
- Chemical reactions in canned foods, indicated by leaks and bulges in the cans

1.2.5 *Personal Hygiene*

Top management and the professional foodservice staff are responsible for determining the standards of sanitation for the foodservice establishment. These standards and the methods of achieving them should be emphasized in an educational program for all the foodservice personnel. Persons who are knowledgeable about sanitation should plan and implement the program. Throughout these sessions, employees should be made aware of their individual roles in the total sanitation program.

Many food-borne illnesses are traced to human contamination of food. These illnesses are frequently caused by employees who are ill or who are careless about their own personal hygiene and food-handling practices. Each employee must understand the principles of sanitation and the causes of food contamination. Furthermore, he or she must know what can be done to prevent contamination of food. Proper techniques of handling food, the importance of good health, and good personal hygiene habits should be stressed through continuous training. The educational program should bring into focus the role of each food handler in protecting his or her own health and the well-being of customers.

Visual aids, such as films, posters, and other educational materials, are effective tools for stimulating interest in good sanitation and reinforcing proper sanitation techniques. Such materials are available through state and federal agencies and through many commercial companies. Other sources include the

National Sanitation Foundation, the National Restaurant Association, the Center for Disease Control in Atlanta, Georgia, and educational-film companies.

The health of employees, their personal hygiene habits, and their food-handling practices reflect the standards of sanitation in the production, manufacture, preparation, storage, packaging, distribution, and selling of food. Training and follow-up supervision by qualified staff members must be continuous and constant to ensure a safe and sanitary foodservice.

Carelessness in body cleanliness or food-handling practices can lead to serious illness. Bacteria are present everywhere—on skin, in mouths, on hands, in hair, in body discharges, on clothing, on utensils and equipment, and on the food itself. Organisms can be passed from the careless worker to the food or utensils and then to the customer.

Persons who work with food must be in good physical condition. Annual physical examinations, semiannual dental checkups, regular eye examinations, and sufficient rest are extremely important to maintain good health. Underweight or overweight conditions should be avoided or corrected. Well-balanced, nourishing meals are necessary to maintain proper weight and good health. While these are practices that everyone should observe, they are especially important for the foodservice worker, who is responsible for protecting his or her own health as well as that of others. In addition to these general practices, every foodservice worker is responsible for adhering to very rigid standards of cleanliness and personal hygiene.

A clean body is the foundation for cleanliness and good appearance. A daily bath, clean teeth, clean and well-groomed hair, and skin free from blemishes are essential. The use of effective deodorants, dental floss, and mouth astringents will aid in avoiding body odors that are offensive to coworkers and customers.

Hands, with short, well-manicured fingernails, must be kept immaculate. Hands should be washed thoroughly with soap and water in a hand sink (sinks for washing dishes or utensils or for the preparation of food should not be used for hand washing) and dried carefully before handling food or equipment, after using toilet facilities, after handling any soiled or contaminated objects, after smoking, and after eating. Disposable towels or a mechanical dryer should be used for drying hands. Communal towels must not be used, as they pose a serious danger of contaminating the hands with bacteria. Jewelry, watches, and nail polish should not be worn in foodservice areas. Jewelry may catch on equipment and cause injury. Pieces of jewelry may break and get into the food, causing injury to the customer. Nail polish may chip off and fall into the food.

Clothing, including uniforms, aprons, undergarments, and hose, must be clean and changed daily. Comfortable and carefully fitted shoes that are in good repair should be worn to prevent discomfort, fatigue, and accidents. Hair nets and/or caps must be worn to protect the food and work surfaces from contact with hair.

People with communicable diseases should not work with food. Germs may be spread by discharges from the respiratory tract and from the intestinal tract. Mumps, meningitis, measles, and the common cold are infections that can be spread by discharges from the nose and throat. Typhoid fever, dysentery, and diarrhea are but a few infections that are associated with intestinal discharges.

Disposable tissues should be used only once and then discarded. Hands should be washed thoroughly after coughing, sneezing, or using tissues. People suffering from eczema, other skin diseases, sores, or infected wounds should not work with food.

1.2.6 *General Sanitation Practices*

Foodservice personnel must observe certain practices when working in foodservice areas to protect the consumer as well as themselves.

Food should be handled, whenever possible, with spoons, tongs, or forks. A clean spoon or fork should be used to taste food, and the utensil should never be put back into the food after it has touched the mouth. Food should never be tasted with the fingers. Hands should never be put into a bin in which ice is stored. Plastic gloves are recommended for mixing foods, making sandwiches, and arranging or dispensing food. Gloves should be replaced after handling raw poultry or meat, after handling any soiled objects, after work has been interrupted, and whenever a glove is torn or punctured. When working with a meat slicer or other equipment, gloves should be removed. The glove may catch on the machine and cause injury.

Hands should be kept away from the areas of dishes, glassware, and silverware that come in contact with the mouth. Plates should be held by placing the palm of the hand underneath the plate with the fleshy part of the thumb on the edge of the plate. Cups should be lifted by the handle, glassware should be held at the base of the glass and only the handles of silverware should be touched.

Household pets (cats, dogs, birds, and fish) should be kept out of all foodservice areas. Animals should never be touched by anyone when working with food.

Leftovers that are intended for reuse have to be in perfect condition and should be processed as quickly as possible. Leftovers from guest tables must not be reused under any circumstances.

Garbage and trash need to be moved from foodservice areas at regular intervals throughout the day and should be stored in a separate room—refrigerated, if possible. Mechanical disposal units and compactors should be cleaned frequently.

Pest control is important for safe sanitation. Clean equipment and good maintenance, elimination of breeding areas, and the assistance of qualified pest control operators are required to eliminate insects and rodents. Consultation with pest control experts is necessary before using any pesticides, poisons, or chemicals in a foodservice area. Foodservice personnel need to be trained to read all labels and to follow proper procedures so that food, utensils, and equipment will not be contaminated with poisonous materials.

Soiled dishes, glassware, silverware, linen, and utensils may be contaminated with disease organisms from users. Unless this ware is handled carefully, employees may pick up the germs on their own hands and transfer them to their mouths or to customers.

Soiled items must be handled with the same care used for clean utensils. After handling dishes and utensils used by others, it is extremely important to wash hands thoroughly with soap and water.

1.2.7 *Food Sanitation*

The kitchen is the most important area of the operation with regard to sanitation. Absolute cleanliness in the processing and storage of food should be maintained at all times. The following practices must be observed in handling the various types of food.

Milk and cream are very perishable and must be stored in the original containers (not plastic) or in containers that have been sanitized. Milk products should be refrigerated at a temperature of 40°F (4°C).

Butter or margarine should be covered and stored in the refrigerator at 40°F (4°C).

Fats and cooking oils should be stored at low temperatures in closed containers that are protected from exposure to light and air to prevent rancidity. Cooking oils that are used for deep-frying have to be drained off and filtered daily. A used supply of cooking oil may not be replenished with fresh oil; it must be exchanged completely.

Eggs must be kept refrigerated. Fresh eggs should be stored between 35° and 45°F (2° and 7°C). Frozen eggs should be held at 0° to 20°F (−18° to −6°C).

Fruits and vegetables should be stored at 50°F (10°C) and should be thoroughly washed before use. Control of humidity and proper covering of the products will reduce loss caused by spoilage. Vegetables should be peeled as near to cooking time as possible. Prolonged soaking in cold water leads to a loss of nutrients.

Canned foods should be stored in areas that are cool, dry, and well ventilated. A temperature of 60°F (16°C) is recommended to retain maximum quality, while humidity control is necessary to prevent rusting of cans. Food in cans with bulged lids, dents, or leaks should not be used. Canned foods that have been opened should be transferred to containers that can be covered.

Ice creams and sherbets are made from ingredients that provide good growing conditions for bacteria.

Extreme cleanliness is necessary while mixes are being prepared. The mix should be heated to 185°F (85°C) for at least one minute and then quickly cooled to below 40°F (4°C). Measuring tools can be dangerous sources of infections: all utensils used in the preparation of ice creams and sherbets should be thoroughly cleaned and sterilized with disinfectant or boiling water.

Cream-filled pastries and custards are highly perishable. After preparation, these products should be refrigerated immediately. Only freshly prepared custards and cream-filled pastries should be served.

Sandwiches and canapés prepared with meats, poultry, fish, eggs, or salad dressings must be refrigerated at 40°F (4°C). Countertops and equipment used for sandwich preparation should be sanitized and dry, and hands should be carefully washed.

Fresh meat, poultry, and seafood, as well as products containing them, must be prepared and stored with caution. Pork should be cooked to at least 150°F (66°C). Cooked foods should not be held at room temperature. They should be stored in shallow pans at 35°F (2°C); 40°F (4°C) is the upper limit. Ground meat and similar raw meat products spoil very quickly and should be kept unfrozen no longer than one day. A greasy layer on the meat, an unpleasant odor, changes in color, and the formation of mold are all typical signs of spoilage in meat or meat products. When in doubt, throw it out!

Fresh mushrooms (except cultivated mushrooms and chanterelles) can be used only after an expert has examined the variety carefully and found them to be edible. Some types are highly toxic. Mushrooms showing signs of decay may harbor poisons, and these should never be used.

Ground grain products should be stored in a dry and well-ventilated place. Bread bins or drawers should not be lined with newspaper. Sliced bread that has been removed from a guest's table may not be served again or used for the preparation of breadcrumbs.

Frozen products should be stored at 0°F (−18°C) and should always be thawed at refrigerator temperature 40°F (4°C). Thawing at room temperature is dangerous.

The U.S. Public Health Service states:

All food, while being stored, prepared, displayed, served, or sold at foodservice establishments, shall be protected from contamination. All perishable food shall be stored at such temperatures as will protect against spoilage. All potentially hazardous food shall be maintained at safe temperatures, 45°F (7°C) or below, or 140°F (60°C) or above, except during necessary periods of preparation and service.

1.2.8 *Sanitation of the Utensils, Equipment, Premises, and Furnishings*

All utensils and equipment that come into contact with food and all areas in which food is processed, especially the kitchen, must be kept clean at all times, by following a well-planned system. See figure 1-3.

The kitchen must be cleaned at least once a day. Floors, ceilings, and walls should have smooth, hard surfaces for easy maintenance. Damaged surfaces, such as crevices, splits, and holes, are hiding places for bacteria and vermin. These surfaces should be repaired and carefully maintained to block the entrances and eliminate the hiding and breeding places for such pests. Floors should be mopped after every service and must be thoroughly washed each day. Floor drains facilitate cleaning and washing equipment and floors. The kitchen should be equipped with effective ventilation and lighting systems.

Refrigerators and freezers require regular inspections. Routine checks of motors, condensers, coils, and all mechanical parts, as well as frequent defrosting, are essential for good maintenance. The shelving and accessories should be removed and cleaned regularly. Inside walls and floors should be properly cleaned once a week. Before restocking, the refrigerator should be thoroughly dry.

Storerooms should be equipped with temperature and humidity controls that will provide optimum conditions for holding various food products. Dry storage areas must be well ventilated, cool, and clean. A systematic plan for the organization and arrangement of the storeroom will facilitate cleaning.

Machines and other equipment should be sanitized with a suitable disinfectant at regular intervals. Dishwashing machines, food mixers, grinders, slicers,

What?	When?	How?	What to Use	Effect			
				cleans	*protects*	*disinfects*	*antibacterial*
Floors	daily	hose, brush, and water	combined cleanser and disinfectant	●		●	
Walls, doors, trolleys	daily	wash and wipe dry	combined cleanser and disinfectant	●		●	
Windows, mirrors	when soiled	wash and wipe dry	window cleaner	●			
Workbenches, tables	after use	wash and dry	detergent	●		●	
Grill, oven, convection oven, deep-fryer	when soiled inside	consult manufacturer's instructions	oven or grill cleaner	●			
	when soiled outside	wash and dry; consult manufacturer's instructions	combined cleanser and disinfectant; stainless-steel cleanser	●	●	●	
Steamer, dishwashing machine, tiltpan	daily	wash and dry; consult manufacturer's instructions	combined cleanser and disinfectant; stainless-steel cleanser	●	●	●	

Figure 1-3. Routine cleaning of the kitchen, equipment, and furnishings is essential for proper sanitation control. A few guidelines: Use a washing powder/detergent that is recommended by the manufacturer of your dishwashing machine. Rinse thoroughly any equipment or machinery that you have cleaned with disinfectant. Wear rubber gloves when you are handling acid or caustic detergents.

What?	When?	How?	What to Use	Effect			
				cleans	*protects*	*disinfects*	*antibacterial*
Cutters, food-transport trolleys	daily, inside and outside	wash and dry; consult manufacturer's instructions	combined cleanser and disinfectant; stainless-steel cleanser	●	●	●	
Small equipment and hand tools	daily; after use	wash and dry	combined cleanser and disinfectant; stainless-steel cleanser	●	●	●	
Meat block and cutting boards	daily	wash and dry; use wire brush and salt on meat block	combined cleanser and disinfectant	●		●	
Refrigerator	when soiled	wash and wipe dry	combined cleanser and disinfectant	●		●	
Cutlery and crockery	after use	in dishwashing machine	dishwashing powder; very hot water	●			●
Ice cream and soft-ice machines	daily	consult manufacturer's instructions	combined detergent and disinfectant	●		●	

Figure 1-3, *continued.*

What?	When?	How?	What to Use	Effect			
				cleans	*protects*	*disinfects*	*antibacterial*
Drains	weekly	consult installer's instructions	acid (lime dissolving)	●			
Hands	several times daily	wash thoroughly	disinfecting hand soap	●		●	●
Refuse and swill bins	after emptying	wash and rinse out	disinfectant			●	
Buckets, mops, and rags	after use	soak and wash	combined cleanser and disinfectant	●		●	
Scullery (pots and pans)	after use	soak and clean	all-purpose detergent; very hot water	●			

Figure 1-3, *continued.*

steamers, ranges, ovens, and other equipment must be cleaned daily or after each use.

Kitchen utensils, containers, knives, and tools constructed of noncorrosive metals (alloys of iron, nickel, and chrome) are durable, easy to clean, and resistant to chemical reactions with foods. Utensils must be fabricated in such a way that there are no traces of poisonous metals, such as zinc or lead, that could come in contact with food. At one time copper and brass were commonly used for cooking utensils. The weight and upkeep of equipment made from these materials have

made them unsatisfactory for institutional use. Enamelware chips and cracks easily and is not suitable for heavy-duty kitchen equipment. Only plastic containers that have been officially certified for use with foods should be used.

Work tables and work surfaces constructed of stainless steel, rubber, or plastic without seams are easily cleaned, nontoxic, and nonabsorbent. Wooden cutting boards should be replaced with hard rubber, plastic, or fiberglass boards.

Deep-fat fryers should be drained each day. The

fryer should then be scrubbed and cleaned with detergents or baking soda and rinsed thoroughly. Oil or shortening should be changed frequently to prevent the accumulation of acid products, which affect the quality of the oil and products fried in oil.

Grills and roasting spits should be cleaned after each use. The heating surface should be brushed with a steel brush to remove any carbonized material.

The systems for oxygenating and for circulating the water in fish tanks require daily inspection. The condition of the fish should be checked daily. Tanks should be cleaned at least once a week and filled with fresh water.

Restrooms must be cleaned as often as is necessary during the day. They should be well ventilated. The walls and floors of the restrooms must have hard, smooth, easy-to-clean surfaces.

Handbasins should be available in the restrooms, dressing rooms, and kitchens. Each should be equipped with hot and cold running water, liquid soap, and single-use towels (paper or roller towels) or air dryers. The handbasins and toilets should be cleaned frequently throughout the day.

Trash containers must be washed and disinfected inside and out. The areas in which they are stored must be cleaned and sanitized daily.

Packing cases can be dangerous sources of bacteria. Vermin find their way into the kitchen via suppliers' packing cases. Such cases should be stored in an area outside the kitchen until they can be unpacked and removed.

Soiled laundry should be stored in laundry carts or containers outside the kitchen.

1.3 Safety

Safety is a major responsibility of all foodservice personnel. The old adage "an ounce of prevention is worth a pound of cure" may be a cliché, but it is nevertheless the key in foodservice safety.

Management must organize safety practices. The Occupational Safety and Health Act of 1970 mandated that management is legally required to protect its employees as well as the public. The act requires each employer to comply with provisions of the law and to provide a place of employment that is safe and free from hazards that may cause physical injuries or fatalities.

Every foodservice establishment should develop an overall safety program that includes firm safety policies and procedures, safety education for staff and employees, and kitchen equipment with built-in safety features. Such a program is necessary to reduce the number of accidents, which cause suffering to the injured, financial loss to the institution, high insurance costs and legal fees, and the loss of business and goodwill through customer injuries on the premises.

The following preventive measures are the responsibility of management:

- Arrange for inspections by qualified safety inspectors
- Follow through on removing and/or correcting potential safety hazards
- Furnish written reports of all accidents
- Provide continuous training programs and supervision by qualified staff that include teaching and enforcing safety procedures
- Keep all equipment, machines, physical structures, and surfaces in good repair
- Specify nonslip materials for floors when planning or remodeling foodservice facilities
- Provide uniform and adequate lighting on work surfaces, in corridors, and at entrances and exits
- Keep all electric wiring in good repair: electric wires and cords must be properly insulated; electric equipment should be grounded properly; safety circuit breakers must be installed; light bulbs should be protected with a guard; electric switches should be located so they can be reached easily in case of an emergency
- Keep correct fire-extinguishing equipment in appropriate locations, and provide a regular maintenance program for the equipment
- Equip the building with an adequate system of smoke and fire detectors to enhance the safety of guests and employees
- Provide equipment required for safety, including ladders for specific uses; special containers, plainly marked, for broken glass; storage racks for knives and sharp tools; covered containers for trash and refuse
- Keep emergency telephone numbers for police,

ambulances, and hospitals posted near the telephone
- Keep first-aid supplies available
- Keep exits clearly marked

The most frequent injuries are the result of accidents caused by burns, cuts, and falls. To avoid such accidents, employees should be aware of specific rules and procedures.

1.3.1 *Prevention of Burns and Fires*

- Know the emergency procedures for reporting fires
- Know the location of fire extinguishers and fire exits and know how to use them
- Keep the hoods over ranges and cooking equipment clean and free of accumulated grease
- Keep oven doors closed except when loading and unloading the oven
- Open and ventilate gas ovens a few minutes before lighting
- Keep ranges, fryers, griddles, and broilers clean and free from accumulated grease
- Use only dry pads to move hot pans or cooking utensils
- Use long-handled hooks to open covers of steam kettles; stir contents with long-handled paddles
- Stand back from equipment when opening doors of pressure steamers and lids of steam-jacketed kettles
- Lift lids from the side of the pan opposite you to allow steam to escape
- Keep handles of pans over the range and away from the direct source of heat, such as over an open flame or burner
- Open valves of steam-jacketed kettles and urns slowly to avoid splashing hot water and steam
- Close all valves and spigots before filling urns or kettles
- Get assistance when moving heavy containers and hot food
- Warn others about hot pans or hot china
- Avoid overfilling pans and containers with hot foods and liquids
- Wear clean uniforms that fit properly; loose sleeves and apron strings may catch on equip-

ment or touch a source of heat; wear shoes with closed toe and heel for protection from spills of hot foods and liquids
- Strike matches in a direction away from you
- Avoid spattering liquids into hot fat
- Keep a supply of salt in an appropriate place to extinguish fires in ovens or on stove tops
- Keep a supply of baking soda in an appropriate place to extinguish fires in fryers
- Keep fire doors closed
- Keep exits, fire doors, and fire escapes free of obstacles and equipment; use these only as directed for emergencies
- Smoke only in designated areas and never leave a burning cigarette unattended
- Do not handle electrical equipment with wet hands or while standing in water
- Report defective electrical wiring
- Test safety circuit breakers at regular intervals to be sure they are working

1.3.2 *Prevention of Cuts*

- Learn the complete instructions for operating meat slicers, food grinders, and food choppers; always read directions
- Keep blades of knives and slicers sharp
- Store knives in safe holders or racks when not in use; knives should never be left in a sink or in an area where they cannot be seen
- Never try to catch a falling knife; move out of its path and let it fall
- Select the appropriate knife for the specific cutting or boning task
- Use knives only for cutting and chopping; never use knives to open lids, cans, or other containers
- Hold knives and sharp tools by the handles
- Use a cutting board; cut away from your body
- Be attentive to the job when using a knife
- Turn the switch to the "off" position before cleaning or adjusting a machine; do not remove food from a machine until the machine stops
- Check switches of electrical equipment and appliances and be sure that they are in the "off" position before plugging the electric cord into the outlet
- Dispose of chipped and broken china and glass-

ware; place them in a container that has no other use; do not put in waste baskets, trash, or garbage receptacles; sweep broken glass or china into a dustpan; use disposable towels and cloths to pick up slivers of glass and china

- Use the proper tool to open crates, boxes, cans, and bottles; remove nails, staples, and wires and put them in a disposable container
- Drain the water from the sink before removing broken glass or china
- Turn the switches of mixers, slicers, and other equipment to the "off" position when the task is completed
- Keep hands away from the edge of the cutting blade while cleaning a slicer; always keep the switch in the "off" position and the blade closed when the slicer is not in use
- Use safety guards when using equipment
- Lock bowls, containers, and attachments in place before starting equipment

1.3.3 *Prevention of Falls*

- Stand on a safe ladder—not on chairs, stools, or boxes—to clean coffee urns, deck ovens, and hoods
- Keep floors and stairs free of grease, spills, and wet spots
- Keep floors, stairways, and traffic lanes free of boxes, cleaning equipment, and other obstructions
- Stack carts and trucks no higher than eye level

1.3.4 *First Aid*

First aid is defined as the immediate care given to the victim of an injury or a sudden illness. The person who administers first aid knows that skill in first-aid techniques can mean the difference between life and death, between temporary and permanent disability, and between rapid recovery and long hospitalization. Everyone feels obliged to help those who have met emergencies, particularly those who are helpless.

The first-aider must think quickly and then act. A physician should be notified whenever a serious accident occurs. Only persons who are qualified should be permitted to administer first aid. The first-aider

should check the victim's respiration and pulse; take the necessary action; and have someone arrange for assistance needed, such as a physician, the police, an ambulance, the fire department, or the rescue squad.

Bleeding

Bleeding rarely represents an immediate threat to the life of the patient; however, severe bleeding from wounds may be fatal. If excessive bleeding occurs, the patient should be positioned so that the wound is elevated above the level of the heart, until medical assistance can be arranged. The wound should be covered with a clean compress, and pressure should be applied with the palm of the hand. The compress can be held in place by use of a pressure pad placed over the compress and tied directly over the pad.

Wounds

A wound is an internal or external break in the skin, tissue, or mucous membrane. Open wounds should be covered with a clean compress. Ointments should not be applied. Cleansing wounds and removal of foreign objects should be left to a physician. Infections may develop following an injury. Symptoms of infection include:

- redness of the affected area
- fever and chills
- pain
- red streaks emanating from the wound
- swollen lymph glands

If such symptoms develop, the person should be referred to a physician at once.

Burns

Burns are injuries caused by heat, radiation, or chemical agents. The degree of burn is usually classified by the depth of the burn. The classifications and their symptoms are:

- first-degree burns—redness or discoloration
- second-degree burns—formation of blisters
- third-degree burns—destruction of cells

First-degree burns seldom require medical attention. Pain will be relieved by submerging the area in cold water. The area should be covered by a clean, dry cloth or gauze.

Second- and third-degree burns require medical care. The first-aid treatment for severe second-degree burns is the same as that required for third-degree burns:

- Obtain medical assistance
- Cover the burned areas with a sterile cloth
- Avoid use of ointments, salt, spray, or home remedies
- Elevate burned feet or legs
- Apply cold packs, not ice water, to burned areas
- Elevate a burned arm above heart level
- Keep a person with facial burns sitting up, and observe breathing
- Avoid breaking blisters or removing shreds of skin
- Give solution of salt and soda water to victim, if he is not vomiting (1 teaspoon salt and ½ teaspoon baking soda per quart of water); allow victim to sip 4 ounces every fifteen minutes

Chemical Burns

Should a corrosive agent get into the eye, the eyelid should be opened fully. The eye should be washed immediately with large amounts of water. Skin that has been burned by chemicals should be washed at once with large quantities of water for ten or fifteen minutes. Clothing should be removed from burned areas immediately. Burned areas may be covered with a sterile bandage.

Poisoning

A poison is a solid, liquid, or gas substance that causes injury or illness on contact with body surfaces or when swallowed or inhaled. Medical aid should be summoned for the victim as quickly as possible. In the meantime, first aid should be administered to dilute the poison, to induce vomiting (except when acids or alkalis have been swallowed), and to maintain respiration.

The label of the poison should be read, and the antidote prescribed should be given to the victim. The label should be given to the physician. Persons who have swallowed roach powder, drugs, or other non-corrosive poisons should be given three or four glasses of water. If this does not induce vomiting, the blunt end of a spoon or a finger should be inserted into the back of the victim's mouth. Medicinal charcoal mixed with water will absorb poison and may be given to the victim; however, the stomach should be flushed or vomiting induced within a short period after the charcoal is swallowed. Victims who are semiconscious should be given artificial respiration, and no attempt should be made to give them liquids.

If acids, alkalis, or other corrosive poisons have been swallowed, milk or water should be given to the victim, and vomiting should not be induced. The victim should be treated for shock, kept from chilling, and be given artificial respiration if necessary. A cloth should be placed over the mouth of the victim before resuscitation is started. This is necessary for the protection of the individual administering the resuscitation.

Foreign Objects

Foreign objects, such as dust, particles of carbon, or sand, are irritating to the eye and may damage it. These precautions should be followed in administering first aid:

- Consult a physician immediately if a substance is embedded in the area of the eyeball
- Avoid rubbing the eye
- Wash hands thoroughly before examining the eye

If an object is embedded under the upper eyelid, pull the upper lid forward and down. Place a cotton swab on top of the cartilage parallel to the edge of the eyelid. The eyelid can then be rolled back over the swab while the patient looks down. The foreign object can be removed with the corner of a clean handkerchief. The eye should be flushed with water from an eyedropper.

Choking is caused by a piece of food lodging in the throat, creating a blockage of the airway, thus making it impossible for the victim to breathe or speak. If the victim shows signs of distress—cannot speak or breathe, turns blue, and/or collapses—the Heimlich Maneuver should be used:

Rescuer Standing (victim standing or sitting)

- Stand behind victim and wrap your arms around his waist; place your fist, thumb side up, against the victim's abdomen, slightly above the navel and below the rib cage
- Grasp your fist with your other hand and press into the victim's abdomen with a quick upward thrust
- Repeat several times if necessary

Rescuer Kneeling (victim lying face up)

- Facing the victim, kneel astride his hips
- With one of your hands on top of the other, place the heel of the bottom hand on the abdomen slightly above the navel and below the rib cage
- Press into the victim's abdomen with a quick upward thrust
- Repeat several times if necessary

Contents of a First-aid Box

- Sterile gauze pads, 4 by 4 inches (10 by 10 centimeters), packaged individually, to stop bleeding (ten pads)
- Heavy dressing, called "ABD pads," for serious bleeding (six pads)
- Two rolls of gauze bandage (Kerlix or Kling) to wrap injuries; these are self-adhering but do not stick to the skin
- Adhesive tape in 1- or 2-inch (2.5- or 5-centimeter) width (one roll)
- Cotton swabs to look under the eyelid for a foreign body (one package)
- Scissors, for cutting bandages
- Flashlight
- Adhesive bandages of assorted sizes
- Hydrogen peroxide for cleaning small wounds (one bottle)
- A 3-inch (7.5-centimeter) elastic wrap for wrapping injured limbs; use carefully according to instructions given by medical personnel
- Eye cup, for rinsing eyes

1.4 Recipe Book and File

The food production system is the key to wholesome and palatable food, controlled food costs, and satisfied clientele.

Standardized recipes are one of the most important tools for assuring high-quality food production. A standardized recipe is one that has been tested and developed to meet the needs of a specific establishment. The available equipment, the skills of the food-service personnel, and the food budget must be considered. The yield is calculated for an exact quantity based on the predicted number of portions required and the specific portion size. The recipe is tested several times, until at least three trials have produced a product of the desired quality and quantity.

One of the most important tasks of a beginning chef involves compiling a file of standardized recipes. Similar files should be maintained for members of the food production staff.

A standardized format should be used for recording all recipes. The form may be on sheets that are 8½ by 11 inches or on cards 5 by 8 inches. The format of the recipe sheet or card should be designed to meet the organization's needs.

Whether a recipe book or a recipe file system is selected, duplicates should be in the manager's office, the kitchen supervisor's office, and in the kitchen.

A recipe rack to which the recipe can be attached and placed over the cook's work station is a convenience that will keep the recipe available and clean.

Recipe Book

A loose-leaf notebook can be used to store recipes, and new recipes can be inserted in the correct place. Although recipe books are convenient and require a minimum of space, more time is required to locate recipes than with a card file.

Recipe Card File

Individual recipe cards are classified, numbered, and filed in a standard-size box under headings such as soups, meats, vegetables, and salads. Colored cards may be used to separate the sections. The recipe cards

Ingredients for:	**Hungarian Goulash (Gulyás)**	File # *17.4.2*
___ persons	Menu text:	*The classic Hungarian goulash made of beef, paprika, and potatoes. Fiery and delicious.*
Date: _____		

Restaurant: *Old Post Inn*
Chef: *Paul Johnson*
Tested by: *Andy Robinson*
Date tested: *11/27/87*
Yield: *10 servings*
Calories per serving: *574*

Ingredients	Ingredients	
_____	*2 ounces*	*fat*
_____	*4½ pounds*	*rump, shoulder OR round, boneless*
_____	*14 ounces*	*onion, chopped fine*
_____	*2 tablespoons*	*paprika, sweet, mild*
_____	*to taste*	*salt*
_____	*1¼ pounds*	*tomatoes, peeled and seeded*
_____	*1¼ pints*	*brown stock*
_____	*1¼ cups*	*red wine*
	1½ pounds	*potatoes, cut into large cubes*

Procedure

1. *Heat the fat in a heavy pan. Cut the meat into 2-ounce chunks. Add the meat and onion. Stew, stirring occasionally, until the juice released by the meat has been completely reduced and a light glaze is formed.*
2. *Add paprika, salt, and tomatoes.*
3. *Pour in the stock and the wine.*
4. *Cover and simmer for 1½ hours. Add the potato cubes and continue cooking until the meat and potatoes are done. Add liquid during the cooking period if too much evaporation occurs. Cook potatoes separately for à la carte.*

Serving Instructions

Four pieces of beef with potatoes per person; with sauce, in brown serving dish #1. Sprinkle chopped parsley over stew.

should be laminated or placed in transparent plastic sleeves to protect the recipes. Recipe cards are easy to locate and can be corrected or revised easily. The files require more storage space than books, however, and there is a greater risk of individual cards being lost.

The format for a recipe sheet or card is, in principle, the same. The following information should be included:

- Exact title or description of the recipe
- Text for the menu
- File number
- Name of the establishment
- Chef's name
- Tester's name
- Date of standardization and/or revision
- Portion size
- Number of portions (yield)
- Ingredients
- Weight or measure of each ingredient
- Equipment to be used (pan size)
- Preparation procedures
- Time and temperature for cooking or baking
- Method or suggestions for serving and garnishes
- Comments

An example of a recipe card or sheet is shown in figure 1-4.

Index

An index is indispensable for either a recipe book or file. The index should be divided into main groups and subgroups. The main groups are annotated on colored section cards with their reference number (decimal) and description. The subgroups are marked with their reference numbers on each of the recipe cards. The system of reference numbers and descriptions then appears again in the index.

Figure 1-4. Example of a recipe card or sheet. The left column is filled in by the head chef when this recipe is used for a different number of servings.

1.5 Menu Book

The beginning and the trained cook alike should keep menu books. A collection of important menus is a good reference that may be very useful in planning. A loose-leaf book is recommended for classification of the individual menus. Two copies of the book, one for the kitchen and one for the office, will simplify menu planning.

Menu Forms

Menu forms should be designed to meet the needs of the particular foodservice. The form should be of sufficient size to include menus that are to be prepared on a specific day. Guides are frequently printed on the menu form to facilitate planning and checking. (See figure 1-5.) The following points should be included:

- Menu number
- Name of establishment
- Name of chef
- Date
- Text for menu
- Text number
- Number of portions prepared
- Number of portions sold
- Retail price
- Notes

Index

An index, divided into main and subgroups, should be included in the menu book. Colored pages, which can be annotated, are used to separate the sections. The individual menus are arranged in order with main and subgroups. Figure 1-6 is an example of an index of a menu book. Figure 1-7 shows how a menu sheet for Hungarian goulash is indexed.

Menu Number: *1.1.1.37*

Establishment: *Old Post Inn*
Chef: *P. Johnson*
Portions prepared: *40*
Portions sold: *21*
Retail price, including service: *$7.95*
Date: *November 27, 1988*

Menu	*Recipe Numbers or Notes*
Soup home style— *Potage bonne femme*	13.2.2.1.
Hungarian goulash— *Gulyàs*	17.4.2.
Salad— *Salade*	Tomatoes & chickory/ Ital. dressing
Caramel custard with Chantilly cream— *Crème caramel Chantilly*	27.1.2

Note: *Cook the potatoes separately and specify on the menu; otherwise, it is difficult to use leftovers.*

Figure 1-5. A menu sheet.

1	Menus for the day	(main group)
1.1	Menus including meat	(subgroup 1 of daily menus)
1.2	Menus including fish	(subgroup 2 of daily menus)
1.3	Menus including poultry	(subgroup 3 of daily menus)
1.4	Menus including game	(subgroup 4 of daily menus)
1.5	Menus for vegetarians	(subgroup 5 of daily menus)
1.6	Drive-in lunches	(subgroup 6 of daily menus)
1.7	Menus for calorie watchers	(subgroup 7 of daily menus)

2	Menus for holidays	(main group)
2.1	New Year's Day	(subgroup 1 of holiday menus)
2.2	Mardi Gras	(subgroup 2 of holiday menus)
2.3	Palm Sunday	(subgroup 3 of holiday menus)
2.4	Good Friday	(subgroup 4 of holiday menus)
2.5	Easter	(subgroup 5 of holiday menus
2.6	Ascension	(subgroup 6 of holiday menus)
2.7	Pentecost	(subgroup 7 of holiday menus)
2.8	Mother's Day	(subgroup 8 of holiday menus)
2.9	Thanksgiving	(subgroup 9 of holiday menus)
2.10	Christmas	(subgroup 10 of holiday menus)

3	Menus for banquets	(main group)
3.1	Smaller banquets (up to 20 persons)	(subgroup 1 of banquet menus)
3.2	Larger banquets (over 20 persons)	(subgroup 2 of banquet menus)
3.3	Special banquets	(subgroup 3 of banquet menus)

4	Buffets	(main group)
4.1	Cold buffets	(subgroup 1 of buffets)
4.2	Hot buffets	(subgroup.2 of buffets)
4.3	Mixed buffets	(subgroup 3 of buffets)
4.4	Brunch buffets	(subgroup 4 of buffets)

Figure 1-6. A menu index.

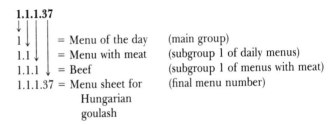

Figure 1-7. Breakdown of menu indexing numbers.

Chapter 2
The Kitchen: Organization and Installation

Foodservice organizations vary in terms of function and size, and each must have its own organizational structure. The needs and sizes of food production units in restaurants, hotels, hospitals, extended-care facilities, and colleges and universities will differ; the organization systems for each, however, are much the same.

The location of the foodservice department in the organizational structure of the facility is significant. The department should be close to top management because of its complex nature and importance. Management may be the responsibility of the owner, a dietitian, or a food-and-beverage manager.

2.1 Kitchen Staff

The kitchen staff is a working team of trained cooks and beginners who produce and complete dishes under the management of the chef or food production manager. The structure and size of the staff, as well as its functions, are usually determined by the following factors:

- Size of establishment
- Type of establishment
- Organization of establishment
- Equipment available
- Foods and dishes to be offered

The allocation of duties depends on the type of kitchen organization chosen and, in the final analysis, determines the tour rosters and duty schedules.

It is erroneous to assume that the need for organizational structure and allocation of duties applies only to large kitchens. Small establishments must also organize their kitchens and allocate duties to be successful. Even a kitchen with four or five cooks may classify the kitchen staff and allocate the duties related to preparation and finishing. In addition to the kitchen organization, the functions of each staff member, the correct allocation of duties, and personnel management are very important.

2.1.1 *Ranks*

The ranks of those in the profession are in principle the same for both conventional and modern kitchens. Only the duties and functions of the cooks differ. The cooking profession employs the following ranks. (See figures 2-1 and 2-2.)

Executive Chef (with diploma or certificate)

This is the highest level possible. The executive chef is in charge of the kitchens of large establishments. He has the overall responsibility for the preparation and service of food in accordance with the standards and practices of the company or facility. He plans menus, meets with management and department heads, and coordinates all kitchen functions.

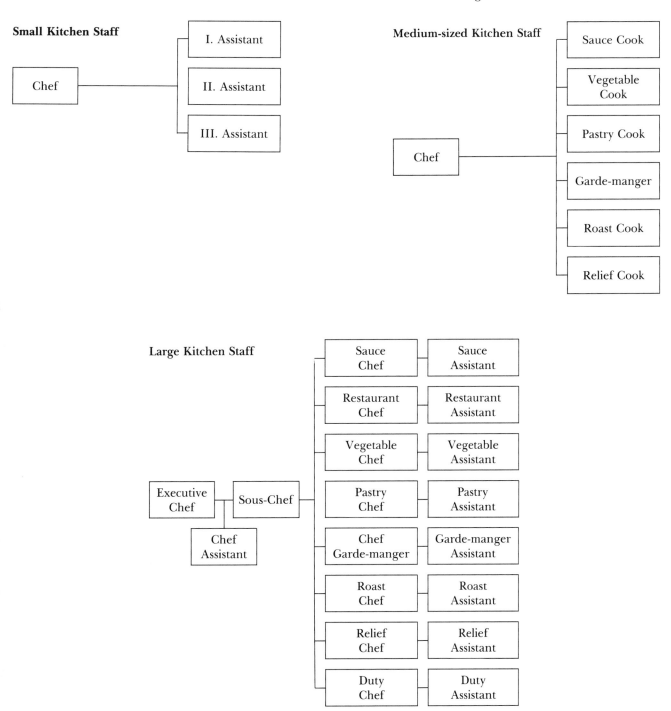

Figure 2-1. Diagrams of conventional kitchen staffs.

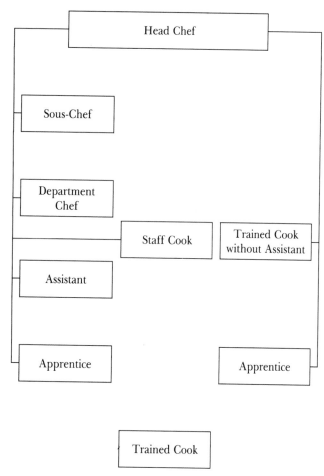

Figure 2-2. Diagram of kitchen ranks.

Head Chef

This title can be used only by those who have professional cooks working for them. The head chef is the authority in the kitchen.

Sous-Chef

The sous-chef, second in command, is responsible for the physical aspect of the kitchen operations, including supervision of the kitchen staff, as well as the preparation and service of the food. This individual is sometimes responsible for training beginners.

Chef Steward

The position of chef steward is used in medium-sized establishments for economic reasons. The person in this role functions as a chef and purchases the food and supplies. In the absence of the chef steward, the sous-chef is in charge. The chef steward acts in a supervisory role during meal hours and banquet service.

Working Chef

The working chef is in charge of the kitchen in smaller foodservice operations. In addition to performing the regular duties of chef, the working chef is responsible for a station or part of a station. Tasks may include preparing the soups, entrées, and sauces; cutting the meat; assisting at stations; and preparing special dishes.

Chef's Assistant

An administrative, technically qualified member of the staff.

Chef de Partie or Department Chef

This person is in charge of a department or section such as fry station, broil station, or roasting station. One or more assistants report to the chef de partie.

Night Chef

The night chef has complete responsibility for the kitchen after the executive chef and sous-chef go off duty. At other times, the night chef acts as an alternate for the the chef garde-manger.

Banquet Chef

The banquet chef is responsible for all parties and banquets. Under the direct supervision of the executive chef, the banquet chef is responsible for all the stations to which party or banquet work has been assigned.

Second Cook

The second cook prepares all soups, stocks, bouillons, jellied consommés, and sauces. Other items prepared by the individual in this position are boiled meats, such as boiled beef, corned beef, boiled and sautéed fish; all braised dishes, such as pot roast, Swiss steak, stews, and goulash; all creamed dishes, such as creamed chipped beef, chicken, and mushrooms; all special à la carte and chafing dish orders, such as seafood Newburg, chicken à la king, and breast of chicken in wine sauce.

Soup Cook

The jobs of the soup cook and the second cook are sometimes combined. The soup cook prepares all soup stocks, consommés, and bouillons.

Broiler Cook

The broiler cook broils steaks, chops, chicken, fish, kebobs, and tomatoes. Frequently, the broiler and roast stations are combined. The cook assigned to this role must have expertise for both jobs.

Fry Cook

The fry cook's work includes deep-fat frying, preparing eggs, omelets, fritters, potatoes, au gratin dishes, and crêpes. Vegetables are cooked at this station if no vegetable cook is on the staff.

Vegetable Cook

The vegetable cook, responsible to the chef, directs the cleaning, preparation, and cooking of all vegetables.

Cook's Assistant

The cook's assistant helps prepare and serve the food.

Relief or Swing Cook

The relief cook relieves the cooks on major stations. Duties include stocking supplies for menus, planning and completing work required for the following day's menu, and maintaining the routine of the day.

Chef Garde-Manger

The chef garde-manger supervises the cold meat department and the breading of meats, fish, and seafood. Other foods prepared in this department include meat, fish, and seafood salads; salad dressings and cold sauces; appetizers, canapés, and sandwiches. All cold foods for buffet service are prepared and decorated by the chef garde-manger.

Pastry Chef

The pastry department is under the supervision of the pastry chef. Duties of this position include planning dessert menus, requisitioning materials and supplies, scheduling the work of assistants, decorating cakes and pastries, and testing and costing recipes.

Assistant Pastry Chef

The assistant pastry chef, under the direct supervision of the pastry chef, is in complete charge of pastry production. All cakes, pies, puddings, cookies, and pastries on the dessert menu are prepared by the assistant pastry chef.

Baker

The head baker has complete responsibility for the bakery department including the production of breads, rolls, and hot breads.

Baker's Assistant

The baker's assistant weighs ingredients, prepares baking sheets and pans, and keeps the bakeshop clean and orderly.

Other Occupations

Additional jobs include assistant cook, butcher, fish butcher, chicken butcher, sandwich maker, salad maker, pantry worker, cake decorator, and food checker.

2.1.2 *Allocation of Duties*

Each department in the kitchen has different areas of responsibility. The classical divisions overlap, however, when the work is separated into two areas, namely, preparation and finishing. For example, it is possible that, in a kitchen used for preparation, the vegetable cook prepares pan-fried or deep-fried foods, and that, in a finishing kitchen, a roast cook finishes and serves vegetable dishes. It is important, however, that no cook serve in the same function in any duty schedule for too long. In a preparation and finishing kitchen, a cook is assigned according to the department requirements, and at the same time, he retains his normal rank. (When this system is used, the conventional names for the different departments are replaced by the title of the overall function.)

The duties of the different positions of the classical French and preparation and finishing kitchens are shown in figures 2-3 and 2-4.

As has been mentioned in earlier, a small kitchen may also be separated into preparation and finishing. The preparation section is responsible for production of pre-prepared sauces and precooked pasta and vegetables.

The modern kitchen with a preparation section and a finishing section does not necessarily have two separate kitchens. In the modern kitchen the preparation of food can be completed without interruption. The chefs can work more rationally and have working hours that are comparable to those in industry. The finishing chefs can concentrate on the orders as they come into the finishing section. Depending upon the type of kitchen, it is possible to assign the chefs who are in the preparation section to the finishing section during peak hours. This system offers great flexibility in the use of professional staff and unskilled labor. This is becoming increasingly necessary because of the continued shortage of qualified staff and because of high labor costs. For example, not only would it be illogical to have a department chef peeling carrots by hand, when this could be done faster with machines and unskilled labor, but the talents and skills of an expert would be lost. The division into preparation and finishing sections, however, poses disadvantages for certain types of kitchens. Those catering for *table d'hôte* (fixed menu) and banquet establishments require a maximum of labor at peak periods. These kitchens will continue to give preference to the conventional system.

Positions	Duties
Head Chef	Manager of the kitchen and kitchen staff.
Chef's Assistant	Administrative and technical kitchen duties, recipe development, and costing.
Sauce Cook	Prepares fish, sautéed dishes, stews, hot hors d'oeuvre, hot entrées, and sauces. (In addition, serves as the deputy head chef where there is no sous-chef.)
Garde-Manger	Processes raw meat, cold dishes, forcemeat, pies, galantines, and cold hors d'oeuvre.
Vegetable Cook	Prepares soups, vegetables, pasta, and foods made of flour, eggs, and cheese.
Roast Cook	Prepares items roasted in the oven and on the spit, deep-fried and grilled foods, baked potato dishes, and gravies.
Restaurant Cook	Prepares à la carte dishes that must be prepared à la minute.
Pastry Cook	Prepares all basic desserts, hot desserts, cold desserts, frozen desserts, and hot and cold pastries.
Relief Cook	Replaces the department chef positions.
Duty Cook	Assumes overall responsibility during a tour of duty. Carries out the extra work of chefs in their absence.
Staff Cook	Prepares the food for the staff.
Assistants	Assist according to their individual skills.

Figure 2-3. The duties of the different positions in the classic French kitchen.

The three basic diagrams presented here illustrate the organizational structure for three different types of kitchens. Figure 2-5 applies to a medium-sized establishment offering many different items on the menu and various portion sizes. There are no preparation and finishing sections, and the work is therefore carried out according to the conventional princi-

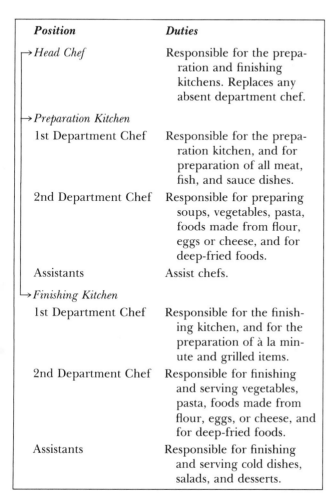

Position	Duties
Head Chef	Responsible for the preparation and finishing kitchens. Replaces any absent department chef.
Preparation Kitchen	
1st Department Chef	Responsible for the preparation kitchen, and for preparation of all meat, fish, and sauce dishes.
2nd Department Chef	Responsible for preparing soups, vegetables, pasta, foods made from flour, eggs or cheese, and for deep-fried foods.
Assistants	Assist chefs.
Finishing Kitchen	
1st Department Chef	Responsible for the finishing kitchen, and for the preparation of à la minute and grilled items.
2nd Department Chef	Responsible for finishing and serving vegetables, pasta, foods made from flour, eggs, or cheese, and for deep-fried foods.
Assistants	Responsible for finishing and serving cold dishes, salads, and desserts.

Figure 2-4. The responsibilities of the various departments in the preparation and finishing kitchen.

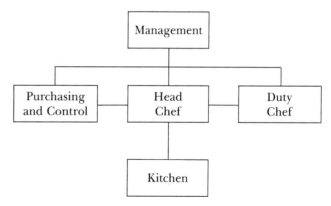

Figure 2-5. Organization chart for a conventional kitchen.

achieved. Figure 2-6 demonstrates that two separate kitchens are not required to effect the division into preparation and finishing. It is possible to allocate almost all the kitchen staff to the finishing section during peak hours, and at the same time avoid having any one cook assigned to the same work for too long. Alternating the cooks from a preparation tour to a finishing tour every week or two assures an all-around training experience equivalent to that provided in a conventional kitchen. In addition to the conditions necessary for the correct functioning of such a

ples for the allocation of duties. Figure 2-6 applies to a medium-sized establishment with a standardized menu and standard portions. Figure 2-7 represents a large establishment that is standardized in terms of both menu and portion size. Regardless of the way in which duties are allocated, the principles of recipe development and menu planning, as described in chapters 1 and 5, should be observed.

Only through organization in the kitchen, including recipe specification, menu planning, tour rosters, and duty schedules, can a uniform quality of food preparation and economic kitchen management be

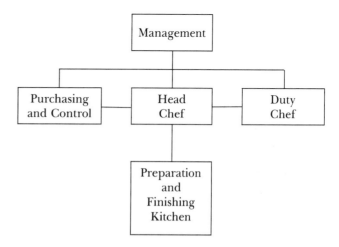

Figure 2-6. Organization chart for combined preparation and finishing kitchens.

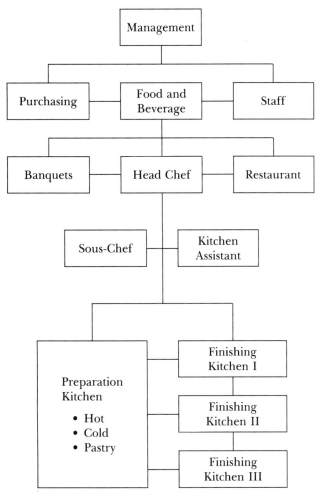

Figure 2-7. Organization chart for separate preparation and finishing kitchens.

kitchen, the importance of teamwork should be stressed. These diagrams cannot be applied without first analyzing the allocation of the duties in a specific kitchen. Figures 2-8 and 2-9 show a shift plan and a duty roster.

2.2 *Mise en Place*

Mise en place is merely organizing and completing in advance all the preliminary tasks involved in the preparation of a meal. Whether the *mise en place* is carried out for a conventional kitchen, a preparation kitchen, or a finishing kitchen, preliminary work must be completed methodically and carefully before further work in the kitchen can be executed. When observing the work of the various cooks on the kitchen staff, it is easy to recognize those who have the ability to organize their work in conjunction with a correct *mise en place*. When a kitchen is properly organized, the routine *mise en place* for the various departments is in written form. Department chefs or cooks should be able to give the assistant exact instructions for the daily *mise en place* on the basis of the recipe and the menu plans. The saying "a good *mise en place* is half the cooking" applies to small kitchens as well as to large preparation and finishing kitchens. The aim of an exact *mise en place* is to complete all the preparatory operations before the actual cooking begins. The cooking process is then simplified, and unexpected orders can be filled easily and promptly. Before the service begins, each member of the cooking staff should allow himself sufficient time to check his *mise en place* thoroughly. Only in this way can a service be completed in an organized manner. The *mise en place* should also include a number of reserve items, and the quality of these should be as good as the quality of the original menu items. Such a plan will prevent dissatisfaction among the guests and will reduce staff frustrations. It is not without reason that a professional French cook once said, "The best cook isn't the one who cooks best, but the one who keeps something just as good in reserve." Cleaning and closing the area are also a part of the *mise en place*. Inventorying supplies on hand, planning and ordering food for reserves, preparing food items in advance, and clearing and cleaning all foodservice areas are duties that must be completed each day. Each of these functions is dependent on the other, and a complete interaction of all the functions is necessary to complete *mise en place*. The general term *mise en place* today means everything from arranging the utensils and linen to preparing a goulash in the preparation kitchen. It should be remembered that the *mise en place* for the finishing kitchen includes taking pre-prepared food and ingredients from the preparation kitchen. The following classifications for the *mise en place* applicable

—— PR = production (07.30–17.30)
- - - - FI = finishing (10.30–23.00)
E = eating

Plan 1: 8 shifts

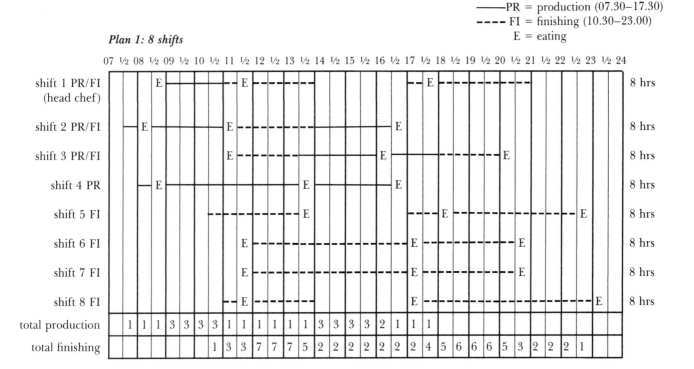

Plan 2: 7 shifts

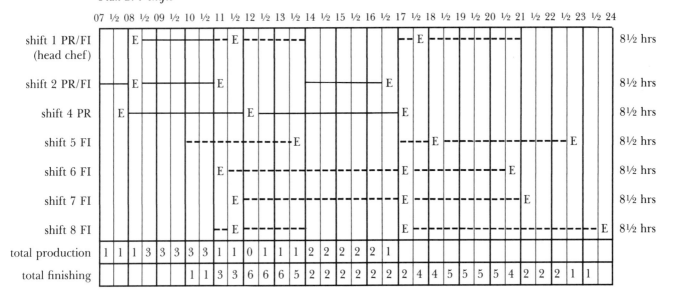

Figure 2-8. A shift plan for a preparation and finishing kitchen.

Duty Roster	Department: *Preparation and Finishing Kitchen*				From *11/6/89* until *11/19/89*		
Employee	*Monday*	*Tuesday*	*Wednesday*	*Thursday*	*Friday*	*Saturday*	*Sunday*
1. Head chef Fisher, Sara	OFF	OFF	Shift 1	Shift 1	Shift 1	Shift 1	Shift 1
2. Chef de partie Burrows, Tim	Shift 1	Shift 1	OFF	OFF	Shift 2	Shift 2	Shift 2
3. Chef de partie Oliver, Bill	Shift 2	Shift 2	Shift 2	Shift 2	OFF	OFF	Shift 3
4. Assistant Simpson, Steve	OFF	Shift 3	Shift 3	Shift 3	Shift 3	Shift 3	OFF
5. Assistant Miller, Donna	Shift 4	OFF	OFF	Shift 4	Shift 4	Shift 4	Shift 4
6. Relief cook Phillpot, John	Shift 5	Shift 4	Shift 4	OFF	OFF	Shift 5	Shift 5
7. Chef de partie Hut, Hank	Shift 6	Shift 5	Shift 5	Shift 5	Shift 5	OFF	OFF
8. Chef de partie Wils, Julie	OFF	OFF	Shift 6	Shift 6	Shift 6	Shift 6	Shift 6
9. Assistant Henderson, Brian	Shift 7	Shift 6	OFF	OFF	Shift 7	Shift 7	Shift 7
10. Assistant Hufton, Leslie	Shift 8	Shift 7	Shift 7	Shift 7	OFF	OFF	Shift 8
11. Assistant Johnson, Michael	OFF	Shift 8	Shift 8	Shift 8	Shift 8	Shift 8	OFF
	Plan 2	Plan 1	Plan 1	Plan 1	Plan 1	Plan 1	Plan 1

Figure 2-9. A duty roster for a preparation and finishing kitchen.

to the various positions and departments should be adapted to the needs of each individual kitchen.

2.2.1 *Basic* **Mise en Place** *of the Cooks' Tools, Cooking Utensils, and Linen*

Regardless of the positions and departments, the cooks' tools, cooking utensils, and linen include the following:

- Kitchen knives
- Meat forks
- Sharpening steels
- Paring knives
- Serrated knives
- Spatulas
- Tongs
- Whips
- Skimming ladles and spoons
- Strainers
- Graters
- Colanders
- Forks

- Meat hooks
- Measuring cups, spoons, ladles, and scoops
- Saucepans
- Stockpots
- Braising pans
- Sauté pans
- Roasting pans
- Baking pans
- Sheet pans
- Counter pans
- Omelet pans
- Pie and tart pans
- Spoons
- Storage containers
- China caps
- Lids
- Molds
- Kitchen aprons
- Towels
- Dish towels
- Range cloths
- Straining cloths
- Dishcloths
- Sponges
- Cleaning products and equipment

Variations of the basic *mise en place* might be necessary for different menus and specialties of the day as well as for planned events such as banquets.

2.2.2 *General* Mise en Place *Duties*

These duties differ according to the kitchen and department, but usually include the preparing and/or the assembling of chopped and peeled onions, whole and chopped parsley, eggs, butter, fats, oil, vinegar, red and white wine, Mediterranean and sweet wines, Cognac, *bouquet garni, mirepoix* (diced vegetables), spices, lemons, and flour.

2.2.3 Mise en Place *for the Sauce Cook—* Saucier

- White veal stock
- Game stock
- Brown veal stock
- Brown veal sauce

- Velouté sauce
- White chicken sauce
- Special white sauces
- Meat extract
- Chicken stock
- Tomato sauce
- Thickened white sauce
- Diced tomatoes
- Duxelles
- Lemons
- *Bouquet garni*
- Chopped onions
- Chopped shallots
- Fat, oil, shortening
- Herbs and spices
- White and red wine
- Fortified wines (Madeira, Marsala)
- Truffle slices
- Sliced mushrooms
- *Mirepoix*
- Parsley sprigs and chopped parsley
- Butter
- Cream
- Flour
- Salt
- Vinegar
- Cognac (brandy)
- Cheese
- Turned mushrooms
- Cornstarch
- Potato starch
- Frying pans
- Saucepans
- Braising pans
- Sauté pans
- Serving dishes (platters)
- China caps
- Straining cloths
- Small casseroles
- Bains-marie (double boilers)
- Gastro-Norm dishes/bowls/containers

2.2.4 Mise en Place *for the Fish Cook—* Poissonnier

In smaller kitchens this is part of the *mise en place* of the sauce cook (*saucier*).

- Fish stock
- Fish velouté
- Turned potatoes
- Cooked potatoes
- Truffle slices
- Turned mushrooms
- All fish sauces
- American sauce
- Chopped onions
- Chopped shallots
- Parsley sprigs
- Chopped parsley
- Capers
- Lemons
- Lemon juice
- Butter
- Cream
- Oil, fat, shortening
- Sliced almonds
- Flour
- Cornstarch
- Herbs and spices
- Frying pans
- Sauté pans
- Oven dishes
- Fish kettles
- Steamers
- Salamander (overhead grill)
- Straining cloths

2.2.5 Mise en Place *for the Vegetable Cook*—Entremetier

- Vegetable stock
- Veal stock
- Meat stock (beef bouillon)
- Chicken stock
- Vegetable soups
- Puree soups
- Cream soups
- Velouté soups
- Special soups
- National soups
- Precooked vegetables
- Precooked rice
- Half-cooked risotto

- Precooked pasta (noodles)
- Cooked potatoes
- Garnish for soups
- Croutons
- Julienne of vegetables
- Brunoise of vegetables
- Mashed potatoes
- Eggs
- Omelet mix
- Poached eggs
- Chopped onions
- Chopped shallots
- Parsley sprigs
- Chopped parsley
- Puff-pastry *fleurons* (prepared by pastry cook)
- Flour
- *Bouquet garni*
- Butter
- Cream
- Fats, oils, shortening
- Lemons
- Herbs and spices
- Omelet pans
- Sauté pans
- Saucepans
- Vegetable dishes
- Bains-marie (double boilers)
- Braising pans
- Gastro-Norm dishes, containers
- Strainers
- China caps
- Straining cloths
- Colanders

2.2.6 Mise en Place *for the Roast Cook*—Rôtisseur

- Sliced lemons
- Turned mushrooms
- All grilling cuts of fish, meat, game, and poultry
- Roasting meat
- Roasting poultry
- Roasting game
- Deep-fried fish
- Breadcrumbs
- Dough

- Flour
- *Mirepoix*
- Whole onions, peeled
- Chopped onions
- Parsley sprigs
- Chopped parsley
- Fried parsley
- Watercress
- Herb butter
- Roasting potatoes
- Turned potatoes
- Small tomatoes (for mixed grills)
- All types of deep-fried potatoes
- Butter
- Milk
- Fat, oil, shortening
- Herbs and spices
- Grilling pans, grills
- Frying pans
- Sauté pans
- Deep-fryers

2.2.7 Mise en Place *for* Garde-Manger

Portioned meat cuts such as:

- Cutlets
- Schnitzels
- Chops
- Mignons
- Tournedos
- Châteaubriand
- Entrecôtes
- Porterhouse steaks
- New York cuts
- T-bone steaks
- Hamburgers
- Mixed grills
- Sausages
- Frying sausages
- Ragouts
- Fricassees
- Stews
- Goulash
- Ballottines
- Galantines
- Pâtés

- Game
- Poultry, trussed or sliced
- Fish, filleted or sliced
- Fish, whole and/or stuffed
- Poultry, stuffed
- Game, stuffed
- Caviar
- Goose liver
- Boiled eggs
- Quail eggs
- Shellfish
- Crustaceans
- Mollusks

All ingredients for preparation of cold hors d'oeuvre:

- Mayonnaise
- Vinaigrette
- Cumberland sauce
- Mint sauce
- Horseradish sauce
- Meat sauce
- Fish sauce
- Cold egg dishes
- Cold roasts
- Cold sausage
- Cold chicken
- All salads
- Salad dressings
- Colanders
- Strainers
- Straining cloths
- China caps
- Gastro-Norm dishes, containers
- Salad plates
- Hors d'oeuvre dishes (*raviers*)

2.2.8 Mise en Place *for the Pastry Cook*—Pâtissier

- All pastry
- All doughs
- Pies/pastries
- Pancakes
- Crêpes
- Creams and caramels
- Tarts

- Flans
- Fruitcakes
- Ice creams
- Soft-ice mix
- Butter
- Cream
- Fat, margarine, shortening
- Candied fruits
- Oranges, mandarins, lemons
- Apples, bananas, apricots, peaches
- Pineapple
- Sugar, salt, flour
- Yeast
- Baking powder
- Meringues
- Fondant
- Icing
- Buttercream
- Sauces
- Glazes
- Small cakes
- Small pastries
- Fruit salad
- Batters
- Raisins, sultanas, currants, peels
- Grated lemon rind
- Liqueurs, such as Curaçao, maraschino, Grand Marnier
- Liquors, such as rum and Kirsch
- Almonds, grated and blanched whole
- Spices
- Vanilla beans and extract
- Chocolate *couverture*
- Gastro-Norm dishes, trays, containers
- Flan rings
- Baking trays
- Jelly-roll tins
- Cream horn molds
- Tartlet pans
- Barquette molds
- Piping bags and tips
- Pastry cutters
- Pastry pincers
- Rolling pins
- Dariole molds
- Pudding molds

- Charlotte molds
- Pie dishes
- Pie molds
- Pie trays
- Copper bowls
- Copper saucepans
- Whisks
- Cooling racks
- Straining cloths

2.2.9 Mise en Place *for the Preparation Kitchen*

The *mise en place* for the preparation kitchen includes preparation of the same items as the general *mise en place* for a conventional kitchen. The items include breadcrumbs, grated cheese, stocks, sauces, raw meat, poultry, game, fish, crustaceans and mollusks, vegetables, potatoes, pasta, pastries, fillings, glazes, sauces, and creams for desserts. Operational duties that are part of the *mise en place* in the preparation kitchen are cleaning and organizing the refrigerators, replenishing the fish chest with ice, and preparing leftover foods.

2.2.10 Mise en Place *for the Finishing Kitchen*

In addition to the general duties, the *mise en place* for the finishing kitchen consists of checking and adjusting the seasonings of the partially and wholly cooked items from the preparation kitchen. Preparation of the ingredients and dishes should be completed if possible, and then the items should be placed in the thermostatically controlled heating cabinets, refrigerators, freezers, or bains-marie. These items and dishes include soups and gravies; fish, crustaceans, and mollusks; meat, poultry, and game; potatoes and pastas; vegetables; salads and aspics; sauces, such as mayonnaise, tartar, vinaigrette; cold entrées and garnishes; glazes and ice specialties; pastries and biscuits; and desserts.

2.3 Kitchen Organization

The organization of the kitchen depends on the following:

- Type of establishment
- Size of establishment

- Type and method of customer service
- Extent of the menu

After this information has been provided, the kitchen can be planned in one of the following ways:

- Conventional
- Combined preparation and finishing
- Separate preparation and satellite
- Convenience food

In selecting one of these types of kitchens, consideration should be given to:

- Number of meals to be prepared at each meal period
- Type of service
- Customer prices
- System for serving the meals
- Serving times for hot meals
- Serving times for cold meals

After determination of these factors, it should be possible to select a kitchen plan that is practical and of the appropriate size. The kitchen plan must also provide:

- Flexibility related to the location and the size of the rooms
- Efficient work flow
- Provision for receiving incoming goods
- Supplies/storeroom
- Adequate refrigeration
- Preparation kitchen (hot, cold, pastry)
- Finishing kitchen
- Sufficient service area
- Warewashing area
- Scullery
- Secure flatware storage

The kitchen staff can be efficient only if the work flow has been properly planned. Figures 2-10 through 2-13 indicate the correct basic arrangement of the various areas and show the relationship of one part of the kitchen to another.

2.3.1 *The Functions of the Kitchen*

Kitchens can be grouped into four main types, reflecting various demands.

Conventional Kitchen

For small *table d'hôte* and banquet kitchens that have flexible standards for menus and portions, all departments are grouped together in blocks. Both preparation and finishing are carried out in the same areas. All hot dishes are served at one counter in the kitchen. (See figure 2-10.)

Combined Preparation and Finishing Kitchen

This is primarily of interest to the medium-sized establishment, open year-round, in which a certain

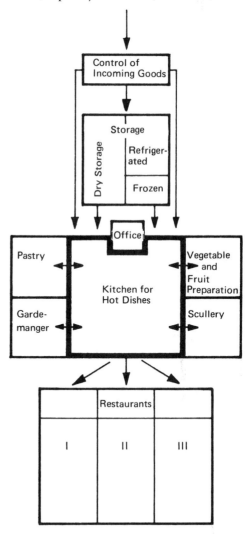

Figure 2-10. Diagram of a conventional kitchen.

amount of standardization of the menu and the portion size is possible. The advantage of this system is that cooks may be assigned to both sections. In principle, preparation and finishing are separated into two blocks. Whether these blocks are totally or partially separated depends on the type of establishment. Each block should accommodate all types of menu items such as hot food, cold food, and pastry. (See figure 2-11.)

Separated Preparation and Finishing Kitchen

This system is preferred for larger establishments. The preparation and finishing blocks (satellite kitchens) are in separate rooms. Each satellite kitchen should consist of one room housing all the departments necessary for the dishes on the menu. Usually, these have no large ranges, frying pans, or steam-jacketed kettles. Instead, there are grills and griddles, microwave and convection ovens, bains-marie, and fryers. The cold and pastry sections generally include only refrigerators for storage of partially and totally finished foods. (See figure 2-12.)

Fast-food Kitchen

This system is of interest to establishments that have no preparation kitchen and purchase only convenience foods. Kitchens of this type require refrigerated and dry storage areas, a preparation section for convenience foods incorporating microwave and convection ovens, and deep fryers. The cold food and pastry section consists only of storage rooms and equipment for refrigerating prepared foods. Space for washing and preparing ingredients is necessary in locations where pre-prepared fresh salads cannot be supplied. (See figure 2-13.)

Figure 2-14 designates the functions of the main kitchen and separate areas.

2.3.2 *Technical Kitchen Planning*

After the type of foodservice and the organizational structure of an establishment have been determined, the planning of the kitchen may begin. Even though an architect may have expertise in kitchen planning, a professional foodservice facility designer should also

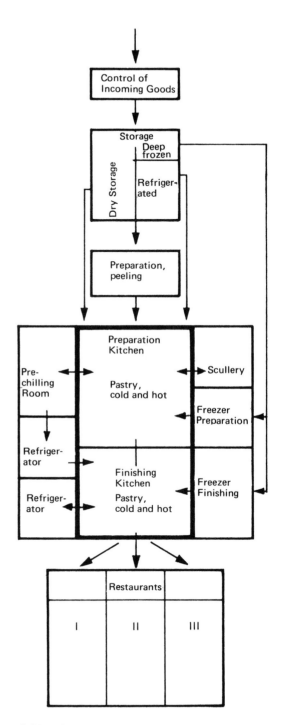

Figure 2-11. Diagram of a combined preparation and finishing kitchen.

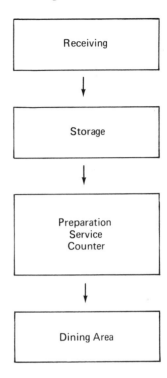

Figure 2-13. Diagram of a fast-food kitchen.

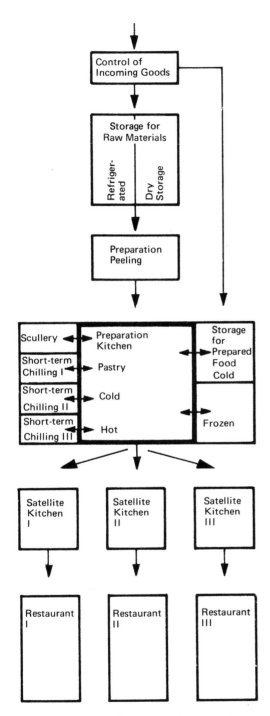

Figure 2-12. Diagram of a separated preparation and finishing kitchen.

be assigned to the job. In addition to standard design concerns, the following areas require additional discussion:

- Optimum size ratio among the individual rooms
- Proper positioning of the equipment in work areas
- Good illumination of the working and cooking surfaces, possibly by positioning near windows or skylights
- Good ventilation for both the hot and cold sections, including installation of range hoods above cooking surfaces to control smoke and steam
- Working diagrams for the utilities, water, and waste installation
- Equipment that conforms to sanitation codes
- Materials for nonslip floors
- Washable wall and ceiling surfaces
- Drainage systems under sinks and washbasins and under cooking equipment where necessary

| MAIN KITCHEN | Hot kitchen: Production and issuing of all hot foods, menus
Garde-manger: Preparation of fish, shellfish, crustaceans and mollusks, meat, poultry and game. Production of all cold dishes. Hors d'oeuvre.
Pastry: Production of all pastry and dough, batters, buttercream, sauces, hot, cold and frozen desserts. Savory pastry dishes (cheese straws, pies, etc.) for the hot kitchen.
* Preparation area: Preparing, cutting, slicing, "turning" (cutting into shapes), and washing of vegetables, potatoes, salads. Also portioning and vacuum packing.
* Scullery: Washing up pots and pans, kitchenware such as sieves, casseroles, trays, Gastro-Norm dishes, and containers
* Silver room: Polishing and burnishing of silverware with silver polish and/or a burnishing/polishing machine
Storeroom: Holding area for nonperishables
Refrigeration area: Walk-in cool rooms/deep freezers and/or freezing chests/refrigerators |

* In small hotels and restaurants, these areas are part of the main kitchen.

Figure 2-14. Functions of the main kitchen and separate areas.

- Conformance to building codes
- Conformance to OSHA (Occupational Safety and Health Administration) and other safety standards

Before kitchen planning can begin, planning checklists must be prepared to ensure that no requirement is left out. Such checklists must contain each and every part of the kitchen(s) and annexes. Figure 2-15 is a sample checklist for kitchen planning.

The professional kitchen consultant or designer is

Storage and Production Units	*Location/Area*	*Space Requirements in ft² or ft³*

	receiving goods:
	  daily
	  periodically
	entrance control
	crates, containers (empty returns)
	waste:
	  food
	  other	

	dry goods, food/nonfood:
	  in the cellar
	  near the kitchen
	refrigeration (for distribution):
	  dairy products
	  eggs
	  vegetables, salads
	  meat, fish
	deep-freeze:
	  meat
	  fish
	  vegetables
	  ice cream and desserts
	other storage:
	  raw vegetables
	  potatoes
	essential cold storage:
	  walk-in cool room
	  refrigerator	

	preparation:
	  vegetables, salads, fruit, fish
	mise en place:
	  hot and cold production
	  hot and cold finishing	

	hot production daily for:
	  finishing
	  banquets
	  bulk production	

Figure 2-15. A checklist for kitchen planning.

Storage and Production Units	Location/Area	Space Requirements in ft² or ft³
	procedures:	
	cooking, steaming	
	deep-frying, blanching	
	grilling, poaching	
	roasting, braising	
	baking, sautéing	
	gratinating, glazing	
	pot-roasting, stewing	
	cold production for finishing and banquets:	
	fish, meat, poultry, game, hors d'oeuvre, fillings, pies, pâtés, terrines	
	distribution:	
	directly to kitchen	
	to control or docket	
	production pastry (baked on premises)	
	daily: cakes, tarts, gâteaux, buttercreams, desserts, sweets, ice cream, fruit salads, meringues, toast	
	bulk production	
	finishing:	
	hot: griddle, grill, deep-fryer, salamander, steamer	
	cold: hors d'oeuvre	
	pastry: finishing cakes, gâteaux, ice gâteaux, coupes, desserts	
	service counter:	
	ice cream desserts	
	cold foods (ready)	
	hot foods (ready)	
	microwave items	
	all buffet foods	

Storage and Production Units	Location/Area	Space Requirements in ft² or ft³
	first aid	
	fire exit/door	
	communication:	
	intercom with external connection	
	paging system (beeper)	
	office:	
	production planning	
	recipes	
	purchasing	
	portion control	
	costing	
	inventory	
	restaurant:	
	with self-help	
	with service	
	number of seats	
	types of service:	
	plate service	
	silver service	
	other	
	dishwashing:	
	by hand	
	machine	
	prerinse	
	waste/garbage	
	glasses	
	silver/copper	
	cutlery	
	crockery	
	handbasin	
	personnel:	
	staff meals	
	cloakroom	
	toilet	
	showers	
	lockers	

Figure 2-15, *continued.*

Storage and Production Units	Location/Area	Space Requirements in ft² or ft³
	transport: Gastro-Norm trolley Gastro-Norm lift Gastro-Norm stacking	
	miscellaneous: air supply air extraction hot water/boiler fat filter water softener unit	

Figure 2-15, *continued.*

responsible for translating the specified requirements into building and installation plans. He or she is also responsible for reconciling the technical requirements of the building, sanitation, heating, ventilation, refrigeration, and utility installation with the relevant official regulations. The state or local codes and standards for foodservice establishments must also be met. Only by seriously planning the kitchen in conjunction with the demands and desires of the professional staff can their needs be satisfied in a kitchen that functions efficiently and economically. Independent foodservice designers and the planning departments of foodservice equipment distributors can recommend building contractors, professional foodservice personnel, and architects who are qualified to assist with planning.

Basic research and a professional kitchen planner are essential in developing kitchen designs and layouts. (See figures 2-16, 2-17, 2-18, 2-19.) The following guidelines should be followed:

- Throughout the stages of planning, you must make sure that the kitchen concept is adhered to. Sometimes portions get lost or changed between the plan and the drawing board.
- Make sure that all regulations are followed.
- Let a professional kitchen planner check your plan; he can save you a lot of worry later.

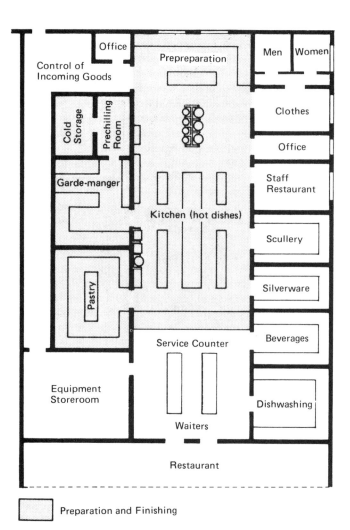

Figure 2-16. Conventional kitchen design and layout.

- Use standard sizes as much as possible when choosing transport, racking, and storage equipment.
- Look at the future when planning kitchens; do not build only for today. Make it your business to know how kitchens should function tomorrow and beyond.
- Think about routing—efficiency through short walking distances for the kitchen staff. Food items should not travel up and down the kitchen,

but go in a logical straight line from storage to preparation to finishing and service.

- Plan for labor saving. Aim for maximum efficiency and production with minimum effort, thus saving labor.
- Good planning will facilitate a good work flow,

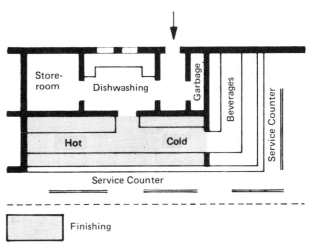

Figure 2-18. Satellite kitchen, design and layout.

from the point of receiving commodities right up to the point where the meal is issued and served.

- After good planning comes choosing the right equipment and correct tools.

2.3.3 *Heating Methods and Equipment*

The following heating methods can be used either directly or indirectly in the cooking process. (See figure 2-20.) The different types of heat are defined by these criteria:

- *Direct contact:* heat conducted by fire, hot plate, griddle plate, pot/pan, or grill
- *Radiation:* heat conducted by infrared heat or mi-

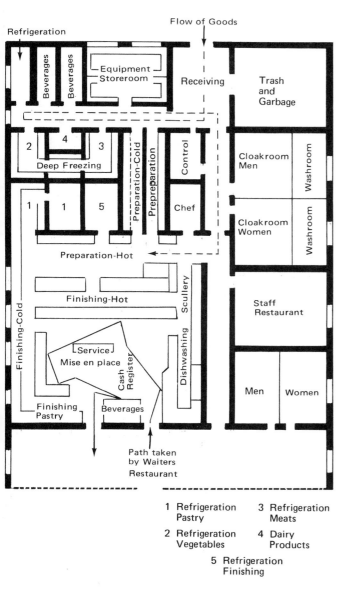

1 Refrigeration Pastry
2 Refrigeration Vegetables
3 Refrigeration Meats
4 Dairy Products
5 Refrigeration Finishing

Figure 2-17. Preparation and finishing kitchen, design and layout.

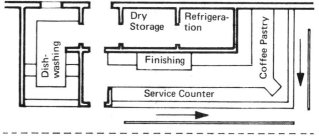

Figure 2-19. Fast-food kitchen, design and layout.

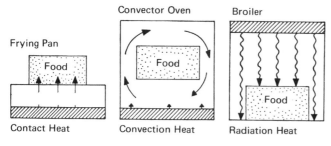

Figure 2-20. Different methods of heating: direct contact, convection, and radiation.

crowaves, as in a broiler, salamander, or microwave oven

- *Convection:* heat conducted by hot air, dry and wet steam, water, and oil, as in a steamer, convection oven, or bain-marie
- *Combination* of the above methods: direct contact, radiation, and convection

Convection Oven

This oven operates on the principle of forced-air convected heat. It is used for primary cooking, roasting, and baking, as well as for reheating prepared foods. The heat is introduced in chambers above, below, or alongside the oven cavity. A fan forces the hot air evenly over all the food. (See figure 2-21 for a comparison of heating in a traditional and a convection oven.) Therefore, it is not necessary to turn the trays. This oven has a number of advantages. It saves both space and cooking time, as compared to a conventional oven. Various dishes can be prepared in the same unit without flavor transfer. Temperature and energy levels can be controlled automatically. Recipes can be prepared with less fat and will lose less weight while cooking. However, the turbulent air limits use with soft, fluffy foods (such as meringue) and tends to make food dry out more quickly than a conventional oven does. (See figure 2-22.)

Steamer

There are three types of steamers—high pressure (15 psi); low pressure (5 psi); and atmospheric (using a convection principle with no pressure). Depending on

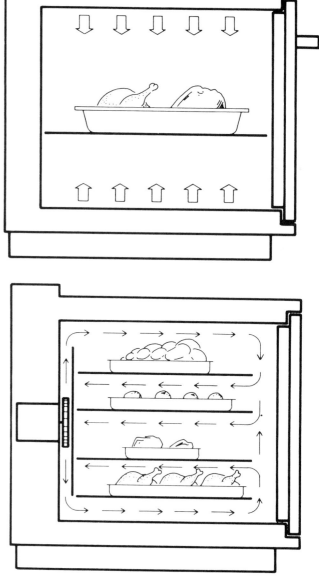

Figure 2-21. The heating principles of a traditional oven (top) and those of a convection oven.

the model, steamers will generate their own steam or obtain it from an outside source. It is important that the steam be injected directly into the chamber. Depending on the food, the cooking time required for

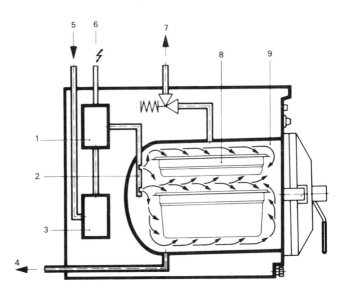

Figure 2-23. Steamer: (1) steam generator; (2) steam supply; (3) water softener; (4) drain; (5) water supply; (6) electrical connection (mains); (7) pressure valve; (8) Gastro-Norm containers; (9) cooking chamber.

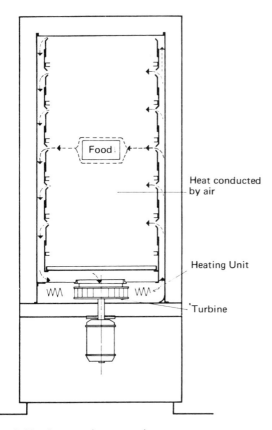

Figure 2-22. Automatic convection oven.

food cooked in a steamer may be reduced by a half to two-thirds. For those foods that are best cooked in moist heat, steaming is a fast method of cooking. It can be used for a variety of foods, from soups to desserts. Because steamed foods are usually low in fat and retain more vitamins, steaming enables you to comply with special requests of guests that have diet restrictions. However, steaming is not suitable for items of irregular size or for thawing blocks of frozen food. (See figure 2-23.)

Microwave Oven

This type of oven generates energy in the form of short microwaves. The heat is not conducted from a heat source, but developed inside the food itself by an electromagnetic field. This field sets the molecules in the food in violent motion so that they repeatedly collide with each other. This friction results in heat, which cooks the food very quickly. Because the heat is created internally, the food is neither encrusted by heat nor does its color change. Metal utensils or containers should never be used in a microwave oven.

Microwave ovens are best used for reheating prepared items or cooking specialties. Because of the way microwave ovens heat foods, their oven cavity is small. Therefore, they are not recommended for the preparation of large quantities of food. Microwaves pass through glass, porcelain, plastics, paper, and similar low-moisture materials without creating heat in them. Most food, depending on the moisture content, will absorb microwaves to some extent and will be heated in this way. (See figure 2-24.)

Since the density and the water content of foods vary, they absorb microwaves differently. Results are most satisfactory in microwave cooking when the cross section or depth of the food is no more than 2 inches. Microwaves are emitted in a steady flow, so that thin areas will be heated more rapidly than thicker sections of the food. Foods with a high mois-

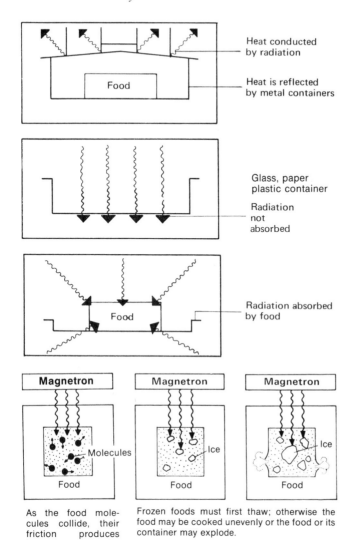

Magnetron | **Magnetron** | **Magnetron**

As the food molecules collide, their friction produces heat that cooks the food.

Frozen foods must first thaw; otherwise the food may be cooked unevenly or the food or its container may explode.

Figure 2-24. Microwave oven. The top three drawings show how various substances react to microwaves: at top, metal containers reflect the microwaves; at center, microwaves pass through glass, paper, and plastic; at bottom, food absorbs microwaves and heats. The drawing at the bottom shows how microwaves cook and thaw food.

ture content require longer cooking, and unless these foods are uniform in size, it will be difficult to have a uniform temperature and degree of doneness in the product.

Frozen food products contain many ice crystals, which the microwaves transform into steam. Best

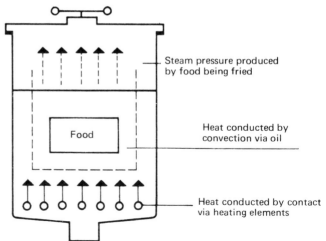

Figure 2-25. Pressure fryer.

results are achieved when the food is defrosted in the microwave oven, removed from the oven cavity, and then put back into the microwave oven and heated to the desired serving temperature. This assures more uniform cooking and avoids cooking the outside of the food before the center thaws.

In the professional kitchen, the microwave oven is a supplementary piece of equipment. When used correctly, it makes wider menu variety possible.

Pressure Fryer

This fryer is heat sealed. The steam pressure is produced by the food itself during deep-frying. This process, known as *broasting,* is suitable for fresh and frozen pieces of chicken and turkey. Advantages of these pressure fryers are increased tenderness, flavor, and moisture content in the product while the cooking time is reduced to less than half the conventional time. These fryers should not be used to cook small quantities of food, because there is not enough moisture given off in the cooking process to build up the necessary steam pressure. Pressure fryers are not suitable for foods with a high moisture content, such as vegetables and potatoes. (See figure 2-25.)

Regeneration Oven

These ovens are used to heat meals already arranged on plates or as individual portions. Some manufactur-

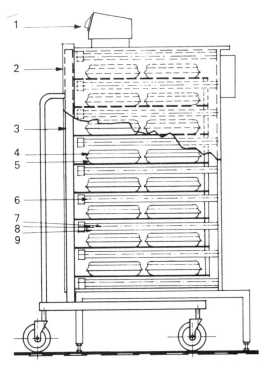

Figure 2-26. Regeneration oven (standard block and mobile unit): (1) switch; (2) standard block 32T; (3) trolley (mobile unit); (4) chrome-nickel-steel lid; (5) dish/plate; (6) infrared radiation; (7) resistor; (8) quartz pipe; (9) protective grill.

ers use heat transmitted by radiation (infrared); others use heat conducted by convection. Both systems, however, are nothing more than heating processes. They are generally used for banquets, self-service restaurants, and convenience food kitchens. (See figure 2-26.)

The advantages of these ovens are:

- Food preparation can be scheduled during slow periods
- Food can be prepared and portioned more carefully during slack periods
- Ovens can be located near the point of service where food may be heated quickly and served to the customer at the proper serving temperature

There are some disadvantages in the use of these ovens. Among them are:

- Menu selections are limited

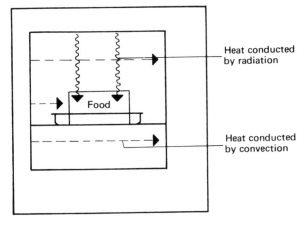

Figure 2-27. Combination microwave-convection oven.

- Equipment and dishware represent a high financial investment
- Portion sizes are limited

Combination Microwave-Convection Oven

The microwave-convection oven is equipped with microwave energy and forced-air convection heating devices. Food can be cooked much faster than in a conventional oven. The oven may also be used for roasting and baking. (See figure 2-27.)

The advantages are:

- Cooking, baking, and roasting times are reduced
- Microwave energy and forced-air heating devices can be applied simultaneously or separately

The disadvantages are:

- Fats and oils used on foods will burn at high temperatures
- Retaining the red color in the interior of roasted meats is difficult

2.3.4 *Kitchen Equipment*

Roasting, Boiling, and Deep-Frying Equipment

- *Bain-marie:* heated by radiation, steam, or hot water; thermostatically controlled; available in sizes that conform to official norms
- *Broiler:* high-temperature top heat via infrared; gas or electric powered

- *Deep-fryer:* heated electrically or with gas, sometimes equipped with automatic fat filter
- *Frypan:* fixed or tilting
- *Griddle:* independent or built-in units; thermostatically controlled hot plates with drip pans for excess fat
- *Grill:* bottom, top, or top-and-bottom contact heat; direct or indirect infrared heat
- *Infrared oven:* available as baking or reheating oven
- *Microwave oven:* for all heating procedures
- *Pizza oven:* heated electrically or by gas; to heat fresh or frozen pizza
- *Pressure cooker:* for all pressure-cooking methods
- *Pressure fryer:* a deep-fryer with a hermetic seal; steam pressure is produced by the moisture from the foods being fried; recommended for large quantities of food, particularly poultry
- *Roasting spit:* thermostatically controlled; preferably a horizontal spit with lateral heating
- *Steamer:* for all pressure steam methods and heating and preparation systems
- *Steam-jacketed kettle:* fixed or tilting, heated either by heat radiation or with direct or indirect steam heating
- *Toaster:* for toasting bread or buns
- *Toaster, conveyor:* conveyor-type model for toasting bread or rolls using either electricity or gas

Chilling and Freezing Equipment

- *Blast-freezer:* for fast-freezing raw products, prepared dishes, and prepared meals
- *Ice cream freezer:* either horizontal or vertical, continuous or batch production
- *Ice machines:* for making ice cubes, cracked ice, and snow
- *Refrigerators:* reach-in and walk-in
- *Soft-freeze machine:* for making soft ice cream and sherbets
- *Storage freezers:* reach-in and walk-in

Kitchen Machines

- *Blender:* for chopping fruits, vegetables, or nuts; for whipping or pureeing food; for mixing cocktails; for making dressings; and for emulsifying small quantities of sauces and creams
- *Bread slicer:* semi- or fully automatic machine with a revolving knife that slices bread; the thickness of the slice can be varied
- *Compactor:* for grinding disposables and glass and metal containers
- *Food chopper:* for preparing forcemeat, vegetable and fish farces, and meat stuffings
- *Food mill:* for making soups, purees, and jams
- *Fruit and vegetable press:* for making fruit and vegetable juices
- *Grating machine:* for making almond or hazelnut powders, for grating cheese, and for making breadcrumbs
- *Grinder:* for grinding meat and vegetables
- *Homogenizer:* for homogenizing creams, sauces, and glazing mixes
- *Meat chopper/slicer:* for chopping meat, poultry, or game
- *Meat saw:* for sawing bones and frozen and dehydrated products
- *Meat tenderizer:* for tenderizing steaks and cutlets
- *Mechanical pastry roller:* for rolling all kinds of pastry dough, piecrusts, and pasta
- *Mixer, food:* for making doughs, fillings, sauces, and creams
- *Pot and utensil washer:* for the cleaning of utensils, saucepans, pots, and bowls
- *Roller machine:* cylindrical marble rollers for grinding almonds to paste, for making marzipan, and for emulsifying fine creams and semiliquid dough
- *Salad draining machine:* for drying fresh lettuce, vegetables, and potatoes
- *Scales:* semi- or fully automatic mechanical or electrical portable or stationary scales; some commercial models can be connected to portioning and cutting machines
- *Sealing apparatus:* for sealing plastic boiling bags used for prepared dishes and meals
- *Silver polishing machine:* for deoxidizing and polishing silverware
- *Slicing machine:* for slicing meat, vegetables, and cheese
- *Vegetable cutter:* for making uniform strips, sticks,

or cubes of vegetables, bread, or potatoes in various sizes and thicknesses

- *Vegetable peeler:* for peeling potatoes and vegetables
- *Vegetable washing machine:* for cleaning vegetables and potatoes
- *Vertical cutter/mixer:* for cutting, chopping, blending, kneading, grinding, and liquefying; for making creams, sauces, salads, and various kinds of dough.

2.3.5 Gastro-Norm

The United States, known for its leadership in technological matters, lags behind the rest of the world in one scientific area: failure to adopt the metric system of weights and measures. The increase in world trade is making a conversion to metrics a necessity. Standardization will pose many problems in some areas.

Fortunately, foodservice has its standards in place. The impetus for standardization came from the Swiss. Representatives of several foodservice organizations in Switzerland met in Zurich to sign a document that would standardize dimensions for "all movable inserts for food dishes and utensils, such as pans, trays, wire racks, drawers, screens and trolleys, and also for kitchen equipment and refrigerators."

Originally, the representatives had planned to create a new Swiss standard. But these plans were dropped in favor of the basic size of 530 mm by 325 mm, already the dimensions of standard American pans. The new standard was named *Gastro-Norm*. This standard has been adopted by foodservice groups and manufacturers throughout Europe.

Antonio Trippi, a Swiss Hotel Association consultant, points out that this dimensional standardization provides for a uniform system throughout the entire foodservice industry. The food can remain in uniformly dimensioned containers from the time it is received throughout the entire operation (preparation, finishing, service, storage).

The standardization has many applications in foodservice:

- Standard packages as well as various combinations of trays and pans will fit standard carts and racks
- Gastro-Norm trays, pans, and sheets will fit steam tables, refrigerated and heated drawers and cabinets, sandwich units, and bains-marie
- Gastro-Norm pans fit steamers and pressure cookers, and the trays become exact inserts for proofing cabinets, ovens, and heated/refrigerated cabinets; after cooking, the same containers may be moved to the service area, since the transport, preparation, storage, and handling are all based on the same common denominator
- Dishwashing racks are standardized, 500 mm by 500 mm (20 by 20 inches), with guide rails on two sides extending to 530 mm; dishware can be stored in or delivered to the serving areas in these racks

It should be remembered that use of all standard 2/1 devices (the 2/1 module corresponds to the 20- by 24-inch pan) can always be achieved by retaining the dimension of 530 mm in one direction. The shapes and dimensions for pans in the Gastro-Norm system are illustrated in figure 2-28 (from the British Standards Institution, London).

The foodservice operator who adopts the Gastro-Norm standards can:

- Speed operating procedures
- Increase stacking volume in small areas
- Simplify internal transportation systems
- Reduce working distances for staff and employees
- Allow universal use of the transport and storage units
- Reduce labor costs
- Standardize service ware
- Permit interchangeability of units

Standardized Equipment

All inserts standardized to Gastro-Norm dimensions can be stacked, and the overall measurements are such that numerous combinations of the various sizes are possible. Standardized bowls and trays are usually made of top-grade stainless steel. This material is un-

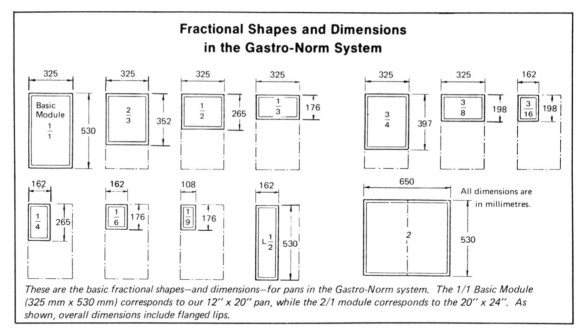

Fractional Shapes and Dimensions in the Gastro-Norm System

These are the basic fractional shapes—and dimensions—for pans in the Gastro-Norm system. The 1/1 Basic Module (325 mm x 530 mm) corresponds to our 12" x 20" pan, while the 2/1 module corresponds to the 20" x 24". As shown, overall dimensions include flanged lips.

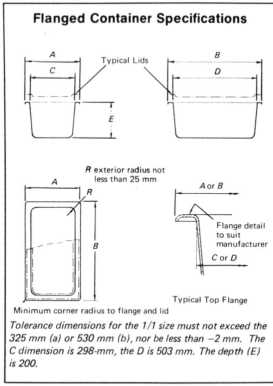

Flanged Container Specifications

Tolerance dimensions for the 1/1 size must not exceed the 325 mm (a) or 530 mm (b), nor be less than −2 mm. The C dimension is 298-mm, the D is 503 mm. The depth (E) is 200.

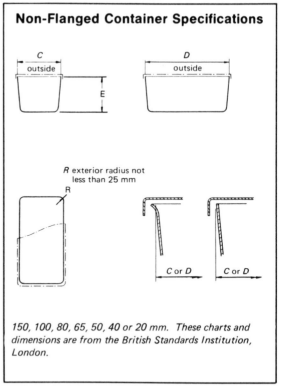

Non-Flanged Container Specifications

150, 100, 80, 65, 50, 40 or 20 mm. These charts and dimensions are from the British Standards Institution, London.

Figure 2-28. Gastro-Norms.

48

affected by heat and cold and can withstand rough treatment. When serving meals, similar units made from different materials (silver, glass, porcelain) can also be used individually or together.

Applications

The Gastro-Norm standards can be used for:

- Pressure-cooking equipment
- Microwave units
- Fryers
- Convection ovens
- Ovens
- Broilers
- Walk-in and reach-in refrigerators and freezers
- Built-in drawers and cupboard units
- Bains-marie and steam tables
- Transporting equipment
- Storage units
- Storage racks
- Food lifts
- Elevators for food carts
- Self-service buffets
- Self-service trays
- Prefabricated units for large banquets
- Portioned prepared-food trays

2.3.6 *Refrigeration*

Refrigerated storage requirements are increasing with the use of more perishable, frozen, and prepared foods. These foods require storage temperatures that will preserve their quality and nutritive value and safeguard against loss from bacterial growth.

Fundamentally, cold is created by removing heat. The principle of mechanical refrigeration is based upon the evaporation of a liquid refrigerant inside a sealed circuit and the recondensation into a liquid. In order to evaporate, the gas removes the heat from the chilling compartment. Every refrigeration and deep-freezing plant should be equipped with an automatic defrosting device. The ice that forms around the cooling element acts as insulation, delaying or even obstructing the transfer of the heat and stopping its pas-

sage to the compressor. Each refrigerated area should be equipped with a thermostat to control its temperature. (See figure 2-29.)

Refrigeration Equipment

There are basically two types of compressors for refrigeration equipment: air cooled and water cooled. Air-cooled equipment must be installed in a well-ventilated room to ensure the fresh flow of air. An automatic ventilation system can act as an aid. Water-cooled equipment requires relatively little space, but the water consumption is in direct ratio to its performance. The choice of one or the other of these two systems cannot be made until the local conditions have been thoroughly examined. Most compressors today are either partially or totally hermetically sealed, so that the electric motors rarely need servicing.

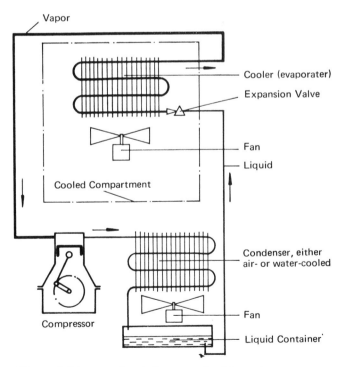

Figure 2-29. Functional diagram of refrigeration technique.

Refrigerated Areas

The design of refrigerated areas is dependent upon the type of establishment: hotel, restaurant, canteen, retirement home, children's home, hospital, college or university, or school foodservice. Each of these has its own specific requirements, and these must be considered when planning the size of the rooms, the length of time the goods will be stored, and the cooling procedure to be used—fast chilling, blast-freezing, and/or frozen storage.

Large establishments must have two zones:

- Zone 1: storerooms and a freezer with large doors to accommodate forklift trucks with pallets
- Zone 2: refrigerators for daily use located near the kitchen, pastry department, ice-cream department, garde-manger, and buffet

Refrigerators and freezers should be constructed in blocks, possibly placing the freezer in the center. This type of construction offers advantages from the technical and insulation standpoint and in terms of construction and costs. The storage rooms for fruit, potatoes, and vegetables should be equipped with humidifiers, and those for meat with a dehumidifier.

Storeroom Temperatures and Humidity

For ideal temperature and humidity levels according to type of food, refer to figure 2-30.

	Temperature		Relative Humidity in %
	°F	°C	
Meat and sausages	30 to 35	−1 to 2	70 to 75
Fish in ice in refrigerator	30 to 35	−1 to 2	80 to 100
Milk, butter, cream	35 to 40	2 to 4	75
Eggs	33 to 45	1 to 7	75 to 85
Fruits and vegetables	40 to 45	4 to 7	80 to 90

Figure 2-30. Ideal temperature levels and humidities for foods.

Walk-in Refrigerators/Freezers

Walk-ins should be long and narrow so that there is sufficient wall space for racks and standardized trays and shelves. Because of humidity requirements, only meat and meat products should be stored in the meat refrigerator. The short-term refrigerator space must be large. Foods such as milk, cheese, fish, and pastry should always be stored separately, if possible, so that the odor of one does not transfer to another. (See figure 2-31.) Shelving dimensions should correspond to accepted norms. The operational system must be determined before planning the walk-ins. These details will be necessary for calculating capacity and performance.

Refrigerators and Standardized Refrigerated Units

All modern refrigerators, refrigerated units, and refrigerated chests are standardized according to the accepted norms. All these units may be fitted with drawers to accommodate the standardized inserts for the safe storage of food. The fan-cooling system is absolutely necessary to achieve sufficient airflow in these very compact units.

2.3.7 *Industrial Food-Freezing Processes*

Freezing refers to the process of preserving fresh or prepared food by quickly reducing the temperature of the food to 0° to 5°F (−18° to −21°C). The technology associated with fast-freezing has made considerable advances. Research proves that fast-frozen food maintains freshness and taste much longer than when it is preserved in any other way. Formerly, food was frozen slowly at 23° to 10°F (−5° to −12°C). In this process, cell fluid turned into ice crystals. Today low temperatures—between −40° and −50°F (−40°C and −45°C)—are used. With this fast-freezing process, known as blast-freezing, the cell fluid is no longer transformed into large ice crystals. It becomes a granular mass that does not damage the cellular tissue. Recommended storage temperatures for frozen foods range between 0° and −10°F (−18° and −23°C). At these temperatures meat, fish, fruit, vegetables, game, poultry, and ice cream products can be preserved over long periods of time without any substantial loss

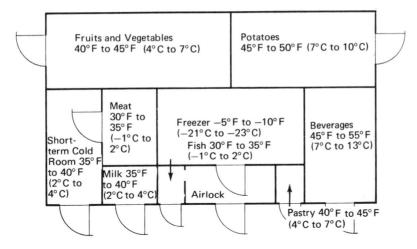

Figure 2-31. Diagram of walk-in refrigerators/freezers.

in aroma, flavor, or vitamin content. There are five different blast-freezing methods.

Multiple-Plate Contact Process

The food is first wrapped and then placed between two hollow plates within which the refrigerant is circulating. If the temperature of the plates is roughly −40° to −60°F (−40° to −51°C), the temperature of a food product measuring 2 inches across can be reduced to −5°F (−21°C) in less that 2 hours. Up to twenty plates can be used in a single unit.

Tunnel Process

The food is placed in a tunnel and subjected to a current of air at −30° to −50°F (−34° to −45°C). The ice-cold air must be circulated by fans so that the surface temperature of the food drops quickly but uniformly.

Blast-Freezer Process

This process involves a small freezing chamber. In addition to the cooling unit itself, two powerful fans are built into the rear. The conditions are the same as in the freezing tunnel. A standardized cart, which is fitted with metal gratings, is filled with flat plastic bags containing prepared meals. The food may be packaged or open, and any shape or consistency of food may be frozen. The unit's high performance within a very small space makes it possible to reduce the temperature of the products to −5°F (−21°C) within 20 to 30 minutes. (See figure 2-32.)

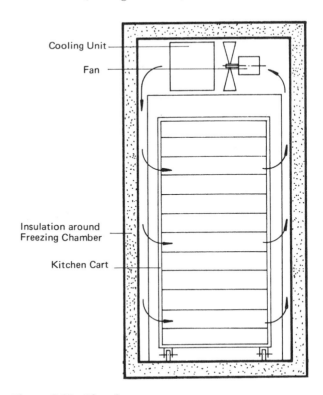

Figure 2-32. Blast-freezer.

Flow-Freezer Process

Large amounts of small items, such as peas, Brussels sprouts, beans, berries, or french-fried potatoes, can be continually frozen in a flow freezer. A stream of cold air at −40°F (−40°C) surrounds and lifts each individual piece. The products are packaged after the freezing process is completed.

Liquid Nitrogen Spraying Process

Liquid nitrogen (N_2) evaporates at −321°F (−196°C), and spraying foods with it produces temperatures of −94° to −130°F (−70° to −90°C), making it possible to freeze food products very quickly. Conventional deep-freezing equipment can finish the job. This rather expensive method of shock-freezing results in

an improvement in the quality of certain foods, such as bakery products, delicate fish, prepared meals, and meat portions. The process can be used in conjunction with specially constructed freezing tunnels and chambers.

2.3.8 *Equipment for Making and Handling Sherbet and Ice Cream*

Ice cream and sherbets are made from mixes frozen by mechanical freezers that have a stirring mechanism that whips air into the products as they freeze. If a commercial ice cream mix is used, the only equipment needed will be a freezer and hardening cabinets. (See figure 2-33.)

The ice cream should freeze fast enough to de-

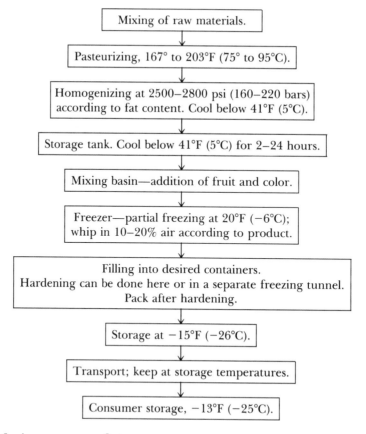

Figure 2-33. Process used for ice cream manufacture.

velop fine crystals, and the beating should be sufficient to retain the fine texture. Fast hardening at low temperatures is also necessary to maintain a fine texture. Two types of ice cream freezers are shown in figure 2-34. Both have advantages and disadvantages. In the horizontal freezer, the large freezing area of the cylinder facilitates fast freezing and the large beating area facilitates greater volume. However, some of the mixture stays on the sides of the cylinder, does not get mixed with the rest, and is difficult to remove. In the vertical freezer, the ingredients get completely mixed; however, the freezing area is fairly small so that freezing takes longer, and less beating action results in a smaller finished volume.

Strict laws govern the production and sale of ice cream. Freezer systems and machines for portioning and packaging must meet high standards of hygiene.

2.4 Kitchenware: Pots and Pans

Pots and pans can be made of various materials. They all have advantages and disadvantages, described below. The materials themselves are described in section 2.4.1. Figure 2-35 shows examples of pots and pans made from these materials.

Copper (tinned)

Advantages:

- Food does not burn easily as a result of sticking at the bottom of the pan
- Good heat conduction

Disadvantages:

- Cleaning is labor-intensive
- High maintenance cost (replacing the linings)
- Acids can affect the material
- The lining can affect the taste of the food

Stainless Steel

Advantages:

- Easy to clean
- Little maintenance
- The color of the food does not change during cooking
- No adverse influence on the taste of the food

Disadvantages:

- Food sticks on the bottom easily if it is not stirred
- Poor heat conduction

Steel

Steel is used only for oven trays, baking dishes, grills, and frying pans.

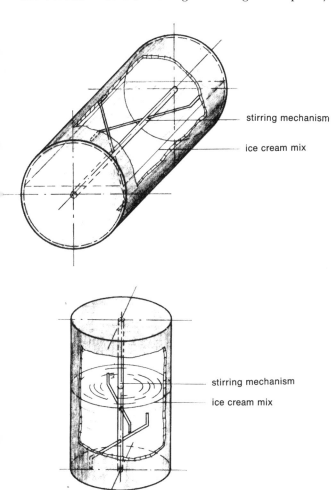

Figure 2-34. Ice cream freezers. *Top:* Horizontal ice cream freezer. *Bottom:* Vertical ice cream freezer.

Advantages:

- Suitable for coloring fried foods (sauté pans)
- Can stand a lot of heat

Disadvantages:

- Rust
- Can affect the taste of the food

Nonstick Materials

Advantages:

- Foods can be fried without using fat or butter
- Food does not stick to the pans
- Material does not affect the taste of the food

Disadvantages:

- The material can scratch easily, especially in commercial use

Aluminum

Advantages:

- Lightweight
- Inexpensive

Disadvantages:

- Aluminum can affect the color and taste of food
- The material is not very strong and can be dented easily
- Handles break off easily

Figure 2-35. Pots and pans: (1) omelet pan, of stainless steel, steel or nonstick material, for sautéing and pan-frying; (2) sauteuse, of copper or stainless steel, for glazing, sautéing, stewing; (3) grill pan, of stainless steel, for grilling; (4) stewing pot, of steel, copper, or aluminum, for braising and stewing chopped foods; (5) sautoir, of steel, copper, or aluminum, for pan-frying and sautéing small pieces of food; (6) rondeau, of steel, copper, or aluminum, for frying, stewing, and braising; (7) and (8) kettles, for making stocks and soups; (9) roasting pan; (10) stewing pan; (11) and (12) bains-marie (water baths); (13) fish kettle.

2.4.1 *Materials for the Manufacture of Kitchenware*

Materials for foodservice equipment should be appropriate for the specific use. The materials must meet certain minimum requirements as established by the Joint Committee on Food Equipment Standards:

> Only such materials shall be used on the construction of foodservice equipment/or appurtenances, as will withstand normal wear, penetration of vermin, the corrosive action of foods or beverages, cleaning compounds and such other elements as may be found in the use environments and will not impart an odor, color, or taste to the food

The basic materials most commonly used in the manufacture of today's equipment are either ferrous, such as iron or steel, or nonferrous, such as aluminum or fiberglass. The material selected will affect the durability, the maintenance, the appearance, the weight, the sanitation, and the cost of the equipment.

Aluminum

Aluminum is a lightweight metal that is less expensive than other materials. It has high thermal and electrical conductivity and is relatively easy to clean. It is used for steam-jacketed kettles, food carts, cooking and baking pans, trays, and utensils.

Foods with high acid and/or alkali content attack pure aluminum. The discoloration in the metal is easily removed with fine steel wool or an aluminum cleaner. Copper scouring pads will scratch aluminum and should not be used. The surface of aluminum can be treated to be more resistant to corrosion, discoloration, and marring. This treatment is called anodizing. Anodized aluminum is lightweight and durable, and it is suitable for portable equipment, such as carts, trucks, dollies, and for storage shelves and cabinets.

Cast Iron

Cast iron is used for large pieces of equipment such as ranges and ovens. It is also used for griddles, Dutch ovens, and frypans. It conducts heat very well, but cast-iron pans are heavy and difficult to clean.

Copper

Copper kitchenware was very popular in the kitchens of long ago. Even today copper-clad kitchenware is used both in the home and in institutional kitchens. Traditional cooks have been reluctant to give up their shining copper kitchenware because of its high conductivity, its attractive appearance, and its resistance to corrosion. Copper-clad cooking utensils must be lined with stainless steel or aluminum to prevent reactions of foodstuffs with the copper. The high initial costs, the heavy weight, the cost of replacing the linings, and the maintenance costs have limited the use of copper-clad utensils in today's institutional kitchens. These utensils are frequently used for display cooking and decorative purposes.

Glass, Porcelain, and Ceramics

These have limited use for commercial kitchen equipment because they are breakable. They are often used as protective linings in equipment to prevent absorption of odors and flavors and metallic contamination. Glass is hard and resistant to acids and very high temperatures. The materials are easily cleaned and attractive.

Silver

Silver is a precious metal, and its cost makes it prohibitive for use in commercial foodservice. Silver plate is also costly; however, it is occasionally used for flatware, such as knives, forks, spoons, and for hollowware including coffee servers, teapots, pitchers, and sugar bowls. These items, often referred to as "hotel silver," are covered with a thick layer of silver plating.

Stainless Steel

Stainless steel is a noncorrosive metal that is used more extensively than any other in the foodservice industry. Alloys of iron, nickel, and chromium are combined with steel and used for the manufacture of all kinds of equipment. Manufacturers may use different trade names, but stainless steel is most known in foodservice. It is made of approximately 70 percent steel, 20 percent chrome, and 10 percent nickel. Manufacturers may vary the formula slightly, but the important elements of the alloys are very similar.

Stainless steel has many outstanding qualities that make its use important in foodservice. Its strength, attractive appearance, permanence, smooth, hard surface, and high weldability make it particularly suitable for fabricated equipment, serving counters, heavy-duty equipment, tables, and machines. It is also used for kitchen utensils, pans, inserts for serving counters, and tableware. Pans made of polished stainless steel are not recommended for certain uses, such as the preparation of omelets, as the food tends to stick to the fine pores of the metal. Other important features of stainless steel are its resistance to stain, scratches, and corrosion, its ease of cleaning, and the availability of different finishes, ranging from dull to bright. It is resistant to any chemical reactions with foodstuffs and may be used for all food preparation processes at any temperature. These characteristics are particularly significant for the foodservice industry, where sanitation and safety are of utmost importance.

Plastics

Plastics are lightweight and have only limited use in the kitchen. There are two main groups: thermosetting and thermoplastic. The former is harder and more resistant to heat; the latter, softer and less heat resistant. At temperatures between 175° and 210°F (82° and 99°C), plastic tends to lose its shape and may even melt. Plastics are most useful for storage and in the *garde-manger*. Since the material is fairly soft, it should not be cleaned with scouring products. Kitchen utensils made of hard metals should not be used with plastics, or the plastics will be scratched.

2.5 Kitchen Utensils

Materials recommended for the following accessories are stainless steel, aluminum, wood, and plastic (or as required for the tool); materials to be avoided are copper and bronze. Figures 2-36 and 2-37 show examples of various kitchen utensils.

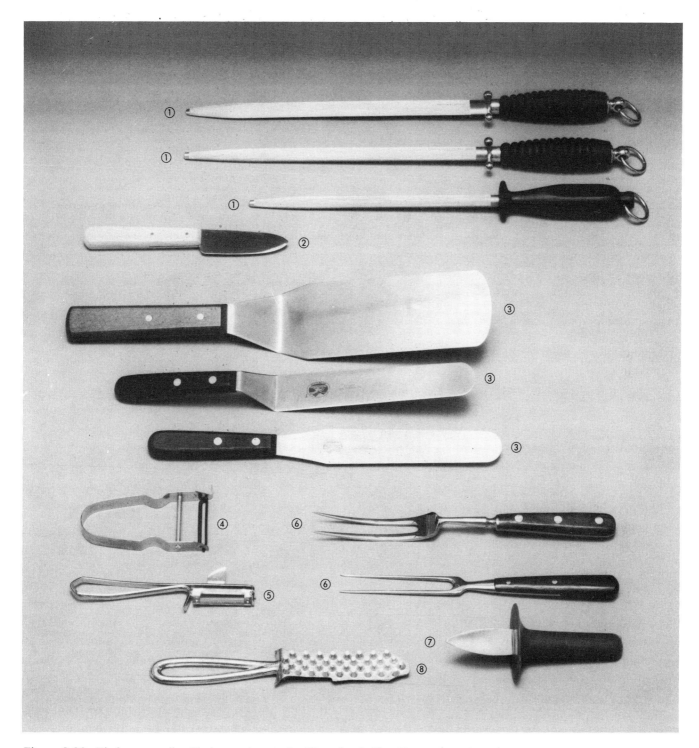

Figure 2-36. Kitchen utensils: (1) sharpening steels; (2) paring knife; (3) spatulas; (4) peeler; (5) asparagus peeler; (6) meat forks; (7) oyster knife; (8) fish scaler.

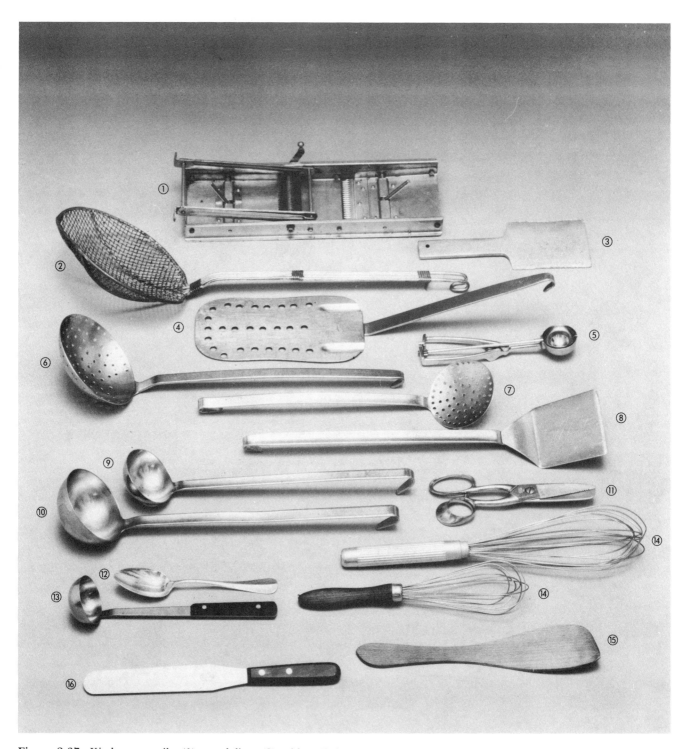

Figure 2-37. Kitchen utensils: (1) mandoline; (2) spider; (3) beater; (4) fish spatula; (5) ice cream scoop; (6) and (7) skimmers; (8) frying spatula; (9) and (10) ladles; (11) fish shears; (12) serving spoon; (13) sauce ladle; (14) whisk; (15) wooden spatula; (16) metal spatula.

- Apple corers
- Bains-marie
- Baking trays
- Bone saws
- Boning knives
- Bread knives
- Bread slicers
- Brushes
- Butcher knives
- Can openers
- Carving knives
- Cheesecloth
- Cheese servers
- Cherry pitters
- China caps
- Choppers
- Citrus presses
- Clam knives
- Cleavers
- Colanders
- Container and pan lids
- Cookie cutters
- Cutlet bats
- Cutting boards
- Deep-frying baskets
- Deep-frying pans
- Dough cutters
- Dressing needles
- Egg slicers
- Fillet knives
- Fish and sausage forks
- Fish cutters
- Fish kettles
- Fish servers
- Flour brushes
- Flour scoops
- Fluting knives
- French knives
- Fruit knives
- Frying ladles
- Frypans
- Funnels
- Garlic presses
- Graters
- Hors d'oeuvre cutters

- Ice cream scoops
- Juice extractors
- Ladles
- Larding needles
- Lemon zesters
- Mallets
- Mandolines (vegetable slicers)
- Measuring cups
- Measuring spoons
- Meat forks
- Meat hooks
- Meat saws
- Meat trays
- Melon ballers
- Mixing bowls
- Mold pans
- Mortars
- Nutmeg graters
- Nozzles
- Olive tongs
- Omelet pans
- Oyster knives
- Paring knives
- Pasta makers
- Paste molds
- Pastry bags
- Pastry knives
- Pitchers
- Poultry shears
- Pudding pans
- Ravioli boards
- Roasting and stewing pots
- Roasting pans
- Roasting shovels
- Rolling pins
- Sauce ladles
- Saucepans with handles
- Sauce pots, shallow and deep
- Sauté pans
- Scales: ingredient, portion
- Serrated knives
- Sharpening steels
- Sieves
- Skimmers
- Spatulas (wooden, metal, and plastic)

- Spice containers
- Spider (wire mesh skimmer for deep frying)
- Springform pans
- Stockpots
- Storage bins and containers
- Strainers
- Sugar sprinklers

- Thermometers: candy, meat
- Truffle cutters
- Trussing needles
- Vegetable peelers
- Whips
- Whisks

Chapter 3
Foods

All phases of marketing, the composition, and the method of handling materials used in the various fields of foodservice by the manager or dietitian, the chef or the cook, and the buyer are discussed in this chapter. The various categories of food will differ in their standards, grades, market forms (fresh, frozen, dehydrated, smoked, canned), units of purchase, costs, storage requirements, and federal and legal regulations. These differences must be known by those responsible for the purchase and preparation of food. The basic principles of the food laws and of sanitation are explained in chapter 1.

There are five main food groups:

- Seafood, meats, and poultry
- Eggs and dairy products
- Edible fats and oils (animal and vegetable)
- Grains, fruits, and vegetables
- Beverages

3.1 Purchasing

Purchasing refers to the task of obtaining the necessary goods with the right quality and in the right quantity at the right time, in the right place, and at the most economical price. With purchasing so defined, and with the aim of bringing about a noticeable cost saving, while at the same time providing the best possible service, careful supervision of the most important elements of the purchasing function can be achieved. (See figure 3-1.)

3.1.1 *Control of the Requirements*

The two extremes that must be avoided in purchasing are the "hand-to-mouth" method, or emergency buying, and buying excessive quantities of goods. Huge stocks of rarely used goods increase operating costs through storage costs (rent, interest, depreciation) and through losses caused by waste and theft. These costs can exceed any savings achieved by purchasing large quantities of one item.

The control of the requirements must be based upon three premises:

- Purchase of the food at the right time
- Purchase of the right kind and quantity of food for the intended use
- Purchase of the food at the right price

3.1.2 *Obtaining the Merchandise at the Right Time*

Planning the requirements in relation to time of need necessitates asking the following questions: What inventory level should be established as the reorder point? What security margin is required? This margin is calculated by determining the maximum number of days a delivery could be delayed. This number is multiplied by the maximum number of units required per day. For example, if the deliveries might be delayed for as many as five days and four cases of the specific item are used each day, the security margin required would be twenty cases. Available storage space will influence the inventory level for which reordering is necessary. Therefore, the maximum quantity that can

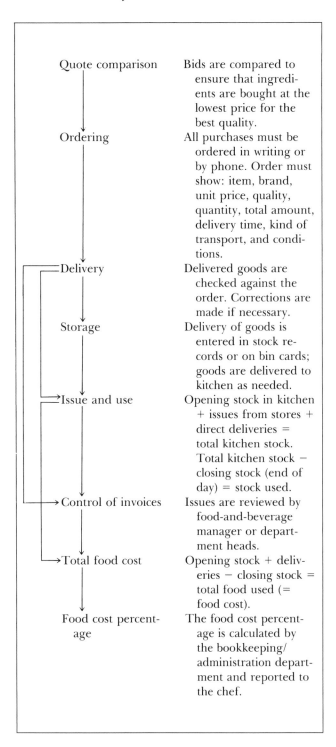

Quote comparison	Bids are compared to ensure that ingredients are bought at the lowest price for the best quality.
Ordering	All purchases must be ordered in writing or by phone. Order must show: item, brand, unit price, quality, quantity, total amount, delivery time, kind of transport, and conditions.
Delivery	Delivered goods are checked against the order. Corrections are made if necessary.
Storage	Delivery of goods is entered in stock records or on bin cards; goods are delivered to kitchen as needed.
Issue and use	Opening stock in kitchen + issues from stores + direct deliveries = total kitchen stock. Total kitchen stock − closing stock (end of day) = stock used.
Control of invoices	Issues are reviewed by food-and-beverage manager or department heads.
Total food cost	Opening stock + deliveries − closing stock = total food used (= food cost).
Food cost percentage	The food cost percentage is calculated by the bookkeeping/ administration department and reported to the chef.

be stored, the average consumption over a given period of time, and the margin of safety must be known for every product used. After this information is determined, a reordering cycle can be calculated for each product.

3.1.3 *Purchasing at the Right Price*

In the foodservice industry, the price at the point of delivery is the critical factor. The purchasing calculation is, therefore, greatly affected by the services provided by the supplier. Transportation costs (including insurance), warehouse charges, and interest and bank charges must be added to the cost of the goods. If the goods are purchased directly from the supplier, then the transport costs are one's own responsibility and usually have to be paid in cash. If the supplier gives credit, then this represents a saving in interest and should not be underestimated. If one transports the goods oneself, then the cost of fuel, auto insurance, and depreciation costs of the vehicle must be considered in calculating the cost per mile. The time involved (wages) and the risk of losing the goods are not included in the calculation. The "cheap" supplier is, therefore, not always the most favorable supplier, nor necessarily the one representing the best value for money.

In order to achieve optimal supply, it is best to use the "ABC analysis." The most important article in terms of turnover is placed first on the list of all articles that are purchased. The second most important article takes the second place, and so on until a list of all articles that are consumed or sold is complete. The list is then divided into three groups (A, B, and C). Group A contains the first 10 percent of the listed articles, group B the next 20 percent, and group C the remainder.

If the percentage share of each article of the overall

Figure 3-1. Purchasing control. Purchased items must be checked and overseen from the moment they are delivered until they are served or otherwise disposed of. Responsibility for purchasing control falls to the manager/owner in a small restaurant, to the chef and the manager/owner in a medium-sized restaurant, and to the food-and-beverage manager in a large restaurant.

turnover is added, you obtain an extremely interesting and informative purchasing aid. For example, you discover that 50 percent of total turnover is accounted for by 10 percent of all the articles, or that 20 percent of all the articles makes up the last percentage point of turnover. "Optimal supply" seen in the light of the "ABC analysis" becomes "optimal supply for the storeroom or warehouse." The quantity ordered of each article necessary for optimal supply of the storeroom is fixed as a function of the purchase price, the requirement over a given period of time, the transport, warehousing, storage costs, and the bank charges. In this way, the optimal quantity to be ordered can be fixed.

3.1.4 *Maintaining an Analysis of the Various Markets*

A knowledge of the market is increasingly important today, not only among the prospective clients, but also the market where the goods are obtained. Only profound knowledge of these markets can protect one from losses. Good suppliers provide their clients with reliable, objective information, and not just brand advertising.

3.1.5 *Supervision of the Ordering of Goods*

Purchasing is an important and challenging function. The buyer for an institution must be knowledgeable about marketing. He must know the kinds and forms of foods available for the specific need, the quantities required, the standards of foods, and market trends, and he must have a knowledge of contracts and their legal requirements. The buyer must be well qualified for the position. He must maintain a high standard of ethics with companies and their sales representatives. Very often it is the director or the manager of the foodservice who assumes responsibility for purchasing certain items such as wine, spirits, and meat. What purchasing alternatives exist? It is important that the buyer not be influenced by cheap prices or other decoys. Merchandise with guaranteed quality (particularly important in the cases of wines and meat), financial soundness, good and dependable service, and sufficient capacity on the part of the supplier increase

the quantitative and qualitative rating the supplier receives when various firms are under consideration. The most important criterion is the quality of the goods. The prices and conditions should be of only secondary importance. The terms of delivery and of payment are also important when making a choice of suppliers. Buying from a wide variety of sources (many suppliers, many small deliveries) in the long run overworks the purchasing office and leads to many time-consuming deliveries of single articles.

3.1.6 *Control of Deliveries*

The acceptance of merchandise (control of deliveries) consists of checking products at entry and storing them or transferring them to the appropriate section of the establishment. First of all, one verifies that an order was made out for the goods that have been delivered and that the delivery conforms with the order in terms of products and quantity. Once the delivery note has been signed, the inventory card must be completed. It is then possible to check the inventory of any product in stock in the storeroom.

3.1.7 *Control of Quality and Quantity*

The checking of quality in the food trade is normally possible only when the merchandise is being used. For this reason, signing the delivery note does not prejudice subsequent claims on a delivery that was not in order. It should be remembered, however, that when a complaint is made, a sample of the objectionable merchandise should accompany the complaint, so that the claim for compensation can be documented. It is quite evident that such an extensive purchasing organization is not suitable for every establishment. Nevertheless, it does seem that in this particular field improvements are necessary for a number of establishments.

The quantities of food to be prepared must be checked against the recipe and a quantity table, which should be clearly displayed in every kitchen. Accurate scales are needed in all departments for exact portion control. The menu plans will also aid in determining the quantities of food to be prepared. (See chapter 5.)

When these controls are used, there will be a minimum of leftovers.

3.1.8 *Control of the Losses*

Losses are caused by poor purchasing practices as related to quality and quantity controls and inadequate supervision. Usually the accounting department identifies the losses when the monthly or annual gross profit is calculated. To avoid losses, recheck the calculation and make a daily calculation of the kitchen's gross profit.

3.1.9 *Stock Control*

The total of food used equals the kitchen food cost. Food used can be either storeroom issues or direct purchases (items delivered directly to the kitchen).

Food should only be issued from the storeroom on requisition, which is a completed docket, signed by the responsible person. Those responsible for food-and-beverage control should make sure that no foods are issued without a signed requisition.

The food/stores requisition should have the following details:

- Date
- Article(s)
- Quantity
- Department or function
- Signature of the person making the requisition

Kitchen Control

Daily food-cost control is important. (See figure 3-2.) By keeping only very small stocks in the kitchens, it is not difficult to work out the daily amount of food used (daily food cost), if issues are made daily from the storeroom and a stocktaking is done at the end of each day. Food cost is part of turnover, and it can be expressed as a percentage of the turnover, because food cost is part of the selling price.

Here is an example of the food cost over three days:

first day:	45%
second day:	50%
third day:	55%
	150%

150/3 = 50 percent average daily food cost

Kitchen Control on 31-08-1988

Food Item	Remark	Quantity				Value of Food Used (food cost)		
		In Stock Yesterday	+ Issued Today	− In Stock Now	= Food Used	Unit Price	Subtotal	Total
Artichoke hearts		000	16	000	16	1.25	20.—	
Artichoke bottoms		1	14	5	10	1.30	13.—	
							33.—	33.—
Beets, sliced		10	10	8	12	.48	5.76	
Beets, julienne		8	12	2	18	.51	9.18	
							14.94	14.94

Figure 3-2. Kitchen control form.

The following is true of this type of food-cost control:

- It is particularly suitable for large businesses
- It can be done daily and/or weekly
- It allows daily/weekly control with percentages
- It can be broken up into various food categories, such as fish, vegetables, meat, poultry, and dairy.

Refer to figure 3-3 for sample storeroom bookkeeping.

3.1.10 Basic Principles of Storage

The following guidelines apply to dry goods, cold storage, and deep-freeze.

Dry-goods Storeroom

- Stores must not be placed on the floor; otherwise the floor of the dry-goods storeroom cannot be properly cleaned
- Dry goods must not be stored near pipes or drains
- Soaps, detergents, disinfectants, and the like

must be stored in a separate room away from foodstuffs

- Contents of opened cartons must be placed on shelves
- The dry-goods storeroom must be kept dry and properly ventilated
- The storeroom must be cleaned at regular intervals
- Stock rotation (first in—first out) must be maintained
- Goods that are most frequently used should be placed as near as possible to the entrance/exit of the storeroom
- Heavy articles should be placed on lower shelves

Cold Storage

- Products that have been taken out of their original cartons should be labeled to be easily identified
- Wrapped/packed foodstuffs should not be stored in water or ice
- The coolroom thermometer should be checked

Article: _Pineapple, can 1/1_   Quality: _fancy_   Brand: _Golden Sun_

Storeroom: _front_   Shelf: _24_   Minimum: _2 ¢_   Max.: _20 ¢_

Supplier: _Johnson & Co., Boston_   Ordering period/time: _variable_

Year: January February March April May June July August September October November December   Sheet:
_1988_   _1_

| Date | No. | Supplier or Receiver | Quantity In/Out | | | Price | Received | Issued | Balance Value |
			In	Issued	Balance				
1-1		Balance			000	$3.—			000
30-1	107	Johnson Ltd.			100	$3.—			$300.—
31-1		Rest. A		10	90			$30.—	$270.—
31-1		Closing Stock			90				$270.—
		January							

Figure 3-3. Storeroom bookkeeping.

frequently; recommended storage temperatures are:

> *meat and meat products:* 32° to 35°F (0° to 2°C)
> *fish and crustaceans on ice:* 30°F (−1°C)
> *dairy products and eggs:* 33° to 38°F (1° to 3°C)
> *fruits and vegetables:* 38° to 44°F (3° to 6°C)

- When storing large pieces of meat and other large food items, allow for air circulation around them; large pieces of meat should be hung
- No food should be placed near or on the floor
- Coolrooms should be cleaned thoroughly at regular intervals
- All food should be issued on rotation basis, first in—first out
- Vegetables and fruits should be checked daily for rot
- Dairy produce should not be stored in the same coolroom with fish and crustaceans
- A coolroom should be subjected to regular maintenance, which means that it will be checked and kept in good order to avoid breakdowns and poor performance

Deep-freeze Storage

- Frozen foods should be stored at 0°F (−18°C)
- Frozen foods must be properly wrapped for storage
- Avoid accumulation of ice on the freezing element in the freezer
- Avoid opening the freezer doors more than necessary; issue frozen foods at set times only, except if sudden shortages occur in the kitchen(s) or production departments, of course
- The freezer (walk-in, chest, or standing model) must be emptied and cleaned out thoroughly at regular intervals; make sure the frozen food does not thaw out completely while the freezer is being cleaned
- Apply the rule "first in—first out" when issuing frozen foods from frozen storage; frozen foods do not keep forever, and the quality deteriorates after a time
- Put date labels on frozen foods kept in storage
- Keep floor and racks in the freezer tidy and clean

- Have a maintenance contract for the freezer (motor, circulation, condenser), to prevent breakdowns

3.2 Seafood—*Poissons, Fruits de mer*

Fish, as well as meat and poultry, is used in large quantities in every foodservice operation. It has high nutritional value and is satisfying when prepared properly. Fish is expensive, and a great deal of care is necessary in appropriate preparation and usage.

Fish are divided into two main groups: freshwater fish and saltwater fish. Both groups are then broken down into species.

There are typical signs of good quality in fish. Fresh fish have bright clear eyes, dark red gills that are free from odor or slime, bright-colored scales that adhere tightly to the skin, and firm flesh that is free from objectionable odors. Fish usually have less flavor immediately preceding and following the spawning period.

3.2.1 *Preservation*

Fresh seafood deteriorates rapidly. These procedures should be followed immediately after seafood is received:

- Pack in ice or store in a refrigerator at 35° to 40°F (2° to 5°C)
- Store in the original moisture-proof wrapper
- Keep fish refrigerated for no longer than one or two days before cooking

Specialized factories in fishing areas conserve fish by the following methods:

- *Marinating:* herrings
- *Smoking:* eel, herrings, salmon, plaice, sprats
- *Salting:* herring, sardines, cod
- *Freezing:* most kinds of fish
- *Drying:* cod, mackerel

Fish tanks used to store live fish require water that is properly circulated and oxygenated. The temperature of the water should be constant at 40° to 55°F (5° to 13°C). The fish tank must be kept clean.

Fresh fish (not previously frozen) must always be kept packed in ice.

3.2.2 *Freshwater Fish*—Poissons d'eau douce

Freshwater fish include eel, perch, pike, grayling, trout, salmon, and sturgeon, among others.

Eel—*Anguille*

Figure 3-4. Eel—*Anguille.*

Origin and occurrence: The eel, a migratory fish, leaves the sea when young and heads for freshwater, where it grows to a maximum length of 5 feet. It then returns to the sea for spawning. It stays there and may grow to a length of 8 feet. (See figure 3-4.)

Species and description: Although the eel is a snakelike fish, it is not related to other snakelike marine creatures, the lamprey, or the conger eel. A related fish is the Moray eel. The slime in its mouth is poisonous, so its bite should be avoided, but the meat tastes like eel and is often used smoked or for bouillabaisse.

Quality characteristics: The fat content of eel is high, and therefore, it is less easy to digest. Medium-sized eels have a pleasant taste. Eels from ponds have an undesirable taste; they should be kept in a fish tank with flowing water before killing.

Usage: The eel should be skinned before preparation. (See chapter 7.) Fresh eel may be used for eel soup or stew, or it may be pan-fried, deep-fried, marinated, or served cold in aspic. Smoked eels are also available.

Perch—*Perche*

Origin and occurrence: The name *perch* is used for a variety of freshwater and saltwater fish; the fish described here are the freshwater European *Perca flu-*

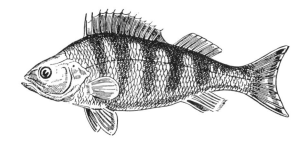

Figure 3-5. European perch—*Perche.*

viatilis and the closely related American *Perca flaviscens.*

Species and description: The European perch grows to a length of between 10 and 15 inches and can weigh over 2 pounds. Its head is conical, its skin is very scaly, and it has spiny fins. The fins on the back are a violet color, while those on the belly are reddish yellow. The back is dark green with black vertical stripes. There is a characteristic dark spot immediately behind the first dorsal fin. (See figure 3-5.) American perch is similar, but the coloring may be different.

Quality characteristics: When cooked, the flesh is firm and white and has a delicate flavor.

Usage: Small perch are usually pan-fried or deep-fried and served whole. Larger perch are filleted and prepared in various ways—steamed, deep-fried, pan-fried with lemon or with almonds, or poached.

Pike Perch—*Sandre*

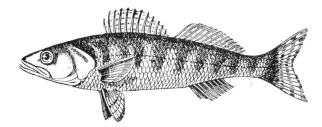

Figure 3-6. Pike perch—*Sandre.*

Origin and occurrence: Although pike perch originated in eastern Europe, it now flourishes in several rivers throughout Europe. The fish requires water with a very low salt content. It is found in Austria and in Lake Balaton in Hungary, where it is called *Fogosch.*

Species and description: The pike perch belongs to the perch family. It is quite thin and ranges from 15 to 20 inches in length, although some 30-inch fish have been reported. Its back is dark green with shiny white sides. (See figure 3-6.)

Quality characteristics: The pike perch spawns between April and July. Its flesh is white, soft and delicate, juicy and tasty. Pike perch is better fresh than frozen, although there is more of the latter on the market, since it is imported from eastern Europe.

Usage: All of the basic preparation methods can be used without affecting the taste.

Pike—*Brochet*

Figure 3-7. Pike—*Brochet.*

Origin and occurrence: Pike is found in rivers, lakes, and large ponds.

Species and description: Pike is a noble fish, a tough hunter, and, for the most part, feeds on smaller fish. It sometimes reaches a length of 4 feet and a weight of 25 pounds. The body is long and thin and the head wide and flat. One-year-old fish are called *jacks.* (See figure 3-7.)

Quality characteristics: The flesh of a pike is tender and tasty and at its best when the fish is two years old and weighs 4 to 6 pounds. Older pike are less tender, and their flesh is full of fine needlelike bones.

Usage: Pike weighing less than 1 pound is usually pan-fried. Otherwise, it should be steamed, poached, baked, or spit-roasted to preserve the delicacy of the fish. The flesh of older pike is generally used for fish stuffing.

Grayling—*Ombre*

Origin and occurrence: A member of the salmon family, grayling are found in rivers and streams throughout the northern hemisphere.

Species and description: Grayling resemble trout, and

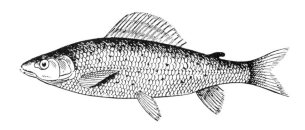

Figure 3-8. Grayling—*Ombre.*

they may reach lengths of 16 inches. (See figure 3-8.)

Quality characteristics: The flesh of the grayling is very delicate and moist and has the flavor of thyme.

Usage: For pan-frying, steaming, poaching, and grilling.

Golden Trout (Saibling)—*Omble chevalier*

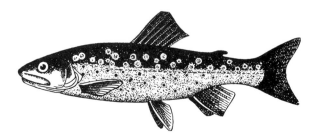

Figure 3-9. Golden trout—*Omble chevalier.*

Origin and occurrence: Several varieties of this salmon are found in lakes north of the Alps, in lakes throughout northern Europe, and in North America.

Species and description: The golden trout may not be golden. The colors vary according to age, sex, and region. (See figure 3-9.)

Quality characteristics: The flesh of golden trout is delicious, and it is popular on many menus.

Usage: Golden trout is usually prepared by the same methods used for preparing river trout; however, methods of preparation vary in different regions.

Lake Trout—*Truite de lac*

Origin and occurrence: Lake trout actually from lakes are a variety of river trout. The trout found in Arctic seas is referred to as "sea trout."

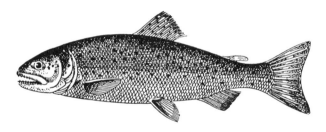

Figure 3-10. Lake trout—*Truite de lac.*

Species and description: A member of the salmon family, this species is a migrating fish that swims up rivers in order to spawn. The fish grows up to 4 feet in length; its back is a gray-blue to black color and is covered with many light yellow and red spots. (See figure 3-10.)

Quality characteristics: Lake trout that are neither too old nor too large have flesh that is relatively easy to digest.

Usage: The fish is best when poached, pan-fried (*à la meunière*), or grilled.

Rainbow Trout—*Truite arc-en-ciel*

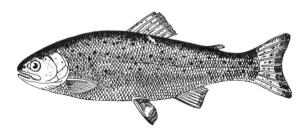

Figure 3-11. Rainbow trout—*Truite arc-en-ciel.*

Origin and occurrence: The rainbow trout, a member of the salmon family, is a native of the Pacific slope of the Sierras, from California to Alaska, and is now found throughout the United States and Europe. It prefers clear, cool, unpolluted water. Because of its voracity and resistance to illnesses (for example, furuncles), it has established itself among many fish breeders.

Species and description: Wild rainbow trout grow up to 2 feet in length. They normally come from breeders in a size suitable for one portion. The rainbow trout is easily identified by the reddish band or rainbow that runs from head to tail on each side of the fish. The back dorsal fin and the tail are covered with a multitude of black spots. The brightness of color will vary depending on the environmental and feeding conditions. (See figure 3-11.)

Quality characteristics: The quality of the flesh depends upon the type of food consumed by the fish. All types of trout are noble fish and are known for their excellent eating quality.

Usage: The fish should be cooked immediately after killing and dressing. The forms of preparation are: poaching, deep-frying, and pan-frying (*à la meunière*).

River Trout (Brown Trout)—*Truite de rivière*

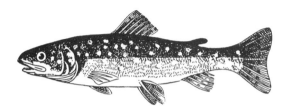

Figure 3-12. River trout—*Truite de rivière.*

Origin and occurrence: River trout are found in streams and rivers throughout the northern hemisphere. They live in cold, clear, fast-flowing water. River trout can become sea trout if they have an opportunity to migrate out to sea.

Species and description: River trout can grow to a length of 15 inches and reach a weight of 6½ pounds. Their color changes according to that of their surroundings. The skin is mostly spotted, and the back is olive green to black. The scales are very small. Not only does the color adapt itself to the local surroundings, but also to the quality of the flesh. This is the reason the fish is given different names, for example, wood trout, mountain trout, or stone trout. They all belong to the same species. (See figure 3-12.)

Quality characteristics: Stone and mountain trout have a delicate, white, easily digestible flesh. However, any trout that feed on the bottom of shallow water have a matt white or slightly reddish flesh characterized by a mossy taste.

Usage: Live trout are especially good for poaching. Trout that have been stored are better pan-fried (*à la meunière*).

Salmon—*Saumon*

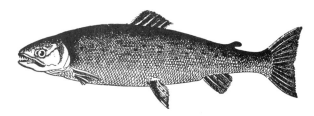

Figure 3-13. Salmon—*Saumon.*

Origin and occurrence: The fish industry divides salmon into four groups: river salmon, Norwegian and Swedish salmon, silver salmon, and American salmon. *River salmon* come from the Rhine, the Loire, and Scottish and Icelandic rivers. Rhine and Loire salmon are highly appreciated for their fine pink flesh and good taste. In recent years these types of salmon have become increasingly rare because of industrial pollution. Today the catch is insignificant. *Norwegian and Swedish salmon* are available on the market from spring until autumn. *Silver salmon* (Bornholm salmon) come from the Baltic and are caught year-round. *American salmon* (real salmon) are found from Alaska to California. There are five species of Pacific salmon that live in North American waters. They are as follows (information taken from *Food Fish Facts No. 8,* Chicago: National Marine Fisheries Service):

- *Chinook salmon or king salmon* are the largest of the Pacific salmon, averaging 20 pounds. They have a blue-green back marked with dark spots and silvery sides. The flesh, rich in oils, ranges from dark salmon red to white in color. It breaks into large flakes and is especially good in salads.
- *Chum salmon* or *keta* grow to an average length of 3 feet and weigh about 10 pounds. They are found in the Sacramento River and in Puget Sound. The flesh has less color and less oil than other species.
- *Coho or silver salmon*, a favorite with sportsmen, weigh from 6 to 12 pounds and are 2 to 3 feet in

length. Coho are abundant in Alaska and Puget Sound. The flesh is a deep salmon color and breaks into large flakes when cooked.
- *Pink or humpback salmon*, common to Alaska, are found as far south as Oregon and California. They range from 3 to 6 pounds in weight. The flesh is a pale pink. They are used in soups, entrées, and sandwiches.
- *Sockeye or red salmon* average about 2 feet in length and weigh between 3 and 5 pounds. The flesh is firm, rich in oil, and is a deep red in color. They are suitable for salads and cold entrées.

Atlantic salmon are found in North American waters from Maine to Labrador.

Species and description: The spawning period of the salmon lasts from October to December. In the spring the fish leave the sea and swim upstream to the river to spawn. In all but Pacific salmon, the fish then return to the sea. The flesh of fish going upstream to spawn is red and fatty, while that of fish returning to the sea after spawning is rather white and of poor quality. After spawning, Pacific salmon die from exhaustion or from fungus disease and thus create food for the young salmon. The young fish remain in the upper reaches of the rivers for 1 to 2 years and then migrate to the sea. Salmon are approximately 5 to 6 feet long and weigh 44 pounds. They have a longish round shape, a relatively small pointed head, a blue-green back, silvery sides with colored spots, and a shiny white belly. The male fish (milter) have a hook-shaped appendix on the lower jaw and are therefore called "hook salmon." They are preferred over the female fish. (See figure 3-13.)

Quality and characteristics: Fish weighing between 15 and 30 pounds are the best quality.

Usage: Fresh salmon is usually grilled or poached in a court bouillon. For *smoked salmon,* the fish is salted and then smoked when cold. It is cut into sides weighing 3 to 9 pounds, and it is packed in long hampers for shipment. On arrival, smoked salmon must be unpacked and hung. During the night, the cut sides should be laid on marble or stone. Smoked salmon should never be stored in the refrigerator, because it turns soft and can no longer be cut. North American packers ship enough *canned salmon* to provide 7 percent of the annual American fish consumption. All species are canned, but the bulk of the product is made from sockeye.

Salmon Trout—*Truite saumonée*

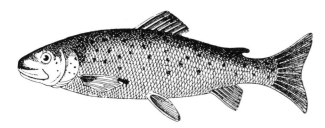

Figure 3-14. Salmon trout—*Truit saumonée.*

Origin and occurrence: This fish is a crustacean-feeding brown trout (lake trout or river trout) that has developed a pink flesh as a result of its diet. Salmon trout is found in rivers and lakes.
Species and description: The salmon trout grows to 2½ feet long and can weigh 17½ pounds. (See figure 3-14.)
Quality characteristics: The flesh is pink in hue and has a pleasant flavor.
Usage: Salmon trout is normally prepared like salmon, either poached in a court bouillon, grilled, or baked.

Whitefish—*Féra*

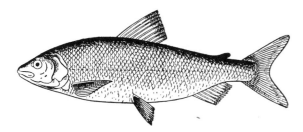

Figure 3-15. Whitefish—*Féra.*

Origin and occurrence: Almost all northern lakes contain whitefish.
Species and description: Whitefish can be grouped by size: large (mostly found near banks), medium, small, and dwarf. Whitefish belong to the salmon family, evident from the small fat fin at the tail end of the fish. (See figure 3-15.)
Quality characteristics: Whitefish have a white, tasty flesh that is rather dry.
Usage: The best way to prepare medium or large whitefish is pan-frying (*à la meunière*). Butter should be added to compensate for the lack of fat in the flesh. Small whitefish and dwarf whitefish are best deep-fried. They are also poached and smoked.

Burbot—*Lotte*

Figure 3-16. Burbot—*Lotte.*

Origin and occurrence: A member of the cod family, burbot is somewhat eel-shaped, with its scales embedded in a heavy skin, so it is usually skinned for preparation. The flesh is firm but oilier than other cod species.
Species and description: Burbot is the only freshwater member of the cod family. It occurs in northern waters in North America, Europe, and Asia. It is found in very deep water, except during spawning periods. (See figure 3-16.)
Quality characteristics: Its flesh is well suited for poaching. The liver of this fish is considered a delicacy by connoisseurs.
Usage: Fried or poached—*en matelote.*

Sturgeon—*Esturgeon*

Figure 3-17. Sturgeon—*Esturgeon.*

Origin and occurrence: The different variations of this fish include the sterlet and beluga, which are most frequently found in the Black and Caspian seas and in the rivers flowing into them.

Species and description: Sturgeon is a member of the cod family. The *sterlet,* a prize breed in Russia, measures up to 5 feet in length and can weigh a maximum of 330 pounds. The *osietr* grows up to 6 feet in length and weighs 440 pounds. The *beluga,* the largest fish in the sturgeon family, grows as large as 13 feet in length and weighs up to 3,000 pounds. The fish has a gray-blue back, silver-gray sides, and whitish belly. The mouth opens like a shovel and underneath are barbels. Since it is born in freshwater, it is considered a freshwater fish. The roe of the different types of sturgeon is used to make caviar. From the air bladder of the beluga is taken the isinglass, fish gelatin, which is used for binding cold dishes. The spinal marrow is called *vesiga,* which, after drying, is used to make Russian fish pies and pâtés. (See figure 3-17.)

Quality characteristics: The flesh has a good flavor.

Usage: Sturgeon is sold smoked, salted, and fresh. The main consumers are the Russians and those living in adjacent countries.

Caviar

Origin and occurrence: Caviar is the salted roe (fish eggs) of various species of the sturgeon family in the Black and Caspian seas. The roe is removed as soon as the fish is caught. It is prepared by removing the cellular tissue around the roe, pressing it through a hemp sieve, and salting the roe. Until 1953, the Russian town of Astrachan, on the Caspian Sea, was the center of the caviar trade. At that time, Iran withdrew the fishing concessions, which it had previously granted Russia, and set up its own trading organization in Bender Pehlevi.

Species and description: Caviar is classified according to the type of sturgeon:

- *Beluga* (*hausen*), the largest variety of sturgeon, produces up to 350 pounds of eggs. The silver-gray coarse caviar obtained from this fish is of first-class quality, and it is preferred in the West.

- *Schip* reaches a weight of 175 pounds and produces up to 25 pounds of excellent caviar.
- *Osietr* (the Russian name for sturgeon) weighs up to 440 pounds, but much larger specimens have been caught. It produces up to 45 pounds of eggs. This caviar is grayish to yellow in color. More of this caviar is produced in Iran and Russia than any other types. Mainly consumed in Russia, Osietr is seldom found in other markets.
- *Sevruga* comes from the smallest but most frequently found sturgeon, weighing between 25 and 120 pounds and producing 2½ to 12 pounds of caviar. The roe is fine textured and has an excellent flavor.
- *Botarga* is the so-called Ketarogen, which is not made from sturgeon, but from the roe of salmon, pike perch, grayling, and tuna. Botarga caviar is red and coarse. It is used for garnishing and for decorative purposes.

Quality characteristics: The larger the individual egg and the lighter its silver-gray color, the more valuable the caviar. The egg should be glassy, well rounded and dry, uniform in size and color, and it should have a mild taste that is neither salty nor bitter. Caviar spoils quickly, and for this reason it must be kept on ice. Caviar packed in cans should be refrigerated.

- *Malosal* caviar is only slightly salted and is considered a special delicacy, since the taste of salt is not evident. This caviar, which contains 3 to 4 percent salt, keeps for only a limited time.
- *Salt-barrel caviar* contains 10 to 12 percent salt. Although the salt prolongs the shelf life, it does lower the quality and affects the taste. This type of caviar is rare.
- *Pausnaya* is pressed caviar, lightly salted, packed in barrels. The eggs are not whole but pressed to a jamlike consistency.

Usage: The nutritional value of caviar is high because of its fat and protein content, but the main reason for its use is pure enjoyment. Caviar is served either in ice or over ice as an hors d'oeuvre. It may be used for garnishing, on toast, as a canapé, or in cold sauces. Caviar butter may be prepared by mixing five parts butter to one part caviar and forcing the mixture through a sieve. Salt-barrel caviar is the most suitable for this use.

Barbel—*Barbeau*

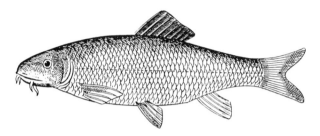

Figure 3-18. Barbel—*Barbeau.*

Origin and occurrence: The barbel lives near the bottom and the banks of European rivers.
Species and description: The barbel is related to the carp. It can grow up to 28 inches and weigh up to 9 pounds. The body is thin, and the back is an olive green color. (See figure 3-18.)
Quality characteristics: The full-flavored flesh ranks low in eating quality because it is very bony. The roe should not be eaten during the spawning period, from May to June.
Usage: This fish can be prepared in the same fashion as carp.

Carp—*Carpe*

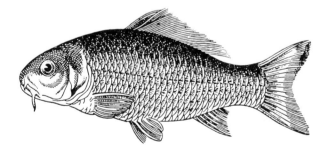

Figure 3-19. Carp—*Carpe.*

Origin and occurrence: A European fish that has been introduced all over North America, carp is found in running or stagnant water and in special breeding ponds.
Species and description: Carp can reach a length of over 3½ feet and weigh up to 33 pounds. (See figure 3-19.) There are pond and river varieties; the body of river carp is somewhat longer. The three types of pond carp are these:

- *Mirror carp* with large shiny scales scattered along the line running down the center of the sides of the fish
- *Scale carp* with regular scales
- *Leather carp*, which has no scales

Quality characteristics: The flesh is soft and easily digested and is at its best in winter. All pond carp should be kept in fresh-flowing water for some time before killing, to eliminate the muddy flavor. Medium-sized carp are best, especially mirror carp. The soft roe of carp (*Laitance de carpe*) is a delicacy.
Usage: Fresh carp is usually stewed or poached, but it may be baked, broiled, or fried, and it is used to a large extent to make gefilte fish.

Catfish

Origin and occurrence: North and South America produce millions of catfish. The largest species are found in the Amazon basin, but North American species can also grow to large sizes. They are found in lakes and rivers. In addition they are raised commercially on fish farms and are sold fresh and frozen.
Species and description: There are twenty-eight species of catfish in North American waters and several in South America. These include bullheads, all rather small fish about 1 pound, and the channel (3 pounds average), white (1 pound average), and blue catfish (30 pounds average). The color varies according to species, from nearly jet black to silvery blue to yellowish brown. Catfish have nasal and lower jaw barbels, the number varying with the species.
Quality characteristics: Blue, channel, and white catfish have firm white flesh and good flavor. The brown bullhead has pink to red flesh, and the yellow bullhead has yellowish flesh. All species are good to eat, but they require care in preparation, since they have

sharp spines on the fins. Follow the same procedure used to skin eels.

Usage: Dress and fillet the fish. Barbecue, basting with a good sauce; or bake or grill *en papillote;* or dip into cornmeal and pan-fry (the classic method).

Sheatfish (Wels)—*Silure*

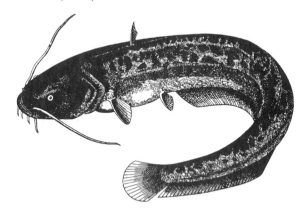

Figure 3-20. Sheatfish (wels)—*Silure.*

Origin and occurrence: This catfish, found in rivers and lakes of central Europe, is, next to the sturgeon, the largest river fish in Europe, weighing 300 to 400 pounds.

Species and description: This fish, frequently 10 feet in length, has a fat body, a flattened head with two long and four short barbels, and is brown in color. It lives in the bottom of rivers and lakes and feeds on fish, crabs, and frogs. It has even been known to eat waterbirds. (See figure 3-20.)

Quality characteristics: Young sheatfish have a good flavor.

Usage: Fillets may be sautéed, deep-fried, or stewed.

3.2.3 *Saltwater Fish*—Poissons de mer

Cod—*Cabillaud*

Origin and occurrence: Cod is found in Atlantic waters from Virginia to the Arctic but is most abundant in the Grand Banks, off Newfoundland. When dried, it is a *stockfish,* and when dried and salted, a *salted cod.*

Species and description: The cod has long been recog-

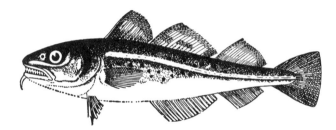

Figure 3-21. Cod—*Cabillaud.*

nized for its value as a food and as an important resource in world trade. An inveterate hunter, cod lives off other fish. It is also a fertile fish. Each female produces some nine million eggs over the spawning period. The cod has a strong, stubby head with protruding upper jaws and long barbels. The light-colored lateral line extending along the sides is a typical characteristic. It can reach a length of 5 feet. Young cod are called *scrod.* (See figure 3-21.)

Quality characteristics: Its flaky, grayish white flesh is rather fragile.

Usage: Fresh cod is usually boiled or poached. Dried or salted cod is soaked in water and then poached in a court bouillon, garnished with parsley and hard-cooked eggs, and served with a sauce. Cod is found on the market in fresh, frozen, and dried forms. Practically all of the fish portions and sticks on the market are produced from domestic and imported cod.

Haddock—*Aiglefin*

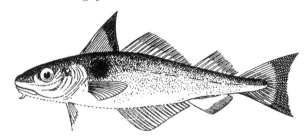

Figure 3-22. Haddock—*Aiglefin.*

Origin and occurrence: This member of the cod family lives in the North Atlantic and the North Sea.

Species and description: Haddock belongs to a large

group known as groundfish. The back is grayish brown, the belly white. Above the lateral fin, there is a black spot, and the line down the middle of both sides is jet black. (See figure 3-22.)

Quality characteristics: The flesh is white, tender, and firm, with a mild and pleasing flavor. It is rich in protein and low in fat.

Usage: It is suitable for stewing, sautéing, and deep-frying; for making fish salads, marinades, and for smoking.

Hake—*Colin* or *Merlu*

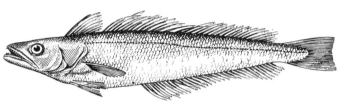

Figure 3-23. Hake—*Colin.*

Origin and occurrence: Hake is caught on both sides of the Atlantic Ocean and in the colder waters of the southern hemisphere.

Species and description: Hake is a thin fish with a pointed head. The lower jaw juts out somewhat. The back is gray-black with black spots. The sides are silvery white and have a black line running the length of the fish. Although hake do grow to over 3 feet in length, the commercial size is between 1½ and 2½ feet. (See figure 3-23.)

Quality characteristics: The flesh is fine and white and very sensitive to pressure; therefore, it should be covered with only a light layer of ice.

Usage: Hake may be prepared in several ways. The preferred method is to sauté thin slices of the fish. It is abundant and inexpensive, and, for this reason, it is often used in medium-sized establishments. Poached fillet of hake is also very good, as is braised hake with tomatoes or peppers.

Whiting—*Merlan*

Origin and occurrence: The whiting or silver hake is found between the Arctic Ocean and the Black Sea. It

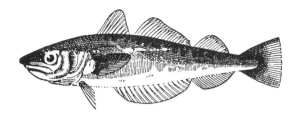

Figure 3-24. Whiting—*Merlan.*

is abundant on the continental shelf of eastern North America, from Newfoundland to Cape Hatteras.

Species and description: The whiting has two dorsal fins and one anal fin, while cod, haddock, and pollock have three dorsal and two anal fins. Although it can grow to 20 inches, it is rarely longer than 12 inches or heavier than 5 pounds. It is light colored with a black dot at the base of the lateral fin. It has a silvery line along its sides. (See figure 3-24.)

Quality characteristics: The flesh of whiting is tender, lean, and flaky. The fish is fragile and cannot tolerate the pressure of ice blocks.

Usage: Whiting adapt readily to poaching, steaming, deep-frying, sautéing, broiling, or baking. The flesh is also used in the manufacture of fish stuffings.

Anchovy—*Anchois*

Figure 3-25. Anchovy—*Anchois.*

Origin and occurrence: Anchovies are netted in the North Sea, the Atlantic, and along the Mediterranean coast, chiefly in winter.

Species and description: This small sea fish grows to a length of about 6 inches. Its projecting snout and large mouth distinguish it from the sardine. (See figure 3-25.)

Quality and characteristics: A good anchovy is selected by size. It has a pleasant, fresh, aromatic taste. Its flesh should be pink, without oil. Its freshness can be determined by the color of its back. It turns from a beautiful green when fresh to a dark greenish blue and then to almost black.

Usage: Anchovy fillets, anchovy rings, and paste are made from these fish. They can also be used for garnishes, sandwiches, and anchovy butter.

Herring—*Hareng*

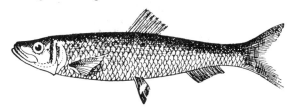

Figure 3-26. Herring—*Hareng*.

Origin and occurrence: The herring lives in large schools in the Arctic Ocean, in the North Atlantic as far south as the Bay of Biscay, and in the North Sea and the Baltic. When spawning, herring migrate to warmer waters, and it is during this period that they are caught.

Species and description: The herring can be 16 inches long. It is a thin fish with silver scales, a blue-gray back, bluish sides, and a shiny, silver-white belly. (See figure 3-26.) In Norway, cases have been reported in which herring have lived as long as fifteen years. The five main types of herring are:

- *Norwegian herring,* a large fish, usually over 12 inches long, that spawns in the spring and is caught year-round
- *Scottish herring,* caught from the beginning of the summer through the fall
- *Skagerrak herring,* caught in the fall and winter
- *Yarmouth herring,* caught from October to December
- *Iceland herring,* caught off the north of Iceland from July to September, the largest and fattest

Quality characteristics: The sea or fall herring is lean but flavorful. The coastal or spring herring is fat, but less desirable in taste. The following two groups of fish are distinguishable by age:

- *White* (*Matjes*) *herring* is the virgin herring in which the roe and the milt have not yet formed

(usually occur after two years). *Matjes* means "girl" in Dutch and, in the context of herring, indicates that the fish is not yet sexually mature.
- *Full herring* is herring that is caught with the milt and roe before spawning.

The herring is an especially valuable fish. Its price is low in relation to its high fat and protein content. The flesh of the fish is white and delicate.

Usage: Green (fresh) herrings are those herrings primarily suited for sautéing and grilling. The surplus herring catch finds its way to the fish processor, where it is preserved in many different ways. The well-known methods of preserving herrings are:

- *Bismarck herrings* have had the heads and bones removed, and the flesh with the skin still left on has been marinated in a mild vinegar solution seasoned with pepper, mustard seeds, bay leaves, and onions
- *Rollmops* are skinned and pickled fillets rolled in black pepper, paprika, onions, and pickles, put on wooden skewers, and placed in a mild vinegar solution
- *Fried herrings* are made from green herrings that have had the head and guts removed and have been placed in vinegar; fried rollmops are made in the same way, except they are rolled before frying
- *Bloaters or kippers* are salted and smoked herrings.

Sardine—*Sardine*

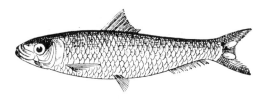

Figure 3-27. Sardine—*Sardine*.

Origin and occurrence: The name *sardine* probably originated from the fact that the tiny fish were first found around the island of Sardinia in the Mediterranean. The Maine sardine is an Atlantic herring.

Species and description: The sardine is similar to the

herring, although considerably smaller. It reaches a length of 9 inches. A sardine is, in reality, a young *pilchard,* a small fish 9 to 10 inches long. The back is bluish green, the belly white. The scales are fairly large. The only true sardines available on the market are those with a maximum length of 5 to 6 inches. (See figure 3-27.)

Quality characteristics: Sardines are rich in protein. They also contain iron, calcium, and phosphorus. Sardines are usually boiled and packed in oil, usually olive oil. The type of oil should be specified on the label. Maine sardines are packed in various types of oil and also in tomato and mustard sauces.

Usage: In coastal regions the sardine is prepared fresh in many different ways, including sautéing and grilling. Sardines that are 5 to 6 inches long are separated for use in the canning factories.

Sprat—*Esprot*

Figure 3-28. Sprat—*Esprot.*

Origin and occurrence: The most important fishing grounds for sprat are off the Norwegian coast, in those parts of the North Sea bordering England, Belgium, Holland, and Germany, and in the Baltic.

Species and description: The sprat belongs to the herring family and resembles a sardine. The maximum length is 7 inches. The back is darkish blue in color, and the sides and belly are white. (See figure 3-28.)

Quality characteristics: The main catches occur during the winter months. The quality is best during November and December.

Usage: Sprats are usually smoked. The fresh fish are marinated with salt, sugar, spices, and herbs under controlled temperatures while they undergo a ripening process. Afterwards, they are packed in glass jars, cans, or small barrels. Only semipreserved, they are not sterilized and will keep for only a limited period of time.

Mackerel—*Maquereau*

Figure 3-29. Mackerel—*Maquereau.*

Origin and occurrence: This fish lives along the North Atlantic coasts. They are hunting fish and swim deep down in the sea during the winter. During the spring, they are caught along with the herrings in large numbers by trawling nets.

Species and description: The mackerel is a very fast fish with a torpedo-shaped body, small scales, and changing colors, with green and blue predominating. Dark blue zebralike stripes cover the back and run halfway down the sides. The lower half of the fish is silvery. Mackerel grow to a maximum length of 2 feet. The average size found on the market is 10 to 12 inches. (See figure 3-29.)

Quality characteristics: The reddish flesh of mackerel is of high quality in texture and flavor. Fresh mackerel is available only for a limited time because of the short fishing season. The fish are preserved to utilize the very large catches.

Usage: Fresh mackerel should be sautéed or grilled. Otherwise fillets of mackerel are preserved in oil, marinated, or prepared in sauce. Mackerel can also be cold- or hot-smoked. It is especially good barbecued and baked with an acid sauce.

Tuna—*Thon*

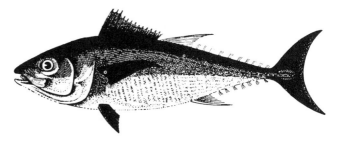

Figure 3-30. Tuna—*Thon.*

Origin and occurrence: The major seas are the home of the tuna fish, where, in springtime, it spawns along the coastlines. During this season, tuna is caught in huge numbers. It is also found in areas where herring is caught.

Species and description: Tuna, a member of the mackerel family, is a hunting fish. It grows to a length of 10 feet and to a maximum weight of ½ ton. The back is dark blue, and the sides are gray with silvery spots. Tuna are very strong, and they often break heavy-duty netting. For this reason they are difficult to catch. (See figure 3-30.)

Quality characteristics: The reddish flesh of the tuna is excellent, and it is prepared while still fresh in the fishing areas. The mode of preparation is similar to that of veal or young beef. In Germany, tuna is consumed either fresh or smoked. Italy, which constitutes one main fishing area, exports high-quality *tonno,* which is usually poached in olive oil. The United States, Portugal, Spain, Yugoslavia, France, and, more recently, Peru and Japan also can tuna in oil. "White" meat is generally the preferred quality, and this is achieved by blanching and cooking the fish in oil. Albacore has the lightest meat of all tuna. A medium-sized tuna, the bonito, yields the darkest flesh.

Usage: Fresh tuna is sautéed, grilled, deep-fried, smoked, or canned. Today tuna ranks as the number one seafood in the United States. Over a billion cans are consumed annually. It is also available in solid pack, chunk style, or grated.

Conger Eel—*Congre*

Figure 3-31.   Conger eel—*Congre.*

Origin and occurrence: This is strictly a marine fish found in European and American waters; it is an entirely different species from the eels in figure 3-4.

Species and description: The conger eel is a snakelike fish of the Congridae family. It lives in coastal waters, where it grows to a length of 8 or 10 feet; it weighs about 85 pounds. (See figure 3-31.)

Quality characteristics: The flesh is full of bones and has little appeal as food.

Usage: The conger eel is rarely available at fish markets. It has limited use unless smoked.

Gray Mullet—*Mulet/Muge*

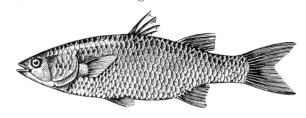

Figure 3-32.   Gray mullet—*Mulet/muge.*

Origin and occurrence: This fish is found along the Mediterranean and as far north as the English and Norwegian coasts. It swims up river estuaries with the incoming tide.

Species and description: The gray mullet of the Mugilidae family reaches a length of approximately 16 inches. Although similar to the freshwater grayling, it has a fuller belly, a longer body, and large round scales. The mouth is wide and blunt. Very fine teeth line the edges of the jaws. The lower jaw has a hook-shaped prolongation, which locks into the upper lip. (See figure 3-32.)

Quality characteristics: The flesh has a distinctive, savory flavor.

Usage: Favorite cooking methods for this fish are poaching, sautéing, grilling, baking, and deep-frying.

Red Mullet—*Rouget/Surmullet*

Origin and occurrence: This fish is found along the Mediterranean coasts of France and Italy, together with their respective islands.

Species and description: This fish grows to an approximate length of 12 inches. Because it has no gall bladder, it is called the "snipe of the sea." (See figure 3-33.)

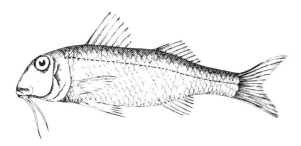

Figure 3-33. Red mullet—*Rouget/Surmullet.*

Quality characteristics: The flesh is white, delicate, and fine flavored.
Usage: Red mullet adapts to sautéing and grilling. Since it has no gall bladder, it is often prepared without removing the entrails. The roe of red mullet is used to make *tarama,* a salted product much used in the Mediterranean.

Brill—*Barbue*

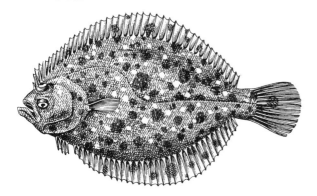

Figure 3-34. Brill—*Barbue.*

Origin and occurrence: Brill are found along the coasts of the North Sea and the Baltic.
Species and description: A member of the flatfish family, the fish has an elliptical body and smooth skin. It grows to a length of 12 to 20 inches. The gray-brown upper side is covered with orange-colored spots. (See figure 3-34.)
Quality characteristics: The white, tasty flesh is highly prized.
Usage: The fish is best poached or deep-fried, since the flesh is too fragile for other preparations.

Flounder—*Flet*

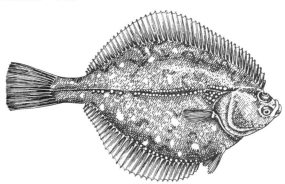

Figure 3-35. Flounder—*Flet.*

Origin and occurrence: This fish, caught both in the North Sea and the Baltic, prefers the less salty Baltic. It migrates up rivers along the coasts bordering these two areas. It also is found along the Atlantic coast, from the Gulf of St. Lawrence to New Jersey, and in the Pacific, from California to Alaska.
Species and description: The flounder, a very thin flatfish, grows up to 20 inches in length and weighs from ½ to 4½ pounds. The skin is brown with red and yellow spots on the top side. The belly is a yellowish white color. (See figure 3-35.)
Quality characteristics: The good-flavored white flesh is similar to that of halibut.
Usage: Flounder is considered one of the finest edible fish. When fresh, it is suitable for pan-frying or deep-frying. It is also smoked. Generally, flounder can be prepared in the same fashion as sole.

Halibut—*Flétan*

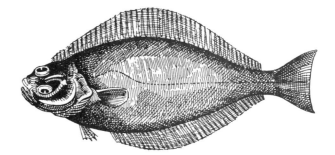

Figure 3-36. Halibut—*Flétan.*

Origin and occurrence: Halibut is found in the Arctic Ocean and is caught off Greenland, Iceland, and in the Barents Sea.

Species and description: Halibut, a member of the flatfish family, may grow to 6 feet in length and weigh over 300 pounds. There are four commercial sizes: 3¼ to 6½ pounds; 9 to 18 pounds; 22 to 44 pounds; and 55 to 110 pounds and over. The head is pointed, the upperside is grayish brown, and the belly white. (See figure 3-36.)

Quality characteristics: The flesh is white and mild in flavor. It freezes well and is suitable for use in institutional foodservice.

Usage: Similar to other large fish, halibut must be filleted or cut into slices before it is poached, baked, or deep-fried. All varieties of flatfish should be poached carefully and slowly over moderate heat to avoid overcooking and loss of protein.

Lemon Sole, Dab—*Limande*

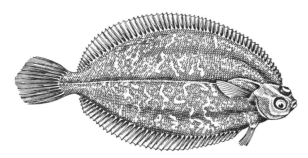

Figure 3-37.   Lemon sole, dab—*Limande.*

Origin and occurrence: This fish ranges from southern California to Alaska, but it occurs in greatest abundance off the coast of New England.

Species and description: Lemon sole, a flounder, resembles Dover sole in appearance, but it is heavier and has stronger fins. The skin of the lemon sole is more difficult to remove than that of the Dover sole. (See illustration in chapter 7.) This fish has a small head, a smooth skin, and a line running down the center, which curves around the breast fin. The color of the fish is reddish brown to blood red, with light and dark marbling. It grows to a length of 15 inches. (See figure 3-37.)

Quality characteristics: The flesh of the lemon sole has an excellent taste, but it is rather fragile and difficult to fillet.

Usage: Lemon sole may be deep-fried, sautéed, or poached.

Plaice—*Plie*

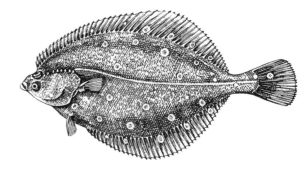

Figure 3-38.   Plaice—*Plie.*

Origin and occurrence: Plaice are found in the North Sea, the Baltic, the Barents Sea, and in the Atlantic.

Species and description: A member of the flatfish family, plaice grow to 3 feet, but the smaller ones are preferred. The body is elliptical, the skin smooth. The upper side is gray-brown with round, reddish yellow dots. The belly is yellowish white. (See figure 3-38.)

Quality characteristics: Plaice are usually consumed when fresh. There are three commercial sizes: large (15 to 19 inches, weighing over 2 pounds), medium (10 to 13 inches, approximately ½ to ¼ pound), and sautéing plaice, which are the smallest. The flesh is very tasty.

Usage: It is usually filleted and poached or sautéed. Plaice is also smoked.

Dover Sole—*Sole*

Origin and occurrence: Sole live in all coastal waters off Europe, to the west of the Baltic Sea.

Species and description: Dover sole grows to a length of 15 inches. It has a thin, flat body. The upper side is brown with small scales, and the belly is white. (See figure 3-39.)

Quality characteristics: Sole is one of the most esteemed of European fish. The flesh is the best and

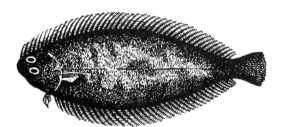

Figure 3-39. Dover sole—*Sole.*

most delicious of all saltwater fish. Those coming from the ocean or the English Channel, also called "Ostend soles," are a light reddish gray on the top side, have a great deal of flesh, and are preferred over the darker sole from the North Sea and Italian waters. The skin is easily removed.

Usage: Dover sole may be prepared in many different ways. Large sections of cookbooks are devoted to preparation ideas for this fish.

Sand Dab—*Carrelet*

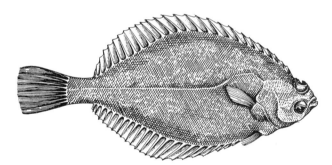

Figure 3-40. Sand dab—*Carrelet.*

Origin and occurrence: The main fishing areas are the Atlantic Ocean, the North Sea, and the Baltic.

Species and description: The sand dab is a flounder also known as *Torbay sole.* Its body is thinner than that of the turbot, and it has small scales instead of the stonelike bony areas. The belly is glassy. (See figure 3-40.)

Quality characteristics: Sand dab is cheaper than turbot, but its flesh is lean, white, and tender.

Usage: It is good poached or pan-fried.

Turbot—*Turbot*

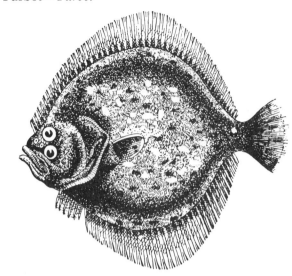

Figure 3-41. Turbot—*Turbot.*

Origin and occurrence: Turbot lives in the Atlantic, in the North Sea, and in the Baltic.

Species and description: Turbot is a large flatfish. Small turbots are called *turbotin.* In the North Sea and in the Baltic, turbot grow to a length of 15 inches; in the Atlantic, to 5 feet. Stonelike bony patches on the outside account for its characteristic appearance. The color is variegated brown with light specks. The belly is white. North Sea and Baltic turbot are rather dark, while those from the Atlantic are light in color. (See figure 3-41.)

Quality characteristics: Turbot is one of the favorite saltwater fish. The flesh is snow-white, very firm, and keeps well. It is at its best between April and September. The light-colored, medium-sized turbot from the Atlantic, also known as Boulogne turbot, is better than the darker variety from the North Sea and Baltic Sea.

Usage: Turbot is usually grilled, poached, or stuffed and baked.

Skate—*Raie*

Origin and occurrence: The skate or ray lives near the bottom of coastal waters and in the open sea. It is caught along the coast.

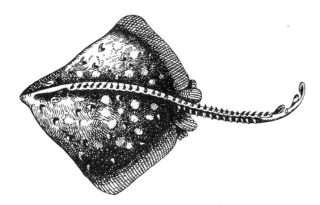

Figure 3-42. Skate—*Raie.*

Species and description: The skate is a cartilaginous fish with a flat, disclike body and usually a long, whip-shaped tail. The breast fins are merged with the body. There are several varieties of skates. Of the two main kinds, stingrays and smooth skates, the former is preferable for cooking purposes. The entire body of the stingray is covered with little thornlike spines with large spines near the eyes and on the back and tail. It grows to a length of about 2½ feet. The smooth skate has a smooth skin, few spines, and a long, pointed jaw. Skates up to 10 feet long are not uncommon. (See figure 3-42.)

Quality characteristics: Only the wing-shaped sides of the body and the breast fins are usable for culinary purposes. Therefore, there is a high proportion of waste. When fresh, skates are considered a real delicacy in France, Belgium, Holland, and Switzerland.

Usage: Skate must be prepared while fresh, and sautéing is especially suitable. Before cooking, the fish must be thoroughly scraped. After cooking, the skin should be removed, because it is often full of sand. It should be filleted before sautéing. Smoked skate is also very good.

3.2.4 *Crustaceans, Shellfish, and Mollusks*—Crustacés, coquillages, et mollusques

Crustaceans include various types of lobsters, barnacles, shrimps, and crabs. They are characterized by their five pairs of jointed legs. The front pair is equipped with pincers or claws. The body is enclosed by a calcium secretion (hardened shell) that is shed from time to time during growth.

Mollusks are invertebrate animals with unsegmented bodies protected by a calcareous shell. In the case of the squid, the shell has been reduced to an internal feather-shaped pen. Many of our edible mollusks, such as clams, mussels, scallops, and oysters, are bivalves, but we also eat univalves, such as abalone, periwinkle, whelk, and the terrestrial gastropod—the snail.

Living animals should be packed in wet wood shavings and shipped as quickly as possible in containers that allow air circulation. They can stay alive out of water for two days if they are kept cool but not on ice.

Crab—*Crabe*

Figure 3-43. Crab—*Crabe.*

Origin and occurrence: There are many different varieties, including the spider crab, hermit crab, and fiddler crab. In the United States three species of crabs dominate the fisheries. The blue crab from Atlantic waters contributes the largest share. The Dungeness crab and the king crab from the Pacific coast and Alaska are also of major importance to the fishing industry. Softshell crabs are molting blue crabs that have shed their hard shells. Snow crabs, belonging to the family of spider crabs, are a new resource for crab meat. Crab lives along sea coasts, where it is caught in nets, pots, and various types of gear.

Species and description: These crabs belong to the short-tailed crustacean family. (See figure 3-43.)

Quality characteristics: The meat of the blue crab is tender, full of flavor, and is adaptable to many cooking methods. The king and Dungeness crabs are less delicate in texture. Since king crab comes into the market only frozen, it tends to be somewhat watery textured. All crab meat is very perishable.

Usage: Crabs are cooked by steaming or boiling for hot and cold dishes. Softshell crabs may be sautéed or deep-fried. In the canning industry, crabs are processed into crab meat and crab extract. The canned meat may be used interchangeably in recipes specifying cooked crab meat, although no canned crab is the equal of fresh in taste or texture. After cooking but before serving, the tail fin should be twisted off to remove the intestines.

Crayfish—*Ecrevisse*

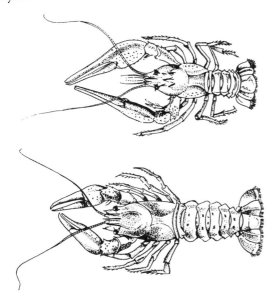

Figure 3-44. Crayfish—*Ecrevisse* (marsh crayfish, top; river crayfish, bottom).

Origin and occurrence: Crayfish live in shallow, calcium-rich rivers, ponds, and lakes.

Species and description: The river crayfish, found in freshwater, is considered a "noble" crayfish. It is blackish brown in color. There is also the Galician pond or marsh crayfish. This crayfish has a bluish green color. The lower part of the pincers is white.

Quality characteristics: The noble crayfish tastes considerably better than the Galician crayfish. Crayfish

are classified by size as soup crayfish, and small, medium, large, and giant crayfish. The taste of the meat depends on the cleanliness of the water and the type of food the crayfish has been eating. Crayfish taste best during the summer months from May to August. The meat is juicy, delicate, and has a distinct sweet taste. (See figure 3-44.)

Usage: Only the tails of crayfish are marketed. There are hot and cold crayfish dishes that are complete in themselves. Crayfish are also used as garnishes for fish dishes and with hors d'oeuvre.

Lobster—*Homard*

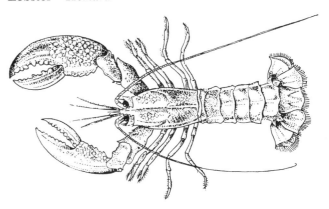

Figure 3-45. Lobster—*Homard.*

Origin and occurrence: Lobster is found off the coast of the state of Maine in the United States; in addition to the Atlantic, it is found in the North Sea and the Mediterranean, but not in the Baltic Sea. It lives over stony ground near the coasts and feeds on small crustaceans.

Species and description: Lobster is similar in shape to a crayfish and has two pincers of different sizes. Lobsters can grow to 45 pounds, and still be tender and edible, but the average size at market is 1 to 5 pounds, with a lobster of 1¼ to 1½ pounds considered an appropriate size for an individual serving. (See figure 3-45.)

Quality characteristics: Lobster is a delicacy that is sold live, boiled, or preserved. After the Maine lobster, the dark brown Swedish and Norwegian lobsters represent the best quality. Live lobsters must be protected against the heat and cold and should be kept moist during transportation. The tail of a live lobster should be curled up tight and should also be elastic. Lobsters, like crayfish, are killed by plunging them into a container of boiling water. Cooked lobster meat and opened cans of lobster are highly perishable and must be consumed quickly. Dead lobsters develop a fish toxin and must not be used.

Usage: Lobster is used for hot and cold dishes. To cut a lobster, see chapter 7.

Lobsterette—*Scampo/Langoustine*

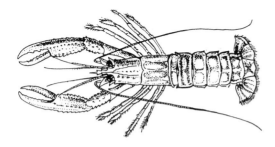

Figure 3-46. Lobsterette—*Scampo/langoustine.*

Origin and occurrence: Scampo is the Italian name for the small lobster found in the Mediterranean, frequently along Danish and Norwegian coasts, and in the western Atlantic and Gulf of Mexico. These lobsterettes are also called "Norwegian lobster," "Danish lobster," and "Dublin Bay prawn."

Species and description: Small members of the lobster family, lobsterettes are pink in color and grow to about 8 inches in length. (See figure 3-46.)

Quality characteristics: The meat corresponds to that of lobster.

Usage: It is usually grilled, steamed, or served in a sauce.

Spiny Lobster (Rock Lobster)—*Langouste*

Origin and occurrence: Spiny lobsters are most frequently found in the Mediterranean, as well as along the coasts of England, Ireland, and South West Africa (Cape crawfish), the Pacific coast of the United States, the east coast of Florida, and the Gulf of Mexico.

Species and description: The spiny lobster is a crusta-

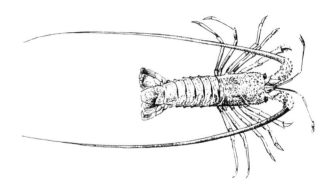

Figure 3-47. Spiny lobster (rock lobster)—*Langouste.*

cean with long feelers, spines over the head and breast, but no pincers. It is reddish violet in color with yellow speckles. It can grow to about 20 inches in length and weigh 13 pounds. (See figure 3-47.)

Quality characteristics: While still alive or when cooked, the strong tail of the spiny lobster must be curled. Those with stretched tails are not good. Since there are no claws, the spiny lobster tail is the main edible portion. The tail is removed, cleaned, and washed. It is then frozen either raw or cooked. The spiny lobster becomes red when boiled. The meat is tasty, but drier and tougher than that of lobster.

Usage: Spiny lobster can be used for both hot and cold dishes. When boiling for cold dishes, the body must be fixed to a piece of wood. For hot dishes, the lobster should be plunged, head first, into boiling water.

Shrimp—*Crevette*

Origin and occurrence: Shrimps are found along all sandy coastlines.

Species and description: A shrimp is a small sea creature belonging to the long-tailed crustacean family. It has a slightly compressed body with long feelers and ten feet, but it does not have pincers. Shrimps grow to between 1½ and 3½ inches. The common varieties are white or common; brown or grooved; pink or coral; red or royal. Prawns are not shrimps; they have more slender abdomens and longer legs. In spite of that, the name is used erroneously for large shrimps. (See figure 3-48.)

Quality characteristics: The meat is tasty, but perisha-

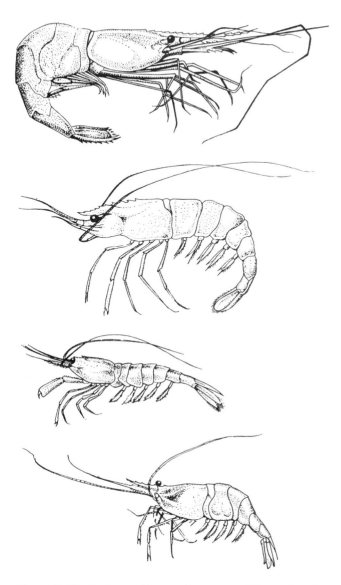

shrimps' tails are removed from their shells and either deep-frozen or sterilized in cans or jars. They can then be used in many different ways as hors d'oeuvre, garnishes, soups, salads, and entrées.

Clams—*Palourdes* or *Praires*

Origin and occurrence: Clams are found on all Atlantic and Pacific coasts, but the species are different in different localities. The most used are the Eastern clams: the softshell and the hardshell quahaug. The quahaug varies in size according to habitat. Razor clams grow on both coasts. Carpet shells, similar to quahaugs, grow in European Atlantic waters and the Mediterranean.

Species and description: Very small quahaugs are called *littleneck clams;* the next larger size is *cherrystones;* quahaugs over 3 inches are called *chowder clams.* Razor clams, with shells like a straight razor, are difficult to dig, since the shell is thin and fragile. The quahaug shell is oval shaped with a purple border in the inside; they are hard enough to use as coquilles for baking.

Quality characteristics: Clams must be gathered from safe environments, approved by local health authorities. Clams are sold live, in the shell, shucked, both refrigerated and frozen, and canned, as well as prepared many different ways. Smoked clams are also on the market. Clam liquor is bottled as juice and broth.

Usage: Tender softshells are used for steamers, served with their own broth and melted butter. Small quahaugs are usually eaten raw on the half shell, but larger hardshells are tough and best used for chowder, stuffed clams, and pancakes. Razor clams are steamed, fried, or used in fritters. New England clam chowder is world famous.

Mussels—*Moules*

Origin and occurrence: The mussel is found in intertidal zones along the European and American coasts. Mussels are bred along the Dutch coast and form huge natural banks in the shallows between the East Frisian Islands and the mainland. They are also cultured along the coasts of France and Spain. Spain produces the largest amount.

Species and description: Mussels are marine bivalves.

Figure 3-48. Shrimp—*Crevette* (deep sea, whipper, North Sea, and Baltic).

ble. Nevertheless, shrimps are now available everywhere fresh, since they can be airlifted in a matter of hours. In some cases shrimps are boiled directly on board the fishing boats.

Usage: Shrimps are available in most areas of the United States either raw or cooked, peeled or unpeeled, and fresh or frozen. After boiling, the

(There are freshwater mussels, but they are not suitable for eating.) The blue or edible mussel is oval, dark blue to lilac brown in color, and whitish blue inside. The size may be small to large, but the mussel inside is not necessarily as large as the shell.

Quality characteristics: Mussels must always be closed and have a fresh sea smell, and they should open only when exposed to heat. The color should be uniform. Live mussels should be clean and free from sand when sold. When purchasing mussels, at least half the purchase should be over 2 inches long.

Usage: When cold, mussels may be marinated or served in a jelly. Hot, they are eaten plain or may be used as a garnish for fish dishes, and fish pies. Mussel shells must be scrubbed with a wire or plastic brush and the beard (byssus) must be removed. Mussel liquid should be strained carefully to remove any sand. Any mussels with unopened shells after steaming should be discarded, as they were either dead before steaming or full of mud.

Oyster—*Huître*

Figure 3-49. Oyster—*Huître.*

Origin and occurrence: Oysters exist along all the coasts of Europe and the United States and are appreciated as a great delicacy. Normally they grow in large numbers on rocks, supporting piles, and other objects. At river estuaries, so-called artificial oyster beds are laid out. A good flow of freshwater into these oyster beds improves the taste of the oysters. The best-known oysters come from the Baltic, the Dutch coast, from Whilstable, Trieste, Venice, and, of course, the Atlantic coast of the United States.

Species and description: The lower shell of the oyster has a concave, bowllike shape, while the upper shell is

flatter. Outside the shells are rough, inside smooth. The age of the oyster can be seen by the number of layers on the shell. (See figure 3-49.)

Quality characteristics: Oysters are of commercial interest when over three to four years old. They are dredged from September to April. All months with an *r* in their names are considered good months for oysters. Oysters gathered between May and August are rather tasteless and spoil easily. Oysters are identified by the surface of the oyster bed—whether it is rock, sand, or clay. Rock oysters are the best. When sold, the country of origin is normally quoted. In Europe, English oysters are considered to be the best, but the Marennes oysters from France are also famous. Oysters taken from the Atlantic, from Canada to Texas, are known as Eastern oysters. The Olympia, a small delicately flavored oyster, is found in Puget Sound. The giant Japanese oyster is taken from the waters of the Pacific. Size and uniformity are the criteria for the classification of oysters: imperial, first class, and second class. These categories are also expressed in zeroes: two zeroes refers to the imperial oysters, four refers to the first class, and six to the second class. Oysters vary in size, texture, and flavor according to the time of year they are harvested. When buying, the oysters must be alive, as indicated by a tightly closed shell. Oysters in open shells are dead and unfit to eat. In the United States oysters must come from beds approved by the U.S. Public Health Service.

Usage: Oysters are a nutritious delicacy. They are consumed raw or cooked. They are used in soups, as filling for pies, and in stews and stuffings. They may be served raw on the half shell, as appetizers, baked on the half shell, or deep-fried.

Scallops—*Coquille Saint-Jacques, Pétoncle*

Origin and occurrence: Scallops are found throughout the world. The sea scallop (*Pecten magellanicus*) is the most commercially important species in the United States. The bay scallop is less plentiful and has a short season, but it is greatly desired by scallop fanciers. A new fishery has been developed for the calico scallop, located off Florida and in the Gulf of Mexico. The discovery of a new and potentially important source

Figure 3-50. Scallop—*Coquille Saint-Jacques.*

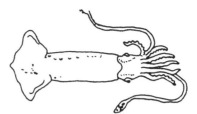

Figure 3-51. Squid—*Calmar.*

of sea scallops in the cold waters of Alaska is particularly interesting. This species, found as far south as Oregon, is different from the sea scallop found in Atlantic waters.

Species and description: Scallop shells become 5 inches long and are connected by muscles. The upper shell is flat, the underneath shell is rounded. In some species both shells are grooved, the more familiar with square-edged grooves, but others have rounded grooves, and there are scallops with smooth shells. (See figure 3-50.)

Quality characteristics: Sea scallops are available all year, but are best from April to October. In European markets the entire scallop in its shell is available, and the entire thing is edible. However, the chief part eaten is the adductor muscle. Fortunate Europeans also have the coral, which adds color and flavor to many scallop dishes. North Americans seldom see coral, as the muscle is removed at sea and the balance of the scallop is discarded. Bay scallops are available from November to April. The tender, succulent meats have a nutty flavor. All scallop meats are excellent sources of protein, vitamins, and minerals. They are low in fat. Both sea and bay scallops are available frozen.

Usage: Scallops can be sautéed, broiled, or baked.

Squid—*Calmar*

Origin and occurrence: Squids are found all over the world; a prolific supply exists off the California coast.

Species and description: Squids have ten arms and a long, cigar-shaped body with fins at the end. They are often confused with octopi, which have 8 arms and a globular body. Though both are cephalopods, they belong to different families and are not related. Squids have no backbone but still retain a rudimentary shell, called a pen, located beneath the mantle of the body. Two fins, at the end opposite to the head, are about half as long as the mantle and are slightly lobed in front. Squids ordinarily have a milky, translucent color, but, when aroused, intense and varied colors ripple through the body, which turns rapidly to red, pink, brown, blue, and yellow, and stays that way for several hours after they have been caught. (See figure 3-51.)

Quality characteristics: Squids are very nutritious, with a large percentage of protein. About 80 percent of the animal is edible. The flavor is delicate. Only brief cooking is needed, and they can be eaten raw. Overcooking makes them tough.

Usage: Any cooking method can be used; sautéing is a good choice. Squids can be stuffed and baked, with the ink used in the sauce.

Cuttlefish—*Seiche*

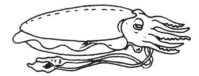

Figure 3-52. Cuttlefish—*Seiche.*

Origin and occurrence: Cuttlefish, also called *inkfish,* are found in the Mediterranean, the Atlantic, and on rocky and sandy bottoms in the North Sea.

Species and description: Cuttlefish are related to squids, but they have a calcified internal shell. The body is more oval than a squid's and is somewhat flattened. It has large fins on the sides and eight arms almost as long as the body. The back is blackish brown, striped like a zebra; the belly is silvery. Like the squid, the cuttlefish can change its color to suit its moods. (See figure 3-52.)

Quality characteristics: Care must be taken when removing the ink sac of the cuttlefish. The dye sepia was originally provided by this ink.

Usage: Small cuttlefish are used whole in stews and pasta sauces; large specimens are cut into rings and may be deep-fried.

Snail—*Escargot*

Figure 3-53. Snail—*Escargot.*

Origin and occurrence: Edible snails are found in various parts of Europe and in North Africa. The best come from wine-growing regions, especially in France, where they nourish themselves on vine leaves.

Species and description: Although mollusks, snails are not shellfish, but terrestrial gastropods. Their closest relatives in the sea are periwinkles. (See figure 3-53.)

Quality characteristics: Snails seal themselves in during the fall season just before the first frosts. They are at their prime at this time. Snail-canning factories purchase land snails throughout the summer and keep them until the fall in so-called snail farms. The snails are then boiled and sterilized in cans. The shells are cleaned and dried. Only small numbers of snails are actually collected in the wild, since the shrinking population is protected by law in many European countries.

Usage: During the winter snail season, the canned snails are put back into the shells, covered with herb butter, and eaten as hors d'oeuvre. Other ways of pre-paring snails include: on the spit, as a salad, marinated with white wine, deep-fried, or sautéed.

3.3 Meat—*Animaux de boucherie*

The term *meat* as used in this text refers to fresh meat only—all animals or parts of animals used as food for human consumption. This includes muscles with the attached tissues, fat, fresh blood, and glandular meats (edible organs and glands). Glandular meats include the tongue, kidney, heart, brain, liver, and pancreas (sweetbread), and the walls of the stomach (tripe). With the exception of chilling, these have not been prepared, processed or preserved, nor have they undergone any other type of treatment, except for tripe, which is scalded after preparation; however, it is still considered uncooked.

Animals slaughtered for meat include:

Bovines

- Calf—*veau*
- Young ox—*bœuf*
- Young cow—*génisse*
- Ox—*bœuf*
- Steer—*taureau*
- Cow—*vache*

Pigs

- Suckling pig—*porcelet de lait/cochon de lait*
- Piglet—*porcelet*
- Pig—*porc*

Sheep

- Suckling lamb—*agneau de lait*
- Lamb—*agneau*
- Ewe—*brebis/mouton*
- Ram—*mouton*

Goat

- Kid—*chevreau*
- Goat—*chèvre*

Frozen Meat

Frozen meat refers to meat that has been preserved through storage at low temperatures. Storing meats at temperatures ranging from 0° to 32°F (−18° to 0°C) inhibits the activity of enzymes and bacteria. The lower the temperature, the longer the meat can be stored without affecting the quality. Lean meats properly wrapped in good-quality paper and stored at zero or lower temperatures will keep well for six to eight months. The maximum storage times for fresh, cooked, and processed meats are shown in figure 3-54.

Processed Meats

These are foods that have been treated with various methods of preservation and/or cooking, such as salt-ing, smoking, drying, roasting, boiling, and canning. Sausages, canned meats, meat marinades, meat pies, meat pâtés, hams, and bacon are a few examples. All food products derived from meat are subject to government regulations.

Purchasing Meat

When purchasing meat, check the amount and the distribution of fat and the amount of meat, fat, and bones. Compare only equivalent cuts, not, for example, sirloin to chuck, since the quality of each piece depends on the type of cut and resulting intended use.

Meat	Refrigerator (38° to 40°F) (3° to 4°C)	Freezer (at 0°F or lower) (−18°C or lower)
Beef (fresh)	2 to 4 days	6 to 12 months
Veal (fresh)	2 to 4 days	6 to 9 months
Pork (fresh)	2 to 4 days	3 to 6 months
Lamb (fresh)	2 to 4 days	6 to 9 months
Ground beef, veal, and lamb	1 to 2 days	3 to 4 months
Ground pork	1 to 2 days	1 to 3 months
Variety meats	1 to 2 days	3 to 4 months
Luncheon meats	1 week	not recom-mended
Sausage, fresh pork	1 week	60 days
Sausage, smoked	3 to 7 days	
Sausage, dry and semidry (unsliced)	2 to 3 weeks	
Frankfurters	4 to 5 days	
Bacon	5 to 7 days	
Smoked hams, whole	1 week	60 days
Smoked hams, slices	3 to 4 days	
Beef, corned	1 week	2 weeks
Leftover cooked meat	4 to 5 days	2 to 3 months
Frozen combination foods		
Meat pies (cooked)	—	3 months
Swiss steak (cooked)	—	3 months
Stews (cooked)	—	3 to 4 months
Prepared meat dinners	—	2 to 6 months

Source: *Lessons on Meat*, National Live Stock and Meat Board.
Note: The range in time reflects recommendations for maximum storage time from several authorities. For top quality, fresh meats should be used in two or three days, ground meat and variety meats should be used in 24 hours.

Figure 3-54. Maximum recommended storage time for fresh, cooked, and processed meats.

Keeping Quality

The following factors determine the keeping quality of the meat:

- Species of the animal
- Quality of the animal feed
- Health of the animal
- Treatment before slaughtering
- Sanitation in the slaughterhouse, packing plant, and foodservice facility
- Bleeding and skinning processes
- Chilling process of the slaughtered carcass
- Sanitation, temperature, and condition of meat-cutting and -processing areas
- Sanitation of equipment and implements or utensils
- Conditions of the distribution system
- Temperature controls of all work, distribution, and storage areas

Beef and mutton dry out on the surface easily and quickly and, for this reason, keep longer than veal or pork. On the other hand, the surface fat may become rancid when exposed to light and oxygen.

Any form of moisture that is in contact with meat impairs its appearance and reduces the keeping quality.

Recommended temperatures and storage times for fresh, cooked, and processed meats are shown in figure 3-54. Microorganisms that can cause food-borne illnesses and infections grow at temperatures between 40° and 140°F (4° to 60°C). Since meat serves as a good medium for growth of organisms, storage temperatures should be below 40°F (4°C). Storage at temperatures between 30° and 32°F (−3° and 0°C) is the most effective for controlling the quality of meat. At this temperature the development of molds and bacteria will be inhibited for a limited period of time. Meat that is to be stored for a longer period should be stored at 0°F (−18°C) or lower. It should be wrapped tightly in a good-quality paper that is greaseproof, vaporproof, and moistureproof. The drugstore method of wrapping provides the best air seal. (See figure 3-55.)

The drugstore or lock-seal wrap is made by placing the food on the center of the sheet of paper large

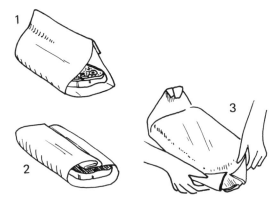

Figure 3-55. Drugstore wrap.

enough so that the ends can be brought together and folded as shown in drawing *1*. The paper is folded down taut against the food, making an interlocking seam, as shown in drawing *2*. The package is then turned over so that the seam lies on the table. A pleat fold is then made on one open end and another fold is made before pressing the folded end against the package. The package is then turned so the folded end is braced against the body, as shown in drawing *3*. Excess air is pressed out of the package, and the other open end is folded. The package is then sealed with freezer tape.

Composition of Meat

The gross structure of carcasses and cuts of animals consists of the edible lean or muscular tissue, the fat in and around the muscles, the bones, and the connective tissue, or gristle, that binds the muscle fibers together. The muscle tissue, the most important meat constituent, contains about 70 percent water, 20 percent protein, 9 percent fat, and 1 percent ash. As the animal is fattened, some of the water and protein of the lean is replaced by fat in the form of marbling. Marbling is the fine network of fat in the muscle fibers. Marbling increases the palatability, juiciness, and tenderness of the meat. Connective tissue contributes to the toughness of the meat. The greater the content of connective tissues, the tougher the meat. The bone aids in identifying the age of the animal and the cut of the meat. Nitrogenous extractives are also found in lean meat. The extractives and the fat are largely responsible for the aroma and flavor of the meat.

The composition of the meat is directly dependent upon the condition of the animal at the moment of slaughtering. Careless handling at this stage may cause spoilage. Meat has a very high moisture content and, therefore, microorganisms can thrive unless high standards of sanitation, cleanliness, temperature, and humidity controls are maintained.

Preparation of Meat

Meat cutting requires skill. The meat cutter must know something of the anatomy of animals and the methods of fabrication. The ability to identify the characteristics of the muscles and the tissues between them, the shape and type of bones, and the location of the layers of fat will help the meat cutter perform his tasks. An understanding of preparation methods for the various cuts of meat is necessary for the person preparing the meat. Proper use of tools and equipment and a knowledge of safety and sanitation practices will protect both the worker and the consumer.

Slaughtered Meat

This term refers to the meat of hogs, cattle, and sheep. Dependent upon the quality, the percentage of bone should not exceed 20 to 25 percent of the carcass weight. Meat carcasses must be thoroughly chilled after slaughtering. To preserve the quality and wholesomeness, meat should be packaged in airproof and moistureproof containers.

Meat Inspection and Grading

Federal inspection and grading provide protection and many benefits to consumers, farmers, processors, and distributors. Meat inspection is a federal requirement in every packinghouse or processing plant in the United States. Rigid standards of processing under sanitary conditions are enforced. Federally inspected meat is marked with a round stamp that reads, "US Insp'd and P'S'D" (United States Inspected and Passed), which indicates fitness for human consumption. (See figure 3-56.)

Grading is a voluntary process. A packer may choose whether he wants the meat in his plant federally graded. The U.S. Department of Agriculture, through its Federal Grading Branch, provides uniform standards to help the producers, packers, distributors, and consumers measure the differences between grades for price/quality comparisons. After the grade has been determined, the official shield identifying the specific grade is stamped with a roller device over the full length of the carcass. USDA initials and the designated grade appear inside the shield. (See figure 3-57.)

3.3.1 Beef

Refer to figure 3-58 and the color insert. The color of young top-quality lean beef should be bright cherry red. The meat of more mature beef will be a darker shade of red. The sirloin and short loin should be sheathed with a thick layer of light-colored fat. Top-quality beef will be marbled with veins of light-colored fat throughout the tender muscles. The meat should be "aged" for 10 to 14 days before cooking, especially meat that is to be used for roasts or steaks. Meat that is to be braised requires only 4 to 8 days of aging.

The wholesale primal loin is composed of two sub-primals, the sirloin and the short loin. The wholesale weight of the sirloin subprimal approximates 5 percent of the live weight and 8 percent of the carcass weight. The sirloin may be cut into steaks that will equal about 3 percent of the live weight and 5 percent of the carcass weight. The top sirloin muscle may be stripped out and used as a boneless top sirloin roast or cut into top sirloin steaks. The wholesale weight of the short loin subprimal equals about 4 percent of the live weight and 7 percent of the carcass weight. Steaks from the short loin are porterhouse, T-bone, top-loin, and club. In another method of fabrication, the tenderloin muscle is removed from inside the short loin and processed as a fillet or cut into steaks, including the chateaubriand, filet mignon, tournedos, and tenderloin tip.

There are two kinds of grading for beef, quality grading and yield grading. Quality grading is based on palatability characteristics: tenderness, juiciness,

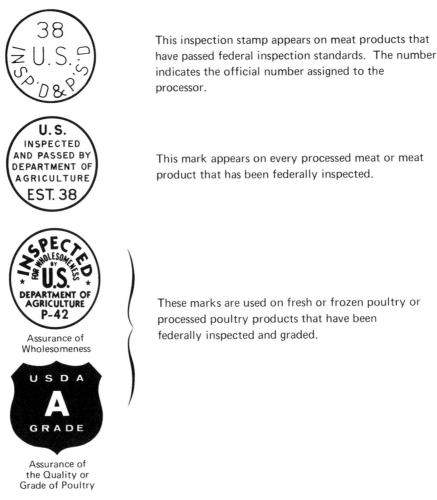

This inspection stamp appears on meat products that have passed federal inspection standards. The number indicates the official number assigned to the processor.

This mark appears on every processed meat or meat product that has been federally inspected.

These marks are used on fresh or frozen poultry or processed poultry products that have been federally inspected and graded.

Figure 3-56. U.S. government inspection stamps. (Courtesy U.S. Department of Agriculture)

and flavor. Yield grading measures the amount of meat a carcass yields. The yield grades are numbered from 1 to 5. Yield grade No. 1 has the greatest percentage of meat compared to fat and bone on the carcass and yield grade No. 5 has the lowest percentage. All graded beef will be graded for both quality and yield.

There are eight grades of quality for beef. Each is a measure of a distinct level of quality. The grades are USDA Prime, USDA Choice, USDA Good, USDA Standard, USDA Commercial, USDA Utility, USDA Cutter, and USDA Canner.

USDA Prime, the highest grade, is produced in limited quantities for use in fine hotels, restaurants, and specialty stores. This beef is well marbled, which enhances both flavor and juiciness. It has a thick covering of firm, creamy white fat, and it is most suitable for aging. The USDA standards were revised in 1976, resulting in reduced marbling requirements in Prime and Choice grades. Consumers are now getting leaner beef than under the previous standards.

USDA Choice is generally the most popular grade in retail markets. The meat is tender, juicy, and well marbled, with less fat than Prime.

Figure 3-57. Stamps of U.S. grades for meat quality and yields. (Courtesy U.S. Department of Agriculture)

Both USDA Good and Standard are considered to be "economy beef." Some markets may sell this quality of beef under a brand name rather than under the USDA grade name. There is less shrinkage because of the lower fat content. Good is quite tender but lacks the flavor and tenderness of Prime and Choice.

USDA Standard has as a high proportion of lean meat and a small amount of fat. It lacks the flavor and tenderness of the higher grades.

USDA Commercial is produced from mature animals. It has a rich, full flavor but requires long, slow cooking to make it tender.

USDA Utility, Cutter, and Canner grades lack the palatability characteristics of the higher grades. These grades are wholesome, nutritious, and economical and are suitable for ground and manufactured items.

3.3.2 Veal

Refer to figure 3-59 and the color insert. A vealer is defined by the U.S. Department of Agriculture as an immature bovine animal 3 months of age or younger that has been fed on milk or milk replacements. The color of its lean meat is light grayish pink. A calf is defined as an immature bovine animal, 3 to 8 months of age that has been fed in part, or wholly, on feeds other than milk. The typical color of the lean meat of the calf is grayish red.

Veal has a high moisture content and a very thin covering of fat. Therefore, it has a short storage life and should be refrigerated at temperatures between 30° and 36°F (−3° and 2°C) for no longer than 5 or 6 days. The same method used for cutting beef into

retail cuts is used for cutting veal. The name of the retail cut is preceded by the term *veal* to differentiate it from beef, lamb, and pork. Veal kidneys should be completely embedded in fat. The flesh of top-quality veal is firm, smooth, and fine grained. The fat is somewhat soft and pliable, and the rib bones are a bright red color. The best veal is delicately flavored. The meat of the very lightweight animals has a tendency to be watery and lacks flavor, whereas the very heavyweight veal or calf may lack the delicate flavor of top-quality veal. The grade of veal is determined by a composite evaluation of conformation and quality. The depth and thickness of flesh, the amount of feathering (fat interlaced with lean between the ribs), the amount and type of kidney and pelvic fat, the amount and quality of external fat, and the texture of the lean flesh are factors that influence the evaluation. The USDA grades for veal are: USDA Prime, USDA Choice, USDA Good, USDA Standard, and USDA Utility.

3.3.3 Pork

Refer to figure 3-60 and the color insert. Pork ranks next to beef in popularity among the American public. Grades are based on quality of the meat and on carcass yields of the four lean cuts identified as ham, loin, picnic, and Boston butt.

The flesh should be whitish pink in color, fine textured, and firm with fat distributed throughout. Pork should be hung for three to four days before use. The five grades based on expected yields of the four lean

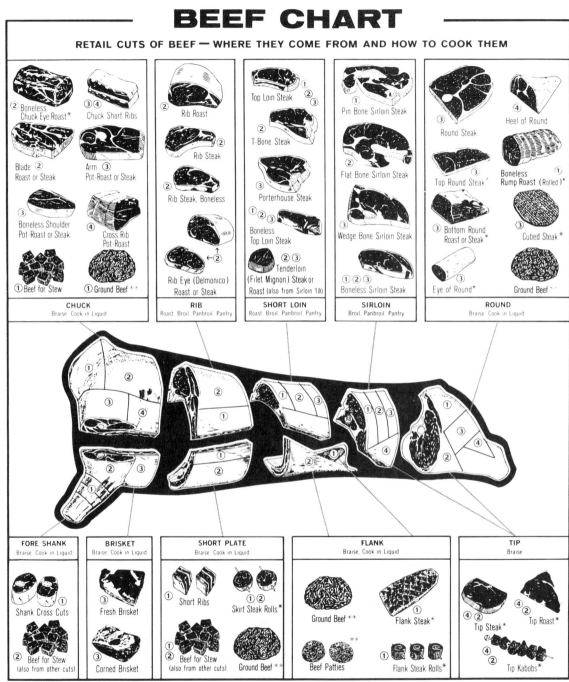

Figure 3-58. Cuts of beef. (Courtesy National Live Stock and Meat Board)

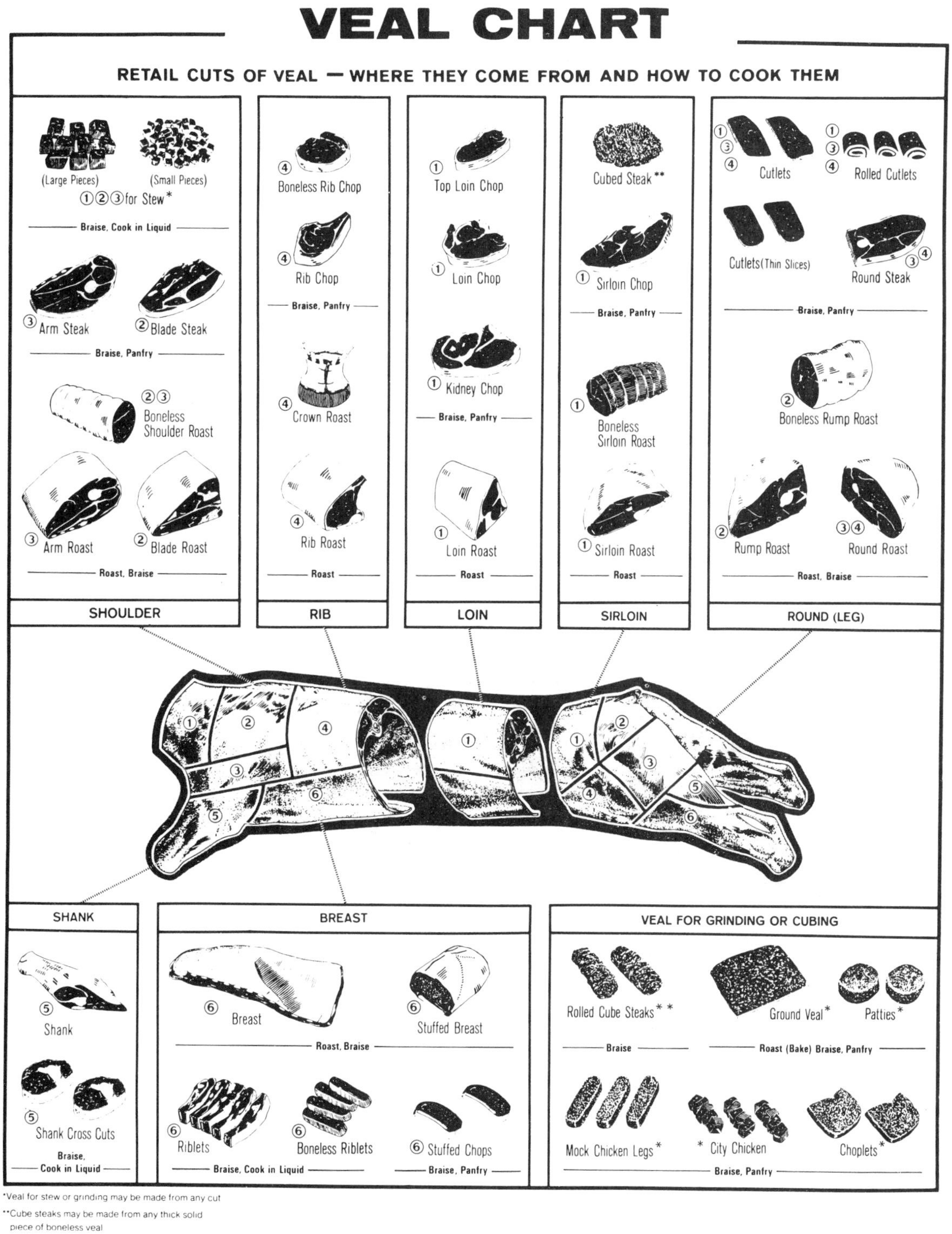

Figure 3-59. Cuts of veal. (Courtesy National Live Stock and Meat Board)

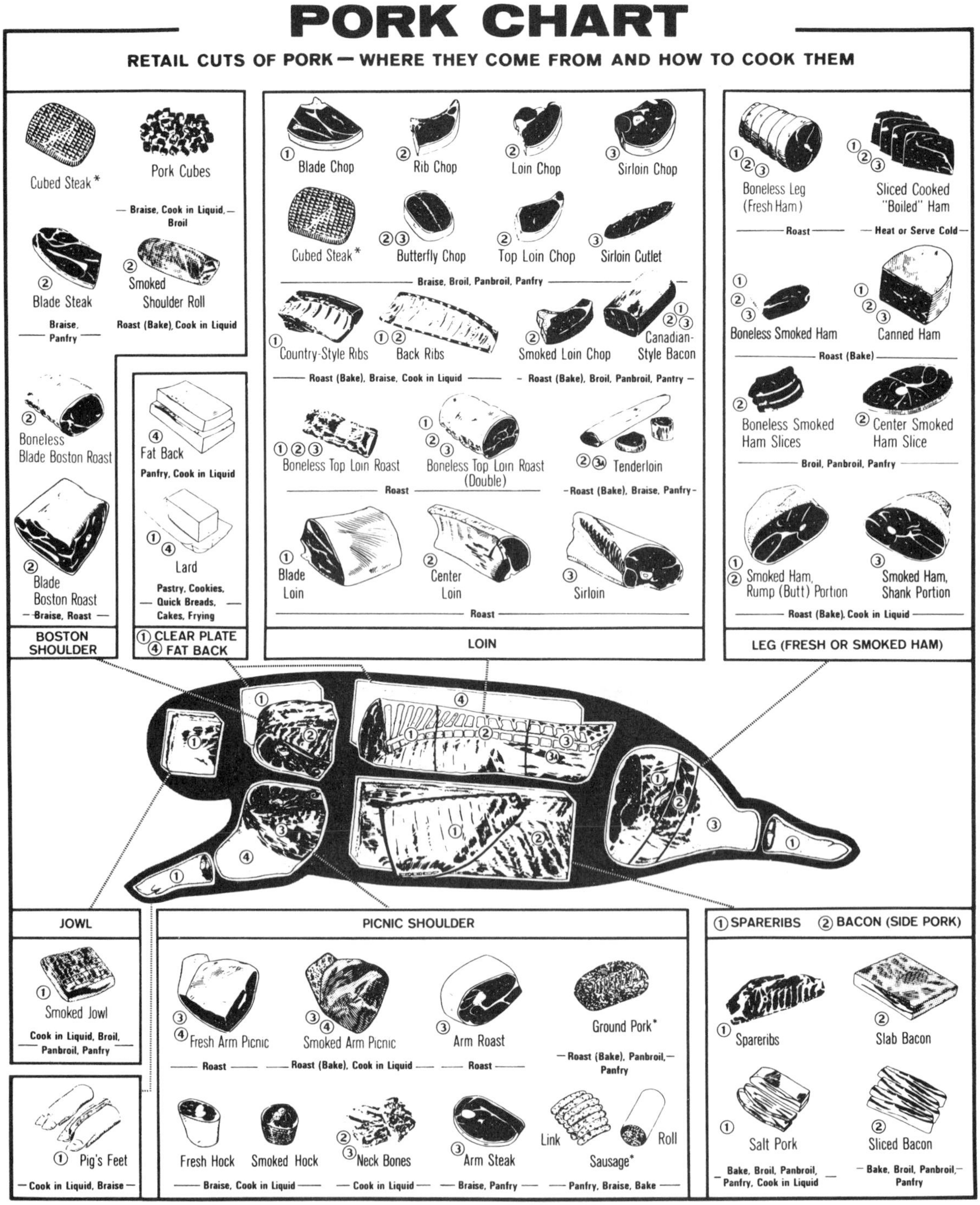

PORK CHART

RETAIL CUTS OF PORK — WHERE THEY COME FROM AND HOW TO COOK THEM

BOSTON SHOULDER

Cubed Steak *

Pork Cubes

— Braise, Cook in Liquid, —
Broil

② Blade Steak

Braise,
Panfry

② Smoked Shoulder Roll

Roast (Bake), Cook in Liquid

② Boneless Blade Boston Roast

② Blade Boston Roast

— Braise, Roast —

① CLEAR PLATE ④ FAT BACK

④ Fat Back

Panfry, Cook in Liquid

① ④ Lard

Pastry, Cookies,
Quick Breads,
Cakes, Frying

LOIN

① Blade Chop

② Rib Chop

② Loin Chop

③ Sirloin Chop

② ③ Cubed Steak *

② ③ Butterfly Chop

② Top Loin Chop

③ Sirloin Cutlet

— Braise, Broil, Panbroil, Panfry —

① Country-Style Ribs

① ② Back Ribs

② Smoked Loin Chop

② ③ Canadian-Style Bacon

— Roast (Bake), Braise, Cook in Liquid —

— Roast (Bake), Broil, Panbroil, Pantry —

① ② ③ Boneless Top Loin Roast

① ② ③ Boneless Top Loin Roast (Double)

② ③ Tenderloin

Roast

— Roast (Bake), Braise, Panfry —

① Blade Loin

② Center Loin

③ Sirloin

Roast

LEG (FRESH OR SMOKED HAM)

① ② ③ Boneless Leg (Fresh Ham)

① ② ③ Sliced Cooked "Boiled" Ham

— Roast —

— Heat or Serve Cold —

① ② ③ Boneless Smoked Ham

① ② ③ Canned Ham

— Roast (Bake) —

② Boneless Smoked Ham Slices

② Center Smoked Ham Slice

— Broil, Panbroil, Panfry —

② Smoked Ham, Rump (Butt) Portion

③ Smoked Ham, Shank Portion

— Roast (Bake), Cook in Liquid —

JOWL

① Smoked Jowl

Cook in Liquid, Broil,
Panbroil, Panfry

① Pig's Feet

— Cook in Liquid, Braise —

PICNIC SHOULDER

④ Fresh Arm Picnic

③ ④ Smoked Arm Picnic

③ Arm Roast

Ground Pork *

— Roast —

— Roast (Bake), Cook in Liquid —

— Roast —

— Roast (Bake), Panbroil,—
Panfry

Fresh Hock

Smoked Hock

② ③ Neck Bones

③ Arm Steak

Link

Sausage *

Roll

— Braise, Cook in Liquid —

— Cook in Liquid —

— Braise, Panfry —

— Panfry, Braise, Bake —

① SPARERIBS ② BACON (SIDE PORK)

① Spareribs

② Slab Bacon

① Salt Pork

② Sliced Bacon

— Bake, Broil, Panbroil, —
Panfry, Cook in Liquid

— Bake, Broil, Panbroil,—
Panfry

*May be made from Boston Shoulder, Picnic Shoulder, Loin or Leg.

Figure 3-60. Cuts of pork. (Courtesy National Live Stock and Meat Board)

cuts are: USDA No. 1, USDA No. 2, USDA No. 3, USDA No. 4, and USDA Utility.

3.3.4 *Lamb and Mutton*

Refer to figure 3-61 and the color insert. The flesh of sheep between 3 and 5 months old is called *baby lamb;* flesh from animals 5 months to a year old is called *lamb.* Mutton is the term used for flesh from sheep over 20 months old.

Lamb carcasses usually weigh between 35 and 65 pounds. The flesh of lamb is lighter in color than that of beef. Mutton flesh is darker. The lean meat of good-quality lamb and mutton has a fine, velvetlike texture; the fat is very firm, brittle, and white. The cut surface of the bones is porous with a reddish color.

Lamb and mutton are graded on quality and yield. The USDA standards for quality are based on conformation, color, and firmness of lean and fat, and texture or grain of flesh. The yield grades reflect differences in the yields of boneless, closely trimmed retail cuts, and in the overall fatness of carcasses and cuts. Yield Grade 1 represents the highest yield of retail cuts and Grade 5 represents the lowest yield.

The quality grades for lamb and yearling mutton are US Prime, US Choice, US Good, US Utility, and US Cull. For mutton the grades are US Choice, US Good, US Utility, and US Cull. Prime and Choice are the grades used most extensively in institutions.

Some of the best-quality lamb comes from New Zealand and Australia. The grading of New Zealand lamb and mutton carcasses for export has been reviewed, and it is reported that overfat lambs were "hidden amongst the Primes." The authors of the study concluded that the New Zealand Prime grade should be divided into two grades, one grade to include the overfat carcasses and the other the leaner, better cutting carcasses. The study is of significance in the United States, as the adoption of these recommendations would perhaps result in the importation of leaner and better-yielding carcasses.

3.3.5 *Sausages*—Charcuterie

Sausage is one of the oldest processed foods. Over the centuries, secret formulas for combinations of meat, spices, herbs, and other ingredients have been handed down from charcutiers, chefs, and families throughout the world, developing sausage making into an art rather than a science.

Today there are over 250 varieties of sausage available in the United States alone. Sausage production has become very profitable in the meat-packing industry. Over 3.8 billion pounds of sausage products are processed in federally inspected plants each year. This is equivalent to 18.4 pounds per person annually.

Federal meat inspection regulations control the ingredients that can be used in sausage products. Only meats that have been federally inspected and approved should be used. The inspection stamp of wholesomeness should be on the products or their packaging.

The differences in the varieties depends on the kind of meat and ingredients used, the combination of the ingredients, the coarseness of the grind, the type of casing, the shape, and whether the product is raw, cooked, dried, smoked, canned, or pickled. Pork, veal, and beef are the meats used in sausages. Fatback trimmings, jowls, and the lean meat from pork; shoulders and shanks from veal; and boneless chucks, plate, shank, briskets, heart, liver, and blood of beef are all suitable for sausage products. Federal regulations permit the addition of liquid, fat, additives, and extenders in specified amounts.

The spices used in sausage, whether in liquid or dry form, should be of excellent quality. Natural spices should be sterilized to prevent bacteria contamination of the meat. Ground pepper, peppercorns, paprika, red pepper, cardamom, cinnamon, and sage are but a few of the spices used. Onions, garlic, parsley, capers, pistachio, truffles, and anchovies are added in varying amounts to impart special flavors to many varieties.

Adequate equipment and general conditions, such as temperature and humidity controls, refrigeration, and storage facilities are necessary for efficient high-quality sausage production. After the sausage is prepared, it is stuffed mechanically into a casing. Natural casings are the intestines of cattle, hogs, and sheep. The stomach and bladder are also used to encase

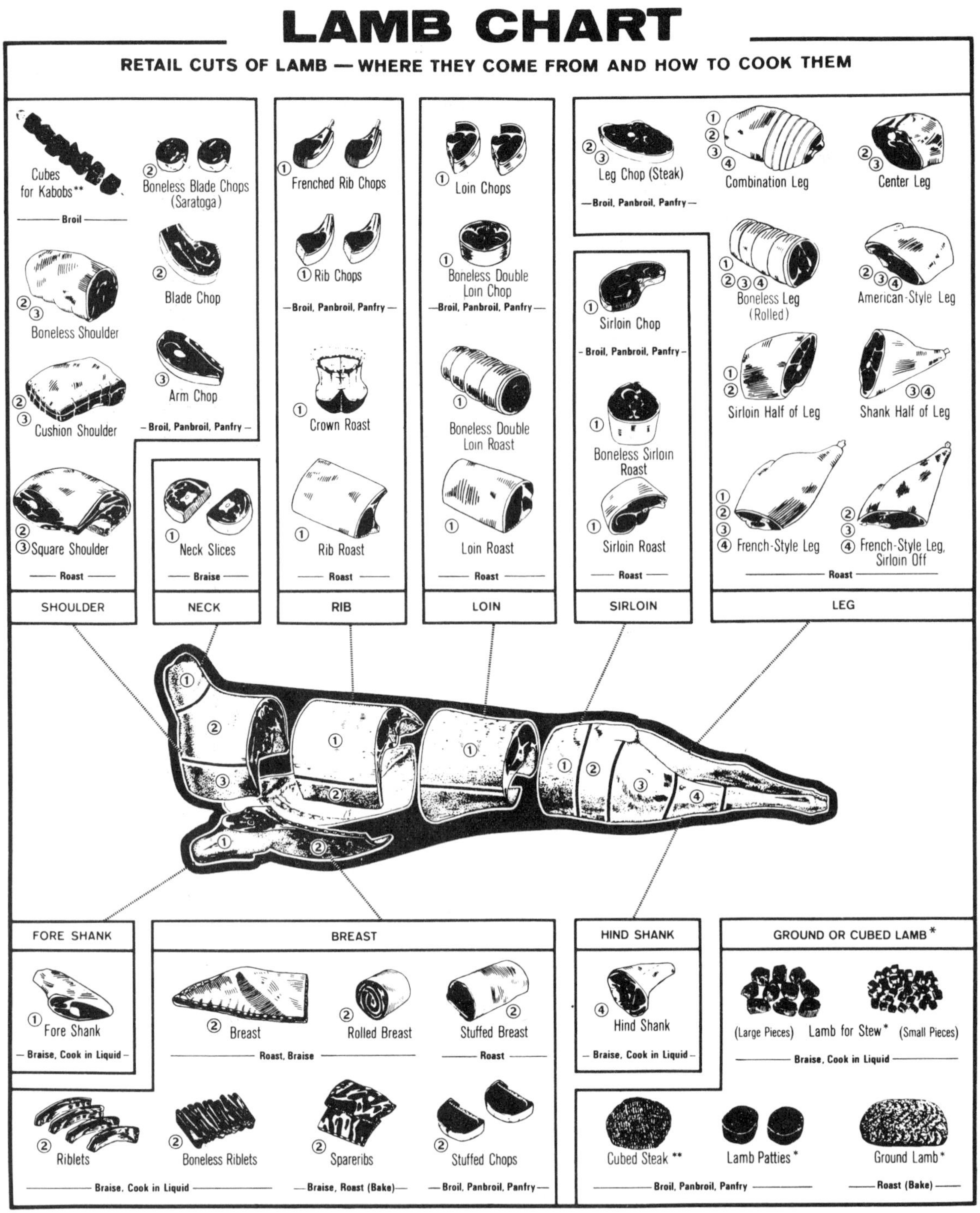

LAMB CHART

RETAIL CUTS OF LAMB — WHERE THEY COME FROM AND HOW TO COOK THEM

SHOULDER

Cubes for Kabobs**

Boneless Blade Chops (Saratoga)

— Broil —

Boneless Shoulder

Blade Chop

Cushion Shoulder

Arm Chop

— Broil, Panbroil, Panfry —

Square Shoulder

— Roast —

NECK

Neck Slices

— Braise —

RIB

Frenched Rib Chops

Rib Chops

— Broil, Panbroil, Panfry —

Crown Roast

Rib Roast

— Roast —

LOIN

Loin Chops

Boneless Double Loin Chop

— Broil, Panbroil, Panfry —

Boneless Double Loin Roast

Loin Roast

— Roast —

SIRLOIN

Sirloin Chop

— Broil, Panbroil, Panfry —

Boneless Sirloin Roast

Sirloin Roast

— Roast —

LEG

Leg Chop (Steak)

— Broil, Panbroil, Panfry —

Combination Leg

Center Leg

Boneless Leg (Rolled)

American-Style Leg

Sirloin Half of Leg

Shank Half of Leg

French-Style Leg

French-Style Leg, Sirloin Off

— Roast —

FORE SHANK

Fore Shank

— Braise, Cook in Liquid —

BREAST

Breast

Rolled Breast

Stuffed Breast

— Roast, Braise — — Roast —

Riblets

Boneless Riblets

— Braise, Cook in Liquid —

Spareribs

Stuffed Chops

— Braise, Roast (Bake) — — Broil, Panbroil, Panfry —

HIND SHANK

Hind Shank

— Braise, Cook in Liquid —

GROUND OR CUBED LAMB*

(Large Pieces) Lamb for Stew* (Small Pieces)

— Braise, Cook in Liquid —

Cubed Steak**

Lamb Patties*

Ground Lamb*

— Broil, Panbroil, Panfry — — Roast (Bake) —

* Lamb for stew or grinding may be made from any cut.

**Kabobs or cube steaks may be made from any thick solid piece of boneless Lamb.

Figure 3-61. Cuts of lamb. (Courtesy National Live Stock and Meat Board)

98

some sausage products. While natural casings are generally preferred, synthetic and collagen casings are widely used. The method of sausage production will, in some instances, influence the type of casing.

The storage of sausage affects the keeping quality. Fresh sausage is highly perishable and should be refrigerated. Smoked and cooked sausages should be held under refrigeration for 4 to 5 days. Semidry sausages are perishable and should be refrigerated or stored in a well-ventilated, dry room at 50°F (10°C) or lower. Sausages are sensitive to changes in temperature and to surrounding odors. When removed from the refrigerator, sweating occurs, producing ideal conditions for the development of molds.

The generally recognized classifications of sausage are fresh sausage, smoked and/or cooked sausages, and dry and semidry sausages.

Fresh Sausage

This is ground raw meat, such as pork sausage, in the form of links or patties or in bulk. Mettwurst is a very fine stuffing made from lean and fat pork. Beef is added to Holsteiner and Berlin mettwurst and frequently to country-style sausage. These products are highly perishable and should be thoroughly cooked before eating.

Smoked and/or Cooked Sausages

These may be made from pork, beef, and veal. Braunschweiger, liver sausage, frankfurters, and bologna are typical examples of this group. Depending upon the particular variety, the sausage is stuffed into a casing and cooked in water at 160°F (70°C) to an internal temperature of 100°F (38°C).

Dry and Semidry Sausages

These are made from pork, beef, or a combination of pork and beef. The uncooked, highly seasoned sausage is stuffed into a casing. Some sausages are dried and smoked, others are only dried. Salami, Thuringer, and Cervelat are well-known varieties. Salami is a hard, raw sausage. Its name comes from the Italian *salame*—"salted meat." Formerly, real salami was made from donkey meat and was merely dried in the air without smoke. Today salami is generally made from pork or from mixtures of lean pork, beef, and bacon fat. In Italy, after the sausages are prepared, they are dipped into a hot flour and water mixture and dried. This leaves a white protective coating around the sausage.

3.4 Poultry—*Volaille*

The word *poultry* refers to the different kinds of domestic and battery-reared fowls that are commercially sold, such as chickens, geese, ducks, turkeys, and pigeons. All other varieties come under the classification of game birds.

The consumption of poultry has increased rapidly in recent years. This increase has resulted from improved production and marketing procedures, year-round availability, moderate costs, and the wide variety of poultry products on the market. Due to the improved methods of processing, freezing, packaging, grading, and distributing, poultry products are available throughout the year, and there is very little fluctuation in price. Immediately after slaughter, poultry should be chilled to 40°F (5°C) and then frozen by rapid freezing and stored at 0°F to −5°F (−18°C to −20°C). The main suppliers of frozen chicken are the United States, Denmark, Holland, and France.

According to United States federal regulations, all poultry must be inspected for wholesomeness before and after slaughter. The approval stamp is attached to the wing or to the package. After inspection the poultry may be graded by a technically trained government grader. Grading service is provided on a voluntary basis to processors and others who request it.

Indicating quality, United States grades apply to the five kinds of poultry: chicken, turkey, duck, goose, and guinea. The highest quality grade is US Grade A. Grade A poultry is fully fleshed and meaty, well finished with no defects, and has an attractive overall appearance.

US Grade B and US Grade C are the other official grades; these grades, however, are seldom found on the retail market. The grade shield may be found on

Species	Description	Usage	Average Weight	Season
Poultry with White Meat				
Chick—*Poussin*	The smallest variety of poultry, age one month.	Roasting	10 to 14 ozs.	Spring
Cockerel—*Coq vierge*	Between a chick and spring chicken. Both sexes are used.	Roasting and grilling	10 to 16 ozs.	Spring
Spring chicken—*Poulet de grain*	Roosters and hens, usually under 10 weeks old. Sleek skin, supple breastbone.	Roasting, grilling, and deep-frying	1¼ to 2 lbs.	Summer
Chicken—*Poulet reine*	Roosters and hens; use of special feed gives good meat and fat layer. Skin sleek and smooth, supple breastbone.	Roasting, grilling, and on the spit	2¼ to 4 lbs.	Summer, fall
Poularde—*Poularde*	Specially bred hens: France—*poularde de Bresse;* Belgium—*poularde de Bruxelles;* Holland—*poularde de Houdan.*	Roasting, pot-roasting, and grilling	4 to 6½ lbs.	Fall, winter
Capon—*Chapon*	A surgically unsexed male chicken (usually under 8 months of age) that has tender meat with soft, pliable, smooth-textured skin.	Roasting, pot-roasting, and grilling	5 to 6¼ lbs.	Fall, winter
Hen—*Poule*	A mature female chicken or fowl (usually over 10 months old) with a nonflexible breastbone. The meat is less tender than that of a rooster.	May be used in many ways: chicken soup, chicken with rice, or fricassee	3¼ to 5½ lbs.	Year-round
Young turkey—*Dindonneau*	A young turkey with white meat, which is, however, drier than that of the poularde. Strong sinews run through the legs of male and female turkeys and must be carefully removed when dressing the birds.	Most suitable for roasting and pot-roasting	4½ lbs.	Fall
Turkey—*Dinde/ Dindon*	Turkeys originated in North America, where they were domesticated by the Indians. Turkeys are in demand in England and North America. Apart from those bred in the U.S., the main suppliers are Argentina, Poland, and Hungary. The turkey has both light and dark meat and little fat.	Smaller turkeys may be roasted or pot-roasted. Larger birds are boned and rolled.	6 to 12 lbs; 11 to 24 lbs.	Winter

Figure 3-62. The different types of poultry.

Species	Description	Usage	Average Weight	Season
Poultry with Dark Meat				
Guinea fowl—*Pintade*	Beside the poularde, the guinea fowl is the most suitable variety of poultry. Its meat is excellent and, after the hunting season, serves as a good replacement for game birds. The breastbone should be supple and the claws sharp.	Grilled or pot-roasted and used for ballottines, galantines, and terrines (cold meat loaves)	1½ to 2¼ lbs.	Fall, spring
Duckling—*Caneton* Duck—*Canard*	The Long Island duckling is best known in the U.S. Nantes duck is famous in France, where the excellent Rouen duck (*caneton rouennais*) is also bred. This variety is especially suitable for roasting "rare." To keep the blood in the duck, it is not slaughtered, but strangled. Young ducks can be recognized by the soft gullet and breast-bone.	Roasting, braising	3 to 3¾ lbs. 3¼ to 5¾ lbs.	August February
Gosling—*Oison* Goose—*Oie*	There are two types—fattened goose and fattened gosling. Goose meat is tasty only during the first year. Fattened goslings should be no older than 5 months. Their weight is approximately 9 lbs. The gullet of young geese can be depressed easily, the webbing of the feet easily torn, and the claws are pointed but soft. The beak can be snapped back easily.	The goose liver is a special delicacy. It can be prepared in many ways (terrines, pâtés, and pies). Geese may be roasted, braised, and stuffed. They are also cut into sections—breast, drumstick.	4½ to 9 lbs. 9 to 13½ lbs.	September January
Young pigeon— *Pigeonneau* Pigeon—*Pigeon*	Pigeons are considered dark meat poultry, although young birds have tender, white meat. The meat of older birds is red and can be used only for soups. The breast should be meaty, the skin smooth, firm, and without colored streaks. Dull, sunken eyes and patchy, hanging wings are signs of excess storage.	Roasting, stuffing, or grilling	1¼ to 1¾ lbs.	Fall

all types of chilled or frozen poultry or poultry parts.

Poultry meat is no different from that derived from mammals. It is, however, generally appreciated for its good taste. White meat from young poultry is easy to digest. It contains animal proteins, fat, vitamins, and minerals (iron, phosphorous). The two groups within the poultry family are poultry with white meat: chicken and turkey; and poultry with dark meat: duck, goose, guinea, and pigeon. The color of the meat has no effect on its quality. (See figure 3-62.)

Quality Determination: It is the class (age) of the bird, not the grade, that indicates the tenderness of the bird. Young birds are more tender than old ones. Young tender classes are best for barbecuing, frying, broiling, or roasting.

Young chickens may be labeled *young chicken, broiler, fryer, roaster,* or *capon.* Young turkeys may be labeled *young turkey, fryer, roaster, young hen,* or *young tom.* Young ducks may be labeled *duckling, young duckling, broiler duckling, fryer duckling,* or *roaster duckling.*

Mature, less tender-meated classes are suitable for stewing or baking. Mature chickens may be labeled *mature chicken, old chicken, hen, stewing chicken,* or *fowl.* Mature turkeys may be labeled *mature turkey, yearling turkey,* or *old turkey.* Mature ducks, geese, and guineas may be labeled *mature* or *old.*

The eating quality of young poultry is superior to that of other birds. Poultry with white meat is supple, without boney breastbones. It has strong feet, sharp claws, a bright red comb, and smooth skin on the legs. Poultry with dark meat has a soft and supple gullet. The same is true of the tip of the breastbone of geese and ducks. It is more difficult to check this, because the lower part of the body is covered with a thick layer of fat that hardens when slightly chilled and responds slightly to finger pressure.

Fresh poultry should always be stored in a refrigerator at a temperature of 34° to 38°F (1° to 3°C) with 70 to 75 percent humidity. The quality of frozen poultry that has been properly handled is equivalent to that of fresh poultry. Inadequate storage practice will affect the quality of the meat. Over longer periods of storage, the temperature should be kept at 0° to −5°F (−18° to −20°C). Poultry should be prepared immediately after thawing. It should not be refrozen.

Poultry can be prepared in the following ways: poached, roasted, grilled, deep-fried, stewed, sautéed, poêler (pot-roasted), spit-roasted. When poaching, use chickens weighing 2 pounds or more, or stewing chickens. When steaming, use chickens weighing 2 pounds or more, but not stewing chickens. When roasting, use any kind of poultry from the largest to the smallest, excluding stewing chickens. When roasting on the spit and grilling, use only tender poultry.

U.S. legislation requires that all meat and poultry sold for public consumption be federally and/or state inspected.

3.5 Game—*Gibier*

Game is the name used for the meat of wild animals.

3.5.1 *Furred Game*—Gibier de poil

Game beasts include the following species: deer (venison), hare, red deer, chamois, wild boar, and wild rabbit. The quality of the meat of game beasts is equivalent to that of domestic animals. It is tender, soft, and easily digested; its nutritional value compares with that of domestic meat. It is at its best during the fall hunting season. If game is to be frozen, it should not be skinned, and should be stored in a vacuum to prevent drying. When butchering game, especially if it is to be used for marinated game stews, the bones should be cut with a meat saw so that they will not splinter. Pieces or splinters of bone in food can cause serious injury.

Red Deer—*Cerf*

The male red deer, weighing between 350 and 500 pounds, can be recognized by his antlers. Red deer live together in herds. In Switzerland, wild red deer are found only in the mountains of the canton of Graubunden.

Animals weighing up to 75 pounds are classified as calf deer and their meat is equivalent to veal. Those weighing 75 pounds to 100 pounds are known as *brockets* and correspond to the meat of young bulls. The meat of red deer weighing over 130 pounds is similar to that of beef. The meat from young red deer is very tender.

The saddle may be used for chops and the leg for cutlets. It can be used for braising and for game stews (*pfeffer*). It is particularly important that the meat of older animals be stored properly.

Chamois—*Chamois*

Chamois is a member of the hoofed game group and usually lives in the mountains (Alps). During the summer, the fur is rusty red with black streaks on the back, and in the winter, it is dark brown. Both sexes carry horns that point backwards.

The meat of young chamois is very tasty, but that of older animals is rather tough and leaves a peculiar aftertaste. Young chamois have thin legs; those of older animals are very bony and covered with hair. Legs can be marinated and braised. Generally the whole chamois is used to make ragout (pfeffer).

Deer—*Chevreuil*

Deer live in herds in the woods. The male animals carry antlers with two beams that have one or more tines. The females are as large as the males but carry no antlers. After an animal has been shot, the entrails are removed, but it is not skinned. The weight of the animal once cleaned is between 30 and 50 pounds. (See figure 3-63.)

The meat of animals three years and younger is tasty and tender, but that of older animals is tough and less easily digestible. Since the meat is generally lean, the leg and saddle must be larded before roasting and should be cooked to the medium or rare stage. Marinating the leg and saddle for approximately 2 hours tenderizes the meat. The remaining parts, which are suitable for ragouts (pfeffer), should be marinated in a good red-wine marinade for 4 to 6 days.

Wild Rabbit—*Lapereau*

Wild rabbits are found in France, England, the United States, and Australia, where they are sometimes so widespread that they become pests. The fur

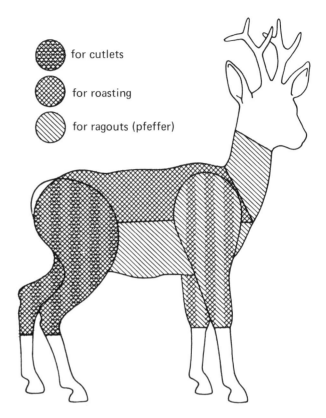

for cutlets

for roasting

for ragouts (pfeffer)

Figure 3-63. Deer—*Chevreuil.*

is grayish in color and the body smaller than the domesticated rabbit.

Rabbit meat is rather dry. It is used primarily in pies and hasenpfeffer.

Hare—*Lièvre*

Hare is a rodent that likes seedlings and cabbage. The male is known as a buck, the female a doe. Hare weigh between 6½ and 13 pounds. The best-quality meat comes from hare that are three to eight months old. They are fattest in November and December. A young hare has long legs and soft ears that bend and tear easily. The meat is quite light and grayish red; that of older animals is dark red. Hare that have been recently killed have clear eyes that glaze over after 2 days and dry out after 8 days. Meat of young hare is very tender, while that of older hare is usually dry.

Hare keeps very well when hung by its feet, unskinned. Hare is cut up into the saddle, leg, neck and breast, and foreleg. The saddle—*rable*—fresh or marinated, with the nerves removed, is larded and roasted to the rare stage. The leg—*cuissot*—is prepared like a saddle or used in hasenpfeffer or ragout. The neck and breast—*cou, poitrine*—are marinated with red wine and *mirepoix* or used in hasenpfeffer. The foreleg—*epaules*—is used as the neck and breast are.

Wild Boar—*Sanglier*

Wild boar weigh a maximum of 450 pounds. Males are called tuskers; females, wild sows. Boars are categorized into three quality groups. Young animals, weighing up to 65 pounds, have yellowish brown coloring. Medium animals, weighing 65 to 80 pounds, have blackish brown coloring. Old animals, weighing over 80 pounds, have tough, wiry hair and tusks.

Connoisseurs appreciate the meat of young wild boar (*marcassins*), especially the saddle and legs. The remaining meat may be used for ragout. Generally, wild boar is prepared by the same methods used for deer.

3.5.2 *Feathered Game*—Gibier de plume

Game birds can be hunted in most countries, usually only during the official hunting season. Game birds include wildfowl (capercaillie, black grouse, pheasant, hazel hen, partridge, grouse, rock partridge, quail), wild pigeon, waterfowl (surface-feeding ducks, diving ducks, wild ducks, wild geese), snipe, and thrush.

The meat of game birds is leaner than that of domestic poultry and is easily digested. Compared with domestic poultry, it has a "gamey" taste. All game birds must be hung in an airy place for a few days before plucking. This is called *gaming*. During this period, a distinctive "high taste" (*haut-gout*) develops. The muscles loosen and the meat becomes tender. Game birds deteriorate quickly after this stage. Wild duck and other waterfowl are very perishable and should not be hung.

Young fowl have soft, smooth-textured, pliable skin; flexible breastbone cartilage; and tender flesh. The meat of older birds is less tender and somewhat darker, with firmer breastbone cartilage. Young birds are usually broiled, sautéed, barbecued, or roasted. Older birds are stewed, braised, or used in combination dishes. The meat of game birds is quite lean and should be barded (see figure 7-42) to prevent excessive browning and drying in the early stages of the cooking process.

Snipe—*Bécassine;* Woodcock—*Bécasse*

There are two types of snipe: the woodcock, which is the same size as the partridge, and the marsh snipe, which is smaller. The former lives in woods, while the latter lives in marshes and moors. The hunting season is usually between September and mid-April.

The woodcock is a migratory bird. It has brownish yellow plumage and long, pointed beak. The marsh snipe also has a long, pointed beak that appears to be split because it is so flat. It has bare legs and a yellow stripe on its back. There are three sizes of marsh snipe, large, common, and small. Large ones are about the size of a partridge; small ones are the size of a lark. Connoisseurs consider the woodcock to be the finest of all game birds. Its meat is very tender with a gamey taste and has the advantage of keeping longer than the other types. It is considered to have reached the appropriate degree of maturity when it takes on a gamey taste.

The unplucked bird should hang in a cool, dry place. Snipe can be roasted or braised. They may be used for hot or cold dishes. The entrails are a specialty—snipe tidbits—when prepared in the following way: the intestines, heart, and liver, and an equal amount of bacon are simmered with shallots, parsley, finely chopped lemon peel, and butter. The mixture is seasoned to taste with salt, pepper, nutmeg, a little brandy, and red wine. The mixture may be bound with breadcrumbs. When cold, blend the mixture with an egg yolk, spread on toast, and heat before using (as garnish for roasts and salmis).

Quail—*Caille*

European quail are migratory birds that cross the Sahara, spend the winter in the northern region of tropical Africa, and return in May to central Europe. The hunting season is in September and October. In Italy, Spain, Greece, and southern Russia, quail are caught with nets. In Britain, quail are protected and cannot be hunted. The American varieties have short wings and can fly only short distances. The best known species is the bobwhite.

Quail is the smallest of the game birds. It is approximately 8 inches long. The plumage is brown with a yellow fleck on the crown of the head and above each eye. The legs are covered with yellowish red feathers. The meat of quail is excellent.

The bird should be hung unplucked. Quail is used in both hot and cold dishes. The best methods for cooking quail are roasting on a spit; poaching in a rich veal stock, or poêler.

Wild Duck—*Canard Sauvage*

Wild duck is a waterfowl found in many different areas. The meat of young ducks, especially teal, is a delicacy. Older birds are tough and usually have an oily taste. Young birds have a flexible breastbone and webbed feet that tear easily. Wild duck should be drawn as soon as possible after the bird is shot and should be chilled quickly.

Pheasant—*Faisan*

Pheasant is the most important quarry for wildfowl hunters. It originally came from the banks of the Black Sea and Asia, but it is found almost everywhere. Exporting countries are Hungary, Rumania, Czechoslovakia, and Denmark.

There are two kinds of pheasant—those with and those without collars. The hunted or noble pheasant does not have a collar. Male birds have a brightly colored plumage. The female pheasant has a short tail, and its plumage is less brilliant than that of a cock. The distinctive feature of the cock pheasant is the shape and the length of its tail. A young pheasant has gray legs with short, stubby spurs and a soft, flexible breastbone. The pheasant is one of the meatiest birds for its size. It weighs from 1 to 2 pounds in the carcass and most of the meat is on the breast.

Pheasant should be hung in a cold, dry place for a few days before it is plucked. This gives the bird its special "gamey" taste. The correct degree of maturity and "gaminess" is reached when a fatty oil starts to come out around the beak. Pheasant may be roasted, braised, or prepared as salmis. Older birds may be made into a soufflé.

Partridge—*Perdreau*

Partridge is usually hunted from the end of August until January. Partridges live in northern, central, and eastern Europe and in North America. Partridge is somewhat larger than pigeon. The younger bird has yellowish legs that are plump and close to the feet. It has a dark, pointed beak, and the feathers are tapered. The older partridge has grayish to grayish yellow legs and a grayish brown plumage. The feathers of the male birds are brightly colored. Partridges live in groups or coveys.

The entrails of partridges are removed immediately after the bird has been killed; the bird is then hung with its feathers. Young birds are roasted; mature birds are made into pies and pâtés and terrines.

3.6 Dairy Products—*Produits laitiers*

3.6.1 *Milk*—Lait

Milk refers to the lacteal secretion obtained from different animals. The milk of many species of animals is used in different parts of the world. In the United States, however, the cow furnishes almost all the milk that is marketed.

Milk appears on today's market in many forms to meet the demands of consumers. In recent years products have been developed to improve keeping quality, to facilitate distribution, to provide for maximum use of all by-products, and to preserve surplus. State and local governments usually determine the standards of composition for all fluid milk products. These governments also are responsible for the sanitation controls. The federal government, however, establishes the standards of identity for evaporated milk, condensed milk, and nonfat dry milk.

Quality specifications for milk are based on flavor, odor, appearance, sediment content, and bacterial count. In appearance it should be smooth and free of any curds, ropiness, or foreign materials. It should have a fresh and sweet odor and taste. Quality milk is high in nutritive value and has good keeping quality. For storage life of milk refer to figure 3-64.

Product	Storage Time	Temperature (°F)
Fresh fluid milk (whole, low-fat, skim, chocolate, and unfermented acidophilus)	8 to 20 days	40°
Sterilized whole milk	4 months	70°
	12 months	40°
Frozen whole milk	12 months	−10°
Evaporated milk	1 month	75°
	12–24 months	70°
	24 months	40°
Concentrated milk	2 or more weeks	30°
Concentrated frozen milk	6 months	−20°
Sweetened condensed milk	3 months	75°
	9–24 months	70°
	15 months	40°
Nonfat dry milk, extra grade (in moisture-proof pack)	6 months	75°
	16–24 months	70°
	24 months	40°
Dry whole milk, extra grade (gas pack: maximum oxygen 2 percent)	6 months	75°
	12 months	70°
	24 months	40°
Buttermilk	2–3 weeks	40°
Sour cream	3–4 weeks	40°
Yogurt	3–6 weeks	40°
Eggnog	1–2 weeks	40°
Ultrapasteurized cream	6–8 weeks	40°

Note: Storage life refers to the length of time after processing—not after purchasing—that the product will retain its quality.

Figure 3-64. Approximate storage life of milk products at specific temperatures.

Average Composition of Milk

The specific gravity of milk is approximately 1.033. Approximately 12.75 percent of the milk is dry solids. The fat content of the milk is approximately 3.7 percent; the total protein content is approximately 3.6 percent; the milk sugar content is approximately 4.7 percent; the mineral content is approximately 0.7 percent; the solids also contain vitamins and enzymes. (See figure 3-65.)

Whole Milk—*Lait entier*

The composition of milk varies among cows and among seasons of the year. Although minimum standards of the composition of milk are established by the individual states, many states define whole milk as milk that contains not less than 3.25 percent milk fat and not less than 8.25 percent milk solids—not fat.

Almost all of the whole fluid milk marketed in the United States is pasteurized and homogenized. Raw milk, or milk that has not been subjected to heat treatment, should be heated or pasteurized before it is consumed.

Certified Milk—*Lait spéciale*

Certified milk, available in only a few areas, originated in 1893 to fulfill the need for safe milk. The certification label on the container means that the raw or pasteurized milk has been produced and distributed under conditions that conform with the standards for cleanliness established by the American Association of Medical Milk Commissions. Certified milk is usually pasteurized; however, it may be raw, and it may be homogenized. It may also be fortified with vitamin D.

Pasteurized Milk—*Lait pasteurisé*

Milk is pasteurized by heating it to 145°F (63°C) and holding it at this temperature for 30 minutes or by holding it at 161°F (71°C) continuously for 15 seconds in equipment that is safe and sanitary. The milk temperature is promptly lowered to 45°F (7°C). Pasteurization destroys all pathogenic organisms in the milk

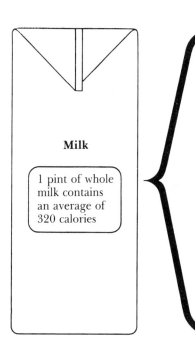

Milk

1 pint of whole milk contains an average of 320 calories

Protein

Content: 3.6% (casein 3.0%, whey protein 0.6%)

Milk protein contains all the essential amino acids and serves an important function in the process of building the body's cells.

Milk Fat

Content: 3.7%

Milk fat is easily digested, contains many vital substances, such as essential fatty acids and vitamins; it is an important source of energy and serves as a protection for certain vital organs.

Milk Sugar

Content: 4.7%

Milk sugar (and therefore milk) provides energy and is necessary for the proper functioning and regulating of certain vital organs and the nervous system.

Minerals

Content: 0.7%

Milk is rich in calcium and phosphorus. These minerals are necessary in human nutrition for building bony structures and for metabolic processes. Calcium is also needed for developing teeth, for muscle contraction, and blood coagulation.

Vitamins

Milk fat contains the vitamins A, D, and E, which are soluble in fat. Milk whey contains vitamins of the B complex and C, which are soluble in water.

Figure 3-65. Nutrient content of milk.

without significantly changing the flavor, odor, or nutritive value. The keeping quality of milk is also improved through pasteurization.

Ultra-heat-treated Milk—*Lait uperisé*

A new process has been developed for treating milk. The milk is heated from 285° to 300°F (140° to 149°C) for a few seconds to destroy the bacteria; it is then immediately cooled. This milk will keep for approximately four months if it is protected from the light. Otherwise the conditions are the same as for pasteurized milk.

Skim Milk—*Lait écrémé*

Skim milk is milk from which the fat has been removed. The fat content is usually 1 percent, although the standards established by various states range from 8 percent to 9.25 percent for the minimum total solids. Skim milk is pasteurized. With the exception of

the milk fat and the vitamin A in the milk fat, the other nutrients in milk—protein, lactose, minerals, and water-soluble vitamins B_1 and B_2—are found in skim milk. Skim milk is frequently fortified with a concentrate of water-soluble vitamin A and vitamin D to replace the vitamins removed with the fat of the whole milk.

Two percent milk, made from skim or whole milk, contains 2 percent milk fat. It is frequently fortified with vitamins and milk solids—not fat.

Mixed Milk Drinks—*Boissons mélangées au lait*

A flavored milk drink is made of pasteurized and homogenized skim or partially skim milk. Syrups or powders with flavoring agents and sugar are added. Chocolate dairy drink consists of skim or partially skim milk flavored with chocolate powder or syrup. Chocolate milk is pasteurized whole milk flavored with sugar and chocolate syrup or powder. Its milk fat content is the same as that of whole milk.

Sour Milk—*Lait aigre*

Sour milk is pasteurized whole milk that is soured through the influence of lactic-acid-building bacteria present in the milk or as a result of adding pure cultured bacteria, vinegar, or lemon juice to heated milk.

Buttermilk—*Babeurre*

Buttermilk may be either a churned or cultured product. Most buttermilk today is not the by-product from churning cream into butter but is made of pasteurized fresh fluid skim milk cultured with streptococcus lactic and incubated at 68° to 72°F (20° to 22°C).

Yogurt—*Yoghourt*

Yogurt is usually manufactured from fresh, partially pasteurized and homogenized skim milk that has been enriched with added milk solids—not fat. The mixture is inoculated and incubated at 105° to 115°F (41° to 46°C). The yogurt coagulates within a two-hour period. The acidifying process is stopped by immediately lowering the temperature to 35° to 40°F (2° to 4°C). The finished product is fine-textured, smooth, semisolid clabbered milk that contains between 11 and 12 percent solids. Fruit concentrates, jams, and whole fruits may be added to the yogurt. A frozen yogurt product is also available in varied flavors. Yogurt can also be made from whole milk with 3.5 percent fat content.

Concentrated Milks

Fresh, frozen, condensed, evaporated, and dried concentrated milks are available on today's market. Varying amounts of water are removed under controlled conditions. The milk may be reconstituted by adding the appropriate quantity of water.

Cottage Cheese—*Fromage blanc*

Cottage cheese may be made from fresh pasteurized skim milk, sour milk, or reconstituted nonfat dry milk. A combination of lactic-acid starter and rennet is used in varying amounts to initiate the coagulation. The milk is further coagulated at temperatures from 70° to 90°F (21° to 32°C) for several hours. Cottage cheese has a mild acid flavor. It is used for salads, with fruits, vegetables, dips, desserts, and pastries.

3.6.2 *Cream*—Crème

Cream is that part of whole unhomogenized milk that rises to the surface. The fat particles are large and less dense than milk. Cream is produced under the same conditions as milk. The U.S. Food and Drug Administration has standards of identity for each of the various types of cream if they are shipped interstate. These standards give minimum milk fat requirements for each type of cream.

Heavy Cream—*Crème entière*

Heavy cream or whipping cream must have at least 36 percent milk fat. It is pasteurized homogenized cream. The stability and volume of the cream are usually increased if the cream has been allowed to stand for twenty-four hours or longer. Air is incorporated into the cream with whipping, which may increase the volume by 80 to 100 percent. To whip cream the utensils should be cold, and the cream should be at 35° to 40°F (2° to 4°C). Cream should not be overwhipped as the product may become grainy and eventually become butter.

Sour Cream—*Crème aigre*

Sour cream must contain a minimum of 18 percent milk fat. It is made by adding about 0.2 percent lactic-acid bacteria culture to pasteurized and homogenized full cream or half-and-half cream. The cream is matured for 24 hours at 68°F (20°C). Sour cream is used for cooking game and pfeffers. It also is used in dips, soups, sauces, salads, and desserts.

Half-and-half Cream—*Demi-crème*

Half-and-half or coffee cream is a mixture of homogenized milk and cream. The federal standards require a minimum of 10.5 percent milk fat.

Ice Cream—*Crème glacée*

Ice-cream products are made of cream, milk, condensed milk, syrup, fresh or frozen or dried fruits, fruit juices and purées, chocolate, sugar, and stabilizers. The mixture is pasteurized (with the exception of some sherbets and ices) and then homogenized. Federal standards state that plain ice cream must contain a minimum of 10 percent milk fat and that the maximum content of stabilizers used is 0.5 percent. The milk fat content of dairy ice cream with fruit, fruit juices, nuts, or chocolate must be a minimum of 8 percent.

3.6.3 *Butter*—Beurre

The origin of butter dates back to ancient times. The early nomadic people used the milk of cows, ewes, goats, and camels to prepare butter. The Aryans introduced butter to the people of India, who considered it a sacred food. According to history, the Scythians brought butter to the Greeks, and from then on its use spread very rapidly throughout the world. See figures 3-66 and 3-67.

The U.S. Department of Agriculture defines butter as "the food product usually known as butter, and which is made exclusively from milk or cream, or both, with or without common salt, and with or without additional coloring matter, and containing not less than 80 percent by weight of milk fat, all tolerances having been allowed for." The USDA has established grades for butter; however, grading is not compulsory. A manufacturer may request inspection and grading. The USDA grade shield (AA, A, B, or C) indicates that the butter has been tested and graded in accordance with the federal specifications for each grade.

Nomenclature and Characteristics of U.S. Grades of Butter

Butter classed as U.S. Grade AA Butter or U.S. 93 Score has a delicate sweet flavor, with a highly pleasing aroma. It is manufactured from high-quality fresh, sweet cream. The butter has a smooth, creamy texture and good spreadability. Salt is completely dissolved in it.

Grade A Butter or U.S. 92 Score has a pleasing flavor, is manufactured from fresh cream, and is fairly smooth in texture. It is very similar to grade AA butter.

U.S. Grade B Butter or U.S. 90 Score may have a slightly acid flavor. It is usually made from selected sour cream. This butter is readily acceptable to many consumers.

U.S. Grade C Butter or U.S. 89 Score has a malty, scorched, or stale flavor and an uneven color.

Average Composition of Butter

Butter is 81.3 percent milk fat, 1.0 percent milk solids, 2.3 percent salt, and 15.3 percent moisture. It is sold in 1-pound, ½-pound, and ¼-pound packages. Ready-cut table butter, cut into 48, 60, 72, or 90 pieces per pound, is also available. The butter is arranged on parchment paper and packed in layers in 5-pound units. It is also packed with individual cuts on a paper server for use in butter dispensers. Sweet butter is unsalted butter made from sweet cream. Clarified butter, or *ghee*, is melted butter with the milk solids removed. Butter should be refrigerated at 35°F (2°C) in its original package or in a covered container, or it may be frozen and stored at 0°F (−18°C).

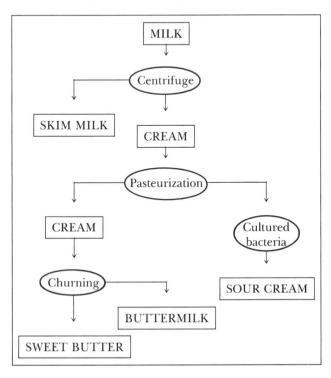

Figure 3-66. Buttermaking.

Buttermaking . . . Then and Now

Butter churns are the oldest dairy equipment, dating from prehistoric days when nomads carried milk in a type of pouch made from an animal's stomach. Slung on the back of a horse or a camel, the pouch bounced as the animal moved, churning the cream or milk within into butter.

Wooden or crockery dasher-type churns used in great-grandmother's day are today's attic treasures. By jouncing a long-handled wooden dasher up and down in the deep churn, the cream was sloshed around until butter particles separated from the remaining liquid, called buttermilk.

Clean cold water was poured into the churn after the buttermilk was drained. The butter granules were washed and drained again. Finally, they were worked or kneaded with a wooden paddle until they became a dense waxy mass. The butter was packed into a fancy butter mold or crock for use.

Buttermaking modernized

New methods of separating cream and of measuring the milk-fat content of milk fostered the industrialization of buttermaking. Two key inventions, both in 1890, were the DeLaval centrifugal cream separator and the Babcock test for butterfat content of milk.

Present-day creameries manufacture butter under rigid requirements for sanitation and quality control. In modern buttermaking, fresh sweet milk is weighed, tested for milk-fat content, and checked for quality. The cream is then separated to contain 30 to 35 percent milk fat for batch churning, 40 to 45 percent milk fat for continuous churning.

Pasteurization of the cream is an essential part of the procedure. The cream must be heated to not less than 165°F (74°C) for not less than 30 minutes, or to 185°F (85°C) for 15 seconds.

In batch churning, the churning principle is essentially the same as in the old dasher-type churn, but the churn is a huge metal cylinder that turns around a horizontal axis. The cream is agitated as the churn rotates. Up to 8,000 pounds of butter can be churned in a batch.

Cream is pumped into the batch churn at 50°F (10°C) or lower. Most butter is not colored (color may be added to meet consumer demand). The churn is rotated for about 45 minutes. After the buttermilk is drained, the butter may be washed with clean, cold water. Salt and additional water are added and then worked in by further rotating the churn.

The butter is removed manually or automatically, then fed into an automatic butter printer-wrapper. The butter is cut, or "printed" into quarter-pound, half-pound, or pound prints. It is then wrapped in wax paper, foil, or parchment and put in cartons. The packaged butter is refrigerated in rooms at 0° to −20°F (−18° to −29°C).

Continuous buttermaking operations, which can produce 1,800 to 11,000 pounds an hour, are an industry trend. New continuous buttermaking processes employ several different scientific principles to form butter.

Generally the pasteurized cream is transported through one or more metal cylinders. Inside, special equipment transforms the cream into butter. Then the salt and coloring, if added, are worked in and the butter is discharged to the printer-wrapper. This is done in one automated operation.

Figure 3-67. Traditional and modern methods of buttermaking. (Courtesy National Dairy Council)

3.6.4 *Cheese*—Fromage

Cheese is defined by the National Dairy Council as "the concentration of all or part of the components of milk obtained through the coagulation of the major milk protein, casein, by suitable enzymes, and/or by acid produced by bacteria. The curd, separated from the whey, is used at once in unripened cheese. In the cheese, the curd is ripened by the action of beneficial bacteria, molds, yeasts, and enzymes."

Natural cheese is made by separating most of the milk solids from the milk by curdling with either a bacterial culture or rennet or both and separating the curd from the whey by heating, agitating, and pressing. Most cheeses made in the United States are made from whole cow's milk; however, some are made from both milk and cream, some from skim milk, and others from whey or combinations of these products. (See figures 3-68 and 3-69.)

The distinctive characteristics such as flavor, texture, aroma, and consistency of the various cheeses result from these factors:

- Kind of milk used
- Type of bacteria or molds used in ripening
- Method used for curdling the milk and for cutting, cooking, and forming the curd
- Amount of salt or seasonings added
- Conditions of the ripening process such as temperature, humidity, and length of time.

All natural cheese should be stored in the original wrapper or covering at refrigerated temperatures. The cut surface of cheese should be covered with aluminum foil, wax paper, or plastic wrapping material to protect the surface from drying. Large pieces that are to be stored over a long period of time may be dipped into melted paraffin. Cheese that has become hard or dried out may be grated and refrigerated in a tightly sealed container. Except for soft unripened cheeses, such as cottage and cream cheese, the flavor and texture of cheese are best when served at room temperature. Cheese should usually be removed from the refrigerator about an hour before serving. Different kinds of cheese should never be served with the same knife.

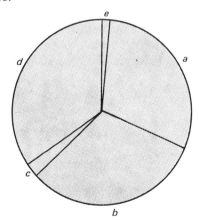

Figure 3-68. Composition of Emmentaler cheese: (a) 30 percent protein; (b) 31 percent milk fat; (c) 2 percent minerals (calcium, phosphorus, copper, and practically all the valuable trace elements); (d) 36 percent water; (e) 1 percent salt; plus vitamins A, D, E, K, the provitamin A, carotene, and B-complex vitamins.

Production of Cheese

The basis of cheese, unless otherwise indicated on the label of the cheese, is cow's milk, which may be adjusted by separating part of the fat or by adding certain milk solids. Thus, various kinds of combinations of milk are utilized in making specific types of cheese. For example, dry-curd cottage cheese is made from skim milk, Cheddar cheese from whole milk, cream cheese from milk enriched with cream, and Swiss and Edam from mixtures of whole and skim milk.

The quality of milk used in cheesemaking as well as that for consumption is of prime importance and is rigidly controlled. Originally most cheese was made from raw milk, but currently most manufacturers use heat-treated milk. Cheeses such as Swiss (Emmentaler) and Gruyère may be produced from heat-treated or pasteurized milk, but they are ripened or cured for at least 60 days for the development of eyes. In those instances where unpasteurized milk is used in the making of cheese, the cheese must be ripened for a period of 60 days at a temperature of not less than 35°F (1.7°C) to ensure safety against pathogenic organisms.

The pasteurization of milk for cheesemaking is not a substitute for sanitation but rather an additional safeguard. The advantages of pasteurization include heat treatment sufficient to destroy pathogenic flora; a higher quality product due to destruction of undesirable gas- and flavor-forming microorganisms; product uniformity; and standardized cheesemaking—easier control of the manufacturing procedure, especially acid development. The disadvantage of pasteurization is the difficulty of developing the full typical flavor in some cheeses such as Cheddar.

The use of heat-treated milk is preferred for ripened cheeses such as Cheddar, Swiss, and provolone to preserve a more typical cheese flavor. Heat-treated milk is usually heated to a temperature short of pasteurization, for example 147°F (64°C), for 16 seconds. Standard high-temperature short-time relationships for this treatment have not been established by industry, thus variability may be expected. The time/tem-

Name	Origin	Consistency and Texture	Color and Shape
American pasteurized process	United States	Semisoft to soft; smooth, plastic body	Light yellow to orange; square slices
Asiago	Italy	Semisoft (fresh), medium, or hard (old); tiny gas holes or eyes	Light yellow; may be coated with paraffin, clear or colored black or brown; round and flat
Bel Paese	Italy	Soft; smooth, waxy body	Slightly gray surface, creamy yellow interior; small wheels
Blue, Bleu	France	Semisoft; visible veins of mold on white cheese, pasty, sometimes crumbly	White, marbled with blue-green mold; cylindrical
Breakfast, Frühstück	Germany	Soft; smooth, waxy body	Cylindrical, 2½ to 3 inches diameter
Brick	United States	Semisoft; smooth open texture; numerous round and irregular-shaped eyes	Light yellow to orange; brick-shaped
Brie	France	Soft, thin edible crust, creamy interior	White crust, creamy yellow interior; large, medium, and small wheels
Caciocavallo	Italy	Hard firm body, stringy texture	Light tan surface, interior; molded into distinctive shapes, typically spindle-shaped or oblong
Camembert	France	Soft, almost fluid in consistency; thin edible crust, creamy interior	Gray-white crust, creamy yellow interior; small wheels
Cheddar	England	Hard; smooth, firm body, can be crumbly	Nearly white to orange; varied shapes and styles
Colby	United States	Hard but softer and more open in texture than Cheddar	White to light yellow, orange; cylindrical
Cottage, Dutch, Farmers, Pot	Uncertain	Soft; moist, delicate, large or small curds	White; packaged in cuplike containers
Cream	United States	Soft; smooth, buttery	White; foil-wrapped in rectangular portions
Edam	Holland	Semisoft to hard; firm crumbly body; small eyes	Creamy yellow with natural or red paraffin coat; flattened ball or loaf shape, about 4 pounds
Feta	Greece	Soft, flaky, similar to very dry, high-acid cottage cheese	White
Gammelost	Norway	Semisoft	Brownish rind, brown-yellow interior with a blue-green tint; round and flat
Gjetost	Norway	Hard; buttery	Golden brown; cubical and rectangular
Gorgonzola	Italy	Semisoft, less moist than blue	Light tan surface, light yellow interior, marbled with blue-green mold; cylindrical and flat loaves
Gouda	Holland	Hard, but softer than Cheddar; more open mealy body like Edam, small eyes	Creamy yellow with or without red wax coat; oval or flattened sphere of about 10 to 12 pounds
Gruyère	Switzerland	Hard, tiny gas holes or eyes	Light yellow; flat wheels
Limburger	Belgium	Soft; smooth, waxy body	Creamy white interior, brownish exterior; rectangular
Monterey Jack	United States	Semisoft (whole milk), hard (low-fat or skim milk); smooth texture with small openings throughout	Creamy white; round or rectangular
Mozzarella	Italy	Semisoft; plastic	Creamy white; rectangular and spherical, may be molded into various shapes
Munster	France	Semisoft; smooth, waxy body, numerous small mechanical openings	Yellow, tan, or white surface, creamy white interior; cylindrical and flat or loaf shaped, small wheels and blocks
Neufchâtel	France	Soft; smooth, creamy	White; foil-wrapped in rectangular portions
Parmigiano Reggiano	Italy	Very hard (grating), granular, hard brittle rind	Light yellow with brown or black coating; cylindrical
Port-Salut, Oka	Trappist monasteries	Semisoft; smooth, buttery	Russet surface, creamy white interior; small wheels, cylindrical flat
Primost	Norway	Semisoft	Light brown; cubical and cylindrical
Provolone	Italy	Hard, stringy texture, cuts without crumbling, plastic	Light golden yellow to golden brown, shiny surface bound with cord; yellow-white interior; various shapes (pear, sausage, salami) and sizes
Queso Blanco	Latin America	Soft, dry and granular if pressed; hard, open or crumbly if pressed	White; various shapes and sizes
Ricotta	Italy	Soft, moist and grainy, or dry	White; packaged fresh in paper, plastic, or metal containers
Romano, Pecorino	Italy	Very hard, granular interior, hard brittle rind	Round with flat sides, various sizes
Roquefort	France	Semisoft, pasty and sometimes crumbly	White, marbled with blue-green mold; cylindrical
Sapsago (Schabzieger)	Switzerland	Very hard (grating), granular frequently dried	Light green; small, cone-shaped
Schloss	Germany, northern Austria	Soft; small, ripened	Molded in small rectangular blocks 1½ by 4 inches long
Stirred Curd, Granular	United States	Semisoft to hard	Varied shapes and styles
Stilton	England	Semisoft to hard; open, flaky texture, more crumbly than blue	White, marbled with blue-green mold; cylindrical
Swiss, Emmentaler	Switzerland	Hard; smooth with large gas holes or eyes	Pale yellow, shiny; rindless rectangular blocks and large wheels with rind
Washed Curd	United States	Semisoft to hard	Varied shapes and styles

Figure 3-69. Common varieties of cheese. (Courtesy U.S. Department of Agriculture)

Flavor	Basic Ingredient	Normal Ripening Period	Mode of Serving
Mild	Cheddar, washed, Colby, or granulated (stirred curd) or mixture of two or more	Unripened after cheese(s) heated to blend	In sandwiches; on crackers
Piquant, sharp in aged cheese	Cow's milk, whole or low fat	60 days minimum for fresh (semisoft), 6 months minimum for medium, 12 months minimum for old (grating)	Table cheese (slicing cheese) when not aged; as seasoning (grated) when aged
Mild to moderately robust	Cow's milk, whole	6–8 weeks	As such (dessert); on crackers; in sandwiches, with fruit
Piquant, tangy, spicy, peppery	Cow's milk, whole, or goat's milk	60 days minimum; 3–4 months usually; 9 months for more flavor	As such (dessert); in dips, cooked foods, salads, and dressings
Strong, aromatic	Cow's milk, whole or low fat	Little or none (either)	As such (dessert); on crackers; in sandwiches
Mild but pungent and sweet	Cow's milk, whole	2–3 months	As such; in sandwiches, salads; slices well without crumbling
Mild to pungent	Cow's milk, whole; low fat, or skim	4–8 weeks	As such (dessert)
Sharp, similar to provolone	Sheep's, goat's or cow's milk (whole or low fat) or mixtures of these	3 months minimum for table use, 12 months or longer for grating	As such; as seasoning (grated) when aged
Mild to pungent	Cow's milk, whole	4–5 weeks	As such (dessert)
Mild to sharp	Cow's milk, whole	60 days minimum; 3–6 months usually; 12 or longer for sharp flavor	As such; in sandwiches, cooked foods
Mild to mellow	Cow's milk, whole	1–3 months	As such; in sandwiches, cooked foods
Mild, slightly acid, flavoring may be added	Cow's milk, skim; cream dressing may be added	Unripened	As such; in salads, dips, cooked foods
Mild, slightly acid, flavoring may be added	Cream and cow's milk, whole	Unripened	As such; in salads, in sandwiches, on crackers
Mild, sometimes salty	Cow's milk, low fat	2 months or longer	As such; on crackers, with fresh fruit
Salty	Cow's, sheep's, or goat's milk	4–5 days to 1 month	As such; in cooked foods
Sharp, aromatic	Cow's milk, skim	4 weeks or longer	As such
Sweet, caramel	Whey from goat's milk	Unripened	As such; on crackers
Piquant, spicy, similar to blue	Cow's milk, whole, or goat's milk, or mixtures of these	3 months minimum, frequently 6 months to 1 year	As such (dessert)
Mild, nutlike, similar to Edam	Cow's milk, low fat but more milk fat than Edam	2–6 months	As such; on crackers, with fresh fruit, in cooked dishes
Mild, sweet	Cow's milk, whole	3 months minimum	As such (dessert); fondue
Strong, robust, highly aromatic	Cow's milk, whole or low fat	1–2 months	In sandwiches; on crackers
Mild to mellow	Cow's milk, whole, low fat, or skim	3–6 weeks for table use, 6 months minimum for grating	As such; in sandwiches, grating cheese if made from low-fat or skim milk
Mild, delicate	Cow's milk, whole or low fat; may be acidified with vinegar	Unripened to 2 months	Generally used in cooking, pizza; as such
Mild to mellow, between brick and Limburger	Cow's milk, whole	2–8 weeks	As such; in sandwiches
Mild	Cow's milk, whole or skim, or a mixture of milk and cream	3–4 weeks or unripened	As such; in sandwiches, dips, salads
Sharp, piquant	Cow's milk, low fat	10 months minimum	As such; as grated cheese on salads, soups, and pasta
Mellow or mild to robust, similar to Gouda	Cow's milk, whole or low fat	6–8 weeks	As such (dessert); with fresh fruit, on crackers
Mild, sweet, caramel	Whey with added buttermilk, whole milk, or cream	Unripened	As such; in cooked foods
Bland acid flavor to sharp and piquant, usually smoked	Cow's milk, whole	6–14 months	As such (dessert) after it has ripened for 6 to 9 months; grating cheese when aged
Salty, strong, may be smoked	Cow's milk, whole, low fat, or skim or whole milk with cream or skim milk	Eaten within 2 days to 2 months or more; generally unripened if pressed	As such or later grated
Bland but semisweet	Whey and whole or skim milk or whole and low-fat milk	Unripened	As such; in cooked foods
Sharp, piquant if aged	Cow's (usually low fat), goat's milk, or mixtures of these	5 months minimum, usually 5–8 months for table cheese, 12 months minimum for grating cheese	As such; grated and used as a seasoning
Sharp, spicy (pepper), piquant	Sheep's milk	2 months minimum, usually 2–5 months or longer	As such (dessert); in salads, on crackers
Sharp, pungent, flavored with leaves; sweet	Cow's milk, skim, slightly soured with buttermilk and whey	5 months minimum	As such; as seasoning (grated)
Similar to, but milder than Limburger	Cow's milk, whole or low fat and/or casein	Less than 1 month, less intensively than Limburger	In sandwiches, on crackers
Similar to mild Cheddar	Cow's milk	1–3 months	Usually used to make pasteurized process cheese
Piquant, spicy, but milder than Roquefort	Cow's milk, whole with added cream	4–6 months or longer	As such (dessert); in cooked foods
Mild, sweet, nutty	Cow's milk, low fat	2 months minimum, 2–9 months usually	As such; in sandwiches, with salads; fondue
Similar to mild Cheddar	Cow's milk	1–3 months	Usually used to make pasteurized process cheese

perature utilized is not quite high enough to give a negative phosphatase reaction (test of pasteurization adequacy), but many undesirable microorganisms are destroyed. In accordance with federal and state regulations, cheese made from heat-treated milk must be held the required length of time (at least 60 days) at a temperature not less than 35°F (1.5°C), thus protecting the safety of public health. More than 90 percent of the Cheddar cheese manufactured in the United States is currently made from either heat-treated or pasteurized milk.

Homogenized milk, cream, or combinations of such are used in soft cheeses such as Brie, Camembert, Neufchâtel, and cream. The advantages of homogenized milk in the production of specific cheeses include: increased surface area of the fat globules, which accelerates hydrolysis of milk fat by mold enzymes; greater yield of cheese per given quantity of milk; less moisture loss during ripening; and reduced fat loss at high storing or curing temperatures. However, homogenization of milk is not desirable for all cheeses. For example, homogenization of milk for hard cheeses results in a product with a brittle body and a tendency to form cracks.

Filtration or clarification of milk for cheesemaking is a desirable safety measure. The clarification process removes extraneous matter that may be held in suspension in milk. Clarification of milk for cheeses such as Swiss and Cheddar improves the body, texture, and flavor by improving size and uniformity of eye formation in Swiss cheese and by increasing the firmness of some cheeses. However, clarification of milk increases the fat loss in the whey and reduces the yield of cheese per given quantity of milk.

Milk used for some natural ripened cheeses may be specially treated for desired effects. The pigment carotene (which exhibits vitamin A activity) gives cheese a yellow color. If the consumer wants white cheese, the milk may be legally treated by bleaching with benzoyl peroxide (in the amount of 0.002 percent by weight of the milk). The label will state that the cheese has been treated with benzoyl peroxide. If any vitamin A is destroyed during the bleaching process, it will be reinstated in the milk.

3.7 Eggs—*Oeufs*

Eggs are a versatile and highly nutritious food. Fresh eggs and processed eggs are available on the market in several different forms. The buyer needs to know the products available, the most suitable uses for each product, and the standards of quality for each product.

Composition of Eggs and Their Nutritional Value

The shell constitutes the outer surface of the egg. A thin membrane made up of the inner and outer layer is on the inside of the shell. The air cell at the large end of the egg forms as moisture is lost. The size of the air cell denotes the age of the egg. The egg white is composed of three layers. Next to the shell is a thin, soft, white layer; the layer next to it is thick, viscous, and white; and a thin white layer surrounds the yolk and separates it from the thick white. The chalazae are strands of white substance on each side of the yolk that keep the yolk near the center of the egg. The yolk is made up of layers and is separated from the white by a very thin membrane. (See figure 3-70.)

Many nutrients required by the human body are found in the egg: water, protein, fat, minerals, vitamin A, thiamine (B_1), riboflavin (B_2), vitamin D, and

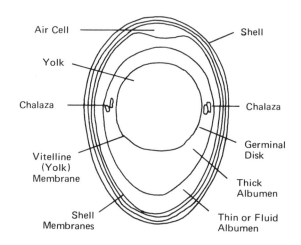

Figure 3-70. Composition of an egg.

niacin. Lecithin, which contains phosphorus, is found in the egg yolk. There are approximately 74 calories in a whole egg.

Grades

Grade refers to the interior quality of the egg and the condition and appearance of the shell. The three consumer grades are US Grade AA (or Fresh Fancy), US Grade A, and US Grade B.

Fresh Fancy quality (or Grade AA) eggs are produced under the USDA Control Program. These eggs reach the market quickly under strictly controlled conditions, guaranteeing the consumer a fresh and premium-quality product. These eggs are especially good for frying, poaching, cooking in the shell, and for uses where appearance is important. Grade B eggs are suitable for most cooking and baking purposes, for scrambling, omelets, and where appearance is not significant.

Quality is based on the cleanliness, shape, and texture of the shell. The color of the eggshell varies with species and breed of poultry, and it has no effect on the grade, quality, or nutritional value of the egg. The interior quality is based on the condition of the white and the yolk and the size of the air cell. Top-quality eggs have a clean, fine textured, unbroken shell, a very small air cell, a thick and firm white, and a yolk that is high, firm, and well centered. Candling is the process used for checking quality. In this process the eggs are held in front of a light to examine the condition of the shell, the yolk, the white, the germ, and the size of the air cell. The presence of blood spots or meat spots can also be detected, and eggs with such defects are sorted out. The time-consuming hand-candling operation is being replaced with electronic equipment that can scan or flash-candle thousands of eggs per hour. A new method of judging quality based on Haugh units is more accurate and objective. Random samples are taken from eggs of a single flock. The eggs are broken out on a flat surface and a Haugh meter measures the height of the thick albumen. The other interior and exterior qualities are also evaluated. The eggs in the lot are scored on the basis of the sampling. A score of 72 based on Haugh units places the lot from which the samples were taken into Grade AA quality.

Egg grading is not mandatory; the Department of Agriculture grading service is provided on a voluntary basis. The service must be requested and paid for by the producer or distributor. The USDA grade shield on a carton or case of eggs certifies that the eggs meet federal standards and have been graded for quality under federal and state supervision. In addition to being marked with the US grade shield, cases and cartons of eggs that score Grade A or above may have another label that states "Produced and Marketed under Federal-State Quality Control Program." Examples of these labels are shown in figure 3-71.

Size and Price

Eggs are marketed by size, based on the minimum weight of a dozen eggs in the shell. These classifications are: *jumbo*, 30 ounces per dozen; *extra large*, 27 ounces per dozen; *large*, 24 ounces per dozen; *medium*, 21 ounces per dozen; *small*, 18 ounces per dozen; and *peewee*, 15 ounces per dozen. (See figure 3-72.) The size is usually indicated on the grade shield, although size and quality are entirely different. Large eggs may be either high or low quality; high-quality eggs may be either large or small.

Egg prices vary by size within the same grade. The amount of price variation is influenced by the supply. Constant price fluctuations pose problems in knowing which size to buy. The Department of Agriculture suggests that if less than a seven-cent difference exists

Figure 3-71. U.S. grade labels for shell eggs. (Courtesy U.S. Department of Agriculture)

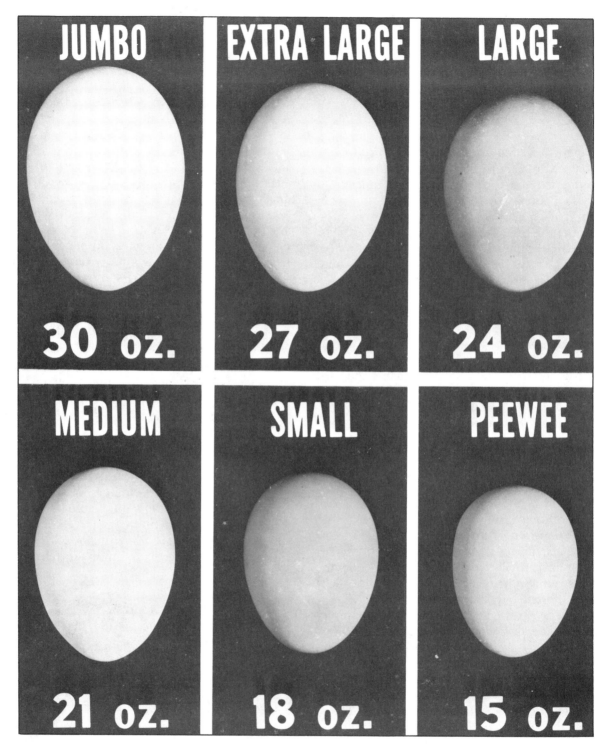

Figure 3-72. Minimum weight per dozen of the different sizes of eggs. (Courtesy U.S. Department of Agriculture)

between one size and the next smaller size in the same grade, the larger size is the better buy. Some food-services have limitations on the sizes they buy for specific purposes. Uniformity in size is important for eggs that are served in a cafeteria or for table d'hôte service. If shell eggs are used for baking and general cooking, the resulting dish will be more standard if its recipe specifies the weight or measure of egg rather than quantity.

Egg Products

The term *products* refers to liquid, frozen, and dehydrated eggs that are obtained by breaking and processing shell eggs. Included in the products are egg whites, egg yolks, mixed whole eggs, and blends of whole eggs and yolks. Sugar, salt, or corn syrup is sometimes added to improve the physical consistency and functional properties. Egg products are convenient to use, require less storage space, and have a longer shelf life than that of shell eggs. Liquid or frozen eggs packed in milk cartons are convenient for use in restaurants and institutions. Bakeries are the largest users of frozen whole eggs and frozen egg whites.

Dehydrated eggs are obtained by removing the water from the same egg products. Chief users of dried egg products are cake mix manufacturers, candy manufacturers, and manufacturers of meringue powders.

Other commercially produced egg products are hard-cooked eggs that are marketed in frozen form, scrambled egg mixes, and dietary foods. Egg products are processed under a strict inspection system under the direction of the Department of Agriculture. All products are pasteurized. Pasteurization is important to control salmonella infection.

3.8 Edible Fats and Oils—*Graisses de huiles comestibles*

Two main groups are defined according to their origin: animal fats and vegetable fats and oils (see figure 3-73).

Animal Origin		Vegetable Origin	
Milk Fats	*Body Fats*	*Fruit Oils*	*Seed Fats and Oils*
Butter	Lard	Olive oil	Coconut oil
	Suet	Palm oil	Palm-nut oil
	Chicken fat		Peanut oil
			Sunflower oil
			Soybean oil
			Rapeseed oil
			Sesame oil
			Cottonseed oil
			Poppyseed oil
			Safflower oil
			Corn oil

Figure 3-73. Edible Fats and Oils.

Labeling

The U.S. Food and Drug Administration requires that certain information be specified on the labels that identify fats and oils. The information must include the common legal name of the product; the ingredients used in the product or the standard of identity; any preservatives, additives, or artificial flavors or color; the net weight or quantity of the product in the container. If the product contains a combination of oils or fats, the specific oils or fats must be listed on the label.

Composition

All fats are chemically classified as esters; that is, combinations of alcohols and acids. Those fats having the most general culinary importance are combinations of the tri-hydroxy alcohol glycerol, more commonly known as "glycerine," with three of the so-called fatty acids—stearic acids, palmitic acids, and oleic acids.

These fatty acids consist of relatively long linear chains of carbon atoms, having, other than their bonds to neighboring carbon atoms, only attachments to hydrogen atoms. The last atom of carbon is attached to the acid radical —COOH, which contains, as well as the hydrogen atom, two oxygen atoms.

An exceedingly important difference between oleic acid and the other two fatty acids, stearic and palmitic, is that oleic acid has, halfway along its molecule, a double bond (where one of the hydrogen atoms is absent from each of the two adjacent carbon atoms). This peculiarity makes fats that contain a high proportion of oleic acid liquid at room temperature; that is to say, at room temperature they are not solid fats, but oils. The greater proportion of oleic acid in the makeup of fat, the more easily digestible it is, particularly by those who have a deficient pancreas or liver. More important still, these high oleic acid fats, or fats having a high proportion of double bonds (known as *polyunsaturated* fats or oils), are particularly recommended in the diet of those who are subject to atherosclerotic degeneration of the arteries, whether or not high blood pressure is present; or indeed for anyone having a blood cholesterol level that is above normal. The more unsaturated the fat (oil), the more satisfactory it is as an article of diet for such conditions. In order of increasing saturation, the culinary oils may be arranged as follows:

- Safflower seed oil
- Sunflower seed oil
- Corn oil
- Sesame seed oil
- Peanut oil
- Olive oil

In order of increasing saturation, the animal fats may be arranged as follows:

- Salmon fat
- Herring fat
- Pork fat
- Mutton fat
- Beef fat

3.8.1 *Animal Fats*

The most frequently used animal fat is butter. (See *Dairy Products.*) It is used as a spread, for frying and sautéing, for sauces, and to improve the flavor of many dishes.

Lard

Lard (*saindoux*) is fat rendered from the fat tissues of hogs. The quality of the lard depends on the parts of the hog from which the fat was obtained and on the method of processing. Leaf lard is the highest quality lard; it comes from the abdominal cavity. Pork fat from other sources must be labeled "rendered pork fat." Moisture rendering is the best process for extracting lard. Lard obtained by this process is known as "kettle-rendered" lard. It is used for frying potatoes, braised vegetables, doughs, and in mixtures of fats for deep-frying. Mutton lard is used for vegetable dishes and fat mixtures.

Beef Fats

The highest quality beef fats come from the abdominal cavities of cattle. Suet fats have limited use in foodservice. These fats may be refined and hydrogenated, a process used to harden liquid oils. Hydrogen is added to the unsaturated carbons joined by double bonds. The process improves the plasticity of the fat, removes objectionable odors and flavors, raises the melting point, and improves the keeping quality.

3.8.2 *Vegetable Fats and Oils*

Most vegetable oils originate from the fruits and seeds of plants. The vegetable oils are easy to handle because they are in liquid form at room temperature and so require no melting.

Storage

Vegetable fats and oils may become rancid when in contact with light, moisture, and high temperatures. They should be stored in airtight containers in an area that is dark, dry, and below 70°C (21°C).

Processing

The method used for processing the oil differs with the various fruits, seeds, and grains. (See figure 3-74.) After cleaning and crushing, the oil is extracted by a cold press treatment or a hot press treatment, depending on the fruit or seed. The cold press treatment is used for olive oil, coconut oil, and sunflower oil. The temperature in the press of the cold press method does not exceed 120°F (49°C). In the hot press treatment, the oil in the plant cells is preheated

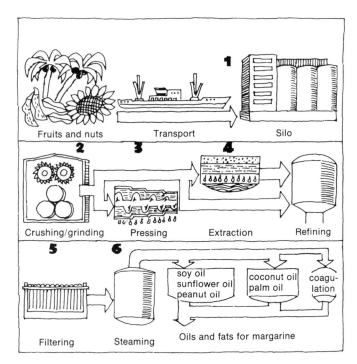

Figure 3-74. The process for making oils and shortenings from oily fruit and nuts: (1) the raw materials (fruits or nuts) are gathered, transported to the plant, and stored; (2) the raw materials are crushed and ground; (3) the crushed mixture is then heated and pressed; (4) the oil is extracted from the mixture and sent to a refinery; (5) the oil is filtered to remove all foreign particles; (6) the oil is steamed to remove all tastes and odors and then collected in containers for further use (such a making margarine).

to approximately 175°F (80°C). Oils processed by this method are thinner and easier to extract. Oils produced by the cold press method are usually more expensive. After the initial pressing, additional oil is extracted from further pressings. Refining is the process used to remove any foreign particles and off-flavors and odors from the oil.

Coconut Oil—*Graisse de coco*

Coconut oil is extracted from the copra, the dried white meat from the nut of the coconut palm tree. These trees are found along tropical and subtropical coastlines.

Peanut Oil—*Huile d'arachides*

Peanut oil is made from the fruit of the peanut plant. Peanuts are found in all the tropical regions of the world; they are grown extensively in the United States and Africa.

Rapeseed Oil—*Huile de colza*

Rapeseed is the only oil-producing plant that is cultivated in any quantity in the temperate areas of Europe. The oil made from this plant is used for brushing loaves of bread before baking and for green salads.

Olive Oil—*Huile d'olive*

Olive oil is obtained by crushing and pressing the ripe fruits of the olive tree, which are up to 22 percent oil. These trees are grown in the Mediterranean regions, Australia, China, and California. Having a very pronounced fruity taste, olive oil of the first pressing, known as virgin oil or *huile vierge,* is of the highest quality.

Palm Oil, Palm Nut Oil—*Huile de palme, Huile de palmiste*

Both oils come from the fruit of the oil palm—the palm oil from the flesh of the fruit, palm nut oil from the kernel.

Sesame Oil—*Huile de sésame*

Sesame oil has been used as a cooking oil for thousands of years. It is also used as a salad oil and for making margarine. The sesame plant is an annual aromatic herb. Sesame oil has a very high content of the essential fatty acids.

Soybean Oil—*Huile de soja*

Soybean oil comes from the seeds of soybeans, a plant originating in China. It is now cultivated in other countries, chiefly in the United States and Brazil.

Sunflower Oil—*Huile de tournesol*

This oil comes from sunflower seeds. Originating in Mexico, the sunflower reached Europe and has spread throughout Spain, France, and the East. The U.S.S.R. is the world's largest producer today. Other major cultivation areas are South America, southeastern Europe, and Africa.

Other Oil-producing Fruits

There are many other important oil-producing plants in the world; the oils derived from their fruits include hemp oil, poppy seed oil, corn oil, wheat oil, linseed oil, and safflower oil.

3.8.3 *Margarine*

Margarine is a widely used product manufactured from one or more of the various approved animal or vegetable fats and other ingredients. The manufacturing process must comply with the quality and health controls of federal and state pure food laws and the federal standard. The product must be la-

beled oleomargarine or margarine. Oleo means beef fat and at one time most margarines were produced from the olein fats of beef. Today, soy oil is used more than any other fat. Margarine is also made from coconut oil, palm nut oil, sunflower oil, corn oil, and palm oil. It is suitable for use as a spread, for baking, roasting, simmering, and for making sauces. Margarines differ from each other in flavor, texture, melting points, and other physical characteristics.

The Manufacture of Margarine

Margarine must by law contain 90 percent fat. It also contains 17 to 18½ percent pasteurized skim milk. It usually contains 1½ to 3 percent salt; however, salt-free margarine is available. Margarine may be graded, and the grades are similar to those for butter. The color should be a light yellow; the flavor and odor should be fresh and pleasing. Margarines should be stored at refrigerated temperatures. (See figures 3-74 and 3-75.)

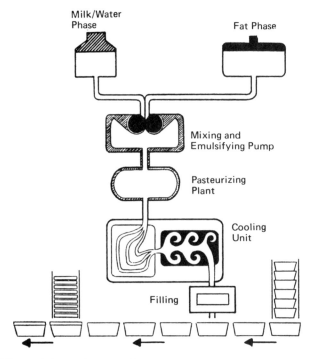

Figure 3-75. The manufacture of margarine.

3.9 Plant Foods

Plant foods are nutritious and inexpensive. High-quality fruits and vegetables are available in both fresh and frozen form throughout the year. Rich in minerals and vitamins, carbohydrates, and proteins, plant foods assist in the performance of many body functions and are essential in human diets. Fresh fruits and vegetables are perishable and should be prepared, stored, or preserved promptly after harvesting to avoid loss of nutrients and to assure maximum eating quality. Baking, steaming, and simmering are the basic cooking methods recommended for minimum loss of nutrients. Freezing fresh fruits and vegetables at 32°F (0°C) or lower for a limited period of time is the best method of preserving their nutrients.

3.9.1 Cereals—Céreáles

Oats—Avoine

Oats (see figure 3-76) and other preparations of rolled oats are popular breakfast foods in many countries. The outer husk is removed from the kernel of the grain, leaving the groat. Scotch or regular oatmeal is made by steaming the groats for a long period of time. Quick-cooking oatmeal is made by cutting, pressing, and drying the groats. "Steel-cut" groats are cut by steel cutters and resemble cracked wheat. Oats, processed into rolled oats, are used for breakfast cereals, porridge, breads, muffins, cakes, cookies, and desserts.

Figure 3-76. Oats—*Avione.*

Wheat—Froment

Wheats produce the most important of all cereal grain foods grown in temperate climates. Next to rice, wheat is used more extensively than any other grain.

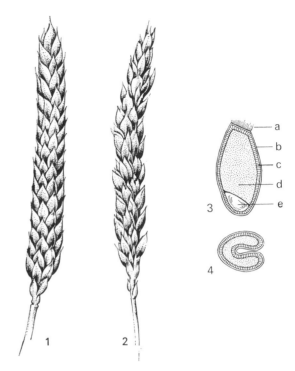

Figure 3-77. Wheat—*Froment:* (1) hybrid wheat; (2) natural wheat; (3) longitudinal section of a grain of *wheat:* (*a*) brush, (*b*) pericarp, (*c*) bran, (*d*) endosperm (nut), (*e*) germ; (4) cross section.

Wheat is the source of flour, which is produced by grinding the grains and sifting out the chaff. Wheats are classified as bread wheats, durum wheat, emer, rivet, or English wheat. Bread wheats include hard wheats and soft wheats. The hard wheats are the source of the highest-quality bread flours because of the high protein content and the high proportion of gluten (the substance in which the starch granules are embedded). In contrast to hard wheats, the soft wheat is high in starch content and mealy in texture. The air pockets between the grains give the wheat a soft, floury appearance. Soft wheats are used to make the highly refined flour used in the preparation of cakes, pastries, and biscuits. Durum, which is amber in color, also contains a high proportion of gluten. It is largely used for the manufacture of semolina, which is then made into pasta products (noodles, macaroni, and

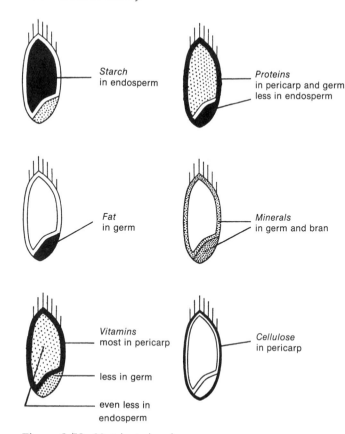

Figure 3-78. Nutrients in wheat.

spaghetti). Flours made from emer wheat or from rivet or English wheat are inferior in quality to those milled from the bread wheats and therefore are generally used as food for livestock. (See figures 3-77 and 3-78.)

Buckwheat is an herb with a triangular-shaped seed. Although buckwheat is not a cereal, the seeds can be ground into a flourlike substance that is called buckwheat flour. This flour is used to make griddle cakes and Russian blini.

Corn—*Mais*

The only cereal crop that is American in origin is corn (see figure 3-79). In the United States, the world's largest producer, corn is grown as food for both people and livestock. Although the United States uses most of its corn for feeding livestock, it is a staple food for the people of South America, eastern Africa, and southeastern Europe. Corn has a high starch content and contains traces of carotene and copper. In addition to its use as a vegetable, corn is ground into a meal and used for cornmeal, corn flour, cornstarch, hominy grits, and corn oil.

Figure 3-79. Corn—*Maïs*.

Millet—*Millet*

The most widely grown millets (see figure 3-80) are sorghum, finger millet, and bulrush millet. Nutritionally, millets have a higher content of minerals than most other grains. This grain is made into golden millet, millet flakes, millet semolina, millet meal, sorghum, and beer.

Figure 3-80. Millet—*Millet*.

Barley—*Orge*

There are two types of barley (see figure 3-81): two-rowed barley and six-rowed barley. Most of the barley grown in Britain is the two-row variety, and the seedlings are dried and used to produce malt for making beer. Pearl barley, used in soups and stews, is made by removing the husks and polishing the grains.

Figure 3-81. Barley—*Orge*.

Rye—*Seigle*

The grain of rye (see figure 3-82) is similar in composition to that of wheat. It is made into rye flour. In Europe, its chief use is for making black bread. Rye is used for making rye bread and whiskey in America.

Figure 3-82. Rye—*Seigle*.

Rice—*Riz*

The history of rice (see figures 3-83 and 3-84) has been traced to a plant called *Newaree,* which was grown in India as early as 3000 B.C. Although rice originated in Asia, the largest exporter of rice today is the United States. Other rice producers are India, Java, Australia, Thailand, Italy, and France.

There are 7,000 or more known varieties of rice. These varieties can be classified into three main groups: long grain, medium grain, and short grain. (See figure 3-85.) Long-grain rice tends to separate

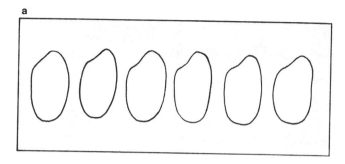

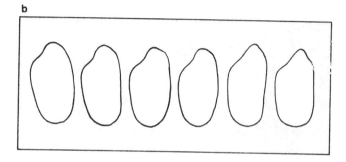

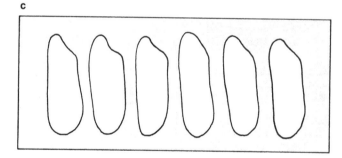

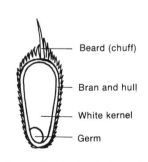

Figure 3-85. Short-, medium-, and long-grain rice. (a) Short-grain rice is usually ¼ inch long, only about 1½ to 2 times its width. The most popular short-grain rice comes from Italy; other types are produced in the Orient. Uses include soups and sweet rice dishes. Originario and cammolino are types of short-grain rice. (b) Medium-grain rice is usually ⅜ inch long, about 2 to 3 times its width. It is produced primarily in Italy, the United States, and Argentina. It is used for a variety of rice dishes, particularly risotto. Stirpe, blue rose, maratelli, vialone, arborio, and roma are types of medium-grain rice. (c) Long-grain rice is usually ½ inch long, about 4 to 5 times its width. It is produced mainly in the United States and Thailand. It is used for a variety of rice dishes, particularly pilau and creole preparations. Lebonnet, labelle, starbonnet, and Siam patna are types of long-grain rice.

Figure 3-83. Rice—*Riz*.

Beard (chuff)

Bran and hull

White kernel

Germ

Figure 3-84. A whole grain of rice.

and is light and fluffy when cooked. It is usually preferred for steamed rice, soups, salads, and for chicken, fish, and meat combinations. Short- and medium-grain rice are moist and tender when cooked. The particles of rice cling together. The flavor of these varieties are preferred by many persons, and they are especially popular for food items that require a tender, easily molded rice, such as rice rings, croquettes, loaves, puddings, and desserts.

Oryza sativa, the botanical name for white rice, is divided into two subspecies, based on grain size. *Oryza sativa Japonica* features a broad kernel with a white center. It absorbs a large amount of water during cooking and swells very much. Therefore, it is used for Asian dishes that call for rice that sticks and for dishes like risottos. It is cultivated in east Asia (China, Korea, Japan), some Arab countries (Morocco, Egypt), the Mediterranean region (Italy, Spain), South America (Brazil, Uruguay, Argentina), Australia, and the west coast of the United States. *Oryza sativa Indica* has a narrower kernel with a milky and transparent appearance. It absorbs less water and swells and sticks less. It is grown primarily in southeast Asia (India, Thailand, Indonesia), Madagascar, South America, the southern states of the United States, and the Caribbean.

Parboiled or converted rice is steamed before it is milled. The process aids in retaining the vitamins and minerals. (See figure 3-86.) Precooked rice is usually fortified with additional vitamins. It has been milled and cooked, and the moisture has been removed through a dehydration process. This instant-type rice is easily and quickly prepared by restoring the moisture with boiling water.

Risotto, Creole rice, rice pilau, Indian rice, jambalaya, and rice pudding are well-known rice dishes.

Wild Rice—*Zizanie*

Wild rice (see figure 3-87) is not a grain but a grass seed gathered from the swamp areas of southern Canada and northern Minnesota, Wisconsin, and Michigan. It is now also being raised in California as well. Its commercial production is very limited. Be-

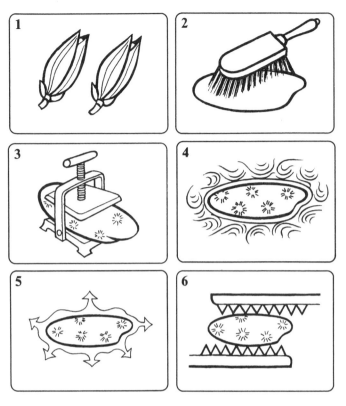

Figure 3-86. Parboiled or converted rice: (1) the rice after harvest; (2) the rice is cleaned to remove dust and dirt; (3) the rice is pressed to force the vitamins and minerals from the hulls into the kernels; (4) steam assists the transfer of vitamins and minerals; (5) the sticky coating is removed; (6) the rice is hulled and polished.

cause harvesting wild rice is labor intensive and the yield is low, wild rice is a rare and expensive commodity. Long, slow cooking is used to develop its nutty flavor.

Figure 3-87. Wild rice—*Zizanie.*

3.9.2 *Legumes*—Légumes

Legumes, or pulses, are the dried seeds of plants that form pods. They contain important nutrients; in fact,

Type	Appearance	Usage	Areas of Origin
White beans	Clear white	Soups, vegetables, purees	Italy, Ethiopia
Breton beans	Roundish, white	Soups, vegetables, purees, salads	France
Flageolets	Longish, green	Soups, vegetables, purees	France, Italy, Spain, Belgium
Butter or lima beans	Yellow	Soups, purees	Germany, Holland, U.S.
Soissons beans	Large, white	Soups, vegetables, purees	Germany, France, Spain
Borlotto beans	Brown	Soups, purees	Italy
Black beans	Black	Salads, soups	U.S., Central and South America
Soybeans	Various colors	Oil, margarine, tofu, meat extender	Asia, U.S., Africa
Yellow peas	Yellow	Soups, purees	Canada, U.S.
Green peas	Green	Soups, purees	Canada, Holland, France
Sweet peas	Green	Soups, vegetables, salads	Spain, Italy, France
Lentils	Olive green, brown, red	Soups, purees, vegetables	Chile, Italy, Argentina, Hungary
Quail beans	Yellow	Soups, purees	Africa, Spain, Greece

Figure 3-88. Legumes—*Légumes*.

they are the best source of plant protein. In addition, they contain carbohydrates and phosphorus. Good legumes must be whole and shiny. Wrinkled surfaces indicate improper or excessive storage; in this condition, legumes will not become soft when cooked.

Legumes may be prepared in many ways, as vegetables, salads, soups, and in combination with other foods. They are available in whole, split, or ground form. With the exception of the soybean, legumes have no fat and therefore are suitable for serving with fatty foods, such as fat bacon or pork. All legumes should be kept in clean containers in a dry, well-ventilated storage area. (See figure 3-88.)

Dried Beans—*Haricots secs*

These are the mature, shelled, and dried garden beans. The best-known type for cooking purposes is the round white Brittany bean or, in the United States, the navy or Boston bean. Other well-known types include the large flat Soissons bean; the long, light green lima bean; the ballet bean; the brown quail-bean; and the Italian Borlotti bean for minestrone soup.

Lentils—*Lentilles*

These are produced in Chile, Italy, Rumania, and Egypt. The best variety is the light green, flat lentil.

Peas—*Pois*

There are two types: yellow peas and green peas.

3.9.3 Ground Products and Starches— Produits moulus et amidons

All flour products must be kept in dry, clean, light, and well-ventilated storerooms. Flour responds to changes in humidity, and it absorbs moisture very quickly. Unless properly stored, flour products may become moldy or rancid. These products are also attractive to many types of insects. These include the flour moth, the flour mite, and the flour beetle. The eggs of the flour moth are sometimes in the filaments of the flour, where they develop into caterpillars (flour worms) and moths that are grayish yellow in color. Related to the spider, the flour mite grows to the length of about .06 inches. This insect, which is hardly visible, is found only in flour that has a high moisture content. The flour beetle is reddish brown to black, approximately ½ inch in length.

Cracker Crumbs—*Brisures*

Dried biscuit and cracker fragments are crushed and sieved and used for lining pastry molds, for gratin dishes, and for making cakes and puddings.

Dunst—*Cendrée*

A type of flour ground to a degree of fineness between that of semolina and flour, dunst is used primarily for making pasta.

Bran—*Egruge*

The product comes from the remnants of ground cereals. It is used for baking whole-grain bread and crisp wafers and in cereals.

Flour—*Farine*

There are 3 types of flours: baking flours, soup flours, and starches and binding flours.

Baking flours include wheat flour and rye flour. Of all the different types of flour derived from the wheat grain, the only kinds used in good cooking are white flour, wheat flour, and premium flour. These are obtained from the lightest, middle part of the grain. Good, glutenous white flour is clinging, and the fineness of the particles is apparent. It should smell fresh and, on tasting, should only taste sweet after chewing for a time. Pastries made from good white flour should quickly form a crust on the outside and should not remain greasy. White flour is used in the kitchen for soups, sauces, and pastries. The flour should be passed through a sieve before use, in order to remove possible filaments, insects, and lumps.

Soup flours are made from rice, oat, barley, green rye, beans, and peas.

Practically the only starches (carbohydrates) used for starch and binding flours are those from cereals and from leguminous tuber or root plants; for example, wheat starch, rice starch, cornstarch (corn flour), potato starch. Arrowroot starch is especially used for children's food.

Flakes—*Flocons*

Oats, rice, and corn can be made into flakes. The raw grains are first cleaned and then treated in a vacuum, which breaks up the starch and makes it digestible. The vacuum-treated grains are then dried and hulled or husked in a suitable machine. Finally, they are crushed between rollers into flakes. Oat flakes are produced by the above process from broken oat grains and are used for soups, health foods, Bircher-muesli, and porridge.

Gruel—*Gruau*

These are broken oat, rice, or barley grains that are mostly used for porridge.

Pot Barley—*Orges mondes*

These are cleaned and polished round barley grains used for soups and desserts. The best varieties are used as food for the sick.

Pearl Tapioca—*Perles de Japon*

This is prepared by washing the starch from the tubers of the cassava plant. The starch is dried in the form of small, round balls or flakes. During cooking, they swell to the size of peas and become glassy and translucent.

Sago—*Sagou*

The sago palm, in the countries of southeast Asia, is the most important source of sago. The pith is scooped from the logs of the tree, and the starch from the pith is washed and dried. When dried at this stage, the starch is used for sago flour. When producing pearl sago, a wet starch paste is pressed through a fine sieve and the grains are dried on an oscillating hot plate. The grains are white or slightly yellow, and they have no taste and no odor.

Semolina—*Semoule*

Semolina is made from flour milled from durum wheat. It is available in fine, medium, and rough forms. Good semolina should be yellowish white (slightly creamy) and dry. A special hard, glutenous wheat semolina is used for making pasta. Semolina is used for soups, gnocchi, pasta, puddings, and dietary dishes.

Tapioca—*Tapioca*

The Brazilian cassava root and certain Indian palms are the source of tapioca and tapioca flour. These products are used for fruit fillings and sauces.

3.9.4 *Bread*—Pain

Ordinary bread is made from wheat flour, and it is designated according to the type of wheat flour used; for example, white bread, whole-wheat bread, graham bread, stone-ground bread. Crisp wafers and pumpernickel are specially prepared whole-meal breads. Diet breads and bread for diabetics are prescribed according to the illness in question.

Storage

Bread products should be stored in well-ventilated, cool, clean areas. Bread refrigerated at 40°F (4°C) will become stale more quickly than bread stored at room temperature. Freezing is the most effective method of retaining the flavor, freshness, aroma, and moisture of bread products. Before freezing, the bread should be thoroughly cooled and then securely wrapped in moisture-proof bags, sealed, labeled, and dated.

Spoilage

Bread may be stored in the refrigerator to inhibit mold growth, particularly during hot weather. Mold may occur if bread is not cooled sufficiently before wrapping, or if it is stored in a humid atmosphere, at a high temperature, or in a poorly ventilated area. The potato mold may develop in breads with a low acid content if the temperature of the storage area is over 70°F (21°C).

Four Stages of Making White Bread

The dough for white bread is first prepared, then fermented, then divided and shaped, and finally is proofed and baked. To prepare dough, sifted wheat flour is mixed with water and salt. To these ingredients yeast is added. Sugar and butter are other ingredients frequently included in bread formulas. Sugar, in controlled amounts, increases the fermentation, and shortening improves the flavor. The dough is thoroughly mixed or kneaded to develop the gluten.

The dough should be placed in a warm and rather humid place to ferment. It should be allowed to rise until doubled in bulk. It is usually desirable to punch the dough down and let it rise a second time.

After the dough has risen, it is divided. It should then be allowed to rest about 10 minutes so that it will be more pliable and easy to handle. The dough is then shaped into loaves or rolls.

Bread products should double in bulk during the proofing period. The bread will continue to rise during the baking period. It should be baked 30 to 50 minutes, depending upon the size and shape of the loaf. Bake the bread in an oven at 390° to 480°F (199° to 248°C). The dough rises rapidly during the early stages of baking. The expansion of the carbon dioxide gas and the enzymatic activity increase at a rapid rate.

Dough Leavening Agents

Yeast: Yeasts are unicellular plant organisms that can only be seen with a microscope. They reproduce by budding. They live primarily on sugars, which they convert into alcohol and carbon dioxide gas. In this way, these organisms can be used for raising dough and for the manufacture of beer, wine, and brandy. Wrap fresh yeast in a damp cloth and store in the refrigerator. Dried yeast is sold in sealed foil packages. Store it in a cool dry place, or refrigerate.

Baking powder: The various kinds of baking powder consist of sodium carbonate, tartar, and starch. In a chemical reaction they produce carbon dioxide, which results in the raising of the dough. Keep baking powder in a dry place.

Salt of hartshorn (ammonium carbonate): This substance is developed when heating carbon dioxide and ammonium hydroxide (a solution of ammonia gas in water is ammonium hydroxide). The salt consists primarily of ammonium bicarbonate and can be manufactured by a number of different processes. Formerly, it was produced by dry distillation of hartshorn. Salt of hartshorn must be stored in hermetically sealed cans in a cool place.

Potash: Potassium carbonate, in contact with acids, produces carbon dioxide. In spice cookies, the acids (formic acid) present in the honey activate the potash.

Alcohol: Brandy, Kirsch, and rum can all be used as leavening agents.

Egg white: Stiffly beaten egg whites can serve as leavening agents.

Cakes, Pies, and Cookies

In addition to wheat flour, other ingredients, especially milk, butter, margarine, sugar, nuts, spices, honey, and fruit are used for making fine baked goods. The more milk and fats (butter) used, the finer and more delicate the resulting product. Yeast, baking powder, salt of hartshorn, honey, and alcohol can all be used for raising the dough.

3.9.5 *Pasta*—Pâtes

Pasta is made with wheat flour products and water. Usually a very finely ground hard wheat semolina is used in industrial production. The high gluten content of the hard wheat flours helps retain the shape, texture, and form of the pasta during cooking. According to government standards, egg noodles must contain 5.3 percent egg in the finished product. Pasta is pressed through a die into the desired shape while still soft and then thoroughly dried so that all the moisture is evaporated. Pasta is also made from whole-wheat flour and soy flour and may be flavored with tomatoes, spinach, broccoli, or Jerusalem artichoke flour. Fresh pasta is not dried completely; it requires only a short cooking time but is perishable and needs refrigeration before cooking. Pasta is used as a first course, as a side dish with meat dishes, or as a main course.

Nutritional Content

Pasta has a high carbohydrate (starch) content. Pasta made from durum semolina has 7 grams of protein in each 2-ounce serving, as well as B vitamins (especially thiamine) and some iron. Pasta is usually combined with other foods such as cheese, meats, vegetables, and sauces, which provide additional nutrients.

Storage

Pasta must be stored in light, dry, well-ventilated areas. Exposure to humidity causes it to mold. Appropriate storage should eliminate the problem of flour mites.

Cooking

Pasta should be cooked in a large quantity of rapidly boiling water—2 gallons (7.6 liters) of water per pound (0.5 kilogram) of pasta. The pasta should be immersed into the water gradually so that the boiling temperature can be maintained. All pasta should be cooked *al dente,* meaning "to the tooth." This denotes a slight resistance to the bite and a chewy, firm texture with no taste of raw flour. When the *al dente* stage is reached, the pasta should be drained. Do not rinse pasta, as that chills it and makes the strands stick together. Instead turn it at once into a serving bowl containing oil or butter, which will help to prevent sticking until the sauce is added. If the cooked pasta becomes chilled, it can be dipped into hot water before serving. The cooking time of pasta varies from 5 to 15 minutes, depending on the variety.

3.9.6 *Vegetables*—Légumes

The term vegetables refers to all plants or parts of plants that are eaten in raw, boiled, or preserved form. Vegetables are important for their nutritional value. Cereals, herbs, and fruits are not classified as vegetables.

Preserved vegetables are vegetables that have been prepared and preserved. These include all canned vegetables, dried vegetables, deep-frozen vegetables, and those that have been preserved with salt and vinegar. Canned vegetables are those that have been processed and sterilized in cans or jars to preserve them.

Fresh vegetables are divided into seven categories. *Root and tuber vegetables (légumes à racines)* include the Jerusalem artichoke, carrot, potato, celery root (celeriac), nettle root, kohlrabi, rutabaga, horseradish, beet, salsify, and turnip. *Stem vegetables (légumes à côtes)* include the cardoon, asparagus, celery, and fennel. *Leafy vegetables (légumes à feuilles)* include Swiss chard, sorrel, and spinach. *Salad vegetables (légumes salades)* include endive, lettuce, romaine, chicory, and watercress. *Cabbages (choux)* are cauliflower, green cabbage, Brussels sprouts, red cabbage, broccoli, white cabbage, Savoy cabbage, kale, and mustard greens. *Fruit and seed vegetables (légumes à graines et à fruits)* include artichokes, eggplant, beans, peas, cucumbers, shell beans, peppers, tomatoes, and zucchini. *Bulbous vegetables* (*oignons*) include garlic, leeks, scallions (green onions), shallots, and onions.

Vegetables should be uniform in size and shape, crisp, firm, and free of defects, mechanical damage, and decay. They should have a fresh appearance and a bright color. Vegetables are important for their minerals, vitamins, trace elements, and essential oils. They are highly versatile in terms of preparation and provide variety to the menu.

Vegetables are perishable and require careful handling. Most vegetables require low storage temperatures and high humidity; however, there are some exceptions. All vegetables should be inspected on receipt and stored promptly at the recommended temperature and humidity. Most vegetables have a limited keeping period and should be used soon after purchase.

Fresh vegetables are available throughout the year; however, they are at their peak during their proper season. Vegetables purchased out of season will most likely be high in price and not of the best quality. Vegetables will most likely be of superior quality and lower in price during the time they are in season. *Spring vegetables* are spinach, carrots, lettuce, dandelions, lamb's lettuce, radishes, sorrel and asparagus. *Summer vegetables* include artichokes, eggplant, beans, peas, cucumbers, cabbages, lettuce, tomatoes, and zucchini. *Fall vegetables* are cardoons, potatoes, cabbages, leeks, parsnips, celery, and all types of bulbous vegetables. *Winter vegetables* are rutabaga, endive, celery root (celeriac), beets, Brussels sprouts, salsify, turnips, and escarole.

Vegetables add flavor, texture, and color to the menu. They are the source of many essential nutrients that are not present in adequate amounts in other foods. They are one of the major sources of vitamins A and C in the diet. Both cooked and raw vegetables are good sources of fiber, or bulk, and many vegetables may be used in quite generous amounts in low-calorie weight reduction diets.

Vegetables are sometimes blanched before undergoing further preparation. Cooking methods include boiling, steaming, sautéing, deep-frying, gratinating, glazing, simmering, and grilling.

Artichoke—*Artichaut*

A thistlelike flowering plant, the globe or French artichoke is a culinary delicacy. (See figure 3-89.) The reddish or blue-brown varieties are superior to the green varieties. The base of the flower and the lower thicker part of

Figure 3-89. Artichoke—*Artichaut.*

the leaves are fleshy and flavorful. They are used for both hot and cold specialty dishes. France is the home of the artichoke, although Spain, the United States, and Italy also supply good-quality artichokes.

Asparagus—*Asperge*

Asparagus is a luxury vegetable that is in season from April to June. (See figure 3-90.) The young asparagus

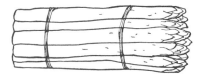

Figure 3-90. Asparagus—*Asperges.*

shoots with their purple or green tips are superior to mature tough and woody asparagus. Among the canned asparagus, the tender California variety is well known; also canned are white asparagus from northern Europe.

Beans, Fresh—*Haricots, frais*

The approximately fifty different varieties of beans are divided into three categories. These are the young *snap bean*, which should contain few, if any, seeds; the larger, light green *French bean* with immature seeds; and the tender light green *runner bean*. Each variety should be well formed, firm, tender, and free of defects. (See figure 3-91.) Beans come onto the market from early summer until October. Mature beans are shelled and used as seeds or as a dry vegetable.

Figure 3-91. Beans—*Haricots*.

Beets—*Betteraves*

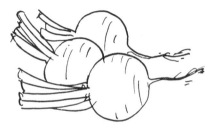

Figure 3-92. Beets—*Betteraves*.

Beets are round or long-shaped root tubers. (See figure 3-92.) The interior of young beets is deep red. The interior texture of mature beets is stringy, and the color is often a pale pink. Beets are prepared in different ways, as side dishes, for salads, for garnishes, and for soups.

Broccoli—*Brocoli*

Broccoli forms a head, looser than cauliflower, of green buds rising from a thick fleshy stalk. There is also a purple-headed variety, very delicate in flavor. Broccoli rabe does not form heads but has the same dark green color and

Figure 3-93. Broccoli—*Brocoli*.

flavor as broccoli, although it is much less tender. (See figure 3-93.) Broccoli is used as a side dish, in salads, soups, and as a garnish.

Brussels Sprouts—*Choux de Bruxelles*

The small, firmly closed green sprouts grow along stalks. (See figure 3-94.) Brussels sprouts are available throughout the year but are most abundant from September to February. They may be boiled, baked, steamed, or French-fried.

Figure 3-94. Brussels sprouts—*Choux de Bruxelles*.

Cabbage—*Chou*

Many vegetables, including kohlrabi, Brussels sprouts, and cauliflower, are members of the cabbage family. Kale, savoy cabbage, white cabbage and red cabbage are the family members popularly known as cabbage.

Figure 3-95. Kale—*Chou vert*.

Kale (*chou vert frisé*) is a variety of cabbage that does not form a head. The leaves are dark green and very curly and wrinkled. (See figure 3-95.) It is generally used for vegetable soup and is a very nutritious variety.

Savoy cabbage (*chou frisé*) is easily identified by the crinkling of the tissues through the greenish yellow leaves. (See figure 3-96.) The heads are loosely formed with a softer and more widely opened bud than white cabbage; the flavor is milder as well.

White cabbage (*chou blanc*) is the vegetable most commonly thought of as cabbage in the United States.

U.S. standards for cabbage provide for two grades: US 1 and US Commercial. The heads of cabbage should be firm or hard with leaves that are tightly closed and finely ribbed. The weight of cabbage heads ranges from 1 to 9 pounds (0.5 to 5 kilograms). (See figure 3-97.) Sauerkraut (*choucroute*) is finely shredded white cabbage mixed with salt and preserved over a long period in barrels or jars, where it undergoes an acidic fermentation. Sauerkraut prepared with vinegar bacteria is artificially acidified and of poorer quality.

Figure 3-96. Savoy cabbage—*Chou frisé.*

Red cabbage (*chou rouge*) is identified by its red or purple color. The heads are very firm and compact. (See figure 3-98.)

Figure 3-97. White cabbage—*Chou blanc.*

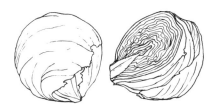

Figure 3-98. Red cabbage—*Chou rouge.*

Cardoon—*Cardon (Carde)*

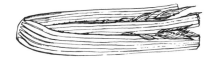

Figure 3-99. Cardoon—*Cardon.*

Cardoon is a French vegetable consisting of a bundle of veined leaves. (See figure 3-99.) The center leaves are very tender. This vegetable, in season in the fall and the winter, grows to a height of 4½ feet. Cardoons are also cultivated in other parts of the world.

Carrot—*Carotte*

Young, tender carrots are available in spring and early summer. The small ones, which are stumpy at the bottom, are the most tender and flavorful. The carrot is a versatile vegetable, good raw or cooked, alone or in combination with other foods. Carrots have a high sugar content and are a rich source of vitamin A. (See figure 3-100.)

Figure 3-100. Carrots—*Carottes.*

Cauliflower—*Chou-fleur*

Cauliflower is a popular vegetable available throughout the year. The large flowerlike head should be firm, white in color, and surrounded by green leaves. (See figure 3-101.) The so-called Paris cauliflower, with its large head, and the Dutch cauliflower are good varieties. Cauliflower became an important crop in the United States in about 1920. Coastal areas, such as those along the Pacific Coast and Long Island, New York, and high altitudes in Colorado are important production centers. The peak of the marketing season is October, and there are relatively large supplies in September and November. The supply is lower from May through August.

Figure 3-101. Cauliflower—*Chou-fleur.*

Celeriac—*Céleri-rave*

Celeriac is grown all over Europe but is less common in the United States. (See figure 3-102.) Closely related to celery, the stem is the edible part of celery, whereas the part of celeriac that is eaten is the swollen base of the stem. Celeriac may be boiled and eaten as a vegetable. It is also used in soups, stews, and salads. If the skins are properly cleaned, it can

Figure 3-102. Celeriac—*Céleri-rave.*

be used in soups. Medium-sized celeriacs are preferred, as the large ones are often hollow and spongy.

Celery—*Céleri en branche*

Figure 3-103. Celery—*Céleri en branche.*

Celery belongs to the Umbelliferae family, frequently referred to as the parsley family. (See figure 3-103.) The characteristic flavor and odor of the plants of this family are the result of the volatile oils found in the stems, leaves, and seeds. Celery varieties are classified by color, green and golden, and by types within the colors. The types of green celery are Utah, crystal, and various types of Pascal. The golden varieties are divided into golden self-blanching, golden plume, and other types. The ribs grow together in a tight bunch; the inner part, the heart, is especially tender. Celery is used in appetizers, salads, and side dishes. It is also used in soups, sauces, stuffings, and relishes. The seeds are used for flavoring.

Chicory—*Chicorée*

There are various types of chicory, all of which are used in salads. Some varieties are grown for their large roots. These are dried, roasted, ground, and blended with some coffees. The best known salad varieties are broad-leafed endive (*chicorée scarol*); chicory (*endive de Bruxelles*), which is called endive or Belgian endive in the United States (see figure 3-104); endive (*chicorée frisée*) which is called curly chicory in the United States (see figure 3-105); and red chicory (*barbe-de-capucin*).

Figure 3-104. Belgian endive—*Endive de Bruxelles.*

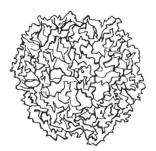

Figure 3-105. Curly chicory—*Chicorée.*

Chinese Artichokes—*Crosnes du Japon*

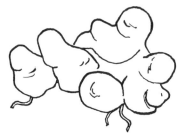

Figure 3-106. Chinese artichokes—*Crosnes du Japon.*

Chinese artichokes are small delicate spiral-shaped tubers, which are usually served à la créme. Originally this was an Oriental vegetable, but it is now grown in most warm climates. It is somewhat like a Jerusalem artichoke. (See figure 3-106.)

Chinese Cabbage—*Chou de Chine*

This name is given to at least three different cabbages developed in China—from north, central, and south China. The best known in the West are Chinese chard (*bok choy*), which has dark green leaves on white stems, some-

Figure 3-107. Chinese cabbage—*Chou de Chine*.

what like a loose Swiss chard; and celery cabbage (*pe-tsai*), with a long, tightly closed head. Both are tender and are more delicately flavored than other cabbages. They are used for stir-fried dishes and in soups. (See figure 3-107.)

Cress—*Cresson*

Figure 3-108. Cress—*Cresson* (watercress—*cresson de fontaine*, left; garden cress—*cresson de jardin*, right).

There are 2 types of cress (see figure 3-108), watercress (*cresson de fontaine*) and garden cress (*cresson de jardin*).

Watercress grows best in running water. It also grows in ditches and along streams, but it is usually cultivated for commercial purposes. It has a very high mineral content, primarily iron, and it is rich in vitamins A and C. It is used in salads, soups, sandwiches, sauces, and as a garnish.

Garden cress is similar to watercress, although less spicy in taste. It is cultivated in gardens and is native to Europe. It is used in the same way as watercress. This cress wilts very quickly and therefore should be prepared just before use.

Corn—*Maïs*

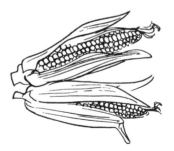

Figure 3-109. Corn—*Maïs*.

Corn is the only cereal crop that has an American origin. It is now grown in most countries throughout the world. It is used as food for both humans and animals. There are many different types of corn. Sweet corn has a sweeter taste than most varieties and is preferred for humans. The cob should be filled with plump and milky kernels and covered with husks that are soft, tender, and green. The grains should be yellow or white, soft, and sweet. Sweet corn is available fresh, frozen, and canned. Fresh sweet corn is at its best from May to September but loses flavor for every hour after picking. There are several types, including long cobs with golden kernels and small cobs with almost white kernels. (See figure 3-109.)

Lye-soaked hulled corn is called *hominy*. It is available dried and canned whole, or dried in ground form as *grits*.

Cucumber—*Concombre*

Figure 3-110. Cucumber—*Concombre*

There are two types of cucumber: those that have been grown in hothouses, known as indoor or long cucumbers, and those grown out-of-doors, known as outdoor or ridge cucumbers. (See figure 3-110.) Cucumbers are used for soups, salads, and as vegetables and garnishes.

Young cucumbers are pickled together with herbs and sugar in vinegar and are sold under one of the following names according to their size, cut, and method of preparation: gherkins, delicatessen pickles, spiced pickles, mustard pickles, dill pickles, and sweet pickles. The main producers are the United States, Holland, Belgium, Germany, and Israel.

Eggplant—*Aubergine*

This is a long or round fruit from the Solanaceae family, violet in color. Eggplant is eaten as a cooked vegetable. It is at its peak in the summer and fall but is available all year long. (See figure 3-111.) There

Figure 3-111. Eggplant—*Aubergine*.

are also white eggplants and red eggplants. Small thin eggplants are sometimes sold as Italian eggplants.

Fennel—*Fenouil*

In its prime in summer and winter, fennel is a tightly closed leafy bulb that grows in temperate climates and has a characteristic fine anise aroma. The leaves are used in sauces, soups, and salads. The fleshy bulbous stem is eaten raw or cooked as a vegetable. The seeds are used in breads and preserves. (See figure 3-112.)

Figure 3-112. Fennel—*Fenouil*.

Garlic—*Ail*

Garlic is a round-shaped bulb formed by several individual cloves enclosed within the skin of the bulb. It is used for seasoning hot dishes, and in cold dishes, salads, dressings, and sauces. (See figure 3-113.) See also

the discussion of garlic under "Spices and Herbs" later in this chapter.

Figure 3-113. Garlic—*Ail*.

Jerusalem Artichoke—*Topinambour*

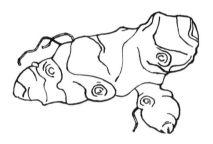

Figure 3-114. Jerusalem artichoke—*Topinambour*.

This vegetable is an irregularly shaped tuber, often covered with wartlike spots. It is about the size of a potato, with a high water content, an earthy odor, and a faint taste of turnips. The tubers can be boiled, baked, and used in soups and stews. The Jerusalem artichoke is not related to the globe artichoke. (See figure 3-114.)

Kohlrabi—*Chou-rave*

Kohlrabi can be distinguished from other cabbages by the bulblike thickening of the stem 1 to 3 inches (2.5 to 7.5 centimeters) above the ground. This is the edible portion of the plant, and it is usually yellow-green or violet in color. (See figure 3-115.) The plant is harvested when the bulblike part is 2 or 3 inches (5 to 7.5 centi-

Figure 3-115. Kohlrabi—*Chou-rave*.

meters) in diameter. It grows larger, but it is then too woody and tough for eating. The name *rabi* means turnip. This bulblike part may be eaten raw or as a cooked vegetable. The young leaves may also be used as a salad, or they may be steamed or cooked like spinach.

Lamb's Lettuce—*Mâche/Doucette/Rampon*

Also called corn salad, lamb's lettuce is a valerian plant generally used for a salad. Today it is often cultivated but also grows wild. Its main season is winter. This plant should not be confused with rampion, which is grown chiefly for its roots. (See figure 3-116.)

Figure 3-116. Lamb's lettuce—*Mâche/doucette.*

Leek—*Poireau*

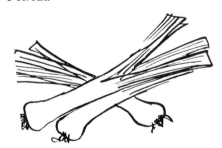

Figure 3-117. Leek—*Poireau.*

The common leek grows from a bulbous root into a long, tightly closed leaf stalk that is green at the top where the leaves are separated. (See figure 3-117.) The blanched, elongated bulb is used as vegetable and for seasoning in soups, sauces, and stews.

Lettuce—*Laitue*

Several varieties of lettuce can be classified as salad vegetables. Loose-leaf or bunching lettuce (*laitue a tondre—couper*) is an open, loosely branched variety that does not form a head. Butterhead lettuce (*laitue pommée*) has soft pliable leaves with a buttery flavor.

Boston and Bibb are principal types of the variety. (See figure 3-118.) Cos lettuce or romaine (*laitue romaine*) has elongated, stiff ribs with dark green leaves. (See figure 3-119.) *Crisphead lettuce* is the ubiquitous salad lettuce often called iceberg. (See figure 3-120.) *Stem lettuce* is an ingredient in many Chinese dishes. The seedstalk is the edible part of this lettuce.

All varieties of lettuce are basic ingredients of most salads. The popularity of tossed salad has increased the demand for cos varieties. Characteristics of good quality are medium to light green color; firm, but not hard heads; fresh and tender leaves. Almost all varieties are cultivated in hothouses and are available on most markets throughout the year. The season is at its peak from June to October.

Figure 3-118. Butterhead lettuce—*Laitue pommée.*

Figure 3-119. Romaine lettuce—*Laitue romaine.*

Figure 3-120. Iceberg lettuce—*Lettuce.*

Okra—*Ladyfinger*

Okra is a pointed, finger-shaped pod that grows to a length of 1¼ to 6 inches (3 to 15 centimeters), but only young pods are tender; when they reach 3 inches they begin to be tough. Okra is cultivated in the southern United States, the West Indies, Africa, Greece, and Turkey. Okra is quite mucilaginous. It is used in soups, salads, stews, and as a vegetable.

Onion—*Oignon*

The real, large onion is round and slightly flattened or pear shaped. It contains a milky juice. Onions should be firm and dry with small necks. Avoid onions with thick woody centers in the neck or with fresh sprouts. There are yellow onions; small white onions called silverskins; large white Bermuda onions, which

Figure 3-121. Onions—*Oignons.*

are mild in taste; Italian red onions; Spanish onions, which have less milk; pearl onions, which are white, yellow, and red. (See figure 3-121.) Scallions or green onions are young onions of the same species; they are pulled before the bulb has formed at the base and sold while still fresh and green and not cured like other bulb onions. The silverskins, *petits oignons,* are used as a garnish for fish, meat, and vegetables. Red onions are often tied on braided strings, the dried tops used for the braids. See also the discussion of onions under "Spices and Herbs" later in this chapter.

Palm Hearts—*Coeurs de palmier*

A tropical delicacy, these are the tender terminal shoots of the cabbage palm tree. Usually sold precooked and canned, they are most often used for salad but can be butter-sautéed. (See figure 3-122.)

Figure 3-122. Palm hearts—*Coeurs de palmier.*

Parsnip—*Panais*

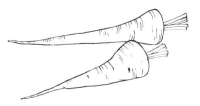

Figure 3-123. Parsnip—*Panais.*

Parsnips are shaped like carrots. The flesh is fine grained, tender, and white. They have a sweet, nutty, spicy flavor similar to that of celery. The roots are used for flavoring, soup, and as a side dish. The best season is September to May, but after the first frost parsnips are sweeter. (See figure 3-123.)

Peas—*Pois*

A favorite vegetable fresh and dried, peas come in many varieties.

Green peas (*petits pois*) are immature shelled peas. These peas are considered the finest flavored. They

Figure 3-124. Green peas—*Petits pois.*

should be picked when young and shelled while fresh, just before cooking. The peak of the crop comes in early spring. (See figure 3-124.) Mature peas are ripened for use as dried peas. When dried, they may be used as seeds or for green pea soup.

Snow peas (*pois mange-tout*) are immature peas with a crisp tender pod. Both pea and pod are eaten. The pod should be green and bright. The peak seasons are spring and summer. These are available frozen, but fresh are far superior. (See figure 3-125.)

Black-eyed peas, pigeon peas, and chickpeas may be eaten fresh but are more familiar in dried form. Yellow peas are sold dried whole and split.

Figure 3-125. Snow peas—*Pois mange-tout.*

Pepper—*Poivron*

Most peppers marketed are sweet green peppers, available in varying amounts throughout the year but most plentiful during the late summer. Fully mature peppers of the same type have a bright red color. Look for medium to dark green color, a

Figure 3-126. Pepper—*Poivron*.

glossy sheen, relatively heavy weight, and firm walls or sides. Avoid peppers with thin walls (shown by light weight and flimsy sides), any that are wilted or flabby with cuts or punctures through the walls, and those with soft, watery spots on the sides (evidence of decay). (See figure 3-126.)

Mature red peppers can be bought fresh and used in soups and salads. Roasted, peeled, and packed in olive oil in jars or cans, they are called pimientos. In addition to green and red peppers, there are bright yellow sweet peppers, which are somewhat milder in taste. Also available are brown, deep purple, and orange peppers, all of which are sweeter than green peppers.

Chile peppers are related to green peppers but are much hotter in taste. There are mild and very hot kinds, in red, green, dark red, and almost black, of various sizes. These are used to flavor foods in the southwestern United States, Mexico, India, and Indonesia. Green chiles, both mild and hot, are available canned.

Potato—*Pomme de terre*

The potato tuber is an enlarged part of the ground stem. The potato has liberal amounts of water, carbohydrates, protein, minerals, and vitamins. (See figure 3-127.)

The types of potatoes generally found on the United States market are classified by their shape and skin color. Potatoes are long or round, and their skin color may be white, red, or russet. The principal varieties of each of these types are the russet Burbank

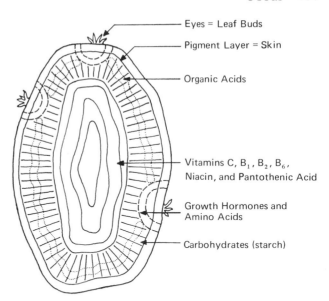

Figure 3-127. Potato—*Pomme de terre*.

(long russet), the white rose (long white), the Katahdin (round white), and red Pontiac (round red). Other varieties are available at different times of the year. The Norgold russet (a long to blocky shape, light russet in color) and the Norland (a round red) are but a few varieties that are becoming increasingly popular.

Potatoes may also be classified by their use. There are new potatoes, general-purpose potatoes, and baking potatoes. New potatoes are best when boiled. Because of their immaturity, they may be skinned easily, and they remain firm when cooked. General-purpose potatoes, both round and long types, are used for boiling, frying, and baking. These potatoes are available year-round, and they are used more than any other type. Potatoes grown specifically for their baking qualities are quite dry and mealy. The best known variety for this use is the russet Burbank.

The Department of Agriculture provides a voluntary grading service as a guide to the purchase of quality potatoes. US Extra No. 1, the premium grade, allows for few defects. The next grade is US No. 1. Minimum sizes and weights of the potatoes are also specified in the grades. Potatoes should be firm, well shaped, smooth, and free from bruises, cuts, sprouts, and decay.

It is important to store potatoes in a cool (45° to 50°F; 7° to 10°C), well-ventilated, dark area.

Radish—*Radis*

Radishes are familiar spring vegetables, usually eaten raw. There are many types, including *daikon*, a large white Oriental root, and the black radish, which is the size of a large rutabaga. The most familiar radishes are the red radish and the white radish.

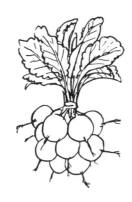

Figure 3-128. Red radish—*Radis.*

Red radishes, available year-round, are most plentiful from May through July. California and Florida produce most of our winter and spring supplies, while several northern states provide radishes the rest of the year. Look for medium-size radishes (¾ to 1⅛ inches in diameter) that are plump, round, firm, and of a good red color. (See figure 3-128.) Avoid very large or flabby radishes (likely to have pithy centers). Also avoid radishes with yellow or decayed tops (sign of overage).

While the wild radish probably originated in southern Asia, white cultivated variations are found in many countries. It is at its best in the spring. Often more pungent than the red radish, it is shaped like a carrot. (See figure 3-129.)

Figure 3-129. White radish—*Radis.*

Rampion—*Raiponce*

Figure 3-130. Rampion—*Raiponce.*

This is a variety of European bellflower with thick, fleshy roots that can be eaten raw or prepared like black salsify. The leaves are used in salads or cooked as a vegetable. (See figure 3-130.)

Rhubarb—*Rhubarba*

Figure 3-131. Rhubarb—*Rhubarbe.*

This highly specialized vegetable is used like a fruit in sweetened sauces and pies. Limited supplies are available during most of the year, with most supplies available from January to June. Look for fresh, firm rhubarb stems with a bright, glossy appearance. Stems should have a large amount of pink or red color, although many good-quality stems will be predominantly light green. Be sure the stem is tender and not fibrous. Avoid either very slender or extremely thick stems, which are likely to be tough and stringy. Also avoid rhubarb that is wilted and flabby. (See figure 3-131.) Use only the stems in cooking; the leaves are poisonous.

Rutabaga—*Chou-navet*

Round-shaped root vegetables, rutabagas are both white fleshed and yellow fleshed; however, commercially, rutabagas are almost always yellow fleshed. (See figure 3-132.) Rutabagas are usually eaten as a cooked vegetable. In the United States they are sometimes called Swedes. They are a fall and winter vegetable.

Figure 3-132. Rutabaga—*Chou-navet.*

Salsify—*Salsifis*

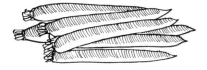

Figure 3-133. Black salsify—*Salsifis.*

Salsify is the name given to two plants from different families. White salsify is also called oyster plant. Black salsify belongs to the *Scorzonera* genus. Their flavors are similar, and the flesh of both is white or oyster colored. This long, fleshy root, ½ to 1 inch (1.2 to 2.5 centimeters) thick, is eaten as a boiled vegetable. (See figure 3-133.) When snapped in two, good fresh black salsify should contain milky juice; older black salsify is woody and spongy. The young leaves are sometimes eaten in salads. Although originally from southern European countries, black salsify is now grown all over Europe and in the United States. Salsify discolors when peeled and exposed to air. Drop at once into acidulated water.

Shallot—*Echalote*

A member of the onion family, every part of this mild and aromatic plant is edible. The crisp green stalks and the small elongated bulb are chopped and used in salads, soups, and meat dishes. They are excellent in fine sauces and for pickles.

Sorrel—*Oseille*

A spring vegetable similar to spinach, sorrel is used as a vegetable and for soup. (See figure 3-134.)

Figure 3-134. Sorrel—*Oseille.*

The young tender vegetable has a pleasant acid taste.

Spinach—*Epinard*

Figure 3-135. Spinach—*Epinard.*

This is a popular vegetable, primarily available in spring and the fall, although it can be obtained throughout the year. Good spinach should have a deep green color with tender young leaves, not stalks. After the seed stalk develops, the spinach is tough, discolored, and bitter. Spinach must be dry and the leaves separated for storage. Spinach is available frozen, in whole leaves or chopped. (See figure 3-135.)

Squash—*Gourde*

American natives, these members of the gourd family include summer squashes, such as yellow crooknecks and straightnecks, pattypans or cymlings, zucchini (see separate entry), and others; and winter squashes, such as acorn, butternut, Hubbard, and turban squashes. Pumpkin is also related. Winter squashes have orange flesh, while the summer vegetables may be yellow, white, or pale green. All grow on vines. Summer squashes are often sautéed or eaten raw, while winter squashes are usually baked.

Swiss Chard—*Côte de blette*

Figure 3-136. Swiss chard—*Côte de blette.*

Swiss chard, or seakale beet, is grown for its foliage. It has a broad, white-leafed stalk and dark green leaves. The young, tender leaves have a milder flavor than spinach. The white stems are prepared like celery or asparagus. There is also variety with red stems and leaves. (See figure 3-136.)

Tomato—*Tomate*

Figure 3-137. Tomato—*Tomate.*

The tomato is a vegetable by cultivation and use, but botanically it is a fruit. (See figure 3-137.) It is native to South America and was brought to Europe and North America by the early Spanish explorers. It is available throughout the year but is at its prime in summer and fall. Good tomatoes are firm, large, and bright red with a smooth skin. Tomatoes are rich in vitamins A and C. In the United States, the small cherry tomato and the pear tomato are very small tomatoes that may be either red or yellow. They are attractive in salads and as garnishes. There is also a green variety that is ripe in spite of its color.

Turnip—*Navet*

This smooth root tuber is round or oblong in shape. (See figure 3-138.) The flavor is slightly bitter. Young, firm vegetables should be chosen. They are good in stews, casseroles, salads, and as a vegetable. Turnips are available throughout the year, but are at their prime between June and February. The mild, oblong Parisian-type turnip is particularly good.

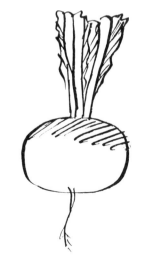

Figure 3-138. Turnip—*Navet.*

Zucchini—*Courgettes*

Figure 3-139. Zucchini—*Courgettes.*

This vegetable, originally from Italy, is a squash. The young vegetables up to 6 inches are the best. They are usually dark green or green and white striped. These squash are delicately flavored and are used as side dishes, in soup, or as an hors d'oeuvre. (See figure 3-139.)

3.9.7 *Mushrooms*—Champignons

Mushrooms, the fruits of higher fungi, belong to the subkingdom thallophyta. All thallophyta—algae, fungi, and bacteria—are characterized by their lack of true roots, stems, or leaves.

Most mushrooms are saprophytes, plants deriving all of their nourishment from the bodies of decaying, dead organisms. They grow wild in the woods and meadows, and their food source is from the organic matter in dead leaves, soil, and rotting logs. The mushroom plant consists of the sporophore and the mycelium. The sporophore is the reproductive portion of the plant. This fruiting body, commonly known as the mushroom, has a stalk and a cap with bladelike gills on the undersurface from which spores are produced and shed. The mycelium is the underground vegetative portion of the plant. It originates from the spores and forms an extensive underground network of filaments, known to commercial growers as spawn. The fruit bodies, or mushrooms, are formed on the mycelium. There are many species and varieties of mushrooms; however, most mushroom experts agree that the *Agaricus bisporus* is the only mushroom cultivated in either the United States or Europe. The *Agaricus campestris* is the ordinary field mushroom. It is often difficult to distinguish between edible and poisonous mushrooms. The commercially cultivated mushrooms are always safe. Mushrooms can be grown in cellars, caves, and tunnels. They require an even temperature for growth.

Mushrooms should be fresh in appearance. The gills, the fluted formation on the undersurface of the cap, should be light colored. Black or dark brown gills are a sign of age. The mushrooms should be white or cream colored and should be free of dirt, wilting, and pitting. The composition of a 3.5-ounce (100-gram) uncooked edible portion of mushrooms includes 90 percent water; 2.7 grams protein; 4.4 grams carbohydrate; 28 calories. In addition, there are small amounts of fat, phosphorus, potassium, and trace minerals.

Fresh mushrooms are perishable and should be refrigerated at 32°F (0°C) to keep them in prime condition. They should not be washed until just before preparing. Mushrooms can be preserved by drying, canning, pickling, or processing into mushroom extract.

Mushrooms can be poached, steamed, sautéed, baked, or broiled. Mushrooms may be used as a main dish, a garnish, an hors d'oeuvre, in sauces, and in salads. Black truffles (périgord) are used as garnishes and for decorating cold dishes.

Bay Boleta—*Bolet bai brun* (*Boletus badius*)

The cap of this edible mushroom grows to a diameter of 4½ inches and is chestnut brown in color. When dry, it is matt and velvety; when wet, it is slimy and shiny. The thick stalk is stringy and lighter in color than the cap. The flesh is yellowish white, firm, and turns blue when broken near the pores. Found in pine forests and occasionally in deciduous woods, this variety avoids chalky soil. These mushrooms are steamed with herbs and served with a cream sauce.

Cèpe—*Bolet-cèpe* (*Boletus edulis*)

The cap of the young cèpe, an edible mushroom, is roundish, rimmed, and moist, and it sits on the stout stalk like a hat. Smooth and bare and shaped like a cushion, it can grow to a diameter of 10 inches. This mushroom becomes slimy with age and when exposed to damp weather. The color may be white, light or dark brown, or reddish brown, depending on the locality. The edges are lighter in color. The pores are first white, then yellowish green, and finally olive-green. They are separated from the stalk, or at least very short at that point. When mature, the pores are as much as 1 inch long. The stalk, first round and later cylindrical, is white to pale brown with a fine network of raised white veins toward the top. The flesh is white, with a wine-red area underneath the skin of the cap in older specimens. The taste is mild, similar to that of nuts.

The cèpe is found in sparse deciduous and pine forests and in meadows. The brownish black-capped cèpe is found in southern climates in sparse oak and beech forests. It has a dark brown velvety cap and saffron-colored stalk.

The cèpe is best when steamed with herbs and served with a cream sauce.

Chanterelle—*Chanterelle* (*Cantharellus caruncopioides*)

The cap of this edible mushroom grows to a width of over 3 inches, is humped and then spreads out and deepens. The edge of the cap is irregular, ragged, indented, and wavy. It is the color of egg yolk but fades after exposure to rain. The gills are like folds that divide and practically form a network running down to the point where the stalk gradually replaces the cap. The flesh of the stalk is firm, thinner at the bottom, and can be split into long fibers. The flesh of the cap is white, yellowish toward the edges, and it has a slight peppery taste and an aroma that is similar to that of apricots.

Found in the woods from June through autumn, chanterelles are often found in clumps. The violet-scaled chanterelle has a thick, violet, scaly skin, which later becomes loose and often disappears. This variety is less irregular when fully grown, and the gills are thicker and less intricate. It is usually found in beech woods in mountainous areas. The corn-colored chanterelle has a cap that is almost white. The gills and stalk are the color of egg yolk; the mushroom, as a whole, is more stumpy and the flesh firmer. It is usually found in beech woods that have a chalky soil.

Chanterelles may be simmered in butter, with herbs, or served in cream sauce or Greek style.

Common Morel—*Morille ronde* (*Morchella esculenta*)

The cap of this edible mushroom is conical, and the color is ocher-yellow to dark brown, or olive to brown. It is pitted with irregular cavities up to 1/2 inch wide. The folds between these cavities are often uneven, and in older plants they are rust colored (not black!). The stalk is thick, often grooved or folded, and the base is sometimes very wide. The point is powdery with a white to yellow color.

The common morel is found on sandy river banks, in sunny damp meadows that are protected from the wind and located near ash trees, near stacked wood, and in fruit gardens, woods, and parks. This morel is in season in April and May.

Used only in dried form, morels may be sautéed in butter with herbs, or they may be served in a brown sauce with meat dishes or as creamed morels (*morilles à la crème*).

Conical Morel—*Morille pointue* (*Morchella conica*)

The cap of this edible mushroom is miter-shaped, always pointed, and a pale gray-yellow-brown color. The folds are thick, fluffy, and matted. The cap on older plants is brown or black. The folds curve regularly from top to bottom of the cap. The transversal folds lie deeper, and the longitudinal cavities are narrow. The stalk is smooth and pale. The top is very fragile with a fine smooth texture. This morel grows in moss in mountain woods, in woody meadows, and on old burned patches of ground. It is in season from April to the end of July. These morels may be sautéed in butter with herbs, or they may be creamed.

Cultivated Mushroom—*Champignon de Paris* (*Agaricus bisporus*)

This mushroom is a whitish brown color with a thick stalk. The meat changes in color from white to slightly red. The cap is 2 to 4 inches in diameter, curved with small scales, and it varies from white to light-brown. It has a faint, nutlike, pleasant odor. The cultivated mushroom, considered to be one of the greatest delicacies among mushrooms, is grown in dark places in soil that has been enriched with horse manure. It requires a constant temperature between 57° and 64°F (15° and 18°C), and a quality spawn is essential. Cleanliness and sanitation are necessary to prevent infestation of insects and vermin. Although originally cultivated in France, this mushroom is grown in many European and North American areas, and in the Far East (especially Taiwan). These mushrooms may be served whole or sliced, in cream sauce, Provence style, with herbs, as a puree, as an hors d'oeuvre, and with cocktail sauce. They are also used as garnishes.

Field Mushroom—*Agaric champêtre* (*Agaricus campestris*)

The cap of this edible mushroom grows to 6 inches in diameter. It varies from white to brown in color; from a silky smooth surface to one that is covered with fibrous scales; from a shape that is round when young to one that is flattened and spread out when older. The rim of the cap hangs over the gills, which are free, close to one another, and quite full. Initially they are light pink, soon turning purplish brown, and finally brown to black. The stalks are quite short and silky smooth with a brown base. There is never a volva. The ring is split at the edges and hangs slightly. The flesh is white but turns to a meat-red color when broken. The flavor is spicy and excellent. It is found in meadows, pastures, and gardens from June to autumn. This variety may be confused with the carbolic champignon. When rubbed or cooked, the carbolic champignon smells strongly of carbolic acid or ink, and the flesh from the base of the stalk turns an intense yellow color.

Gyromitra (*Gyromitra esculenta*)

The cap is irregular, with thick, indented, waxy, brown folds that are very fragile. The appearance is similar to that of brains. The interior is grayish white, fine in texture, and pocketed. The stalk is short, fat, and shaped in folds. Initially, the stalk is solid but subsequently becomes hollow. The flavor is very strong. A scarce variety, gyromitra are found in sandy, nonchalky pine forests, in clearings, burned areas, and in areas where logs are stacked. They are imported to the United States from Europe.
GYROMITRA ARE POISONOUS WHEN RAW. Boil for 5 to 10 minutes and dispose of the water, which contains the water-soluble poison. In Central Europe these mushrooms are sorted according to size, strung on threads, and dried over heat. Gyromitra are dried and used like morels.

Horn of Plenty—*Corne d'abondance* (*Craterellus cornucopioides*)

The cap of this edible mushroom can reach a width of 3 inches and is grayish brown. It consists of thin, irregular-shaped, wavy-sided funnels with crinkled edges. The gills are a dirty yellow, which turn to gray, and they run down the stalk. The stalk itself is hollow, yellowish, and often flattened and grooved. The flesh is yellowish, with a strong and sometimes earthy smell and taste.

The horn of plenty is often found in masses in fir tree forests, in moss, and near huckleberry bushes. It is usually dried and used in sauces and as a substitute for truffles.

Pholiota—*Pholiota ridée* (*Pholiota caperata*)

The cap of this edible mushroom is up to 4 inches wide, initially bell shaped and then slanted outwards. It is straw yellow to ocher brown and rimmed with white in the middle. The rim is shriveled, torn, and pitted. The gills are often wrinkled and close to each other; they are initially a pale yellowish color, then later turn to rusty brown. The edges of the gills are white and notched. The stalk is first silky white, strong and firm, but later becomes white and flaky. The flesh is whitish yellow and usually permeated with water. It is mild and tender. The smell is spicy and the flavor good. These mushrooms are found in the moss in spruce and pine forests and occasionally under deciduous trees. They may be sautéed or stewed.

St. George's Mushroom—*Mousseron de Saint-Georges* (*Tricholoma georgii*)

The cap of this edible mushroom grows up to 6 inches wide, first hemispherical and then flattening out; the edge is rolled inward; the color is white to ocher yellow; it sometimes splits open. The gills are thin and narrow and very close together. They can either grow right up to the stalk or be separated from it. They are fragile. The thick stalk is the same color as the cap. The flesh is white, and the odor resembles that of flour. This variety is found in fields and meadows from the end of April until June. It tends to grow in groups, even in circles, or in so-called fairy rings. This excellent edible mushroom occurs in many different forms and colors. It is usually identified by its odor. It is possible to confuse it with the poisonous red-staining inocybe, which also appears in the spring. These mushrooms may be prepared by the same methods suggested for cépes.

Saffron Milk Cap/Orange Agaric—*Lactaire delicieux* (*Lactarius deliciosus*)

The cap of this edible mushroom can grow to 4 inches in diameter and is between a reddish and yellowish orange with dark concentric circles. It is sticky and slimy and has a tightly curled rim. Later on it becomes funnel shaped and frequently has green spots. The gills reach down the stalk. They are orange-red and delicate. If damaged, green spots develop. The stalk, firm and solid when young, later becomes hollow, and is the same color as the cap. The flesh is fragile and white, but when broken open, it releases an orange-colored milk that turns carrot red. The flavor is usually mild, but it can be bitter and spicy, especially in dry areas. Very frequently, these are found in damp pine forests and in fields. They may be deep-fried, sautéed, stewed, or used in mixed mushroom dishes.

Tawny Grisette—*Amanite vineuse* (*Amanita spissa, excelsa*)

The cap of this edible mushroom is curved initially in a hemispherical shape, which later flattens. It is 3 to 5 inches wide, grayish brown with flaky gray remnants. The rim is smooth and moist. The gills are white and closely bunched. The solid stalk is cylindrical, with a white hanging ring. The ring, high up on the stem, is white; beneath the ring, it is gray. The flesh is white and mild. This mushroom is found in deciduous and evergreen woods from spring to autumn. It is sometimes confused with the poisonous panther cap. The latter, however, has a sack-shaped volva and white scales on the cap. These mushrooms are best when stewed with onions and herbs.

Black Truffle—*Truffe du Périgord* (*Tuber meinosporum*)

Black truffles are ½ to 3 inches wide, dark brown to black in color, and covered with small warts. (See figure 3-140.) They are shaped like a tuber and pitted with cavities. The flesh of this edible mushroom is marbled with black veins, and it has a strong and aromatic odor. These truffles are found in France below the soil surface, usually under oak trees in deciduous woods. They are ripe from November to March. The

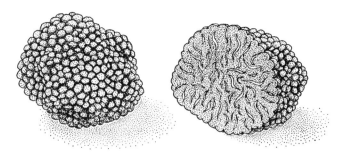

Figure 3-140. Black truffle—*Truffe du Périgord.*

Périgord truffle is preferred over all truffles and is very expensive. Raw truffles are used in soups, sauces, salads, and meat dishes. They may be sautéed in butter or simmered in wine. They are a choice garnish or decoration for many dishes.

Summer Truffle—*Truffe d'été* (*Tuber aestivum*)

Shaped like a tuber, these edible truffles are 1 to 4 inches wide and are usually covered with bumps. They are blackish brown with a thick skin and large warts. The flesh varies from grayish white to yellowish brown, with light-colored veins. This variety is found from August to March in deciduous woods. It grows 1 to 6 inches below the surface of the soil and is found in Italy, France, Switzerland, and Germany. Raw summer truffles are used for salads and garnishes. They may be sautéed or stewed with spices.

White Truffle—*Truffe blanche* (*Choiromyces maeandriformis*)

This edible mushroom is 2 to 3 inches wide, usually the size of a duck's egg, but it can grow much larger. It is round and looks like a potato covered with large bumps. The skin is like leather, firm, smooth, and without warts. Initially it is grayish white, with cracks, and then turns yellowish brown. White truffles are grown in Italy, in Piedmont, and in central Europe. They are on the market from July to September. Raw white truffles are used for salads and hors d'oeuvre. They may be sautéed or used in casseroles or as a seasoning.

Death Cap—*Amanite phalloide* (*Amanita phalloides*)

This mushroom is DEADLY POISONOUS. The cap, which grows to a width of 5 inches, is a light or dark olive brown with dark fibers radiating out to the rim. When dry, the cap has a silky sheen; when damp, it becomes sticky. The gills are pure white, with a greenish shimmer. They are quite close together and free. The long, thin stalk is bulbous at the base and is white with pale green lateral bands. The stem has a large hanging ring, which is enclosed in a wavy volva. The flesh is white, and when young, it has a faint but pleasant odor that develops into a repugnant smell. This is the *most dangerous* of all mushrooms. The death cap is found in deciduous forests, especially under oak trees, from July to September. The majority of deaths caused by eating mushrooms can be traced to this variety. It can be confused with the green *Russula* species and the rusty-striped *Tricholoma portentosum*. Neither of these possesses a ring or a volva.

Destroying Angel—*Amanite vireuse (Amanita virosa)*

This mushroom is DEADLY POISONOUS. The cap, as wide as 4 inches, is conical or bell shaped; it is white, although when old the center turns to an ivory color. It is sticky and slimy in wet weather. The gills are white, free, and narrow near the rim of the cap. The stalk is slim with fine streaks above the tattered ring. Shreds hang from the margin of the cap. The thin volva surrounds the base. The flesh is white and has an unpleasant chlorine odor. The destroying angel is found throughout damp woods. Similar to the *Amanita verna*, the cap of the destroying angel is bell shaped with a ragged margin and the ring is tattered. Both are found in the same localities.

Devil's Boletus—*Bolet de satan (Boletus satanas)*

This mushroom is POISONOUS. The cap, a firm, thick, spongy mass, grows to 10 inches in width. It is yellowish white with a greenish tint, changing to an ocher yellow. It has smooth texture, and during dry periods, it splits open. The tubes can be either free or fixed. Originally yellow, these tubes are blood red to orange yellow at their pores. Broken or pressed areas turn blue green. The stalk is short and bulging; the upper part is yellow, the middle carmine red. There is a delicate red network over the upper part of the stalk. The flesh is whitish and firm, although it later becomes spongy. The odor of older fungi is unpleasant. Young specimens can be mistaken for cèpes.

Fool's Mushroom—*Amanite printanière (Amanita verna)*

This mushroom is DEADLY POISONOUS. The cap, growing to 4 inches in width, is white or slightly ocher colored in the center. It is sticky when wet, otherwise shiny. The gills are free, pure white, and run to the rim of the cap. The thin stalk tapers upward and is slightly flaky beneath the hanging ring. The tight ring is finely streaked and attached high on the stalk. The thin volva hugs the bulbous base. The flesh is white and soft, and in older specimens the odor is very offensive.

Panther Cap—*Amanite panthère (Amanita pantherina)*

This mushroom is VERY POISONOUS. The cap grows up to 5 inches wide. It is colored from grayish yellow to brown and is darker in the center. The rim is skirted. The cap is covered with small pure white flakes in concentric circles. The gills are shining white and set close together, and the edge is striated. The stem is white, and the upper part, above the hanging, heavily fringed ring, is smooth without streaks. The bulbous base of the stalk stands in a tightly fitting volva, and bears two or three circular ridges. This mushroom is found in deciduous and pine forests. The panther cap cannot be confused with the circular-shaped gray amanita (tawny grisette). These gray amanitas have grayish scales on the cap, a smooth or slightly skirted rim, and a streaked ring. The stem has a club-shaped base, but there is no volva. The tawny grisette is not poisonous.

Red-Staining Inocybe—*Inocybe lobée (Inocybe patouillardii)*

This mushroom is VERY POISONOUS. The cap is white and 1 to 3 inches in diameter. When the mushroom is young, the rim of the cap is rolled inward. Later, the cap turns yellowish brown and opens into a conical or bell shape, with streaks radiating from the center. The stalk is stout and white with reddish spots. The gills are free, set close together, and uneven. Initially white, they later turn to a rusty tinge. The flesh is firm, fibrous, and white, becoming red with age or on contact with the air. Parts that are broken or pressed turn red. The mushroom has an acid odor and only a faint taste. This mushroom grows in groups in deciduous woods during spring and summer. It may be confused with the St. George's mushroom or the Pholiota (*Pholiota caperata*).

Tiger Tricholoma—*Tricholome tigre* (*Tricholoma tigrinum*)

This mushroom is VERY POISONOUS. The cap can grow to 6 inches wide. It is grayish in color with violet shading and dark gray and brown scales. The cap is initially bell shaped and gradually slants irregularly outward. It is firm and fleshy and turned inward at the edges. The gills are dirty white, with a greenish tinge, dense and almost free at the stem. Often water droplets hang from the edges of the gills. The compact stalk is 1¼ inches wide; its base is club shaped. Water droplets often collect at the top of the stalk. The flesh is whitish with the exception of the gray area under the skin of the cap. The base of the stalk is whitish to a light ocher color. It has a faint flour odor. The taste is mild to bitter. This species is found in groups in chalky soils in hilly areas. Unless the scales on the cap are properly developed, it is difficult to identify this species. It is easily confused with the Pholiota, although the robust nature of the fungus is different. The poison of the tiger tricholoma causes serious stomach and intestinal disorders.

3.9.8 *Fruit—Fruit*

Fruit, in food terminology, is the collective term for all edible fruits of cultivated or wild plants and for certain kinds of seed nucleii, such as nuts. Most fruits may be eaten raw.

The fresh produce market generally divides fruits into six groups. Berries (*baies*) include blackberries, strawberries, blueberries, raspberries, currants, cranberries, gooseberries, and wine and table grapes. Citrus fruits (*agrumes*) are oranges, grapefruits, kumquats, limes, mandarins, and lemons. Exotic fruits (*fruits du midi*) include pineapples, avocados, bananas, dates, figs, kiwis, pomegranates, persimmons, mangoes, melons, olives, okra (also used as vegetable), papayas, passion fruit, pistachios, peanuts, and sultanas. Hard-shelled fruits (*fruits à coque*) include hazelnuts, chestnuts, almonds, and walnuts. Seed fruits (*fruits à pépins*) are apples, pears, and quinces. Stone fruits

Retail Cuts of Beef and Their Uses
(see color photo opposite)

Name of Cut	Usage
A. *Neck*	Ground meat
B. *Brisket*	
B1. Clod tip	Boiled beef
B2. Clod	Boiled beef
B3. Lower brisket	Boiled beef
C. *Shoulder*	
C1. Plate	Boiled beef
C2. Uncovered plate	Boiled beef
D. *Chuck and ribs*	
D1. Prime ribs of beef	English roast beef, braised beef, boiled beef
D2. *Pot roasts*	Ragout, goulash, boiled beef, braised beef
E. *Foreshank*	
1. Shank	Ground meat
2. Hock	Ragout, braised
3. Shoulder filet	Ragout, braised
4. Knuckle soup bone	Ragout, braised
5. Thick shoulder	Ragout, braised
6. Chuck	Ragout, boiled
F. *Rump and round*	
F1. Top round	Braised beef, roast beef
F2. Round steak	Ragout, goulash, London broil
F3. Bottom round	Carbonnade, stew, braised beef
G. *Flank*	
Flank	Boiled beef, London broil
H. *Sirloin and short loin*	
Porterhouse steak	Broiled steak
T-bone steak	Broiled steak
Club steak	Broiled beef, sautéed beef
Roast loin, roast beef	Roast beef, sirloin steak
Tenderloin	Roast; châteaubriand, tenderloin steak, tournedos, filet mignon
Rump roast	Braised beef, carbonnade, ragout
Other cuts	
Tongue	Salted, smoked
Muzzle	Salad
Stomach	Tripe
Liver	Slivers, slices, dumplings
Kidneys	Small slices, braised
Feet	For thickening sauces
Oxtail	Soup, stew

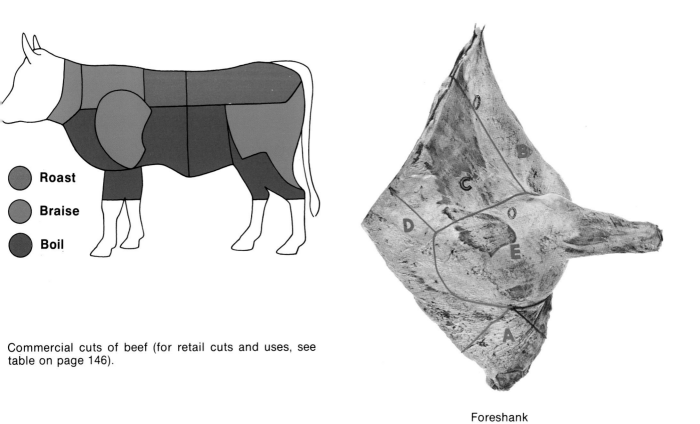

Commercial cuts of beef (for retail cuts and uses, see table on page 146).

Foreshank

Round, sirloin, short loin, and flank

Chuck

Shoulder

Commercial cuts of veal.

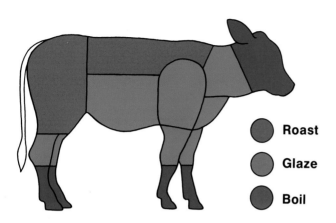

Roast

Glaze

Boil

Inside   Outside

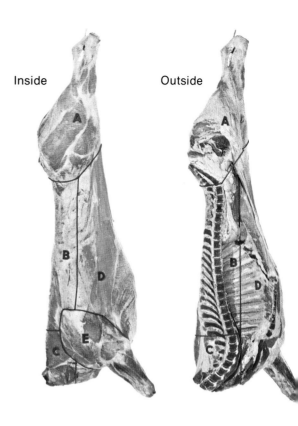

Retail Cuts of Veal and Their Uses

Name of Cut	Usage
A. *Leg*	
Rump roast	Roast, cutlets, sliced
Heel of round	Roast
Round roast	Roast, sliced
Top round	Roast, scallops, sliced
Shank	Osso buco, ragout
B. *Saddle, back*	
Loin	Roast, steaks, chops
Filet	Roast, piccata, sliced
Rib	Roast, cutlets
C. *Neck*	Roll roast, ragout
D. *Breast*	Roast, cutlets, ragout, fricassee
E. *Shoulder*	
Shank	Osso buco, ragout
Arm	Roast, ragout
Blade	Ragout
Other cuts	
Head	Boiled, with vinaigrette sauce
Ruffle	Deep-fat fried, busecca style
Brains	Poached, deep-fat fried
Tongue	Boiled
Sweetbreads	Braised, poached, as stuffing
Liver	In thin slices
Kidneys	Thin slices, grilled
Feet	Braised, deep-fat fried, for headcheese

Commercial cuts of pork.

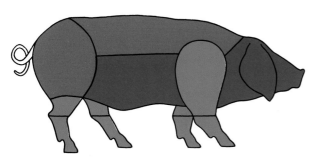

 Roast

 Glaze/braise

 Boil

Retail Cuts of Pork and Their Uses

Name of Cut	Usage
A. *Ham*	In brine, smoked
Roast	Roast, cutlet
Top round	Roast, cutlet
Butt	Roast
B. *Loin*	
Loin	Roast, steaks
Filet	Roast, mignons, thin slices
Rib	Roast, chops
Neck	Roast, ragout
C. *Spare ribs*	Salted lean bacon, smoked, grilled, broiled
D. *Shoulder*	Roast, stews, smoked
E. *Belly*	Lard
Other cuts	
Head	In brine
Tongue	In brine, boiled
Brains	Poached
Liver and kidneys	In thin slices
Feet, trotters	Salted and boiled, braised
Shank	Glazed, salted
Ears, muzzle, tail	Salted

Inside

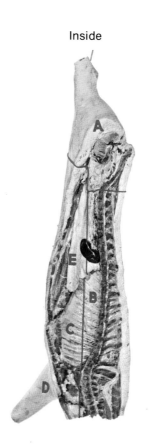

Outside

Commercial cuts of lamb.

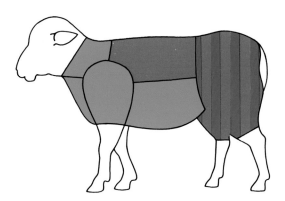

 Roast

 Braise/glaze

 Boil

Inside

Outside

Retail Cuts of Lamb and Their Uses

Name of Cut	Usage
A. *Leg*	Roast, braise, boil
B. *Saddle, rack*	
Whole, and saddle with legs (baron)	Roast
Loin	Roast, chops
Rib chops	Roast, cutlets
C. *Breast*	Ragout, Irish stew, curry
D. *Shoulder*	Ragout, Irish stew, curry, rolled and boiled, roast
E. *Neck*	Ragout, Irish stew, curry
Other cuts	
Liver	Slivered, sliced
Kidneys	Grilled, sliced
Feet	Stuffed

Fresh vegetables (for identification, see last page of this color section).

Exotic fruits (for identification, see last page of this color section).

►
Useful herbs (for identification, see last page of this color section).

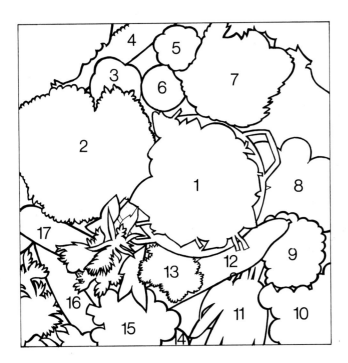

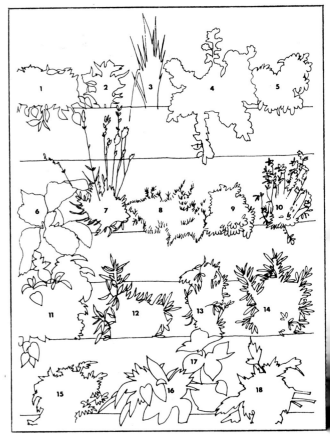

Fresh vegetables: (1) spinach; (2) Savoy cabbage; (3) yellow pepper; (4) corn; (5) green pepper; (6) beet; (7) red cabbage; (8) tomatoes; (9) cauliflower; (10) Brussels sprouts; (11) carrots; (12) cucumber; (13) parsley; (14) onion; (15) mushrooms; (16) zucchini; (17) eggplant.

Useful herbs: (1) peppermint; (2) English or red peppermint; (3) chives; (4) burnet; (5) marjoram; (6) borage; (7) lavender; (8) thyme; (9) oregano; (10) winter savory; (11) lemon verbena; (12) tarragon; (13) savory; (14) rosemary; (15) parsley; (16) sage; (17) basil; (18) lovage.

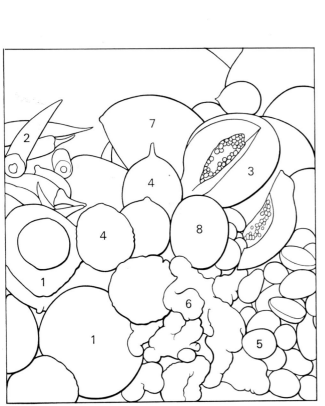

Exotic fruits: (1) avocado; (2) okra (actually, okra is a vegetable); (3) papaya; (4) passion fruit; (5) kumquat; (6) ginger root; (7) mango; (8) lime.

(*fruits à noyau*) include apricots, cherries, peaches, and plums.

Fruits differ in quality, flavor, texture, and appearance. They are usually priced according to their quality and size. U.S. grade standards have been established for most fresh and processed fruits. The top grades of fresh fruits may be either US Fancy or US No. 1. The Grade A or Fancy is for fruit with excellent color and uniform weight, size, and shape, with few or no blemishes. US Grade B canned fruits are very good quality and only slightly less perfect than Grade A. US Grade C canned fruits may contain some broken and uneven pieces. These fruits are good and wholesome and particularly suitable for jam, frozen desserts, puddings, gelatin salads, and desserts.

Fresh fruits are highly perishable and should be purchased only for a specific use, in the quantity needed. They should be stored in well-ventilated areas at the proper temperature. Nuts are perishable, and only the current year's crop should be purchased. Canned fruits should be stored in a well-ventilated area no warmer than 75°F (25°C). To maintain the quality of frozen fruits, they should be stored at 0°F (−18°C). Nutmeats should be stored in airtight containers at refrigerated temperatures.

Fresh, canned, and frozen fruits are used for salads, sauces, garnishes, desserts, and other dishes. Fruit is an important and economical food in terms of its nutritional value. Most fruits contain carbohydrates, minerals, and vitamins.

All domestic and imported varieties of fresh fruits can be classified as cooking fruit, fallen or damaged fruit, or table fruit. Cooking fruit is ripe, clean, and undamaged fruit suitable for cooking, drying, or preserving. Fallen or damaged fruit is any fruit that is not ripe or that is overripe or damaged. Table fruit is completely ripe, undamaged, clean fruit that corresponds to the accepted standards for the variety in terms of size and color.

Almond—*Amande*

Almonds may be classified as sweet, bitter, or shell; the sweet and bitter almond are the two varieties of economic value. Grown for its edible nuts, the sweet almond is used for snacks, desserts, and garnishes and

Figure 3-141. Almond—*Amande*.

is used by confectioners and bakers. (See figure 3-141.)

The bitter almond is used for flavoring and in cosmetic skin preparations. The kernels and the crude oil of the bitter almond contain prussic acid (HCN, a poisonous acid); however, the bitter flavor tends to deter anyone from eating these almonds in amounts that would cause poisoning. The term *mixed* means that about 1 percent of bitter almonds is added to sweet almonds to give a spicy flavor.

Originally from southern France and Italy, shell almonds have a brittle shell, and are served on many fruit trays as a dessert.

Apple—*Pomme*

The cultivated apple of commercial value is of the genus *Malus* and of the species *sylvestris*. Apples have been grown for at least 3,000 years, and until the twentieth century, they were about the only fresh fruit available during the winter months. Although there are innumerable varieties of apples, only seventeen or eighteen varieties represent most of the commercial production in the United States. More Red Delicious apples are produced than any other variety. McIntosh ranks second, and Golden Delicious, third. Other well-known varieties in the United States are Rome Beauty, Jonathan, Winesap, Baldwin, Stayman, York, Astrachan, Starr, Newton, Northern Spy, and Rhode Island Greening.

The flavor of apples is a combination of sweetness, acidity, and bitterness. There is a great variation in these qualities that affects the flavor. There is also a difference in the texture. Some varieties are soft and mealy; others are crisp and hard.

Apples may be eaten out of the hand, peeled or unpeeled. They can be used in compotes and salads, as baked, spiced, pickled, fried, or candied apples; in pies, cobblers, strudels, pastries, and pudding; and in chutney, mincemeat, jellies, and jams. Apples are made into cider and vinegar. They are also used as a garnish for many dishes and are available in canned, dried, and frozen form.

The storage requirements of apples differ with the variety. The fruit must be carefully handled and stored under conditions compatible with their needs. Storerooms should be well ventilated; the storage temperature for most varieties is 30° to 32°F (−1° to 0°C) at 80 to 90 percent relative humidity.

Apricot—*Abricot*

The apricot varies in color from pale yellow to deep orange with a red blush. The fruit is slightly flattened, with a smooth surface, and has a smooth, flat kernel. It grows in warm or temperate climates. Apricots are used for table fruit, baking, stewing, compotes, salads, and garnishes. They are excellent in preserves and pastries. Apricots are available canned, dried, and frozen.

Avocado—*Avocado*

The avocado is a tasty tropical fruit grown in the United States, Central America, South Africa, Israel, and Italy. When ripe, avocados are halved, the stone is removed, and the fruit is eaten plain or served as an hors d'oeuvre, entrée, salad, main dish, or dessert. The best varieties are those with a small kernel, weighing 7 to 10 ounces. Avocados are rich in protein, fat, and vitamins A and B.

Banana—*Banane*

Bananas are grown in hot, humid, tropical climates; Ecuador is the leading supplier. Bananas ripen after they are harvested and develop their best eating qualities during the ripening process. They should be stored at 60° to 70°F (15° to 20°C) and should never be refrigerated. Ripe bananas are golden yellow. Black spots on the skin indicate that the fruit is overripe; however, these bananas may be used in cakes, pie fillings, breads, and puddings.

Blackberry—*Mûre*

The many varieties of blackberries grow on bushes in shady woods and in sunny groves. The berries should be purplish black, fresh, dry, and free of mold. They may be eaten fresh or canned and are used in compotes, desserts, yogurt, jam, jelly, syrup, and sherbet.

Blueberry—*Myrtille*

The blueberry bush, common throughout Europe and the United States, bears pea-sized berries, bluish black in color and very juicy. Blueberries grow in dry woods in central Europe, in the pre-Alpine regions in Europe, and in North America. Most of the blueberries that reach the fresh food market are cultivated. At their peak in June and July, blueberries are available from May through August. Fresh blueberries are eaten as a dessert with cream and are used in blueberry pie and blueberry muffins. They can be made into preserves, jelly, and a topping or syrup to serve over ice cream or pancakes.

Cherry—*Cerise*

Cherries originated in Persia. Like all stone fruits, cherries can be stored for only one or two days. There are many varieties of cherries, but of all the species, only the sour or pie cherry and the sweet cherry have been domesticated. Bing, Royal Ann, and Lambert are three of the popular sweet cherries grown in the United States. The sour cherries are Montmorency, which is the most popular of cherries grown in America; Early Richmond, a dark red cherry that is good for all cooking purposes; and the English Morello, a very dark red cherry excellent for all culinary uses. Cherries are used for table fruit, in pies, pastries, cakes, tarts, jams, and jellies.

Chestnut—*Marron*

Chestnuts found their way from Persia to Greece and Rome, and from there to the Alps. The shiny chestnuts are especially suitable for cooking purposes, since they are easy to peel. The skin of the gray-flocked chestnut is more difficult to remove. Chestnuts are used in stuffings or combined with vegetables, such as cabbage and Brussels sprouts.

Cranberry—*Airelle rouge*

The fruit of a wild, low, evergreen bush, cranberries are native to the peat and bog areas of North America, Europe, and Asia. The large American cranberry, native to America, is exported in large quantities. The acid taste changes after cooking with sugar to a delicate and pleasing one. Maturity is indicated by color, which ranges from bright red to almost black. Cranberries are used in jams, jellies, cakes, relishes, ices, salads, and for making fruit juices. They are a good accompaniment for game and poultry dishes. November is the peak month for cranberries in the United States, and large amounts are used at Thanksgiving and Christmas with the traditional roast turkey.

Currant—*Groseille à grappe*

These are the berries of the currant bush. There are three main varieties, red, white, and black. Black currants are known as *cassis*. *Blanc de cassis*, a French aperitif, should not be confused with the black currant. Currants are grown in Germany, England, Switzerland, and in subtropical countries. The berries can be eaten fresh or canned, or they may be processed into syrup. They are used in many different ways for desserts, ice cream, sherbet, sauces, and jellies.

Date—*Datte*

This is the fruit of the date palm. Dates are usually classified into three types: the soft dates generally sold in pressed masses and eaten raw or used in making candies; the semidry date from North Africa with the fruit still attached to the strand; and dry dates, which are quite hard, important in the diets of the Arab countries. The world's most popular date, Deglet Noor, is a semidry date. Good-quality dates are fat and full with a soft interior flesh. The main exporting areas are Iraq, North Africa, and Egypt. Dates are eaten as a confection and are used for making pastries and desserts.

Fig—*Figue*

The fig tree is one of the most important commercially grown plants in the Mediterranean countries. It is also found in California. The Smyrna figs that come from Turkey are well known. Greece supplies the fan-shaped Calmata figs as well as other varieties. The California varieties are Calimyrna, Black Mission, and Kadota. Figs are extremely perishable and must be handled carefully and cooled immediately after harvesting. Figs are eaten fresh, canned, or dried, and are used for desserts and garnishes.

Gooseberry—*Groseille verte*

This berry of the gooseberry bush exists in some 500 varieties. The fruits are also classified according to color (red, yellow, green, and white). They are grown in Europe, North Africa, and western Asia. Ripe gooseberries are used as table fruit and for tarts and jam. Unripe gooseberries may be made into an excellent compote.

Grape—*Raisin*

The grape is a member of the vine family, and the most important species for dessert and wine grapes is the *Vitis vinifera*. Grape growing is the world's largest fruit industry. Grapes are grown throughout the world, except in regions with extremely cold temperatures. Depending on their use, grapes are classified into five groups: table grapes, raisin grapes, wine grapes, juice grapes, and canning grapes. The following European types are well-known table grapes: Thompson seedless, Emperor, Tokay, Ribier, and Red Málaga. The American types are Concord, Niagara, Catawba, and Delaware. In the United States, Emperor, Thompson seedless, Tokay, Cardinal, and Ribier are well-known table grapes. Grapes used for dry wine must be of high quality and have moderate sugar content; those used for sweet wine should have a high sugar content and moderately low acidity. Most grape juice and jellies are made from Concord grapes. Most varieties should be stored at 30°F (1°C), at a relative humidity of 90 to 95 percent.

Grapefruit—*Pamplemousse*

This citrus fruit grows chiefly in tropical or subtropical countries. In Europe, the very juicy, white-fleshed Jaffa grapefruit from Israel is best known. In the United States, grapefruit is available throughout the year, with the most abundant supplies from January through May. While Florida is the major producer of grapefruit in the United States, other states known for their grapefruit are Texas, California, and Arizona.

There are several varieties of grapefruit, but the principal distinctions are between those that are seedless (few or no seeds) and seeded and among those with differences in the color of the flesh. The white-flesh grapefruit is most common, but the pink-flesh varieties are also popular. Grapefruit is used for juice, appetizers, salads, cocktails, garnishes, desserts, and sherbets.

Hazelnut and Walnut—*Noisette et noix*

Hazelnuts (filberts) are grown in large quantities in the areas along the coasts of the Black Sea and the Mediterranean; they are also grown in the United States. Those from Italy and the eastern Mediterranean countries are sold as Levantine nuts. Walnuts are found in many varieties all over the world. The thin-shelled types are best for desserts. Green, unripe walnuts are often pickled. Hazelnuts and walnuts are perishable and may easily become rancid or infested with insects. Only nuts from the current year's crop should be purchased, and they should be purchased in limited quantities and for the specific use, either whole, chopped, or broken. Hazelnuts and walnuts are eaten out of hand, in salads, pastries, and desserts. Nuts in the shell are sometimes served as a dessert.

Kiwi Fruit

These berries are an exotic tropical fruit grown commercially only in New Zealand. The vines also grow naturally on the fringes of forests in the Yangtze Valley of China. The kiwi is the size and shape of a lime. It has a brown, fuzzy, thin skin. The outer flesh is a light translucent chartreuse and the flavor is often described as a composite of the gooseberry, strawberry, banana, and peach. Kiwis are eaten out of hand, in fruit salads, on ice cream, and as garnishes.

Kumquat—*Cumquat*

This is a type of dwarf orange that comes from China. Chinese kumquats grow on a small evergreen shrub with dark green leaves. They are also grown in California. Unlike other citrus fruits, they are eaten with the skin. Good kumquats are firm, bright, and glossy. They may be sliced for salads and compotes, ground with cranberries for a relish, pickled, or made into preserves. Preserved kumquats are a good accompaniment with pork, poultry, and game.

Lemon—*Citron*

Southern Asia is the home of the lemon, although it is grown in the Mediterranean countries, California, and Florida. Lemons that are to be exported are picked when green and then stored in hothouses at 120°F (49°C) for two or three weeks until the skin turns yellow. The common lemon has a thin skin, and it is fleshy and juicy. The thin-skinned lemon, known as the *premiere fleur*, is available from the late fall to January.

Lime—*Limon*

This citrus fruit looks like a small lemon; however, it has a thin green skin. Although originally from the Himalayan valleys, it is now cultivated in America, Asia, and Africa. The lime is largely used for lime juice to enhance the flavor of foods or as an additive in drinks. Lime juice is sometimes mixed with beer, used in cocktails, or made into sherbet.

Lychee—*Lychee*

This fruit resembles a nut or a pine cone. At harvest its color is dark red; later it turns various shades of brown. The flesh is white and its taste is reminiscent of strawberries. The kernel in the middle is unedible, as is the shell. Lychees are available during the winter months from tropical countries. Peeled, they can be used as dessert fruits, especially after Chinese meals.

Mango—*Mango*

Mangoes are one of the most popular fruits of the tropics. They grow on mangifera or mango trees in all areas near the equator. There are green and yellow-to-orange varieties. Mangoes are best when eaten fresh. The fruit is halved, the kernel removed, and the flesh eaten out of the skin with a spoon. Mangoes may also be used in salads, fruit cups, and desserts. Mango chutney is the preserved product made from the unripe fruit. It is served with Oriental and Indian dishes, particularly curry.

Melon—*Melon*

Melons belong to the Cucurbitaceae family, which includes pumpkins, squashes, watermelon, and muskmelons. There are many varieties of *cantaloupe.* Hales Best is the most important commercial variety in the United States, and the Bender and Hearts of Gold are other excellent melons. The characteristics of good cantaloupe are thick, sweet, and juicy flesh with a rich aroma. California is the main source of cantaloupes in the United States. Most cantaloupes are eaten fresh as appetizers or desserts. They are also used in salads, compotes, ice cream, toppings, and some are pickled.

The *honeydew* melons are related to the cantaloupe. They have a smooth, light green to yellow rind. The flesh should be thick, fine textured, and juicy with a sweet flavor. The *Persian* melon is similar in external appearance to the cantaloupe. The dark green rind is covered with a fine netting. The thick orange flesh is sweet, juicy, and rich in flavor. The *Crenshaw* melon is a late variety. It has a smooth rind mottled with gold and green color with very little ribbing and netting. The flavor of this melon is rich, sweet, and mellow. The *casaba* is another late variety. The rind is deeply furrowed, and the flesh is soft and white with a delicate sweet flavor.

The *watermelon* is especially popular during the summer months. There are many varieties, but the Charleston Gray ranks as the most popular in U.S. markets. The melon, about 24 inches long and weighing up to 35 pounds, has a grayish green rind with darker green veins. The bright red flesh is crisp, sweet, and rich in flavor. The seeds are black. Other important varieties of watermelon are Black Diamond (Cannonball or Florida Giant), Jubilee, Klondike, and Congo. Seedless varieties have been developed. They are round and weigh between 8 and 10 pounds.

Olive—*Olive*

Figure 3-142. Olive—*Olive.*

The fruit of the olive tree is used as a food and as a source of edible oil. The flesh contains about 22 percent oil, and the seed also has a high oil content. Although the olive originated in the Mediterranean region, with Spain, France, and Italy important producers, the tree is also grown in China, southern Australia, the United States, and North Africa. The fruit is a drupe. It contains a single hard seed surrounded by firm flesh. The skin changes from green to dark blue or purple when ripe. The fruits are picked when ripe or when fully grown and are then processed and packed in brine. Fresh olives can be processed into ripe, green, Sicilian-style green or salt-cured, or oil-coated olives. (See figure 3-142.)

Orange—*Orange*

The word *orange* is derived from the Arabian word *nāranj* and the Persian *nārang.* Oranges are divided into sour and sweet types. The sour orange is important in the United States as a rootstock and in Spain and other countries for its bitter or sour fruits. The sweet orange species is grown in the United States and elsewhere for commercial use. The sweet orange can be divided into four varieties, the common orange, such as the Valencias from Florida and California; the blood or pigmented orange, such as the Ruby; the acidless orange grown in some Mediterranean areas; and the navel orange, such as the Washington navel of California.

Good-quality oranges have a fine-textured skin and

good color for the specific variety. They are firm and heavy for the size. Sweet oranges are used as a table fruit and for juice; in salads, desserts, and as garnishes. The skin of the bitter orange is suitable for confections, particularly in the form of candied orange peel. Oranges are grown in the Mediterranean countries and in California, Arizona, Texas, Florida, and Washington.

Papaya—*Papaya*

The papaya is native to tropical America; however, it is also grown in Africa, Sri Lanka, India, Malaya, and Australia. It is spherical to oblong in shape, with a thin smooth skin that turns from green to yellow or orange when ripe. The flesh, yellow to orange in color, has a sweet delicate flavor. Black seeds are packed in the center of the fruit and must be removed before eating. Papaya is cut into slices or served with cocktails, drinks, or as a garnish for meat. It is often served at breakfast. The juice of unripe papaya contains an enzyme that is an excellent natural meat "tenderizer" and is sold commercially for this purpose.

Passion Fruit—*Passionfruit*

This is the fruit of several varieties of the passionflower. It has a yellow to brownish yellow hard skin. This tropical creeper flourishes most frequently in South America and in other tropical and subtropical areas of Africa and the Far East. The juice of the fruit is drunk pure, mixed as a soft drink, or added to punches. The pulp is used in ice cream and dessert recipes and also for jam.

Peach—*Pêche*

The peach is a small- to moderate-size deciduous tree that grows to a height of 30 feet. The fruit's name is derived from *persica,* the species name. China is the original home of the peach, but it is now grown in central Europe and in the United States. The fruit is one of the finest table fruits. Good peaches are quite firm with a velvety skin and yellow color.

There are many varieties of peaches in the United States, but the general classifications are freestone, with flesh that readily separates from the pit, and clingstone, with flesh that clings tightly to the pit.

Freestones are used for freezing and eating fresh; clingstones are used primarily for canning. Peaches are used for hot and cold dishes, garnishes, and desserts.

Peanut—*Arachide*

Figure 3-143. Peanut—*Arachide.*

Peanuts are of South American origin, but today they are an important crop all over the tropics and in India, Africa, and America. The plant is a bushy annual. After pollination, the short flower stalks lengthen downward and push the fruits, which are on the end of the stalks, into the ground, where they ripen 2 to 3 inches below the surface. (See figure 3-143). A neutral-tasting oil, pressed out of the ground nuts, is used as cooking and salad oil and for making margarine. The peanuts, containing 40 to 50 percent oil, are pressed. The residue left after extracting the oil is used for animal feed. Peanuts are also eaten as snacks, are used as garnishes, and can be ground into a paste that becomes peanut butter.

Pear—*Poire*

Pears are of the genus *Pyrus,* which includes twenty to twenty-five species native to Europe, Asia, and northern Africa. Commercial varieties in the United States are derived from the *Pyrus communis* varieties of Europe. In the United States, the pear-growing centers are in the dry valleys of Oregon, Washington, and California.

Of the 3,000 varieties known in the United States, only a few are of commercial value. The Bartlett pear is now the world's leading commercial variety. It is on the market from July until October. This pear is yellow when ripe, the flesh is white, and the flavor is sweet with a rich muscatel flavor. There is also a red-skinned Bartlett. The Beurre d'Anjou is the principal winter pear and is on the market from October to May. The Anjou is yellowish white in color, is juicy, and has a spicy sweet flavor. The Bosc pear is another popular winter pear and is known for its unique shape and color. This variety has a long, tapering neck and its skin is dark yellow with an overlay of brownish russet. The flesh of the Bosc is yellowish white and very juicy. It is a popular dessert pear. Other well-known varieties include the Comice, Kieffer, Hardy, Clapp, and Seckel.

Fresh pears are eaten out of the hand; in salads and compotes; they may be stewed, baked, glazed, and pickled. Great quantities of pears are canned, and some are dried.

Persimmon—*Kaki*

Persimmon, which is a delicacy, grows on the persimmon tree in Italy, southern Europe, and the United States. The regions around Naples, Emilia, and the Ligurian coast are well known as exporters of this special fruit. The yellowish red fruits, which have the appearance of tomatoes, are ripe in the late fall. The fruit is eaten fresh, dried, or stewed.

Pineapple—*Ananas*

The pineapple, belonging to the orchid family, comes from the West Indies and Central America and flourishes in the tropics. The main areas of cultivation are Hawaii, California, Jamaica, Mexico, Puerto Rico, the Bahamas, and the Canary Islands. In Europe, pineapples are grown in hothouses, but these are inferior in both taste and aroma. The pineapple is a multiple fruit. All parts of the flower, including the axis, bracts, sepals, petals, and ovaries, coalesce and become very fleshy and aromatic. The fruit's aroma comes from the pineapple ether. Fully ripe, mature pineapples are golden yellow or reddish brown, firm, and heavy. The eyes or pips are glossy, and the leaves can be pulled out easily. Pineapple is used in many different ways, as dessert, in fruit bowls, in salads, and as a garnish.

Pistachio—*Pistache*

Figure 3-144. Pistachio—*Pistache.*

These small, green, almondlike kernels are from a small tree of the cashew family. They grow in the Mediterranean countries and in Asia Minor. The main trade brands are Tunis, Aleppo, and Sicily. The nuts are used for decorating cakes, ice cream, desserts, for cold meat pies, galantines, and delicatessen sausages. They are also eaten salted and as a confection. (See figure 3-144.)

Plum—*Pruneau*

An excellent table fruit, plums are also good in pies, puddings, cakes, tarts, jellies, and jams. They may be stewed, poached, or served in salads and compotes.

Pomegranate—*Grenade*

The fruit of the pomegranate tree has a hard brownish to red shell and is the size of an apple. It is cultivated in Cyprus, the Canary Islands, North Africa, Sicily, and Spain. A light-colored, sweet, juicy, and winelike layer of fruit flesh surrounds numerous seeds. This is eaten fresh, or made into syrup, ices, and sherbets.

Quince—*Coing*

Originally grown in the Kydone district of Crete, the quince was brought to Central Europe by the Romans. There are both apple- and pear-shaped quinces. The ripe, golden fruits have a greenish felt-like skin, and although hard and very acid, the flesh turns dull pink when cooked with sugar. It makes a delicious jelly.

Raisin—*Raisin sec*

These are dried vine berries, coming from southern Europe, Asia Minor, South Africa, Australia, and the United States in various sizes and colors. The best known variety is the Smyrna raisin; it is the real raisin and is large, yellow skinned, with or without seeds. The Málaga raisin is large, blue in color, and excellent in flavor. The Sultana raisin is either light yellow or blue. The fine Sultana is small, light yellow in color with a delicate skin. The Corinthian raisin is a small, almost black, dried grape with a pleasant taste. Raisins must be kept dry and cool in closed containers.

Raspberry—*Framboise*

This is the fruit of the raspberry bush, which grows both wild in the woods and is cultivated in gardens. There are three groups of cultivated raspberries in North America, red raspberries, black raspberries or blackcaps, and purple canes. Raspberries are usually consumed fresh or as a jelly, jam, or syrup. They are also used in bavarians, pies, mousse, punch, and ices. Raspberry juice is fermented and distilled and sold as a brandy. These berries are in season in June and July.

Strawberry—*Fraise*

The strawberry, king of all berries, is a favorite fruit throughout the world. It is an aggregate fruit, since the bottom of the flower develops into an aromatic, sweet berrylike structure on which the actual fruits, in the form of seedlings, are attached. Wild strawberries abound in Europe, and the ever-bearing strawberry is derived from them. The large garden strawberry and the large Chile or giant strawberry are of the same origin. The cultivated strawberry is native to America. Strawberries are used in desserts, jams, as breakfast fruit, and as garnishes.

Tangerine—*Mandarine*

A somewhat flattened orangelike fruit, the tangerine has loose skin that is easily peeled from the fleshy part of the fruit. Good-quality tangerines are smooth-skinned, shiny, segmented, and not too small. They are used as table fruit and for special desserts. Tangerines and oranges belong to the citrus family, and originally came from southern China, Burma, and the southern regions of the Himalayas. Today the chief areas of production are the southeastern United States, Central America, and the Mediterranean countries. The California and Arizona tangerine varieties are divided into four categories. Mandarins are lighter in color than other varieties and have a mild sweet flavor. Tangelos are a cross between a grapefruit and tangerine, combining the best of both fruits for a tangy, sweet flavor. Tangerines are a brighter orange color than any of the varieties. Temple oranges are larger than the others and have a sweet-tart distinctive flavor. Tangerines should be stored in well-ventilated areas at approximately 45°F (7°C).

Fruit Products

Fruit pulp (*pulpe de fruits*) is made from crushed or broken and strained soft fruits, such as strawberries, raspberries, and apricots. It is used in fruit bavarians, fruit ice, sorbets, sherbets, and fruit sauce.

Fruit nectar (*nectar de fruits*) is pressed fruit, almost like liquid fruit pulp, that is thinned with water or seltzer and sometimes sweetened with sugar or honey. It is not strained and may have pieces of fruit flesh in it. It is used as a refreshing drink.

Fruit juice (*jus de fruits*) is made from pressed fruits, such as oranges, lemons, and grapefruits. Fruit juices are used as breakfast drinks, mixers for tall drinks, appetizers, and as cool refreshing drinks.

Candied fruits (*fruits confits*) are fruits cooked and preserved with sugar. Usually orange and lemon peels are candied. These confections are used for puddings, cakes, and pastry.

Marmalade (*marmelade*) is a jam made from citrus fruits and sugar and sometimes with other fruits as well. Marmalade makes a delicious spread for toast and biscuits; it is used in the bakery and as a filling for pancakes.

Jam (*confiture*) is traditionally made from soft fruits, whole fruits, and/or the pulp. The fruit is cooked with sugar until it forms a firm set. Examples are strawberry jam, raspberry jam, and plum jam. Jams are used as spreads for toast and biscuits and as filling for pancakes. They have many uses in the bakery.

Fruit jellies (*gelée de fruits*) are cooked in a manner similar to jams, but the juice is strained and cooked with sugar before being allowed to set. They have a much greater clarity than jams, as only the juice of the fruit is used.

Fruit purees (*purée de fruits*) are made from cooked or uncooked pureed fruit, with or without sugar added. Applesauce is an example of a pureed fruit.

3.9.9 *Sugar*—Sucre

Sugar is an energy-producing food. When more sugar than the body needs is consumed, it is converted to fat. The basic unit of all carbohydrates is simple sugar. There are two types of raw sugar: sugar obtained from sugar cane and sugar obtained from sugar beet. (See figure 3-145.) The two types vary only slightly in their cooking qualities. After processing in a sugar factory, a refined sugar is derived, from which the various commercial products are manufactured.

Corn Syrup (Glucose and Dextrose)

Glucose, as well as fructose, is found in honey and in the juice of most sweet fruits, such as grapes, cherries, and plums. This sugar is generally extracted from potato or cornstarch by boiling the starch with diluted sulphuric acid. The action of the acids or enzymes changes the cornstarch to glucose. Corn syrup is used in the manufacture of candies and jams.

Invert Sugar

When sucrose is hydrolyzed or inverted, equal parts of glucose and fructose are formed. This product is called invert sugar.

Molasses

Sulfured molasses is the term used to describe the syrup that is a by-product of the manufacture of the

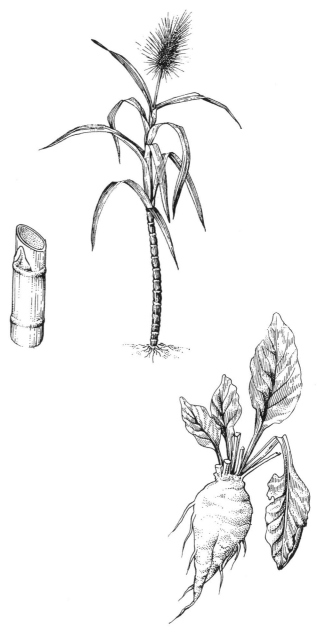

Figure 3-145. Sugar cane (top) and sugar beet (bottom).

sugar from sugar cane. It is a brown or brownish black mass. The molasses remaining after sugar is extracted from the sugar beet is too bitter for human consumption. It is used for making alcohol. Sugar-cane molasses is an unsulfured molasses made from the sun-ripened sugar cane. It can be used as a syrup or in the manufacture of imitation honey.

Maltose (Malt Sugar)

Maltose is available in sugar or syrup form. Real malt products are made from germinated barley using the so-called maltin process. The barley starch is converted into malt sugar by diastasis. Maltose has a distinct flavor and may be used for making many yeast products, such as breads and rolls.

Lactose

Lactose is a sugar found in milk and is derived by evaporation of the whey and subsequent crystallization and purification of the sugar. It is also called milk sugar.

Vanilla Sugar

Vanilla sugar is made by keeping one or two vanilla beans in a closed container with two cups of sugar. It originally consisted of the vanilla crystals that formed when vanilla was stored in closed barrels.

Caramelized Sugar

If sugar is heated to between 350° and 400°F (177° and 204°C), the sucrose breaks down, gives off water, and forms a brown viscous mass known as caramel. When the caramel is dissolved in diluted alcohol or water, a dark brown liquid with a definite odor and a bitter flavor is formed. It is a very strong coloring agent, used to color and flavor many different kinds of foods and candies.

Honey—*Miel*

The general term *honey* refers to the mature, sweet substance that bees gather from the nectar of flowers or from other natural plant secretions and store in the honeycombs. Honey is marketed in two basic forms: extracted and comb. Extracted honey has been removed from the comb by centrifuge, and it is sold in either liquid or crystallized form. Comb honeys are creamed, candied, or spread. The light-colored May and blossom honeys, or even the honey that is made primarily from the blossom of linden trees, are superior to the darker forest honey. Honey should be stored in a dry place at room temperature.

Imitation Honey—*Miel artificiel*

Products that contain sugar and are similar to honey in terms of appearance and consistency should be labeled as imitation honey, specifying the actual ingredients. Glucose is the main ingredient in imitation honey.

Saccharin

Saccharin, an artificial sweetener, is a white crystalline compound extracted from coal tar. Chemically pure saccharin is about 550 times sweeter than sugar. The commercial product is the soluble powder pressed into tablets that are about 110 times sweeter than sugar crystals.

Cyclamates

Cyclamates, also artificial sweeteners, must be labeled as drugs and should be used only under a physician's order. They are extracted from a chemical substance. Neither saccharin nor cyclamates has any nutritional value.

Aspartame

Aspartame, marketed under the trade name Nutrasweet, is a recent addition to the artificial sweetener group. A naturally occurring protein that is sweeter than saccharin, aspartame can only be added to already cooked or raw foods. Heating aspartame destroys its sweetening ability.

3.9.10 *Spices and Herbs—Les épices et les herbes*

Spices and herbs are aromatic substances obtained from the dried parts of plants, such as the roots, shoots, fruits, leaves, and bark. These substances are marketed as whole or ground spices, whole or crushed herbs, seeds, and blends of spices, herbs, and seasonings. The aromatic substances that give the spice its particular aroma and flavor are the etheric oils. The flavor of the essential oil or flavoring compound will vary depending on the quality and freshness of the spice. The oils of spices are volatile, and the flavors may be lost rapidly if the spices are stored in open containers or in warm or humid areas.

Fresh herbs have a better flavor than dried herbs do. The plants should be cleaned and washed. Such plants as parsley, chives, and chervil are usually chopped and added to or sprinkled over salads, soups, and other foods. The stems are frequently used in *bouquet garni.*

Dried herbs and spices, such as whole leaves, twigs, seeds, or finely chopped root vegetables, are often used in foods that are to be cooked for a long period of time. These spices and herbs should be added at the beginning of the cooking. The spices can be removed only if they are wrapped and tied in a piece of cheesecloth.

Ground spices release their flavors quickly. When they are to be used in a dish that requires a long cooking time, they should be added at the end of the cooking period. Ground spices must be stored in airtight containers in a cool, dry place. Containers should be tightly closed after each use to avoid loss of the volatile oils.

Allspice—*Poivre de Jamaïque*

Figure 3-146. Allspice—*Poivre de Jamaïque (Pimenta dioica).*

Allspice is produced from the berries of a small tropical evergreen tree that grows in Jamaica. It is also grown in Mexico, the Antilles Islands, and South America. Allspice is also known as pimento, pimenta, and Jamaica pepper. The red or dark brown to yellowish berries are about ¼ inch in diameter and contain dark brown seeds. (See figure 3-146.) The odor and flavor are reminiscent of several spices—cloves, nutmeg, and cinnamon. Allspice is used in the preparation of sausages, fish, pickles, relishes, and desserts.

Anise—*Anis*

Figure 3-147. Anise—*Anis (Pimpinella anisum).*

The herb anise should not be confused with the vegetable anise or with star anise. The vegetable can be distinguished by its bulb. The star anise is from a tree belonging to the magnolia tree of China. The herb is thought to be native to the Orient, but it has been long established in Mexico, Spain, Morocco, Mediterranean countries, Yugoslavia, Turkey, and Russia. A plant of the parsley family, it is similar to burnet. The plant grows to a height of 18 inches. It has fine leaves and clusters of small white flowers. (See figure 3-147.) The seeds, used for flavoring, are small, hard, and a greenish brown color. The Spanish Málaga aniseed, with large, green-tinged seeds, which is very sour, is the best variety. The Russian aniseed is superior for its aroma. Aniseed is a raw material for the liqueur industry. The liqueur anisette, as well as other beverages, are flavored with anise. The oil of anise is used in cough medicines. Aniseeds are added to pastries, cookies, breads, candies, and pickles. The oils are very volatile, and therefore the seeds should be stored in sealed tins. Anise is marketed as aniseed, ground anise, and oil of anise.

Artemisia (Wormwood)—*Armoise*

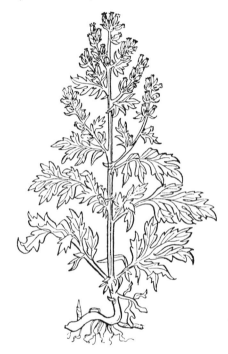

Figure 3-148. Artemisia (wormwood)—*Armoise* (*Artemisia absinthium*)

Wormwood belongs to the daisy family and is a native of Europe. A perennial herb, it grows to a height of 3 feet with grayish green, silklike stems and leaves and aromatic flowers. (See figure 3-148.) Wormwood is used in the preparation of roast goose and eel dishes. It is also used for making absinthe liqueur and vermouth wine. With the stalks removed, it can be boiled or simmered with food.

Basil—*Basilic*

A native of eastern Asia and central Europe, basil belongs to the mint family. It is grown all over the world. This annual plant grows to a height of 18

Figure 3-149. Basil—*Basilic* (*Ocimum basilicum*)

inches. The flowers and leaves have long been used as a culinary herb. (See figure 3-149.) The plant also has many folklore associations with love, hate, and royalty. The leaves add flavor to fish and meat dishes, soups, sauces, salads, and especially to tomatoes and dishes flavored with tomatoes. It is the chief ingredient in pesto, a Genoese sauce with many uses. The herb can be simmered with food or can be minced and used as a garnish.

Bay Leaf—*Laurier*

The bay laurel, an evergreen shrub or tree, is native to the Mediterranean countries, especially Italy, Yugoslavia, Crete, Greece, and Turkey. The leaves of this tree are dried and used for bay leaves. The bay leaves, dark green in color, are approximately 2 to 4 inches long. (See figure 3-150.) The color turns to an olive green as the leaves dry. The pungent flavor and distinct aroma make this an ideal herb for many dishes. Bay leaf is used for oxtail soup, meat stews, roast wild boar, leg and rib of lamb, minced or ground meat, hasenpfeffer, carp in beer, marinated herrings, soups, sauces, and tomato dishes. Bay leaves should be washed carefully before using.

Figure 3-150. Bay leaf—*Laurier* (*Laurus nobilis*).

Borage—*Bourrache*

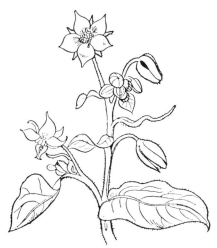

Figure 3-151. Borage—*Bourrache* (*Borago officinalis*).

Borage, originally from the Mediterranean area, is now cultivated as a garden herb. This plant has blue flowers with hairy leaves and stems. (See figure 3-151.) The fresh, young leaves of borage are used to flavor salads, the blue flowers to color vinegar. Dried borage can be used to season cabbage by simmering it with the vegetable. Borage flowers can be candied for decorating desserts.

Burnet—*Pimprenelle*

Figure 3-152. Burnet—*Pimprenelle* (*Sanguisorba minor*).

Burnet is grown in Germany and central Europe. A wild plant of the rose family, burnet has clustered flowers. There are over 200 varieties. In addition to oils, the plant contains bitter essences. When crushed, the leaves have a taste similar to that of cucumber. The roots are 4 to 8 inches long, yellow on the inside and brown to grayish yellow on the outside. (See figure 3-152.) Burnet is used for seasoning soups, sauces, and vegetable and fish dishes. The young leaves can be used in salads; the dried roots are used as a drug.

Caper—*Câpre*

Capers are grown in the Mediterranean countries—France, Spain, Italy, Malta, and Majorca. Capers are the buds of the caper bush. They are similar to the buds of the marsh marigold and the nasturtium. (See figure 3-153.) The fruits are sorted according to size, the smallest being the best quality and the largest the most inferior. They are stored, shipped in brine, then drained and preserved in vinegar in the country

Figure 3-153. Caper—*Câpre* (*Capparis spinosa*).

where they are to be packed in consumer units. They are available in the following qualities: nonpareilles (small), surfines (medium), capucines (large). There are also capers packed in salt; they need to be rinsed before being added to foods. Capers are used in meatballs, stews, meat pies, tartare steaks, salads, sauces, and pickled herring. Capers should not be cooked with the food but added to the finished product.

Caraway—*Carvi*

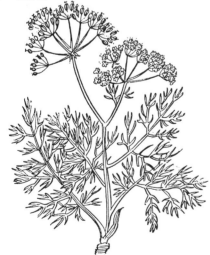

Figure 3-154. Caraway—*Carvi* (*Carum carvi*).

This plant has been grown for its seeds since very early times. It is generally believed that it originally came from Asia Minor. Caraway is cultivated from Europe to Siberia, northern Persia, and the Himalayas. The many-branched hollow-stemmed biennial herb grows up to 2 feet high and has small white flowers. The fruit (seed), approximately ⅛ inch long, is grayish brown when ripe, and each carpel has five thin ridges. (See figure 3-154.) Caraway, added to food during cooking, is used in rye bread, sauerkraut, beef stews, soups, and candy. Caraway seed, along with cumin and anise, gives kümmel, the popular liqueur, its distinctive flavor.

Note: Although cumin (*Cuminum cyminum*) and caraway are both members of the parsley family, there is a distinct difference in their flavors. The Germans call both seeds *kummel;* the Spanish call caraway *carvi,* and their word for cumin is *comino.* The French, however, call caraway *cumin de près* or *carvi,* and both caraway and cumin are known as *cumin* in France. Cumin is used in curry powder and chili powder. Whole or ground cumin is used commercially in the preparation of sausages, pickles, cheese, meats, and breads.

Cayenne Pepper—*Cayenne*

See Pepper (*Capsicum* species).

Chervil—*Cerfeuil*

Figure 3-155. Chervil—*Cerfeuil* (*Anthriscus cerefolium*).

Chervil is native to western Asia, Russia, and the Caucasus. Chervil, grown as a garden plant, has aromatic curled leaves and hemlocklike flowers. (See figure 3-155.) It has the flavor of mild parsley. Fresh chervil is used in soups and salads. Dried chervil is used for seasoning in sauces and with roast lamb.

Chives—*Ciboulette*

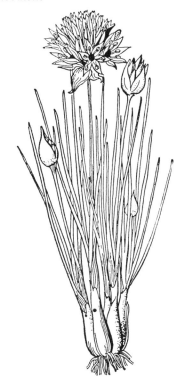

Figure 3-156. Chives—*Ciboulette (Allium schoenoprasum).*

Chives are widespread in Europe, the United States, Russia, and Japan. Related to leeks, chives have bright green, tuber-shaped, mild-flavored leaves and reddish blue clusters of flowers. (See figure 3-156.) Chives are often grown as potted plants. The leaves are snipped and used for garnishes and in salads, fish dishes, soups, cream cheese, and omelets.

Cinnamon—*Cannelle*

Cinnamon is ground from the dried bark of trees in the evergreen or *Cinnamomum* genus. The true cinna-

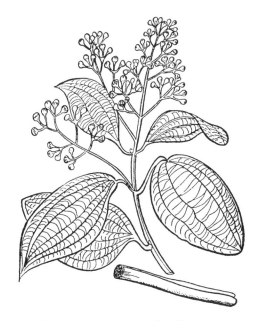

Figure 3-157. Cinnamon—*Cannelle (Cinnamomum zeylanicum).*

mon (*Cinnamomum zeylanicum*) is imported from the Seychelles Islands and Sri Lanka. It is known as "Ceylon cinnamon." Most of the cinnamon used in the United States is derived from the trees of the *Cinnamomum cassia* species. The term *cassia* is used to identify this cinnamon that is native to China, Indonesia, and Southeast Asia.

The cultivated Ceylon cinnamon tree resembles an evergreen laurel bush and reaches a height of approximately 30 feet. In Sri Lanka, the tree is pruned back to a height of 6 feet so that the plant will produce a maximum number of branches. The outer bark is yellowish brown, and it is removed from the tree after two years of growth. The shoots are cut off close to the ground, and the bark is pulled off in two strips. The outer skin of the bark is scraped off, and the pale brown strips are placed concentrically inside one another and slowly dried into "quills." The thinnest varieties are the best. The quality diminishes with increased thickness. The flavor of this bark is milder and the color lighter than the bark of the cassia tree. (See figure 3-157.) Most countries use Ceylon cinnamon; however, cinnamon from cassia trees that have a higher oil content is in greater demand in the

United States. The higher the oil content, the stronger the flavor and aroma. Saigon cinnamon, with the highest oil content of all species, is the finest quality of cassia cinnamon.

Cinnamon may be ground for use in pastries, breads, puddings, cakes, candies, and cookies. Stick cinnamon is used for preserved fruits, pickles, fruit soups, compotes, and hot beverages. Oil of cinnamon, distilled from broken bark, is used for flavoring and for medicinal purposes.

Coriander—*Coriandre*

Figure 3-158. Coriander—*Coriandre* (*Coriandrum sativum*).

Coriander is found in Morocco, southern France, and the Orient. It is a solid-stemmed plant approximately 2 feet high with white flowers. It is a member of the parsley family. The dried fruits, which are about the size of small peppercorns, are rippled on the outside and are a reddish brown color. The leaves of coriander are cilantro, also known as flat or Italian parsley. (See figure 3-158.) The plant is susceptible to damage by beetles.

Clove—*Clou de girofle*

Figure 3-159. Clove—*Clou de girofle* (*Eugenia caryophyllata*).

Cloves are the dried, unopened flower buds of a tropical tree that is native to Indonesia. These trees are grown commercially on Zanzibar, Madagascar, and Pemba. These countries are leading producers and exporters. The source of the word *clove* is the French word *clou,* which means "spike" or "nail." Zanzibar and Pemba alone have half a million 40-foot clove trees, which are bright crimson during the flowering season. The bright red flower buds are broken off the trees with bamboo poles and dried either in the sun or near a fire. The nail-shaped clove is dark brown. (See figure 3-159.) The clove is characterized by its spicy aroma and strong pungent flavor. Whole cloves are used in marinades, leg of lamb, red cabbage, game of all kinds, meat stews, soups, hasenpfeffer, carp in beer, eels in beer, marinated herrings, pickles, and mustard fruits. Ground cloves are used in fruit cakes, gingerbread, honey cakes, pepper cakes, hot punches, cookies, and breads.

Curry—*Cari*

India produces curry powder, but since it is a mixture of spices, it is possible to make it anywhere. Most of the ingredients are grown in Indonesia and Southeast

Figure 3-160. Spices for curry powder.

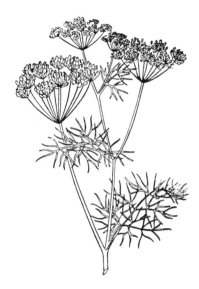

Figure 3-161. Dill—*Aneth* (*Anethum graveolens*).

Asia, where it is also used extensively. Curry is a blend of several ground spices according to traditional and jealously guarded formulas. The main spices include turmeric, coriander, ginger, fenugreek, caraway, pepper, and paprika, but cardamom, cumin seed, mustard seed, and many other spices are used in various recipes. Curry powder may be mild, medium, or fiery, depending on the amount of ginger and chile peppers used. The kind prepared in southern India is very hot. Turmeric gives it the bright yellow color; powders with less turmeric may be less yellow. (See figure 3-160.) Curry powder is used in curried rice, chicken curry, curry sauce, eggs, vegetables, and fish dishes. The flavor of many foods can be enhanced by the addition of curry.

Dill—*Aneth*

A native of Europe, dill is also grown in the United States and the West Indies. Dill is a German garden plant, similar in form and taste to that of caraway. A parchmentlike skin is found on each side of the seed. It is available as fresh dill, the upper part of the stalks bunched together like parsley, as dried dill, which is called dillweed, and as dill seed. (See figure 3-161.) It is used for pickling, in salads, sauerkraut, soups, and sauces. Dill is also used in poaching salmon and other

fish and is part of a classic dish from Apicius—chicken with dill—that can be adapted for any small bird.

Garlic—*Ail*

Figure 3-162. Garlic—*Ail* (*Allium sativum*).

Garlic is a plant that has been cultivated for thousands of years and is grown everywhere. Like the onion, it is a member of the lily family. The garlic bulb is surrounded by several layers of skin. Each bulb is made up of several smaller white or purplish cloves that are enclosed in a membrane. (See figure 3-162.) The most distinctive characteristic of garlic is its odor. Dehydrated garlic is marketed as instant garlic powder, instant minced garlic, and garlic salt. There is also garlic juice. Garlic is used in meat dishes, soups, salads, dressings, pasta dishes, sauces, pickles, and goulash. The use of this pungent flavoring is characteristic of the foods of Provence.

Ginger—*Gingembre*

Figure 3-163. Ginger—*Gingembre* (*Zingiber officinale*).

The ginger plant is a native of Asia. It is grown in Japan, China, India, Jamaica, and Africa. Ginger is produced from plants with leaves similar to reeds. The ginger used for food comes from the rhizome (root). (See figure 3-163.) The roots of the young plants (ten months old) are used for the best-quality crystallized ginger. The flavor is pungent and spicy. Ground ginger is produced from the more mature rhizomes. It is a yellowish brown color. Ground ginger is used as a spice in pickles, stews, eggs, mustard, fruits, fruit cakes, ice cream, pepper cakes, ginger milk, and vermouth. Candied ginger is used as a garnish and in pastries and confectionery. Fresh (green) gingerroot is used in many Oriental and Polynesian dishes and in marmalades and confections. Ginger is also used in making ginger ale and ginger beer.

Horseradish—*Raifort*

Figure 3-164. Horseradish—*Raifort* (*Armoracia lapathifolia*).

Horseradish is a member of the wallflower family. It is a perennial herb that originated in central Europe and Asia. It is now cultivated throughout Europe and the United States. The brownish yellow root is approximately 18 inches long. The interior of the root is an off-white color. (See figure 3-164.) The distinctive flavor is very strong and pungent. The root is peeled, grated, and simmered with vinegar and milk. Fresh horseradish is grated for sauces and for fish and meat dishes. It is available in fresh or dehydrated form, also mixed with vinegar.

Juniper—*Genièvre*

Figure 3-165. Juniper—*Genièvre* (*Juniperis communis*).

The juniper tree is grown in Italy, Czechoslovakia, and Rumania. In America the juniper berry was used by the Indians. The trees are still grown extensively but usually as ornamentals rather than for the berries. The juniper is a small evergreen tree belonging to the cypress family. The blue black fruits are about the size of peas, and they are picked the second season the berries appear. (See figure 3-165.) Italy, where the berries are handpicked, produces the finest quality. Juniper berries are used to flavor sauerkraut, roast wild boar, gin, liqueurs, and cordials. The berries should be cooked with the food.

Lovage—*Livèche*

Lovage is native to southern Europe. Scotch lovage is a native plant in northern Britain. This garden plant grows about 6 feet high with clusters of aromatic yellow flowers. The stem and roots are used as an herb. (See figure 3-166.) The herb is used in roasts, soups, and sauces. It should be cooked with the food. The

Figure 3-166. Lovage—*Livèche* (*Levisticum officinale*).

plant is also used as a vegetable. The young stems may be candied.

Mace—*Macis*

Figure 3-167. Mace—*Macis* (*Myristica fragrans*).

Mace is a product of the nutmeg tree that is native to the Molucca Islands in Indonesia. Mace is the reddish yellow coating around the nutmeg called aril. The mace, a highly aromatic spice with a taste more delicate than that of the nutmeg, is best when it is thin and brittle and reddish yellow in color. (See figure 3-167.) Mace is used in the preparation of pickles, preserves, sauces, pound cakes, breads, puddings, and pastries. It is used in large quantities in the meat-processing industry.

Marjoram—*Marjolaine*

Figure 3-168. Marjarom—*Marjolaine* (*Marjorana hortensis*).

The sweet or knotted marjoram is the best known, and it is native to the Mediterranean region. It is also grown in Britain, Germany, France, and Czechoslovakia. They are small plants, related to the oregano plant, with light rose flowers. The plants are often cut after flowering and dried. The leaves are a gray-green color, and they are sold as marjoram leaves or ground marjoram. (See figure 3-168.) Marjoram is used for seasoning potato soup, stuffed goose, liver dumplings, snails in sauce, roast rabbit, ham and meat dumplings, and herb sauces. The leaves lose their color unless stored in sealed containers.

Mint/Peppermint—*Menthe*

Figure 3-169. Mint—*Menthe* (*Mentha spicata, M. piperita*).

Peppermint is cultivated throughout Europe and the United States. Spearmint, a native of Europe, is cultivated throughout England and the United States. Peppermint can be identified by is characteristic odor, its short leaves, and its flowers. The spear-shaped leaves of spearmint are spicy and contain menthol. The plant has spikes of lilac-colored flowers with stamens that extend beyond the corolla. The most popular variety is English spearmint, which has a red stem. (See figure 3-169.) Peppermint is used in liqueurs, cordials, candies, and beverages. It is also used for oil of peppermint. Spearmint is used as a flavoring for lamb, vegetables, fruit soups, potatoes, and for mint sauce and mint ice cream.

Mustard—*Moutarde*

Mustard comes from a plant of temperate and tropical zones that grows all over the world. The leaves, called mustard greens, are used as a vegetable, raw or cooked. More significant are the seeds, chiefly from the black and white mustard plants. The seeds are tiny, light brown, with a rather hard shell. They are sold whole or ground as dried mustard. Prepared mustard, used as a condiment, is a mixture of the ground seeds and water. Chinese and English mustards are very sharp. Mustard made from ground seeds mixed with ground turmeric, vinegar, glucose, and salt is mild. Mustard from ground seeds mixed with herbs and white wine (Dijon type) is pungent, but smooth. Mild prepared mustard mixed with grated horseradish (horseradish mustard) is sharp. There are also a mild German-style mustard, a sweet Austrian-style mustard, fiery Jamaican and Bahamian mustards, and a sharp Dutch mustard. Whole mustard seeds are used in pickling; ground seeds are used to flavor sauces, cheese dishes, and salad dressings.

Nutmeg—*Noix de muscade*

Figure 3-170. Nutmeg—*Noix de muscade* (*Myristica fragrans*).

The nutmeg tree is a native of the Moluccas (Spice Islands) in Indonesia. It is also grown in the West Indies, Banda Isles, Papua, and Brazil. The nutmeg tree averages between 32 and 38 feet in height. The fruit is similar to the peach. Between the fleshy outside skin and the kernel itself, there is a reddish yellow seed coating (mace). Nutmeg is the kernel or seed of the fruit, and its flavor is sweet and spicy. (See figure 3-170.) There are approximately 60 large nuts or 150 very small nuts in 1 pound. Nutmeg may be purchased in whole or ground form. Whole nutmeg may be grated as needed. Nutmeg is used extensively in custards, eggnogs, and cream puddings and desserts. It is also used in aspics, meat pies, soups, fried brains, shelled vegetables, chicken soups, chicken fricassee, breast of veal, mushroom dishes, and spinach.

Onion—*Oignon*

Figure 3-171. Onion—*Oignon* (*Allium cepa*).

Holland, Egypt, the United States, Italy, and Bermuda are the main onion producers. An onion is a 2½-foot-tall plant with a bulb, a hollow stalk, and whitish green clumps of flowers. (See figure 3-171.) Onions that are allowed to grow to full size may be dried and processed into instant chopped onions, instant onion powder, onion salt, onion flakes, and onion juice. Spring onions are used in salads and as garnishes. Dehydrated onions are a convenient form to use in the preparation of soups, stews, meat dishes, sauces, and dressings. Onions are the favorite flavoring herb all over the world and have been used for thousands of years.

Oregano—*Oregano*

Oregano grows in Mexico, Italy, and the United States. A member of the mint family, it has a strong,

Figure 3-172. Oregano—*Orégano* (*Origanum vulgare*)

aromatic, and pleasant taste. The dried leaves are a dull green color. (See figure 3-172.) The taste is similar to marjoram, but oregano is much stronger and coarser. This herb is used to season Mexican and Italian dishes, such as pizza and pasta. It is an ingredient in chili powder.

Paprika—*Paprika*

Figure 3-173. Paprika—*Paprika* (*Capsicum annuum*).

Paprika is produced in Spain, southern France, Italy, Yugoslavia, and Hungary. It is made from the sweet pepper *Capsicum annum*. The bright red fruits are conical-shaped and 2 to 3 inches long. The rather flat yellow seeds are inside the fruit. (See figure 3-173.) The peppers are eaten as a vegetable, as pickles, and in salads. The red peppers are ground after the seeds and membranes are removed. Spanish-grown paprika is a brilliant red color with a sweet mild flavor. Paprika is essential to Hungarian cooking. The Hungarians have developed the peppers and the methods of processing them to have a spice that ranges from delicate to noble sweet to semisweet to hot. Noble sweet is pungent, but hot is extremely hot. Paprika is used to add color as well as flavor to foods. It is used in risotto, Hungarian goulash, carp with paprika, and on canapés.

Parsley—*Persil*

Figure 3-174. Parsley—*Persil* (*Petroselinum crispum*).

Parsley is native to the Mediterranean countries. A small garden herb, the leaves are usually curled, crisp, and bright green. The plant can be harvested several times a year. The characteristic odor is due to the presence of volatile oils in the stems and leaves. The leaves may be dried. There are several kinds. Curly parsley has very curly leaves (see figure 3-174); Italian, or flat-leaf, parsley, also called cilantro, has flat leaves, but a more pronounced flavor (see coriander); Hamburg parsley is grown for its roots, which are used to flavor soups and stews. When fresh, the herb is used with fish, meat, vegetables, salads, soups, and for garnishing all dishes. Dried parsley leaves are excellent for seasoning and garnishing. When dried, parsley loses its color, especially if exposed to light. When preserved in brine, it loses its aroma. It is always best to use fresh parsley. The stems are more flavorful than the leaves, so use them in *bouquet garni*.

Pepper—*Poivre* (*Piper nigrum*)

Figure 3-175. Pepper—*Poivre* (*Piper nigrum*).

Pepper is native to southeast Asia, chiefly on the Malabar coast, Borneo, Java, and Sumatra. The *Piper nigrum* is a climbing plant that forms its fruits on long hanging spikes. The fruits, called peppercorns, turn red when ripe. (See figure 3-175.) Pepper is available as whole black pepper, ground black pepper, coarse-ground black pepper, whole white pepper, and ground white pepper. For black pepper, the unripe peppercorn is sundried until the outer skin becomes wrinkled and changes to a black color. Black pepper has a stronger and more pungent flavor than white pepper. The best quality comes from the Malabar coast, where the peppercorns are properly sieved and cleaned. Black pepper from Borneo (Sarawak) and

Indonesia is inferior to the Malabar standard. White pepper is produced from the mature peppercorn of the same plant. It is fermented after the harvest and the outer covering is separated from the seed. The small white seeds are dried. The flavor is hotter but less pungent than that of black pepper. Whole peppercorns are used to flavor soups, meats, and pickles. Ground pepper is used to season foods. White pepper is often preferred for light-colored foods.

Pepper—*Poivre* (*Capsicum* species)

Figure 3-176. Red chile pepper—*Chili* (*Capsicum frutescens*).

Capsicum peppers are native to tropical America but were carried to Spain by early explorers and from there spread to India and Indonesia. Today they are grown in Africa, the West Indies, and Japan as well. In addition to the sweet bell peppers, which we use as a vegetable, this genus includes many species, which may be red, green, yellow, almost white, or almost black. Among them is the cayenne pepper (*poivre de cayenne*), made by grinding pods and seeds together to make a very hot spice; red chile peppers, including mild *ancho* and fiery *pequín* (see figure 3-176); green chile peppers, including *serrano* and *jalapeño*, both hot; and some milder species. There are also some sweet green chiles. Cayenne is available ground; red and green chiles are sold fresh, dried, and ground. It is essential to use rubber or plastic gloves when handling any chile, as their strong oils can burn the hands. These spicy peppers are used to flavor Mexican foods and the foods of the southwestern United States, India and Indonesia. They are often used as an ingredient in curry powder and are added to other spices for pickling and marinating.

Poppy—*Pavot*

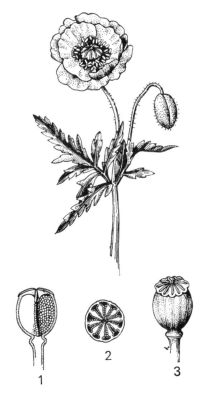

Figure 3-177. Poppy—*Pavot* (*Papaver orientale*): (1) longitudinal section of the seed capsule, empty and full; (2) cross section of the seed capsule; (3) whole seed capsule.

The poppy plant comes from the Far East and the Netherlands. Poppy seeds are from the perennial poppy plant, which grows to a height of about 5 feet. Poppies are cultivated for the seeds in the fruit capsule that contain oil. Immature capsules contain the milk juice, which is the source of opium. The ripe dried seeds have a crunchy mintlike flavor. (See figure 3-177.) When dried, poppy seeds are used on bread and rolls, cakes, cookies, in salads, in mild dishes such as cabbage and noodles, and in fillings for pastries.

Rosemary—*Romarin*

Figure 3-178. Rosemary—*Romarin* (*Rosmarinus officinalis*).

Rosemary is a native of the Mediterranean area. It is a tall, bushy shrub with silvery green leaves, resembling pine needles, and violet flowers. (See figure 3-178.) The herb is available as whole leaves or ground rosemary. Fresh or dried rosemary is used to flavor meat and poultry dishes and salads. It is also used in stews and soups. It is especially good with lamb and pork.

Saffron—*Safran*

A member of the iris family, saffron is a native of Asia. It is also grown in Spain, France, Italy, and North Africa. The three stigmas of the flower of the autumn crocus are the only part of the plant used in the production of saffron. (See figure 3-179.) They are picked by hand and carefully sorted by color, which varies from yellow to red. Saffron gives a strong

Figure 3-179. Saffron—*Safran* (*Crocus sativus*).

yellow coloring to foods. It has a distinctive mild bittersweet flavor. It is a very expensive spice. Saffron is used for sauces, soups, rice dishes, potato dishes, breads, and pastries.

Sage—*Sauge*

Figure 3-180. Sage—*Sauge* (*Salvia officinalis*).

Sage, a native of Europe, is grown in Britain and the United States. Sage is a garden plant that grows about 3 feet tall and has blue flowers and grayish green leaves. (See figure 3-180.) Fresh and dried sage are sold in bunches, although the leaf is the only part of the plant used. The flavor is spicy and somewhat bitter. It is used as poultry seasoning, in stuffings, and in veal dishes, such as *saltimbocca*.

Savory—*Sariette*

Figure 3-181. Savory—*Sariette* (*Satureia hortensis*).

Summer savory was originally grown as a garden herb in the Mediterranean countries. This very fragrant herb has spicy leaves and pale-colored lilac flowers. (See figure 3-181.) Fresh or dried savory is used in beans, sauerkraut, sausages, stuffings, vegetables, soups, and roast lamb. It should be cooked with the food.

Tarragon—*Estragon*

The plant is native to Europe and was grown as a garden plant in Russia and Mongolia. A perennial herb, tarragon has long, thin, olive-green leaves and

Figure 3-182. Tarragon—*Estragon* (*Artemisia dracunculus*).

small, button-shaped flowers. (See figure 3-182.) Tarragon loses much of its flavor when dried and is best used fresh. The leaves are used in pickles, soups, salads, and sauces, and for making tarragon vinegar.

Thyme—*Thym*

Figure 3-183. Thyme—*Thym* (*Thymus vulgaris*).

Thyme, originally a Mediterranean plant, is now grown in France, Spain, Yugoslavia, Czechoslovakia, Great Britain, and the United States. This herb is a low-growing plant with small, aromatic, rolled-up leaves and reddish lilac labiated flowers. (See figure 3-183.) Thyme is used as a seasoning in roast rabbit, roast game, game stews, ragouts, stuffed duckling, venison pie, hasenpfeffer, sauces, roasts, and soups. This herb should be cooked with the food.

Turmeric—*Curcuma*

Figure 3-184. Turmeric—*Curcuma* (*Curcuma longa*).

Turmeric is grown in eastern Asia, India, Africa, and Australia. It belongs to the ginger family. The flavor is mild and sweet, and it has a strong aroma. The roots have a distinctive yellow color due to the pigment curcumin. (See figure 3-184.) Ground turmeric is one of the main ingredients in curry powder and in prepared mustard. It is imported by Sweden and England for making their well-known sauces. It is also used to produce a yellow dye used in India.

Vanilla—*Vanille*

Vanilla is produced from an orchid native to Central America. The plant has been transplanted to other parts of the world. Madagascar is the primary source

Figure 3-185. Vanilla—*Vanille* (*Vanilla plantifolia*).

of vanilla today. The vanilla beans from Madagascar are cured by dipping them into boiling water and then drying slowly. The cured pods should be black in color. (See figure 3-185.) They are packed in airtight boxes or tins. Vanilla is also grown in Réunion, formerly called "Bourbon," in the Mascarene Islands. The vanilla from there is still known as Bourbon vanilla. This and the vanilla from Mexico are superior in quality. A more economical and efficient method of curing has been developed. The harvested beans are ground without drying. They are cured in a brine and then dehydrated. Imitation vanilla extracts are made from a colorless crystalline synthetic compound called vanillin. Pure vanilla extract is superior to imitation vanilla. Vanilla beans or vanilla extract is used to flavor creams and desserts, cold fruit soups, compotes, cookies and cakes, tarts, rice pudding, ice cream, roasted almonds, and candies. The pod of the vanilla bean should be slit open, cooked with the food, and removed before serving.

3.10 Cooking Aids—*Produits auxiliares*

Monosodium Glutamate—*Glutamal*

Monosodium glutamate (MSG) is a sodium salt of glutamic acid derived from protein. It is an ingredient that enhances the taste of food, which is a plus. On the negative side, however, the almost pure glutamate is rapidly absorbed in the bloodstream and can cause bad reactions—severe headaches, increased salivation. It is no longer allowed to be used in infant foods. If you do use it, do so with a gentle hand; it is frequently used in Oriental foods.

Salt—*Sel*

A number of salts are described below.

For *brine salt,* deep holes, 450 to 900 feet, are bored into the earth so that the salt strata dissolves in the ground water. The brine is then pumped to the surface, purified, and evaporated.

Kitchen salt (*sel de cuisine*) is a white, crystalline substance, sodium chloride, that is found in natural beds in sea water. It is added to food to improve flavor. All varieties of kitchen salt come either directly or indirectly from the sea. There are different kinds of salt, depending upon the method of extraction.

Rock salt is extracted from sea water by natural evaporation. It is a nonedible, unrefined salt that is used in freezing ice cream or as a base for heating oysters on the half shell.

Saltpeter is sodium nitrate, used in some meat processing. The chemical gives a red color to the meat. It is a suspected carcinogen.

Kosher salt is also known as coarse salt. It is sometimes sprinkled over pretzels or rolls before baking or over meat just before serving. Since kosher salt is absolutely pure, containing no iodide or silicoaluminate, it is the salt required for all pickling and for making such food as sauerkraut. It is also used for scrubbing chopping blocks.

Table salt consists of especially small salt crystals or finely ground salt. For some cooking purposes, coarse salt crystals may be dried slowly in the oven and then ground. Good salt should dissolve completely in water. The reddish commercial salt contains iron oxide and carbon and should not be permitted in the kitchen. Iodized salt is table salt to which a very small quantity of potassium iodide has been added. Most table salt contains an ingredient to make it free flowing.

Vinegar—*Vinaigre*

Comestible vinegar is a condiment or a dilute solution of acetic acid, which is extracted from wine, fermented fruits or grains, or other alcoholic liquids. The strength of vinegar is specified by the percent of acid. There are four different varieties of vinegar. Fermentation vinegar is formed naturally by the action of vinegar bacteria on dilute alcohol. Flavored vinegars are made of cider or wine vinegar to which herbs, spices, or honey are added. Lemon vinegar is made up of equal parts of well-flavored vinegar and lemon juice. Vinegar essence is manufactured in several different ways, including purely chemical processes.

Agar—*Agar*

Agar is a vegetable substance extracted from red seaweed that is gathered by divers off the coasts of Sri Lanka, Japan, and California. The salt is removed by repeated washing in clear fresh water. The seaweed is then cooked to yield a solution, which is bleached, filtered, and poured into molds. When cool the gelatinlike mass is cut into strips or slabs. It is also available in powdered form. Good agar dissolves in hot water and is colorless. Its jellifying capacity is eight times as strong as that of ordinary gelatin. It is used for gelatin products that require a strong jellifying power.

Food Coloring—*Colorants*

Many coloring agents are used in cooking or baking. They are made from plants, flowers, fruits, and officially approved synthetic colors.

Gelatin—*Gelatine*

Gelatin is made from bones, connective tissue, and skins of animals. The calcium is removed with dilute hydrochloric acid. The remaining substance is soaked in cold water for a period of time and then heated to 100° to 140°F (38° to 60°C). The liquid is then partially evaporated, defatted, and coagulated on stone or glass plates and poured into special molds. The solid blocks are cut into slices and dried on wire nets. Gelatin is marketed as plain, unflavored gelatin and may be purchased in sheets, granules, powder, or flakes. The quality of gelatin depends on the method of processing and manufacturing. Good-quality gela-

tin is odorless and tasteless, and it produces a strong, soft, and tender gel.

Pectin—*Pectin*

A substance from the fibrous parts of most fruits, pectin is used to gel cooked fruits and juices used in the preparation of jellies, jams, and preserves.

3.11 Seasonal Calendar

The following fresh foods are generally at their peak during the months indicated.

Almond	July–November
Anchovy	October–May
Apple	September–April
Apricot	May–September
Artichoke	January–September
Asparagus	April–June
Banana	January–December
Barbel	October–March
Beans	May–October
Beef	January–December
Beluga	May–December
Blackberry	June–September
Blueberry	June–September
Boston lettuce	June–October
Broccoli	October–March
Brussels sprouts	September–March
Burbot	January–December
Cabbage, red	August–December
Cabbage, Savoy	July–October
Cabbage, white	January–December
Cardoon	October–March
Carp	January–December
Carrot	May–November
Cauliflower	July–May
Caviar	January–December
Celery root (celeriac)	September–February
Chamois	July–September
Chanterelle	July–September
Cherry, sour	May–August
Cherry, sweet	June–July

Chestnut	January–December	Mushroom, cultivated	January–December
Chicken	January–December	Mussel	August–April
Chicory	April–October	Mutton	January–December
Chives	March–November		
Clams	August–April	Nectarine	July–October
Cod	January–December	Nut	September–April
Corn	August–September		
Crab	September–March	Onion	January–December
Cranberry	September–October	Orange	October–July
Crayfish	May–September	Oyster	September–April
Cucumber	June–November		
		Parsley	January–December
Duck, domestic	March–October	Partridge	September–March
Duck, wild	August–April	Pea	May–August
		Peach	July–October
Eel	January–December	Pear	July–February
Eggplant	July–October	Perch	January–September
Endive	April–October	Pheasant	November–February
		Pigeon	January–December
Field mushroom	July–October	Pike	July–April
Fig (green)	July–November	Pike perch	January–December
Frogs' legs	March–October	Pineapple	January–December
		Plaice	April–November
Golden trout	February–October	Plum	August–October
Goose	January–December	Pork	January–December
Gooseberry	June–August	Potato	January–December
Goose liver	October–April	Potato, new	June–July
Grapes	September–October		
Grouse	October–November	Quail	May–October
Guinea fowl	March–October	Quince	October–January
Haddock	January–December	Rabbit, domestic	January–December
Hare	September–March	Rabbit, wild	September–April
Hazel grouse	September–January	Radish	February–September
Hazelnut	January–December	Raspberry	June–October
Herring	May–January	Ray	January–December
		Red currant	June–August
Lake trout	February–August	Red deer	September–March
Lamb	March–June	Rhubarb	February–October
Leek	January–December	Rock lobster	February–October
Lettuce	June–October	Romaine lettuce	April–November
Lobster	April–September	Rutabaga	May–September
Mackerel	April–December	Salmon	August–March
Melon	June–October	Salmon trout	February–October
Morel	April–May	Salsify	December–March
Morel, conical	April–May	Sardine	June–October

Scallops	January–June
Shrimp	March–September
Snail	October–April
Snipe	August–March
Snow grouse	October–March
Sole	January–December
Sorrel	March–July
Strawberry	May–August
Sturgeon	May–October
Tomato	July–October
Trout	February–November
Truffle, black	November–April
Truffle, summer	June–August
Truffle, white	July–September
Tuna	May–October
Turbot	January–December
Turkey	January–December
Veal	January–December
Venison	September–March
Walnut	August–September
Watermelon	August–December
Whitefish	May–November
Wild boar	January–December

3.12 Beverages

The beverages described here contain substances that have either a stimulating or a calming effect on the brain and nerves—caffeine, theine, and theobromine. All stimulants must undergo fermentation or low or high temperature roasting.

3.12.1 *Coffee—Café*

Coffee originally came from the mountainous Kaffa region in Ethiopia, and the coffee tree was transplanted from there to Arabia. Pilgrims traveling to Mecca in the seventeenth century brought the first fertile beans to east India; the Dutch brought coffee to Dutch East India in 1696 and, soon afterwards, to the West Indies. The earliest recorded evidence of coffee plantations in Brazil dates back to 1727. The French were highly successful in establishing coffee plantations on Haiti and Santo Domingo. Today coffee is cultivated in South America, Central America, the West Indies, Asia, and Africa. The Moslem religion prohibits the consumption of alcoholic drinks; however, coffee is in great demand, and drinking it has become a habit throughout all Arab countries. In Turkey, the first coffeehouses opened in Constantinople in the middle of the sixteenth century. At the siege of Vienna in 1683, the Turks fled, leaving 500 sacks of coffee as part of the booty for the victors. Thus, the first coffeehouses opened in Vienna, and, as time went by, coffee drinking became a custom throughout the world.

Coffee Varieties

Coffee beans are classified according to their origin, method of preparation, size, and ripeness. There are considerable differences in terms of shape, color, purity, consistency, reaction upon roasting, and brewing. The different varieties of coffee are, in some cases, named after the producing country, in other cases, after the port of shipment.

Leading producers of commercial coffees are:

- South America: Brazil (Brasília, Santos, Paraná, Rio, Bahia, Minas), Colombia, Venezuela (Caracas)
- Central America: Guatemala, Costa Rica, El Salvador, Mexico, Nicaragua
- West Indies: Haiti, Santo Domingo, Cuba
- Asia: India (Malabar coast), Java, Sumatra, Celebes
- Africa and Arabia: Kenya, Uganda, Ethiopia, Angola, Yemen (Arabian Mocca, port of shipment, Hodeida)

Cultivation of Coffee

Growing wild, the coffee tree, with its 3- to 4-inch dark evergreen leaves, similar to bay leaves, can reach a height of 20 to 24 feet. In plantations it is cultivated in bushes about 7 to 9 feet tall. The trees are pruned to keep the height within the reach of the pickers. The flowers are white and have a fragrance similar to

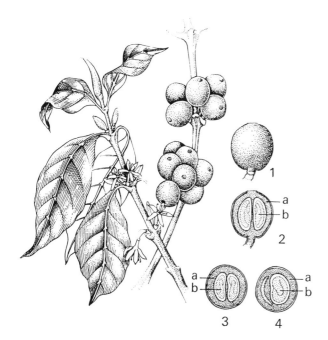

Figure 3-186. Coffee—*Café:* (1) fruit; (2) longitudinal section of the fruit, (*a*) flesh, (*b*) coffee bean; (3) cross section of the fruit, (*a*) flesh, (*b*) coffee bean; (4) cross section of a pearl bean, (*a*) flesh, (*b*) coffee bean.

that of jasmine. The bush flowers two or three times a year and the blossoms, the ripe and the unripe fruits often appear on the bush at the same time. The ripe fruits look like cherries and are a dark red to bluish black, depending upon the variety. The flesh of each berry holds two beans, which are surrounded by a silvery skin and a horn shell. After the shell has been removed, the contents are referred to as shelled coffee. The size of the coffee bean contained in the fruit varies between ⅙ and ⅔ inch long, ⅒ to ⅓ inch wide, and ⅒ to ⅐ inch thick. If the fruit produces only one bean, then it is round or roller shaped and is known as pearl coffee. These pearl beans are removed and sold separately. Their quality is not superior to that of normal coffee beans. (See figure 3-186.)

Processing of the Coffee Berries

Coffee berries are processed by either the dry or the wet process. In the dry process, unwashed coffee or whole berries are placed in heaps and undergo fermentation. They are then spread out and dried in the sun. The dried fruit flesh, shell, and silver skin are removed mechanically. These beans are known as hard coffee. In the wet process, the berries are opened by a pulping machine, the fruit flesh is removed by water during washing, and the beans are fermented in water for a short time. Thereafter, they are dried and taken out of the silver skin. The washed coffee is usually considered higher in quality than the unwashed.

Coffee Roasting

Roasting is necessary to develop the flavor of coffee. During the roasting process, the beans change in color from green to light or dark brown, depending on the degree of roast. Coffee may be roasted to the light stage, which is a light brown color; medium roast, a dark brown color; or dark roast, a very dark brown color. Roasting causes a 20 percent loss in weight. Roasted coffee attracts moisture and should be stored in airtight containers. The aroma of freshly roasted coffee is easily lost because of the volatility of the flavor esters. Since ground coffee loses its aroma and flavor much faster than the bean, coffee should be ground just before use.

Decaffeinated Coffee

Coffee contains the stimulant caffeine. Decaffeinated coffee is popular with those persons who are sensitive to caffeine. Approximately 97 percent of the caffeine is removed before roasting. Neither the aroma nor the taste is absolutely dependent upon the caffeine, therefore decaffeinated coffee has become popular. The caffeine is usually extracted from the raw coffee with ether, benzene, and other solvents. The caffeine content of normal coffee is between 1.1 and 2.5 percent, that of caffeine-reduced coffee 0.2 percent, and that of so-called decaffeinated coffee is 0.08 percent.

Powdered Coffee (Instant Coffee)

Instant coffee consists of coffee extract that is spray-dried or freeze-dried. The quality of the powders on the market varies with the quality of the coffee bean and the processing methods. This product is convenient to store and easily prepared. Boiling water is poured over the coffee powder to prepare the beverage.

Coffee Substitutes

Even though the term *coffee substitute* is frequently used, there is really no such thing as imitation coffee. The stimulating effect of coffee and the fragrance of its fine aroma cannot be imitated. Nevertheless, many products have been used as replacements to make a drink similar to coffee. The most popular are barley and the malt produced from it, rye, chicory and sugar beet, figs, or types of sugar. The consumption of imitation coffees varies with the price of coffee. As prices increase, the consumption of coffee substitutes increases; as prices decrease, the consumption declines.

3.12.2 *Tea*—Thé

Figure 3-187. Tea—*Thé:* (1) flowery orange pekoe; (2) orange pekoe; (3) pekoe; (4) pekoe Souchang.

Tea comes from the leaf buds and young leaves of a tropical evergreen plant. The terminal bud and the next two leaves are usually hand plucked; however, the terminal bud and the first leaf are used for tea of superior quality. The tea plant is grown in the form of a bush and flourishes in subtropical and tropical climates. (See figure 3-187.) After plucking, the tea is withered, rolled, fermented, dried, sifted, and graded. The best-known tea-producing countries are Sri Lanka (Ceylon), China, Java, Sumatra, India (Assam), Japan, and Formosa.

During the processing, the leaf turns from green to black, but in some countries green tea is preferred. It is produced by heating the leaf to prevent fermentation. Immediately after plucking, the leaves are either treated with steam or they are placed in heated pans to induce evaporation of the juice contained in the leaves. Leaves for black tea are laid out on wire netting until they wilt. After 12 to 20 hours, the now somewhat elastic leaves are mechanically rolled under increasing pressure and then fermented. The fermentation causes the tea leaves to oxidize, develop flavor, and turn a bright copper red color. After fermentation, the leaves are either roasted or dried in hot air, at which point the rolled tea leaves take on their black color.

Darjeeling tea, which grows at a height of 7,000 feet in the Himalayas, has a delicate and distinctive flavor. Tea grown at high altitudes is of better quality than that grown at lower heights. The Indian tea varieties, the so-called "plantation teas," usually give a full, pleasant infusion. Assam tea is the strongest, Darjeeling the most aromatic. The tea from Ceylon, particularly that from mountainous regions, is also very aromatic. It is especially known for its light brown color. Chinese and Japanese teas, weaker flavored than Indian varieties, have an especially aromatic mild taste. Consumption of tea from Ceylon (Sri Lanka), India, Java, and Sumatra has increased substantially over the last few years.

Leaf Tea

Tea is classified by the leaf from which it is made. *Flowery orange pekoe* is made from the finest, most delicate leaf tips, which are slightly fluffy with a silky down. *Orange pekoe* tea comes from delicate, rolled leaves that sometimes have whitish gray or golden tips. *Pekoe* tea is made from the second leaves down from the tip of the branch. *Pekoe Souchong* tea comes from the third rough leaf, which is long and open.

Souchong tea is from large, conically shaped leaves, rolled roughly. *Broken* tea is used as a filler in blends. It is made by repeatedly rolling the leaves, so that the enlarged surface area speeds up the preparation of the infusion. *Scrap* tea is dust and fannings. This is the waste and is less valuable. Most scrap tea is used to fill tea bags.

3.12.3 *Cocoa—Cacao*

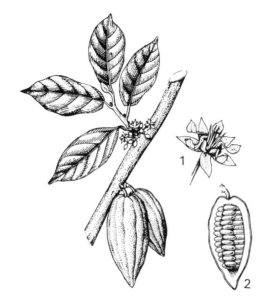

Figure 3-188. Cocoa—*Cacao:* (1) flower; (2) longitudinal section of the fruit.

The term cocoa refers both to the dried roasted or unroasted seeds of the cacao tree and to the product resulting from the grinding of the original or partially defatted cocoa mass, which is then known as cocoa powder. Cocoa powder should contain a minimum of 10 percent cocoa fat for regular cocoa and up to 22 to 24 percent for breakfast cocoa. Dutch-process cocoa has a higher fat content. The cocoa mass is the basis of cocoa powder and the raw material for the manufacture of chocolate. Cocoa is not only a stimulant, but also a food. Raw cocoa beans contain 12.5 percent protein, 50 percent fat, 11 percent starch, and 12 percent other carbohydrates.

Cocoa comes from the evergreen cacao tree, of the genus *Theobroma.* The tree is native to Central America and the northern part of South America. It is now found in Africa, where Nigeria and Ghana have become major suppliers. The cacao tree can reach a height of 45 feet and carries flowers at the same time as fruits. The fruit is a pod with a leathery shell that contains several rows of seeds. The trees require much care and an average temperature of 70° to 75°F (21° to 24°C). There are many varieties, and their quality is affected by the soil, climate, and method of processing. (See figure 3-188.)

After picking, the beans are stacked in heaps and fermented for a few days at 120°F (50°C). After fermentation, they are dried and packed in sacks for shipment to Europe or North America. On arrival in the chocolate factories, the beans are washed and then roasted at 210° to 300°F (100° to 150°C) to develop flavor and aroma. After roasting, they are shelled and cracked into small nibs. Depending upon the quality and the prevailing price, crushed cocoa beans are blended by the same method used for coffee and tea. These blends are then ground into a smooth liquid mash. The finer the cocoa is ground, the better the quality. The cocoa mass consists of 50 percent fat, or cocoa butter. Part of the fat is then removed under hydraulic pressure. The remaining residue is pulverized into a fine powder. The fat content of cocoa is about half that of chocolate. Cocoa should be stored in sealed containers in a dry area.

Chapter 4
Nutrition

4.1 Basic Principles of Nutrition

Balanced nutrition is necessary for maintaining the human body. The body is continuously using the substances that make it up, and these must be replaced by absorbing food. A number of important factors must be considered if the process of alimentation is to be carried out correctly. Daily consumption of minimum servings of important food groups and recommended allowances for essential nutrients provide the basis for balanced nutrition. Other factors, such as food preparation procedures, affect the nutritive value of food.

4.2 Digestion

Digestion is a complicated physical and chemical process. It can be compared to a huge laboratory, where any malfunction can bring the whole process to a standstill.

Digestion starts in the mouth. The food is broken up and chewed with the teeth, while simultaneously being mixed with saliva from the salivary glands. Proper chewing is extremely important for good digestion. Food is then swallowed and transported to the stomach via the esophagus.

"Carry-over" digestion from the mouth continues in the stomach. Further digestion occurs in the stomach when the food mass is mixed with gastric juice from the gastric glands by gastric contractions, a mechanical action.

The partially liquefied and dissolved food mass, or chyme, is mixed with bile, intestinal juice, and pancreatic juice in the small intestine by additional mechanical action. The bile is prepared by the liver and concentrated and stored by the gallbladder. Intestinal juice is secreted by the small intestine and pancreatic juice by the pancreas. Digestion in the small intestine results in the complete breakdown of the food mass to the end products of digestion.

The food-absorbing villi of the small intestine absorb the nutrients and transport them to the cells via the blood or lymph circulation. In the large intestine, or colon, the water is extracted from the chyme, which partially solidifies. The rectum stores the feces or stool prior to discharge from the bowels.

The following substances are excreted from the body: water, salt, nitrogenous waste, carbon dioxide, cellulose, and other undigested food substances, as well as intestinal bacteria. These substances leave the body via exhalation, perspiration, urination, and defecation. Regular bowel movements are important for health. Regularity can often be achieved by appropriate food and adequate fluid intake, as well as by a healthy way of life, including exercise.

The diagram of the gastrointestinal tract identifies the major segments of the digestive tract and the organs and glands concerned with digestion. (See figure 4-1.)

4.2.1 *The Digestibility of Foods*

Recognizing that many foods and food preparation methods are tolerated differently by individuals, the following food lists attempt to illustrate foods that may be classified as easy or difficult to digest.

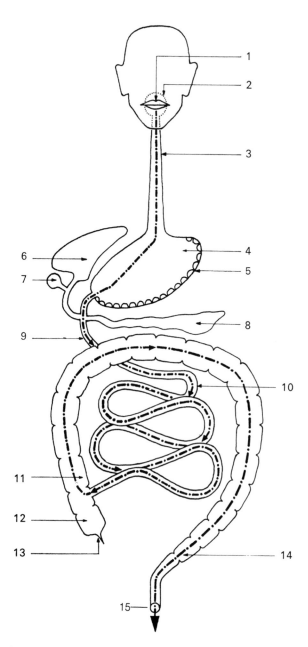

Figure 4-1. The gastrointestinal tract: (1) teeth and tongue; (2) salivary glands; (3) esophagus; (4) stomach; (5) gastric glands; (6) liver; (7) gallbladder; (8) pancreas; (9) duodenum; (10) small intestine; (11) large intestine (colon); (12) cecum; (13) appendix; (14) rectum; (15) anus.

Easily Digested Foods

- Refined bread, crackers, and cereal
- Tender, lean, or ground beef, veal, pork, lamb, poultry, fish, liver, and sweetbreads prepared by baking, roasting, broiling, stewing, or creaming
- Eggs prepared any way except fried
- Cooked vegetables, such as asparagus tips, green and wax beans, beets, carrots, white and sweet potatoes, spinach, winter squash
- Vegetable purees and juices
- Ripe peeled fruits, such as avocado, banana, peach, pear, grapefruit, and orange sections
- Cooked or canned apples, apricots, cherries, peaches, and pears
- Fruit purees and juices
- Milk and milk products including mild-flavored cheese and yogurt
- Simple plain desserts, such as cakes and cookies, custard, fruit whip, gelatin, ice cream, and pudding
- Cream soup
- Butter, margarine, cream, smooth peanut butter, cooking fat, and vegetable oils
- Some seasonings, such as salt, sugar, and flavoring extracts in moderate amounts
- Decaffeinated coffee, cereal coffees, tea, milk beverages, cocoa, and hot chocolate in moderate amounts

Difficult-to-digest Foods

- Coarse or whole-grain bread, crackers, and cereal products
- Tough, fatty meats
- Salted and smoked meats, fish, and poultry
- Fried eggs
- Raw and fried vegetables
- Gas-forming vegetables, such as broccoli, Brussels sprouts, cabbage, cauliflower, and onions
- Raw apples, unripe fruits, fruits with tough skin and seeds, such as berries
- Strong-flavored cheese
- Rich desserts, such as cake, pie, and other pastries
- Doughnuts

- Desserts with coconut and/or nuts
- Salad dressings
- Excessive amounts of garlic, onion, pepper, or other herbs and spices
- Alcohol, carbonated beverages, caffeinated coffee, and chocolate drinks
- Foods with high fat contents

4.3 Metabolism

The organism normally absorbs all the necessary substances from the chyme in the stomach and intestines. The remainder that cannot be digested is evacuated as waste. The nutrients taken from the chyme reach the various cells, tissues, and organs and undergo many complicated changes. Once these changes are complete, the residual products are excreted via the kidneys, lungs, intestines, and sweat glands. All these changes and conversions that the nutrients undergo during their journey through the cells of the body are collectively referred to as *intermediary metabolism*. It is extremely important that these processes maintain a state of equilibrium if the organs, tissues, and cells are to function normally and the organism as a whole is to remain healthy. A malfunction or blockage in the metabolic pathways disrupts the normal state of balance and can result in pathological symptoms. Insufficient or excessive quantities of certain substances can be formed. If, for example, the body is not receiving enough iron, the required number of red blood corpuscles is not produced, and anemia may develop.

Human beings must ingest air (oxygen), water, and substances of animal and vegetable origin to ensure building and maintenance functions. Instinct, experience, tradition, habit, and a subjective sensitivity guide human beings in food selection. Foods are chosen from the available raw materials that, on the one hand, contain the necessary quantities of nutrients, and, on the other hand, provide a certain amount of enjoyment.

4.4 Nutrients and Other Food Components

Nutrients provide energy, enable the body to build and replace the cells that make up the organs and

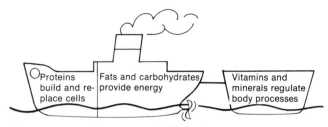

Water acts as a transport and disposal agent

Figure 4-2. The nutrients that power the human "vessel."

tissues, and help to regulate body processes. (See figure 4-2.) Foods contain the following basic nutrients: proteins, carbohydrates, fats, minerals, vitamins, and water. Food also contains substances that promote the perception of taste and that act as stimulants. Although these latter substances cannot actually be classified as nutrients, they are nevertheless important for total enjoyment of the diet and, hence, indirectly for the nutrition of the body.

4.4.1 *Proteins*

The primary function of dietary protein is the building and repairing of body tissue. Without the proteins contained in food, the cells could neither be built nor continuously replaced as they wear out. Protein also has important regulatory functions. Protein foods have energy value. The food intake therefore must always contain a certain amount of protein. However complete the diet might be, if no protein were included, the result could only be emaciation and finally a slow death. The American diet is rich in protein. Mean per capita consumption is over 100 grams (3.5 ounces) of protein per day. However, it cannot be assumed that intake is equally distributed among different population groups. Any extra protein is burned in the metabolic process as energy, and does not have its usual body-building effect. Liberal protein intake is not generally considered hazardous to health, except under certain circumstances, such as the presence of some forms of kidney disease. Extra protein intake is uneconomical.

Almost all animal and vegetable products contain protein, but animal protein, found in meat, fish, eggs, milk, cheese, and poultry, is more complete than vegetable protein. Vegetable protein is usually consumed in the form of bread, flour, and cereal products; vegetables, including legumes; and nuts. Two basic measures must be considered in establishing the daily protein requirement: quality and quantity. The quality of protein is based on the essential amino acid requirement in relation to the total nitrogen, the variations in different types of food, and the availability of amino acids in foods. The quantity of protein recommended is based on the U.S. standard for adults, established as approximately 0.9 gram (0.032 ounce) per kilogram (2.2 pounds) of body weight per day. This becomes about 45 grams (1.6 ounces) daily for a person weighing 50 kilograms (110 pounds) or 65 grams (2.3 ounces) for a person weighing 70 kilograms (143 pounds).

4.4.2 Carbohydrates

The major function of carbohydrates is to provide energy for muscular activity and the creation of warmth. The greater the physical demands on the body, the higher the energy need and therefore the carbohydrate requirement. Carbohydrates occur mainly as sugar and starch in vegetable foods (flour and cereal products, fruits, and vegetables). Milk is the only animal food contributing to the daily carbohydrate intake. Pure sugar, syrups, jellies, jams, honey, and candy are sources of concentrated carbohydrates. Carbohydrates must be broken down into glucose, fructose, and galactose in preparation for absorption within the walls of the small intestine. For example, cane sugar and beet sugar (disaccharides) must first be split into glucose and fructose by the digestive juices.

The carbohydrates in refined flours and cereals, sugars, and sweets are completely or almost completely digested, whereas those from fibrous vegetables, fruits with seeds, and whole-grain flours and cereals are less completely digested. This is partially explained by the presence of nondigestible components, such as cellulose, in the latter group of foods. Cellulose, which occurs in almost all vegetable products, is classified as a carbohydrate but, unlike starch and sugar, cannot be digested by man. In spite of this, cellulose, as part of the total dietary fiber, is necessary for normal gastrointestinal function. No specific requirements have been established for the amount of carbohydrates needed in the diet. However, a normal diet including at least 100 grams (3.5 ounces) of carbohydrates daily will maintain metabolic processes.

4.4.3 Fats

Dietary fats are chiefly true fats or simple lipids. These include the animal and vegetable fats and oils that consist of fatty acids and glycerol. These are rendered more accessible to digestive and absorptive processes by the bile from the gallbladder. Generally speaking, vegetable sources contain more unsaturated fatty acids. Some vegetable oils reduce the cholesterol content of the blood when consumed in high polyunsaturated fatty diets and are therefore recommended for people with heart or liver disorders or as a preventive measure. Fats are potent carriers of energy in the body and thus constitute valuable reserves for the body. Fats have the highest calorie value of the nutrients supplying energy. Fats are also important in the process of body maintenance and regulation. Extra fat in the diet is partially stored away in fat deposits. During periods of undernutrition, the body lives mainly on these deposits of fat. Fat comes from animal and vegetable foods: milk and milk products; animal fats in such foods as meat, poultry, fish, and egg yolk; and vegetable fats including margarine, seed and vegetable oils, fruits or vegetables (avocados, olives); and nuts. Many prepared foods, such as salad dressings, cakes, pastries, gravies, and sauces, contain fat. No precise levels for either the quantity or type of fat needed in the normal diet have been established. However, many Americans could probably benefit by decreasing their fat intake.

4.4.4 Calories

Protein, carbohydrates, and fat create warmth during the process of metabolism. This warmth is measured in calories, 1 calorie representing the amount of warmth necessary to increase the temperature of 1 kilogram of water 1°C. The more physical work a man does, the more nutrients are burned. Different foods produce varying amounts of energy, and for this reason it is important to know their caloric values. Caloric evaluation of foods is based on the fact that 1 gram of protein creates 4.1 calories, 1 gram of carbohydrate creates 4.1 calories, and 1 gram of fat creates 9.3 calories of warmth.

The daily calorie requirement, by occupation, is as follows. Those in sedentary occupations—nonmanual workers, office workers, clerks, officials, and supervisors—require 2,200 to 2,400 calories daily. People employed in moderately active occupations, such as shoemakers, bookbinders, doctors, and postmen, require 2,800 to 3,000 calories daily. Those involved in active occupations, including metal workers, painters, and carpenters, need 3,000 to 3,200 calories daily. People who perform tasks involving heavy manual labor—bricklayers, blacksmiths, soldiers, farm laborers, diggers, and longshoremen, for example—need 3,600 calories and more each day.

4.4.5 *Vitamins*

Vitamins are nutrients that are vitally important in the prevention of disease and in the regulation of body processes. A wide range of different vitamins is required; if one is missing from or inadequate in the diet, deficiency diseases, such as scurvy, result. Vitamin deficiencies may be secondary to other diseases. In the initial stages, such illnesses may be cured by taking the vitamins that were previously missing. For this reason, special vitamin preparations are widely available. However, in general, if healthy persons consume an adequate diet, nutritional supplementation is unnecessary. Hypervitaminosis, causing toxic signs and symptoms, is caused by overdosage, or metabolic disease, or other disturbances producing a vitamin intolerance. The daily vitamin requirement is quantitatively low, but this is no reflection on the importance of these nutrients.

Vitamins are present in most animal and vegetable foods, provided losses during growth, food storage and handling, food processing, and food preparation and preserving are minimal. Some vitamin losses occur in such food processing techniques as the milling of flour and cereal products, the canning and drying of fruits and vegetables, and the pasteurization of milk. Of the roughly thirty known vitamins, the following are especially important to include in the daily diet.

Vitamin A

Vitamin A deficiency results initially in night blindness or diminished vision in dim light, and later, in eye diseases, skin changes, reduced rate of growth, and a lowering of resistance to infection. Vitamin A is fat soluble and fairly heat stable but is sensitive to light and air. It is found only in animal foods, mainly fish liver oils, milk, whole milk cheese, fortified margarine, butter, liver, and egg yolks. However, in many vegetable products there is a provitamin, carotene, which easily converts into vitamin A in the liver. Therefore, plant foods with carotene are considered vitamin A sources. All leafy green vegetables, green stem vegetables (asparagus and broccoli), yellow vegetables (carrots, sweet potatoes, pumpkin, and winter squash), tomatoes, and yellow fruits (apricots, peaches, and cantaloupe) are rich in vitamin A. White and red cabbage, celery ribs, and white root and bulb vegetables have a low vitamin A content. The daily recommended allowance for adults is 5,000 International Units.

Vitamin D

Infants, growing children, adolescents, pregnant and lactating women, and persons who have limited exposure to sunlight are most susceptible to some form of vitamin D deficiency. It is characterized by such problems as insufficient or delayed calcification of the bones and teeth (rickets), slow rate of growth, predisposition to dental caries, and muscle twitchings and cramps.

Vitamin D is fat soluble and resistant to heat. In the human skin, a substance is present that is converted into vitamin D by the action of the ultraviolet light of sunshine. For this reason, it is not absolutely necessary for the total vitamin D allowance to be contained in the food consumed. Practically the only natural vitamin D sources are milk, cream, fatty fish, fish liver oils, liver, and egg yolk.

The recommended daily allowance of Vitamin D for infants, children, adolescents, pregnant and lactating women is 400 International Units. Although no recommended allowance is indicated for adults, a dietary intake of 400 International Units for healthy adults of all ages will not produce risk.

Thiamine (Vitamin B₁)

Chronic deficiency of thiamine leads to serious disorders and damage to the nervous system and heart— beriberi disease, which is prevalent in the Orient. A mild deficiency is characterized by such symptoms as loss of appetite, nausea, apathy, fatigue, dizziness, and numbness. Thiamine-deficiency states are found in the alcoholic. Thiamine is water soluble and therefore is often lost in food processing, preparation, and cooking. Preparation and cooking losses depend upon preparation methods, such as soaking, amount of water used in cooking and retained after cooking, length of cooking period, and amount of surface area exposed. Thiamine is extremely sensitive in an alkaline medium. The addition of baking soda or bicarbonate to a food very quickly destroys the vitamin. Thiamine is comparatively heat-resistant in dry form and in solution in an acid medium. Little loss occurs in cooking procedures, such as baking bread and cooking breakfast cereal, because the water used in preparation is absorbed.

Thiamine is naturally present in an exceptionally wide range of foods, such as whole-grain and enriched bread, cereal, and flour products; lean meat, especially pork, organ meats, and sausage; eggs; green leafy vegetables and legumes; and nuts. A daily allowance for adults of 0.5 milligrams per 1,000 calories is recommended. Older persons should maintain an intake of 1 milligram per day, even if the intake is less than 2,000 calories daily. Requirements increase during pregnancy and lactation.

Riboflavin (Vitamin B₂)

A severe riboflavin deficiency disease in human beings has not been identified. However, lack of riboflavin does produce symptoms involving the skin and mucous membranes, especially the mouth and eyes.

Typical eye changes include inflamed eyelids, itching and watering, inability to focus properly, sensitivity to light, and rapid tiring.

Like thiamine, riboflavin is water soluble and reasonably heat resistant for short periods, but it is very susceptible to light. Small losses may occur in food processing and preparation. In general, when cooked in liquid form, precautions taken to conserve thiamine will protect riboflavin. Riboflavin is found in significant quantities in organ meats, such as liver and kidney, lean meat, milk, cheese, eggs, whole-grain bread and cereal products, and leafy green vegetables.

Riboflavin allowances are computed as 0.6 milligrams per 1,000 calories for people of all ages. Recommended levels increase during pregnancy and lactation.

Niacin

Pellagra, the deficiency disease caused by lack of niacin, is characterized by changes in the skin and mucous membranes, diarrhea, and mental disturbances. Pellagra is practically nonexistent today in the United States. However, incidence of the disease has been reported among chronic alcoholics and is secondary to other illnesses.

Niacin is the most stable of the vitamin B group, but because it is water soluble, some may be lost in cooking water and meat drippings. Both animal and plant foods are good sources of both niacin and the dietary factor tryptophan that converts to niacin. The chief sources are liver, lean meat, poultry, fish, milk, eggs, whole-grain and enriched bread and cereal products, legumes, and nuts.

The niacin allowance recommended for adults, is 6.6 milligrams per 1,000 calories, with a minimum of 13 milligrams regardless of caloric intake. Increases are recommended for pregnancy and lactation.

Vitamin B₁₂

Lack of vitamin B₁₂ is seldom seen in the United States because of the high protein diet consumed. However, individuals on borderline diets, such as food fad diets, and vegetarians may show signs of lack of this vitamin. Nervous disorders and changes in mucous membranes may result. An absorption defect in some persons may cause pernicious anemia, a blood disease. Other illness may decrease vitamin B_{12} absorption and produce vitamin deficiency.

Vitamin B_{12} is water soluble and could be washed out of food that is soaked too long. It is not especially sensitive to heat or air, but does lose its potency on exposure to light, strong acids, and alkali.

Vitamin B_{12} is present in large quantities in liver and kidney. Meat, fish, eggs, milk, and cheese also supply good amounts. There is very little, if any, of the vitamin in vegetable foods. The recommended daily dietary allowance for this vitamin is 3 micrograms for adolescents and normal adults. Four micrograms per day is the recommended allowance for pregnant and lactating women.

Ascorbic Acid (Vitamin C)

The classic illness that results from deficiency of vitamin C is scurvy. Lack of ascorbic acid results in abnormalities in the supporting or intercellular tissues, which could result in hemorrhage, bleeding gums, malformed and weak bones, degeneration of muscle fibers, and anemia. Ascorbic-acid deficiency is a factor involved in reduced resistance to infection and retarded wound healing. Mild deficiency produces vague symptoms, such as weakness, irritability, weight loss, and pain in muscles or joints. Ascorbic acid is water soluble and chemically unstable. Therefore, undue exposure to oxygen, alkali, copper and iron (copper utensils and carbon-steel knives), and prolonged cooking at high temperatures accelerate the rate of vitamin loss. If vegetables are finely cut up or chopped, ascorbic acid is very quickly destroyed by exposure to oxygen (oxidation) and light. If potatoes are cooked after being peeled, more ascorbic acid and B vitamins are lost than when cooked in the jackets. Baking soda also reduces the ascorbic-acid level if added to green vegetables. Proper preparation and cooking methods, such as short soaking and cooking times, moderate heat exposure, and minimum holding periods, will reduce losses of all water-soluble vita-

mins. Consumption of raw fruits and vegetables helps ensure adequate daily vitamin intake.

Ascorbic acid is present in fair to good quantities in potatoes, vegetables, and fruits. The largest amounts are found in citrus fruits, cantaloupe, guavas, pineapple, rose hips, strawberries, broccoli, Brussels sprouts, cabbage, green peppers, kale, spinach, tomatoes, and turnips. In nearly all cases, dried products contain no ascorbic acid. Milk and meat are practically devoid of the vitamin.

An allowance of 45 milligrams per day is recommended as an adequate supply for health in normal adults. An increased intake is recommended during pregnancy and lactation and may be appropriate during periods of continued stress or drug therapy.

4.4.6 *Minerals*

Minerals, mineral salts, mineral elements, or inorganic nutrients are present in the cells, tissues, and fluids, soft tissues, and hard skeletal structures, such as blood, muscles, and bone. Minerals are vitally important, even if they are only necessary in minute quantities. One cannot replace another, as is the case with some nutrients. Minerals are interrelated and do not play independent roles in general body function. Any deficiency of certain minerals can, over a long period of time, be fatal. Minerals are grouped into two categories: major minerals or macronutrients, needed in the diet at levels of 100 milligrams per day or more, and trace minerals or micronutrients, needed in amounts no higher than a few milligrams per day. About thirteen different minerals are known to be needed by the body, and all must be derived from the diet.

Minerals are present in all basic food groups. Some food processing and food preparation methods reduce mineral content. For example, soaking foods and cooking in large quantities of water may decrease the mineral contribution to the diet. Therefore, the use of the liquid in which vegetables have been cooked for making dishes such as soup and sauces is recommended. The minerals whose supply is most likely to be critical are calcium, iron, and iodine.

Calcium (Ca)

A variety of illnesses, such as rickets, osteomalacia (adult rickets), osteoporosis (bone thinning), and periodontal disease are associated with deficiencies of calcium. Milk and milk products are the richest sources of calcium. Certain other foods make contributions to the daily diet: leafy green vegetables, fruit, eggs, canned fish, and shellfish. Drinking water also contains some calcium, but this varies with the water supply. The allowance of 800 milligrams per day ensures an adequate supply of calcium in the diet for adult men and women. Additional dietary calcium should be consumed during pregnancy and lactation.

Iron (Fe)

Iron-deficiency anemia is fundamentally a dietary disease. This is probably the most widespread form of malnutrition in the United States. In iron-deficiency anemia, lack of iron produces defective red blood cells and results in faulty body functioning. Good to excellent sources of iron are liver and other organ meats, lean meat, egg yolk, leafy green vegetables, dried fruit, whole-grain and enriched cereal products, legumes, shellfish, and molasses. Adult males have an allowance of 10 milligrams of iron per day. The allowance for adult females and during lactation is 18 milligrams; during pregnancy the allowance exceeds 18 milligrams.

Iodine (I)

Iodine is necessary for the proper functioning of the thyroid gland and regulation of basal metabolism. Lack of iodine results in enlargement of the thyroid glands and a condition known as simple goiter. Cretinism, caused by an iodine deficiency, at birth or during infancy, is characterized by physical and mental retardation. An increased incidence of thyroid cancer is associated with iodine deficiency. Food and water sources of iodine are variable depending upon the soil content and composition of animal feed. Soil in coastal regions is generally richer in iodine than soil in inland areas. Seafood is the only excellent, consistent source of the mineral. Therefore, the regular use of iodized salt in food preparation and at the table is a better safeguard to assure nutrient adequacy. The daily requirement for adults is 50 to 75 micrograms. Growing children, as well as pregnant and lactating women, need more. Iodine may be restricted if certain skin conditions, such as acne, exist.

Phosphorus (P)

A phosphorus deficiency does not result in the failure of vital functions. Nevertheless, phosphorus assumes many widely varying roles, giving rigidity to the bones and teeth; serving as an essential component in many metabolic processes, including brain and nerve metabolism, particularly in regulatory processes; and being a constituent of substances that control heredity. Phosphorus is present in many foods, especially high-protein foods. Good to excellent sources are meat, milk and milk products, eggs, legumes, nuts, and whole-grain bread and cereal products. The recommended dietary allowance of 800 milligrams for adults has been established. Higher levels are set for pregnancy and lactation.

Magnesium (Mg)

Magnesium deficiency is likely to occur in association with a number of diseases or stressful conditions when food intake and/or absorption are altered. Since magnesium is necessary for regulatory functions, such as transmission of nerve impulses and muscle contractions, a deficiency state produces neuromuscular dysfunction. Major food sources of magnesium are dairy products, whole-grain breads and cereals, dry beans and peas, soybeans, nuts, and green leafy vegetables. Adults have an allowance of 300 to 350 milligrams magnesium per day. Allowances are higher for pregnancy and lactation.

Sodium (Na)

Sodium deficiency in humans is unlikely, but excessive retention or excretion usually related to disease or extreme environmental conditions leads to sodium imbalance. The principal source of sodium is table salt, sodium chloride, and many sodium compounds are used in food processing and preparation. Animal foods, specifically milk, eggs, meat, poultry, and fish, are natural sources.

Potassium (K)

Potassium regulates osmotic pressure in the body cells, activates enzymes, and plays a role in the transmission of nerve impulses. Potassium is also necessary for muscle functions. It is available from vegetables and fruits, especially peaches, apricots, and oranges, as well as from meat. A balanced diet supplies the daily requirement of 400 milligrams.

Fluorine (F)

Fluoride, a compound that contains fluorine, is necessary for healthy bones and teeth and for the prevention of cavities. The recommended daily allowance is 1 to 2 milligrams. Fluoride is frequently added to the water supply in the United States. Fluoride supplement tablets are also available.

4.4.7 *Water*

The water content of the human body varies with age, weight, sex, and physical condition. About 65 percent of body weight of lean adults is water. Human beings consume between 4¼ to 7 pints of water daily, either in the form of liquid or food. Water is necessary as the medium in which all chemical and physical processes of the body operate. The amount of water required is dependent upon environmental conditions, physical work, and the food intake. Intake is normally regulated by the sensation of thirst.

4.4.8 *Taste Agents and Stimulants*

These are generally present in small quantities in food. Their function is nevertheless important: they stimulate the digestive glands, the appetite, and/or the metabolic process. This is the role played by the aromatic substances present in spices or created by special ways of preparing food (steaming, grilling, roasting, frying).

4.4.9 *Dietary Fiber*

During digestion most foods are not entirely utilized, and indigestible substances remain. These substances most frequently occur in plant foods and chiefly consist of cellulose. In spite of indigestibility, they are very important for the peristaltic action of the digestive organs and, above all, ensure a rapid passage of the chyme into the intestine. If food contains insufficient roughage, constipation can result. Where there is too much roughage, the food passes through the intestines too quickly and cannot be properly used by the body.

4.5 Biological Agents

4.5.1 *Enzymes*

Enzymes regulate the activities of the living cell and make metabolism possible. While enzymes control construction and destruction of various substances in the body, they do not change during the process. Chemically all enzymes are proteins. They do not have to be ingested, since the human body can produce its own supply. The action of different enzymes is limited to specific situations. They can only function in a temperature range of 50° to 104°F (10° to 40°C); higher temperatures destroy enzymes.

Important enzymes include pepsin, erepsin, and trypsin, which break down proteins; saliva, which breaks down starch; and lipase and amylase, which break down fats.

4.5.2 *Hormones*

Hormones are produced in central organs of the body such as the pituitary gland, the thyroid gland, and the gonads. They specifically regulate, activate, or slow down body functions.

4.6 Applied Nutrition

The experience gathered during the period of classical cooking, as practiced in the eighteenth and nineteenth centuries, shows that eating food that is too luxurious and heavy can lead to early death. Since the beginning of this century, many nutritional experts have tried to identify those kinds and quantities of foods that are the most suitable for people in different age groups and in varying states of health. This work has resulted in great advances in knowledge concerning the availability of suitable nutrition in normal and disease states.

4.6.1 *Normal Diet*

A normal diet generally uses both classical and modern cooking techniques. It should be varied and made up of both animal and vegetable foods. Special care should be taken to assure proper proportions of the key nutrients, with emphasis on calorie, vitamin, and mineral content. Those methods of preparation that promote nutrient retention should be given priority. Food selected with high vitamin and mineral content that has been prepared with care to retain nutrients for a total diet, which includes raw vegetables and fruits, offers a good guarantee of proper nutrition. Figure 4-3 is a food value chart. It is by no means complete. Complete food value charts are issued by the U.S. Department of Agriculture.

4.6.2 *Lenten Diets*

Lenten diet restrictions were originally decreed by Roman Catholic Church regulations. All types of meat are generally prohibited; fish is usually an acceptable replacement. Fish dishes are complemented with fresh vegetables and fruits. Milk products are recommended because of the protein, vitamin, and mineral content. The use of vegetable fat is preferable to animal fat.

4.6.3 *Vegetarian Diet*

A total or strict vegetarian diet excludes not only meat, but also foods that are derived from animals, such as milk and milk products, eggs, and in some cases, even a few nonanimal foods. The main elements of this type of diet are vegetables, legumes, nuts, seeds, bread and cereal products, fruits, and fats and oils. These are carefully cooked, using vegetable fats and oils. Since a wide range of vegetable and meat

analogs exist, it is possible to achieve a fairly balanced form of nutrition. In certain cases, this type of food can be used for special dietary purposes. Care should be taken to supplement these diets, since certain essential forms of protein are missing in vegetable foods.

4.6.4 *Food for Modified Diets*

This is specially prepared food for those suffering from various illnesses or as a preventive measure against certain disorders. The food must meet the requirements of the disorder and should never adversely affect metabolism. Many regular foods are used for dietary cooking. Special precautions, such as cooking without added salt or fat, may need to be taken. The main therapeutic adaptations of the normal diet are as follows:

- Provide change in consistency of foods
- Increase or decrease caloric level
- Modify nutrient content
- Increase or decrease fiber content
- Provide foods bland in flavor
- Include or exclude specific foods
- Modify quantity and frequency of meals and snacks

Special dietary foods are prescribed for a variety of conditions: overweight or underweight; protein deficiency; fevers and infection; disturbances of the gastrointestinal tract; liver, gallbladder, and pancreatic malfunctions; cardiovascular and renal disorders; surgical conditions; metabolic and nervous disorders; anemias; allergic and skin disturbances; and children's diseases.

4.6.5 *Calculating the Calorie Content of a Meal*

To be as accurate as possible, it is wise to calculate calories in quantities for ten servings and then divide by ten to get the calorie count per portion. The exact food quantities (see chapter 7 for portion sizes and quantities) and the exact number of calories per food item (see figure 4-3) are required to determine calorie counts. This is how you calculate:

- Determine the number of calories as shown on the food value chart (figure 4-3).
- With deep-fried food, always add a fifth or a quarter of the weight of the deep-fried food as fat.
- Do not include herbs and vegetables that are going to be strained out of the food (soups and/or sauces).
- It is always better to calculate a little on the generous side. That way the guests get fewer calories rather than more than is stated.

4.6.6 *Modified Diets*

Many illnesses lead to disturbances in the metabolism and thus are harmful to the body; on the other hand, certain illnesses may be controlled or cured by altering the metabolic process. The regulation of the food consumed by the patient is important under these circumstances. The choice of food and mode of preparation depends upon the type of illness and general condition of the patient.

Dietetics is the name given to the application of the science and art of human nutrition in helping people select and obtain food for the primary purpose of nourishing their bodies in health or disease throughout the life cycle.

The term *modified diet* refers to the choice of food as a preventive, supportive, or key therapeutic measure to meet the patient's nutritional, psychological, and aesthetic needs. In this way, the diet can be considered as part of, or the principal, medical treatment. The physician and dietitian determine the patient's dietary needs and prescribe the diet modification. The dietitian translates the diet order into palatable menus, directs the mode of preparation, evaluates the patient's response to the diet, and counsels the patient and family. The kitchen chef prepares the special dietary food according to specifications established by the dietitian and receives feedback concerning patient acceptance of the diet.

The normal menu serves as the basis for planning daily modified diets. The main principles of special dietary cooking are the same as those for preparation of the normal diet. The difference lies in the selection of food and ingredients most appropriate for the individually planned modified diet. Strict sanitation must be practiced in every respect. Only a few types of food are specially prepared for dietary purposes, such as salt-free foods. The physician and dietitian determine the type and quantity of food. The diet of each patient is dependent upon the type and stage of illness, the patient's condition, and food preferences. Therefore, the diet selected for patients all suffering from the same illness can vary considerably. Nevertheless, there are certain basic medical principles that form the basis for planning diets for some of the main types of illnesses.

Diets for Gastrointestinal Conditions

Many special dietary recommendations are made for the management of a number of digestive tract disorders. Traditionally, many diet modifications have been of questionable value. There should be a sound rationale and scientific basis for using a restricted diet. If not, a liberal diet modification, which is likely to be nutritionally adequate and well accepted by the patient, is advised. The conservative approach has been to allow foods described as easily digested and non-stimulating, such as bland, smooth, and low-fiber foods. Cooking methods that minimize chemical, mechanical, and thermal irritation to the digestive tract are recommended. Therefore, some major considerations in menu planning and food preparation would be to identify individual food intolerances; vary daily menu plans to improve patient acceptance and nutritive content of diet; cook foods, especially raw fruits and vegetables; avoid strong-flavored foods and highly seasoned dishes; use methods of preparation least likely to cause digestive disturbances, such as poaching, simmering, and steaming; use methods of preparation for maximum nutrient retention; and avoid serving food at extreme temperatures.

The more liberal approach to dietary management has been to recommend a normal diet with a few modifications primarily based on avoidance of foods poorly tolerated and on flexibility to meet individual requirements. The quantity of food and meal spacing may be as important as the type of food consumed. A

Food	Measure U.S.	(g)	Calories	Protein (g)	Fat (g)	Saturated Fat (g)	Carbohydrates (g)	Calcium (mg)	Iron (mg)	Vitamin A (I.U.)	Thiamine (mg)	Riboflavin (mg)
Dairy Products												
Cheese, Cheddar	1 oz.	(28)	115	7	9	6.1	T	204	0.2	300	0.01	0.11
Cheese, cottage, small curd	1 cup	(210)	220	26	9	6.0	6	126	0.3	340	0.04	0.34
Cheese, cream	1 oz.	(28)	100	2	10	6.2	1	23	0.3	400	T	0.06
Cheese, Swiss	1 oz.	(28)	105	8	8	5.0	1	272	T	240	0.01	0.10
Cheese, American pasteurized process spread	1 oz.	(28)	82	5	6	3.8	1	159	0.1	220	0.01	0.12
Half-and-half	1 Tbsp.	(15)	20	T	2	1.1	1	16	T	20	0.01	0.02
Cream, sour	1 Tbsp.	(15)	25	T	3	1.6	1	14	T	90	T	0.02
Milk, whole	1 cup	(244)	150	8	8	5.1	11	291	0.1	310	0.09	0.40
Milk, skim	1 cup	(244)	85	8	T	0.3	12	302	0.1	500	0.09	0.37
Buttermilk	1 cup	(245)	100	8	2	1.3	12	285	0.1	80	0.08	0.38
Milkshake, chocolate	10.6 oz.	(300)	335	9	8	5.0	63	396	0.9	260	0.14	0.67
Ice cream	1 cup	(133)	270	5	14	8.9	32	176	0.1	540	0.05	0.33
Sherbet	1 cup	(193)	270	2	4	2.4	59	103	0.3	190	0.03	0.09
Yogurt, fruit-flavored	8 oz.	(227)	230	10	3	1.8	42	343	0.2	120	0.08	0.40
Eggs												
Fried in butter	1	(46)	85	5	6	2.4	1	26	0.9	290	0.03	0.13
Hard-cooked	1	(50)	80	6	6	1.7	1	28	1.0	260	0.04	0.14
Scrambled, with milk, in butter	1	(64)	95	6	7	2.8	1	47	0.9	310	0.04	0.16
Fats and Oils												
Butter	1 Tbsp.	(14)	100	T	12	7.2	T	3	T	430	T	T
Margarine	1 Tbsp.	(14)	100	T	12	2.1	T	3	T	470	T	T
Salad dressing, blue cheese	1 Tbsp.	(15)	75	1	8	1.6	1	12	T	30	T	0.02
Salad dressing, French	1 Tbsp.	(16)	65	T	6	1.1	3	2	T	—	—	—
Salad dressing, Italian	1 Tbsp.	(15)	85	T	9	1.6	1	2	T	T	T	T
Mayonnaise	1 Tbsp.	(14)	100	T	11	2.0	T	3	0.1	40	T	0.01
Meat, Poultry, Fish												
Clams, raw	3 oz.	(85)	65	11	1	—	2	59	5.2	90	0.08	0.15
Crabmeat, white or king, canned	1 cup	(135)	135	24	3	0.6	1	61	1.1	—	0.11	0.11
Salmon, pink, canned	3 oz.	(85)	120	17	5	0.9	0	167	0.7	60	0.03	0.16
Sardines, Atlantic, canned in oil	3 oz.	(85)	175	20	9	3.0	0	372	2.5	190	0.02	0.17
Shrimp, french-fried	3 oz.	(85)	190	17	9	2.3	9	61	1.7	—	0.03	0.07
Tuna, canned in oil	3 oz.	(85)	170	24	7	1.7	0	7	1.6	70	0.04	0.10
Bacon, broiled or fried crisp	2 slices	(15)	85	4	8	2.5	T	2	0.5	0	0.08	0.05
Ground beef, broiled, 10% fat	3 oz.	(85)	185	23	10	4.0	0	10	3.0	20	0.08	0.20
Roast beef, lean	3 oz.	(85)	165	25	7	2.8	0	11	3.2	10	0.06	0.19
Beef steak	3 oz.	(85)	330	20	27	11.3	0	9	2.5	50	0.05	0.15
Beef stew with vegetables	1 cup	(245)	220	16	11	4.9	15	29	2.9	2,400	0.15	0.17
Lamb chop	3.1 oz.	(89)	360	18	32	14.8	0	8	1.0	—	0.11	0.19
Liver, beef	3 oz.	(85)	195	22	9	2.5	5	9	7.5	45,390	0.22	3.56
Ham, light-cure	2.7 oz.	(85)	245	18	19	6.8	0	8	2.2	0	0.40	0.15
Pork chop	1 slice	(78)	305	19	25	8.9	0	9	2.7	0	0.40	0.15
Bologna	1	(28)	85	3	8	3.0	T	2	0.5	—	0.05	0.06
Frankfurter, cooked	1	(56)	170	7	15	5.6	1	3	0.8	—	0.08	0.11
Sausage, pork link, cooked		(13)	60	2	6	2.1	T	1	0.3	0	0.10	0.04
Veal cutlet, braised	3 oz.	(85)	185	23	9	4.0	0	9	2.7	—	0.06	0.21
Chicken drumstick, fried	1.3 oz.	(38)	90	12	4	1.1	T	6	0.9	50	0.03	0.15
Chicken, half-broiler, broiled	6.2 oz.	(176)	240	42	7	2.2	0	16	3.0	160	0.09	0.34

Figure 4-3. Nutritive values of foods.

Food	Measure U.S.	(g)	Calories	Protein (g)	Fat (g)	Saturated Fat (g)	Carbohydrates (g)	Calcium (mg)	Iron (mg)	Vitamin A (I.U.)	Thiamine (mg)	Riboflavin (mg)
Fruits and Fruit Products												
Apple, raw, 2¾-in. diam.	1	(138)	80	T	1	—	20	10	0.4	120	0.04	0.03
Apple juice	1 cup	(248)	120	T	T	—	30	15	1.5	—	0.02	0.05
Applesauce, sweetened	1 cup	(255)	230	1	T	—	61	10	1.3	100	0.05	0.03
Apricots, raw	3	(107)	55	1	T	—	14	18	0.5	2,890	0.03	0.04
Banana, raw	1	(119)	100	1	T	—	26	10	0.8	230	0.06	0.07
Cherries, sweet, raw	10	(68)	45	1	T	—	12	15	0.3	70	0.03	0.04
Grapefruit, raw, medium, white	½	(241)	45	1	T	—	12	19	0.5	10	0.05	0.02
Grapes, Thompson seedless	10	(50)	35	T	T	—	9	6	0.2	50	0.03	0.02
Cantaloupe, 5-in. diam.	½	(477)	80	2	T		20	38	1.1	9,240	0.11	0.08
Orange, 2⅝-in. diam.	1	(131)	65	1	T	—	16	54	0.5	260	0.13	0.05
Orange juice	1 cup	(249)	120	2	T	—	29	25	0.2	540	0.23	0.03
Peach, raw, 2½-in. diam.	1	(100)	40	1	T	—	10	9	0.5	1,330	0.02	0.05
Pear, raw, Bartlett, 2½-in. diam.	1	(164)	100	1	T	—	25	13	0.5	30	0.03	0.07
Raisins, seedless	1 cup	(145)	420	4	T	—	112	90	5.1	30	0.16	0.12
Strawberries, whole	1 cup	(149)	55	1	1	—	13	31	1.5	90	0.04	0.10
Watermelon, 4 × 8 in. wedge	1	(926)	110	2	1	—	27	30	2.1	2,510	0.13	0.13
Grain Products												
Bread, raisin	1 slice	(25)	65	2	1	0.2	13	18	0.6	T	0.09	0.06
Bread, white, enriched	1 slice	(25)	70	2	1	0.2	13	21	0.6	T	0.10	0.06
Bread, whole-wheat	1 slice	(28)	65	3	1	0.1	14	24	0.8	T	0.10	0.06
Oatmeal or rolled oats	1 cup	(240)	130	5	2	0.4	23	22	1.4	0	0.19	0.05
Cake, angel food, 1/12 cake	1	(53)	135	3	T	—	32	50	0.2	0	0.03	0.08
Boston cream pie, 1/12 cake	1	(69)	210	3	6	1.9	34	46	0.7	140	0.09	0.11
Fruitcake, dark, 1/30 loaf	1	(15)	55	1	2	0.5	9	11	0.4	20	0.02	0.02
Pound cake, 1/17 loaf	1	(33)	160	2	10	2.5	16	6	0.5	80	0.05	0.06
Doughnut, cake type	1	(25)	100	1	5	1.2	13	10	0.4	20	0.05	0.05
Muffin, corn	1	(40)	125	3	4	1.2	19	42	0.7	120	0.10	0.10
Noodles, enriched, cooked	1 cup	(160)	200	7	2	—	37	16	1.4	110	0.22	0.13
Pancake, plain	1	(27)	60	2	2	0.5	9	27	0.4	30	0.06	0.07
Pie, apple, 1/7 pie	1	(135)	345	3	15	3.9	51	11	0.9	40	0.15	0.11
Pie, cherry, 1/7 pie	1	(135)	350	4	15	4.0	52	19	0.9	590	0.16	0.12
Pie, lemon meringue, 1/7 pie	1	(120)	305	4	12	3.7	45	17	1.0	200	0.09	0.12
Pie, pecan, 1/7 pie	1	(118)	495	6	27	4.0	61	55	3.7	190	0.26	0.14
Pie, pumpkin, 1/7 pie	1	(130)	275	5	15	5.4	32	66	1.0	3,210	0.11	0.18
Pizza, cheese, 1/8 of 12-in. pie	1	(60)	145	6	4	1.7	22	86	1.1	230	0.16	0.18
Rice, white, enriched, cooked	1 cup	(165)	180	4	T	T	40	5	1.3	0	0.10	*
Beans and Nuts												
Beans, Great Northern, cooked	1 cup	(180)	210	14	1	—	38	90	4.9	0	0.25	0.13
Peanuts, roasted in oil, salted	1 cup	(144)	840	37	72	13.7	27	107	3.0	—	0.46	0.19
Peanut butter	1 Tbsp.	(16)	95	4	8	1.5	3	9	0.3	—	0.02	0.02
Sugars and Sweets												
Caramels	1 oz.	(28)	115	1	3	1.6	22	42	0.4	T	0.01	0.05
Chocolate, milk	1 oz.	(28)	145	2	9	5.5	16	65	0.3	80	0.02	0.10
Honey	1 Tbsp.	(21)	65	T	0	0	17	1	0.1	0	T	0.01
Jams and preserves	1 Tbsp.	(20)	55	T	0	—	14	4	0.2	T	T	0.01
Sugar, white, granulated	1 Tbsp.	(12)	45	0	0	0	12	0	T	0	0	0

Vegetables

Vegetables												
Asparagus, canned, spears	4	(80)	15	2	T	—	3	15	1.5	640	0.05	0.08
Beans, green, from frozen	1 cup	(135)	35	2	T	—	8	54	0.9	780	0.09	0.12
Beans, lima	1 cup	(170)	170	10	T	—	32	34	2.9	390	0.12	0.09
Beets, canned, diced/sliced	1 cup	(170)	65	2	T	—	15	32	1.2	30	0.02	0.05
Broccoli, cooked	1 stalk	(180)	45	6	1	—	8	158	1.4	4,500	0.16	0.36
Cabbage, raw, shredded	1 cup	(70)	15	1	T	—	4	34	0.3	90	0.04	0.04
Carrots, raw, 7½ × 1⅛ in.	1	(72)	30	1	T	—	7	27	0.5	7,930	0.04	0.04
Cauliflower, raw	1 cup	(115)	31	3	T	—	6	29	1.3	70	0.13	0.12
Celery, raw	1 stalk	(40)	5	T	T	—	2	16	0.1	110	0.01	0.01
Corn, sweet, cooked	1 ear	(140)	70	2	1	—	16	2	0.5	310	0.09	0.08
Cucumber, with peel	6–8 slices	(28)	5	T	T	—	1	7	0.3	70	0.01	0.01
Lettuce, iceberg, chopped	1 cup	(55)	5	T	T	—	2	11	0.3	180	0.03	0.03
Mushrooms, raw	1 cup	(70)	20	2	T	—	3	4	0.6	T	0.07	0.32
Onions, raw, chopped	1 cup	(170)	65	3	T	—	15	46	0.9	T	0.05	0.07
Peas, frozen, cooked	1 cup	(160)	110	8	T	—	19	30	3.0	960	0.43	0.14
Potatoes, baked, peeled	1	(156)	145	4	T	—	33	14	1.1	T	0.15	0.07
Potatoes, french-fried	10	(50)	110	2	4	1.1	17	5	0.9	T	0.07	0.01
Potatoes, mashed, with milk	1 cup	(210)	135	4	2	0.7	27	50	0.8	40	0.17	0.11
Potato chips	10	(20)	115	1	8	2.1	10	8	0.4	T	0.04	0.01
Sauerkraut, canned	1 cup	(235)	40	2	T	—	9	85	1.2	120	0.07	0.09
Spinach, chopped, from frozen	1 cup	(205)	45	6	1	—	8	232	4.3	16,200	0.14	0.31
Squash, summer, cooked	1 cup	(210)	30	2	T	—	7	53	0.8	820	0.11	0.17
Sweet potatoes, baked in skin, peeled	1	(114)	160	2	1	—	37	46	1.0	9,230	0.10	0.08
Tomatoes, raw	1	(135)	25	1	T	—	6	16	0.6	1,110	0.07	0.05

T = trace
* = varies by brand
Source: *Home and Garden Bulletin No. 72,* U.S. Department of Agriculture

Figure 4-3, continued.

few foods such as coffee and alcohol may be avoided or restricted.

Diets for Liver, Gallbladder, and Pancreatic Disorders

Dietary management varies considerably depending upon the specific disease, acute or chronic stage, disease complications, such as fluid retention or hemorrhage, condition of the patient, such as nutritional deficiency or overweight, and food tolerance, including loss of appetite, nausea, and vomiting.

In liver disease the aim is to protect the liver from stress and to aid in its proper functioning. Generally, a diet high in calories, protein, and carbohydrates with a moderate fat content is recommended. Other modifications with changes in food consistency, size and frequency of meals, sodium content, and vitamin supplements will depend upon the individual case. In the final stages of liver disease, protein intake is reduced because nitrogen-containing substances are not metabolized by the liver.

In gallbladder disease, a fat-restricted, bland diet reduces symptoms. If the individual is overweight, a low-calorie diet is prescribed.

Dietary treatment in pancreatic disorders depends upon the nature and extent of digestive impairment. A typical diet in chronic pancreatis is of soft consistency with high-calorie, high-protein, and low-fat levels divided into six small meals.

Loss of appetite may be a significant problem for patients with any of these conditions. Therefore, every effort should be made to encourage the patient to eat. For example, attractive food served in a pleasant, calm atmosphere will stimulate the appetite. Simply prepared foods that are poached, steamed, or simmered will not overtax the digestive processes.

Diets for Cardiovascular Conditions

Dietary management for cardiovascular disorders varies depending upon the emphasis as a preventive or therapeutic measure, acute or chronic stage of illness, and complications.

Frequently, calorie-controlled diets are formulated to meet individual needs. The type and quantity of fat are adjusted. Usually total fat consumption is reduced, cholesterol intake restricted, and the ratio of unsaturated fats (mainly vegetable oils) to saturated fats (mainly animal fats) is increased. For some individuals, it may also be necessary to restrict total carbohydrate intake moderately and limit dietary sources of sugar.

In acute situations, such as heart attack or complications with infection, obesity, high blood pressure, constipation, and/or fluid retention, additional restrictions modify the diet prescription:

- Sodium restriction, if there is fluid and sodium retention
- Fluid restriction, if there is poor circulation and fluid retention
- Liquid, soft, or bland diet

Diet for Diabetes Mellitus

Diabetes is a malfunction of the metabolism. It is caused by poor utilization of carbohydrates because of insufficient or total lack of functioning insulin, a hormone secreted by the pancreas. The metabolism of protein and fat is also altered. When the disease is uncontrolled, the blood sugar becomes elevated, sugar spills over into the urine, and excessive amounts of urine are excreted to remove the sugar.

Dietary management controls, but does not cure, the disease. Dietary control is the central therapeutic measure. A dietary prescription is planned and adjusted periodically to control the calorie, carbohydrate, protein, and fat content of the food intake. When planning and preparing the diet, these quantities must be calculated exactly, served in measured quantities, and adhered to by the patient. The rule about choosing a preparation method that least affects the nutritive content of food and controls caloric content is applicable for this dietary modification.

In some cases, insulin therapy or oral hypoglycemic (blood-sugar lowering) agents will be prescribed in addition to dietary control. A regular, normal diet with emphasis on calorie control and liberal protein intake is recommended for the diabetic. The carbohydrate content of the milk, bread and cereal, fruit, and starchy vegetable food groups is calculated to control quantity and plan for carbohydrate distribution throughout the day. Low-calorie foods, such as low-carbohydrate vegetables and salads without sauces, or with controlled amounts of salad dressing, are encouraged. Simply prepared foods and raw fruits and vegetables are recommended. Mixed dishes, such as casseroles, are acceptable, but more difficult to include in the menu plan, unless an accurate estimate of nutrient content per serving is feasible.

Diabetics are prone to early signs of heart disease. Recent trends in the dietary management of these patients include such measures as fat control. A current theory stresses calorie control and fat control rather than undue concern with carbohydrate restriction in the dietary management of diabetics. However, the traditional, conservative approach recommends the reduction or avoidance of foods with high sugar content, such as concentrated sweets, rich desserts, and alcoholic beverages.

Chapter 5
The Menu

5.1 Menu Planning

Menu planning is an art and a science that requires an extensive knowledge of foods and their basic methods of preparation and service as well as an understanding of the nutritive value of food combinations. It was Carême who said that the success of a dinner depends on the composition of the menu, assuming, of course, that the preparation of the food is flawless.

As in any other art, menu making requires careful planning and the observance of a few principles that are basic to meeting the objectives of the management: satisfying the customer, patient, or guest; and utilizing the skills and abilities of the available personnel. One must consider the following:

- Type of institution
- Nutritional principles
- Physical facilities
- Personnel
- Variety of foods
- Combination of flavors
- Season of the year
- Budget
- Menu terminology
- Long-range planning

The type of institution is the first consideration in planning menus. The objective or purpose of a hospital will differ from that of a hotel or restaurant, while neither of these will be the same as that of a fast-food establishment or a university residence hall. The menus of each should focus on the people to be served. For those persons who receive all their meals in a hospital, extended-care facility, retirement home, or residence hall, the menus must be planned to meet the total nutritional requirements of the group to be served.

Restaurants, hotels, fast-food establishments, industrial cafeterias, and school lunchrooms usually provide only part of the daily food intake of the client or student. Although these operations do not have responsibility for fulfilling the total daily dietary requirements of the individual, the menu should include foods that will provide selections that will meet nutritional needs.

Satisfying the guests requires knowing them. The successful menu maker will know the age, sex, occupation, and economic status of the intended patrons, because these factors are significant in their acceptance of certain foods. Food habits and preferences are sometimes the result of family attitudes and practices, ethnic backgrounds, regional preferences, and religious traditions and restrictions. There is a difference in planning a menu for Americans or Germans; for a physicians' association or a butchers' trade organization; for a country wedding or for one in a large city. The life-styles of the clients must be considered—their national dishes, the methods of preparation, and the seasoning must be harmonized to suit their tastes.

Nutritional principles, as applied to menu planning, are the same throughout the life cycle. The activity level and the metabolic processes vary with individuals depending on age, sex, and activity and, therefore, caloric requirements differ. Persons with physical illnesses may require a modified diet. These diets are planned by a dietitian who is qualified to adjust the normal diet to meet the nutritional needs of the patient.

In recent years considerable attention has been given to the nutrition of the elderly. Their needs differ from younger adults' only in terms of calories required. The general slowing down of body processes and activity in older persons usually reduces the need for high-calorie foods, such as sweets and fats. Many older people lack the physical strength and interest to prepare foods that are nutritionally balanced and easily assimilated. When an elderly person enters a retirement home or an extended-care facility, the change from a familiar environment to one that is strange often causes feelings of depression, loneliness, and insecurity. As a result of these disturbances, the clients often complain about the food and refuse to eat. Planning menus that are nutritionally adequate and appealing for this group offers a real challenge. Loss of teeth or poorly fitting dentures makes chewing difficult. Individuals suffering from paralysis or blindness may have problems handling foods. It should not be assumed that people with these and other handicaps must have only ground, soft, and liquid foods. Many individuals will adjust surprisingly well and enjoy a variety of foods that differ in texture, particularly if the foods are carefully prepared and attractively presented in a form that can be handled easily.

The physical facilities available will also influence the menu pattern. The amount of space and the type and capacity of the equipment will determine the variety of the products that can be prepared and the number of persons that can be served. The menu must be planned to distribute the work load between the various pieces of equipment and to utilize all the equipment.

The number of employees available and their skills and abilities, the total number of man-hours, and the number of employees scheduled at any specific time are controlling factors in menu planning. In the small establishment, where only one or two cooks are employed, the menus must obviously be quite simple with limited selections. In a larger commercial enterprise, the skill and size of the labor force affect the number of selections that can be offered on the menu. Spiraling food and labor costs in recent years have prompted the development of more simplified menus and quality-controlled food production systems.

The trend toward the use of more prepared foods, preportioned meats, poultry, and fish products, processed vegetables, mixes, and frozen foods aids the menu planner in balancing the work load between production units. The wise menu planner will avoid overloading an individual or a department with a large number of menu items that require time-consuming tasks and last-minute preparation. A well-balanced work schedule is important to control the standard of quality and to maintain the morale of the work force.

Variety in the menu should be introduced not only through the food items, but also in terms of methods of preparation, and the texture, color, form, and shape of the food. The planner must have a vast knowledge of foods and must also be able to plan and visualize interesting combinations of each. Variety can be achieved on the menu by offering entrées that have been roasted, fried, and braised; vegetables that have been steamed, baked, and sautéed; salads in the form of raw vegetables, molds, and combinations of fresh or canned fruit; desserts that have a good balance between pastries, puddings, and frozen items. The basic forms of preparation must offer variety not only on the single menu; the methods of preparation should differ from day to day and from menu to menu. A cauliflower cream soup followed on the next day by a potato cream soup does not offer the required variety, since both are thick soups. Regardless of whether the food item is fish, meat, poultry, game, or vegetables, there must be variety in the food items and in their presentation.

Monotony can be avoided by providing foods of different sizes, shapes, and heights on the same menu. Potatoes and some vegetables may be served whole, or in cubes, diced, shredded, julienne, or thick or thin slices.

Every course in a menu must be fundamentally different from the others in terms of appearance and preparation. If the first course consists of a cold entrée, the foods used in the preparation should not be repeated in any form in the courses that follow. The different kinds of sauces, which are either served with the food or separately, must differ from each other in color, taste, and seasoning. Butter sauces (hollandaise, béarnaise, and mousseline) are similar and should occur only once in a menu. Nor should two brown sauces that have been prepared in the same way appear in the same menu. Fish served in a white-wine sauce should not be followed by an allemande sauce (thick white sauce) in the next course. A balance of red meats and white meats should be offered. Leg of lamb or mutton and beef should never be featured on the same menu, nor should the dark meat of poultry and game be served after a red meat. Whenever a soup is prepared with vegetables, the following course should include a variety of vegetables different from those in the soup. The use of fresh fruits and vegetables will add color, texture, and flavor to every menu. Deep-fried dishes should never appear more than once on a menu.

Variety may also be introduced through color. A menu that provides an assortment of foods with rich natural colors will have more eye appeal and be easier to merchandise than the menu that is composed of foods all of one color or colorless foods. Artificial coloring should not be used. Menus should include items with contrasting textures and consistencies. A fresh green salad served with a pasta or a cream of tomato soup with a crisp cheese wafer will increase the appeal of each item. Only one creamed dish should be offered in the same meal.

Combination of flavors is perhaps the most significant factor affecting palatability of foods. The skillful menu planner will consider not only the sweet, salty, bitter, and sour flavors, but also those of spicy and highly seasoned foods. A variety of these flavors that complement each other will be far more interesting than a duplication of the same flavors.

In the past, soups were never served after a cold hors d'oeuvre, but now that fewer courses are served, a highly seasoned soup, such as spiced tomato soup, would be appropriate.

The flavors of certain vegetables and accompaniments combine with certain meats, and some combinations have become traditional. The wise planner will use initiative and imagination in planning to avoid monotonous repetitions. Endives with roast veal, chestnuts with ham, and risotto with veal and chicken are appropriate combinations. Pasta is excellent with braised beef, roast veal, and stews; it would never be served, however, with a steak or with roast beef or leg of lamb or mutton. Fried and baked potatoes are suitable with grilled or fried meats; steamed potatoes with braised meats, roasts, and stews; and boiled potatoes are a favorite with poached fish and boiled meats. A chocolate sauce would ruin an apple dish, but it is excellent with pears. Crisp cookies are good with ice cream, but a soft cookie is better with stewed fruit.

The season of the year exerts an influence on food preferences. During cold weather, greater quantities of heavy foods, such as chowders, roasts, and rich pastries, will be consumed. On a hot summer day, cold soups, cold hors d'oeuvre, crisp cool salads, chilled and frozen desserts, and cold buffets are usually popular. One or more hot items should also be included on the menu for those who prefer hot food.

In some locations the availability of certain foods will vary with the seasons. Improvements in transportation and distribution systems have made it possible, however, to perk up a menu with off-season foods. Maximum use should be made of perishable foods when they are on the local markets. During this time, they are usually at their peak of quality and at their lowest price.

Fish is of poorer quality after swimming upstream to spawn and during the spawning period. It should therefore not be featured on the menu during this time.

Fresh game is at its peak during the fall months. It is best to avoid serving frozen game, particularly that from furred animals.

Featured traditional foods and appropriate themes on holidays and for special events add interest to a menu. Many novel and interesting ideas can be promoted on Valentine's Day, Easter, Thanksgiving, and other holidays.

The budget will stipulate the projected income and

the amount of this income that can be used for the purchase of food. Food sales, the major source of the potential income, must also cover labor and operation costs. The percentage of income that can be spent for each of these expenses should be determined by management.

The menu must be planned in accordance with the established food cost percentage. To maintain this percentage it is necessary to calculate daily food costs, provide and use standardized recipes, know raw food and portion costs, and adjust prices and menu selections as costs fluctuate. The daily food cost is based on storeroom requisitions and purchases.

A standardized recipe system is essential for successful food cost control. The recipes should list the total raw food cost and the individual portion cost. The menu planner must know and keep these costs up to date. Failure to use such a system will lead to major inconsistencies in quality and cost controls. Portion control is necessary from aesthetics and cost

standpoints. Portions should be standardized in relation to cost and appetite so that a variety of foods can be enjoyed in a meal without excessive cost or waste.

A diagram of a menu schedule appears in figure 5-1.

5.1.1 *Framework of the Menu*

The courses of the menu should be arranged on the menu in the same sequence that they will be ordered and consumed. Appetizers and other light dishes such as soup, cold and hot hors d'oeuvre, and fish are served as separate courses preceding the main course (*grosse pièce*). This course is followed with more light dishes. Technically, the complete menu framework usually includes the following courses:

1. Cold hors d'oeuvre—*Hors d'oeuvre froid*
2. Soup—*Potage*
3. Hot hors d'oeuvre—*Hors d'oeuvre chaud*
4. Fish—*Poisson*

Plan from _____ to _____	Sunday, May 15, 19XX	Menu No.	Number Portions		Price	Monday, May 16, 19XX	Menu No.	Number Portions		Price
			Prod.	Sold				Prod.	Sold	
1st course	Mushroom Omelet	1.4.2.17	10	8						
Menu A	Consommé Sévigné Chicken Sauté with Chambertin wine Homemade Noodles Stuffed Tomatoes, Provençe Style Florida Salad	1.3.1.4	50	35						
Menu B	Consommé Sévigné Sirloin Steak with Pepper French-fried Potatoes Stuffed Tomatoes, Provençe Style Green Salad	1.1.1.15	87	85						
Dessert	Coupe Melba	1.3.1.4	30	30						
Menu alterations	Menu B/Soup from	1.3.1.4				Menu Schedules for 7 to 10 days				
Speciality of the day 1 2 3	Sliced Veal, Zurich Style Beef Stew, Farmer's Style Veal Rib Roast Lorette	17.1.3.24 17.4.2.3 18.3.4.7	10 15 15	8 10 5						
Season	Asparagus (10 varieties)	Special	14	11						
Staff lunch Staff evening meal	Veal Cutlet Cordon Bleu Noodles, salad Coffee, toast Cheese Potatoes in their jackets	— —	45 40	40 38						

Figure 5-1. A menu schedule.

5. Main course—*Relevé/Grosse pièce*
6. Hot entrée—*Entrée chaude*
7. Cold entrée—*Entrée froide*
8. Sherbet—*Sorbet*
9. Roast and salad—*Rôti, salade*
10. Vegetable—*Légume*
11. Sweet dish—*Entremet*
12. Savory—*Savoury*
13. Dessert—*Dessert*

The classical framework differs slightly:

1. Cold hors d'oeuvre—*Hors d'oeuvre froid*
2. Soup—*Potage*
3. Hot hors d'oeuvre—*Hors d'oeuvre chaud*
4. Fish—*Poisson*
5. Main course—*Relevé/Grosse pièce*
6. Entrée—*Entrée*
7. Sherbet—*Sorbet*
8. Roast and salad—*Rôti, salade*
9. Cold roast—*Rôti froid*
10. Vegetable—*Légume*
11. Sweet dish—*Entremet*
12. Savory—*Savoury*
13. Dessert—*Dessert*

1. *Cold hors d'oeuvre:* Literally translated, *hors d'oeuvre* means "outside of the main work." In earlier times, hors d'oeuvre were served separately from the menu proper in France: canapés and various tidbits of garnished vegetables were served in the foyer or in the salon together with a light white wine. The ingredients for these snacks were not repeated in the main menu, which was served in the dining room. Much later hors d'oeuvre were incorporated in the menu and served before the soup or the bouillon.

Hors d'oeuvre are small servings decoratively arranged that are chosen to complement the courses that follow. Examples are: oysters, caviar, fish, shellfish, sausages and meat products, venison, eggs, vegetables, mushrooms, fruits, pâté, and jellied meats.

2. *Soups:* Soups frequently are considered the prelude to a meal and act as the "business card" of the kitchen. They should be served hot (except if they are intended to be eaten cold as for gazpacho or vichy-

ssoise) and complement the dishes to follow. In first-rate establishments the menu frequently offers a choice of both clear and thick soups. From the Middle Ages to the seventeenth century the soup constituted the main course of a meal and included meat or vegetables. The clear and thick soups we know today were developed from these dishes.

3. *Hot hors d'oeuvre:* Hot hors d'oeuvre are always served after the soup. In France this course is sometimes called *Entrées volantes ou petites Entrées*—"flying or small entrée." In earlier times this course, like cold hors d'oeuvre, was considered an aperitif, not part of the menu proper.

4. *Fish:* This course used to consist of a whole fish served with vegetables and sauces. Today fish can be used as a hot hors d'oeuvre or as an entrée. Fish, like meat, is now usually portioned before cooking.

5. *Main course:* These courses of meat, venison, or poultry were originally served whole and cut at the table. Preparation and serving required much time. Today raw products are divided into individual portions, except under special circumstances. These individual portions, cut before preparation, are what we now call entrées. Historically the first dish considered part of the menu proper was this main course.

6. *Hot entrées:* Always served after the main course, these dishes are portioned as raw materials. They can be divided into six categories:

- Butchered meat
- Poultry
- Venison
- Mousses
- Soufflées
- Precooked dishes such as meat in pastry, filled tartlets, sausages, galantines, pies, fricassees, ragouts, goulashes, and carbonades

Hot entrées often take the place of the main course.

7. *Cold entrées:* This course includes: cold meat, poultry and venison; meat jellies; galantines; mousses; pies, tarts, terrines, and other kinds of cold charcuterie.

8. *Sherbets:* Served as a refreshment between

courses (to clean the palate in preparation for later courses) or as part of the dessert, sherbets consist mainly of ice with hints of lemon juice, Champagne, or spirits.

9. *Roast and salad:* Roasts for this course are prepared from poultry or fowl, venison, or from red butchered meats such as beef. To accompany roasts, one should choose simple salads in season or mixed salads of light ingredients that are easy to digest.

10. *Cold roast:* The name for this course is misleading since it actually most often resembles a cold hors d'oeuvre, such as truffled goose liver pâté, served without salad to preserve the delicate flavor. Other choices include shellfish, mousses, cold chicken, and fish dishes. Modern menus generally omit this course.

11. *Vegetables:* In the short menu schedule, vegetables are served together with the main course. Potatoes should always be served before other vegetables, frequently even at the same time as entrées or roasts. Experts used to disagree on whether to serve vegetables before or after the roast, and finally decided on the latter. Vegetables used to be part of the dessert course, hence the title *entremetier* for the vegetable cook.

12. *Sweet dishes:* These preparations can be warm, cold, or frozen. The word *entremet* or dessert can be used to describe this course. When vegetables were still part of the *entremets,* the sweet dish only was called *plat de douceur.*

13. *Savory:* This course is omitted from modern menus. It was a separate warm course between the sweet dish and the dessert, especially favored in England. It consisted mainly of hot spicy tidbits very similar to hot hors d'oeuvre.

14. *Dessert:* Cheese, fruit, and nuts constitute the last course of the meal and replace the old-fashioned serving of enormous *pièces montées,* towering arrangements of cakes and pastries.

The fourteen-course menu (see figure 5-2) conforms to every aspect of the classical menu framework. Menus today, however, seldom offer such an extensive number of courses and dishes. The menu illustrates the kinds of food served in each course and the proper sequence of service. The sherbet, which is

Cold hors d'oeuvre	*Oysters*
Soup	*Consommé Princess*
Hot hors d'oeuvre	*Marrow on Toast*
Fish	*Blue River Trout*
	Whipped Butter
Main course	*Beef Tenderloin with Vegetables*
Hot entrée	*Breast of Chicken with Truffles*
Cold entrée	*Mousselines of Ham with Paprika*
Sherbet	*Champagne Sherbet*
Roast	*Roast Pheasant*
Salad	*Salad*
Vegetable	*Asparagus au Gratin*
Sweet dish	*Blancmange with Hazelnuts*
	Pastries
Savory dish	*Emmentaler Cheese Sticks*
Dessert	*Fruits—Dessert*

Hors d'oeuvre froid	*Natives*
Potage	*Consommé princesse*
Hors d'oeuvre chaud	*Croûte à la moelle*
Poisson	*Truite au bleu*
	Beurre fouetté
Grosse pièce	*Filet de bœuf jardinière*
Entrée chaude	*Suprêmes de poulet aux truffes*
Entrée froide	*Mousselines de jambon au paprika*
Sorbet	*Sorbet au Champagne*
Rôti	*Faisan rôti*
Salade	*Salade*
Légume	*Asperges en branches au gratin*
Entremets	*Bavarois aux noisettes*
	Pâtisserie
Savoury	*Paillettes d'Emmental*
Dessert	*Fruits—Dessert*

Figure 5-2. A classical menu, in English and French.

shown within the framework, is not treated as a separate course. It serves as a refreshing dish, and it also provides an opportunity for brief greetings or announcements without interfering with the continuity of service. It would be inappropriate to serve a frozen drink in the middle of a short menu or to have speeches or toasts at that time. This menu lists all the possible courses in a menu. Choices of foods are seldom offered within a course. Occasionally, there may be a choice in the method or preparation for the sweet dishes, soups, and fish, such as a clear and a thick soup, a fried and a poached fish course, a hot and a cold sweet dish.

Changes in the order of courses are permitted and sometimes recommended, provided the general rules are not broken. Thus, the hot entrée is often served before the main course. The methods of preparation of the fish course and the main course then become extremely important.

In recent years there has been a trend toward simplification of menu patterns and fewer menu selections. The discriminating guest does not demand a large choice of foods and courses. A menu of three to six carefully selected delicacies that have been expertly prepared is more likely to be considered a culinary treasure than an extensive list of different foods. Courses are traditionally served in the order of the menu framework as shown in two examples below.

Soup—*Potage*
Main course—*Grosse pièce*
Vegetable—*Légume*
Sweet dish—*Entremets*

Soup—*Potage*
Fish—*Poisson*
Main course—*Grosse pièce*
Vegetable—*Légume*
Sweet dish—*Entremets*

Menus arranged as those in the four examples below may begin with a salad. In these menus, fruit and cheese may be served instead of a sweet dish.

Cold hors d'oeuvre—*Hors d'oeuvre froid*
Soup—*Potage*
Fish—*Poisson*
Main course—*Grosse pièce*
Roast—*Rôti*
Vegetable—*Légume*
Sweet dish—*Entremets*

Cold hors d'oeuvre—*Hors d'oeuvre froid*
Soup—*Potage*
Fish—*Poisson*
Main course—*Grosse pièce*
Cold entrée—*Entrée froide*
Roast—*Rôti*
Vegetable—*Légume*

Sweet dish—*Entremets*
Dessert—*Dessert*

Cold hors d'oeuvre—*Hors d'oeuvre froid*
Soup—*Potage*
Fish—*Poisson*
Main course—*Grosse pièce*
Hot entrée—*Entrée chaude*
Cold entrée—*Entrée froide*
Roast—*Rôti*
Vegetable—*Légume*
Sweet dish—*Entremets*
Desserts—*Dessert*

Cold hors d'oeuvre—*Hors d'oeuvre froid*
Soup—*Potage*
Hot hors d'oeuvre—*Hors d'oeuvre chaud*
Fish—*Poisson*
Main course—*Grosse pièce*
Hot entrée—*Entrée chaude*
Cold entrée—*Entrée froide*
Sherbet—*Sorbet*
Roast—*Rôti*
Vegetable—*Légume*
Sweet dish—*Entremets*
Dessert—*Dessert*

If a savory dish were added to the menu in the last example above, the framework of the classical menu would be complete. The savory dish is served after the sweet dish (*entremets*).

The shortened version of the classical menu, as shown in figure 5-3, shows how some of the courses in the longer menu can be combined or omitted. The courses should be arranged in the proper order; however, there is greater flexibility in the menu and a greater variety of foods can be offered. A cold entrée, such as a mousse, may serve as a cold hors d'oeuvre; a chaud-froid or pâté may be substituted for the meat dish. In more elaborate menus, fish or light hot entrées may be used as the hot hors d'oeuvre. In simple luncheon menus, the more extensive entrées with vegetables are frequently used as the meat dish rather than as a main course. A roast served with appropriate vegetables may also replace the *grosse pièce*. Frozen sherbets and the savories are omitted in the shortened

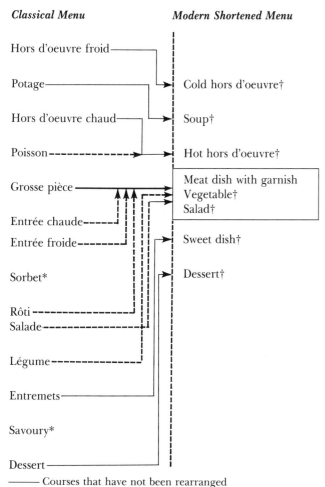

Classical Menu

Hors d'oeuvre froid

Potage

Hors d'oeuvre chaud

Poisson

Grosse pièce

Entrée chaude

Entrée froide

Sorbet*

Rôti

Salade

Légume

Entremets

Savoury*

Dessert

Modern Shortened Menu

Cold hors d'oeuvre†

Soup†

Hot hors d'oeuvre†

Meat dish with garnish
Vegetable†
Salad†

Sweet dish†

Dessert†

———— Courses that have not been rearranged
– – – Courses that have been rearranged
   * Omitted from short menus
   † Need only be offered as alternatives in modern lunch
     menus

Figure 5-3. Menu framework.

menu, but all the other courses maintain their traditional function.

5.1.2 Types of Menus

The following are six types of menus.

The Lunch Menu

This is the midday meal, and it is generally composed of light food. Fruit juice or vegetable juice is often served instead of soup.

The Brunch

The name is derived from combining the words breakfast and lunch, and the brunch menu is usually a combination of the two. Some brunch menus include foods that are traditional breakfast favorites. Others provide a wide choice of fruits, hot breads, eggs, meats, coffee, and tea.

The Dinner

This is the evening meal, and includes three to five courses. The dinner usually represents the main meal of the day.

The Gala Menu

This is a menu for festive evenings. The menu should be carefully planned for the specific occasion, and the food and service must be flawless.

The Light Menu

This menu is for midday or evening meals for days of fasting. Although meat is generally omitted from this menu, fish, eggs, milk and cheese products, vegetables, pasta, rice, fruit juices, and fruits may be served.

The Vegetarian Menu

Foods of animal origin are not permitted in this type of menu; however, eggs and milk products are used under some conditions. All kinds of plant foods and vegetable and fruit juices are of special importance in these menus.

5.1.3 Examples of Menus

The menu shown in figure 5-4 was selected for a dinner for twelve persons. It is appropriate for a small group; however, it would be extremely difficult to serve the same menu to a large group of people, as it would be impossible to maintain the quality and proper temperature of the mixed grill. Crêpes for a small group can be prepared at the table quite easily, but it would be impractical to serve this dessert to a large group. Figure 5-5 shows an example of a menu that could be served to a group of 100 or more persons.

Clear Oxtail Soup with Marsala
Fillet of Sole, Home Style
American Mixed Grill
Puffed Potatoes
Cardoons with Beef Marrow
Mimosa Salad
Crêpes Suzette
Fruit Basket

Figure 5-4. Menu for twelve guests.

Clear Oxtail Soup with Marsala
Roast Rib of Beef, American Style
French-Fried Potatoes
Cardoons with Beef Marrow
Mimosa Salad
Iced Vacherin with Fruits

Figure 5-5. Menu for 100 guests.

Figure 5-6 is a menu for a conference of 800 persons. The individual courses were selected for fast service. A slice of game pâté and a piece of melon were arranged on each plate, and these were placed on the table before the guests arrived. The Cumberland sauce was also placed on the table. The waiters served half a spring chicken and green beans on the prewarmed plate of each guest. The potatoes and salad were served separately on the table. The fruit, garnished with whipped cream, was served in small individual glass bowls.

The dinner menus in figures 5-7 and 5-8 represent holiday offerings for fine restaurants or hotels. The New Year's Eve Supper menu in figure 5-9 is suitable for a supper following festive occasions or at gala balls. On such occasions light cold buffets, like that shown in figure 5-10, are also popular.

Game Pâté—Melon with Kirsch
Cumberland Sauce
Clear Soup with Diced Vegetables
Roast Spring Chicken
Potato Chips
Buttered Green Beans
Salad
Chilled Fruit with Whipped Cream

Figure 5-6. Menu for 800 guests.

Medallions of Rock Lobster on Tomato Mousse, Duchess Style
Red Turtle Soup with Sherry
Baby Chicken Stuffed with Goose Liver in Casserole
Truffle Sauce—Pearl Potatoes
Asparagus Tips and Green Peas with Butter and Parsley
Endive Salad
Christmas Pudding with Cognac
or
Frozen Soufflé
Fruit Basket

Figure 5-7. Christmas dinner menu.

Birds' Nest Soup with Port
Slices of Poached Turbot—Riche Sauce
Duckling with Orange in Cocotte
Bigarade Sauce—Mirette Potatoes
Sautéed Brussels Sprouts
Hearts of Lettuce Salad
Chocolate Blancmange
or
Biscuit Tortoni with Maraschino Cherries
Cookies, French Style
Assorted Fruit

Figure 5-8. New Year's Day dinner menu.

Clear Soup, Princess Style
Beef Wellington
Red-wine Sauce
Straw Potatoes—Tomatoes Clamart with Peas
Endive Salad
Ice Cream Charlotte-Melba Sauce
Candies

Figure 5-9. New Year's Eve supper menu.

Lobster Cocktail with Caviar
Medallions of Salmon, Norwegian Style
Pâté of Venison—Mousse of Goose Liver
Poularde with Truffles
Assorted Salads
Ice Coupe—Cassata, Naples Style
Plum Cake—Candies
Fruit Basket

Figure 5-10. Cold-buffet menu.

5.2 Types of Meals

The classical and formerly common types of meals such as breakfast (*petit déjeuner*), lunch (*déjeuner*), dinner (*dîner*), and supper (*souper*) have, as a result of changing life-styles, been altered both in composition and in terms of the hour at which they are consumed. The most important types of meals are, therefore, reclassified.

Breakfast—*Petit déjeuner*

Depending upon nationality and local custom, breakfast may be anything from a cup of black coffee or tea with biscuits to a full-scale English breakfast. The English breakfast is considered a main meal and may include fruit juices, fresh fruits, tea, marmalade and toast, cold cereals or porridge, egg dishes, fish dishes (haddock and kippers), ham, chicken, or lamb chops.

Lunch—*Déjeuner*

Usually served at midday, lunch consists of simpler foods and fewer courses than dinner. The luncheon menu often includes a light main course, fruit juice, salad, and fruit. A hearty soup served with bread and fruit or a sandwich is also a popular midday meal. Salads and fruit juices are sometimes served instead of a soup. Cheese, fruits, or a light frozen specialty are the usual desserts.

Snacks

Small hot or cold dishes that can be combined with salads, fruits, yogurt, or cottage cheese are favorite snack items. Small portions of all kinds of sausages, cold meats, and sandwiches are also eaten as snacks.

Dinner—*Dîner*

Dinner, served in the evening, is usually the principal meal of the day in most restaurants and hotels. At this time of day, the customer has more time for leisurely dining. Most dinner menus will consist of three to five of the following courses:

- Cold hors d'oeuvre
- Soup
- Fish or hot hors d'oeuvre
- Main course with garnishes
- Sweet dish or dessert

The Midnight Supper

This generally refers to a gala menu of four to six courses served late in the evening on festive occasions. The food should always be of excellent quality, easy to digest, and carefully served.

Buffet

Cold buffets in the past were usually identified with after-theater performances, balls, and other late evening occasions. Today cold, warm, and combination buffets are served at lunchtime and in the evening. Buffets provide the opportunity for the ultimate in culinary art, decor, color, variety of food, and fast service. A large group of people can be accommodated easily with a minimum of service. Cold buffets are especially popular during the summer months.

5.3 Menus for the Day

The printed menu is an important merchandiser. The customer frequently forms his first impression of the restaurant from the menu presented to him. It should be designed to harmonize with the decor and atmosphere, and it should be planned to function as a promotion tool that will increase sales through customer satisfaction. Whether a simple menu that lists the menu for the day or one that is more complex with a wide selection of courses and dishes, the menu should be written in a clear style and arranged on the card so that the guest can make his choices easily.

Menu formats differ widely among establishments; there are, however, certain fundamentals that are basic to any menu design regardless of the format (see figure 5-11):

- The menu should be on durable paper stock that is stain resistant.
- The size should permit easy handling at the table.
- The format should be simple with adequate margins and spacing for easy reading.

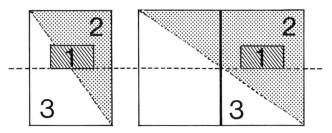

Figure 5-11. The eye-catching points on a menu. Area 1 is where the guest looks first; area 2, second; area 3, last. Print the specialties and high-profit items in area 1, the popular items in area 2, and the low-profit items in area 3.

- The size and style of the print should be legible.
- Food items should be listed in the classical order or in the sequence that the food will be ordered (small cold, small hot, large cold, and large hot dishes).
- Specialties on the menu may be printed in bold-face type, in colored print, underlined, or attached on a colored rider or sticker.
- Descriptions of menu items should be worded to give a clear and interesting visual image of the food item; misleading terminology and information should be avoided.
- The grammar, spelling, prices, and other information should be accurate.
- The menu should be spotlessly clean, free of marks and corrections.
- The name, address, telephone number, and days and hours of service should be listed on the menu.

The order of dishes on the following menu is not quite identical to that of the menu framework. Since the specialties for the day can consist of either the hot entrées or the main courses (taken from the full menu card), this group of dishes is listed after the entrées rather than after the main courses.

Cold hors d'oeuvre—*Hors d'oeuvre froids*
Soups—*Potages*
Hot hors d'oeuvre—*Hors d'oeuvre chauds*
Fish—*Poissons*
Hot entrées—*Entrée chaudes*
Specialties of the day—*Plats du jour*

Roasts—*Rôtis*
Vegetables—*Légumes*
Sweet dish—*Entremets*
Dessert—*Dessert*

Certain establishments offer a choice of vegetables, and the guest selects the one he wants with the meat he has ordered. In other restaurants the vegetables and garnishes that accompany the meat are indicated on the menu.

If the hot dishes must be prepared in advance because of the required preparation time, then these dishes and the main dishes on the menu for the day (also previously prepared) should follow the hot entrées in a separate group as "Specialties of the day"—*Plats du jour*. These dishes are usually less expensive than the so-called made-to-order dishes. The menu in figure 5-12 is an example of a menu of the day.

The menu style should be simple, attractive, and easy to read. It may be designed so that specialties or daily features can be added in the form of a clip-on or sticker. Menu items are sometimes identified with a number, which simplifies ordering.

5.4 Presentation of the Food

The saying "the eye eats too" is fully justified. The meal service or presentation of the food has an important effect on customer acceptance. The table settings should be coordinated with the foodservice, so that the food, china, glassware, table linens, and silver are both attractive and functional. The food must be of excellent quality and at the proper temperature for palatability and safety. The table appointments should be attractive, and the food should be served by personnel who are efficient, courteous, and sensitive to the customers' needs. Serving food at the proper temperature is perhaps the greatest factor in controlling the quality of food that has been carefully prepared. Practices that will aid in maintaining hot foods at the proper temperature are these:

- Heat food to the proper temperature before serving.
- Heat plates, bowls, and serving dishes before dishing food into them.
- Heat sauces and gravies before pouring over food or into sauceboat.

Cold hors d'oeuvres
Mixed hors d'oeuvres
Malossol caviar
Goose liver pâté
Russian eggs

Hors d'oeuvres froids
Hors d'oeuvres variés
Caviar Malossol
Pâté de foie gras
Oeufs à la russe

Soups
Cup of consommé
Clear oxtail soup
Cream of asparagus soup

Potages
Consommé double en tasse
Oxtail clair
Crème Argenteuil

Hot hors d'oeuvres
Pastry shells garnished with chicken
Emmentaler cheese omelet
Fried eggs Meyerbeer

Hors d'oeuvres chauds
Bouchée à la reine
Omelette emmentaloise
Oeufs au plat Meyerbeer

Fish
Blue river trout—Hollandaise sauce
Whitefish, meunière style
Fried perch—Tartar sauce

Poissons
Truite au bleu—Sauce hollandaise
Féra meunière
Perches frites—Sauce tartare

Entrées
Tournedos Rossini
Sirloin steak with béarnaise sauce
Veal cutlets, hunter style
Lamb chops with green beans
Calf's liver, English style

Entrées
Tournedos Rossini
Entrecôte béarnaise
Côte de veau chasseur
Côtelettes d'agneau aux haricots verts
Foie de veau á l'anglaise

Specialties of the day
Osso buco, Milanese style
Breast of veal, bourgeois style

Plats du jour
Osso buco milanaise
Tendron de veau bourgeoisie

Roasts
Spring chicken with vegetables
Saddle of hare Mirza

Rôtis
Poulet de grain en casserole
Râble de lièvre Mirza

Vegetables
Asparagus with melted butter
Green peas with mint
Sautéed green beans
Tomatoes, Provençe style
Boiled potatoes
Sautéed potatoes
French-fried potatoes
Mixed salad

Légumes
Asperges en branches—Beurre fondu
Petits pois à la menthe
Haricots verts sautés
Tomates provençale
Pommes nature
Pommes sautées
Pommes frites
Salades diverses

Figure 5-12. A menu for the day, including specialties.

Sweet dishes
Soufflé Rothschild
Crêpes Suzette
Mixed fruits with Kirsch
Stewed fruits
Assorted cakes
Ice creams
Peach sundae

Entremets
Soufflé Rothschild
Crêpes Suzette
Macédoine de fruits au kirsch
Compotes
Gâteaux divers
Glaces
Coupe Melba

Dessert
Fruits and cheeses

Dessert
Fruits et fromages

Our Specialties
Scotch smoked salmon on toast
Goose liver medallions—Chilled melon
Pheasant terrine, gourmet style
Clear oxtail soup with diced vegetables
Bouillabaisse, Marseilles style
Rock lobster Thermidor
Stuffed sole, chef's style
Mixed grill special
Veal cutlet en papillote
Stuffed leg of chicken Louisette
Saddle of venison Baden-Baden
Paella Valenciana
Chicken curry, Bombay style
Porterhouse steak, Mexican style
Grand Marnier frozen soufflé
Pears with chocolate sauce
Pineapple crepes flambé
Baked alaska

Nos Specialites
Toast de saumon fumé d'Ecosse
Médaillons de foie gras—Melon rafraîchi
Terrine de faisan à la façon des gourmets
Oxtail clair brunoise
Bouillabaisse marseillaise
Langouste Thermidor
Sole farcie à la mode du chef
Mixed grill spécial maison
Côte de veau en papillote
Jambonneau de poularde Louisette
Selle de chevreuil Baden-Baden
Paëlla valenciana
Curry poulet Bombay
Porterhouse steak mexicana
Soufflé glacé Grand Marnier
Poires Williams Suchard
Crêpes à l'ananas flambées
Omelette norvégienne

Figure 5-12. *continued.*

- Serve food to guests immediately after it has been dished.
- Cover all hot foods with a warm plate cover after dishing on the plate.
- Prepare deep-fried foods just before serving, drain, and serve on a dish covered with paper.
- Avoid serving portions that are too large.

The dishes in which the food is served must be appropriate for the particular food item. Not only does the properly designed serving dish enhance the appearance of the food, it also simplifies the service.

Today earthenware dishes are available in shapes and sizes to suit the character of the particular food, and food served in these dishes will retain the heat better than in almost any other serving dish. Rich soups, beef broths, and gratinated soups are especially attractive when served in earthenware or copper dishes. The soup should be stirred gently from the bottom so that the vegetables and other contents can be distributed evenly into the serving dish. Croutons, puffs, and crisp biscuits are usually served in a separate dish and added to the soup at the table.

If boiled potatoes are served on the same plate with

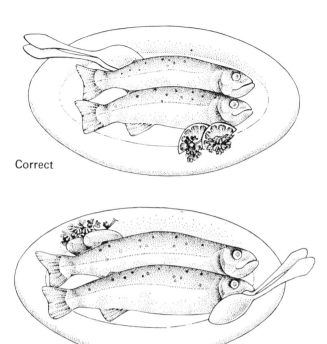

Correct

Incorrect

Figure 5-13. Presentation of fish.

poached fish, the potatoes should be arranged attractively in small quantities, or they should be served separately in a vegetable dish. Blue fish should always be served with the court bouillon in a special casserole or earthenware dish to prevent changing color or cooling.

Egg dishes should be served on porcelain or glass, but not on silver, because it will discolor on contact with egg.

Vegetables served as garnishes should be served on a plate large enough to arrange them attractively.

Fish, meat, and vegetables that are served in a sauce should not be disguised by the sauce. Roasted meat should never be covered with a sauce or gravy. If the meat is sliced and arranged on a platter, the connoisseur can admire the artistry of the cook. Since even the best sauces and gravies will change the color and appearance of the meat, they should be served separately in a sauceboat.

A bouquet of fresh watercress is an attractive garnish when a roast is served without vegetables. Meat

scallops, steaks, and cutlets should be served with lemon and parsley if no other garnishes are available. A whole fish should be garnished by placing a cluster of parsley and lemon wedges beside the head of the fish; the garnish is placed near the bone of a chop. (See figure 5-13.)

The cook needs to know how the waiter will present and serve the dish to the guest. He can then arrange the food on the dish so that the waiter can serve the food simply or the guest can help himself easily. The waiter should always stand to the left of the guest and present the correct side of the platter to him. For example, when serving a whole fish, it will be the side of the dish toward which the tail is pointing; and, when serving slices of fish or meat, it should be the side of the dish with the last or top slice that is nearest the guest. If garnishes or vegetables are placed on only one side of the dish, they should be arranged in such a way that the guest does not have to reach over the meat to serve himself vegetables. The guest should always be served from the left side. (See figure 5-14.)

Soufflés should be prepared and timed so that they can be served without delay when removed from the oven. The alert waiter will place the necessary plates in front of the guests and serve the soufflé immediately. Otherwise, the soufflé will collapse. Soufflé puddings and gnocchi, Parisian style, are also delicate items and should be served in the same way.

The preparation and presentation of cold dishes is an art that requires culinary skill and imagination. Complete organization of the work, an adequate supply of appropriate serving dishes, and sufficient quantities of perfectly prepared clear gelatin are basic essentials. Bases made from semolina, rice, and butter are sometimes used. However, to be most effective, they should be a pure white color. Finely diced aspic is more attractive than plain aspic. There should always be complete harmony between the garnishes and the entrée. This harmony concerns the use of the garnish, as well as the content of the garnish itself.

Only edible substances, such as truffles, leeks, sweet peppers, eggs, pickles, capers, and radishes, should be used for decorating food. The so-called *pièces montées* or pompous culinary structures are now

Figure 5-14. Serve the guest from the left side.

considered out of date and are no longer used for decorating. Today, decorations and centerpieces for tables and buffets often include ice sculptures, floral arrangements, elaborate creations made with royal icing, and artistically garnished arrays of food.

The presentation of cold dishes requires a sensitivity for the combination of colors, shapes, and textures to achieve complete harmony between the appearance of the food, the table appointments, and the decorations.

5.5 The Service

There are many types of service. Each differs from the other, and each type will differ among establishments. The goal of each is to serve quality food attractively and efficiently. To achieve this goal, certain basic requirements must be met, regardless of the type of service.

5.5.1 *Rules of Service*

Good service is dependent upon the *mise en place,* or the preliminary preparation. This requires organizing the work. The cutlery, glasses, silence cloths, tablecloths, napkins, serving dishes, coffee and tea services, plate warmers, banquet carts, and the serving cart for flaming should be in place and ready for use.

Certain rules for serving guests are valid for any type of service:

- *Presenting the food:* The waiter should stand to the left of the guest and hold the serving dish close to the guest's plate, with the serving cutlery pointing toward the guest, so that he can serve himself more easily.
- *Serving the food from the dish:* The food is always served from the guest's left. The waiter should ask the guest what he would like before serving the food onto his plate.
- *Serving the food using a service table:* The dishes are served from a service table using plate warmers. This enables the waiter to have both hands free so that he can serve the food onto the plates more quickly and efficiently.
- *The placement:* The glasses, empty plates, or plates with the food, and cups and saucers are placed on the table from the right, with the exception of the bread plates, salad plates, and finger bowls. The latter are used on the left and are, therefore, placed from the left.
- *Clearing:* Plates are also cleared from the right. Serving dishes, bowls, sauceboats, and salad bowls are removed first, then the plates and glasses. Each time the table is cleared, any soilage or breadcrumbs should be removed.

5.5.2 *Types of Service*

The types of service were formerly named after their country of origin. Thus, one used to talk about English, French, and Russian service. Now the services are named more objectively.

The Banquet Service

This service is used for a given number of people who are to be served a predetermined menu simultaneously. The appetizer is often on the table before the guests are seated. The food is usually dished onto warm plates in the kitchen. The plates are then taken into the dining room in heated carts or on trays. The waiter removes the appetizer dishes from the table and then serves the dinner plates to the guests. In another type of banquet service, the food is prepared and arranged on heated serving platters and dishes in the kitchen. The waiter takes the platters of food and the heated dinner plates into the dining room. The waiter places an empty dinner plate in front of each guest and then serves the food from each of the serving dishes onto each guest's plate.

The waiter clears the dinner plate, salad plate, bread and butter plate, and silver from each guest before the dessert is served. The coffee cups and saucers are sometimes placed on the table before the meal is served. The waiter fills the cups from a coffee server.

Efficiency and planning are essential when organizing banquets and/or catering for functions. The first move in the right direction is a good booking/reservation system, of which an example is shown in figure 5-15. Obviously, each booking form has to be made to suit the situation; it is impossible to show an example that suits every establishment. The form shown contains every relevant detail for a jubilee dinner for 100 persons.

The following points are important:

- Copies must be sent to all parties involved (kitchen, celler, etc.).
- Special wishes of the client must be noted (such as diets).
- The ordered wines must be in stock.

- The menu must be arranged within the scope and possibilities of the establishment, the available staff, and equipment. (No use putting a suckling pig on the menu if you do not have an oven large enough to cook it.)
- The banquet manager must discuss all details with the kitchen chef and the restaurant manager before completing the booking with the client.

The *Table d'Hôte* Service

Table d'hôte refers to the simultaneous service of the same menu at an established price. It may offer no choices, or it may provide a limited selection of items within categories, such as a juice, soup, or fruit cup for the appetizer. Each waitress or waiter should be able to serve ten or twelve guests.

The *à Part* Service

Contrary to the *table d'hôte* service, with the *à part* service the guests are served individually. Although all the guests have the same menu, they do not all have to appear for the meal at the same time. The dishes are placed on the tables so that the guests can help themselves, or they are offered and either served by the waiter or merely held while the guest helps himself. The dish is then placed on the table.

The *à la Carte* Service

The guest selects items from the selection offered on the menu. Each item is given a separate price. The *à la carte* service is most often employed in restaurants. In some establishments, the dishes are placed on plate-warmers within reach of the guest, so that he can help himself; in others, the food is shown to the guest and then dished onto the plate and served by the waiter.

Self-Service

The guest selects his own food and beverage and collects his tray and cutlery from a service counter. He usually then pays the cashier and goes to a dining table. The cafeteria is a well-known example of this

BANQUET RESERVATION

Name___*John Adams*___

Address___*923 Water Street*___

___*Ourtown, Maine 56789*___

Phone___*555-6789*___

Booking date___*10/3/XX*___

Event___*Company banquet*___

Room___*Conference*___

Time___*1:00–4:00 PM*___

Number___*100*___

Note___*VIP*___

Music *Hussey & Lange duo, phone 555-8910*

Menu cards

number___*100 + 15*___

function___*jubilee*___

text___*Congratulations*___

___*to Adams and Sons on*___

___*their first 50 years*___

Kitchen order

Time___*12:15 P.M.*___

Number of persons___*100*___

Area___*4*___

Tidbits___*crudités, nuts, chips*___

Table arrangement

Service	Menu
Plates (100)	Asparagus
Sauceboats (10)	Hollandaise sauce
Soup bowls (10)	Oxtail soup with sherry
Cocottes (10)	Spring chicken périgourdine
Vegetable dishes (10)	Parisian potatoes
Vegetable dishes (10)	Glazed carrots
Cheese platters (5)	Vacherin Mont-d'Or
Dessert platters (10)	Charlotte royale

Number of waiters___*10*___

Particulars
  Decorations, music, dais, projector, wines, soft drinks, liqueurs, coffee, cigars, flowers, candles, menu cards, name cards

Predinner drink _105 Pommerol brut 1976_

Wines:
207	*Rüdesheiner*	1982
222	*Fendent Sion*	1982
515	*Maienfelder Beerli*	1981
521	*Vosne-Romanée*	1978
533	*St-Emilion*	1972

Account to___*C. Jones, Adams & Sons*___

Food___*See kitchen order*___

Predinner drinks___*$1.50 per*___

Decorations___*$100*___

Music___*$500*___

Completed by___*Sara Green*___

Date___*5/6/XX*___

Distribute to: Manager; control; kitchen; restaurant; cellar, banquet manager; office

Figure 5-15. Banquet reservation form.

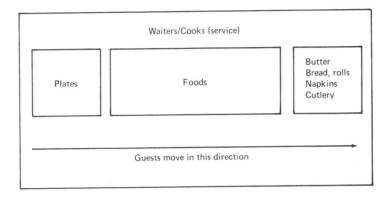

Figure 5-16. The organization of a cold buffet.

type of service. Self-service is popular in establishments where large numbers of guests arrive at the same time and a large turnover is experienced. There are several types of cafeterias, but most specialize in fast service and low cost. Some smaller establishments also use the self-service system.

The Buffet Service

The best known is the cold buffet, although this type of service may also include a complete meal from the soup to the dessert. The various foods, usually elaborate presentations, are placed upon a table from which the guests make their choice. (See figure 5-16.) Plates and cutlery are also on the buffet table, or on a separate table. The guests serve themselves, or the food is placed on their plates by service personnel. The guest usually pays a flat rate price, which is based on the number of choices offered.

5.6 Menu Spelling

The standard references for menu spelling are:

- French: *Larousse Gastronomique* and *Larousse*
- English: *The Concise Oxford Dictionary* and *Webster's International Dictionary*

The rules for spelling that are contained in these works should be followed. The so-called international menu language, in which the first letter of nouns and fantasy names must be written in capitals, should, in the interest of standardization, no longer be used.

French Spelling

In French menus, except at the beginning of a line, all words are written in lowercase, except the first letter. Proper names, fantasy names, geographical areas, and place names are spelled with a capital letter only when used as nouns, as shown below:

> *Potage parisienne*
>   but
> *Asperges du Valais* (area name)
> *Entrecôte Café de Paris* (place name)
> *Emincé Touring* (fantasy name)
> *Coupe Melba* (proper name)

The phrase *à la* or *à la mode de,* as it should be written, is used as little as possible, in order to keep repetition in the menu to a minimum. The phrase *à la* is only used in the sense of:

- *à la façon de* (du, de la)—in the fashion of
- *à la mode de*—in the style of
- *à la manière de*—in the manner of

It should also be used when naming foods:

> *Epinards à la crème* (name of the food)
> *Risotta à la turque* (à la manière)
> *Sole à l'italienne* (à la mode)
> *Truite à la bernoise* (à la façon)

The use of *à la* should be maintained where the name

concerned begins with a vowel, and when its omission would result in a phonetic dissonance:

> *Ravioli à l'italienne*
> *Pêche à l'impératrice*

À la is not used with proper names when used as a dedication or honor to a person:

> *Tournedos Rossini*
> *Pêche Melba*
> *Poularde pochée Demidoff*

The term *à la* is sometimes used with names of places or regions:

> *à la mode de Caen*
> *Ravioli à la milanaise*
> or
> *Ravioli milanaise*

When in doubt, *à la* should be omitted.

It should be remembered that *à la* changes to *au* or *aux* depending on the noun concerned:

> *Spaghetti à la crème*
> *Spaghetti au fromage*
> *Spaghetti aux morilles*

When *à la* is omitted, the adjectives are expressed in the feminine, since *à la* is being used instead of *à la mode*, as in *Potage parisienne*. If it is the name of a food, however, then the adjective is expressed in the same gender as the noun, as in *Saumon fumé suédois*—Swedish smoked salmon, but *Saumon fumé à la suédoise (à la mode)*—Smoked salmon, Swedish style.

Spelling of Russian Proper Names

In order to ensure a common way of spelling Russian proper names, those ending with *ov* or *of* will all take the ending *off*: Demidoff, Malakoff, Stroganoff. In proper Russian spelling, these words end in *ow*. If the menu is written in French, *ov* should be used.

English Spelling

Everything is written in small letters, except for proper names and geographical names: Swiss cheese, Peter the Great. All adjectives derived from proper names are written with a capital letter: English style, French dressing, Parisian steak, Victorian pies. The *à la* or *à la mode de* are normally translated into English as "style": Russian style, Milanese style, Viennese style, Charterhouse style.

Drinks

All drinks in English and French are written with small letters, except for brand names, such as Grand Marnier, Campari, Canadian Club, Courvoisier, Martell; for example, omelet with rum—*omelette au rhum*, but omelet with Grand Marnier—*omelette au Grand Marnier*.

Rules Applicable to All Languages

Spelling mistakes can be avoided by using the dictionaries and reference books already mentioned.

The menu should be written in the language of the country concerned; in international establishments the language is French.

The layout and spelling should be without errors. The words should either be positioned symmetrically, or every new line should begin at the lefthand margin.

Generally the first letter of a new line will be a capital letter, except where it is a continuation of the name of a dish.

> *correct*
> Roast saddle of venison
>   with game sauce—
> *Selle de chevreuil rôti*
>   *chasseur*

> *incorrect*
> Roast saddle of venison
>   With game sauce—
> *Selle de chevreuil rôti*
>   *Chasseur*

The menu texts are always based upon one guest. If several persons can be served from one piece of food, it should still be described in the singular. For example, the correct term would be Leg of lamb, boulangère style—*Gigot d'agneau boulangère*, not Legs of lamb, boulangère style—*Gigots d'agneau boulangère*.

If at least two pieces of the food are to be served to each person, then the dish should be expressed in the plural. For example, Fillets of golden trout, home style—*Filets de rouget bonne femme*—is correct; Fillet of golden trout, home style—*Filet de rouget bonne femme*—is incorrect.

Each course should be clearly separated from the next by means of a space or a line. Descriptive terms that belong together should not be split up at the end of a line.

> *correct*
> Fillets of sole,
>   home style—
>   *Filets de sole*
>   *bonne femme*

> *incorrect*
> Fillets
>   of sole, home style—
>   *Filets*
>   *de sole bonne femme*

No abbreviations should be used within the text of the menu, for example *sc.* instead of *sauce,* or *fr.* instead of *fresh.*

Proper names that refer to a classical type of preparation should not be translated, nor should the *à la* or "style" form of description be used. For example, Ice coupe Melba—*Coupe Melba*—is correct; Ice coupe Melba style—*Coupe à la Melba*—is incorrect.

Well-known national dishes can be written in their original fashion: minestrone, not Italian vegetable soup; ravioli, not stuffed noodle squares; welsh rarebit, not Welsh cheese cream.

If the basic form of preparation is included in the description of a dish, there is no need to repeat it: *Fèra meunière,* not *Fèra dorée à la meunière;* Irish stew, not Irish stew à l'irlandaise; Roast prime rib of beef, not Roast prime rib of beef rôti.

The following menus illustrate French spelling and English translation:

FRENCH	ENGLISH
Déjeuner	**Lunch**
Cocktail de crevettes	Shrimp cocktail
Côtelettes de chevreuil	Venison cutlets
Baden-Baden	Baden-Baden
Pommes dauphine	Dauphine potatoes
Choux de Bruxelles aux marrons	Brussels sprouts with chestnuts
Soufflé au citron	Lemon soufflé
Sauce aux abricots	Apricot sauce
ou	or
Fromage et beurre	Cheese with butter
Dîner	**Dinner**
Consommé à la paysanne	Clear soup, peasant style
Perches frites	Deep-fried perch
Sauce tartare	Tartar sauce
Filet de boeuf Parmentier	Fillet of beef with potatoes
Chou-fleur à la crème	Cauliflower with cream sauce
Salade	Salad
Coupe Melba	Peach sundae

5.7 History of European Cookery

Cookery, the most ancient of the arts, dates back to the prehistoric age. Although little is known about prehistoric cookery, the discovery of the use of fire for culinary purposes during this period had a great influence on the diet of man. After fire was discovered, men gathered around the hearth and shared their meat and game. Other staple foods in the diets of these ancient peoples included roots, grains, fruits, honey, fish, milk, and eggs. Roasting was probably the first method of cooking. Meat was roasted on the hot embers of an open fire or on spits above the open flame.

Boiling, another mode of cookery in primitive times, was practiced before pottery and other cooking vessels were known. The hides and stomachs of animals were made into bags. Filled with food, water, and hot pebbles, the bags were dropped into a pit that was lined with stones and filled with water. Hot pebbles were added to the pit to maintain the cooking temperature throughout the cooking process.

More is known about cookery in Egypt than any other ancient civilization. Although there are no books or manuscripts of this period, pictorial records of bakers and cooks at work and inscriptions in hieroglyphics were found in tombs and on pyramids and clay tablets. Vegetables, fruit trees, vines, chicken, fish, and eggs were plentiful along the Nile. The Egyptians were known for their breadmaking and confections, and bakers were held in high esteem.

The Persians were notorious for their lavish banquets and feasts. The Assyrian king Sardanapalus introduced the first cooking contests, offering thousands of gold pieces and other rewards to those who produced a new dish. Marmalades made from the fabulous fruits of Persia, delicate sweets, and fine wines, served in elaborate vessels of gold, were in abundance at every feast. Some of the foods introduced by the Persians continue to be featured on menus throughout the world today.

It was from the Persians that the Greeks learned the art of cooking and dining. Until the middle of the fifth century B.C., there was little difference in the diets of the rich and poor in Greece. Barley pastes, barley gruel, and barley bread were the basic fare. The early Greeks ate four meals a day—breakfast or *acratisma;* dinner, *ariston* or *deiphon;* relish, *hesperisma;* and supper, *dorpe.* Later, luncheon replaced the midday dinner, and dinner was served at a later hour. The dinner soon developed into banquets or feasts for religious or social purposes. The best chefs of Greece, including Thimbron, Themacides, and Archestratus, were trained in Syberius, a city famous for its cuisine. Many recipes that have been handed down to us through the Romans and French were created in this city.

The Roman cuisine was based on the recipes and methods of cooking learned from the Greeks and from *De Re Coquinaria,* the first known book on cookery. This book was supposedly written by Apicius in the first century A.D.; however, the only known copies date from the eighth and ninth centuries. The Romans soon developed their own cuisine, which was more elaborate and more delicate than that of the Greeks. The magnificence of their banquets and gastronomical splendors continued to flourish until the end of the fourth century.

The fall of the Roman Empire brought a decline in the development of cookery, literature, and the arts. The monasteries, however, assumed an active role in keeping these arts alive. Large monasteries were complex communities with farms, trade schools, and commercial centers, as well as religious foundations. St. Gall in Switzerland, known for its culinary delicacies, was one of the first training centers for cooks.

The Romans took many of their traditions of cookery with them to England. It was the Germanic invaders, however, who had the greatest influence on English cookery. The dishes of the Celts, Saxons, and Normans became basic culinary fare. The majority of people in England were farmers and laborers. Their food was simple and hearty. The English banquets and feasts of the Middle Ages were extravagant affairs with an abundance of food and ale. It was during the Middle Ages that Christmas became a time of feasting. Great preparations were made for the twelve-day period from Christmas Eve to Epiphany. Throughout the Elizabethan period, there was an attitude of indifference toward the preparation of food, and this continued until many years later when hotels and clubs employed chefs from France.

Until early in the sixteenth century, the cooking of France was as unimaginative as that of England. In 1533, the Duke of Orleans married Catherine de Médicis of the well-known Florentine family. She took many of the famous chefs and pastry cooks of Italy with her to France. The French learned from these Italian masters and skillfully developed their own school of cooking. The cuisine of France continued to grow, and by the end of the seventeenth century, France was known throughout the world for its classic cuisine. The classic French cuisine implies a perfectly planned menu; fresh and superior ingredients; talented cooks; simple, artistic, and perfect presentations; subtle and balanced tastes; and an appreciative audience.

Chapter 6
Kitchen Accounting

Cost control is one of the prime functions of sound management in any foodservice operation. Effective cost control requires a system of procedures and records that serve as guidelines for effective and successful operation within the limits of the budget.

Prior to developing a system of procedures and records, certain management functions must be in effect to ensure achieving the highest possible gross profit. These functions include:

- Establishing purchasing methods in accordance with real needs
- Establishing methods for receiving food and supplies, including checks on quality, quantity, packaging, and portioning
- Establishing methods for menu planning, food production, storage control, and service
- Establishing selling prices (initial calculation)

The calculation of the gross profit of the kitchen (final calculation) acts as a barometer of good kitchen management. Where gross profit is too high, either too much is being saved in terms of quality or quantity, or the selling price is excessive. In both cases the result may be declining sales volume. If, on the other hand, the gross profit is too low, then inadequate purchasing practices, lack of quantity control, improper utilization of purchased goods, or low selling prices are probably the causes. To achieve a balance between maintaining profitability and good quality requires knowledge and skill. Only those who understand this relationship will be rewarded with good profits and satisfied guests. Obviously, the profitability of a

kitchen must be firmly based and calculated exactly and honestly.

It is not the intention here to explain accounts payable, inventories, accounts receivable, or balance sheets. The following principles for the establishment of the cost of food items have purposefully been kept simple and practical. Comprehensive teaching of this subject is a matter for the professional schools.

6.1 Initial Calculation of the Selling Price

The cost of raw materials includes the food cost of all goods necessary for preparing the dish. The additional charge to the raw material cost includes the overhead, all cost and expenses over and above those of the raw materials that are necessary for operation of the establishment. These operational costs include:

- Salaries in cash and kind
- Fringe benefits
- Energy, heating, lighting, and cleaning
- Marketing, promotion, office expenses, and supplies
- Repair and maintenance costs
- Interest and mortgage costs or rent

A predetermined net profit is included in the additional costs. An example of this calculation is shown in figure 6-1.

As a rule, management will determine the ratio of operational expenses to the raw material costs, which is then expressed as a percentage of the material cost. In figure 6-1, the figure was 190 percent, so that 190

Cost of raw material	100% base	$5.00
Additional operating costs, determined by management	190%	$9.50
Selling price	290%	$14.50

Figure 6-1. Raw material cost plus operating costs (including profit) equal selling price.

	$ Value	Percentage
Selling price	14.50	100% (base)
Raw costs	5.00	34.48% (5.00/14.50)
Gross profit	9.00	65.52% (9.50/14.50)

Figure 6-2. Gross profit equals selling price minus raw cost, divided by selling price.

percent of the raw cost ($5.00) of this dish is attributed to additional (operating) expenses: $9.50. The selling price is the sum of the raw cost and the operational cost, $14.50, and is equal to 290 percent of the raw cost.

A simplified calculation eliminates the need to add operational expenses repeatedly. The cost is obtained by multiplying the raw material costs by a constant. This constant is equal to one-hundredth of the selling price, which is expressed as a percentage of the raw material costs. For example, 290 (the total percentage) divided by 100 equals 2.9, the constant you can now multiply any raw cost by to determine total cost. You can also divide this constant into any total cost to calculate the raw material cost.

6.2 Calculation of Gross Profit

If the initial calculation of the selling price is a responsibility of the chef, he must be informed of the actual cost results so that he can modify his management techniques or his initial selling price calculation if necessary. In certain cases, particularly in small establishments, the calculation of the gross profit actually obtained is the responsibility of the chef.

Applying the same figures to one serving at $14.50, we obtain the results shown in figure 6-2. The gross profit obtained should correspond to the operational expenses.

6.3 Price Calculations for Menus and Dishes

To calculate food cost, taking into account the loss of weight after cutting, trimming and/or portioning (unless purchased already trimmed and portioned), the following formula is used:

$$\frac{\text{Price per pound} \times 100}{100\% - \text{trimmings }\%} = \text{Food cost}$$

For example, the actual food cost for 2 pounds cold roast beef must be determined. A piece of sirloin weighing 7 pounds was purchased for $28.00 ($4.00 per pound).

Trimmings:

Sinew and muscle	6%
Fat	6
Weight loss during roasting	20
	32% = 2.24 pounds
	(32% of 7 pounds)

The cost of the price *per pound* of cold roast beef is:

$$\frac{\$4.00 \times 100}{(100\% - 32\%) = 68\%} = \$5.88$$

For 2 pounds: 2 × $5.88 = *$11.76*

Figure 6-3 is an example of price calculations for a menu.

Dishes	Name of Raw Materials	Quantities for 10 Persons	Cost Per Unit as Purchased	Cost Per Item	Cost Total
Scrambled eggs with tomatoes	Toasted bread	1¾ pounds	.69/pound	1.21	
	Butter	1 ounce	.90/pound	.06	
	Eggs	20	.07/each	1.40	
	Cream	6 ounces	.98/pint	.36	
	Spices, salt	—	—	.01	
	Tomatoes, fresh	1 pound	.45/pound	.45	
	Oil	1 ounce	.90/pint	.06	
	Onion	1 ounce	.12/pound	.01	
	Parsley	1 ounce	.50/pound	.03	$ 3.59
Cold consommé with sherry	Beef, slices	2¼ pounds	2.50/pound	5.62	
	Egg whites	2	.04/each	.08	
	Leeks	1 ounce	.50/pound	.04	
	Celery	1 ounce	.29/pound	.02	
	Carrots	1 ounce	.16/pound	.01	
	Tomato paste	1 ounce	.45/pound	.03	
	Onion	1 ounce	.12/pound	.01	
	Stock	5¼ pints	2.32/gallon	.73	
	Spices, salt	—	—	.01	
	Vegetable brunoise	3½ ounces	—	.10	
	Sherry	6 ounces	2.10/quart	.42	$ 7.07
Veal chops with mushrooms	Rib of veal	4 pounds	3.00/pound	12.00	
	Spices, salt	—	—	.04	
	Flour	1 ounce	.105/pound	.01	
	Shortening	2 ounces	.75/pound	.09	
	White wine	6 ounces	2.10/quart	.42	
	Cream	12 ounces	.98/pint	.74	
	Mushrooms	2¼ pounds	1.20/pound	2.70	
	Butter	1 ounce	.90/pound	.05	
	Flour	1 ounce	.105/pound	.01	$16.06
Baked potatoes	Potatoes	5 pounds	.23/pound	1.15	
	Butter	2 ounces	.90/pound	.10	
	Flour	½ ounce	.105/pound	.003	
	Parsley	1 ounce	.50/pound	.03	
	Chives	1 ounce	—	.03	
	Nutmeg, spices, salt	—	—	.04	
	Clarified butter	6 ounces	.75/pound	.29	$ 1.64
Green salad	Lettuce	3 heads	.29/head	.87	
	Salad dressing	1 pint	3.65/gallon	.46	$ 1.33
Strawberries and cream	Strawberries	3¼ pounds	.65/pound	2.11	
	Sugar	2 ounces	.18/pound	.02	
	Cream	1 pint	.98/pint	.98	$ 3.11
Rolls	Rolls	10	.02/each	.20	$ .20
	Cost of raw material				$33.00
	Selling price = Raw material costs × constant: *2.9*				$95.70
	Selling price per person				$ 9.57

Figure 6-3. Food-cost calculation of a menu.

Part II
Cooking

Chapter 7
Basic Principles

7.1 The Art of Cooking

What does the art of cooking mean? It means that one knows a great deal about the practical aspects of cookery and cooking techniques. It presupposes a full and precise knowledge of food; a well-developed sense of taste and smell; a sensitivity for color, texture, and shape or form; and the ability to coordinate all major elements into complete harmony.

According to John Ruskin, a nineteenth-century English writer and art critic, the art of cooking includes a grandmother's thrift, a knowledge of modern chemistry, a Frenchman's sense of artistry, and an Arab's hospitality. In summary, the art of cooking means providing high-quality food and service to the complete satisfaction of the guest.

7.1.1 *Classical Cooking*

Classical cooking refers to French cookery that reached its zenith in the kings' palaces during the seventeenth and eighteenth centuries. French cookery is subject to continuous change and is closely linked with changes occurring in other art forms. The goal to be achieved today is the combination of classical dishes coupled with artistic but simple, decorative foods. Only by understanding cookery in this sense is it possible to achieve perfection in the practice of culinary art.

Classical cookery includes all the basic dishes together with those specialties and dishes adapted from the old French and international cookery. On the other hand, those historical monstrosities, with their pompous and unaesthetic structures or pretentious ornamentation are not a part of classical cooking. Only attractive presentations that satisfy the palate and the eye are classical. This is especially true when the name of the dish also corresponds to its actual ingredients. The names *Rossini, Colbert, à la bordelaise, à la portugaise, à la florentine,* and *Argenteuil* are recognized classical names, and recipes for these dishes require specific ingredients.

7.1.2 *Plain Cooking*

Unlike classical cookery, plain cooking originally started in private kitchens. The food is simpler but nevertheless nutritionally adequate and carefully prepared. Many regions and local areas have their own particular cuisine. The climate and geographical conditions, the background of the people, and the traditions and customs of the area often influence the eating patterns and nutritional needs of the people. Many of the dishes unique to a specific region have gained widespread acceptance, as more and more emphasis is placed on nutritional and health needs of the people.

7.1.3 *Modern Cooking*

Although classical cookery must constitute the basis of all innovations, the trend today is toward safe and efficient storage, simplification of food preparation methods and service, and improved nutrition. The classical art of cooking and modern cooking depend on one another. Only those innovations and classical dishes that conform to basic nutritional principles in terms of ingredients, methods of preparation, and all other culinary rules can be considered modern.

The increasing interest in nutrition and in the nutritive value of foods has greatly influenced food choices. These choices are based on foods that are rich in nutrients, low in calories, and free of synthetic additives. In an effort to reduce fat consumption, whole milk and cream are being replaced by low-fat milk and yogurt; herbs are replacing butter as seasoning for vegetables; more fish and fresh vegetables are being consumed; and fresh fruits are substituted for desserts that are high in calories. The use of basic methods of preparation, such as blanching, poaching, steaming, and grilling, that will conserve nutrients is as important as providing variety. Synthesizing classical cookery with those principles that lead to the health and well-being of the individual is basic to modern cooking.

7.1.4 *Dietary Cooking*

A specific diet is based on the modifications of the nutritional components of the normal diet. Included in these changes are modifications in the number of calories; modifications in one or more of the nutrients (proteins, fats, carbohydrates, vitamins, and minerals); and modifications in texture and seasoning (liquid, bland, or low residue). Although most of the normal foods are used, they must be tailored to meet the needs of the individual and be prepared so that none of the nutritional content is lost or damaged.

7.1.5 *Nouvelle Cuisine*

The French introduced the so-called *nouvelle cuisine*, meaning "the new kitchen." The essence of this cooking trend is to use fresh ingredients and to retain as much as possible the natural taste of the ingredients. This means shorter cooking times and fewer additives. Fatty roux (flour and fat) is avoided; soups and sauces are thickened, if necessary, without using flour. *Nouvelle cuisine* dishes are never heavy and/or rich. The food is cooked *à la minute* (to order) as much as possible; vegetables must remain crisp.

The following well-known French kitchen-masters are followers or initiators of the new cooking trend and have published their recipes in various books:

- Paul Bocuse
- Michel Guérard
- Jean and Pierre Troisgros
- Roger Vergé
- Alain Chapel
- Henri Lévy
- Alfred Girardet
- Jean-Claude Vrinat

7.2 Cooking Techniques

The term *cooking techniques* refers to the skills and methods required for the preparation of high-quality hot and cold dishes. These techniques may vary to some extent depending on the types of food and the serving system, but in principle they are the same. Knowledge progresses through the following categories, with understanding of one prerequisite for understanding those that follow.

1. *Basic information:* different preparation, cutting, dressing, carving, and preservation techniques; proper cooking and storage temperatures; portion control
2. *Basic methods of preparation:* blanching, poaching, boiling, steaming, deep-frying, sautéing, grilling, broiling, gratinating, baking, roasting, braising, glazing, stewing
3. *Mise en place:* preparation and finishing of hot and cold dishes and pastries
4. *Basic preparations:* marinades, meat jellies, breadings, stuffings, stocks, sauces, soups, seasoned butters, doughs, creams
5. *Basic elements of dishes and their garnishes:* sauces, soups, hors d'oeuvre, egg dishes, fish dishes, entrées, main dishes, salads, vegetables, potatoes, pasta and rice, desserts
6. *Basic elements of meals:* menus

Knowledge of basic information, basic methods of preparation, *mise en place,* and basic preparations is absolutely necessary. This fundamental methodology and a knowledge of the basic types of preparation and of recipes are prerequisites for the preparation of quality food. The basic elements of meals incorporate all these cooking techniques. The individual who is responsible for the preparation of food must appreciate and understand all the techniques to ensure efficiency and quality in food preparation.

7.2.1 *The Cooking Process*

Cooking generally means conducting heat into the food to change and improve it in terms of palatability, bacteriological content, and taste. If moist heat, such as water, is used, the soluble substances in the food are transferred into the fluid, for example, infusing herbs, tea, and coffee. With dry heat, such as the oven, a part of the water evaporates, and the food taste becomes stronger and more concentrated. The cooking process begins at about 140°F (60°C). Many biochemical processes start at this temperature. Most microorganisms, such as bacteria and fungi are killed between 140°F (60°C) and 150°F (65°C), provided that the product is held at this temperature for sufficient time. Toxic byproducts of their metabolism are usually not destroyed under 212°F (100°C). Most proteins (simple proteins) alter their characteristics or lose moisture at about 145°F (63°C). Coagulation takes place between 165°F (74°C) and 175°F (80°C). This means that at about 175°F (80°C) the collagen in meat is transformed into gelatin. By softening the collagen, the meat becomes most tender and more easily digestible. Proper cooking will also destroy pathogenic organisms and make meat safer for consumption. Foods cooked at higher temperatures, such as in a pressure steamer, will require a shorter cooking time. Figure 7-1 shows the effects of various temperatures on the cooking and storage of food.

The air pressure at sea level is about 29.9 inches, and decreases with increasing height. Water also evaporates at a lower temperature above sea level and, therefore, a longer cooking time is necessary.

Microwave ovens are suitable for heating precooked or frozen foods. In regular ovens the outer layer of food is cooked first and is changed faster by cooking than the inside. Microwave ovens are preferable for reheating because they cook foods from the inside out. Most cooked foods can thus be reheated without dehydration or loss of flavor. Porous foods, such as rare roast beef, will, however, have greater cooking losses and become dry and tough when cooked by microwave.

Results of excessive cooking include:

- The proteins (simple proteins) toughen; food is less palatable and less digestible.
- Several nutrients are partially or totally destroyed (vitamins C, B_1, B_{12}).
- The structure of some foods is reduced to a porridgelike mass.
- Taste and aroma are partially or totally destroyed.
- Chlorophyll (the green in leaves) and other natural coloring substances sometimes undergo major color changes.
- Sugar and other substances burn or caramelize and acquire a bitter taste.
- Moisture and fat content are reduced excessively, resulting in dry, tasteless products.
- Excessive shrinkage occurs.

Special Problems: Boiling Potatoes and Sweet Rice Dishes

To boil potatoes, cover them with water and bring them to the boiling point immediately. When tender, the potatoes should be drained thoroughly. If they are left too long in hot water, the starch jells on the surface and forms a hard, insulating layer that prevents the inside from becoming soft.

Cooking sweet rice dishes also requires special precautions. Since sugar turns into a syruplike solution at high temperatures, it thickens the mixture. When boiling rice or semolina dishes, the sugar should be added at the end of the cooking process. Otherwise, the sugar inhibits the hydration, or absorption of water, and the grains of rice or semolina neither swell properly nor become soft.

7.2.2 *Poaching*

Poaching is a method of moist-heat cookery. Foods are immersed in liquid that is between 150° and 195°F

545° to 580°F (285° to 304.5°C)	Broiler heat (gratinating)
490°F (254.5°C)	High oven heat
340°F (171°C)	Medium oven heat
320° to 475°F (160° to 246°C)	Sautéing
320° to 355°F (160° to 179°C)	Deep-frying
300° to 490°F (149° to 254.5°C)	Grilling
300° to 390°F (149° to 199°C)	Glazing
285° to 490°F (141° to 254.5°C)	Baking
285° to 390°F (141° to 199°C)	Braising in oven
285° to 320°F (141° to 160°C)	Pot-roasting
265° to 300°F (129.5° to 149°C)	Blanching in oil
250° to 285°F (121.5° to 141°C)	Stewing
230° to 390°F (110° to 190°C)	Roasting
230°F (110°C)	Low oven heat
230°F (110°C)	Steaming in pressure cooker (6.5 psi)
212°F (100°C)	**Boiling point of water**
212°F (100°C)	Blanching in water
200°F (93°C)	Natural starches jell: potatoes, cereals, rice, flour, arrowroot, tapioca, sago
195°F (91°C)	Starch binding agents lose some of their thickening power
194° to 208°F (90° to 98°C)	Simmering
190° to 195°F (88° to 91°C)	Herb tea, coffee infusions
185°F (85°C)	Rinsing temperature for dishwashing machines, killing of bacteria
175° to 185°F (79° to 85°C)	Internal meat temperature of pork and poultry
165°F (74°C)	Internal meat temperature of well-done veal
160°F (71°C)	Regeneration temperature for fast food
160°F (71°C)	Egg yolk coagulates
160°F (71°C)	Internal meat temperature for well-done red meat
150°F (65°C)	Starch binding agents jell
150° to 190°F (65° to 90°C)	Poaching
150°F (65°C)	Egg white coagulates
140° to 150°F (60° to 65°C)	Killing of pathogenic agents after a certain period of time (pasteurizing)
140°F (60°C)	Internal meat temperature of large medium-done beef roasts
120°F (49°C)	Serving temperature for most hot dishes
120°F (49°C)	Internal meat temperature of large rare beef roasts
50° to 120°F (10° to 49°C)	Bacteria flourishes (with moisture)
45° to 48°F (7° to 9°C)	Optimal storage temperature for potatoes
39° to 43°F (4° to 6°C)	Optimal storage temperature for vegetables and fruits
37° to 41°F (3° to 5°C)	Optimal storage temperature for boiled products
32°F (0°C)	**Freezing point of water**
32° to 37°F (0° to 3°C)	Optimal storage temperature for meat, fish, and milk products
−8° to 0°F (−22° to −18°C)	Optimal storage temperature for frozen products
−76° to −40°F (−60° to −40°C)	Optimal temperature for shock freezing

Note: Water boils at sea level at 212°F (100°C). With increasing altitude, there is lower air pressure and so water has a lower boiling point; food will require longer cooking times.

Figure 7-1. Temperatures for various cooking and storage methods.

(65° and 90°C). The temperature is maintained throughout the cooking period. The liquid barely bubbles, and the bubbles do not break the surface of the water.

Cooking Stocks

The basic stocks are obtained by immersing meat, poultry, or fish bones in water and heating in an uncovered container to the boiling point. The heat is immediately reduced so that the liquid barely simmers. To retain clarity and nutritive value, stocks should never be boiled. High temperatures may cause cloudiness. Stock may be clarified in two ways:

- *Clarifying with ice:* The opaque substances clump together and precipitate to the bottom of the container.
- *Clarifying with egg white:* One slightly beaten egg white, a crumpled egg shell, and some ice water are mixed together for each quart of stock. The mixture is stirred into the stock, and it is heated very slowly. The heavy foam that accumulates is pushed to one side and the stock is simmered (never boiled) for 10 to 15 minutes. The stock is removed from the heat and after standing for 1 hour, it is strained through a cloth.

7.2.3 *Gelatinization with Starch*

Most starches are derived from cereal grains or roots. Starches are important in food preparation, and because of their different characteristics, they differ in their thickening power, clarity, and viscosity. When combined with liquid and heat, the cellulose softens and the starch granules begin to swell and absorb the liquid. This process is called gelatinization. When heated, the mixture thickens. Natural cereal, potato, sago, tapioca, and arrowroot starch begin to gelantinize or swell at 150°F (65°C). The first stage of binding or thickening begins at 160°F (70°C). At this temperature only part of the starch grains is broken and the texture of the mass is still quite grainy. Unless the starch is cooked longer, it may have a raw taste. Certain starches, such as waxy maize, reach maximum thickness at about 160°F (70°C). If this starch is heated above 200°F (93°C), the starch granules of the mixture will rupture, and the mixture will become thin.

Starch should be mixed thoroughly with cool or warm liquid before heat is applied. Most kernels can absorb up to thirty times their volume in liquid. It may also be mixed with fat before dispersing in water. For foods with a high sugar content, such as puddings and pie fillings, the starch should be mixed with sugar before adding to the liquid. Most starch mixtures should be heated to the boiling point and then cooked at a lower temperature to obtain the maximum viscosity and a cooked flavor.

7.2.4 *The Gelatinization Process with Flour*

Flours differ in their thickening power depending on the gluten and starch content. Pastry and cake flours thicken better because they have a higher starch content and less gluten than bread flour. Because of the starch content, flour mixtures must be heated to 200°F (93°C). After reaching this temperature, the heat should be reduced and the cooking continued for 20 to 30 minutes to achieve full viscosity and to remove the starch taste.

7.2.5 *Boiling and Evaporating*

Boiling, in its technical sense, refers to the conversion of liquid to gas at the initial boiling point of a liquid; for example, water boils at 212°F (100°C), when the bubbles break on its surface. Evaporation is the conversion of liquid to gas below the initial boiling point, for example, a street drying off in the winter after rain has fallen. Sublimation is the conversion of a solid directly into a gas at sufficiently low pressure. An example occurs when icy streets dry off when it is windy and the temperatures are low.

What the eye sees as steam is not vapor, but finely distributed water droplets or fog. Energy is necessary to produce vapor pressure and is measured in calories. A large calorie corresponds to the amount of energy needed to increase the temperature of 1 kilogram of water at 59°F (15°C) by 34°F (1°C). The greater the pressure, the higher the temperature at which the vapor forms. At a vapor pressure of 6.5 psi, required for a high-pressure steamer, the initial boiling point is 230°F (110°C). The higher the temperature, the faster the food cooks. It should be remembered that the total mass of food, the size of the food pieces, and the temperature of the food at the onset of the cooking process will all affect the length of cooking time. Food that is to be cooked in a pressure steamer should be of uniform size. See *Heating Methods and Equipment* in chapter 2. Almost 80 calories are necessary to convert 1 kilogram of ice into water at 32°F (0°C). Steam contains more heat than hot water. Pressure steamers are suitable for thawing and cooking pieces of food that are small enough for the heat to penetrate rapidly and evenly. If the pieces are too large, the exterior may be overcooked before the heat penetrates the inside of the food.

Freeze-Drying

As air pressure is lowered, the boiling point of liquid drops. (At the top of a high mountain, water boils at a lower temperature than at sea level.) In a vacuum, which has zero air pressure, water boils at a temperature below the normal freezing point of 32°F (0°C).

Freeze-drying is a process where prefrozen food is put into a vacuum chamber and heated. The ice crystals of the food boil immediately and are converted to steam. The steam must be removed as rapidly as it is formed. The food dries and is vacuum packed.

The Rising of Dough

The substance that causes a dough to rise is called a *leaven*. Dough is leavened by the formation of gas in the dough. Water expands 1600 times its original volume when converted to gas. The ratio of water to flour in the dough will determine the extent of leavening that is possible with steam.

The process involving baking powder and yeast is one of fermentation. The volume increase caused by fermentation is far lower, however, than that induced by the water converting into steam. When slightly heated, the fermentation agents create carbon dioxide gas. If the temperature exceeds 140°F (60°C), the fermentation process stops, and any further rising of the dough is caused by the production of steam from the remaining water. For this reason, dry dough will not rise properly even if large amounts of baking powder and yeast are added.

The Rising of Puff Pastry

Properly made puff pastry is folded so that a layer of shortening or butter always separates the layers of pastry. There are often hundreds of layers. These layers should never be damaged by improper handling; butter and shortening contain water, which is converted to steam during baking. A steam cushion develops between each layer and causes the pastry to rise. This is the reason a puff pastry such as *vol-au-vent* rises to 2 or 3 inches with hundreds of thin, tender, and crisp layers.

The Beating of Egg Whites

Stored or older eggs have greater ability and are better for beating than fresh eggs. The egg whites become thicker during storage, and the foaming ability and stability increase with age. Unless eggs are at least three days old, they cannot be whipped to maximum volume. The beaten egg whites should be folded into a mixture immediately after whipping. If allowed to stand or if improperly stirred, the air bubbles created by beating will burst. These little bubbles, like miniature balloons, are filled with air. When heated in the oven, steam is created in each balloon, which then expands. This is the reason a dish containing beaten egg whites rises during baking. If the heat is reduced on a soufflé, or it is suddenly chilled, the steam in the little balloons condenses, the balloons shrink, and the entire mass collapses.

7.2.6 *Roasting*

The basic principles of roasting are fully described later in this chapter. From a chemical and bacteriological standpoint, the following aspects are very important.

Salt should be added after roasting has begun and browning is completed. Salt is hygroscopic; that is, it absorbs water. After salting, the water in the meat is attracted to the surface, and browning is delayed.

Meat is tenderized for roasting and braising in two ways: by mechanically destroying the cell fibers (elastin) with sharply pointed wooden meat mallets or special machines (tenderizers), or by chemically altering the collagen (the basic substance forming the connective tissues). Collagen can be changed into gelatin either by moist heat, marinating in an acid solution, or by adding a chemical tenderizer. Chemical tenderizers contain certain enzymes that break down the connective tissue; the basic substance, however, is usually papain, which comes from the papaya fruit. In tropical countries, where this fruit is abundant, meat is often marinated with fresh papaya juice. The recommended quantity of chemical tenderizer should not be exceeded.

7.2.7 *Frying*

The frying process as discussed here refers to deep-frying. This process is used extensively in large food-service establishments because of the ease and speed of preparation. The food is immersed in fat in deep-fryers that are heated with gas or electricity and thermostatically controlled.

Edible fats and oils with a high smoke point (heat resistant) are used since they can be heated to nearly 475°F (245°C) without breaking down. When deep-frying, the high temperature of the fat converts the water content of the food into steam. A good-quality fat will have large white bubbles on its surface, which break rapidly during the frying process. Fats with a high percentage of free fatty acids have low smoke temperatures. Foods fried in fat with a low smoke temperature will absorb more fat than those fried in fat with a high smoke temperature will. Hydrogenated vegetable fats and vegetable oils are lower in free fatty acids and have a higher smoke temperature than do butter, animal fats, and olive oil. Vegetable fats are, therefore, generally used for frying.

Fats are high in cost and should be kept in good condition. Recommended cooking temperatures and times should be followed. After the frying is completed, the heat should be reduced to 200°F (93°C). Suggested temperatures for deep-frying are given in chapter 8. The temperature and time will vary depending on the type of equipment, the quantity of food in the fryer, and the sizes of the pieces of food.

Decomposition of fat because of excessive heating produces undesirable flavors and indigestible substances. A white smoke known as acrolein forms as the fat breaks down. Excessive foaming and smoking of the fat and deterioration of flavor in fried foods indicate a high content of free fatty acids. When this occurs, the fat should be discarded. The following practices are necessary to preserve the frying life of the fat:

- Avoid salting foods over the fryer or griddle, as salt will break down the fat.
- Replace fat lost during frying process with fresh fat.
- Keep equipment clean. Sediment in the fat or on the equipment can break down the fat.
- Avoid adding fresh oil to rancid oil.
- Avoid use of steel wool on thermostats.
- Avoid use of metal tools, and repair any exposed iron on the equipment. Metals cause a breakdown of the fat.
- Dry the food before immersing in fat.
- Store fats in a dark, dry, cool area. Rancidity develops on exposure to air or light.

Frying Potatoes

Young potatoes contain little starch, and they are usually moist and good for salads and steamed or creamed potatoes. Older, dry potatoes have a higher specific gravity, and they are low in sugar and high in starch. These are good for baking, whipping, or deep-frying. The sugar in young potatoes has not converted into starch, and therefore, the potatoes are unsuitable for deep-frying. The potatoes will stick together and develop dark stripes on the surface because of carmelization of the sugar.

7.2.8 *Acidity in Cooking*

Acidity is expressed in pH. Water has neutral pH, with a value of 7. The lower the pH value, the higher the acid content. The strongest acid is indicated by 0 and the strongest alkali by 14. Since the chlorophyll of green vegetables is destroyed by acidity, it is better retained by cooking vegetables in a small amount of tap water, which is usually alkaline, or by using a waterless method. Baking soda should never be added to green vegetables. The alkalinity produced by baking soda destroys some of the B vitamins and the ascorbic acid, and it also has a detrimental effect on the texture and flavor of vegetables.

In order to maintain the white or light color of food, a small amount of acid may be added during the

	pH	
Highest acid	0	
	1	Hydrochloric acid
	2	Lemons, vinegar
High acid	3	Rhubarb, grapefruit
Medium acid	4	Oranges, cherries
	5	Bananas, asparagus, spinach, potatoes, coffee
Low acid	6	Many vegetables, butter, milk, salmon, meat
Neutral	7	Pure water
Low alkali	8	Ripe olives, egg white, hard water
	9	
	10	
	11	
	12	
	13	
Highest alkali	14	

Figure 7-2. The pH scale.

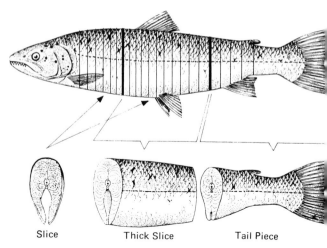

Figure 7-3. Salmon can be cut into slices (steaks), thick slices, and/or the tail piece before cooking.

last half of the cooking period. By adding citric acid to mushrooms, the bright white color can be maintained. Effects of acids and alkalis on the color of food can sometimes be offset by addition of artificial colors.

Figure 7-2 shows that most foods are acidic. The most important point to remember is that foods with low acidity are more susceptible to attack by bacteria than those with a high acid content.

7.3 Methods of Preparation, Cutting, and Dressing

The illustrations that follow demonstrate techniques for preparing, cutting, and dressing fish, meat, poultry, vegetables and potatoes.

7.3.1 *Fish*—Poissons

Figures 7-3 through 7-15 show ways of skinning and otherwise preparing various fish.

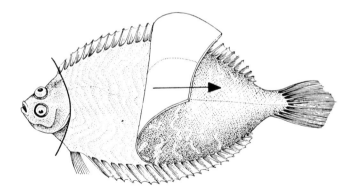

Figure 7-4. Lemon soles are skinned from head to tail.

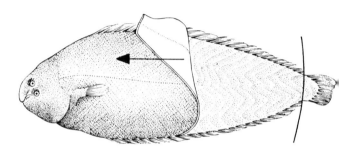

Figure 7-5. Dover sole is skinned from the tail to the head.

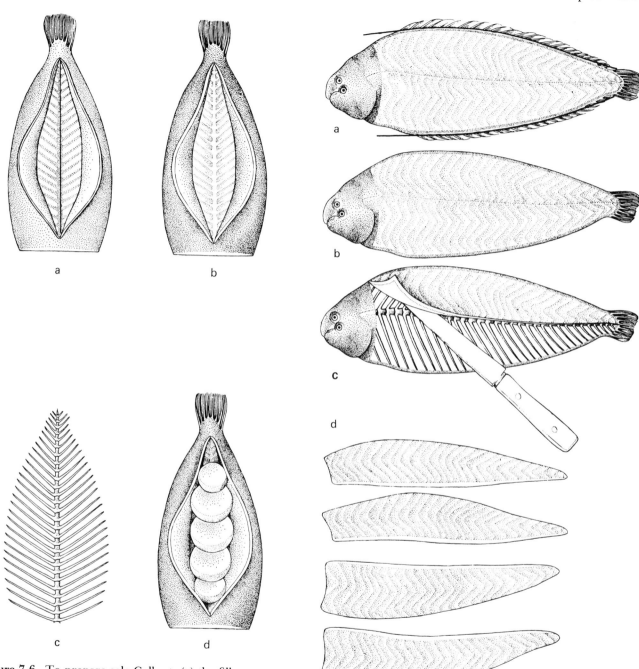

Figure 7-6. To prepare sole Colbert: (a) the fillets are separated from the skeleton at the center of the fish; (b) the fish is then deep-fried; (c) the skeleton is removed after deep-frying; (d) the sole is then filled with Colbert butter.

Figure 7-7. Always fillet sole from head to tail: (a) the skinned sole; (b) the sole after trimming; (c) filleting; (d) the four quarter-fillets ready for use.

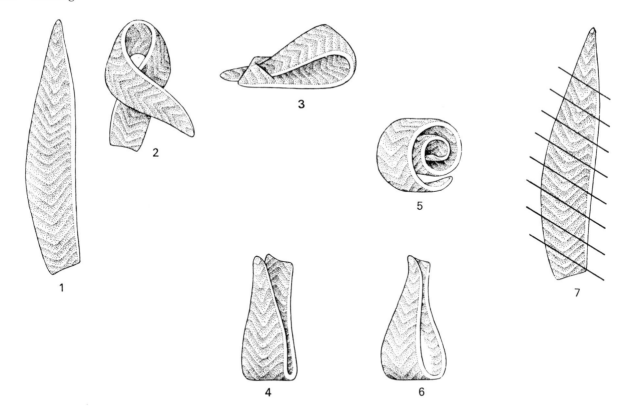

Figure 7-8. Fillets of sole or flounder can be shaped and cut in a number of ways for different preparations: (1) whole; (2) collar-shaped; (3) foulard-shaped; (4) folded; (5) rolled (*en paupiette*); (6) stuffed; (7) goujons (strips).

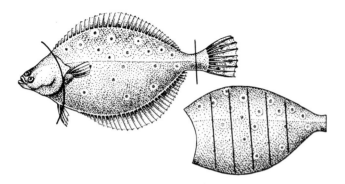

Figure 7-9. The head and tail of small plaice should be cut off *without* removing the skin. The fish should then be carved.

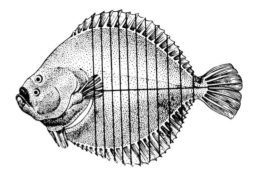

Figure 7-10. When cutting turbot, the slices should be cut thicker at the tail end. Only raw turbot should be cut in this way.

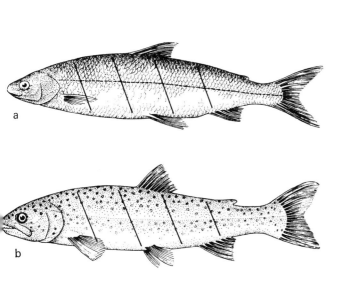

Figure 7-11. Fish can be cut and shaped in various ways for different preparations: (a) carved whitefish for sautéing; (b) carved trout for sautéing; (c) trout in a ring shape for poaching *au bleu;* (d) whiting, English style.

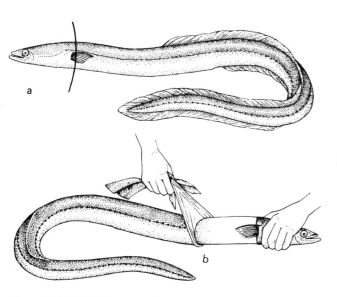

Figure 7-12. To skin an eel: (a) loosen the skin behind the neck fins; (b) pull off the skin, using a towel to hold it.

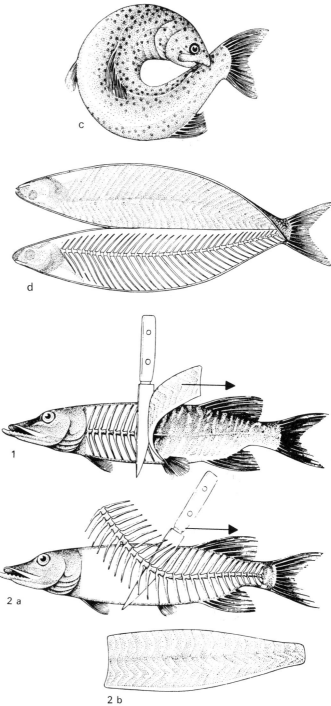

Figure 7-13. To fillet freshwater fish: (1) remove the fillets from the head toward the tail; (2a) remove the backbone; (2b) the fillet is ready for use.

233

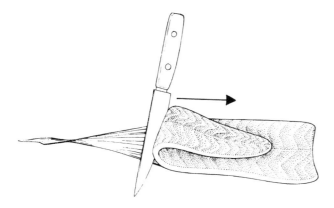

Figure 7-14. When skinning fish fillets, the skin is worked from the tail forward.

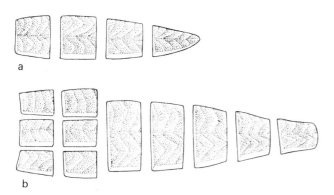

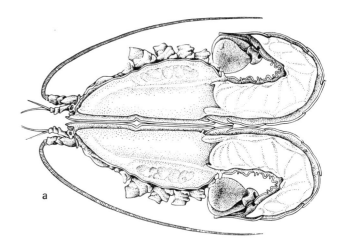

Figure 7-15. Fish fillets are cut according to their size: (a) cutting small fillets; (b) cutting larger fillets.

7.3.2 *Crustaceans and Shellfish*—Crustacés et Coquillages

See figures 7-16 through 7-19 for information on how to prepare oysters and lobsters.

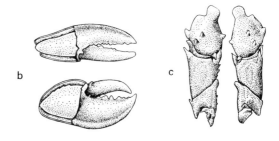

Figure 7-16. Lobster is often cut in half for hot and cold dishes: (a) the two halves of the lobster; (b) the claws cut open; (c) the claw meat.

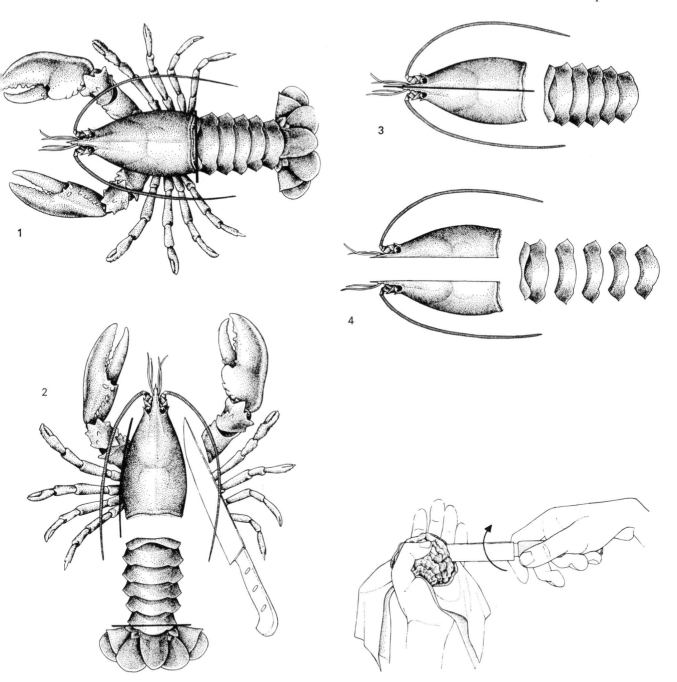

Figure 7-17. To prepare lobster, American style (*homard à l'américaine*): (1) separate the tail from the body; (2) cut off the claws and legs; (3) split the body; (4) the split body and the pieces of tail.

Figure 7-18. To open an oyster, hold the oyster firmly in a double layer of thick cloth. Insert the blade of an oyster knife near the hinge. Push it in, then move it around to cut the muscle that holds the shell together.

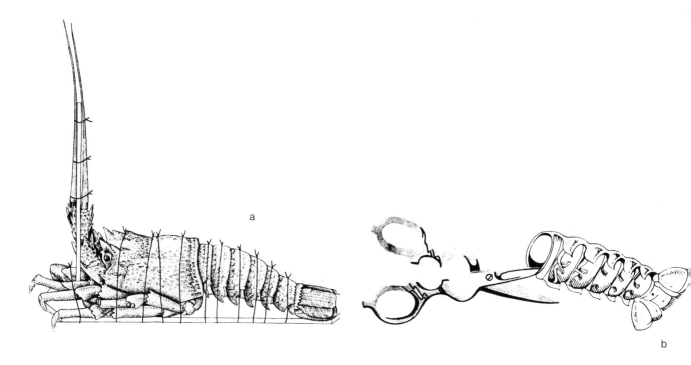

Figure 7-19. Before cooking, the body of a rock lobster is bound horizontally to a board, and the antenna are bound vertically to a stick (a); after cooking, the shell is cut (b) and removed from the tail meat (c).

7.3.3 *Meat*—Viande de boucherie

Figures 7-20 through 7-32 depict ways of handling beef, veal, and lamb, as well as information about larding, birds, and roasting in aluminum foil.

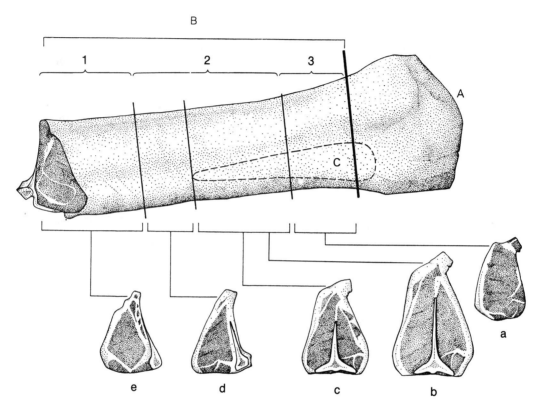

Figure 7-20. Beef may be butchered into: (A) the round or rump; (B) the ribs (1), short loin (2), and sirloin (3); (C) the tenderloin (see figure 7-21). The following pieces are then cut from the loins and ribs (including the bone): (a) sirloin steaks (may be boneless); (b) porterhouse steak and tenderloin cut at the thickest point of the short loin; (c) T-bone steak, cut further forward on the short loin and thus smaller than the porterhouse steak; (d) club steak, cut at the tip of the tenderloin, but not including the tenderloin; (e) rib steak with the bone—rather than dividing into separate rib steaks, the whole piece may be used as a standing rib roast.

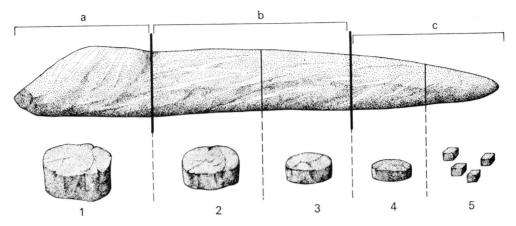

Figure 7-21. Beef tenderloin is cut from the boneless portions of the short loin and sirloin. It is further cut into: (a) the head, which is sliced into (1) châteaubriand; (b) the center piece, which is sliced into (2) filet steaks and (3) tournedos; and (c) the end, which is sliced into (4) small fillet steaks, also known as filet mignon, and cubed (5) for goulash.

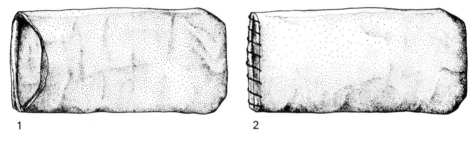

Figure 7-22. To prepare stuffed breast of veal (*poitrine de veau farcie*): (1) open the deboned breast at one end; the pocket opening should extend to the other end; (2) stuff the breast and sew it closed.

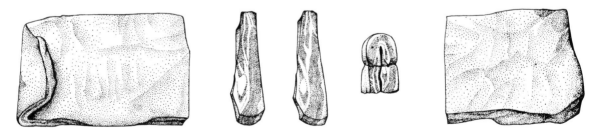

Figure 7-23. In veal breast riblets (*tendrons de veau*), the riblets are cut through across the breast and folded into a U shape; the two ends are then bound together.

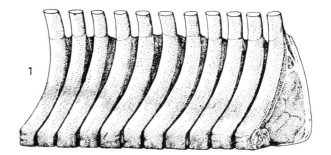

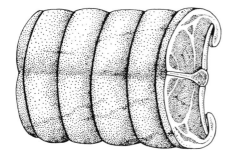

Figure 7-24. Saddle of lamb (*selle d'agneau*) is formed by
the two loin pieces. The thin ends should be pressed
inward and bound.

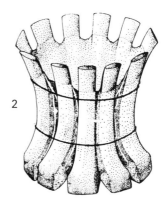

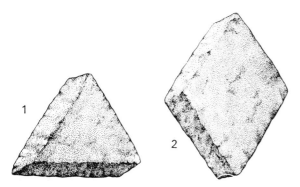

Figure 7-26. For lamb épigrammes (*épigrammes d'agneau*),
breast of lamb is first boiled, then deboned. The meat is
cut into pieces, breaded, and panfried in butter. The
meat may be in (1) a triangular shape; or (2) a square
shape.

Figure 7-25. A lamb crown roast (*couronne d'agneau*) is a
popular form of preparation in English-speaking
countries. Other meats can also be prepared as crown
roasts. To make it: (1) prepare the meat as for roasting,
paring the ribs to uncover about ¾ inch of the bone and
cutting slightly with the saw between the ribs from the
inside of the rack; (2) shape the whole piece into a crown,
with the inside facing outward, and bind. After roasting,
remove the string and fill the cavity as desired.

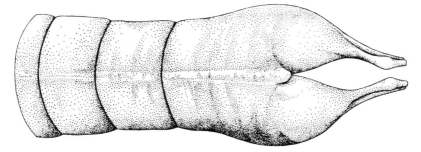

Figure 7-27. A baron of lamb (*baron d'agneau*) is the saddle and two legs of lamb. Mutton may also be prepared this way.

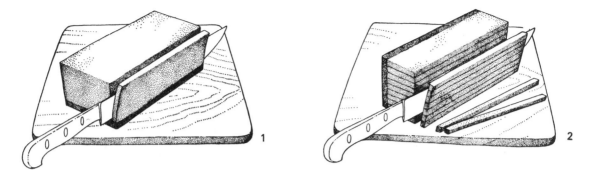

Figure 7-28. To cut larding strips: (1) cut the slices of lard down to the rind; (2) place the rind on the left and cut the strips.

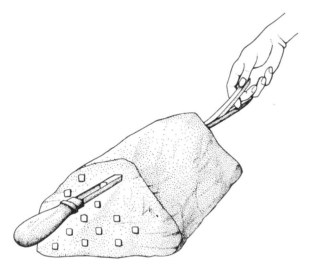

Figure 7-29. To lard large pieces of meat, a larding needle (*lardoire*) is used to insert strips of lard (¼ to ½ inch thick) completely through the meat.

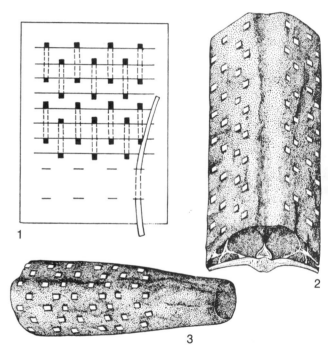

Figure 7-30. The method for interlarding depends on the type of meat. Unlike larding, in interlarding, the rows are shorter and staggered (1). To interlard small saddles (venison and red deer), two rows of interlarding are sufficient; for larger saddles (veal and mutton), more rows are necessary (2). Interlarding tenderloin and legs of lamb or mutton is done lengthwise (3).

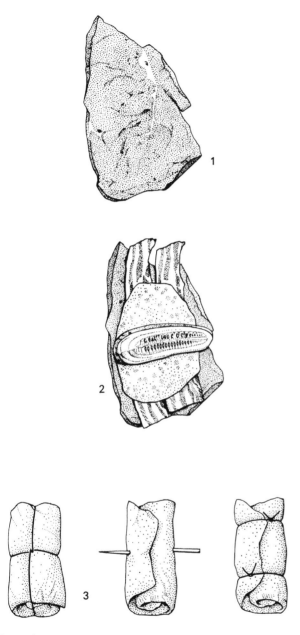

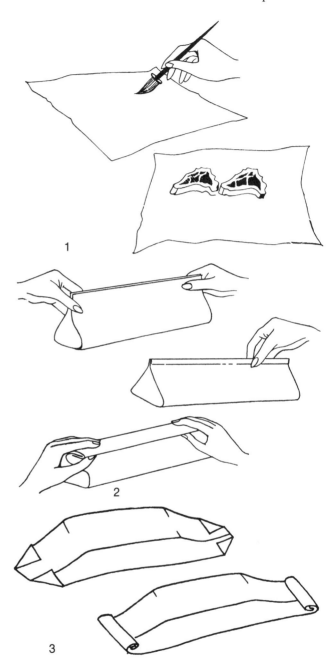

Figure 7-31. To prepare meat birds (*paupiettes*): (1) meat for the birds is cut from the rump, top pieces, or shoulder depending on the animal and the quality; (2) beef slices are taken from the rump and spread with bacon slices, pork stuffing, and slices of gherkin; (3) the birds are then bound; a number of binding methods can be used, as shown.

Figure 7-32. To roast meat in aluminum foil: (1) season the meat, coat the foil with oil, and place the meat on the foil; (2) wrap loosely, folding the foil over twice at the top; (3) turn the packet over, turn the four corners in, and fold each end over twice.

7.3.4. *Poultry*—Volaille

Figures 7-33 through 7-40 depict ways of preparing poultry.

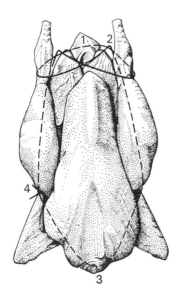

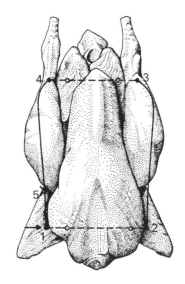

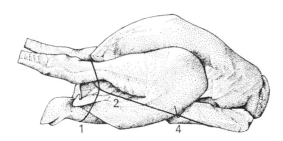

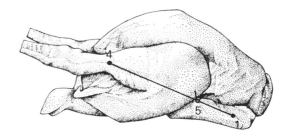

Figure 7-33. To truss poultry by hand: (1) pass the string under the tail end, crossed above the legs; (2) pass the two crossed ends of the string between the legs; draw the string over the left wing; (3) after covering the end of the neck with the breast skin, hook the string between the end of the neck and the shoulders; (4) knot the two ends of the string on the right-hand side. Note that it is possible to begin at *3*, but the string cannot be pulled as tight as when one begins at *1*.

Figure 7-34. To truss poultry with a needle: (1) push the needle through the wing and pass it through the breast skin and neck stump; (2) pull the needle out through the other wing; (3) push the needle through the end of the leg and through the breast; (4) pull the needle through the end of the other leg; (5) tie the two ends.

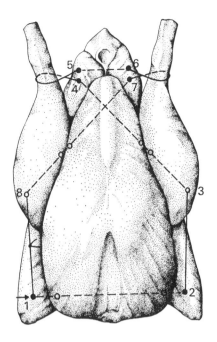

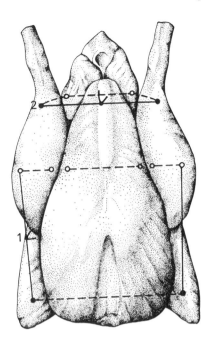

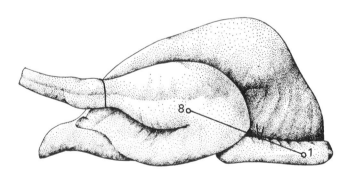

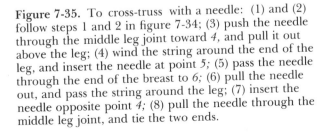

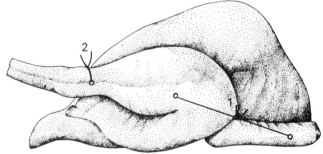

Figure 7-35. To cross-truss with a needle: (1) and (2) follow steps 1 and 2 in figure 7-34; (3) push the needle through the middle leg joint toward *4*, and pull it out above the leg; (4) wind the string around the end of the leg, and insert the needle at point *5;* (5) pass the needle through the end of the breast to *6;* (6) pull the needle out, and pass the string around the leg; (7) insert the needle opposite point *4;* (8) pull the needle through the middle leg joint, and tie the two ends.

Figure 7-36. To double-truss with a needle: (1) first perform the simple trussing technique shown in figure 7-34, except, at the third point of entry, the needle should be inserted through the middle joint of the leg, not the end of the leg; (2) pierce and bind the two ends of the legs and the end of the breast separately. Goose and turkey are usually trussed in this way.

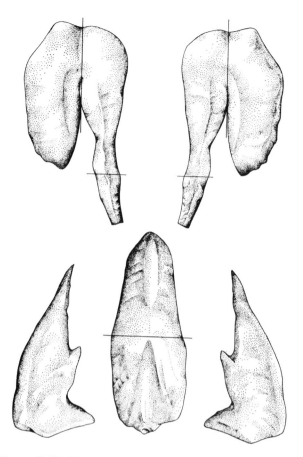

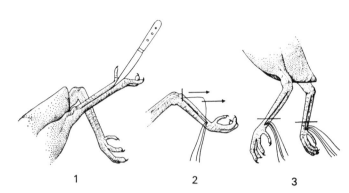

Figure 7-39. To remove the tendons from a freshly killed turkey: (1) cut the legs along the back; (2) pull out the tendons; (3) cut off the feet and tendons.

Figure 7-37. To cut a chicken for sautéing, first slit the back of the chicken and remove the backbone. Remove the legs and separate into two thigh and drumstick. Separate the wings from the breast, and cut the breast into two halves.

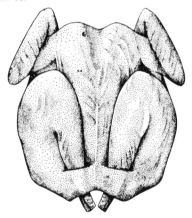

Figure 7-38. To prepare a chicken for grilling, slit the back of the chicken and loosen the whole backbone. Press the chicken flat, and insert the legs through two holes cut in the skin.

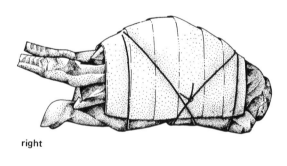

right

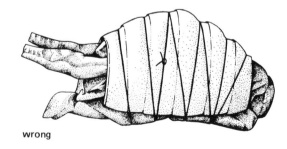

wrong

Figure 7-40. To bard poultry and feathered game, cut fine slices of unsalted bacon or fatback, cover the whole breast, and bind as shown.

244

7.3.5 *Vegetables*—Légumes

Figures 7-41, 7-42, and 7-43 show how vegetables, including potatoes, can be prepared.

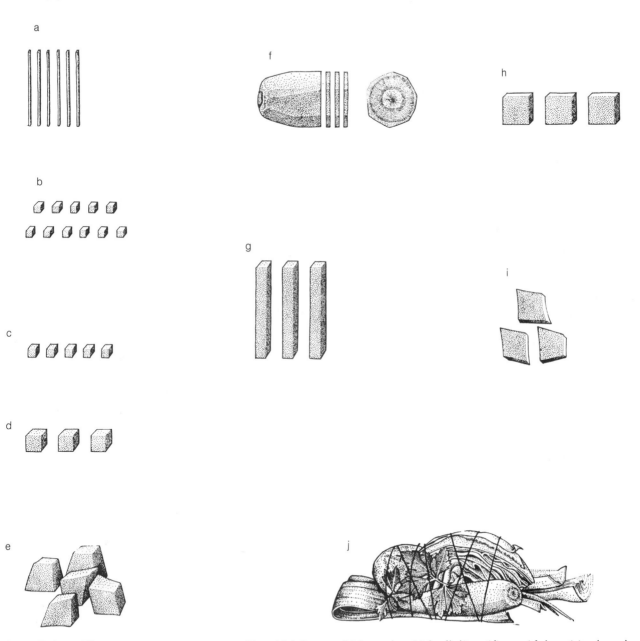

Figure 7-41. Different ways to prepare vegetables: (a) julienne; (b) brunoise; (c) jardinière; (d) macédoine; (e) mirepoix; (f) vichy (carrots); (g) sticks (bâtonnets); (h) dice (for paysanne style, croûte au pot, fermière style, and minestrone; (i) matignon (j) bouquet garni.

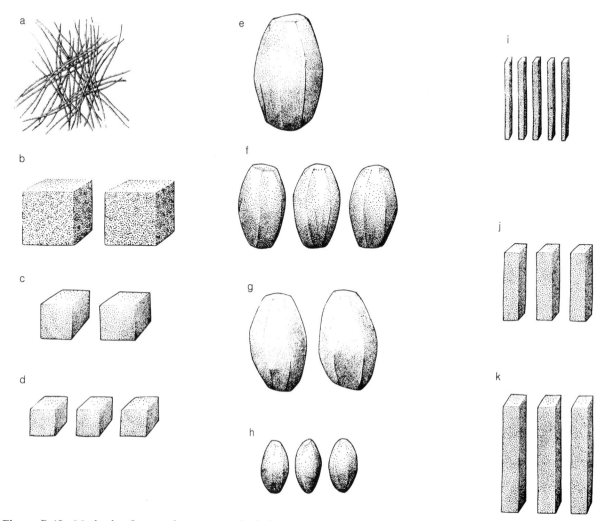

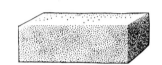

Figure 7-42. Methods of preparing potatoes include:
(a) chiffonade; (b) Maxim; (c) rissolé (fried in hot fat);
(d) Parmentier; (e) fondante; (f) château (sautéed in
butter); (g) natur (plain); (h) olivette; (i) allumettes
(shoestrings); (j) mignonettes; (k) french fries (*frites*);
(l) steak fries (*Pont-Neuf*); (m) savoyarde (baked with
bouillon, egg, cheese, and spices); (n) chips; (o) soufflé;
(p) Chatouillard; (q) Berny; (r) Saint-Florentine;
(s) duchess; (t) Parisian (sautéed in butter); (u) noisette
(nut-shaped; browned in butter); (v) waffle or ridged
chips (*gaufrette*); (w) William; (x) Lorette; (y) croquettes;
(z) Anna.

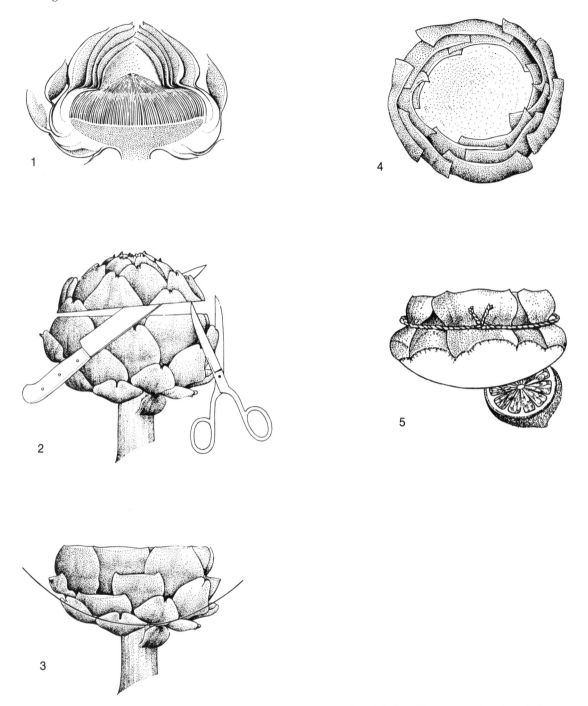

Figure 7-43. To prepare artichokes: (1) a cross section of unprepared artichoke; (2) remove the tips of the outer leaves; (3) remove the stalk and bottom leaves; (4) remove the choke in the center; (5) rub the heart with lemon and bind.

7.3.7 *Miscellaneous*—Divers

See figures 7-44 through 7-48 for demonstrations of various preparation techniques.

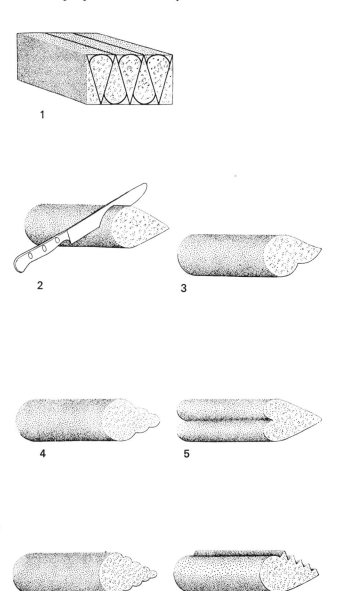

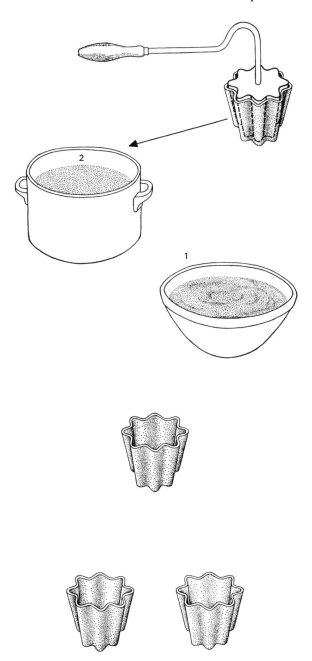

Figure 7-44. To cut bread croutons: (1) cut the bread into wedges; (2) slice into croutons of the desired shape (3 to 7).

Figure 7-45. To make croustades, or shells: (1) dip the iron, previously heated in oil, into the batter, up to ⅛ inch from the top edge; (2) finish cooking the croustades in a deep fryer.

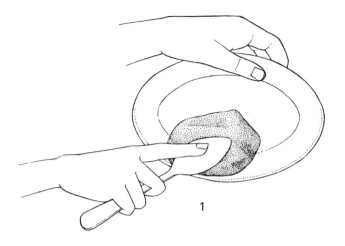

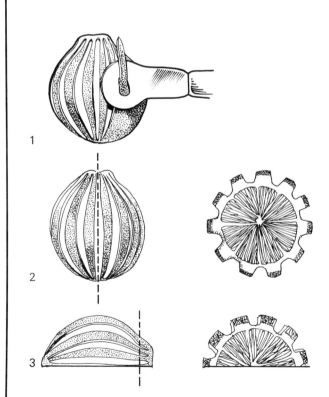

Figure 7-46. The size of quenelles (forcemeat dumplings) is determined by the size of the spoon (coffee, dessert, or soup) used to form them, as well as the way the quenelles are formed. To make quenelles; (1) spoon up the forcemeat, trimming on the rim of the bowl; (2) for small quenelles, force the mixture out of the spoon lengthwise; (3) for larger quenelles, as well as potatoes dauphine (deep-fried dumplings of potato puree and pâte à choux), force the mixture from the spoon sideways.

Figure 7-47. Citrus fruit can be decoratively grooved, sliced, and used as garnish. To make decorative slices: (1) use a special knife to remove strips of peel from the fruit; (2) if half-slices are required, halve the fruit before slicing; (3) cut the ends off the fruit and slice.

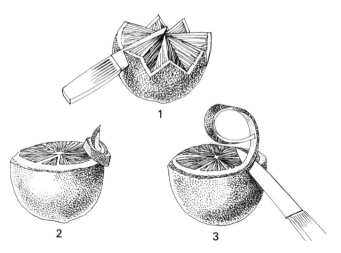

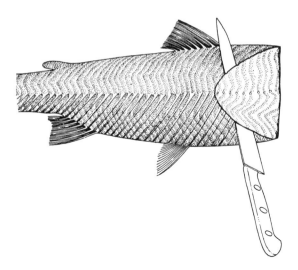

Figure 7-48. Citrus fruit halves can also be used as decorative garnish. (1) Cut off both ends so the halves will sit flat. Cut the fruit in half and stand each half on the cut end. Cut wedges into the top of the half. (2) Cut off both ends so the halves will sit flat. Cut the fruit in half and stand each half on the cut end. Cut a strip of peel loose. Tie a knot in the end of the strip. (3) Cut off both ends so the halves will sit flat. Cut the fruit in half and stand each half on the cut end. Cut a strip of peel loose and curl it.

Figure 7-50. When carving smoked salmon (*saumon fumé*), remove the fins and bones first. The slices are then cut on a bias down to the skin.

7.3.8 *Carving*

Figures 7-49 through 7-58 show how to carve cooked fish, meat, and poultry.

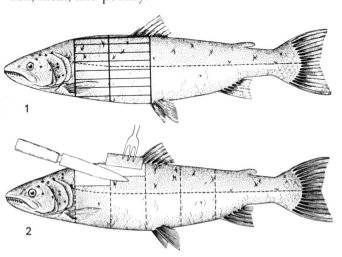

Figure 7-49. To carve cooked salmon (*saumon*): (1) make deep cuts along the back and across the side; (2) remove the slices with a fish knife and fork.

Figure 7-51. Slice cooked turbot horizontally. After the top half is removed, the backbone must be cut through and lifted off.

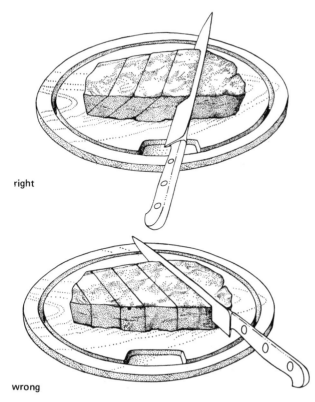

right

wrong

Figure 7-52. Double sirloin steak, rib steak, châteaubriand, porterhouse, and T-bone steak should always be cut diagonally. If possible, use a cutting board to collect the meat juices.

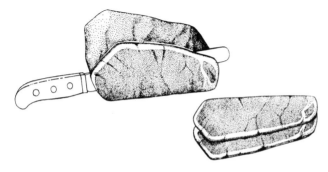

Figure 7-53. Roast beef should always be cut vertically with a carving knife.

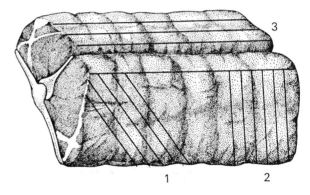

Figure 7-54. Saddles (*selles*) can be cut in a variety of ways: (1) diagonal cut; (2) cross cut; (3) longitudinal (English) cut.

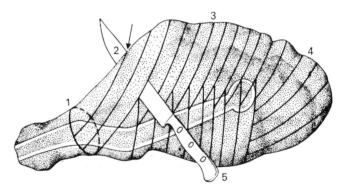

Figure 7-55. To carve leg of lamb or mutton: (1) loosen the meat around the bone and cut four slices; (2) place the leg so that the hump (3) is uppermost and carve slices; turn the leg and remove the final slices (4) and (5).

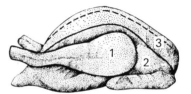

Figure 7-56. To carve a chicken: (1) remove and divide the legs and thighs; (2) remove the wings; (3) carve both sides of the breast lengthwise and remove the breastbone.

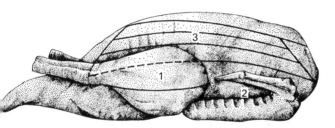

Figure 7-57. To carve duck: (1) remove and divide the legs and thighs; (2) remove the wings; (3) cut each side of the breast lengthwise into four fillets.

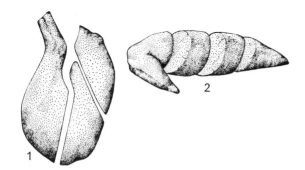

Figure 7-58. To carve a large roaster chicken (*poularde*): (1) remove the legs and cut into three pieces; (2) separate the breast meat and wings from the breastbone, cut in half lengthwise, and carve diagonally.

7.4 Food Preservation

Most fresh foods are highly perishable and have a natural tendency to deteriorate. Food spoilage is caused by the microorganisms, such as bacteria, yeasts, and molds; by the enzymes within the food itself; and by insects. This deterioration can be controlled by using only fresh foods that have been cleaned and stored properly. Foods can be preserved to avoid deterioration over a period of time. Modern methods of food preservation include refrigerating, dehydrating, freeze-drying, salting, smoking, and pickling. Canning, freezing, and the Nacka system are special methods of preservation discussed in more detail. See figure 7-59.

Refrigerating

The action of microorganisms and enzymes can be retarded for short periods of time by refrigerating foods at temperatures as low as 32°F (0°C). Meats that have been partially or completely prepared can be preserved for a short time by refrigerating the food in plastic bags from which the air has been removed.

Dehydrating

Dehydration removes the water from foods. Artificial drying processes that are more efficient, more sanitary, and faster have replaced sundrying. Among the common dried foods are fruits, vegetables, legumes, whole and nonfat milk, buttermilk, and egg solids. Dehydration is not only a method of preserving food, it also reduces the weight of the food and eliminates the need for refrigeration. These foods require much less storage space than in the natural state and have gained acceptance in the military service, in institutions, and by campers.

Freeze-Drying

Foods that are freeze-dried are frozen and then dried. This process is one of sublimation. The frozen food is put into a vacuum and sufficient heat is provided to change the ice crystals to a vapor without going through a liquid phase. Approximately 98 percent of the moisture is removed from the food, reducing the weight to one tenth of the original. Fruits, vegetables, shrimp, coffee, and certain meats are freeze-dried, and these foods can be rehydrated easily. The change in flavor, texture, and color of freeze-dried foods is minimal.

Salting

Another mode of preservation is salting, which is also called curing or salt-curing. Food with a salt content of above 5 percent resists deterioration and that with an 8 percent content is preserved. Cod is the most familiar salted food; the amount of salt used varies with different cures, some cod becoming stiff as boards, others remaining softer and flexible with less salt. Salt pork and cured but unsmoked bacon are

Preserving Method	How It Works	Products
Dehydration: air-drying, freeze-drying, spray-drying, radiant heat	Water is extracted from the food. Bacteria cannot grow on dry materials.	Dried meat (jerky), dried sausages, potato products, instant products
Drying: with hot air, in the sun, in the oven	Water is evaporated with heat from the food. Bacteria cannot grow in dried food.	Vegetables, fruit (apricots, prunes, apples), herbs
Smoking	Smoke (and curing salts) retard food deterioration.	Bacon, ham, sausage, turkey, chicken, fish (fatty)
Pickling/curing	The acid reaction inhibits food deterioration.	Meat, pigs' knuckles, herring
Preserving in sugar	Sugar syrup prevents deterioration.	Candied fruits, citrus peel, gingerroot
Marinating in vinegar or alcohol	Acids and alcohol retard food deterioration.	Fish (herring), meat (game, beef), vegetables (gherkins, onions), salads (beets), fruits (cherries)
Fermenting: milk acid (rennet), yeast, acid	Chemical change induced by the action of bacteria.	Yogurt, sauerkraut, alcoholic beverages, vinegar preserves
Cooling: refrigerator, vacuum-packed	Refrigeration stalls bacterial growth. Vacuum packing stalls bacterial growth for a longer period.	Dairy produce, meat, fish, meat products, fish products, precooked foods
Freezing: deep-freeze	Stops bacterial growth.	All deep-freeze products
Freeze-drying	Water is removed by sublimation. Bacteria cannot grow on dry food.	Instant foods (coffee), milk powder, citrus fruit juices, vegetables, mushrooms
Heating: pasteurization below 212°F (100°C); canning at 212°F (100°C); sterilizing above 212°F (100°C)	Heat kills germs	Fruit juices, some milk products are pasteurized. Jams, marmalade, fruits, vegetables, and many other products are canned. Meat, vegetables, ready foods (prepared meals) are sterilized.
Chemical preservation (subject to regulation)	Chemicals kill some germs	Half-preserves: fish and meat products

Note: For many products more than one preserving method is used.

Figure 7-59. Methods of preserving food.

salted. Chipped beef is both salted and dried. Only pure salt is used for curing.

Smoking

Foods to be smoked are first cured with salt or brine. They may be hot-smoked for a short period to make a flavored product that still requires refrigeration or other storage; or cold-smoked for longer periods, which preserves the food for some time. Actual smoke from special woods is still used, but today smoke flavor is also used for a quicker processing. Salmon and haddock, hams, turkey, sausages, and cheese are smoked.

Pickling

Vegetables such as cucumbers, beets, cabbage, okra, and carrots, herring, corned beef, pigs' feet, and game are examples of foods that can be preserved by a pickling process. The food is immersed in a solution of vinegar and other preservatives. The acid reaction inhibits deterioration.

7.4.1 Canning

Foods to be canned are sealed in containers and heated. The heat cooks the food and destroys the microorganisms. Storage in sealed containers prevents further contamination. Vegetables, fruits, mushrooms, fish, and meat can be preserved by this method.

Canning Fresh Vegetables

Since vegetables have a low acid content, the only safe way to can them is to process them under 10 pounds (4.5 kilograms) of pressure using a steam pressure canner. The U.S. Department of Agriculture recommends the following procedure for canning vegetables:

- Use fresh, young, tender vegetables of uniform size.
- Wash thoroughly in several changes of water. Do not soak in water.
- Pack either raw or cooked vegetables using raw-pack or hot-pack methods.

Raw pack: Pack cold raw vegetables (except corn, lima beans, and peas) as tightly as possible in a sterile jar. Cover with boiling water, leaving ½ inch (1.2 centimeters) of space at top of jar. Add ½ teaspoon (3 grams) of salt to each pint (½ liter) jar.

Hot pack: Cover vegetables with water and heat to boiling point, or cook as long as required for specific vegetable. Pack cooked vegetables loosely in sterile jars. Vegetables should be near the boiling point when packed. Add ½ teaspoon (3 grams) of salt to each pint (½ liter) jar; 1 teaspoon (6 grams) to quart (liter) jars. Cover with boiling liquid from the vegetables or with boiling water. Leave headspace in jars as recommended in specific recipe.

Insert a long spatula around the jar between the sides of the jar and the vegetables to release any air bubbles. Add liquid to cover vegetables if necessary. Keep jars in very hot water while filling remainder of jars. Screw ring bands on jars tightly by hand. Follow the directions of the manufacturer of the canner being used. These pointers apply to any steam pressure canner. Fill bottom of canner with 2 to 3 inches (5 to 7.5 centimeters) of boiling water. Place filled glass jars on rack so that steam can circulate around each container. Use a rack between each layer of jars. Fasten canner cover securely so that no steam can escape except through the vent. When steam pours steadily through the vent, let it escape for 10 minutes or more until all air is driven from the canner. Close pet cock or put on weighted gauge. Let pressure rise to 10 pounds (4.5 kilograms). At this moment start counting processing time. Keep pressure constant by regulating heat under the canner. Do not open pet cock. Remove canner from heat as soon as processing time is completed. Remove jars from canner.

Canning Fresh Fruits

Fresh fruits, fruit juices, and tomatoes are canned by the boiling water method. A canning kettle and lid are required for this process. The kettle must be deep enough so that the tops of the jars are covered by at least 1 inch (2.5 centimeters) of boiling water. Either the raw-pack or hot-pack method may be used. The U.S. Department of Agriculture recommends the following procedure:

- Use fresh firm fruits without defects.
- Wash fruit thoroughly and pare if necessary.
- Cut fruit directly into a solution of 2 tablespoons (30 milliliters) each of salt and vinegar to 1 gallon (3.79 liters) of water. Do not leave fruit in solution more than 20 minutes. Rinse the fruit before putting in jars.
- Pack either raw or cooked fruit using the raw-pack or hot pack methods.

Raw Pack: Put cold, raw fruit into sterile jars and cover with boiling-hot syrup, juice, or water to within ½ inch (1.2 centimeters) of rim of jar. The syrup improves the appearance of most fruit and keeps it firmer. Put jars into canner containing hot but not boiling water.

Hot pack: Heat syrup or other liquid to boiling point in a large pan; add the prepared fruit, and cook as directed for specific fruit. Remove fruit from syrup and pack in sterile jars; pour syrup into jars to within ½ inch (1.2 centimeters) of rim of jar, or as directed in specific recipe; put jars into canner containing boiling water.

Add boiling water to bring water in canner an inch or two (2.5 centimeters or 5) over tops of jars; never pour boiling water directly on glass jars. Put lid on canner. As soon as water in canner comes to a rolling boil, start to time the processing. Boil gently and steadily for the time required for the specific fruit. Keep covered with water throughout processing. Remove jars from the canner as soon as processing time is completed.

The proportions for sugar syrup are as follows:

- 4 cups (10 deciliters) water or juice to 2 cups (454 grams) sugar equals 5 cups (12.5 deciliters) of thin syrup.
- 4 cups (10 deciliters) water or juice to 3 cups (680 grams) sugar equals 5½ cups (13.8 deciliters) of medium syrup.
- 4 cups (10 deciliters) water or juice to 4¾ cups (1080 grams) sugar equals 6½ cups (16.2 deciliters) of heavy syrup.

7.4.2 *Freezing*

The flavor, color, texture, and nutritional values of many foods are preserved by freezing at temperatures as low as −60°F (−52°C). Vegetables, fruits, poultry, game, meats, and fish are some of the foods that can be frozen.

Freezing is a three-step process that requires chilling, sharp freezing, and holding at low temperatures. As soon as the food is thoroughly chilled, it is frozen at −10°F (23°C) or below. After the food is frozen, it can be stored at a temperature of 0°F (−18°C) for a long period.

Frozen foods offer a number of advantages. Freezing preserves natural flavors, colors, and nutrients. The organisms that cause spoilage and the enzymes that cause further ripening are not destroyed by freezing, but they become inactive. They do become active when the foods are thawed. No preservatives, taste additives, or artificial colors are required to freeze foods. Foods for freezing should be fully ripe, firm, and as fresh as possible.

Freezing offers cost and labor savings to foodservice operations. Most preparation tasks (cleaning, washing, and peeling) are done by the commercial processor. Fewer foodservice employees are therefore needed if frozen foods are purchased, and less supervision is required when preparation tasks are reduced. Freezing also simplifies the calculation of costs because the preparation costs do not have to be calculated for frozen foods. Each portion cost can be easily calculated, and prices can be determined on the basis of exact costs.

Portion control is also easier with frozen foods. Frozen products are packaged in standard-sized containers in either bulk or individual portions. The number of portions required can be determined easily, and the problems of overproduction and underproduction are reduced.

The use of frozen foods can reduce cooking time. The cooking time of frozen products as compared to equivalent fresh products is generally reduced by 30 to 50 percent. Frozen prepared dishes require even less cooking time.

Finally, using frozen foods can simplify menu planning. A wider selection of menu items can be offered because of extensive inventory of a variety of frozen foods. Seasonal foods are available throughout the year in frozen form. Greater variety can be offered on the menu without increasing staff or workload.

The freezing process involves freezing the water in food. Water is the main constituent of all perishable foods. This water is not pure, but an unsaturated solution of salts, sugars, acids, and other soluble substances and is, in part, found free in the cells or in the intercellular spaces. The water should be frozen as quickly as possible so that small ice crystals are formed. After the water in the food has been transformed into ice, the damaging activities of the microbes and enzymes are stopped; the gradual degeneration of the vitamins and nutrients ceases.

Only food of the best possible quality should be frozen. The freezing process maintains the original quality of the food prior to freezing; that is, if the product was initially poor, then freezing will not improve it.

The food must be frozen through to the center as fast as possible. Both low temperatures and good freezing performance are necessary. If the freezing process is slow, large ice crystals will form and rupture the cell tissue. Instructions from the manufacturer will specify the amount of food that can be frozen at one time. In case of power failure or mechanical breakdown, dry ice can be placed in the freezer to help keep food frozen. The dry ice should be added as soon as possible after the power goes off.

Frozen foods must be correctly packaged if they are to keep well. Wax-lined cardboard boxes with plastic liners; heavy plastic bags with wire tape; heavy-duty aluminum foil; coated, moisture-vaporproof, laminated freezer paper; polyethylene sheets; and clear plastic wrap are good packaging materials that will protect the food from exposure to air, odors, and dehydration.

It is necessary to maintain a temperature of 0° to −12°F (−18° to −25°C) from the time the food is frozen until it reaches the user. The lower the temperature, the longer the quality can be maintained.

Basically, frozen products are cooked by the same method as their fresh counterparts. Partially or fully thawed frozen food must be consumed quickly. Thawed food should never be refrozen.

Freezing Raw Products

Most vegetables and fruits can be frozen. Some varieties freeze better than others. Fresh meat, game, poultry, feathered game, and freshwater fish can also be frozen. The food products are first blanched, boiled, fried, or otherwise prepared and then frozen.

To freeze vegetables, wash, peel, blanch quickly in boiling water, chill, drain, and pack. The following should not be blanched: cucumber, zucchini, peppers, tomatoes, and kitchen herbs.

Fruits and berries can be frozen without added ingredients, or with the addition of sugar or syrup (possibly with a little ascorbic acid); stone fruits must be blanched.

Only fresh lean meat from young animals should be frozen. The USDA inspection stamp guarantees wholesomeness and the shield-shaped USDA grade mark indicates quality. The meat should be in ready-to-use portions.

Freshwater fish, either whole or filleted, should be kept cold after being caught. The fish should be frozen and glazed. After freezing starts, dip the fish into cold water and complete the freezing process.

Polyethylene bags (odorless, minimum thickness 0.05 mm) and sheets, plastic containers, aluminum foil (extra strong), and aluminum containers are all suitable for packing the food. All frozen products must be *carefully* packed in moisture-vaporproof paper, preferably hermetically sealed, and marked with the date, contents, and weight or number of units. Freezer-proof sealing tape and labels should be used.

Rules for freezing:

- The freezer should be set at the minimum temperature.
- Consider the capacity of the freezer; process only an amount that can be frozen within 24 hours.
- The food should be packed as flat as possible.
- Place the packages against the chilling walls or next to the freezing plates.
- Leave space between the packages so that the cold air can circulate freely.
- Stack packages after they are completely frozen.

The length of time frozen food can be stored depends upon the type of food and its fat content. All frozen food must be stored at 0°F (−18°C) or lower.

- *Fruits and vegetables:* 6 to 12 months
- *Lean meat:* 6 to 10 months
- *Fatty meat:* 2 to 4 months
- *Poultry:* 8 to 10 months
- *Freshwater fish:* 2 to 3 months
- *Baked products:* 2 to 4 months

When cooking frozen raw products, the following points apply to both commercial and home-produced frozen food.

- *Vegetables:* Boiling and steaming times are reduced by one-third to one-half; a minimum of liquid should be added.
- *Fruits:* Fruits for cooking and baking purposes can be used in the frozen state; fruits for salads and desserts are best when partially thawed.
- *Meat, poultry, game:* Thaw large pieces at refrigerator temperature. Thaw small pieces at refrigerator temperature or use in the the frozen or partially thawed state.
- *Fish:* Whole or filleted fish should be thawed until it can be sliced or separated. Breaded fish products should be cooked while still frozen.

Frozen Prepared Foods

Technological developments resulting from both food and equipment research have led to the use of more prepared foods in foodservice establishments in recent years. The shortage of skilled foodservice personnel, spiraling labor costs, and the increasing number of persons eating away from home have augmented the demand for new types and forms of foods that can be served easily with a limited labor force. The ever-increasing number of prepared foods on the market makes it possible to supplement menus and offer greater variety. Some foodservice systems are designed around foods that are prepared on the premises and then frozen and stored for later use.

The extensive use of these partially and fully prepared foods has increased the demand for new types of equipment for processing, storing, finishing, and serving the food.

Although there is a growing trend to produce prepared foods on the premises, there are many problems related to the production techniques: the development of recipes for products that require ingredients, such as antioxidants, emulsifiers, tenderizers, and other unfamiliar products; and the equipment required for processing, packaging, storing, and reconstituting. Because of the high cost of the equipment and the technical knowledge needed for such a system, the more common practice is to purchase commercially prepared products to meet specific needs.

The finishing method for frozen prepared foods depends on the type of dishes, the packaging, and the methods of heating available in the kitchen. All dishes can be further seasoned or garnished. A limited *mise en place* should always be available so the prepared dishes can be finished with a flair and merchandised attractively.

A work sheet with specific directions for thawing, heating, and garnishing should be written for each item. Using such guidelines, even auxiliary personnel can prepare the dish so that it can be served at any time.

Depending on the packaging, the dishes are prepared as follows:

Boiling bags: These are polyethylene packs that are resistant to both very low and very high temperatures. Foods in boiling bags are prepared by placing them, still frozen, into boiling water and heating for the prescribed length of time (15 to 20 minutes). No losses occur, and since they are heated indirectly via the hot water, there is less danger of overcooking. Since the package is hermetically sealed, several different menu items can be heated in the same water.

Alutrays: The heating or final stage of cooking takes place in an oven, a broiler, or in an automatic convection oven. Alutrays cannot be used in microwave ovens. They are generally used for dishes which are to be glazed or gratinated.

Porcelain and plastic containers: When heating in microwave ovens, materials that allow microwaves to pass through and penetrate into the food should be used. China, ceramics, and opaque glass may be used if there is no metal trim or metal base glaze. Plastics, such as plastic wrap or freezer containers, are only suitable for warming food. Only plastics that are labeled "dishwasher proof" or "may be placed in boiling water" should be used. The cover of the containers should be placed loosely on the container to avoid splitting or bursting.

Ready-to-cook dishes: Gnocchi, ravioli, french-fried potatoes, and pommes dauphine should be finished in a frying pan, an oven, or in a deep-fryer depending upon the cooking instructions. The following must be remembered for all dishes: do not cook excessively large quantities at one time; keep the heating equipment hot, so that the temperature does not drop when the food is placed inside.

Meat dishes: Meat dishes that have been frozen with the meat juices or a sauce should be heated slowly in the pan, adding a little liquid. If necessary, the meat juices should be bound as soon as the meat has thawed.

Vegetable dishes: Fully precooked vegetable dishes should be slightly thawed and then heated with a small amount of liquid.

Soups and soup ingredients: Fish soups or specialty soups should be thawed in the pan with a little water and then heated. Soup ingredients, such as shredded savory pancakes (Célestine), marrow, semolina, and liver dumplings should be cooked while still frozen.

7.4.3 *Nacka System*

This method of preservation is a chilling system used in preparation kitchens. The preparation kitchens are located away from the main establishment and are supplied on a daily basis with the appropriate quantities of raw materials. Since this system has only limited use in the hotel and restaurant business, the description here is purposely brief.

This system of preservation was originally developed in Sweden for the personnel of mining companies and was adopted and improved by the Nacka hospital—hence the name. Before freezing, the raw materials are first prepared and cooked. The foods, which are 80 percent precooked, are then packed in vacuum-sealed plastic bags (in individual or up to five portions). A subsequent pasteurizing process is necessary for certain delicate dishes. The prepared foods must then be chilled as quickly as possible to 37° to 39°F (3° to 4°C) either in ice water or in a freezing tunnel. If then stored at the same temperature, the food keeps for about three weeks. For this reason, exact dating is mandatory. Opened bags must be used immediately and must not be refrozen. Any food preserved using this system must be kept chilled until it is to be prepared and served. The following dishes can be prepared using this system: soups, meat with sauce, vegetables, vegetable salads, whipped and fried potatoes, pasta, rice, and corn.

The food is heated by placing the bags in boiling water. Depending upon the size of the bag, the food is either served directly onto the plates or kept warm in bain-marie units. The main advantages of this system are independent preparation; possibility of storage for a few days in a refrigerated storeroom; no expensive finishing equipment required; and no containers to wash. Some disadvantages are limited choice; additional fresh vegetables required to accompany the main dish; limited storage; and danger of scalding oneself when opening multiportion bags.

7.5 Cooking Temperatures of Fats and Oils

Knowledge of the temperature ranges of various fats is necessary to be able to select the correct fat to use. When the smoke point of a fat is reached, chemical changes occur that affect the usability of the fat. Smoke indicates that the fat is breaking down and the product being fried will absorb fat because the proper frying temperatures cannot be maintained. Rancidity in the fat affects the flavor, odor, and usability of the fat and the food fried in the fat.

Maximum Temperature of Fats and Oils

Butter, fresh	300°F (150°C)
Clarified butter	320°F (160°C)
Margarine	300°F (150°C)
Lard	375° to 400°F (180° to 200°C)
Coconut oil	350° to 400°F (180° to 200°C)
Peanut oil	445° to 455°F (230° to 235°C)
Olive oil	400°F (200°C)
Sunflower oil	440°F (220°C)
Palm oil	440°F (220°C)

Required Fat Temperatures for Sautéing

Hamburger	initially 340°F (170°C), then 265°F (130°C)
Sirloin steak	initially 340°F (170°C), then 265°F (130°C)
Châteaubriand	initially 320°F (160°C), then 255°F (125°C)
Tournedos	initially 340°F (170°C), then 285°F (140°C)

Veal cutlet	initially 285°F (140°C), then 265°F (130°C)
Veal chop	initially 285°F (140°C), then 250°F (120°C)
Pork chop	initially 285°F (140°C), then 265°F (130°C)
Mutton chop	initially 340°F (170°C), then 265°F (130°C)
Breaded cutlet	initially 265°F (130°C), then 240°F (115°C)
Fish à la meunière	initially 285°F (140°C), then 230°F (110°C)

Deep-Frying

Only very *heat-resistant, nonfoaming fats* should be used for deep-frying. Fats should not be mixed with oils, since this inevitably leads to foaming. Hydrogenated fats and natural fats are resistant to oxidation changes that cause breakdown. Overheating the fat can be prevented by correct adjustment of the heat controls and periodic checks of the thermostats. The fat in the deep-fryer should be filtered after each use. The deep-fryer should be covered when cool to protect it from the effects of light and oxygen. Deep-fryers should not be overloaded. It is better to use two or more of them. Oils with a high polyunsaturated fatty-acid content are not suitable for deep-frying, since these acids combine very quickly with the oxygen in the air and oxidize. For example, sunflower seed oil should not be used for deep-frying, in spite of its high smoke point, because of its more than 50 percent content of polyunsaturated fatty acids. Soybean oil, corn oil, sesame oil, and rapeseed oil are not suitable for deep-frying. The following list indicates required fat temperatures for deep-frying.

Small fish, for one-step frying	350°F (180°C)
Larger fish or pieces of fish, for blanching	265° to 285°F (130°C to 140°C)
Larger fish or pieces of fish, for frying	350°F (180°C)

French-fried potatoes	350°F (180°C)
Croquettes	320°F (160°C)
Choux, beignets, doughnuts	320° to 340°F (160°C to 170°C)
Vegetables, for frying	320° to 340°F (160°C to 170°C)

7.6 Basic Principles of Roasting

Roasting refers to the process of cooking in an uncovered container without water, the dry heat surrounding the food.

7.6.1 *Roasting Meats*

Roasting is recommended for large tender cuts of beef, veal, pork, lamb, and for some poultry and game. The length of time of roasting must be controlled or the product will dry out. Only tender, top-grade, and fine-quality meats are suitable for roasting. Well-marbled and fat-covered meats provide better roasts. Lean meats must be larded or barded before roasting since they have little or no fat content.

7.6.2 *Roasting Equipment*

There are two methods for roasting meat: the spit (see figure 7-60), and the oven. Domestic ovens incorporating a spit are also available. Roasting on the spit involves only heat conducted by radiation. Oven roasting involves heat conducted by radiation, by direct contact, or by convection. The roasting pan or other container must be of an appropriate size for the piece of meat to avoid burning the fat and meat juices on the exposed surfaces not covered by the meat.

When roasting in the oven, the following rules should be followed:

- Place roasts fat side up and poultry breast side down in an open shallow roasting pan or on a grill placed on a pan to retain the fat and juices.
- Insert a meat thermometer in the meat so the bulb is in the center of the largest muscle. The bulb should not touch the bone or fat.
- Do not cover; add no liquids.
- Roast fat-covered meats (lean meats may need to

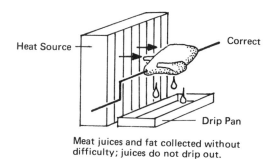

Heat Source — |→ → →| — Correct

— Drip Pan

Meat juices and fat collected without difficulty; juices do not drip out.

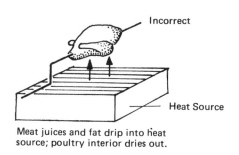

— Incorrect

↑ ↑ — Heat Source

Meat juices and fat drip into heat source; poultry interior dries out.

Figure 7-60. Roasting on a spit.

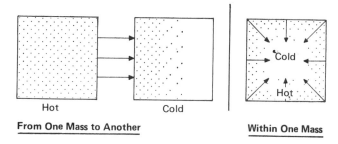

Hot   Cold

From One Mass to Another   Cold   Hot   **Within One Mass**

Figure 7-61. Heat moves from hot to cold areas. When meat is roasted, the cold exterior is heated first and then the interior is heated.

be barded or larded) in a preheated oven at 300°F (150°C) and maintain this temperature throughout roasting process. Roast small roasts at 350°F (175°C). Sear roasts with little fat covering in an oven preheated to 475°F (245°C). Leave at this temperature until browned, then reduce temperature to 300°F (150°C) and complete roasting.

- Remove the roast from the oven when the proper internal temperature has been reached. If the roast is allowed to stand before carving, remove it from the oven when the thermometer registers five to ten degrees below the desired degree of doneness.
- Allow the roast to stand 15 to 20 minutes in a warm place after removing from oven.

7.6.3 The Roasting Process

Roasting occurs with the penetration of heat from the exterior of the meat toward the interior. (See figure 7-61.) The amount of time that the meat will be exposed to heat penetration depends upon the type of

meat and the degree of roasting required. The roasting time is determined by the thickness of the meat and the weight. Should the thickness of the meat not be uniform, it must either be cut into two pieces, or the thinner part must be protected from the heat with aluminum foil. Meat should be at room temperature before roasting.

Our ancestors had neither thermometers nor thermostats, nor was it possible to adjust the oven and spit temperatures by operating a switch or turning a tap. Nevertheless, they were excellent at roasting meat, since they carefully controlled the flow of the heat from the oven or spit to the roast itself. The same degree of care and attention is necessary today. The size of the oven, its heating capacity, and the heat conduction techniques used must be considered. It is not possible to roast a large amount of meat in a small oven, nor in one that heats too slowly because its burners are too small. If the voltage has dropped or the gas pressure has been lowered, it will also be difficult to roast the meat properly. On the other hand, an oven can be equipped with a very fast and powerful heating system that needs to be carefully controlled. The oven can also be too large for the size of the piece of meat. The art of roasting requires coordination of all these factors to achieve the correct heat flow. Constant checking permits the roast cook to recognize whether the degree of heat is insufficient or excessive and enables him to make the appropriate adjustments. The temperatures used for roasting sometimes tend to be too high because of the old theory that all the juices would be lost if the meat was not seared. It is true that meat without a fat covering may be seared. If roasting begins at 450° to 500°F (235 to 255°C), the temperature should be lowered to 300°F (150°C) as soon as the meat is brown. The beginner will soon notice that the thicker the meat, the lower the temperature required, and that the highest temperature, 500°F (255°C), is used only for the smallest pieces. High temperatures during roasting cause the fat to melt and much of the meat juice to evaporate, leading to a reduction in weight and volume and resulting in the formation of a bitter and inedible crust. It is, therefore, important to check and maintain this equilibrium of heat throughout the roasting process.

The roasting time depends on the thickness, weight, size of the piece of meat, and upon the degree of roasting desired. There is no definite rule for the time required for roasting. However, extensive research has made it possible to provide guidelines for average roasting times, which every cook should know. (See figures 7-62 to 7-65). It is, of course, necessary to differentiate between roasting white meats, including poultry, which many people prefer well done, and red meats, which are often served more rare. If the bone is left in the meat, or the spit is used, the roasting time will be longer.

A number of methods are used for determining the degree of roasting necessary. The needle test is an old, well-proven method for measuring the degree to which meat of any kind is roasted. A needle is inserted into the middle of the roast. The color of the meat juices shows the degree to which the meat has been roasted. (See figure 7-66.) There is another method

Type	Approximate Roasting Time per Piece
Leg of venison	30 to 40 min.
	Per lb.: 8 to 10 min.
Saddle of venison	20 to 30 min.
	Per lb.: 6 to 8 min.
Saddle of hare	15 to 20 min.
Wild boar	As for pork, well done
Woodcock	12 to 15 min.
Quail	8 to 10 min.
Wild duck	15 to 20 min. (rare)
Pheasant: 1¾ to 2½ lb.	20 to 25 min. depending upon the size
Partridge	12 to 18 min.

Figure 7-63. Roasting times for game, cooked medium to medium rare. Sear if desired at 450° to 500°F (232° to 255°C) before roasting at 350° to 400°F (171° to 200°C).

for determining the degree to which poultry is roasted. The poultry is held above a white plate with the legs toward the plate. If the juices are clear and light, the bird is well done. (See figure 7-67.)

The temperature of the meat is measured using a meat thermometer. The newest and most reliable roasting method works on the principle that each stage of the cooking process results from a definite meat temperature. The tip of the thermometer is equipped with a heat-sensitive point. Therefore, the tip should be inserted into the thickest part of the meat and should not be in contact with any bones, fat,

Type	Thin (1½ in.)	Thick (2½ to 3 in.)	Extra-thick (4 in. plus)
Beef tenderloin, whole	5 to 6 min. per lb.	8 to 10 min. per lb.	roast at 425°F (220°C) for 50 min.
Beef sirloin	8 min. per lb.	10 to 13 min. per lb.	—
Rib roast	—	—	15 to 18 min. per lb.
Saddle of lamb	8 min. per lb.	10 min. per lb.	—
Leg of lamb	8 min. per lb.	13 min. per lb.	15 to 20 min. per lb.

Figure 7-62. Roasting times for beef and lamb, cooked medium. Roast at 300°F (150°C) or sear first at 500°F (225°C) before roasting at 300°F (150°C).

Type	Thin (1½ in.)	Thick (2½ to 4 in.)
All cuts	10 min. per lb.	18 to 20 min. per lb.

Figure 7-64. Roasting times for veal and pork, cooked well-done. Sear if desired at 400° to 450°F (210° to 227°C) before roasting at 300° to 325°F (150° to 163°C).

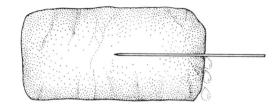

Figure 7-66. Insert a needle into a roast and check the color of the juices to determine the degree of roasting.

or equipment. The thermometers pictured in figure 7-68 are used as follows:

- Move the arrow until it is set to the desired degree of doneness.
- Insert the thermometer into the meat before starting the cooking process.
- When the temperature-indicating needle points to the arrow, the required degree of doneness has been reached.

Meat temperatures for all types of roasts:

- *Rare:* Only for red meat, meat temperature of 125°F (50°C); meat juices are dark red

- *Medium rare:* Only for red meat, meat temperature of about 130°F (55°C); meat juices are red
- *Medium:* Only for red meat and game, meat temperature of about 140°F (60°C); meat juices are pink
- *Well-done:* For red meat, about 160°F (70°C); for veal and lamb, about 170°F (77°C); for fresh pork, about 170°F (77°C); for fresh poultry, 170° to 185°F (77° to 85°C); meat juices are clear and light

Type	Weight	Approximate Roasting Time per Piece	Per Pound
Capon	4 to 6 lb.	70 to 90 min.	
Roaster	3 to 4 lb.	50 to 70 min.	
Chicken	2 to 2½ lb.	35 to 45 min.	
Spring chicken	1½ to 1¾ lb.	25 to 35 min.	
Chick	14 oz.	15 min.	
Turkey	8 to 12 lb.		18 min.
Young turkey	5 to 8 lb.		15 to 18 min.
Guinea fowl	1½ to 2 lb.	30 to 35 min.	
Nantes duckling	3 to 4 lb.	35 to 40 min.	
Duck	4 to 5 lb.		15 to 18 min.
Gosling	3 to 6 lb.		15 to 18 min.
Goose	6 to 12 lb.		18 to 20 min.
Young pigeon	½ to ¾ lb.	12 to 15 min.	
Pigeon	14 to 16 oz.	15 to 20 min.	

Figure 7-65. Roasting times for poultry, cooked well-done but juicy. Sear if desired at 400° to 450°F (210° to 227°C) before roasting at 325° to 350°F (160° to 171°C).

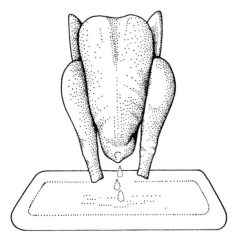

Figure 7-67. Hold poultry over a white plate, legs down, and check the color of the juices to determine the degree of roasting.

7.6.4 *Presentation of Roasts*

After roasting is complete, large roasts should stand in a warm place for 10 to 15 minutes. The roast should be removed from the oven when the thermometer registers five to ten degrees lower than the desired degree of doneness, as the meat continues to cook upon removal from the oven. The roast is allowed to rest so that the juices that accumulate in the center spread throughout the entire piece of meat. Furthermore, the meat will be easier to carve and juices will not be lost during carving. Small pieces of feathered game or roast poultry must be served immediately.

When roasted meat has been carved, it should be served at once. The gravy obtained by deglazing is served separately in a sauceboat.

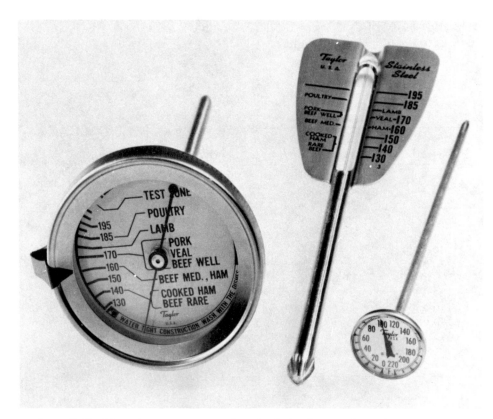
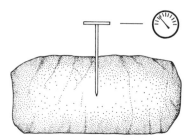

Figure 7-68. Meat thermometers used to check the degree of roasting.

7.7 Portion Sizes

The type of establishment and the clientele exert a significant influence upon portion sizes and the quantities needed. The information in figure 7-69 should be considered as a general guideline. For example, whether a braised meat dish forms part of a menu together with an hors d'oeuvre, dessert, and an entrée or of a menu with a soup as the only other dish makes a great difference in terms of the quantity of braised meat required. Every establishment should prepare a table of quantities for its own requirements, expressed in gross weights for the kitchen records, and in ready-to-cook weights for the preparation kitchen.

	Per Person	
	Menu	à la Carte
Soups		
Portion	—	½ pint
Plate	⅓ pint	⅓ pint
Cup	½ pint	½ pint
Small cup	2 fluid ounces	2 fluid ounces
Pasta to be added per quart	1 ounce	1 ounce
Egg dishes	2 units	2 units
Sauces		
Brown and white sauce	2 fluid ounces	4 fluid ounces
Hollandaise	2 fluid ounces	4 fluid ounces
Melted butter	¾ ounce	1 ounce
Fish (ready to cook)		
Perch	5½ ounces	9 ounces
Grayling	5½ ounces	9 ounces
Trout	5½ ounces	9 ounces
Pike	5½ ounces	9 ounces
Salmon	5½ ounces	9 ounces
Sole	5½ ounces	9 ounces
Turbot	7 ounces	10½ ounces
Pike-perch	5½ ounces	9 ounces
Prepared fillets	3½ ounces	6½ ounces

	Per Person	
	Menu	à la Carte
Beef (ready to cook)		
Tenderloin steak	4¼ ounces	6½ ounces
Sirloin steak	4¼ ounces	6½ ounces
Rump steak	4¼ ounces	6½ ounces
Boiled beef	5½ ounces	9 ounces
Tenderloin goulash	4¼ ounces	6½ ounces
Roast beef	4¼ ounces	6½ ounces
Braised beef/goulash	5½ ounces	7 ounces
Tongue	4¼ ounces	6½ ounces
Tripe	4¼ ounces	6½ ounces
Veal (ready to cook)		
Cutlet	4¼ ounces	5½ ounces
Cutlet for breading	3½ ounces	4¼ ounces
Roast	5½ ounces	6½ ounces
Chop	5½ ounces	6½ ounces
Sliced	3½ ounces	5½ ounces
Liver, kidneys	3½ ounces	5½ ounces
Head (without bone)	5½ ounces	9 ounces
Stew	5½ ounces	9 ounces
Pork (ready to cook)		
Chop	5½ ounces	6½ ounces
Chop, smoked, cured	5½ ounces	6½ ounces
Roast	5½ ounces	6½ ounces
Ham	3½ ounces	5½ ounces
Bacon	3½ ounces	5½ ounces
Lamb/Mutton (ready to cook)		
Chop	4¼ ounces	7 ounces
Stew or Irish stew	5½ ounces	9 ounces
Roast	5½ ounces	6½ ounces
Goat (ready to cook)	9 ounces	12½ ounces
Game (ready to cook)		
Leg of venison	6½ ounces	9 ounces
Saddle of vension	8 ounces	12½ ounces
Game stew (without bones)	5½ ounces	7 ounces
Rabbit stew (without bones)	5½ ounces	7 ounces
Saddle of hare	7 ounces	10½ ounces

Figure 7-69. Suggested guidelines for portion sizes.

	Per Person	
	Menu	*à la Carte*
Pheasant	7 ounces	10½ ounces
Partridge	7 ounces	10½ ounces
Poultry (ready to cook)		
Chicken	10½ ounces	14 ounces
Duck	10½ ounces	14 ounces
Goose	12½ ounces	1 pound
Turkey	10½ ounces	12½ ounces
Guinea fowl	7 ounces	10½ ounces
Pigeon	7 ounces	10½ ounces
Pasta	2 ounces	3½ ounces
Rice	2 ounces	3 ounces
Potatoes (peeled)	5½ ounces	7 ounces
Vegetables (ready to cook)	3½ ounces	5½ ounces
Asparagus	7 ounces	10½ ounces
Tomato salad (ready to serve)	3½ ounces	5½ ounces

	Per Person	
	Menu	*à la Carte*
Cold Meat Dishes		
Mixed cold cuts	—	5½ ounces
Ham (without bone)	—	5½ ounces
Salami	—	3 ounces
Bacon, Canadian	—	3½ ounces
Open-faced sandwich with beef	—	3½ ounces
Open-faced sandwich with ham	—	3 ounces
Open-faced sandwich with salami	—	2 ounces
Cheese and Cheese Dishes		
Cheese	—	3½ ounces
Cheese slices	2 ounces	4¼ ounces
Fondue	—	5½ ounces

Figure 7-69. *continued.*

Chapter 8
The Basic Cooking Methods

The basic cooking methods are used separately or in combination to prepare all cooked food items. This chapter tells how the heat is initiated and controlled for each method of preparation. There are eleven basic methods. Each must be thoroughly understood and properly executed for perfect cooking—cooking that will ensure highest quality in terms of flavor, color, appearance, and nutritional value.

8.1 Blanching—*Blanchir*

Blanching is often a preliminary cooking method; when done in hot oil, it is equivalent to a prefrying process.

Two procedures can be used to blanch foods. For the first, place the food in a large quantity of cold water (1 part food to 10 parts water). Bring to a boil (212°F/100°C) slowly, uncovered, and boil for a short time. Plunge the food into cold water quickly to prevent further cooking if the food is not to be used immediately. This method is used primarily to blanch bones and certain cuts of meat. It helps open the pores and leech out excess salts from cured ham and salt pork, as well as excess blood from some meats.

For the second blanching procedure, place a small amount of food in a large quantity of rapidly boiling water (1 part food to 10 parts water). Return to a boil, and boil uncovered for a short time. Plunge the food into cold water quickly to prevent further cooking, drain, and refrigerate if the food is not to be used immediately. This method is used mostly for vegeta-bles and potatoes. It closes pores and helps retain color and nutrients.

Fish, vegetables, and potatoes can also be blanched in hot oil; the procedure is similar to that for the second blanching procedure, with hot oil, about 275°F (130°C), used in place of water.

8.2 Poaching—*Pocher*

Poaching is a gentle cooking process that prevents food from drying out. Food may be poached in water, court bouillon, or stock in a saucepan, or it may be poached in a water bath (bain-marie) or double boiler. In either case, the water should be between 150° and 175°F (65° to 85°C), and the vesicle should remain uncovered.

Fish (wrapped in aluminum foil) and poultry are often poached in stock or court bouillon. Dumplings, variety meats, smoked pork, sausages, and eggs are poached in water. Note, when poaching eggs, that the water temperature must stay below 175°F (80°C), or albumin (protein) will be lost. Farces, stuffings, puddings, potatoes, vegetables, timbales, sweets, and custards are placed in molds or glass containers and poached, without stirring, in water baths. Creams, sponge cake batters, and sauces are poached, with stirring, in water baths.

8.3 Boiling and Simmering—*Bouillir et mijotir*

A variety of foods are boiled or simmered in a variety of ways, for a number of reasons. Potatoes, dried vegetables, and bones should be placed in cold water, covered, and brought to a boil; boiling in this way allows them to absorb water and cook evenly, while preventing tough or hard exteriors. Clear stocks, broths, and meat jellies (aspics) should be simmered, *not* boiled, uncovered, to prevent cloudiness. Vegetables are placed in boiling water, covered, to help them cook more quickly and thus retain nutrients and color. Pasta and rice are cooked in rapidly boiling water, uncovered. Rapid boiling is needed because starch on their exteriors gelatinizes; the boiling water prevents the pieces from sticking to each other. Blanched meat and poultry, such as beef, veal, mutton, lamb, and chicken, are placed in water or stock that is just boiling, uncovered, for a few minutes, to close the pores. The temperature should then be reduced to a gentle simmer; add more liquid if necessary.

8.4 Steaming—*Cuire à vapeur*

Steaming reduces cooking time, so that more nutrients remain in the food. Because the food is not immersed in water, the food can be used without draining; moreover, the food is not disturbed during cooking.

Steaming can be done without pressure or with pressure. To steam without pressure, use a heavy container with a perforated base, grating, or basket, and a heavy cover. Keep the level of the boiling water below the food. The heat should be very high, 400° to 425°F (200° to 220°C). Replace any water that is lost by evaporation. Some soups, meats, poultry, vegetables, potatoes, legumes, and rice are steamed this way. Soups, most rice dishes, and cereals are steamed in liquid that is superheated. This method of steaming is also used for canning.

Steaming under pressure requires a pressure cooker, for wet heat, or a high-speed steam cooker, for dry heat. This method of steaming cooks food very quickly. The best working pressure is 5.5 to 7 pounds per square inch (psi). Follow the equipment manufacturer's instructions carefully when steaming under pressure.

8.5 Deep-fat Frying—*Frire*

Fish, meat, poultry, vegetables, potatoes, fritters, beignets, doughnuts, and other desserts are prepared by deep-fat frying. Place the shortening or oil in a deep-fat fryer; if using solid shortening, keep the temperature at 200°F (93°C) until the fat has melted. The fat must not foam; if it does, it should be discarded. Do not use polyunsaturated fat for deep-frying, as it will break down under the high temperatures (fat that breaks down will smoke at low temperatures [below 340°F/170°C], will foam, and will have a dark color and unpleasant odor). After the fat has melted, set the thermostat to the temperature required for the food being cooked, usually between 325° and 350°F (160° and 180°C). Food should be dry and at room temperature before frying (frozen, blanched potatoes and shrimp are exceptions). Shake off any loose breading or crumbs before frying foods. Fry only small quantities of food at a time to avoid absorption of fat and drops in the fat's temperature. Do not salt over the fryer, as salt breaks down fat. Do not use a cover in deep-frying; the steam trapped by the cover will make crisp foods soggy. Drain the grease from fried foods before serving.

8.6 Sautéing—*Sauter*

Sautéing is the quick cooking of food in a small amount of fat. Medium to high heat, 325° to 475°F (160° to 240°C) is used to cook the food quickly. The term *pan-frying* is often used interchangeably with sautéing; this is incorrect: pan-frying is principally used for poultry, large fish, and other foods that are sometimes finished by slow cooking in the oven.

Sautéing is used for two purposes: to cook small pieces of food, such as diced or cut-up meat and poultry, fish, vegetables, and potatoes, quickly, or to sear and cook chops, cutlets, steaks, poultry and small fish or fillets, as well as some sliced vegetables.

When sautéing small pieces of food, use a sauté pan (*sauteuse*). Add a small amount of fat, heat, add the food, and sauté quickly by shaking the uncovered pan constantly. Blanched, dried vegetables can be sautéed in this way. Small pieces of meat are also sautéed this way; after they are cooked, remove them from the pan and keep them warm, add a bit more fat and some stock or wine to the remaining juices, reduce the liquid, and return the meat to the reduced sauce.

A large sauté pan (*sautoir*) is used to sauté larger pieces of meat. Heat a small quantity of fat, add the food, and quickly brown each side. Do not shake the pan; simply flip the food frequently until browned. The pan should not be covered. Vegetables, such as raw slices of eggplant, zucchini, or potatoes, can also be sautéed in this manner.

An omelet pan is sometimes used for sautéing, as is a griddle, though a griddle is not suitable for finely cut meats.

8.7 Broiling/Grilling—*Griller*

Meat, such as chops, cutlets, and steaks; poultry; sausages; fish; and shellfish can all be prepared by broiling or grilling. Vegetables and potatoes may also be prepared in this manner if first wrapped in aluminum foil.

Place the food to be grilled or broiled on a rack. The heat source may be from above, below, or both. Use high heat, 425° to 475°F (220° to 250°C) at the beginning to sear the meat, then lower the temperature to between 300° and 400°F (150° and 200°C) and cook to the desired degree of doneness. Use high heat and a short cooking time for small pieces; larger pieces should cook longer at a more moderate temperature. Do not use a fork to test for doneness, as piercing the meat will allow meat juices to escape. Instead, use a spatula. Meat that is rare (*bleu*) will be soft, spongy, and bloody. Medium-rare (*saignant*) meat will be springy and bloody. Medium-done (*à point*) meat is slightly springy. Well-done (*bien cuit*) meat is firm and does not spring back. Red meat is usually cooked medium or medium rare, whereas white meat is almost always cooked until well done.

Meat, fish, and poultry that are to be grilled are often marinated beforehand. Marinating provides flavor and can help tenderize by softening and moistening the food. A marinade usually consists of seasonings and acid, such as vinegar or wine. Steep the food in the marinade for at least 30 minutes before grilling or broiling.

8.8 Gratinating—*Gratiner*

Food that is prepared au gratin has a topping of crumbs (such as breadcrumbs or crushed crackers, corn-flake crumbs, or crushed potato chips) combined with a high-fat product such as butter, cheese, cream, or eggs. To prepare fish, meat, poultry, vegetables, potatoes, pasta, casseroles, or escalloped dishes au gratin, place the food in a dish, top with the gratin, and place uncovered under a salamander or broiler or in an oven, with high heat, 475° to 550°F (250° to 300°C), until a golden brown crust forms. Flat fish, thin slices of meat, and vegetables with a high moisture content, such as tomatoes, are prepared au gratin in the same manner but require lower heat.

This same basic procedure is used to caramelize sugar sprinkled on sweet desserts; the sugar replaces the gratin.

8.9 Oven-baking—*Cuire au four*

A wide variety of foods are baked in an oven, including potatoes, pasta dishes, many desserts and pastries, fish, and ham. Set the oven's thermostat to the desired temperature, which can range from 275° to 475°F (140° to 250°C), depending on the food being cooked. Place the food on a greased sheet pan or rack, or use molds without covers. Bake to the desired degree of doneness. Some preparations require the oven heat to be increased or decreased after a certain period of time. The oven, at a low temperature, may also be used to dry, rather than cook, certain foods, such as meringues.

A convection oven may also be used for baking. Fans force heated air into the oven cavity, resulting in more rapid baking. A slightly higher temperature is required in a convection oven than in a conventional oven. Any food that can be baked in a conventional oven can also be baked in a convection oven. In addition, convection ovens are often used to heat already-prepared convenience foods, which should be covered while baking.

8.10 Roasting—*Rôtir*

Foods can be roasted in an oven in two ways. Top grades of meat with fat covering, such as prime rib, rib eye, sirloin rump roast, and turkey, are not seared but are roasted at a constant temperature. Insert a meat thermometer so the heat sensor (the tip) is in the center of the largest muscle of the meat. Roast the meat, fat side up, at 300° to 350°F (150° to 175°C) until the thermometer registers the desired degree of doneness (see chapter 7 for recommended roasting times). Do not cover, and do not add liquid.

Large pieces of fish, poultry, game, and meat without fat covering, as well as potatoes, are seared before roasting. Sear meat in the oven in an uncovered dish at 400°F (200°C). Then insert a meat thermometer into the food so that the heat sensor (the tip) is in the center of the largest muscle. Place in a 300°F (150°C) oven and roast, basting frequently, until the thermometer registers the desired degree of doneness (see chapter 7 for recommended roasting times). Sear fish in the same way, but roast at 225°F (110°C). Sear poultry, game, and potatoes in this way as well, but roast at 325° to 400°F (180° to 200°C).

Food that is roasted on a spit is also seared, but at a higher temperature than oven-roasted foods, 475° to 525°F (250° to 280°C). Spit-roasted food also requires more frequent basting. The larger the piece of meat, the lower the temperature required after searing.

8.11 Braising, Glazing, Pot-roasting, and Stewing—*Braiser, glacer, poêler, et étuver*

Braising, glazing, pot-roasting, and stewing are all similar methods of preparation. Each is a gentle form of cooking in which the food is covered and heated in liquid. The more tender the food, the lower the heat and the less liquid required.

8.11.1 *Braising*—Braiser

Red meat, fish, and vegetables are often braised. To braise red meat, such as beef, mutton, or lamb, cover and sear the meat with a *mirepoix* with fat at 400°F (200°C). Add red wine or marinade to the pan and reduce, uncovered, at a temperature of about 350°F (180°C). Add stock to one-quarter of the meat's height, cover, and braise in the oven at 350°F (180°C), basting and turning the meat frequently. Remove the meat, reduce the stock over high heat, 425°F (220°C), strain, and degrease. Return the meat to the pan and braise, uncovered, at 400°F (200°C), basting regularly, until tender.

Vegetables, including green beans, cabbage, lettuce, and fennel, are also often braised in the oven. Begin by stewing the vegetables, covered, with a small amount of liquid, in the oven set at a low temperature, 275°F (140°C). Add broth or other liquid to one-third the depth of the vegetables, cover, and braise, basting occasionally, in the oven at about 325°F (160°C). Remove the vegetables, reduce the liquid, and serve it as a sauce.

Fish, such as salmon, carp, trout, and turbot, are braised like vegetables are. Add a *matignon* to the fish while stewing. Then add a mixture of half white wine and half fish stock. Cover and braise in the oven, basting frequently. Remove the fish, reduce the liquid, and serve as a sauce.

8.11.2 *Glazing*—Glacer

Glazing is similar to braising but is used for white meat and poultry, as well as some vegetables. To glaze white meat, such as veal, and poultry, such as turkey or chicken, begin by searing, with a *mirepoix*, covered, in the oven at 350°F (170°C). Add wine or marinade to deglaze the pan, reduce, and baste—or glaze—the meat. The glaze will coat the meat to prevent loss of juices. Add stock until it reaches one-sixth the depth of the meat. Braise, covered, at 325°F (160°C), basting frequently, until almost tender. Increase the oven temperature to 400°F (200°C), and cover the meat with the strong glaze, which has been produced by the high gelatin content of the meat combined with the stock and wine. Remove the meat, add white wine and stock to the mixture, reduce, strain, and degrease.

To glaze vegetables, such as carrots, parsnips, turnips, and pearl onions, as well as chestnuts, blanch first and then place in a saucepan with a small quantity of stock or water. Add a little butter and sugar, cover, and stew at 300°F (150°C). Uncover, increase the temperature to 400°F (200°C), and glaze by shaking the pan to coat the vegetables. Add a little more sugar toward the end of the cooking time to increase the glazing effect.

8.11.3 *Pot-roasting*—Poêler

Poultry, such as chicken, turkey, goose, or duck, and meats, including veal and beef, may be pot-roasted. (Poultry may require barding first.) Place the meat or poultry in a pan with a little butter, cover, and roast in the oven at 275° to 325°F (140° to 160°C), basting regularly. Uncover, increase the heat to 325° to 350°F (160° to 180°C), and cook until golden. Remove the meat, deglaze the pan, and reduce the liquid.

8.11.4 *Stewing*—Etuver

Some foods, such as fish, small pieces of meat, high-moisture vegetables, and fruits, are cooked, or stewed, in their own liquids. Place the food in a saucepan with a bit of fat and a very small amount of—or no—liquid, and simmer, covered, on the stove over low heat, 250° to 275°F (120° to 140°C). When the food's liquid has been released and the food is cooked, remove the food and reduce the liquid.

Chapter 9
Convenience Foods

The term *convenience foods,* of American origin, has spread throughout the world. The definition of convenience foods is simple: all raw materials that are in any way processed constitute convenience foods. Hundreds of years ago, and even to this day among certain African tribes, families transformed their grains of corn into semolina or flour using mortars or other primitive grinding implements. Even these simple processes may be described as resulting in convenience foods. The same is true for fermenting and drying tea, for roasting and grinding coffee. Be it roasted coffee, ground cereals, peeled carrots, filleted fish, portioned and breaded cutlets, ready-to-use meats, or prepared meals, all may be classified under the general heading convenience foods. Recently a more specific term, *ready foods,* has come into use. This term refers to preserved, prepared dishes and prepared meals manufactured ready to use. It would appear that even in earlier times people sought to make certain foods available in a semiprepared condition; nevertheless, there has been a meteoric expansion in the use of convenience foods over the last few decades.

The application possibilities for convenience and ready foods are practically unlimited. It is important to choose applications that increase, rather than decrease, productivity and, at the same time, lower overhead costs. We must, therefore, be aware of where, how, and when convenience foods can be used.

Where

- All hotel and restaurant establishments
- Canteens and institutions
- Hospitals and health-care centers
- The military
- At home
- Schools and colleges

How:

- Partially processed products
- Ready-to-cook products
- Ready-to-heat dishes
- Ready-to-serve products

When:

- Staff is limited
- Storage space is insufficient
- Raw products are unavailable
- Raw products cannot be stored
- Processing equipment is inadequate
- Preparation and finishing areas and equipment are inadequate
- Time is limited

Purchasing, storing, serving, and merchandising these food products require a sound knowledge of basic food production and service. Unless the appropriate techniques and knowledge are used in handling and evaluating these products, great losses in food quality and costs can be incurred.

A continuous education program should be in effect to provide instruction to food production and service employees. There must first be an understanding of the basic principles of purchasing, food production and service, menu planning, storage, and merchandising. A knowledge of these principles is required before new systems, techniques, and methods can be understood and effectively applied to the use of these new food products.

9.1 Degrees of Preparation

As figure 9-1 shows, there are four different degrees to which food can be prepared. A simple example

illustrates the structure of the different degrees or stages and how they are partially interdependent. A whole roaster chicken is purchased. It must then be cleaned, and when this is completed, the product is partially processed. If it is then cut into portions, it becomes a ready-to-cook product. When further prepared by applying one of the basic forms of preparation, such as braising, it becomes a ready-to-heat

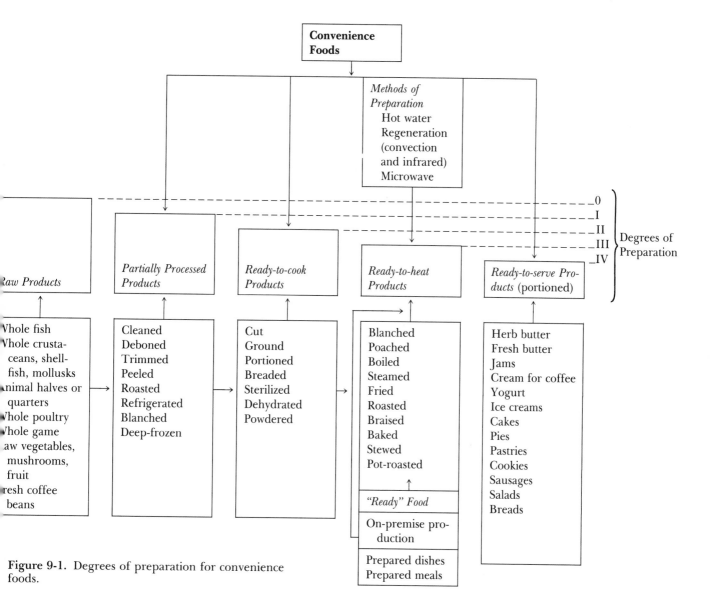

Figure 9-1. Degrees of preparation for convenience foods.

product, such as *poulet sauté* or braised chicken. If the same food is garnished with mushrooms, vegetables, potatoes, or noodles, it is a ready-to-heat meal. Products that are ready-to-serve can also be partially prepared from the basic raw materials but are usually served "as is" to the guest. The chronological order shown in figure 9-1 illustrates the possibility of purchasing many products from industrial suppliers at any degree of preparation desired. The organization of the establishment and its kitchens will determine whether the products should arrive in raw condition or partially or completely prepared. A knowledge of the methods of preservation of food, as described in chapter 7, is necessary. These can be briefly recalled as: drying, hot-packing, salting, smoking, dehydrating, marinating, pickling, sterilizing, vacuum packing, refrigerating, freezing, and freeze-drying. The most important method of preservation in the hotel and restaurant business is freezing. Other processes used in the industry include pasteurizing, steaming, chemically acidifying, and the Nacka system.

9.2 Methods of Preparation

Convenience foods may be heated by several different methods. The heating process should have no detrimental effect on the quality, degree of doneness, or appearance of the food. An instruction sheet, including the following information, should be prepared for each item:

- Product
- Unit, weight, number of portions
- Supplier
- Equipment to be used for preparation
- Length of time and temperature for preparation
- Additional ingredients
- Presentation

Hot water, regeneration, and microwave heating are most frequently used to prepare preserved convenience foods.

Hot Water

Preparation in hot water is usually used with the boiling bag process. A large quantity of water is heated to

185° to 195°F (85° to 91°C) in a bain-marie, in a fixed or tilting steam-jacketed kettle, or in a simple open pot. The ratio of hot water to boiling bag should be at least 20 : 1 by volume. When dipping the usually chilled or frozen boiling bag into the hot water, the temperature of the water should never be allowed to drop more than 10°F (5°C). The length of the heating period depends upon the size and characteristics of the product in the bag. Several components of the menu can be heated at the same time. Care must be taken to avoid burning oneself when opening the bag after heating. Depending on the size of the units, the products are either served directly or held in bains-marie.

Microwave

The principles of microwave heating is described under *Heating Methods and Equipment* in chapter 2. This is a heating process and not a basic form of preparation. Frozen prepared foods should usually be thawed before heating. Certain precautions should be taken when using a microwave oven. These include:

- Metal objects should never be put in the cooking chamber
- Sauces should be heated separately when possible
- Sauced dishes may splatter, so the crockery should be covered with paper toweling or a paper plate
- Sealed boiling bags or closed plastic containers should be pierced before placing in the oven to allow steam to escape during cooking
- Dishes or containers used in the oven should be: heat-tempered, ovenproof clear glass containers without metal trim; china, ceramics, pottery without metal trim or metal base glaze; paper dishes
- The preserving method used for the food can cause taste changes during the heating process; therefore, each dish must be seasoned to taste before serving
- The microwave oven must be kept spotlessly clean
- The oven should be turned on only when the

door is closed and when there is food in the oven to avoid damaging the Magnetron tube

Almost all products need to be prepared, using one of the basic forms of preparation, before heating in the microwave oven. Microwave ovens are particularly suitable for preparing convenience foods.

Regeneration Equipment

As explained in chapter 2, regeneration ovens function using either convected hot air or infrared heat. They are suitable for heating quantities of food for large groups, banquets, or parties. The previously prepared meals are portioned on plates or unitized platters, which are individually covered. The plates, arranged on mobile oven racks, can be rolled from the preparation area into the oven and from the oven to the serving area. Depending on the size of the oven, between thirty-two and seventy-two meals can be heated simultaneously in about 15 minutes. These ovens reduce cooking time and the multiple shelves spaced close together increase the oven capacity. They are useful for banquets of all sizes, for canteens, and for groups of people arriving at undetermined times, such as road, rail, and air travelers.

9.3 On-Premise Production of Convenience Foods

As previously stated, the term convenience foods refers to prepared dishes and prepared meals. In principle, they are portioned and ready-to-serve. The possible preserving techniques and methods of preparation are limited. The methods of preservation are:

- Refrigerated, ready-to-serve, packed in clear foil, keeping period of 12 to 48 hours
- Refrigerated, vacuum packed, ready-to-serve, keeping period of roughly 6 days
- Frozen, packed in a partitioned boiling bag, to be served only after preparation, keeping period roughly 3 months

The conditions governing all on-premise production of convenience foods are these:

- Hygenically impeccable processing and serving conditions
- Standardized recipes
- Observation of rules concerning storage periods
- Clear marking of production and expiration date on each pack
- Safe and appropriate preparation (heating) methods
- Availability of essential equipment such as blast freezers, adequate refrigeration for safe storage, and the necessary equipment for reheating the food

Examples of foods for on-premise production include:

- Farm-style sausages with onions
- Meat loaf with mushrooms
- Fricassee of veal, home style
- Beef, modern style, with buttered potatoes
- Sliced beef with mashed potatoes
- Stuffed beef birds with pasta
- Beef tongue in Madeira sauce with noodles
- Chicken curry with rice
- Beef stew with red cabbage and creamed potatoes
- Pork stew with vegetables and homemade noodles
- Pork stew, bourgeois style, with noodles
- Chopped steak with pepper sauce
- Roast pork with boiled potatoes and beans
- Tripe à la mode de Caen with buttered potatoes
- Piccata, Milan style, with spaghetti
- Ham in Madeira sauce with ratatouille
- Goulash with buttered potatoes
- Lobster bisque
- Bouillabaisse
- Lasagne
- Cannelloni with cream sauce
- Liver dumplings with onion sauce and mashed potatoes
- Veal and ham pie
- Macaroni and cheese
- Creamed chicken
- Apple pie

9.4 Profitability

As shown in figure 9-2, the purchase price increases progressively in relation to the degree to which the product is prepared. On the other hand, losses incurred from waste, labor, and overhead costs may be reduced. Since less space and fewer machines are required, investments, running costs, interest, and depreciation can be limited. The preparation costs of ready-to-serve foods are reduced to zero. The following comparison serves as a simple example. Establishment A makes a raspberry ice-cream pie, a job that includes the following stages: cleaning and sorting the fruit, mixing a dough, preparing the ice cream and garnish, baking the crust, filling and garnishing the pie, freezing, and portioning. Establishment B buys the finished preportioned raspberry ice-cream pie directly from the supplier. This product can be placed directly into the freezer compartment of the service counter, where it is plated and served.

In theory, it should be possible to eliminate the kitchen and base the menu on convenience foods and ready-to-serve products. The overall costs of such a system should be thoroughly analyzed. The advantages of a totally ready-to-serve food system would include reduction in labor costs; reduction in operating costs, such as power, gas, water, and steam; reduction of waste; possible reduction in size of plant required; equalization of food production over a given period of time; built-in portion control; reduction in investment and depreciation of equipment.

Disadvantages of such a system include these: choice of menu items limited to availability of products; lack of control over the quality of food served; lack of control of nutritional content of specific items. For example, the ingredients in a specific entrée may not meet the protein requirements for a patient or those of a school lunch program.

Convenience foods can maintain or increase profits only if they are used methodically as a solution to a specific problem. The above comments could lead one to the erroneous conclusion that cooks will become redundant in the future. As figure 9-1 shows, even convenience products must be produced at some time, using one or more of the basic forms of preparation. It is even more evident that with the continuously increasing labor costs for skilled personnel, the latter must be assigned to the preparation and finish-

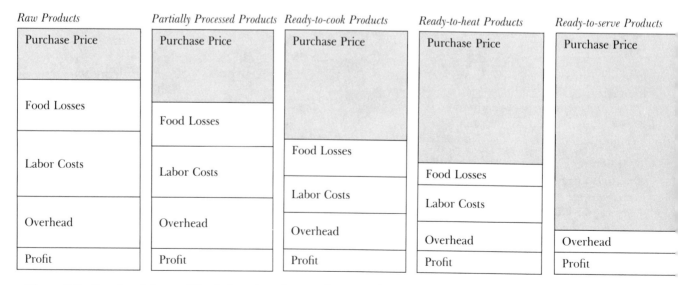

Figure 9-2. Cost breakdown of foods, based on degree of preparation.

ing of the more important and more expensive foods. Cooks should not devote time to preparing products that can be easily produced on an industrial basis or by less skilled personnel. A good basic training program is absolutely necessary for all foodservice personnel.

Chapter 10
The Recipes: Basic Preparations

10.1 Bases and Ingredients—*Bases et ingrédients*

10.1.1 *Marinades*—Marinades

Marinades are liquids that usually contain acid such as lemon juice, vinegar, or wine; various seasonings and spices; and oil. Marinades may be cooked or uncooked. A marinade will

- Add flavor and aroma
- Tenderize the fibers of certain pieces of meat
- Ensure the preservation of the product over a longer period of time

Instant Marinades—*Marinades à la Minute*

Ingredients *for fish:* Lemon juice, chopped herbs, and spices; *for meat pâtés, galantines, and terrines:* pâté seasoning mixtures and Madeira wine and brandy; *for grilled meat:* salt and spice mixes, oil for basting; *for lamb and mutton:* various herbs and a small amount of crushed garlic mixed with oil. To prepare, marinate the pieces of fish or meat for 15 to 30 minutes.

Uncooked Marinade for Meats and Game—*Marinade crues pour les viandes de boucherie et le gibier*

Yield
U.S.—5 quarts
Metric—5 liters

Ingredients	U.S. Weight or Volume	Metric Weight or Volume
Wine, red or white	4½ quarts	4.5 liters
Vinegar	16 fluid ounces	5 deciliters
Mirepoix:		
Onion, chopped	14 ounces	400 grams
Carrots, chopped	7 ounces	200 grams
Celery, chopped	5 ounces	150 grams
Garlic, crushed	2 cloves	2 cloves
Bay leaves	2	2
Cloves	3	3
Peppercorns, crushed	¾ ounce	20 grams
Juniper berries (for game only)	¾ ounce	20 grams
Rosemary	1 sprig	1 sprig
Thyme	1 sprig	1 sprig
Salt	½ teaspoon	3 grams

Procedure
1. Combine wine and vinegar.
2. Sauté all the mirepoix ingredients lightly and add to the wine and vinegar. Mix thoroughly.
3. Place meat in a stainless steel container, crock, or bowl and add marinade. Cover with a weight to keep meat submerged.
4. Refrigerate for several days.

Variations

Cooked Marinade

This marinade is the same as the uncooked marinade except the ingredients are heated to the boiling point, then cooled to 120°F (50°C). Pour it over the meat and keep refrigerated for 1 to 3 days.

Other Marinades

Other liquids that can be used as marinades include barbeque sauces for grilled meats and brine for pickling pork, beef, or fish.

10.1.2 *Aspics or Jellies—Gelées*

Meat Aspic or Jelly—*Gelée de viande*

Yield
U.S.—5 quarts
Metric—5 liters

Ingredients	U.S. Weight or Volume	Metric Weight or Volume
Veal bones, chopped	8 pounds	4 kilograms
Calves' feet	6 pounds	3 kilograms
Bacon rind	1 pound	500 grams
White stock, cold	7 quarts	7 liters
Bouquet garni	1	1
Salt	1 ounce	30 grams
Cloves	½ teaspoon	3 grams
Clarification:		
Lean beef, chopped	28 ounces	800 grams
Egg whites	2 or 3	2 or 3
Spice sachet:	1	1
Parsley stems, chopped	1 teaspoon	5 grams
Thyme	¼ teaspoon	½ gram
Bay leaf	1	1
Peppercorns, crushed	½ teaspoon	3 grams
Garlic, crushed	¼ teaspoon	2 grams

Procedure
1. Blanch the bones, calves' feet, and bacon rind. Add the cold stock and heat to the boiling point. Add the *bouquet garni,* salt, and cloves, and simmer 4 to 5 hours, uncovered.
2. Skim and remove fat as it collects.
3. Strain through cheesecloth.
4. Tie ingredients for spice sachet in cheesecloth.
5. Add the chopped beef, egg whites, and spice sachet. Simmer for 1 to 1½ hours. Strain. Adjust seasoning and color.

Note: If the jelly does not set properly, add gelatin (allow 1½ teaspoons unflavored gelatin per pint of stock). Madeira wine may be added to the jelly.

Variations of Meat Aspic or Jelly

Fish Jelly—*Gelée de poisson*

Mix ground, inexpensive sliced whitefish with chopped onions, the whites of leeks, egg whites, and a small amount of white wine; add cold fish fumet; stir carefully until boiling point is reached and remove from fire immediately; allow to steep for 30 minutes. Skim and strain carefully through a cloth.

Poultry Jelly—*Gelée de volaille*

Chicken stock is substituted for white stock.

10.1.3 *Panadas—Panades*

Panadas are used for binding, extending, and improving stuffings. They are always used cold. The ingredients for the various panadas are all based on 1 quart (1 liter) of liquid.

Flour Panada—*Panade à la farine*

Yield
U.S.—2 pounds
Metric—1 kilogram

continued

Ingredients	U.S. Weight or Volume	Metric Weight or Volume
Water	1 quart	1 liter
Butter	5 ounces	150 grams
Salt	¾ ounce	20 grams
Flour	20 ounces	600 grams

Procedure

1. Combine water, butter, and salt in a saucepan. Heat to the boiling point.
2. Add the flour, stirring constantly with a wooden spoon. Cook until the mixture does not adhere to the sides of the pan.

Variations

Bread Panada—*Panade au pain*

Follow the recipe for flour panada, substituting 1 quart (1 liter) of milk for water and 28 ounces (900 grams) of white bread for flour. Remove crust from the bread and soak in hot milk. Squeeze and break up the bread. Stir constantly over heat until the mixture becomes thick and quite dry.

Rice Panada—*Panade au riz*

Follow the recipe for flour panada, substituting 1 quart (1 liter) of stock for water and 12 ounces (350 grams) of rice for flour, and reducing the amount of butter to 1 ounce (30 grams). Cook the rice in the stock and butter, stirring until the mixture is thick and dry.

10.1.4 *Forcemeats*—Farces

Forcemeat is a mixture of finely chopped meat, fish, or poultry that is combined with seasonings and spices and bound with panadas and/or eggs. Forcemeats are used to stuff fish, poultry, meat, or vegetables. They are also used in the preparation of mousses, terrines, timbales, and pâtés. The ingredients for forcemeats should be cool when mixed to avoid curdling. Forcemeats may be made into quenelles.

Fish Mousseline Forcemeat—*Farce mousseline de poisson*

Yield
U.S.—1 pound
Metric—1 kilogram

Ingredients	U.S. Weight or Volume	Metric Weight or Volume
Fish, skinned and boned	8 ounces	500 grams
Cream	1 cup	5 deciliters
Eggs, whole	2	2
Salt	½ teaspoon	3 grams
Pepper	¼ teaspoon	2 grams
Parsley	1 tablespoon	15 grams
Chives	1 tablespoon	15 grams
Egg whites, beaten	2	3

Procedure

1. Grind fish very fine.
2. Combine fish with cream and eggs. Mix thoroughly.
3. Add seasonings and herbs.
4. Fold in beaten egg whites.
5. Refrigerate until ready to use.

Forcemeat for Fish Dishes—*Farce de poisson*

Yield
U.S.—1 pound
Metric—1 kilogram

Ingredients	U.S. Weight or Volume	Metric Weight or Volume
Fish, skinned and boned	8 ounces	500 grams
Flour panada	4 ounces	200 grams
Parsley	1 tablespoon	15 grams
Chives	1 tablespoon	15 grams
Cream	½ cup	2 deciliters
Salt	½ teaspoon	3 grams
Pepper	¼ teaspoon	2 grams
Egg whites, beaten	2	3

Procedure
1. Chop fish very fine and mix thoroughly with the panada.
2. Add the parsley, chives, cream, herbs, and seasonings to the fish. Blend thoroughly.
3. Fold in the egg whites.

Forcemeat for Game—*Farce de gibier*

Yield
U.S.—1 pound
Metric—1 kilogram

Ingredients

	U.S. Weight or Volume	Metric Weight or Volume
Game meat, ground	7 ounces	400 grams
Lard	4 ounces	200 grams
Pork	2¾ ounces	150 grams
Ice cubes	5 ounces	250 grams
Goose liver	2¾ ounces	150 grams
Apple, chopped	1	1
Shallots, chopped	1 ounce	50 grams
Salt	½ teaspoon	5 grams
Pepper	¼ teaspoon	2 grams
Madeira	2 tablespoons	30 milliliters
Brandy	¼ cup	60 milliliters

Procedure
1. Grind the game meat, lard, and pork with the ice cubes. Mix thoroughly.
2. Sauté the goose liver, apple, and shallots. Add seasonings. Add Madeira and flambé with brandy. Cool.
3. Combine the two mixtures and correct seasoning.

Forcemeat for Hot Meat Dishes—*Farce de viande*

Yield
U.S.—1 pound
Metric—1 kilogram

Ingredients

	U.S. Weight or Volume	Metric Weight or Volume
Veal, ground	5 ounces	250 grams
Pork, ground	5 ounces	250 grams
Ice cubes	5 ounces	250 grams
Lard	4 ounces	200 grams
Egg yolks	2	3
Salt	½ teaspoon	5 grams
Pepper	¼ teaspoon	2 grams
Cream	¼ to ½ cup	150 milliliters

Procedure
1. Dice all the meat. Put the meat and the ice cubes through the meat grinder two or three times.
2. Blend the lard and egg yolks. Add to the meat and mix thoroughly.
3. Add seasonings.
4. Blend cream into the mixture until the right consistency is attained.
5. Chill until ready to use.

Note: Chopped mushrooms, diced tongue, truffles, goose liver, or chicken liver may be added to the forcemeat to enhance the flavor and the color.

Mousseline Forcemeat—*Farce mousseline*

Yield
U.S.—1 pound
Metric—1 kilogram

Ingredients

	U.S. Weight or Volume	Metric Weight or Volume
Veal	8 ounces	500 grams
Ice cubes	4 ounces	200 grams
Cream	½ cup	3 deciliters
Egg whites	3	5
Salt	½ teaspoon	3 grams
White pepper	⅛ teaspoon	1 gram

Procedure
1. Remove fat and sinews from meat. Dice meat.
2. Attach the finest blade to the meat grinder and put

meat and ice cubes through the grinder several times.
3. Add the cream, egg whites, and seasonings slowly. Mix thoroughly.
4. Refrigerate until ready to use.

Plain Forcemeat for Hot Dishes—*Farce simple*

Yield
U.S.—1 pound
Metric—1 kilogram

Ingredients	U.S. Weight or Volume	Metric Weight or Volume
Pork	4 ounces	200 grams
Ice cubes	5 ounces	250 grams
Bacon	¾ ounce	50 grams
Bread or flour panada	5 ounces	250 grams
Egg	1	2
Egg yolks	3	5
Pepper	¼ teaspoon	2 grams
Salt	½ teaspoon	3 grams
Cream	3 tablespoons	45 milliliters

Procedure
1. Grind the pork with the ice cubes.
2. Grind the bacon and mix thoroughly with the pork.
3. Combine the panada, eggs, egg yolks, and seasonings with the pork and mix thoroughly.
4. Add the cream gradually and stir until the mixture is very smooth. Add more cream if necessary.

10.1.5 *Duxelles*

There are two types of duxelles: dry duxelles, a form of mushroom hash, used to stuff tomatoes, mushrooms, and other vegetables; and duxelles with added liquids, tomato sauce, stock, fish fumet, or wine, combined with other ingredients and used in forcemeats, stuffings, and sauces.

Dry Duxelles—*Duxelles sèches*

Yield
U.S.—8 ounces
Metric—225 grams

Ingredients	U.S. Weight or Volume	Metric Weight or Volume
Mushrooms	4 ounces	115 grams
Onion, chopped	½ onion	½ onion
Shallots, chopped	2	2
Butter	3 tablespoons	40 grams
Salt	½ teaspoon	3 grams
Pepper	⅛ teaspoon	1 gram
Nutmeg	few grains	few grains

Procedure
1. Clean and trim the mushrooms. Chop very fine. Put in cheesecloth, twist, and extract as much liquid as possible.
2. Sauté chopped onion and shallots in melted butter until slightly brown. Stir frequently.
3. Combine remainder of the ingredients with the mushrooms, add to the onions and shallots, and stir over high heat until all the liquid has evaporated.
4. Refrigerate.

Variation

Duxelles for Tart Shells—*Duxelles pour tartelettes farcies*

Combine an equal quantity of dry duxelles and either mousseline forcemeat or finely chopped ham.

Duxelles for Stuffed Vegetables—*Duxelles pour légumes farcis*

Yield
U.S.—1 pound
Metric—1 kilogram

Ingredients	U.S. Weight or Volume	Metric Weight or Volume
Mushrooms	4 ounces	115 grams
Onion, chopped	½ onion	½ onion
Shallots, chopped	2	2
Butter	3 tablespoons	40 grams
Salt	½ teaspoon	3 grams
Pepper	⅛ teaspoon	1 gram
Nutmeg	⅛ teaspoon	1 gram
Tomato puree	2 tablespoons	30 milliliters
White wine	¼ cup	60 milliliters
Brown sauce	2 tablespoons	30 milliliters
Breadcrumbs	¼ to ½ cup	85 grams

Procedure

1. Clean and trim mushrooms. Chop very fine. Put in cheesecloth, twist, and extract as much liquid as possible.
2. Sauté chopped onion and shallots in melted butter until slightly brown. Stir frequently.
3. Combine remainder of the ingredients with the mushrooms, add to the onions and shallots, and stir over high heat until all the liquid has evaporated.
4. Refrigerate.

10.1.6 *Ingredients for Stocks, Sauces, and Soups*—Ingredients pour fonds, sauces, et potages

Herb Bouquet—*Bouquet Garni*

Bouquet garni refers to a combination of parsley stems, thyme, and bay leaf. If fresh herbs are used, the parsley is folded around the other sprigs and all are tied with a string. Tarragon, rosemary, basil, fennel, garlic, or celery are sometimes added to the bouquet, depending on the specific recipe. Bouquets for very light stocks and sauces are made of only white vegetables. Bouquets are often specified as small, medium, or large.

A *bouquet garni* for light stocks includes leeks, split lengthwise; peeled carrots; some celery; and one onion spiked with bay leaf and cloves, tied together with a string. A *bouquet garni* for bouillon includes the same ingredients, but cabbage is added and the onion is cut in half and its peel is browned. The outer layer of celery can be used but must be washed thoroughly. Use cabbage leaves sparingly, since they can cause a gray coloring. Prepare 1 to 2 ounces per quart of liquid to be flavored.

Matignon

Matignon, a type of *mirepoix*, is a combination of finely minced vegetables used for garnishing meats. The choice of the vegetables is determined by the use. This version of mirepoix is used when the cooking time of the liquid is short. Chopped ham sautéed in butter can be added.

Mirepoix

Mirepoix is a mixture of vegetables, herbs, and spices with or without pork rind, or diced fresh pork fat or ham, used to enhance the flavor of meat, fish, and shellfish dishes. Onions, celery, carrots, leeks, garlic, peppercorns, bay leaves, cloves, thyme, and rosemary are used in various combinations. If for use in brown sauces, omit the leek and garlic, since they could turn bitter.

Spice Sachet—*Sachet d'épices*

Various spices and herbs are tied in clean cheesecloth. The spice sachet is cooked with meats, game stews, sauerkraut, pickled beets, beans, and in soups and sauces.

10.1.7 *Seasoned (Compound) Butters*—Beurres composés

Seasoned butters are butters that have been mixed with one or more flavoring substances. The butters are melted or cooked for varied periods of time and used as accompaniments to meat, fish, and vegetables. They are also used in sauces or as garnishes.

Seasoned Butter—*Beurres composés*

Yield
U.S.—1 pound
Metric—1 kilogram

Ingredients	U.S. Weight or Volume	Metric Weight or Volume
Butter	1 pound	1 kilogram
Lemon juice	2 ounces	1 deciliter
Salt	½ teaspoon	3 grams
White pepper	⅛ teaspoon	1 gram

Procedure
1. Stir butter till smooth, without melting it.
2. Add other ingredients and mix thoroughly.

Other Flavored Butters

Anchovy Butter—*Beurre d'anchois*

Add 5 ounces (300 grams) of minced anchovy fillets. Omit salt.

Basil Butter—*Beurre au basilic*

Add 2¾ ounces (150 grams) of minced basil.

Café de Paris Butter—*Beurre Café de Paris*

Add 5 cloves garlic, 9 anchovy fillets, ¾ ounce (50 grams) of parsley, ¾ ounce (50 grams) of chives, all minced. Mix thoroughly. Add 6 beaten eggs, 2 tablespoons (50 milliliters) of Madeira, and 2 tablespoons (50 milliliters) of brandy.

Caviar Butter—*Beurre de caviar*

Add 2¾ ounces (150 grams) of caviar. Omit salt.

Colbert Butter—*Beurre Colbert*

Add ¾ ounce (50 grams) of meat extract and ¾ ounce (50 grams) of minced tarragon to the recipe for maître d'hôtel butter.

Dill Butter—*Beurre d'aneth*

Add 2¾ ounces (150 grams) of finely chopped dill.

Garlic Butter—*Beurre d'ail*

Add 4 ounces (200 grams) of crushed garlic.

Horseradish Butter—*Beurre de raifort*

Add 4 ounces (200 grams) of finely grated horseradish.

Lobster Butter—*Beurre de homard*

Add 5 ounces (250 grams) of cooked chopped lobster sautéed and 2 tablespoons (50 milliliters) of brandy.

Maître d'Hôtel Butter—*Beurre maître d'hôtel*

Add 4 ounces (200 grams) of chopped parsley and ⅛ teaspoon (2 grams) of white pepper.

Mustard Butter—*Beurre à la moutarde*

Add 2¾ ounces (150 grams) of prepared mustard.

Pimiento Butter—*Beurre de piment*

Sauté 5 ounces (300 grams) of pimientos in butter. Cool and puree. Combine with butter mixture. Add 1¾ ounces (100 grams) of diced pimiento.

Shrimp Butter—*Beurre de crevettes*

Add ½ ounce (350 grams) of chopped cooked shrimps and 2 tablespoons (50 milliliters) of brandy.

10.1.8 *Thickening Agents*—Liaisons

Thickening agents are used to thicken or bind a liquid, to make soups and sauces creamier, and to improve taste.

Cornstarch

Use cornstarch for thickening soups and sauces. Mix with cold stock, wine, milk, or water, and then add to near-boiling liquid, stirring constantly, to thicken. Liquids thickened with cornstarch, potato starch, or rice starch remain transparent.

Flour and Fat—*Roux*

There are three basic types of *roux:*

- White roux, used for béchamel sauce, basic white sauce (velouté), and some soups
- Blond roux, which is always made with butter
- Brown roux, used to thicken brown sauces

For a white roux, the butter or fat must *not* be browned. For a blond roux, the flour and butter may be cooked a little longer than for a white roux, over a slightly higher heat (do not let it brown, however). A brown roux is cooked longer and over a higher heat. The longer cooking time required for a brown roux will affect the thickening qualities of the flour; therefore, you need to use a bit more flour. White and blond roux are made with butter, but brown roux may be made with other fats. Flour browns to a better color in fat, because most fats withstand high temperatures. The longer cooking time required for brown sauces may cause the starch in the roux to break down. The roux should be stirred constantly over a moderate heat for 5 to 15 minutes.

Roux—*Roux*

Yield
U.S.—thickener for 1 quart soup or sauce
Metric—thickener for 1 liter soup or sauce

Ingredients	U.S. Weight or Volume	Metric Weight or Volume
For soup:		
Butter	1 ounce	30 grams
Flour	1¾ ounces	50 grams
For sauce:		
Butter or fat	2 ounces	60 grams
Flour	2¾ ounces	80 grams

Procedure
1. Melt the butter or fat in saucepan.
2. Remove pan from heat and add sifted flour. Mix well.
3. Cook the flour with the butter or fat over very low heat to eliminate the taste of uncooked flour and allow starch granules to swell.
4. Before adding liquid, allow the roux to cool.

Kneaded Butter—*Beurre manié*

Kneaded butter is used to thicken sauces if, for example, a sauce is too thin. Kneaded butter is also used for sauces that are prepared *à la minute* (short order). To prepare kneaded butter, measure equal quantities of butter and flour. Mix the softened butter with the flour and knead to a paste that does not stick to the fingers or the bowl. Kneaded butter has to be cooked for a time to avoid giving a mealy taste to the dish to which it is added.

Cream

Cream is used to thicken and flavor both sauces and soups. For sauces, add the cream to the sauce and reduce together; or reduce the sauce first and add the cream afterward. For soups, add the cream to the ready soup; do *not* cook the cream with the soup.

Egg Yolks

Egg yolks are used to thicken and enrich a variety of dishes. For sauces, salpicons, potato croquette mixture, and the like, add the egg yolks to the warm mixture and stir well. Sauces with a high starch content can be brought to almost boiling after adding the egg yolks. (*Do not boil.*)

For crème anglaise, bavarian cream, custards, and the like, mix the egg yolks with the specified ingredient (usually with sugar—see specific recipes). Add the boiling liquid (usually milk) to the beaten egg yolks, stirring vigorously. Do not heat the mixture higher than 180°F (80°C).

Egg Yolks and Cream—*Liaison*

Yield
U.S.—liaison for 1 quart soup or sauce
Metric—liaison for 1 liter soup or sauce

Ingredients	U.S. Weight or Volume	Metric Weight or Volume
For soup:		
Egg yolks	1	1
Cream	½ cup	1 deciliter
For sauce:		
Egg yolks	2 to 4	2 to 4
Cream	¾ cup	2 deciliters

Procedure

1. Mix the egg yolk(s) with the cream; this is called a *liaison*.
2. Add the *liaison* to a small part of the hot soup or sauce and mix well.
3. Strain through a strainer or cloth.
4. Add the strained mixture to the rest of the soup or sauce.
5. Do not heat the soup or sauce higher than 180°F (80°C).

Blood

In some recipes, usually jugged hare or other jugged game, blood is prescribed. It must be noted here that blood is not always available. If blood is used, it is usually mixed with cream. This mixture is then added to the hot jugged hare or game. Do not boil the sauce after adding the blood and cream, or the blood will curdle.

10.2 Basic Stocks—*Fonds*

A carefully prepared basic stock is essential to any quality sauce or soup. A good chef who really knows and loves his profession can best demonstrate his abilities in the preparation and in the use of basic stock.

Stocks must always be cooked slowly and should not be covered. Scum and fat should be removed as they accumulate.

Bones used for making brown stock should be cut into small pieces with a meat saw. After browning the bones, only a small amount of liquid need be added. This is initially reduced to a glaze to ensure that the stock has a rich brown color. Only at this point should the full measure of liquid be added and simmered gently for 4 to 6 hours. If the stock is not going to be used immediately, to prevent spoilage, it should be cooled as quickly as possible by placing the container in cold running water. It should then be refrigerated.

10.2.1 White Stock—*Fond blanc*

Yield
U.S.—10 quarts
Metric—10 liters

Ingredients	U.S. Weight or Volume	Metric Weight or Volume
Bones, veal	10 to 12 pounds	5 to 6 kilograms
Water	12 quarts	12 liters
Onion, chopped	1 pound	455 grams
Celery, chopped	½ pound	225 grams
Thyme	½ teaspoon	3 grams
Parsley	1 teaspoon	5 grams
Bay leaf	1	1
Cloves, whole	½ teaspoon	3 grams
Peppercorns, crushed	½ teaspoon	3 grams

Procedure
1. Cut bones with a meat saw. Wash in cold water.
2. Place bones in stockpot and cover with cold water. Heat to the boiling point (blanch).
3. Drain.
4. Cover bones with fresh water. Add vegetables and spices.
5. Simmer for 2 to 3 hours. Remove scum as it accumulates.
6. Skim and strain.

10.2.2 Brown Stock—*Fond brun*

Yield
U.S.—10 quarts
Metric—10 liters

Ingredients	U.S. Weight or Volume	Metric Weight or Volume
Veal or beef bones, chopped	12 to 16 pounds	6 to 8 kilograms
Fat	4 ounces	110 grams
Water	12 to 15 quarts	12 to 15 liters
Mirepoix:		
Onions, chopped	8 ounces	200 grams
Celery, chopped	4 ounces	100 grams
Carrots, chopped	4 ounces	100 grams
Tomato puree (optional)	1 pint	5 deciliters
Pork rind	4 ounces	110 grams
Salt	1 teaspoon	15 grams

Procedure
1. Place bones and fat in a roasting pan.
2. Brown in oven at 375°F (191°C).
3. Turn bones occasionally to brown uniformly.
4. Add *mirepoix* to partially browned bones and brown both together to final stage. Tomato puree is optional.
5. Drain fat from pan and reserve.
6. Deglaze roasting pan with small amount of water.
7. Cover bones with deglazing liquid and water, add pork rind and salt, and heat to the boiling point. Simmer for 3 to 4 hours.

8. Skim surface and add more water if necessary.
9. Strain through cloth.

10.2.3 Game Stock—*Fond de gibier*

Yield
U.S.—10 quarts
Metric—10 liters

Ingredients	U.S. Weight or Volume	Metric Weight or Volume
Game bones, chopped	12 to 16 pounds	6 to 8 kilograms
Pork rind	5 ounces	140 grams
Fat	4 ounces	110 grams
Juniper berries	6	6
Mirepoix:		
Onion, chopped	8 ounces	200 grams
Celery, chopped	4 ounces	100 grams
Carrots, chopped	2 ounces	55 grams
Water	12 to 15 quarts	12 to 15 liters
Salt	1 teaspoon	15 grams

Procedure
1. Place the bones, rind, and fat in a pan and brown.
2. Add the *mirepoix* and continue browning.
3. Remove bones and *mirepoix* and place in a stockpot.
4. Deglaze the pan with a small amount of liquid.
5. Pour all the ingredients into the stockpot and simmer slowly for 2 to 3 hours.
6. Skim the fat frequently and add more water if necessary.
7. Strain through cloth.

10.2.4 Chicken Stock—*Fond de volaille*

Yield
U.S.—10 quarts
Metric—10 liters

Ingredients	U.S. Weight or Volume	Metric Weight or Volume
Chicken and veal bones	10 to 12 pounds	5 to 6 kilograms
Water	12 quarts	12 liters
Bouquet garni:		
Onion, chopped	1 pound	455 grams
Celery, chopped	8 ounces	225 grams
Thyme	½ teaspoon	3 grams
Parsley	1 teaspoon	5 grams
Bay leaf	1	1
Cloves, whole	½ teaspoon	3 grams
Peppercorns, crushed	½ teaspoon	3 grams

Procedure
1. Wash bones in cold water.
2. Place bones in stockpot and cover with cold water. Bring to a boil (blanch).
3. Drain.
4. Cover bones with the 12 quarts of fresh water. Add *bouquet garni* and spices.
5. Simmer for 4 hours. Remove the scum as it accumulates.
6. Strain through cloth.

10.2.5 Fish Stock—*Fond de poisson*

Yield
U.S.—10 quarts
Metric—10 liters

Ingredients	U.S. Weight or Volume	Metric Weight or Volume
Fish bones	10 to 12 pounds	5 to 6 kilograms
White mirepoix:		
Onion, chopped	4 ounces	110 grams
Celery, chopped	2 ounces	55 grams
Garlic	2 cloves	2 cloves
Mushroom trimmings	4 ounces	115 grams
Bay leaves	2	2
Cloves	3	3
Butter	3 ounces	85 grams
Water	10 quarts	10 liters
Wine, white or red	1 pint	5 deciliters
Salt	1 tablespoon	15 grams

Procedure
1. Chop and wash fish bones.
2. Sauté the *mirepoix* in butter.
3. Combine the fish bones, *mirepoix,* and water.
4. Heat to the boiling point. Remove scum as it accumulates.
5. Add wine and salt to the stock and simmer for 30 minutes. Strain.

10.2.6 Fish Fumet—*Fumet de poisson*

Yield
U.S.—10 quarts
Metric—10 liters

Ingredients	U.S. Weight or Volume	Metric Weight or Volume
Fish bones	10 to 12 pounds	5 to 6 kilograms
White mirepoix:		
Onion	4 ounces	110 grams
Celery	2 ounces	55 grams
Garlic	2 cloves	2 cloves
Cloves	3	3
Bay leaves	2	2
Mushroom trimmings	4 ounces	110 grams
Butter	5 ounces	150 grams
Fish stock	10 quarts	10 liters
White wine	1 pint	5 deciliters
Salt	1 tablespoon	15 grams

Procedure
1. Chop and wash fish bones.
2. Mince the vegetables for *mirepoix* and the mushrooms.

3. Sauté the *mirepoix* in butter.
4. Combine the *mirepoix*, mushroom trimmings, fish bones, fish stock, wine, and salt. Simmer slowly for 30 minutes. Strain through cloth.

Note: The reduced stock of poached fish, such as that from *filets de sole au vin blanc*, is also referred to as *fumet de poisson*.

10.2.7 Vegetable Stock—*Fond de légumes*

Yield

U.S.—10 quarts
Metric—10 liters

Ingredients	*U.S. Weight or Volume*	*Metric Weight or Volume*
Fat	5 ounces	150 grams
Onions, chopped	10 ounces	300 grams
Leeks, sliced	10 ounces	300 grams
Celery, diced	5 ounces	150 grams
Cabbage, shredded	5 ounces	150 grams
Tomatoes, sliced	4 ounces	100 grams
Fennel	4 ounces	100 grams
Garlic	1 clove	1 clove
Bay leaf	1	1
Clove, whole	1	1
Water	12 quarts	12 liters
Salt	1 tablespoon	15 grams

Procedure

1. Sauté the onions and leeks in the fat for a few minutes. Add other vegetables and sauté until translucent.
2. Add 12 quarts of water and the salt and simmer for approximately 1 hour.

3. Strain through cloth, pressing on vegetables to release as much liquid as possible.

Note: This stock is used primarily for vegetarian and fish items.

Second Cooking of Basic Stock—*Rémouillage*

The second cooking of a basic stock is called *rémouillage*. It is used in the preparation of meat extract. The cooked chicken and game are added to the basic stock and a *mirepoix*. The stock is simmered for 5 hours.

Meat Extract—*Glace de viande*

Meat extract is prepared by reducing brown stock to a gelatinous consistency. The glaze is used to improve the flavor of sauces and to coat certain meats, game, poultry, and aspics.

Meat extract is made by straining the *rémouillage* or brown stock into a heavy stockpot. The stock is allowed to simmer over low heat to a syrupy consistency. Toward the end of the cooking time, the remaining liquid should be strained into a smaller, heavy-bottomed saucepan. The heat should be very low, and the glaze should simmer until thick enough to coat a spoon. The hot glaze should be poured into containers, covered tightly, and refrigerated.

Fish extract and game extract are obtained by reducing a fish fumet and a game stock, respectively.

Roast Juices—*Jus de rôti*

To preserve the typical flavor of a roast, deglaze the pan in which it was cooked with water or wine. In the case of poultry or game roasts, the appropriate stock can be used for deglazing. The resulting juice is usually served unthickened but degreased.

Chapter 11
Sauces—*Sauces*

The foundation of a good sauce is, in most instances, a stock that has been skillfully prepared, although there are some sauces that do not require stock, such as hollandaise and béarnaise. Sauces are used to add richness and color and to enhance the flavor of certain foods. A sauce should have a smooth texture and a flavor and consistency that complement the food it accompanies; it should never mask the flavor of the food. There are many different preparations for sauces, and there are distinct differences in their flavors, textures, and appearances. (See figure 11-1.)

Sauce espagnole was considered, at one time, the basic ingredient of all brown sauces, and as a result, the flavor and consistency of all brown sauces were very similar. The quality of the sauce was further affected by the practice of not reducing the stock sufficiently in order to obtain a greater yield. In recent years *Espagnole* has been replaced by the delicate, reduced, and partially bound veal stock, *fond brun lié*. In addition to the *fond brun,* there are other basic sauces with many variations. Special seasonings, garnishes, and other ingredients may be added to provide an even greater variety. The strength of the sauce is increased and the flavor improved by reducing the volume.

The preparation of fine sauces is an art, and it is usually assigned to the cooks who have had an extensive background of training and experience.

11.1 Brown Sauces—*Sauces brunes*

Figure 11-2 shows the basic brown sauces and their most important derivatives.

11.1.1 Basic Brown Sauce—*Fond brun lié*

Yield
U.S.—10 quarts
Metric—10 liters

Ingredients	U.S. Weight or Volume	Metric Weight or Volume
Brown stock	20 quarts	20 liters
Arrowroot *or* cornstarch	4 to 5 ounces	100 to 150 grams

Procedure
1. Dissolve arrowroot or cornstarch in 2 cups (4 deciliters) of cold stock.
2. Reduce the remainder of the stock to half its volume.
3. Stir dissolved arrowroot or cornstarch into the reduced stock.
4. Stir and cook until slightly thickened.

Variations on Basic Brown Sauce

Meatless Brown Sauce—*Fond brun maigre*

Substitute fish stock with red wine for the brown stock to prepare a meatless brown sauce.

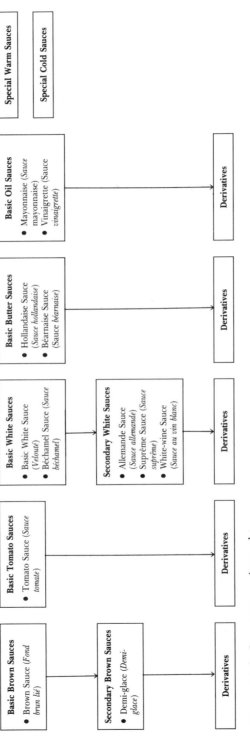

Figure 11-1. Sauce categories and types.

Basic Ingredient	Basic Sauce	Secondary Sauce	Primary Derivatives
Brown stock	Basic brown sauce	Demi-glace	Bigarade orange sauce
			Bordelaise wine sauce
			Brown chaud-froid sauce
			Brown cream sauce
			Charcutière sauce
			Colbert sauce
			Deviled sauce
			Diane sauce
			Duxelles sauce
			Gratin sauce
			Hunter's sauce
			Italian sauce
			Madeira sauce
			Marrow sauce
			Onion sauce
			Périgueux sauce
			Port wine sauce
			Robert sauce
			Roebuck sauce
			Salmi sauce
			Tarragon sauce
			Wine merchant's sauce
			Zingara sauce

Figure 11-2. Brown sauces—*Sauces brunes.*

11.1.2 Demi-Glace I

Yield
U.S.—10 quarts
Metric—10 liters

Ingredients	U.S. Weight or Volume	Metric Weight or Volume
Veal bones	13 to 18 pounds	6 to 8 kilograms
Mirepoix:		
Carrot	3 ounces	100 grams
Celery	2 ounces	50 grams

Ingredients	U.S. Weight or Volume	Metric Weight or Volume
Mirepoix:		
Onion	2 ounces	50 grams
Bay leaf	¼ leaf	¼ leaf
Thyme	1 sprig	1 sprig
Oil	½ cup	1 to 2 deciliters
Tomato puree	4 ounces	100 grams
White wine	1 quart	1 liter
Brown stock	20 quarts	20 liters
Flour	12 ounces	300 grams
Salt	1 tablespoon	20 grams

Procedure

1. Brown the cut veal bones with the *mirepoix* in oil. Add tomato puree and cook until vegetables are tender.
2. Deglaze the sauté pan with wine.
3. Add the flour. Pour brown stock and deglazing into a stockpot. Add vegetable mixture.
4. Simmer for 30 minutes, reducing by half. Skim while cooking and degrease.
5. Strain.
6. Adjust seasoning.

11.1.3 Demi-Glace II

Yield
U.S.—10 quarts
Metric—10 liters

Ingredients	U.S. Weight or Volume	Metric Weight or Volume
Butter or margarine	5 ounces	150 grams
Veal bones, chopped fine	12 to 16 pounds	6 to 8 kilograms
Mirepoix:		
Carrot	3 to 4 ounces	100 to 150 grams
Celery	2 to 3 ounces	50 to 75 grams
Onion	2 to 3 ounces	50 to 75 grams

Ingredients	U.S. Weight or Volume	Metric Weight or Volume
Mirepoix:		
Bay leaf	¼ leaf	¼ leaf
Thyme	1 sprig	1 sprig
Tomato puree	4 ounces	100 grams
Flour	4 ounces	100 grams
White wine	1 quart	1 liter
Brown stock	20 quarts	20 liters
Arrowroot *or* cornstarch	5 ounces	150 grams
Salt (optional)	1 tablespoon	20 grams

Procedure

1. Brown the bones in melted butter or margarine.
2. Add *mirepoix* and continue to brown.
3. Add tomato puree.
4. Dust with flour and brown for a few minutes.
5. Deglaze the browning pan with wine.
6. Pour brown stock and deglazing into a stockpot. Add bones and *mirepoix*.
7. Reduce volume by half.
8. Strain.
9. Bind with arrowroot or cornstarch if necessary.
10. Skim off fat and adjust seasoning.

Derivatives of Demi-Glace

Bigarade Orange Sauce—*Sauce bigarade*

This sauce is prepared with a reduction of red wine, orange juice, and fine strips of orange and lemon zest. These ingredients are covered with a demi-glace, and the mixture is simmered and then flavored with Curaçao and a dash of cayenne pepper.

Bordelaise Wine Sauce—*Sauce bordelaise*

This wine sauce is made with a reduction of red wine, chopped shallots, crushed peppercorns, thyme, and bay leaf; demi-glace is added to the reduction and it is simmered for a few minutes. It is then strained. The sauce may be garnished with sliced or diced blanched beef bone marrow.

Brown Chaud-froid Sauce—*Sauce chaud-froid brune*

This sauce is prepared by reducing 1 quart (1 liter) of demi-glace and a few drops of truffle essence to half its volume. Then 1 pint (5 deciliters) of meat aspic and ½ cup (1 deciliter) of Madeira are added. The sauce is strained through cheesecloth and cooled. Basic brown sauce may be used instead of the demi-glace. The giblets and backbones of poultry may be used with the veal to prepare the basic brown sauce; the bones and trimmings of game may be used for game dishes.

Brown Cream Sauce—*Sauce crème*

For meat dishes only, this sauce is prepared by draining the fat from the pan and deglazing with white wine. Demi-glace is added and reduced to half the volume. The sauce is bound with equal parts of basic white sauce and cream.

This sauce may also be made for *mise en place*. Approximately 5½ quarts (5½ liters) of demi-glace are reduced to half the volume. The demi-glace is bound with 2½ quarts (2½ liters) of veal white sauce. When ready to use, ¼ cup (1 deciliter) of white wine is added to 1 quart (1 liter) of the basic sauce. The sauce is heated to the boiling point and 1 pint (5 deciliters) of cream, a few grains of cayenne pepper, and the juice of half a lemon are added.

Charcutière Sauce—*Sauce charcutière*

This sauce is prepared by combining a reduction of vinegar and white wine, shallots, and peppercorns with demi-glace. It is simmered for a few minutes and strained. Julienne of pickles, mustard, Worcestershire sauce, and meat glaze are added. It is usually served with pork.

Colbert Sauce—*Sauce Colbert*

This sauce is a reduction of chopped shallots, crushed peppercorns, white wine, and demi-glace. The sauce is simmered for a few minutes and then strained. After the sauce is removed from the heat, softened butter, chopped herbs, and lemon juice are added.

Deviled Sauce—*Sauce diable*

This sauce is made from a reduction of white wine, shallots, peppercorns, demi-glace, and tomato puree. The sauce is heated to the boiling point, strained, and bound with butter. It is seasoned with cayenne pepper and chopped herbs.

Diane Sauce—*Sauce Diane*

This is a demi-glace that has been well peppered and prepared with cream. It may be a pepper sauce that has been prepared with double cream. It is usually garnished with hard-cooked egg whites and truffles cut into half-moon shapes.

Duxelles Sauce—*Sauce duxelles*

This sauce is prepared by sautéing a quantity of chopped shallots in butter and deglazing the pan with white wine. Demi-glace and tomato puree are added. Dry duxelles are added. The sauce is heated to the boiling point, the temperature is reduced, and the sauce is simmered slowly. Chopped parsley is added before serving.

Gratin Sauce—*Sauce au gratin*

Fish fumet is reduced with chopped shallots. Dry duxelles and brown sauce are added, and the sauce is heated to the boiling point. It is garnished with chopped parsley.

Hunter's Sauce—*Sauce chasseur*

This sauce is made by sautéing sliced shallots and mushrooms in butter and deglazing with white wine. After reducing, a demi-glace and a small amount of tomato puree are added. The sauce is simmered for a few minutes, and the butter and parsley are added.

Italian Sauce—*Sauce italienne*

This sauce is made by sautéing chopped shallots, ham, and mushrooms in butter and deglazing the pan with white wine. Demi-glace and tomato sauce or tomato puree are added. The sauce is then boiled for a few minutes, and chopped parsley and tarragon leaves are added.

Madeira Sauce—*Sauce Madère*

This is a demi-glace sauce made with Madeira wine.

Marrow Sauce—*Sauce à la moelle*

This sauce is prepared by the same method used for bordelaise wine sauce. It is served with blanched cubes of beef marrow, chopped parsley, and some slivers of fresh butter.

Onion Sauce—*Sauce lyonnaise*

For this sauce finely chopped onions are sautéed in butter, deglazed with demi-glace, and seasoned with white wine and a dash of vinegar.

Pepper Sauce—*Sauce poivrade*

See Roebuck Sauce.

Périgueux Sauce—*Sauce Périgueux*

To prepare this sauce, a reduction of Madeira wine and chopped truffles are added to demi-glace. The sauce is bound with butter.

Piquant Sauce—*Sauce Piquante*

This sauce is a reduction of white wine, vinegar, and chopped shallots added to demi-glace and seasoned with cayenne pepper. It is garnished with chopped pickles, herbs, and tarragon.

Port Wine Sauce—*Sauce au porto*

This is a Madeira sauce using port instead of Madeira.

Robert Sauce—*Sauce Robert*

This sauce is prepared from a reduction of chopped onions, white wine, and demi-glace. It is simmered for a short time and strained. Mustard and lemon juice are added. It is especially good with pork chops.

Roebuck Sauce—*Sauce chevreuil*

This game sauce is prepared by sautéing a *mirepoix*, bacon trimmings, crushed peppercorns, and juniper berries in butter. It is deglazed with a small amount of game marinade made with red wine. Veal and game stock are added, and the sauce is reduced to half its volume. It is slightly bound with cornstarch. The sauce is strained and seasoned with cayenne pepper, lemon juice, and butter.

Salmi Sauce—*Sauce salmis*

The chopped carcasses, neck, and skin from the game being cooked are sautéed in butter with a *mirepoix*. It is deglazed with a little white wine and reduced. Demi-glace is added. It is simmered for 30 minutes and strained. The sauce is further diluted with game stock and boiled down to the desired thickness. Truffle essence and reduced mushroom stock are added.

Tarragon Sauce—*Sauce à l'estragon*

This sauce is a reduced demi-glace with a little white wine and a sprig of tarragon. It is strained and garnished with chopped tarragon leaves.

Tortue Sauce—*Sauce tortue*

This is Madeira sauce with herbs (such as thyme, bay leaf, parsley, sage, rosemary, and basil), a little tomato sauce, and a pinch of cayenne pepper. It is garnished with diced calf's tongue, pickles, quartered mushrooms, pitted olives, and veal quenelles.

Wine Merchant's Sauce—*Sauce marchand de vin*

This is a reduction of red wine and shallots that have been deglazed with demi-glace and reduced.

Zingara Sauce—*Sauce zingara*

This is a reduction of shallots and white wine. Demi-glace and a little tomato sauce are added and the sauce is simmered for a short time. It is seasoned with paprika and garnished with julienne of beef tongue, truffles, and mushrooms.

11.2 Tomato Sauce—*Sauce tomate*

Yield
U.S.—10 quarts
Metric—10 liters

Ingredients	*U.S. Weight or Volume*	*Metric Weight or Volume*
Oil	¾ cup	2 deciliters
Bacon trimmings	5 ounces	150 grams
Mirepoix:		
Carrots	6 ounces	200 grams
Celery	4 ounces	100 grams
Onion	4 ounces	100 grams
Bay leaf	½ leaf	½ leaf
Thyme	2 sprigs	2 sprigs
Tomato puree *or* fresh tomatoes	70 to 88 ounces *or* 4 to 5 pounds	2 to 2.5 kilograms
Flour	4 ounces	100 grams
White stock	12 quarts	12 liters
Sugar (optional)	¼ cup	80 grams
Salt	1 tablespoon	20 grams

Procedure
1. Heat oil. Fry bacon trimmings and *mirepoix*.
2. Add the tomato puree or chopped fresh tomatoes. Continue frying and stir in the flour.
3. Add the white stock.
4. Simmer for 1 to 1½ hours. Add more white stock if necessary.
5. Strain. Add sugar if necessary and salt. Adjust seasoning.

Variations of Tomato Sauce

Portuguese Sauce—*Sauce portugaise*

Peeled, seeded, and diced tomatoes are added to crushed garlic and onions that have been sautéed in oil. The mixture is simmered and combined with some reduced meat juices, a little tomato puree, and chopped parsley. It is heated to the boiling point and a few slivers of butter are added.

Provençale Sauce—*Sauce provençale*

This sauce is made from a reduction of white wine, shallots, and garlic. Peeled and chopped tomatoes and tomato puree are added and simmered. It may be garnished with chopped parsley, olives, and mushrooms.

11.3 White Sauces—*Sauces blanches*

The basic white sauce (*velouté*) is used in the preparation of many sauces. Some white sauces are derived from veal stock, some from fish stock, and others from stock made from poultry or vegetables. The sauces should always be derived from the corresponding stock, for example, tarragon sauce to be used for fish should be made with fish stock. Figure 11-3 lists the main and secondary white sauces with their most important derivatives.

11.3.1 Basic White Sauce—*Velouté*

Yield
U.S.—10 quarts
Metric—10 liters

Ingredients	*U.S. Weight or Volume*	*Metric Weight or Volume*
Butter	1¼ pounds	600 grams
Flour	1¾ pounds	800 grams
White (veal) stock, chicken stock, *or* fish stock	12 quarts	12 liters
Salt	1 tablespoon	20 grams

Procedure
1. Melt butter.
2. Add flour; stir, and cook without coloring.
3. Add the cold stock.
4. Simmer for 1 to 1½ hours, stirring occasionally. If necessary, add more stock.
5. Adjust seasoning.
6. Strain through cheesecloth.

Note: If the stock used has a weak flavor, sauté a *mirepoix* in the butter before mixing in the flour.

Basic Ingredient	*Basic Sauce*	*Secondary Sauce*	*Primary Derivatives*
White stock	Basic white sauce—veal (velouté)	Allemande sauce	Caper sauce Chaud-froid, blond Chaud-froid, white Chive sauce Chivry sauce Curry sauce Horseradish sauce Mushroom sauce Poulette sauce Tarragon sauce Villeroi sauce
Chicken stock	Basic white sauce—chicken (velouté)	Suprême sauce	Albuféra sauce Mushroom sauce Tarragon sauce Toulouse sauce
Fish stock	Basic white sauce—fish (velouté	White-wine sauce	Anchovy sauce Bercy sauce Caper sauce Cardinal sauce Diplomat sauce Fine-herb sauce Oyster sauce Riche sauce Shrimp sauce Victoria sauce
Milk	Béchamel sauce	Cream sauce	Aurora sauce Chantilly sauce Horseradish sauce Mornay sauce Nantua sauce

Figure 11-3. White sauces—*Sauces blanches.*

Derivatives of Basic White Sauce

Chaud-froid Sauce, Meatless—*Sauce chaud-froid maigre*

Combine 1¾ cups (350 milliliters) of basic white sauce made with fish stock and 1¾ cups (350 milliliters) of fish aspic. Cook slowly until about 2 cups (4 deciliters) of liquid remain; continue to cook over high heat for a few minutes. Add ¼ cup (50 milliliters) of cream. Add a few drops of lemon juice. Yield: 2½ cups (5 deciliters).

Normandy Sauce—*Sauce normande*

Combine 1 cup (2 deciliters) of basic white sauce made of fish fumet from poached fish with ½ cup (1 deciliter) of mushroom stock, and ½ cup (1 deciliter) of fish stock. Boil until about 1 cup (2 deciliters) remains. Mix 2 beaten egg yolks with 3 tablespoons (45 grams) of cream. Add to sauce. Add 3 tablespoons (45 grams) of butter. Yield: 1½ cups (3 deciliters).

11.3.2 Allemande Sauce—*Sauce allemande*

Yield
U.S.—10 quarts
Metric—10 liters

Ingredients	*U.S. Weight or Volume*	*Metric Weight or Volume*
Basic white sauce (veal)	12 quarts	12 liters
Egg yolks	8 to 10	8 to 10
Cream	1 quart	1 liter
Lemon juice	½ cup	60 milliliters

Procedure
1. Reduce the sauce to the desired consistency while stirring.
2. Blend egg yolks and cream.
3. Add the hot sauce slowly to the egg yolk/cream mixture, stirring constantly. Heat the sauce almost to boiling point to bind.
4. Add lemon juice to taste.

Derivatives of Allemande Sauce

Caper Sauce—*Sauce aux câpres*

Add capers and a dash of vinegar to allemande sauce.

Chaud-froid Sauce, Blond—*Sauce chaud-froid blonde*

Combine 1¾ cups (3½ deciliters) of allemande sauce and 1¾ cups (3½ deciliters) of chicken or meat aspic. Cook slowly for 15 minutes. Add ¾ cup (1½ deciliters) of cream and ½ teaspoon (2 grams) of salt. Cook slowly until the sauce coats the spoon. Strain the sauce and beat until cool. Yield: 2½ cups (5 deciliters).

Chaud-froid Sauce, White—*Sauce chaud-froid blanche*

Follow the recipe for Chaud-froid Sauce, Blond, with these exceptions: substitute basic white sauce for allemande sauce and add ¼ cup (½ deciliter) of cream.

Chive Sauce—*Sauce à la ciboulette*

This sauce is prepared by adding finely chopped chives to allemande sauce.

Chivry Sauce—*Sauce Chivry*

This is an allemande sauce with blanched and chopped herbs, such as tarragon, spinach, parsley, and/or chervil.

Curry Sauce—*Sauce curry*

Sauté a small vegetable *mirepoix* in 2 tablespoons (30 grams) of butter. Add ½ teaspoon (2 grams) of salt, 1 teaspoon (5 grams) of curry powder, 1 grated garlic clove, ⅛ teaspoon (0.5 gram) of thyme, and a sprig of parsley. Deglaze with 1½ cups (3 deciliters) of basic white sauce made with veal stock. Cook slowly for 30 minutes. Strain. Add ½ cup (1 deciliter) of cream. Add juice of a half lemon. Yield: 2 cups (4 deciliters).

Horseradish Sauce—*Sauce raifort*

Add 1 tablespoon (15 grams) of grated horseradish to 1 cup (2 deciliters) of allemande sauce. Yield: 1 cup (2 deciliters).

Mushroom Sauce—*Sauce aux champignons*

Sauté 8 ounces (100 grams) of peeled mushrooms in butter. Add the mushrooms to 1½ cups (3 deciliters) of allemande sauce. Yield: 2 cups (4 deciliters).

Poulette Sauce—*Sauce poulette*

Add 1 tablespoon (10 grams) of chopped parsley, 1 tablespoon (15 grams) of butter to 1 cup (2 deciliters) of allemande sauce. Add ¼ teaspoon (1 gram) of lemon juice. This sauce is served with vegetables or variety meats. Yield: 1 cup (2 deciliters).

Tarragon Sauce—*Sauce à l'estragon*

This is an allemande sauce seasoned with tarragon vinegar and chopped tarragon leaves.

Villeroi Sauce—*Sauce Villeroi*

Cook 1 cup (2 deciliters) of allemande sauce, ¼ cup (½ deciliter) of ham stock, and a few drops of essence of truffle until the sauce coats a spoon. Strain and garnish with julienne of chicken, sliced mushrooms, and truffles. Yield: 1 cup (2 deciliters).

11.3.3 Suprême Sauce—*Sauce suprême*

Yield
U.S.—10 quarts
Metric—10 liters

Ingredients	U.S. Weight or Volume	Metric Weight or Volume
Basic white sauce (chicken)	10 quarts	10 liters
Cream	1 quart	1 liter
Butter	9 ounces	250 grams

Ingredients	U.S. Weight or Volume	Metric Weight or Volume
Lemon juice	of one-half lemon	of one-half lemon

Procedure
1. Reduce the sauce to the desired consistency.
2. Add the cream, a little at a time.
3. Add butter and lemon juice.
4. Adjust seasoning.
5. Strain through cheesecloth.

Derivatives of Suprême Sauce

Albuféra Sauce—*Sauce Albuféra*

This is a suprême sauce to which meat extract (*glace de viande*) has been added.

Mushroom Sauce—*Sauce aux champignons*

Mushroom stock is reduced and added to mushroom caps. The mushrooms are then added to suprême sauce.

Tarragon Sauce—*Sauce à l'estragon*

This is a suprême sauce with blanched and chopped tarragon leaves.

Toulouse Sauce—*Sauce Toulouse*

This is a suprême sauce seasoned with truffle essence, lemon juice, and melted butter.

11.3.4 White-wine Sauce—*Sauce au vin blanc*

Yield
U.S.—10 quarts
Metric—10 liters

Ingredients	U.S. Weight or Volume	Metric Weight or Volume
Basic white sauce (fish)	10 quarts	10 liters

Ingredients	U.S. Weight or Volume	Metric Weight or Volume
Fish stock (from poached fish)	1 quart	1 liter
Egg yolks	4 to 6	4 to 6
Cream	1 quart	1 liter
Butter	9 ounces	250 grams
Lemon juice	of one-half lemon	of one-half lemon

Procedure
1. Reduce sauce and stock to desired consistency.
2. Blend egg yolks and cream.
3. Add the hot sauce slowly to the egg yolk/cream mixture, stirring constantly.
4. Reduce slightly.
5. Mix in butter and lemon juice.
6. Strain through cheesecloth.

Derivatives of White-wine Sauce

Anchovy Sauce—*Sauce aux anchois*

Add 2 tablespoons (30 grams) of anchovy butter to 1 cup (2 deciliters) of white-wine sauce. Yield: 1 cup (2 deciliters).

Bercy Sauce—*Sauce Bercy*

Sauté 1 tablespoon (15 grams) of chopped shallots in butter. Add ½ cup (1 deciliter) of white-wine sauce and ½ cup (1 deciliter) of fish stock. Boil slowly until about ½ cup (1 deciliter) of liquid remains. Add 1 cup (2 deciliters) of white-wine sauce, 1 tablespoon (15 grams) of butter, and 1 tablespoon (15 grams) of chopped parsley. Yield: 1 cup (2 deciliters).

Caper Sauce—*Sauce aux câpres*

This is a white-wine sauce garnished with capers.

Cardinal Sauce—*Sauce cardinal*

This is a white-wine sauce flavored with lobster butter and truffle essence.

Diplomat Sauce—*Sauce diplomate*

This is a white-wine sauce mixed with lobster butter. It is garnished with diced lobster and truffles and dusted with cayenne pepper.

Fine-Herb Sauce—*Sauce aux fines herbes*

This is a white-wine sauce with added chopped parsley and tarragon leaves.

Oyster Sauce—*Sauce aux huitres*

Combine ½ cup (1 deciliter) of oyster stock and 2 cups (4 deciliters) of white-wine sauce. Add ⅛ teaspoon (0.5 gram) of cayenne, ½ teaspoon (2 grams) of salt, and ⅛ teaspoon (0.5 gram) of pepper. Cook for 10 minutes. Garnish with 12 poached oysters. Yield: 2 cups (4 deciliters).

Riche Sauce—*Sauce riche*

This white-wine sauce is mixed with crayfish butter, truffle essence, and sliced mushrooms.

Shrimp Sauce—*Sauce aux crevettes*

This is a white-wine sauce seasoned with shrimp butter and cayenne. It is garnished with diced shrimps.

Victoria Sauce—*Sauce Victoria*

This is a white-wine sauce seasoned with lobster butter. It is garnished with diced lobster meat and truffles.

11.3.5 Béchamel Sauce—*Sauce béchamel*

Yield
U.S.—10 quarts
Metric—10 liters

continued

Ingredients	U.S. Weight or Volume	Metric Weight or Volume
Roux:		
Butter	20 ounces	600 grams
Flour	28 ounces	800 grams
Milk	10 quarts	10 liters
Nutmeg, grated	¼ teaspoon	1 gram
Bay leaf	1	1
Onion, studded with cloves	1	1
Salt	1 tablespoon	15 grams

Procedure

1. Melt butter and mix in flour. Cook for a few minutes.
2. Allow roux to cool.
3. Scald milk and gradually add to the roux.
4. Add nutmeg, bay leaf, and onion.
5. Simmer for at least 30 minutes. Add more hot milk if necessary.
6. Adjust seasoning.
7. Strain through cheesecloth.

Note: If the sauce is to be used to coat fish, meat, or vegetables, the consistency should be thicker than normal.

Derivatives of Béchamel Sauce

Aurora Sauce—*Sauce aurore*

This is a béchamel sauce seasoned with tomato puree.

Chantilly Sauce—*Sauce Chantilly*

This is a béchamel sauce blended with whipped cream.

Cream Sauce—*Sauce crème*

Mix a small amount of cream into a béchamel sauce (1 part cream to 9 parts béchamel).

Horseradish Sauce—*Sauce raifort*

This sauce may be prepared from a thick cream sauce or from a basic white sauce. Horseradish is added to the sauce.

Mornay Sauce—*Sauce Mornay*

This is a cream sauce with grated cheese, butter, and cayenne added.

Nantua Sauce—*Sauce Nantua*

This is a béchamel sauce flavored with crayfish butter. It is garnished with diced crayfish. As an alternative to crayfish, the sauce may be flavored with shrimp butter and shrimp. This sauce can also be prepared as a derivative of white-wine sauce.

11.4 Butter-based Sauces—*Sauces au beurre*

The basic butter sauces and their derivatives are shown in figure 11-4.

11.4.1 Hollandaise Sauce—*Sauce hollandaise*

Yield
10 servings

Ingredients	U.S. Weight or Volume	Metric Weight or Volume
Water	⅔ cup	1.5 deciliters
Lemon juice	2 tablespoons	28 grams
Salt	1 teaspoon	6 grams
White pepper	½ teaspoon	2 grams
Egg yolks	6	6
Unsalted butter, melted	1 pound	450 grams
Water	¼ cup	100 milliliters
Cayenne (optional)	few grains	few grains

Procedure

1. Mix the ⅔ cup (1.5 deciliters) water, lemon juice, salt, and white pepper and reduce to ¼ cup (50 milliliters).
2. Add egg yolks and whisk over very low heat until the mixture expands and is very thick.
3. Remove from heat and add the melted butter in a thin stream, a little at a time, adding 1 teaspoon of the remaining ¼ cup (100 milliliters) water after adding each ounce (30 grams) of the butter.
4. Add cayenne if you wish. Strain sauce into a warmed bowl and keep warm over water heated to 140°F (60°C).
5. If sauce needs more acidity, add lemon juice at serving time.

Derivatives of Hollandaise Sauce

Maltese Sauce—*Sauce maltaise*

This is a hollandaise sauce flavored with orange juice and garnished with strips of blanched orange zest. It is a specialty sauce for asparagus. Ideally the oranges should be the blood oranges grown in Malta and Sicily.

Mousseline Sauce—*Sauce mousseline*

This is a hollandaise sauce to which whipped cream is added just before serving.

Basic Sauce	Primary Derivatives
Hollandaise sauce	Maltese sauce
	Mousseline sauce
Béarnaise sauce	Choron sauce
	Foyot sauce
	Rachel sauce

Figure 11-4. Butter-based sauces—*Sauces au beurre.*

11.4.2 Béarnaise Sauce—*Sauce béarnaise*

Yield

10 servings

Ingredients	U.S. Weight or Volume	Metric Weight or Volume
Shallots, chopped	2 ounces	50 grams
Tarragon vinegar	¼ cup	50 milliliters
Peppercorns, crushed	10 to 15	10 to 15
White wine	¼ cup	50 milliliters
Egg yolks	6	6
Butter, melted and clarified	20 ounces	600 grams
Salt	⅛ teaspoon	1 gram
Cayenne pepper	few grains	few grains
Lemon juice	of one-half lemon	of one-half lemon
Tarragon leaves, chopped	1 leaf	1 leaf

Procedure

1. Reduce the chopped shallots, tarragon vinegar, and crushed peppercorns until almost dry.
2. Add wine and egg yolks. Beat the mixture to the consistency of a thick cream, over low heat or in a water bath.
3. Using very low heat, mix in melted butter very slowly, beating constantly.
4. Add seasoning (with caution if salted butter is used) and lemon juice.
5. Strain through cheesecloth.
6. Garnish with chopped tarragon leaves.
7. Keep at a moderate temperature in a water bath.

Note: The container used for serving this sauce should be warm, never hot.

Derivatives of Béarnaise Sauce

Choron Sauce—*Sauce Choron*

This is a béarnaise sauce mixed with a little tomato puree.

Foyot Sauce—*Sauce Foyot*

This is a béarnaise sauce mixed with meat extract (*glace de viande*).

Rachel Sauce—*Sauce Rachel*

This is a béarnaise sauce mixed with both tomato puree and meat extract (*glace de viande*).

11.5 Oil-based Sauces—*Sauces à l'huile*

The basic oil sauces and their most important derivatives are shown in figure 11-5.

11.5.1 Mayonnaise—*Sauce mayonnaise*

Yield
U.S.—10 quarts
Metric—10 liters

Ingredients	U.S. Weight or Volume	Metric Weight or Volume
Egg yolks	40	40
Salt	2 ounces	50 grams
Mustard	4 ounces	100 grams
Cayenne pepper	¼ teaspoon	2 grams
Vinegar	1½ to 2 cups	3 to 5 deciliters
Oil	8½ quarts	8½ liters
Lemon juice	4 ounces	120 milliliters
Worcestershire sauce	1 ounce	30 milliliters

Procedure
1. Beat egg yolks on second speed of mixer until well beaten.
2. Mix dry ingredients with one-half of the vinegar and add to beaten egg yolks.
3. Add oil to the eggs *gradually*, while beating constantly.
4. After all the oil is added, add remainder of vinegar. Continue beating for 5 minutes.
5. Season with lemon juice and Worcestershire sauce.

Note: Mayonnaise should never be frozen.

Basic Sauce	Primary Derivatives
Mayonnaise	Bagration sauce
	English sauce
	Green sauce
	Gribiche sauce
	Rémoulade sauce
	Russian sauce
	Tartar sauce
	Tyrolian sauce
Vinaigrette	Fisherman's sauce
	Norwegian sauce
	Ravigote sauce

Figure 11-5. Oil-based sauces—*Sauces à la huile.*

Derivatives of Mayonnaise

Bagration Sauce—*Sauce Bagration*

This is a mayonnaise with anchovy puree and caviar added.

English Sauce—*Sauce anglaise*

This is a mayonnaise with English mustard added.

Green Sauce—*Sauce verte*

This is a mayonnaise mixed with puree of blanched spinach, parsley, and tarragon.

Gribiche Sauce—*Sauce gribiche*

This is a sauce made by beating crumbled hard-cooked egg yolks with vinegar and oil as for mayonnaise. It is seasoned with salt, pepper, and mustard and garnished with chopped cornichons, capers, parsley, tarragon, chives, and julienne of hard-cooked egg whites.

Mayonnaise Sauce, Russian Style—*Sauce mayonnaise à la russe*

This is a sauce made by beating equal parts of liquid meat aspic and mayonnaise. A dash of tarragon vinegar and some finely grated horseradish are added to the mixture, which is beaten over ice until it thickens. The sauce must be used immediately. It is especially suitable for molded vegetable salads, for timbales, and for coating slices of shellfish and fish.

Rémoulade Sauce—*Sauce rémoulade*

This is mayonnaise with chopped cornichons, capers, parsley, and anchovy paste added.

Tartar Sauce—*Sauce tartare*

This is mayonnaise with chopped egg whites, cornichons, capers, parsley, and onion added.

Tyrolian Sauce—*Sauce tyrolienne*

This is mayonnaise with tomato puree and chopped parsley added.

11.5.2 Vinaigrette—*Sauce vinaigrette*

Yield
U.S.—1 quart
Metric—1 liter

Ingredients	U.S. Weight or Volume	Metric Weight or Volume
Onion, chopped	5 to 7 ounces	150 to 200 grams
Herbs: parsley,	5 ounces	150 grams
chives,		
tarragon,		
basil		
Vinegar	½ cup	1½ deciliters
Oil	2 cups	5 deciliters
Salt	½ teaspoon	4 grams
Pepper	⅛ teaspoon	1 gram

Procedure
1. Combine all ingredients and mix well.
2. Adjust seasoning.

Note: The sauce should always be stirred before serving.

Derivatives of Vinaigrette Sauce

Fisherman's Sauce—*Sauce à la pêcheur*

This is a vinaigrette sauce mixed with chopped crab meat.

Norwegian Sauce—*Sauce norvégienne*

This is a vinaigrette sauce mixed with egg yolks and anchovy fillets, both chopped.

Ravigote Sauce—*Sauce ravigote*

This is a vinaigrette sauce mixed with chopped shallots, herbs, and capers. It is also frequently made with a base of mayonnaise instead of vinaigrette.

11.6 Special Hot Sauces—*Sauces spéciales chaudes*

Applesauce

This sauce is an apple puree seasoned with sugar and lemon juice. It is served hot with roast goose, duck, or pork.

Bread Sauce

This is a sauce made from milk boiled for 20 minutes with a clove-studded onion, breadcrumbs, butter, nutmeg, salt, and pepper. Remove onion before serving. (Especially suited for feathered game.)

Curry Sauce—*Sauce curry*

For this sauce, sauté chopped onion, celery, leek, parsley stems, and apples in some oil. Add curry powder. Deglaze with bouillon or stock and cook for 20 to 30 minutes. Puree and thicken with cornstarch. Season with mace, coriander, and pepper.

Mustard Sauce—*Sauce moutarde*

This sauce is prepared by adding hot water to white roux to which butter and the desired quantity of mustard are added. The finished sauce should be heated carefully.

Onion Sauce—*Soubise*

Combine 1 pound (500 grams) finely cut and blanched onion, 7 ounces (200 grams) blanched rice, approximately 2 cups (5 deciliters) milk or white stock, 1 bay leaf, 1 clove, and seasoning. Cook covered in a water bath in the oven. Strain. Thicken with egg yolks and cream. (This sauce is served with lamb and mutton roasts, saddle of veal or mutton, or lamb cutlets.) Yield: approximately 1 quart (1 liter). As a variation, combine equal amounts of onions and béchamel sauce, cover, cook, stirring occasionally, and strain.

Sour Cream Sauce—*Sauce smitane*

This is a sauce made from sautéed chopped onion moistened with white wine, reduced, and added to sour cream. It is simmered, strained, and seasoned with butter and lemon juice. (Especially suitable for game.)

11.7 Special Cold Sauces—*Sauces spéciales froides*

Cranberry Sauce—*Sauce cranberry*

Combine 2 cups (5 deciliters) of sugar and 2 cups (5 deciliters) of water. Stir to dissolve sugar. Heat to boiling. Add 1 pound (500 grams) fresh cranberries. Cook until skins pop, about 5 minutes. Remove from heat. Serve warm or chilled. (Usually served with roast turkey.) Yield: 1 quart (1 liter).

Cumberland Sauce—*Sauce Cumberland*

Whisk together 1 pound (500 grams) red currant jelly, 1¼ cups (3 deciliters) port wine, ½ cup (1 deciliter) of both orange juice and lemon juice, a little English mustard, a pinch each of cayenne pepper and ginger. Add blanched julienne zests from 2 lemons and 2 oranges. (Usually served with cold game and pâtés.) Yield: 1 cup (1 liter).

Horseradish Sauce Chantilly—*Sauce raifort Chantilly*

Mix with a wooden spoon 1½ pints (8 deciliters) of whipped cream, 4 to 5 ounces (100 to 150 grams) of grated horseradish, lemon juice, and a little cayenne pepper. Adjust seasoning. Yield: 1 quart (1 liter).

Mint Sauce—*Sauce menthe*

Combine 2 cups (5 deciliters) vinegar, 2 cups (5 deciliters) water, 2 ounces (50 grams) chopped peppermint leaves, and ⅓ cup (85 grams) sugar. Cover and bring to a boil. Allow to cool. (This is usually served with hot or cold lamb dishes.) Yield: 1 quart (1 liter).

Chapter 12
Soups—*Potages*

Clear soup refers to the various kinds of bouillons and consommés. Thick soups are broths and/or stocks thickened with flour, grits, groats, barley, semolina, or with pureed vegetables. (See figure 12-1.)

12.1 Clear Soups—*Potages clairs*

This term generally refers to bouillons or consommés made from beef. Special consommés, such as poultry or fish, should be identified as such on the menu. One portion normally consists of ¾ to 1¼ cups (2 to 3 deciliters).

12.1.1 Meat Bouillon—*Bouillon de viande*

Yield
U.S.—10 quarts
Metric—10 liters

Ingredients	U.S. Weight or Volume	Metric Weight or Volume
Beef bones, chopped	10 to 12 pounds	5 to 6 kilograms
Lean beef	2 pounds	1 kilogram
Water	12 quarts	12 liters
Bouquet garni:		
Parsley	1 teaspoon	5 grams
Thyme	½ teaspoon	3 grams
Bay leaf	1	1
Celery, chopped	½ pound	225 grams
Onion, chopped	½ pound	225 grams
Onions, browned	2	2
Salt	1 teaspoon	5 grams
Pepper	⅛ teaspoon	1 gram

Procedures
1. Put bones and meat in *cold* water. Bring to a boil and skim.
2. Add remaining ingredients.
3. Simmer for 4 hours, skimming off foam and fat occasionally.
4. Strain through cheesecloth.

Note: If the bouillon is being prepared for a dish with boiled beef, the meat should be put into *boiling* water. First brown the onions and add them with skins in order to give the bouillon a good color.

12.1.2 Petite Marmite—*Petite marmite*

Yield
10 servings

Ingredients	U.S. Weight or Volume	Metric Weight or Volume
Meat	3 pounds	1.5 kilograms
Chicken	2 pounds	1 kilogram
Leeks	7 ounces	200 grams
Carrots	7 ounces	200 grams
Celery	5 ounces	150 grams

continued

Ingredients	U.S. Weight or Volume	Metric Weight or Volume
Cabbage	7 ounces	200 grams
Turnips	3½ ounces	100 grams
Stock	3½ quarts	3.5 liters
Parsley, chopped	1 tablespoon	15 grams
Chervil, chopped	1 teaspoon	5 grams
Salt	1 teaspoon	5 grams
Pepper	⅛ teaspoon	1 gram
Marrowbones, rinsed	2 to 3 pounds	1 to 1.5 kilograms

Procedure
1. Blanch the meat and the chicken.
2. Peel vegetables and cut into sticks or thin slices.
3. Combine blanched meat and chicken with vegetables, stock, and herbs.
4. Simmer slowly. Test the meat with a fork from time to time. When it slips off the fork easily, remove it. Cut the meat into smaller pieces and return to the soup.
5. Season to taste.
6. Poach marrowbones separately. Put them in the soup just before serving.
7. Garnish with chopped parsley.

Note: Fried slices of bread, cranberries, dill pickles, or grated cheese can be used as garnish. Petite marmite should always be served in special earthenware casseroles.

Variations on Petite Marmite

Petite Marmite, Henri IV—*Petite Marmite, Henri IV*

Made like Petite Marmite, this version uses more chicken than beef.

French Beef Broth—*Pot-au-feu*

For many years this was the name given to a Petite Marmite made only with beef. Today, smoked ribs, bacon, and pork sausages are often used. The use of strongly smoked pork or smoked sausages, however, spoils the excellent taste of the beef broth.

12.1.3 Consommé

Yield
U.S.—10 quarts
Metric—10 liters

Ingredients	U.S. Weight or Volume	Metric Weight or Volume
Lean beef, minced	3 to 4 pounds	1.5 to 2 kilograms
Mirepoix:		
Leeks, minced	8 ounces	225 grams
Carrots, minced	4 ounces	110 grams
Celery, minced	4 ounces	110 grams
Egg whites	4 to 6	4 to 6
Water	2 quarts	2 liters
Brown stock, cold	10 quarts	10 liters

Procedure
1. Mix minced beef and *mirepoix*. Add egg whites and water. Cover and let stand in a cool place for about an hour.
2. Add stock.
3. Heat to the boiling point, stirring occasionally.
4. Simmer slowly for 2 hours.
5. Strain through cheesecloth and skim off any fat.
6. Adjust seasoning.

Note: The green parts of leeks and celery should be included in the *mirepoix*.

Photo opposite: hors d'oeuvre, diplomat style. At the center is a lobster, with the tail meat sliced into medallions. In the raviers, from top left, counterclockwise: paupiettes of sole stuffed with salmon mousse; quail terrine; poached salmon; smoked eel; smoked salmon; medallions of rock lobster; eggs stuffed with caviar on a bed of Russian salad; goose liver pâté in aspic.

Avocados
with shrimp.

Grilled halibut.

Grilled shrimp
kebabs.

►
Paella Valenciana
(see page 452).

Ballottine of mutton carcassonaise. A shoulder of lamb is stuffed with a farce of pork, lamb, mushrooms, peppers, and truffles; then it is wrapped in bacon and slowly roasted in the oven. At the end of the cooking time, the bacon is removed, cut up, and combined with the juices. Garnishes are potato cakes (*pommes galettes*) and halved eggplant filled with ratatouille.

Saddle of lamb imperial. A four-pound saddle of lamb is bound and spit-roasted until medium done. It is garnished with artichokes that have been halved vertically, braised in white wine and butter, stuffed with broccoli, and sprinkled with pine nuts. Artichoke halves are also covered with tomatoes stuffed with peas, topped with poached marrow rounds, half a black olive, and a small mushroom. Pepper barquettes filled with onion sauce (*Soubise*) and gratinated until golden brown top the lamb.

Partridge with
cabbage.

Summer vegetable
platter.

Celery with
marrow sauce.
(see page 412).

A variety of potato dishes.

Potato croquettes (see page 420)

Bernese potatoes (see page 419)

Puff or soufflé potatoes (see page 423)

Shoestring potatoes (see page 423)

Potato cakes (see page 420)

Duchess potatoes (see page 420)

French-fried potatoes (see page 421)   Gratinated potatoes (see page 421)   Potatoes dauphine (see page 420)

Top, from left to right: gnocchi, Roman style (see page 429); gnocchi, Piedmont style (see page 429); gnocchi, Parisian style (see page 429). *Bottom:* cheese soufflé (see page 429).

Soup-filled pastry,
Lucerne style.

Busecca
(see page 320).

Top: savarins with rum and fruit, baba with rum (see page 429). *Bottom:* éclairs and cream puffs (see page 507).

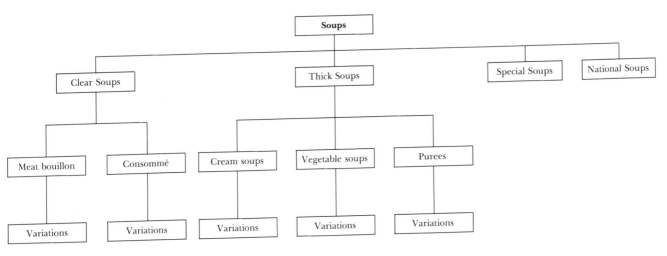

Figure 12-1. Soup categories and types.

Variations on Consommé

Cold Consommé—*Consommé froid*

This soup is prepared from double consommé (see below) that has had the fat carefully skimmed off. It is seasoned with Madeira, port wine, and cayenne pepper. It is portioned into cups while still warm and allowed to cool. Either a mixture of sautéed vegetables or diced, seeded, and peeled tomatoes can be used as garnish. It can be served without any further additions. Cheese straws are often served separately. A cold consommé should always be strong and spicy. When cold, it should gel slightly.

Chicken Consommé—*Consommé de volaille*

This soup is prepared using the simple consommé recipe, adding to the meat chopped chicken trimmings (carcasses, necks, and wings) that have been lightly roasted to give a good poultry flavor.

Double Consommé—*Consommé double*

This is prepared like consommé but the quantity of meat is doubled and a richer *mirepoix* used.

Photo opposite: at top, apples with meringue (see page 500); at bottom, apple charlotte (see page 499).

Game Consommé—*Consommé de gibier*

This soup is prepared using the simple consommé recipe, with the addition of chopped game bones and trimmings that have been cooked for a short time.

12.1.4 Fish Consommé—*Consommé de poisson*

Yield
10 servings

Ingredients	*U.S. Weight or Volume*	*Metric Weight or Volume*
Fish, ground	36 ounces	600 grams
White *mirepoix:*		
Onions, chopped	2 ounces	55 grams
Leeks, chopped	2 ounces	55 grams
Celery, chopped	3 ounces	85 grams
Thyme	½ teaspoon	3 grams
Bay leaf	1	1
Egg whites	2 to 3	2 to 3
Water, cold	1 pint	5 deciliters
White wine	¾ to 1¼ cups	2 to 3 deciliters
Fish stock, cold	2½ quarts	2.5 liters

continued

Procedure

1. Combine fish, *mirepoix*, egg whites, water, and white wine. Mix well.
2. Pour fish stock over the mixture.
3. Bring to a boil and simmer for 30 minutes.
4. Strain through cheesecloth.

Note: Fish dumplings, diced shellfish, vermicelli, rice, or croutons can be used for a garnish.

Other Bouillons and Consommés

Bouillon with Beef Marrow—*Bouillon à la moelle*

Meat bouillon garnished with cubed or sliced beef marrow, previously blanched.

Bouillon with Pearl Barley—*Bouillon à l'orge perlé*

Meat bouillon garnished with boiled barley.

Bouillon with Semolina—*Bouillon à la semoule*

Meat bouillon garnished with boiled semolina.

Consommé, American Style—*Consommé américaine*

Consommé with tomato puree, flavored with cayenne pepper and Madeira, and garnished with tapioca.

Consommé, Andalusian Style—*Consommé andalouse*

Consommé blended with tomato puree and garnished with a julienne of lean ham and rice.

Consommé with Asparagus Tips—*Consommé aux pointes d'asperges*

Consommé thickened with tapioca and garnished with asparagus tips.

Consommé Aurore—*Consommé aurore*

Consommé with tomato puree and tapioca.

Consommé, Bavarian Style—*Consommé bavaroise*

Consommé garnished with small semolina dumplings (quenelles).

Consommé with Beef Marrow—*Consommé à la moelle*

Consommé garnished with poached slices of beef marrow. Slices of bread fried in butter are served separately.

Consommé, Belle Fermière—*Consommé belle fermière*

Consommé with sautéed julienne of cabbage and green beans garnished with pasta.

Consommé, Brunoise Style—*Consommé brunoise*

Consommé with sautéed, finely diced leeks, carrots, celery, cabbage, and turnips.

Consommé Carmen—*Consommé Carmen*

Consommé blended with tomato puree and garnished with strips of sweet peppers and dry cooked rice.

Consommé Caroline—*Consommé Caroline*

Consommé garnished with dry cooked rice.

Consommé Célestine—*Consommé Célestine*

Consommé garnished with a julienne of thin pancakes.

Consommé Chantilly—*Consommé Chantilly*

Chicken consommé garnished with a julienne of cooked egg whites and dry-cooked rice.

Consommé with Cheese Straws—*Consommé aux paillettes*

Consommé or chicken consommé served with cheese straws, seasoned with paprika.

Consommé with Cheese Toast—*Consommé aux diablotins*

Chicken consommé with small round slices of bread that have been covered with cheese, seasoned with paprika, and browned.

Consommé Demidoff—*Consommé Demidov*

Consommé garnished with tiny chicken dumplings (quenelles) and finely diced, sautéed vegetables.

Consommé Dubarry—*Consommé Dubarry*

Consommé garnished with cauliflower and molded custard.

Consommé Duchess Style—*Consommé duchesse*

Chicken consommé garnished with julienne of chicken.

Consommé with Egg Drops—*Consommé aux oeufs filés*

A consommé boiled with beaten eggs.

Consommé with Egg Yolk—*Consommé à l'oeuf*

Consommé served with 1 egg yolk per cup of soup.

Consommé, French Style—*Consommé pot-au-feu*

Consommé with vegetables (see below) garnished with small cubes of boiled meat. It is served in a special pot with small slices of fried bread offered separately.

Consommé with Fried Puff Pearls—*Consommé aux pois frits*

Consommé with fried puff pearls served separately. (Thick pancake batter is poured through a colander over hot fat to make puff pearls.)

Consommé, Hungarian Style—*Consommé hongroise*

Consommé flavored with paprika and Madeira and garnished with sautéed tomatoes that have been peeled, seeded, and diced.

Consommé, Hunter's Style—*Consommé chasseur*

Consommé garnished with sliced mushrooms and tiny puff shells.

Consommé Julienne—*Consommé julienne*

Consommé with a julienne of cooked vegetables: carrots, leeks, celery, and turnips.

Consommé Léopold—*Consommé Léopold*

Consommé with semolina, garnished with julienne of Boston lettuce and chervil.

Consommé with Liver Dumplings—*Consommé aux noques de foie*

Consommé garnished with tiny liver dumplings.

Consommé Lucullus—*Consommé Lucullus*

Chicken consommé garnished with slices of boiled chicken and truffles, green peas, and asparagus tips.

Consommé Madrilène—*Consommé madrilène*

A double chicken consommé flavored with Madeira, brandy, and cayenne pepper. It is garnished with diced tomatoes. It can be served hot or cold.

Consommé Monte Carlo—*Consommé Monte Carlo*

Chicken consommé garnished with stuffed pancakes (crêpes with goose liver filling are rolled and sliced into thin circles).

Consommé, Paris Style—*Consommé parisienne*

Consommé garnished with sautéed, finely diced vegetables, molded custard, and chervil.

Consommé with Pasta—*Consommé aux pâtes*

Consommé garnished with fine noodles.

Consommé with Pearl Tapioca—*Consommé aux perles du Japon*

Consommé garnished with cooked pearl tapioca.

Consommé, Peasant Style—*Consommé paysanne*

Consommé garnished with very finely sliced and cooked vegetables: leeks, carrots, celery, turnips, and cabbage.

Consommé with Poached Eggs—*Consommé à l'oeuf poché*

Consommé or chicken consommé garnished with small poached eggs.

Consommé, Princess Style—*Consommé princesse*

Chicken consommé garnished with molded custard, cooked pearl barley, and julienne of cooked chicken.

Consommé with Profiteroles—*Consommé aux profiteroles*

Consommé or chicken consommé with profiteroles—small pâte à choux puffs—served separately.

Consommé with Quenelles—*Consommé aux quenelles*

Consommé or chicken consommé garnished with meat or chicken dumplings.

Consommé with Ravioli—*Consommé au ravioli*

Consommé garnished with very small ravioli.

Consommé Royale—*Consommé royale*

Consommé garnished with molded custard.

Consommé with Sago—*Consommé au sagou*

Consommé garnished with cooked sago (a starch similar to tapioca).

Consommé with Semolina—*Consommé à la semoule*

Consommé garnished with cooked semolina.

Consommé with Spring Vegetables—*Consommé printanière*

Consommé or chicken consommé with slightly cooked small cubes of carrots, turnips, and celery, and strips of beans and sorrel.

Consommé with Tapioca—*Consommé au tapioca*

Consommé garnished with cooked tapioca.

Consommé with Three Fillets—*Consommé aux trois filets*

Consommé garnished with julienne of chicken, tongue, and truffles.

Consommé with Vegetables—*Consommé croûte au pot*

A petite marmite with finely sliced leeks, carrots, turnips, cabbage, and celery. Croutons fried in butter are served separately.

Consommé with Vermicelli—*Consommé aux vermicelles*

Consommé garnished with cooked vermicelli (fine noodles).

Consommé Viennese Style—*Consommé viennoise*

Consommé garnished with square egg noodles and potato dumplings.

Consommé Xavier—*Consommé Xavier*

Consommé with egg drops and chopped parsley.

Queen's Consommé—*Consommé à la reine*

Chicken consommé thickened with tapioca and garnished with molded custard and julienne of chicken.

12.2 Thick Soups—*Potages liés*

Cream Soups—Potages crèmes et veloutés

Several decades ago two basic methods were used to prepare cream soups. Cream soups were made with a béchamel sauce combined with the appropriate purée and thickened with cream. The other type of cream soup was made with velouté sauce combined with the appropriate purée and thickened with cream and egg yolk (*liaison*) and butter. Today, with the availability of very fine quality thickening flours, from many different cereals, cream soups can be prepared by one method and are all called cream soup. (Other thick soups are vegetable soups and purees.)

12.2.1 Cream Soup

Yield
U.S.—10 quarts
Metric—10 liters

Ingredients	U.S. Weight or Volume	Metric Weight or Volume
Shortening	10 to 14 ounces	300 to 400 grams
Rice flour	14 to 16 ounces	400 to 500 grams
Stock (white, chicken, fish, or other), cold	10½ quarts	10 liters
Butter	2 ounces	55 grams
Cream	1 quart	1 liter
or		
Liaison:		
Cream	1 pint	5 deciliters
Egg yolks	2	2

Procedure
1. Melt shortening. Add flour and blend. Cook slowly and stir. Do not let flour brown.
2. Add cold stock and simmer for about 30 minutes. If too much evaporates, add more stock.
3. Bind with cream and butter or with the *liaison*.
4. Strain.
5. Season to taste.

6. Do not allow the soup to boil again if thickened with a *liaison*.

Note: An alternate method is to dissolve the rice flour in cold milk or white stock. Add this to the boiling stock. The soup is then finished with the ingredients in the basic recipe.

Variations

Barley Soup—*Orge perlé*

Sauté 4 ounces (100 grams) of barley and 1 teaspoon (5 grams) of flour in butter. Add 3 quarts (3 liters) of white stock and a *bouquet garni*. Cook soup until barley is tender. Bind with cream and butter.

Thick Semolina Soup—*Semoule liée*

Sauté 5 ounces (120 grams) of semolina in butter. Add 3 quarts (3 liters) of white stock and a *bouquet garni*. Cook for 20 minutes and bind.

Other Cream Soups

Cream Soup Agnès Sorel—*Crème Agnès Sorel*

Cream soup made with chicken stock and sautéed mushrooms, garnished with julienne of mushrooms, beef tongue, and chicken.

Andalusian Cream Soup—*Velouté andalouse*

Blend 3 quarts (3 liters) of cream soup with ¾ cup (2 deciliters) of tomato puree and 1¼ cups (3 deciliters) of onion puree. Without letting soup boil, bind with a *liaison* of egg yolks and cream. It can be garnished with diced tomatoes, strips of sweet peppers, and dry-cooked rice.

Cream of Asparagus Soup—*Crème Argenteuil*

Cream soup made with equal parts of asparagus stock and white stock, garnished with asparagus tips.

Cream Soup Bagration—*Crème Bagration*

Cream soup made with white stock, garnished with cut macaroni.

Cream of Barley Soup—*Crème d'orge*

Cream soup with barley flour instead of rice flour.

Cream Soup Canoness—*Velouté chanoinesse*

Cream soup made with cream sauce made from fish stock, mushrooms, parsley, and crayfish butter. It is garnished with poached slices of fish milt.

Cream Soup Carmen—*Velouté Carmen*

Cream soup flavored with tomato puree and garnished with diced tomatoes and dry-cooked rice.

Cream Soup Caroline—*Velouté Caroline*

Cream soup blended with almond milk and cooked rice.

Cream of Cauliflower Soup—*Crème Dubarry*

Cream soup made with equal parts of cauliflower stock and white stock, garnished with tiny florets of cauliflower.

Cream Soup Choisy—*Crème Choisy*

Cream of lettuce soup (see below) with croutons served separately.

Cream Soup Dame Blanche—*Velouté dame blanche*

Add ¾ cup (2 deciliters) of almond milk to 3 quarts (3 liters) of cream soup made with chicken stock. Adjust thickening. Garnish with small quenelles of chicken and diced chicken.

Cream Soup Derby—*Crème Derby*

Cream soup made with onion, seasoned with curry, and garnished with dry-cooked rice, chopped truffles, and, if desired, chicken dumplings.

Cream Soup Jackson—*Crème Jackson*

A soup made by mixing equal parts of cream soup and cream of potato soup (see below). It is garnished with vermicelli or cooked tapioca and julienne of the white part of leeks.

Cream of Lettuce Soup—*Crème de laitue*

Cream soup garnished with sautéed, chopped, blanched Boston lettuce.

Cream Soup Mary Stuart—*Velouté Marie Stuart*

Cream soup made with barley flour and chicken stock, garnished with sautéed finely diced vegetables and chervil leaves.

Cream Soup Milanese—*Crème milanaise*

Add ¾ cup (2 deciliters) of tomato puree to 3 quarts (3 liters) of cream soup. Cook and bind. Garnish with elbow macaroni, julienne of white truffles, tongue, and ham.

Cream of Morel Soup—*Crème de morilles*

Add 3½ ounces (100 grams) sautéed morels to 3 quarts (3 liters) of cream soup. Strain and bind. Garnish with finely cut morels.

Cream of Nettle Soup—*Crème d'ortie*

Add 10 ounces (300 grams) of blanched young nettle leaves to 3 quarts (3 liters) of cream soup. Strain and bind. Garnish with croutons.

Cream of Oatmeal Soup—*Crème d'avoine*

Cream soup made with oat flour instead of rice flour.

Cream Soup Portuguese—*Crème portugaise*

Cream soup blended with tomato puree and sliced bacon, strained, and garnished with dry-cooked rice.

Cream of Rice Soup, German Style—
Crème allemande

A soup made with sautéed rice, stock, and *bouquet garni*. After boiling for 10 minutes, the *bouquet* is removed, and the soup is thickened.

Cream Soup Rossini—*Velouté Rossini*

Add 7 ounces (200 grams) of goose liver butter to 3 quarts (3 liters) of cream soup made with chicken stock. To make goose liver butter, blend 3½ ounces (100 grams) of goose liver trimmings or puree with 3½ ounces (100 grams) of butter until smooth.

Cream of Sorrel Soup—*Crème d'oseille*

Add 7 ounces (200 grams) of sautéed sorrel to 3 quarts (3 liters) of cream of oatmeal soup. Strain and garnish with croutons.

Queen's Cream Soup—*Crème à la reine*

Cream soup made with chicken stock and garnished with diced chicken.

Vegetable Soups—Potages aux légumes

These soups are composed of one or more types of vegetables and usually include onions, leeks, and diced bacon, which are first sautéed and then boiled, but not strained. If a vegetable soup consists of several different vegetables, only small quantities of those vegetables with a strong flavor, such as cabbage and turnip, should be used. All vegetable soups are garnished with chopped parsley, chives, or chervil. Flour or potato is used for binding.

12.2.2 Vegetable Soup

Yield
U.S.—10 quarts
Metric—10 liters

Ingredients	U.S. Weight or Volume	Metric Weight or Volume
Fat *or* butter	3½ ounces	100 grams
Leeks	3 pounds	1.5 kilograms
Carrots, sliced thin	1 pound	500 grams
Onions, diced fine	2 pounds	1 kilogram
Celery, sliced fine	1 pound	500 grams
Potatoes *or* turnips, chopped	1 pound	500 grams
Stock	7 to 8 quarts	7 to 8 liters
Cream *or* milk (optional)	1 pint	5 deciliters
Cabbage, shredded fine	½ pound	225 grams
Salt	1 teaspoon	6 grams
Pepper	¼ teaspoon	2 grams
Fried bread	to garnish	to garnish
Parsley, chopped	to garnish	to garnish

Procedure
1. Sauté leeks, carrots, onions, and celery.
2. Add potatoes or turnips and continue to sauté.
3. Add stock and simmer until ingredients are well cooked and soup is bound.
4. Add cream or milk (optional).
5. Add cabbage and simmer for 10 minutes.
6. Adjust seasoning.
7. Garnish with fried bread and parsley.

Note: If potatoes are not used, the vegetables must be dusted with flour or rice flour before adding stock. Acidic vegetables, such as leeks and cabbage, must be well cooked. If not, the soup will curdle if bound with cream.

Other Vegetable Soups

Cultivator Soup—*Potage cultivateur*

Use 3½ ounces (100 grams) of butter, 7 ounces (200 grams) of diced bacon, 7 pounds (3.5 kilograms) of finely sliced vegetables (leeks, onions, carrots, celery, turnips, and potatoes), 7 to 8 quarts (7 to 8 liters) of stock, and seasoning. Follow method for vegetable soup. When portioned, serve grated cheese separately.

Fermière Soup—*Potage fermière*

Cultivator soup served with fried slices of bread.

Flemish Soup—*Potage flamande*

Use 3½ ounces (100 grams) of butter, 14 ounces (400 grams) of onions and leeks, 28 ounces (800 grams) of chopped Brussels sprouts, 5 pounds (2.5 kilograms) of finely sliced potatoes, 7 to 8 quarts (7 to 8 liters) of stock, and seasoning. Follow method for vegetable soup. Garnish with small Brussels sprouts. Yield: 10 quarts (10 liters).

Home-style Soup—*Potage bonne femme*

Use 3½ ounces (100 grams) of fat, 3 pounds (1.5 kilograms) of leeks, 5 pounds (2.5 kilograms) of finely sliced potatoes, 7 to 8 quarts (7 to 8 liters) of stock, and 1 pint (5 deciliters) of cream. Follow method for vegetable soup. Adjust seasoning. Garnish with fried bread and chopped parsley. Yield: 10 quarts (10 liters).

Leek Soup—*Potage aux poireaux*

The same ingredients and method as for home-style soup but with an increased quantity of leeks.

Peasant Soup—*Potage paysanne*

Use 3½ ounces (100 grams) of butter, 10 ounces (300 grams) of diced lean bacon, 7 pounds (3.5 kilograms) of finely sliced vegetables (onions, leeks, carrots, turnips, celery, cabbage, and potatoes), 3½ ounces (100 grams) of flour, and 7 to 8 quarts (7 to 8 liters) of stock. Follow method for vegetable soup. Serve grated cheese separately. Yield: 10 quarts (10 liters).

Purees—*Potages purées*

Soups made from dried or fresh vegetables and then put through a sieve or food mill are known as purees. Vegetables with a high-starch content, or potatoes, rice, and flour can be used to bind purees. Cream is used to enrich them. These soups are garnished with chives, parsley, or croutons.

12.2.3 Vegetable Puree

Yield
U.S.—10 quarts
Metric—10 liters

Ingredients	U.S. Weight or Volume	Metric Weight or Volume
White *mirepoix* of onions and leeks	2½ pounds	1.2 kilograms
Fat	4 ounces	120 grams
Potatoes	6 pounds	3 kilograms
Ham and bacon rinds	2 pounds	1 kilogram
Vegetable stock	8 quarts	8 liters
White wine (optional)		
Cream (optional)	1 pint	5 deciliters
Salt	1 teaspoon	6 grams

Procedure
1. Lightly sauté the *mirepoix* in the fat.
2. Add potatoes and ham and bacon rind, and continue to sauté.
3. Add stock, a little white wine if desired, and seasoning.
4. Bring quickly to a boil, stirring occasionally.
5. Cook slowly for 2 hours and strain.
6. Bind, if desired, with cream.
7. Adjust seasoning.

Other Vegetable Purees

Carrot Puree—*Purée Crécy*

Use 3½ ounces (100 grams) of fat, 28 ounces (800 grams) of onions and leeks, approximately 6 pounds (3 kilograms) of carrots, 10 ounces (300 grams) of rice, 8 quarts (8 liters) of stock, and seasoning. Follow method for vegetable puree. Yield: 10 quarts (10 liters).

Carrot Puree with Tapioca—*Purée velours*

Combine 7 quarts (7 liters) of carrot puree and 3 quarts (3 liters) of stock. Garnish with 7 ounces (200 grams) of tapioca. Yield: 10 quarts (10 liters).

Cauliflower Puree—*Purée Dubarry*

Use 3½ ounces (100 grams) of fat, 20 ounces (600 grams) of white *mirepoix,* approximately 6 pounds (3 kilograms) of cauliflower, 2 pounds (1 kilogram) of potatoes, 8 quarts (8 liters) of stock, and seasoning. Follow method for vegetable puree. Garnish with cooked cauliflower. Yield: 10 quarts (10 liters).

Fresh Pea Puree—*Purée de pois frais*

Use 4 ounces (120 grams) of fat, 2½ pounds (1.2 kilograms) of leeks, 1 pound (500 grams) of lettuce, 6 pounds (3 kilograms) of fresh peas, a little chervil, sugar, 8 quarts (8 liters) of stock, and seasoning. Follow method for vegetable puree. Garnish with fresh peas and chervil leaves. Yield: 10 quarts (10 liters).

Fresh Pea Puree Lamballe—*Purée Lamballe*

To 10 quarts (10 liters) of fresh pea puree, add 6 to 7 ounces (150 to 200 grams) of tapioca. Yield: 10 quarts (10 liters).

Health Soup—*Purée santé*

Add 1¼ pounds (500 grams) of shredded sorrel simmered in butter until water in vegetable has evaporated (chiffonade of sorrel) to 10 quarts (10 liters) of potato puree Parmentier.

Lentil Puree—*Purée Conti*

Use 3½ ounces (100 grams) of fat, 28 ounces (800 grams) of *mirepoix,* 7 ounces (200 grams) of bacon rinds, 2 pounds (1 kilogram) of soaked lentils, 1 pound (500 grams) of potatoes, a little chervil, 10 quarts (10 liters) of stock, and seasoning. Follow method for vegetable puree. Yield: 10 quarts (10 liters).

Pea Puree Saint-Germain—*Purée Saint-Germain*

Use 4 ounces (120 grams) of fat, 28 ounces (800 grams) of onion and leek, 7 ounces (200 grams) of bacon rinds, 2½ pounds (1.2 kilograms) of soaked, dried split green peas, 3 pounds (1.5 kilograms) of potatoes, 10 quarts (10 liters) of stock, and seasoning. Follow method for vegetable puree. Yield: 10 quarts (10 liters).

Potato Puree Parmentier—*Purée Parmentier*

Use 4 ounces (120 grams) of fat, 2½ pounds (1.2 kilograms) of onions and leeks, 6 pounds (3 kilograms) of potatoes, 8 quarts (8 liters) of stock, ham and bacon rinds, and seasoning. Follow method for vegetable puree. Yield: 10 quarts (10 liters).

Potato Puree with Tapioca—*Purée argentée*

Add 3 to 5 ounces (100 to 150 grams) of cooked tapioca to 10 quarts (10 liters) of potato puree Parmentier. Yield: 10 quarts (10 liters).

Potato and Tomato Puree Malakoff—*Purée Malakov*

Use 3½ ounces (100 grams) of fat, 2½ pounds (1.2 kilograms) of leeks, 3 pounds (1.5 kilograms) of potatoes, 3 pounds (1.5 kilograms) of potatoes, 3 pounds (1.5 kilograms) of tomatoes, 8 quarts (8 liters) of stock, and seasoning. Follow method for vegetable puree. Garnish with 20 ounces (600 grams) of sautéed, blanched, chopped spinach. Yield: 10 quarts (10 liters).

Red Bean Puree—*Purée Condé*

Use 3½ ounces (100 grams) of fat, 28 ounces (800 grams) of *mirepoix,* 5½ ounces (160 grams) of bacon rind, 2 pounds (1 kilogram) of red beans, 1 pound (500 grams) of potatoes, 1 quart (1 liter) of red wine, 10 quarts (10 liters) of stock, and seasoning. Follow method for vegetable puree. Yield: 10 quarts (10 liters).

Spinach Puree—*Purée florentine*

To 10 quarts (10 liters) of potato puree Parmentier, add 2 pounds (1 kilogram) of blanched chopped spinach. Yield: 10 quarts (10 liters).

Sport Soup—*Potage sport*

Garnish 10 quarts (10 liters) of pea puree Saint-Germain with 1 pound (500 grams) of sorrel shredded in a fine julienne and simmered in butter (chiffonade of sorrel), 10 ounces (300 grams) of cooked and cut noodles, and chopped parsley. Yield: 10 quarts (10 liters).

Béarnaise Vegetable Puree—*Purée garbure*

Use 5 ounces (150 grams) of fat, 20 ounces (600 grams) of onions, 20 ounces (600 grams) of leeks, 7 ounces (200 grams) of bacon trimmings and rind, 7 ounces (200 grams) of turnips, 7 ounces (200 grams) of cabbage, 28 ounces (800 grams) of carrots, 4 pounds (2 kilograms) of potatoes, 8 quarts (8 liters) of stock, and seasoning. Follow method for vegetable puree. Yield: 10 quarts (10 liters).

Watercress Puree—*Purée cressonnière*

Use 3½ ounces (100 grams) of fat, 2½ pounds (1.2 kilograms) of white *mirepoix*, 6 pounds (3 kilograms) of potatoes, 28 ounces (800 grams) of watercress, 8 quarts (8 liters) of stock, and seasoning. Follow method for vegetable puree. Garnish with sautéed, chopped watercress leaves.

White Bean Puree Faubonne—*Purée Faubonne*

Use 3½ ounces (100 grams) of fat, 28 ounces (800 grams) of white *mirepoix*, 7 ounces (200 grams) of bacon rind, 2½ pounds (1.2 kilograms) of soaked white beans, 2 pounds (1 kilogram) potatoes, 8 quarts (8 liters) of stock, and seasoning. Follow method for vegetable puree. Yield: 10 quarts (10 liters).

Yellow Pea Puree Victoria—*Purée Victoria*

Use 3½ ounces (100 grams) of fat, a few bacon rinds, 2½ pounds (1.2 kilograms) of onions and leeks, 2½ pounds (1.2 kilograms) of soaked, dried yellow peas, 3 pounds (1.5 kilograms) of potatoes, 10 quarts (10 liters) of stock, and seasoning. Garnish with 3½ ounces (100 grams) of cooked rice. Yield: 10 quarts (10 liters).

12.3 Special Soups—*Potages spéciaux*

Special soups are those made with unusual ingredients and/or prepared by a distinctive method. The following are classified as special soups.

12.3.1 Crayfish Bisque—*Bisque d'écrevisses*

Yield
10 servings

Ingredients	U.S. Weight or Volume	Metric Weight or Volume
Fat	2 ounces	50 grams
Crayfish, rinsed and cleaned	3 to 4 pounds	1.5 to 2 kilograms
Mirepoix, chopped fine	7 ounces	200 grams
Diced tomato *or* tomato puree	2¾ ounces	80 grams
Brandy	¼ cup	500 millimeters
White wine	¾ cup	2 deciliters
Fish stock	1½ quarts	1.5 liters
Stock	1 quart	1 liter
Rice flour	2¾ ounces	80 grams
Egg yolks	2	2
Cream	¾ cup	1 to 2 deciliters

Procedure
1. Sauté the crayfish and *mirepoix* in fat until the crayfish turn red.

2. Add tomato and continue to sauté.
3. Flame with the brandy.
4. Add the wine and reduce.
5. Add the fish stock and plain stock and simmer for 10 minutes.
6. Remove the tails of the crayfish. Pound the carcasses and put them back in the soup. Simmer.
7. Bind the soup with the rice flour. Strain.
8. Thicken with egg yolks and cream. Adjust seasonings, and garnish with diced crayfish tails and cubed tomatoes.

Variations of Crawfish Bisque

Lobster Bisque—*Bisque de homard*

Substitute live lobster for crayfish.

Shrimp Bisque—*Bisque de crevettes*

Substitute shrimp for crayfish.

Other Special Soups

Fish Velouté—*Velouté de poisson*

Use 3 quarts (3 liters) of basic white sauce made with fish stock thinned with milk. Thicken with 2 egg yolks and 1¼ cups (3 deciliters) of cream. Adjust seasoning. Garnish with cubes of fish or fish quenelles. Yield: 10 servings.

Germiny Soup—*Potage Germiny*

Sauté 7 ounces (200 grams) of sorrel shredded in a fine julienne in 1 ounce (30 grams) of butter. Add 2½ quarts (2.5 liters) of consommé. Just before serving, thicken with 4 egg yolks and 1¾ cups (4 deciliters) of cream. Do not allow soup to boil. Garnish with chopped chervil leaves.

Chicken Puree, Queen's Style—*Purée à la reine*

Poach 1 chicken in 3½ quarts (3.5 liters) of chicken stock with 7 ounces (200 grams) of *bouquet garni*. Puree the chicken meat, reserving the breast. Bind the stock with 3½ ounces (100 grams) of rice flour. Add the puree and 1¼ to 1¾ cups (3 to 4 deciliters) cream. Adjust seasoning. Garnish with diced breast of chicken. Yield: 10 servings.

Game Puree—*Purée de gibier*

Boil 1 pound (½ kilogram) of game meat (preferably venison) with 14 ounces (400 grams) of lentils in 3 quarts (3 liters) of game stock with 1 onion studded with cloves and a bay leaf. Cook until meat is tender and grind. Flame with brandy. Add ½ to ¾ cup (1 to 2 deciliters) of cream. Adjust seasoning. Garnish with cubed game meat.

Real Turtle Soup, Lady Curzon

Heat 1½ quarts (1.5 liters) of real turtle soup (available canned) with a little sherry. Whip ¾ cup (2 deciliters) of cream. Pour soup into heated cups. Garnish with whipped cream sprinkled with curry powder. Glaze under the broiler. Yield: 10 servings.

Real Turtle Soup, Londonderry

Heat 1½ quarts (1.5 liters) of real turtle soup (available canned). Thicken with 3 egg yolks and ½ cup (1.5 deciliters) of cream. Add a little sherry and Madeira. Do not let soup boil. Yield: 10 servings.

12.4 National Soups—*Potages nationaux*

The methods for preparing these soups are quite varied. The name of the soup should appear on the menu in the language of the country of its origin.

12.4.1 *Basler Zwiebelsuppe*—Basel Onion Soup (Swiss)

Yield
10 servings

Ingredients	U.S. Weight or Volume	Metric Weight or Volume
Onion, chopped	16 to 20 ounces	500 to 600 grams
Fat	2¾ ounces	80 grams
Flour, browned	7 ounces	200 grams
Stock	3 quarts	3 liters
Croutons	5 ounces	150 grams
Cheddar cheese, diced fine	5 ounces	150 grams

Procedure
1. Brown onion in fat. Add browned flour and blend with fat.
2. Add the stock gradually and simmer for 1 hour.
3. Adjust seasonings.
4. Garnish soup with croutons and cheese just before serving.

12.4.2 *Bauern-Chrutsuppe*—Bernese Health Soup, Peasant Style (Swiss)

Yield
10 servings

Ingredients	U.S. Weight or Volume	Metric Weight or Volume
Spinach, chopped fine	1¾ pounds	800 grams
Green onion, chopped	7 ounces	200 grams
Chervil, chopped fine	5 ounces	150 grams
Marjoram, chopped fine	1 sprig	1 sprig
Fat	1¾ ounces	50 grams
Stock	3 quarts	3 liters
Egg yolks	3	3
Cream	1¾ cups	4 deciliters
Bread, toasted	10 slices	10 slices
Chives	3 ounces	75 grams

Procedure
1. Sauté spinach, green onion, chervil, and marjoram in fat.
2. Add stock and simmer for 30 minutes.
3. Thicken with egg yolks and cream.
4. Place toasted bread in bowls and cover with soup. Garnish with chives.

Note: Sorrel may be used in the spring.

12.4.3 *Berner Topf*—Bernese Soup (Swiss)

Yield
10 servings

Ingredients	U.S. Weight or Volume	Metric Weight or Volume
Stock	3½ quarts	3.5 liters
Salt pork *or* hocks	28 ounces	800 to 900 grams
Yellow peas, dried	1 pound	500 grams
Leeks, fine strips	7 ounces	200 grams
Carrots, fine strips	3½ ounces	100 grams
Celery, fine strips	3½ ounces	100 grams
Chives	5 ounces	150 grams

Procedure
1. Simmer stock, salt pork or hocks, yellow peas, leeks, carrots, celery, and chives for 1½ hours. Add more stock if necessary.
2. Remove pork, and puree the soup.
3. Cut pork into small pieces, add to soup, and heat.
4. Serve in soup bowls and garnish with chives.

12.4.4 *Borscht Polonais*—Polish Borscht

Yield
10 servings

Ingredients	U.S. Weight or Volume	Metric Weight or Volume
Leeks	7 ounces	200 grams
Savoy cabbage	7 ounces	200 grams
Red beets	10 ounces	300 grams
Onions	3½ ounces	100 grams
Celery	3½ ounces	100 grams
Parsley roots	2	3
Butter	1¾ ounces	50 grams
Stock	2½ quarts	2.5 liters
Fennel	1¾ ounces	50 grams
Salt	2 teaspoons	10 grams
Cloves	2	2
Bay leaf	1	1
Soup meat	1 pound	500 grams
Duck, browned and disjointed	1	1
Bacon	7 ounces	200 grams
Chipolata sausage, sliced	10	10
Sour cream	¾ cup	2 deciliters
Red beet juice	1¼ cups	3 deciliters

Procedure

1. Cut all vegetables into julienne pieces and sauté in butter.
2. Add stock, fennel, seasoning, soup meat, duck, and bacon.
3. Simmer until meat is tender. Remove meat and cut into pieces.
4. Add meat and chipolatas to soup. Adjust seasoning.
5. Bind with sour cream and red beet juice.

Note: Meat and sour cream may be served separately.

12.4.5 *Bouillabaisse à la Provençale*—Provençal Bouillabaisse (French)

Yield
10 servings

Ingredients	U.S. Weight or Volume	Metric Weight or Volume
Fish (combination of red snapper, turbot, halibut, scallops, perch, pike, trout, whiting, red mullet)	7 pounds	3.5 kilograms
Olive oil	½ cup	1 deciliter
Onions	8½ ounces	250 grams
Leeks	5 ounces	150 grams
White wine	1 pint	5 deciliters
Fish stock	2½ quarts	2.5 liters
Tomato, peeled	4	4
Garlic cloves, grated	2	2
Parsley, chopped	2 ounces	50 grams
Saffron	⅛ teaspoon	1 gram
Fennel powder	⅛ teaspoon	1 gram
Fennel leaves	¼ teaspoon	2 grams
Spice sachet:		
Clove	1	1
Bay leaf	1	1
Savory	1 sprig	1 sprig
Thyme	pinch	pinch
Pernod	few drops	few drops
Salt	2 teaspoons	12 grams
Bread slices	10	10
Butter	5 ounces	150 grams

Procedure

1. Divide the fish (large ones in slices, smaller ones whole) into two groups, according to the cooking time required.
2. Sauté the onions and leeks in the olive oil.
3. Combine all the ingredients except the fish and simmer for 20 minutes. Remove spice sachet.
4. Add fish requiring the longer cooking time and simmer for 10 minutes.
5. Add fish requiring shorter cooking time and continue to simmer for 5 minutes.
6. Toast bread and brush with garlic butter, place on bottom of soup terrine, and pour the soup into the terrine.

Note: The fish may be served separately on a hot platter.

Variation of Bouillabaisse

Bouillabaisse à la Marseillaise—Marseilles Fish Soup (French)

Use recipe for bouillabaisse à la provençale, using water in place of white wine. When served, place slices of bread in the bowl.

12.4.6 *Bundner Suppe*—Soup of Dried, Cured Beef (Swiss)

Yield
10 servings

Ingredients	U.S. Weight or Volume	Metric Weight or Volume
Onions	5 ounces	150 grams
Leeks	5 ounces	150 grams
Carrots	3½ ounces	100 grams
Celery	1¾ ounces	50 grams
Dried beef	3 ounces	80 grams
Westphalian ham	3 ounces	80 grams
Fat	1¾ ounces	45 grams
Flour	1 ounce	30 grams
Pearl barley	3½ ounces	100 grams
Navy beans	1¾ ounces	50 grams
Stock	3 quarts	3 liters
Egg yolks	2	2
Cream	1¼ cups	3 deciliters

Procedure
1. Cut vegetables, dried beef, and Westphalian ham very fine. Sauté in fat and add flour.
2. Add pearl barley and navy beans and continue to sauté.
3. Add stock and simmer for 1½ hours.
4. Thicken with egg yolks and cream. Adjust seasoning.

Note: A special sausage, beinwurst, may be substituted for the dried beef. It should be cooked with the soup, removed, diced, and added to the soup before serving. The dried beef used by the Swiss, known as *grisons*, is an air-dried beef similar to jerky; the Westphalian ham is similar to prosciutto.

12.4.7 *Busecca*—Tripe Soup (Italian)

Yield
10 servings

Ingredients	U.S. Weight or Volume	Metric Weight or Volume
Onions, chopped fine	5 ounces	150 grams
Leeks, chopped fine	5 ounces	150 grams
Fat	2 ounces	60 grams
Potatoes	14 ounces	400 grams
Carrots	5 ounces	150 grams
Cabbage	3½ ounces	100 grams
Tomatoes	3½ ounces	100 grams
Borlotto beans, precooked	2 ounces	60 grams
Veal tripe	1 pound	500 grams
Tomato puree	¼ cup	50 milliliters
Stock	3½ quarts	3.5 liters
Bacon	1½ ounces	40 grams
Garlic cloves	2	2
Marjoram	⅛ teaspoon	1 gram
Parmesan cheese	3 ounces	100 grams

Procedure
1. Sauté onions and leeks in fat. Add potatoes, carrots, cabbage, and tomatoes and continue to sauté.
2. Add beans, tripe, and tomato puree.
3. Add stock and simmer until all ingredients are cooked, for about 1½ hours.
4. Chop and pound bacon, garlic, and marjoram.
5. Add bacon, garlic, and marjoram to soup.
6. Serve grated Parmesan cheese separately.

12.4.8 Chicken Broth (British)

Yield
10 servings

Ingredients	U.S. Weight or Volume	Metric Weight or Volume
Chicken, blanched	2 to 3 pounds	1 to 1.5 kilograms

continued

Ingredients	U.S. Weight or Volume	Metric Weight or Volume
Carrots, julienne	5 ounces	150 grams
Celery, julienne	3½ ounces	100 grams
Leeks, julienne	7 ounces	200 grams
Turnips, julienne	1¾ ounces	50 grams
Chicken stock	3½ quarts	3.5 liters
Bread, sliced and toasted		

Procedure
1. Poach chicken with vegetables.
2. Season chicken stock and add poached, skinned, and disjointed chicken.
3. Serve toasted slices of bread separately.

12.4.9 *Gazpacho* (Spanish)

Yield
10 servings

Ingredients	U.S. Weight or Volume	Metric Weight or Volume
Cucumbers, peeled and diced	3	3
Tomatoes, diced	2 pounds	1 kilogram
Onions, diced	3½ ounces	100 grams
Green peppers, diced	3½ ounces	100 grams
Garlic, chopped fine	2	2
White breadcrumbs	3½ ounces	100 grams
Ice water	1 quart	1 liter
Red-wine vinegar	½ cup	1 deciliter
Salt	½ teaspoon	3 grams
Pepper	¼ teaspoon	2 grams
Olive oil	½ cup	1 deciliter

Procedure
1. Combine the vegetables and breadcrumbs.
2. Add water, wine vinegar, salt, and pepper.
3. Puree the mixture.
4. Add the olive oil gradually, whipping constantly until a smooth mixture is formed.
5. Refrigerate for at least 2 hours.
6. Whip before spooning into cups or soup terrines.

12.4.10 *Geflügelkleinsuppe*—Cream of Chicken Soup (German)

Yield
10 servings

Ingredients	U.S. Weight or Volume	Metric Weight or Volume
Necks, wings, hearts of chicken, blanched	2½ pounds	1.2 kilograms
Fat	1 ounce	30 grams
Carrots, julienne	3½ ounces	100 grams
Celery, julienne	3½ ounces	100 grams
Leeks, fine strips	7 ounces	200 grams
Turnips, diced	1¾ ounces	50 grams
Pearl barley	2 ounces	60 grams
Stock	3 quarts	3 liters
Cream	1¼ cups	3 deciliters

Procedure
1. Sauté chicken pieces in fat.
2. Add carrots, celery, leeks, turnips, and barley, and continue to sauté until tender.
3. Add stock and simmer.
4. Bind with cream and adjust seasoning.

12.4.11 *Gulyás Leves*—Goulash Soup (Hungarian)

Yield
10 servings

Ingredients	U.S. Weight or Volume	Metric Weight or Volume
Beef shoulder	2 pounds	1 kilogram
Onions, sliced thin	12 ounces	350 grams
Fat	1¾ ounces	50 grams
Sweet Szegedi paprika	¾ ounce	15 grams
Salt	½ teaspoon	3 grams
Pepper	¼ teaspoon	2 grams
Stock	3 quarts	3 liters
Potatoes, diced	2 pounds	1 kilogram

continued

Ingredients	U.S. Weight or Volume	Metric Weight or Volume
Tomatoes, diced	3½ ounces	100 grams
Spaetzle	7 ounces	200 grams

Procedure

1. Cut beef shoulder into ¾-inch (2-centimeter) cubes.
2. Sauté the onions and beef in fat.
3. Add paprika, salt, and pepper.
4. Add stock and simmer until meat is tender.
5. Add potatoes and tomatoes. Simmer until the vegetables are done. Adjust seasoning.
6. Add spaetzle before serving.

12.4.12 *Kerbelsuppe*—Chervil Soup (Swiss)

Yield
10 servings

Ingredients	U.S. Weight or Volume	Metric Weight or Volume
Fat	1¾ ounces	50 grams
Leeks, chopped fine	1 pound	500 grams
Potatoes, sliced thin	28 ounces	800 grams
Marjoram	⅛ teaspoon	1 gram
Cream	1¼ cups	3 deciliters
Stock	3 quarts	3 liters
Salt	½ teaspoon	3 grams
Pepper	¼ teaspoon	2 grams
Chervil	5 ounces	150 grams
Croutons	5 ounces	150 grams
Cheese, grated	5 ounces	150 grams

Procedure

1. Melt fat in a saucepan. Add leeks and sauté until light brown.
2. Add potatoes and marjoram and cook until potatoes are tender.
3. Stir vigorously with a whisk until potato is broken into pieces.
4. Add cream, salt, pepper, and chervil. Heat and adjust seasoning.
5. Serve croutons and grated cheese separately.

12.4.13 *Krautsuppe*—Cabbage Soup (Austrian)

Yield
10 servings

Ingredients	U.S. Weight or Volume	Metric Weight or Volume
Fat	1¾ ounces	50 grams
Onions, chopped	5 ounces	150 grams
Savoy cabbage, julienne	28 ounces	800 grams
Stock	3½ quarts	3.5 liters
Rice flour or wheat flour	3½ ounces	100 grams
Salt	½ teaspoon	3 grams
Egg yolks	3	3
Sour cream	¾ cup	2 deciliters
Paprika	⅛ teaspoon	1 gram

Procedure

1. Sauté onions in fat. Add cabbage and 1 pint (500 milliliters) of the stock.
2. Prepare a cream soup with the flour, salt, and remainder of the stock.
3. Add the sautéed cabbage to the soup and heat to boiling.
4. Thicken the soup with egg yolks and sour cream. Adjust seasoning and add paprika.

12.4.14 *Leberknödelsuppe*—Liver Dumpling Soup (German)

Yield
10 servings

Ingredients	U.S. Weight or Volume	Metric Weight or Volume
White bread rolls	4	4
Milk	1½ cups	350 milliliters
Beef liver	9 ounces	250 grams
Beef marrow or veal kidney fat	2 ounces	60 grams

continued

Ingredients	U.S. Weight or Volume	Metric Weight or Volume
Eggs	2 to 3	2 to 3
Flour	1¾ ounces	50 grams
Onion, chopped	2 ounces	60 grams
Garlic	1 clove	1 clove
Salt	1 teaspoon	6 grams
Pepper	½ teaspoon	2 grams
Bouillon	3 quarts	3 liters
Parsley, chopped	½ cup	80 grams

Procedure
1. Soak the bread rolls in the milk.
2. Grind liver, beef marrow or kidney fat, and soaked rolls.
3. Add eggs, flour, onion, garlic, and seasoning. Stir vigorously. Let stand for 30 minutes or longer.
4. Shape mixture into small dumplings.
5. Poach the dumplings in 3 quarts (3 liters) of simmering strong bouillon.
6. Serve the liver dumplings in the bouillon. Garnish with chopped parsley.

12.4.15 *Mehlsuppe mit Käseschnitten*—Flour Soup with Toasted Cheese (Swiss)

Yield
10 servings

Ingredients	U.S. Weight or Volume	Metric Weight or Volume
Flour	7 ounces	200 grams
Fat	4 ounces	120 grams
Onions, chopped	4 ounces	120 grams
Leeks, chopped	3 ounces	80 grams
Stock	3½ quarts	3.5 liters
Bread, toasted	10 slices	10 slices
Emmentaler cheese	7 ounces	200 grams
Butter, melted	2 ounces	60 grams

Procedure
1. Brown the flour in the fat. Add chopped onions and leeks immediately.
2. Add stock, stirring constantly until blended. Simmer for 1 hour. Remove floating fat frequently.
3. Add more stock if needed. Adjust seasoning.
4. Sprinkle cheese and drops of melted butter on toast. Float the toasted cheese slices on the soup when serving.

12.4.16 *Minestrone* (Italian)

Yield
10 servings

Ingredients	U.S. Weight or Volume	Metric Weight or Volume
Bacon, diced	3½ ounces	100 grams
Onions, sliced thin	3½ ounces	100 grams
Leeks, finely sliced	5 ounces	150 grams
Fat	1¾ ounces	50 grams
Carrots, sliced thin	3½ ounces	100 grams
Celery, sliced thin	3½ ounces	100 grams
Savoy cabbage, sliced thin	7 ounces	200 grams
Tomato puree	1½ ounces	40 grams
Stock	3 to 4 quarts	3 to 4 liters
Potatoes, sliced	7 ounces	200 grams
Rice	1 ounce	30 grams
Spaghetti, broken pieces	1 ounce	30 grams
Tomatoes, diced	3½ ounces	100 grams
Borlotto beans, precooked	1¾ ounces	50 grams
Pesto:		
Bacon fat	1¾ ounces	50 grams
Garlic	3 cloves	3 cloves
Marjoram	⅛ teaspoon	1 gram
Basil	⅛ teaspoon	1 gram

Procedure
1. Sauté bacon, onion, and leeks in the melted fat until tender.
2. Add the carrots, celery, and cabbage, and sauté.
3. Add tomato puree and stock and simmer for 1 hour.

continued

Procedure

4. Add potatoes, rice, spaghetti, tomatoes, and borlotto beans, and continue to cook for 20 to 30 minutes.
5. Make a *pesto* by combining the bacon fat, garlic, marjoram, and basil. Pound the ingredients together until a smooth paste is formed. Adjust the seasoning of the soup.
6. Add pesto to the soup before serving.

12.4.17 Mock Turtle Soup (British)

Yield
10 servings

Ingredients	U.S. Weight or Volume	Metric Weight or Volume
Calf's-head stock	2 quarts	2 liters
Basic brown sauce	1½ quarts	1.5 liters
Madeira	¼ cup	50 milliliters
Sherry	¼ cup	50 milliliters
Calf's head, diced	10 to 14 ounces	300 to 400 grams

Procedure

1. Simmer clear calf's-head stock, basic brown sauce, and seasoning for approximately 30 minutes. Bind if necessary.
2. Add Madeira and sherry and adjust seasoning.
3. Add diced calf's head.

Note: Small chicken dumplings may be used as a garnish.

12.4.18 Mulligatawny Soup (British)

Yield
10 servings

Ingredients	U.S. Weight or Volume	Metric Weight or Volume
Onion, chopped	5 ounces	150 grams
Fat	2 ounces	60 grams

Ingredients	U.S. Weight or Volume	Metric Weight or Volume
Curry powder	½ to ¾ ounce	10 to 20 grams
Basic white sauce (chicken)	2½ to 3 quarts	2.5 to 3 liters
Cream	¾ to 1¼ cups	2 to 3 deciliters
Rice	4 ounces	120 grams
Chicken	8 ounces	225 grams

Procedure

1. Sauté the chopped onion in melted fat.
2. Add curry powder and continue to sauté.
3. Make basic white sauce with chicken stock. Strain and add to onion mixture.
4. Add cream and adjust seasoning.
5. Garnish with cooked rice and julienne of chicken.

12.4.19 Mutton Broth (Scottish)

Yield
10 servings

Ingredients	U.S. Weight or Volume	Metric Weight or Volume
Fat	1¾ ounces	50 grams
Leeks, chopped	7 ounces	200 grams
Celery ribs, diced	3½ ounces	100 grams
Carrots, diced	3½ ounces	100 grams
Turnips, chopped	1¾ ounces	50 grams
Onions, chopped	1¾ ounces	50 grams
Mutton stock	3 to 3½ quarts	3 to 3.5 liters
Mutton neck *or* mutton breast	14 to 16 ounces	400 to 500 grams
Pearl barley, blanched	3½ ounces	100 grams

Procedure

1. Sauté vegetables in melted fat.
2. Add mutton stock, mutton neck or breast, and pearl barley.

3. Simmer for 1 to 1½ hours. Remove mutton from the broth and dice.
4. Garnish the broth with the diced mutton.

Note: Lamb may be substituted for mutton.

12.4.20 *Nudelsuppe mit Huhn*—Chicken Noodle Soup (German)

Yield
10 servings

Ingredients	U.S. Weight or Volume	Metric Weight or Volume
Chicken, blanched	2 pounds	1 kilogram
Chicken stock	3½ quarts	3.5 liters
Bouquet garni:		
Bay leaf	½	½
Celery, leaves	2 tablespoons	25 grams
Thyme	½ teaspoon	3 grams
Parsley	4 sprigs	4 sprigs
Cloves	2	2
Leeks, white portion	1	1
Egg noodles	3½ ounces	100 grams

Procedure
1. Poach blanched chicken in chicken stock with *bouquet garni.*
2. Cook egg noodles in salted water and drain.
3. Remove cooked chicken and *bouquet garni* from stock.
4. Cut chicken into small pieces.
5. Add chicken and noodles to the soup. Adjust seasoning.

12.4.21 *Olla Podrida* (Spanish)

Yield
10 servings

Ingredients	U.S. Weight or Volume	Metric Weight or Volume
Mutton breast	10 ounces	300 grams
Veal knuckle	10 ounces	300 grams
Oxtail	1 pound	500 grams
Chicken or pigeon	28 ounces	800 grams
Smoked sausage (chorizos)	10 ounces	300 grams
Ham	7 ounces	200 grams
Chick-peas	9 ounces	250 grams
Vegetables, sliced fine: leeks, carrots, celery, Savoy cabbage	2 pounds	1 kilogram
Stock	3½ quarts	3.5 liters
Salt	1 teaspoon	5 grams
Garlic	2 cloves	2 cloves
Parsley, chopped	1 tablespoon	15 grams

Procedure
1. Simmer mutton breast, veal knuckle, oxtail, chicken or pigeon, sausage, ham, and chick-peas with the sliced vegetables in the stock until the meat is tender.
2. Remove meat and cut into small pieces.
3. Add meat and salt to soup. Flavor with garlic and parsley.

Note: When serving, the soup can be presented in a bowl and the meat and vegetables on a separate platter.

12.4.22 Oxtail Soup (British)

Yield
10 servings

Ingredients	U.S. Weight or Volume	Metric Weight or Volume
Oxtail slices	2 pounds	1 kilogram
Fat	3 ounces	75 grams
Bacon trimmings	2 ounces	50 grams

continued

Ingredients	U.S. Weight or Volume	Metric Weight or Volume
Mirepoix:	10 ounces	300 grams
Onions, chopped		
Celery, chopped		
Carrots, chopped		
Tomato puree	1 to 1¾ ounces	30 to 50 grams
White wine	1¼ cups	3 deciliters
Brown stock	3 quarts	3 liters
Flour, browned	4 ounces	120 grams
Brandy	¼ cup	50 milliliters
Madeira	½ cup	1 deciliter
Potatoes, cooked, diced	5 ounces	150 grams
Carrots, cooked, diced	5 ounces	150 grams

Procedure

1. Season oxtail slices and brown in fat with bacon trimmings. Add *mirepoix* and continue to sauté.
2. Add tomato puree, white wine, and brown stock. Simmer slowly for 2 to 3 hours. Remove oxtail from soup and discard bones. Press meat pieces and chill.
3. Bind soup with browned flour.
4. Skim the fat and add more stock if necessary.
5. Strain through a fine sieve. Adjust seasoning.
6. Add brandy and Madeira.
7. Garnish with chilled oxtail meat and cooked diced potatoes and carrots.

Note: For clear oxtail soup, do not use flour.

12.4.23 *Minestra con Pesto* (Italian)

Yield
10 servings

Ingredients	U.S. Weight or Volume	Metric Weight or Volume
Leeks	5 ounces	150 grams
Onions	3½ ounces	100 grams

Ingredients	U.S. Weight or Volume	Metric Weight or Volume
Carrots	2¾ ounces	80 grams
Potatoes	3½ ounces	100 grams
Celery	1¾ ounces	50 grams
Cabbage	1¾ ounces	50 grams
Fat	1¾ ounces	50 grams
Stock	3 quarts	3 liters
Tomatoes, peeled and diced	3½ ounces	100 grams
Egg noodles, fine	3½ ounces	100 grams
Pesto:		
Fat	1¾ ounces	50 grams
Garlic	1 clove	1 clove
Marjoram	¼ teaspoon	2 grams
Basil	¼ teaspoon	2 grams

Procedure

1. Chop leeks, onions, carrots, potatoes, celery, and cabbage into very fine pieces.
2. Sauté leeks and onions in fat. Add other chopped vegetables and continue to sauté.
3. Add stock and tomatoes. Simmer for 1 hour.
4. Add egg noodles and continue cooking for 20 minutes.
5. Prepare *pesto* by combining fat, garlic, marjoram, and basil and pounding into a smooth paste.
6. Add *pesto* to soup. Adjust seasoning.

Note: During simmering, check thickness of soup continuously, adding stock if necessary. In Italy, the soup is served quite thick. If desired, bacon rind or ham bones can be added during the cooking.

12.4.24 *Potée à la Vaudoise* (Swiss)

Yield
10 servings

Ingredients	U.S. Weight or Volume	Metric Weight or Volume
Stewing beef	2 pounds	1 kilogram
Leeks	10 ounces	300 grams
Carrots	7 ounces	200 grams

Ingredients	U.S. Weight or Volume	Metric Weight or Volume
Celery	7 ounces	200 grams
Savoy cabbage	3½ ounces	100 grams
Turnips	3½ ounces	100 grams
Onions, small	3½ ounces	100 grams
Stock, boiling	3½ quarts	3.5 liters
Vaudois sausage	14 ounces	400 grams
Chives	2 ounces	60 grams
Chervil	2 ounces	60 grams

Procedure

1. Blanch the beef.
2. Combine the vegetables and beef and add to the boiling stock.
3. Simmer slowly until the meat is tender.
4. Remove meat and cut the meat and sausage into small pieces.
5. Add meat and sausage to the soup. Adjust seasoning.
6. Garnish with chives and chervil.

12.4.25 *Rahmsuppe*—Cream Soup (German)

Yield

10 servings

Ingredients	U.S. Weight or Volume	Metric Weight or Volume
Fat	3½ ounces	100 grams
Flour	5 ounces	150 grams
Stock	2 quarts	2 liters
Milk	1½ quarts	1.5 liters
Bouquet garni:		
Bay leaf	2	2
Celery leaves	4 tablespoons	50 grams
Parsley	12 sprigs	12 sprigs
Leek, white portion	2	2
Caraway seeds	⅛ teaspoon	1 gram
Cloves	4	4
Thyme	1 teaspoon	6 grams

Ingredients	U.S. Weight or Volume	Metric Weight or Volume
Cream	1¼ cups	3 deciliters
Butter	2 ounces	50 grams
Bread, sliced and fried		

Procedure

1. Make a roux with the fat and flour.
2. Add the stock, milk, *bouquet garni*, caraway seeds, cloves, and thyme.
3. Simmer for 1 hour. Strain.
4. Add cream and butter. Adjust seasoning.
5. Serve slices of fried bread separately.

12.4.26 Vichyssoise (American)

Yield

10 servings

Ingredients	U.S. Weight or Volume	Metric Weight or Volume
Fat	1¾ ounces	50 grams
Leeks, chopped fine	20 ounces	600 grams
Onion	1	1
Cloves	6	6
Bay leaf	1	1
Potatoes, diced	2½ pounds	1.2 kilograms
Stock	2½ quarts	2.5 liters
Cream	1¾ cups	450 milli-liters
Chives, snipped	3 tablespoons	40 grams
Croutons	5 ounces	150 grams

Procedure

1. Melt fat and sauté leeks. Add onion studded with cloves, and bay leaf.
2. Add potatoes and stock. Cook until potato is soft.
3. Puree.
4. Add cream and adjust seasoning.
5. Garnish with chives.
6. Serve croutons separately.

12.4.27 *Zuppa Mille-Fanti*—Soup of a Thousand Infants or Egg-Drop Soup (Italian)

Yield
10 servings

Ingredients	U.S. Weight or Volume	Metric Weight or Volume
Breadcrumbs, white	3½ ounces	100 grams
Parmesan cheese	1¾ ounces	50 grams
Eggs	3	3
Parsley, chopped	1 ounce	30 grams
Stock, boiling	3 quarts	3 liters

Procedure
1. Blend breadcrumbs, Parmesan cheese, eggs, and parsley.
2. Add small amounts of the bread mixture gradually to the boiling stock, stirring constantly with a whisk.
3. Cover and let stand for 5 to 6 minutes.
4. Stir before serving.

12.4.28 *Zuppa Pavese*—Eggs in Broth, Pavia Style (Italian)

Yield
10 servings

Ingredients	U.S. Weight or Volume	Metric Weight or Volume
Beef bouillon, strong boiling	3 quarts	3 liters
Eggs	10	10
Bread slices, toasted	10	10
Grated cheese	5 ounces	150 grams

Procedure
1. Portion boiling beef bouillon into individual bowls.
2. Break 1 egg into each bowl.
3. Place toasted slice of bread that has been sprinkled with grated cheese on top of soup and gratinate.

Chapter 13
Hors d'Oeuvre—
Hors d'oeuvre

13.1 Cold Hors d'Oeuvre—
Hors d'oeuvre froids

Cold hors d'oeuvre should stimulate the appetite and therefore should always be served as the first course. Soup is often omitted to make way for the hors d'oeuvre. If a soup is served after the hors d'oeuvre, it should be a spicy, clear soup, such as consommé or clear oxtail soup, in order to stimulate the palate again.

Formerly, the cold hors d'oeuvre were divided into three main groups: *hors d'oeuvre à la suédoise* (Swedish-style hors d'oeuvre), *hors d'oeuvre à la russe* (Russian-style hors d'oeuvre), and *hors d'oeuvre à la parisienne* (Parisian-style hors d'oeuvre). Today cold hors d'oeuvre are classified into the following categories:

Canapés and small sandwiches—*canapés, amuse-bouche*
Cocktails—*cocktails*
Shellfish—*crustacés et coquillages*
Fruit—*fruits*
Puff pastry and cream puff pastry—*feuilletés et pâte à choux*
Vegetables—*légumes*
Mousses—*mousses*
Cold egg dishes—*oeufs froid*
Stuffed dishes—*galantines, pâtés froid, terrines*
Cold fish dishes—*poisson froids*
Miscellaneous—*divers*

Because the modern art of cooking is simplicity itself and the world is becoming increasingly more calorie conscious, often only a dish from only one of these categories is served, such as melon or a meat or fish cocktail. It is better to offer one quality product, presented in a simple way, than several cold hors d'oeuvre made from a variety of poor-quality products. Whether single or many, simple or really luxurious, hors d'oeuvre must be attractively presented. If a variety of hors d'oeuvre are to be served, several classical presentations may be used: *hors d'oeuvre sur assiette* (plate), *hors d'oeuvre variés* (assorted), and *hors d'oeuvre riches* (opulent). Toast and butter should be served separately with all hors d'oeuvre.

Hors d'Oeuvre Plate—Hors d'oeuvre sur assiette

This is a nicely arranged plate with a limited choice of simple or more expensive foods. The basic rule here is "small in quantity, but big in quality" and at the same time attractively served. (See figure 13-1.)

Assorted Hors d'Oeuvre—Hors d'oeuvre variés

These can be served on special portioned platters, in *raviers,* on large silver platters, or even from the serving cart. A choice of six to ten different items, including a spicy salad, is quite sufficient. When presenting and, particularly, when serving, care must be taken to

Figure 13-1. Plate of hors d'oeuvre—*Hors d'oeuvre sur assiette.*

ensure that the colors of the different items harmonize. (See figure 13-2.)

Opulent Hors d'Oeuvre—Hors d'oeuvre riches

This is a classical form of presentation. Lobster or rock lobster (*à la parisienne*) should always be in-

cluded. *Raviers* on a silver platter may be used, but it is also possible to arrange the center pieces on a silver platter covered with meat aspic and to serve the accompaniments in small separate bowls. Opulent hors d'oeuvre should, as the name suggests, include exquisite specialties, such as rock lobster, lobster, smoked salmon, poached salmon, caviar, goose liver pâté, and shrimps. (See figure 13-3.)

Canapés and Small Sandwiches— Canapés, amuse-bouche

Canapés are small pieces of toast sliced in decorative shapes that are spread first with butter and then with some form of meat or fish mixture and glazed with aspic or jelly. Small sandwiches are similar to canapés but smaller and are held together with toothpicks. A variety of canapés and small sandwiches can be ar-

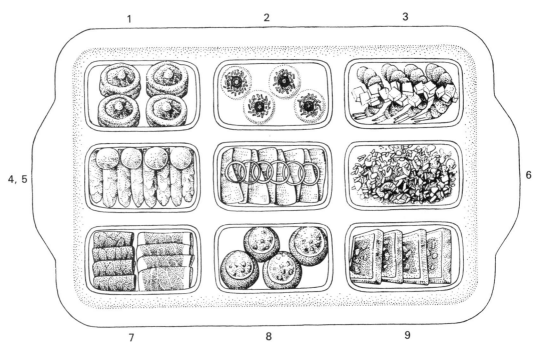

Figure 13-2. Assorted hors d'oeuvre—*Hors d'oeuvre variés:* (1) puff pastry shell (*bouchée*) with goose-liver mousse; (2) artichoke bottoms with Waldorf salad; (3) shrimps with aspic; (4) asparagus tips with mushrooms; (5) sardines with onion rings; (6) Italian vegetable salad; (7) cured, dried beef (Bündnerfleisch) and Westphalian ham; (8) tomatoes stuffed with Russian salad; (9) chicken pâté.

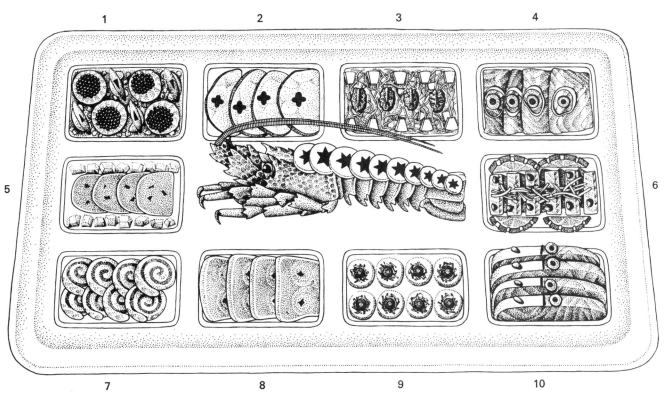

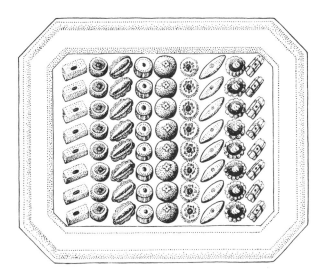

Figure 13-3. Opulent hors d'oeuvre—*Hors d'oeuvre riches:* (1) tartlets with caviar; (2) beef tenderloin, London house style; (3) Waldorf salad; (4) Smoked salmon; (5) goose-liver pâté with aspic; (centerpiece) rock lobster decorated with lobster slices; (6) smoked eel with lemon; (7) rolled fillets of sole; (8) terrine of game; (9) artichoke bottoms filled with chicken salad; (10) cold poached salmon slices.

ranged on a platter for an attractive presentation (see figure 13-4).

Admiral's Canapés—*Canapés amirale*

Small toasts are spread with shrimp butter and garnished with shrimp.

Anchovy Canapés—*Canapés d'anchoise*

Small toasts are spread with anchovy butter and garnished with anchovy fillets and chopped hard-cooked eggs.

Figure 13-4. Assorted canapés—*Canapés variés.*

Caviar Canapés—*Canapés de caviar*

Small toasts are spread with caviar butter and garnished with caviar.

Crayfish Canapés—*Canapés d'écrevisses*

Small toasts are spread with crayfish butter and garnished with crayfish tails.

Goose-liver Canapés—*Canapés de mousse de foie gras*

Small toasts are spread with goose liver mousse and garnished with truffles.

Ham Canapés—*Canapés de jambon*

Small toasts are spread with butter and garnished with slices of ham.

Ox-tongue Canapés—*Canapés à l'écarlate*

Small toasts are spread with mustard butter and covered with fine slices of ox tongue.

Smoked Salmon Canapés—*Canapés de saumon fumé*

Small toasts are spread with butter and garnished with strips of smoked salmon.

Tartare Canapés—*Canapés tartare*

Small toasts are spread with butter and then with prepared steak tartare.

Cocktails—Cocktails

Crispi Cocktail—*Cocktail Crispi*

Pieces of peeled pears, oranges, and grapefruit are mixed with mayonnaise containing a little orange juice, orange rind, and brandy and served in Champagne glasses, garnished with a pitted cherry and walnuts.

Fruit Cocktail—*Cocktail de fruits*

Fresh ripe fruit (pears, oranges, peaches, and apricots) are cut into pieces, mixed with mayonnaise seasoned with ketchup, brandy, and orange rind, and served in Champagne glasses, garnished with fruit.

Lobster Cocktail—*Cocktail de homard*

This cocktail is prepared in the same way as shrimp cocktail, mixing the tail meat into the sauce and using the opened claws for decoration.

Rock Lobster Cocktail—*Cocktail de langouste*

Rock lobster tails, prediced and prepared like the shrimp cocktail, are placed in a Champagne glass, smothered with the sauce, and topped with a slice of rock lobster, covered with a slice of truffle surrounded with chopped hard-cooked egg.

Shrimp Cocktail—*Cocktail de crevettes*

Cooked shrimps are marinated in brandy and lemon juice. The shrimps are placed in a cup or Champagne glass, which is filled two-thirds full with sauce. The cocktail is garnished with shrimp tails, half-moon slices of hard-cooked egg, and truffles. To make *cocktail sauce:* mix 1¼ cups (3 deciliters) of thick, strongly seasoned mayonnaise with a julienne of celery, 2 tablespoons (40 grams) of tomato ketchup, a little Grand Marnier, a few pinches of cayenne pepper, and a few drops of orange juice. If desired, grated horseradish and lemon juice can be added.

In the United States shrimp cocktail is often served as follows: the cooked, peeled, chilled shrimps are arranged on the edge of a special glass cup that fits into another dish containing crushed ice. In the center is a small deep cup containing a highly spiced sauce, which is made of tomato ketchup, lemon juice, and cayenne pepper. Other ingredients may be added to the sauce, such as grated horseradish, diced celery, caviar, or mango chutney. The shrimps are dipped into the sauce one by one.

Sole Fillet Cocktail—*Cocktail de sole*

Cocktail sauce (recipe given with shrimp cocktail, but prepared without orange juice) is portioned into either a wide flat Champagne glass or a glass bowl to a depth of ½ inch (12 millimeters). A soft-cooked egg is placed in the center and encircled by half slices of poached paupiettes of sole (fillets of sole spread with fish forcemeat and rolled). The cocktail is garnished with truffles.

Shellfish—Crustacés et coquilages

Crayfish—*Ecrevisses*

Crayfish or crayfish tails are served with mayonnaise.

Lobster—*Homard*

Fresh lobster is boiled, cut into halves, garnished, and served cold. Mayonnaise is served separately.

Oysters—*Huîtres*

Freshly opened oysters are served on a bed of crushed ice with a lemon wedge. Buttered slices of bread are served separately.

Rock Lobster—*Langouste*

Rock lobster or rock lobster slices are garnished and glazed with aspic. Mayonnaise is served separately.

Shrimp Aspic—*Aspic de crevettes*

Shrimp tails are placed in a mold coated with aspic and decorated with truffles. They are covered with more aspic and allowed to cool and gel.

Fruit—Fruits

Cantaloupe—*Cantaloup*

Cantaloupe is cut in halves, the seeds are removed, and the fruit is served on crushed ice.

Grapefruit—*Pamplemousse*

Unpeeled grapefruit halves are sectioned, using a special serrated knife, and sprinkled with sugar and a few drops of Kirschwasser. The grapefruit is served cold on a napkin.

Puff Pastry and Cream Puff Pastry— Feuilleté et pâte à choux

Anchovy Sticks—*Bâtons d'anchois*

Puff pastry strips are spread with anchovy fillets, covered with second strips of puff pastry, brushed with egg wash and baked.

Anchovy Straws—*Allumettes d'anchois*

Puff pastry strips are covered with anchovy puree or fillets and baked.

Bouchées—*Bouchées*

Small puffs made from puff pastry are stuffed with a mousse of goose liver, venison, or poultry, or with caviar.

Caviar Profiteroles—*Duchesse au caviar*

Small round puffs made from cream puff pastry, called *profiteroles,* are stuffed with caviar and glazed with aspic.

Cheese Straws—*Allumettes au fromage*

Puff pastry strips are rolled in egg and cheese, twisted, and baked.

Eclairs—*Eclairs*

Fingers of cream puff pastry filled with a mousse of goose liver, poultry, or venison.

Profiteroles—*Duchesse*

Small round puffs made from cream puff pastry are filled with goose liver, chicken, or game mousse and glazed with aspic as desired.

Tartlets—*Tartelettes*

Very tiny patty shells are filled with mousse of goose liver, game, or poultry, with caviar, or with fish mayonnaise.

Vegetables—Légumes

Artichokes, Greek Style—*Artichauts à la grecque*

Blanched artichoke hearts are cooked in white wine, oil, lemon juice, fennel, salt, pepper, thyme, and bay leaf and allowed to marinate in the liquid.

Asparagus Tips—*Pointes d'asperges*

Blanched or raw asparagus tips are marinated in a vinaigrette sauce and garnished with hard-cooked eggs.

Avocado Stuffed with Shrimps—*Avocats aux crevettes*

Avocado cups are prepared by cutting a ripe avocado lengthwise, gently twisting the halves apart, and removing the stone. Marinated baby shrimps are mixed with a well-seasoned cocktail sauce containing a little brandy. Avocado cups are filled with shrimp mixture, garnished with hard-cooked eggs, truffles or olives, and lemons. Toast is served separately.

Cauliflower—*Chou-fleur*

Cauliflower are cooked, marinated, and served with mayonnaise.

Celery Hearts, Greek Style—*Céleri à la grecque*

Blanched celery hearts are cooked in white wine, oil, lemon juice, fennel seed, salt, pepper, thyme, and bay leaf and allowed to marinate in the liquid.

Fennel, Greek Style—*Fenouil à la grecque*

Blanched fennel is cooked in white wine, oil, lemon juice, fennel seed, salt, pepper, thyme, and bay leaf and allowed to marinate in the liquid.

Marinated Mushrooms—*Champignons marinées*

Very small, white, firm mushrooms are sliced and sautéed in oil with chopped shallots and lemon juice. Vinegar, white wine, salt, pepper, oil, garlic, sugar, fennel seeds, and thyme are added, and mushrooms are cooked and marinated in this liquid.

Stuffed Olives—*Olives farcies*

Pitted olives are stuffed with anchovy or crayfish butter.

Tomatoes—*Tomates*

Tomatoes are peeled, seeded, and sliced to use for a salad or halved to stuff with a vegetable salad.

Mousses

See chapter 24.

Cold Egg Dishes—Oeufs froids

Cold eggs, prepared in many different ways, are generally served as part of an hors d'oeuvre assortment. They can also accompany cold fish, meat, and poultry if cold or marinated vegetables or salads are served at the same time.

Egg Tartlets—*Oeufs en tartelettes*

Pastry shells are filled with Italian salad, topped with a medium-soft-boiled egg, garnished, and glazed in aspic.

Poached Eggs on Artichoke Hearts— *Oeufs pochés mascotte*

Ham or goose-liver mousse is spread on artichoke hearts, each topped with a poached egg, garnished with truffles or tarragon sprigs, and glazed in aspic.

Poached Eggs on Tomatoes—*Oeufs pochés sur tomates*

Tomatoes are halved, and the pulp is carefully scooped out. The shells are filled with Italian salad topped with a poached egg, garnished with truffles or tarragon sprigs, and glazed in aspic.

Russian Eggs—*Oeufs à la russe*

Seven-minute eggs are arranged on Russian salad, then covered with a well-spiced mayonnaise and garnished with pieces of smoked salmon, anchovy fillets, or capers. In a variation of this dish, Russian salad is blanketed with rémoulade sauce and topped with hard-cooked eggs stuffed with caviar.

Stuffed Eggs—*Oeufs farcis*

Hard-cooked eggs are stuffed with a mousse of goose liver, chicken, or game, and with caviar or with a butter mixture, and glazed with aspic.

Stuffed Dishes—Galantines, pâtés froid, terrines

See chapter 24.

Cold Fish Dishes—*Poissons froids*

Anchovy Fillets—*Filets d'anchois*

Anchovy fillets are arranged attractively, garnished with capers.

Bismarck Herring

Fresh herrings are marinated in wine, vinegar, seasoning, and onion rings and served with sour cream.

Caviar—*Caviar*

Caviar is served in bowls on ice with toast and fresh butter as accompaniments.

Fish Mayonnaise—*Mayonnaise de poisson*

Skinned and boned fish are arranged on a bed of lettuce, coated with a thick mayonnaise, and garnished with anchovy fillets, capers, and slices of hard-cooked egg.

Herring Salad—*Salade de hareng*

Marinated herring fillets are arranged on a platter, coated with sauce, and garnished with apple slices. The sauce may include sour cream, yogurt, possibly mayonnaise, mustard, olive oil, sliced onions, wine vinegar, chives, parsley, paprika, and salt.

Salmon with Mayonnaise—*Saumon en mayonnaise*

Salmon is coated with mayonnaise and garnished.

Sardines—*Sardines*

These fish are served in oil with chopped hard-cooked eggs, onions, and capers as a garnish.

Smoked Salmon—*Saumon fumé*

Smoked salmon is sliced thin, garnished with lemon and onion, and served with toast and butter separately.

Trout—*Truites*

Small poached trout are served in or coated with fish aspic or mayonnaise.

Tuna—*Thon*

Water-packed tuna is arranged on a platter, dressed with a little oil, coated with a salad dressing or vinaigrette, and garnished.

Miscellaneous—Divers

Goose Liver—*Foie gras*

This is served in either sausage or block form. Butter and toast are served separately.

Mortadella Sausage

Mortadella, an Italian pork sausage, is sliced and arranged attractively.

Ox Muzzle Salad—*Museau de boeuf*

Cooked ox muzzle (*ochsenmaul*) is thinly sliced and served with a vinaigrette sauce.

Prosciutto—*Jambon cru*

Prosciutto, an Italian ham, is sliced very thin and rolled up. It is served with melon slices or fresh figs.

Salads—*Salades*

Salads are prepared with fish, tongue, ham, chicken, or vegetables (beets, cucumbers) attractively cut and seasoned with a thin, spicy mayonnaise, a vinaigrette, or an ordinary salad dressing. See chapter 19.

Salami

The meat is cut into fine slices and attractively served.

13.2 Hot Hors d'Oeuvre— *Hors d'oeuvre chauds*

At large dinners, tiny, spicy, hot hors d'oeuvre are served between the soup and fish course. In today's shortened menus, they are often served instead of the hot entrée. The size and richness depends upon the composition of the menu. Many hot hors d'oeuvre are suited for serving as small à la carte dishes and are usually described as hot snacks. Many dishes classified in other categories can be served as hors d'oeuvres; in addition to those listed below, consider crêpes, other quiches, gnocchi, fondue, pasta dishes, raclette, ramekins, risotto, and various grilled sandwiches, recipes for which appear in later chapters.

Well-known Hot Hors d'Oeuvre

Anchovy Sticks—*Bâtons d'anchois*

Preparation is described under cold hors d'oeuvre dishes. Serve hot.

Barquettes—*Barquettes*

Boat-shaped molds lined with short crust paste are filled with a salpicon (a combination of small diced ingredients bound with a sauce), with a puree of shellfish or sole, or with chicken puree, and garnished with truffles.

Brochettes—*Brochettes*

Tender pieces of liver, kidneys, sweetbread, or tenderloin cubes, and bacon are threaded on a metal or wooden skewer, dipped into butter and breadcrumbs, and grilled. When served, the meat can be transferred to a silver skewer. The brochette is topped with maître d'hôtel butter.

Buckwheat Pancakes—*Blini*

The batter is made with yeast, milk, wheat and buckwheat flours, salt, and egg yolks. It is allowed to rise, and beaten eggs whites and cream are added. Pancakes are served with fresh caviar and sour cream.

Calf's Brain Fritter—*Beignets de cervelles*

Poached calf's brain is cut into large cubes, dipped into batter, and deep-fried. Tomato sauce is served separately.

Canapés with Cheese—*Canapés fromage*

Grated processed cheese is mixed with some cream and seasoned with paprika and nutmeg. Depending on the name to be given to the canapé, it is garnished with chopped ham, anchovy, caraway seed, or chopped salami. The canapés are gratinated for a few moments until browned.

Cassoulets with Goose Liver, Aiglon— *Cassoulets à l'aiglon*

Small earthenware pots are filled with a salpicon (ingredients diced fine and bound with a sauce) made from goose liver and mushrooms and bound with a Madeira sauce. A goose-liver soufflé mix is put on top, and the cassoulet is baked in a water bath in the oven.

Cassoulets, Modern Style—*Cassoulets moderne*

Small earthenware pots are filled with a salpicon (ingredients diced fine and bound with a sauce) of veal dumplings, chicken breast, and mushrooms, bound with Madeira sauce. Cassoulets are baked in a water bath in the oven.

Cassoulets Suzanne—*Cassoulets Suzanne*

Small earthenware pots are filled with alternate layers of asparagus tips and chicken fillets and topped with a suprême sauce and a slice of truffle.

Cheese Fritters—*Beignets de fromage*

Cream puff pastry is mixed with grated cheese and a little paprika and deep-fried. Tomato sauce is served separately.

Cheese Soufflé—*Soufflé au fromage*

Prepare a white roux using 3½ ounces (100 grams) of butter and 4 ounces (110 grams) of flour. Cool slightly and add 1 pint (5 deciliters) of boiling milk. Stir vigorously over heat until mixture is smooth. Cool slightly and add 8 egg yolks, 1¾ ounces (50 grams) of grated cheese, 1¾ ounces (50 grams) of diced cheese, ¼ ounce (5 grams) of potato flour, and seasoning (salt, pepper, and nutmeg). Just before putting into the oven, fold in 8 to 9 stiffly beaten egg whites. Fill buttered and floured soufflé molds with soufflé mixture. Place molds in a hot water bath and cook over low heat until soufflé mixture is warmed thoroughly. Place molds on a sheet pan in the oven, and allow the soufflé to rise with increasing heat. If a soufflé mass is

properly prewarmed, it will require approximately the following baking time: large molds—30 minutes; single-portion molds—7 to 8 minutes. A soufflé must be served immediately after it is cooked. To test soufflé for doneness, stick a long needle into the center. If the needle is dry when removed, the soufflé is ready.

Chicken Croquettes—*Croquettes de volaille*

Sauté some shallots in butter, add 20 ounces (600 grams) of cooked chicken, 3½ ounces (100 grams) of ham, and 7 ounces (200 grams) of sautéed mushrooms, all minced. Add 2 to 2½ cups (5 to 6 deciliters) of thick suprême sauce, stirring well. Bind with 4 to 6 egg yolks and adjust seasoning. Spread mixture to a depth of about ¾ inch (20 millimeters) on an oiled sheet pan and allow to cool. Cut into shapes as desired. Roll pieces in flour, dip into egg wash, roll in fine breadcrumbs, and deep-fry. Serve with an appropriate tomato sauce or brown sauce. Yield: 10 servings.

Fish, lobster, and game croquettes can be made in the same way, except that a different sauce is used for binding the croquettes.

Chicken Cutlets—*Côtelettes de volaille*

Chicken croquette mixture is shaped into chop form, breaded, and fried in butter. Fish and game cutlets can also be made in the same way. A sauce is served separately.

Chicken Fritters—*Cromesquis*

Chicken croquette mixture is shaped into sausages, rolled inside thin slices of lean bacon, dipped into frying batter, and deep-fried. Tomato sauce is served separately.

Croustades—*Croustades*

The shells are made of duchess potatoes, rice, semolina, or tart pastry. Fillings for bouchées can be used.

Eggs—*Oeufs*

See chapter 14.

Filled Pastries, Homemade Style—*Petits pâté à la bourgeoise*

A small amount of meat or mushroom salpicon (ingredients diced fine and bound with a sauce) is centered on a small circular layer of puff pastry. Another small circular layer of puff pastry is placed on top. The edges are sealed, brushed with egg wash, and baked.

Fritots—*Fritots*

Fritots is a type of fritter. Calf's brain, sweetbreads, calf's head, cauliflower, and black salsify are cooked. Halved tomatoes are added and the ingredients are dipped into batter and deep-fried. French-fried potatoes are arranged around the fritots, and a tomato sauce is served separately.

Ham Soufflé—*Soufflé au jambon*

Finely pounded and strained (pureed) ham is blended with a béchamel sauce. Egg yolks and stiffly beaten egg whites are folded in together with a little paprika, and the soufflé mixture is baked. Chicken and game soufflés can be made in the same way.

Meat on a Skewer—*Attereaux*

Tender pieces of meat are threaded on wooden skewers, dipped into a thick villeroi sauce, breaded, and deep-fried. They can be served on a silver skewer.

Pancakes—*Pannequets*

Pancakes made with unsweetened batter are stuffed with fillings for bouchées.

Pastry Shells Diane—*Bouchées Diane*

Puff pastry shells are filled with a salpicon of feathered game, truffles, and mushrooms, bound with a salmis sauce, and garnished with a slice of truffle.

Pastry Shells Joinville—*Bouchées Joinville*

Puff pastry shells are filled with a salpicon of shrimp tails, mushrooms, and truffles, bound with a Joinville sauce, and garnished with a slice of truffle.

Pastry Shells Montglas—*Bouchées Montglas*

Puff pastry shells are filled with a salpicon (small diced ingredients bound with a sauce) made from goose liver, mushrooms, tongue, and truffles, and bound with a Madeira sauce.

Pastry Shells, Queen's Style—*Bouchées à la reine*

Sauté chopped shallots in butter, deglaze with ¾ cup (2 deciliters) of white wine, and reduce. Add a salpicon of 14 ounces (400 grams) of veal dumplings, 14 ounces (400 grams) of chicken breast, and 7 ounces (200 grams) of cooked mushrooms, all minced. Bind with 2½ cups (6 deciliters) of suprême sauce. Add a little cream and lemon juice, and adjust seasoning. Fill puff pastry shells with mixture.

Pastry Shells, Saint-Hubert Style—*Bouchées Saint-Hubert*

Puff pastry shells are filled with game puree in a pepper sauce. A mushroom cap is placed on top.

Quiche Lorraine—*Quiche Lorraine*

Make dough from 10 ounces (300 grams) short crust paste. Line tart ring with dough, puncturing the bottom in several places with a fork. For filling, use 3½ ounces (100 grams) of diced bacon (reserve some bacon slices, which can be cooked and rolled to garnish quiche) and 3½ ounces (100 grams) of diced onion. Sauté bacon and onion and spread them over tart shell bottom. Distribute 10 ounces (300 grams) of grated Gruyère cheese evenly over the bacon and onion. Mix 1¾ ounces (50 grams) of flour, ¾ cup (2 deciliters) of milk, ¼ cup (1 deciliter) of cream, and 2 egg yolks. Fold in 2 beaten egg whites. Spread this mixture over the cheese. Bake the quiche at medium heat for approximately 25 minutes. Garnish with bacon. Yield: 1 quiche.

Rice or Noodle Rings—*Bordures*

Rings are formed by pressing cooked rice or noodles bound with egg into a buttered ring mold. The center can be filled with salpicon (a combination of finely diced ingredients bound with a sauce) or diced meat in sauce.

Rissoles—*Rissoles*

These are deep-fried small pastries made from puff pastry cut in various shapes (circles or half-moons) and filled with a cooled salpicon (ingredients diced and bound with a sauce) of shellfish, fish, chicken, goose liver, or game bound with appropriate sauce. The filling used determines the name of the rissole.

Sardine Fritters—*Beignets de sardines*

Canned sardines are dipped into batter and deep-fried. Sauce is served separately.

Swiss Tartlets—*Tartelettes suisse*

Same as tartlets, Oberland style, but filled with cheese and a fine royale sauce.

Tartlets and Dumplings—*Tartelettes aux gnocchi*

Small tart shells are filled with gnocchi, Parisian style, bound with a cream sauce, sprinkled with cheese and a few drops of melted butter, and baked in the oven.

Tartlets, Oberland Style—*Tartelettes oberlandaise*

Small molds lined with short crust paste are filled with a mixture of equal parts of diced cheese and ham. They are covered with royal cream (*crème royale*) and seasoned with paprika. The tartlets are then baked in the oven. *Royal cream (Crème royale):* 1 pint (5 deciliters) cream, mixed with 4 eggs, seasoned and strained.

Timbales—*Timbales*

Well-buttered timbale molds, each of which has a round slice of truffle placed on the bottom, are filled with fish, chicken, or game forcemeat. They are filled with an appropriate salpicon (ingredients diced fine and bound with a sauce). The name is determined by the ingredients. The salpicon is covered with forcemeat, and the timbale is poached in a water bath in the oven. There are also timbales formed with yeast dough, which are hollowed out after baking. These are filled with a bound salpicon and the pastry lid is replaced on top.

Vol-au-Vent, Cardinal Style—*Vol-au-vent cardinal*

Large puff pastry shells are filled with fish dumplings, slices of rock lobster, mushrooms, and truffles and bound with a cream sauce.

Vol-au-Vent, Toulouse Style—*Vol-au-vent toulousaine*

Large puff pastry shells are filled with chicken breast, calf's brain, sweetbreads, mushrooms, and truffles, and bound with an allemande sauce.

13.3. Savories—*Savouries*

The term savories or savory, traditionally English, refers to a course served between the sweet dish and the dessert. These are usually highly seasoned small dishes, similar to those described under hot hors d'oeuvre, and include oyster tarts, cheese straws, cheese fritters, and fish roe. Today savories are seldom served as a separate course; they are more commonly used for cocktail parties, buffets, and snacks.

Chapter 14
Hot Egg Dishes—*Oeufs chauds*

Eggs are prepared in many different ways for breakfast or luncheon dishes, for hors d'oeuvre, snacks, and buffets. Eggs are sometimes served between the soup course and the main course. An à la carte portion usually includes three eggs, while an allowance of one or two eggs is sufficient for an hors d'oeuvre.

The cooking methods for eggs are these:

Eggs cooked in the shell—*oeufs à la coque*
Soft-cooked eggs—*oeufs mollets*
Poached eggs—*oeufs pochés*
Scrambled eggs—*oeufs brouillés*
Fried eggs—*oeufs sur le plat*
Eggs in a mold—*oeufs moulés*
Eggs in cocotte—*oeufs en cocotte*
Deep-fried eggs—*oeufs frits*
Omelets—*omelettes*

14.1 Soft- or Hard-cooked Eggs in the Shell—*Oeufs à la coque*

Yield
U.S.—10 eggs
Metric—10 eggs

Ingredients	U.S. Weight or Volume	Metric Weight or Volume
Eggs	10	10
Water	2 quarts	2 liters

Procedure
1. Bring eggs to room temperature so that shells will not crack during cooking.
2. Place the eggs in boiling water.
3. Reduce heat and cook to desired degree of doneness. If eggs are cooked too long, a green color forms around the egg yolk because of the formation of ferrous sulfide on the edge of the yolk.
4. Serve hot in the shell.

Note: Soft-cooked eggs are cooked to order for 3 to 5 minutes; medium-cooked eggs, for 6 to 8 minutes; and hard-cooked eggs, for 8 to 10 minutes. If the eggs are being used for garnishes, they are simmered for 10 minutes. Hard-cooked eggs should be plunged into cold running water immediately to stop the cooking process.

14.2 Soft-cooked Eggs—*Oeufs mollets*

Yield
U.S.—10 eggs
Metric—10 eggs

Ingredients	U.S. Weight or Volume	Metric Weight or Volume
Eggs	10	10
Water	2 quarts	2 liters

Procedure
1. Cover the eggs with boiling water.
2. Simmer for 6 minutes and remove from hot water.
3. Cool the eggs in cold water until they can be handled.
4. Tap the eggs gently on a hard surface to break the shells. Peel carefully under a stream of water.

5. Warm the peeled eggs for a minute in hot water.

Note: Soft-cooked eggs and poached eggs can be served in the same way. They are simply placed on puff pastry shells, on bread croutons, or on stuffed tartlets. A tomato sauce or a spicy brown sauce is served separately.

14.3 Poached Eggs—*Oeufs pochés*

Yield
U.S.—10 eggs
Metric—10 eggs

Ingredients	*U.S. Weight or Volume*	*Metric Weight or Volume*
Eggs, fresh	10	10
Water	2 quarts	2 liters
Vinegar	¾ cup	2 deciliters

Procedure
1. Carefully crack the eggs into simmering water and vinegar.
2. Simmer for 3 to 4 minutes.
3. Remove eggs with a skimmer. Trim off any trailing bits of white.
4. Place eggs in cool water until needed.
5. To reheat, place in hot salted water for about 30 seconds.

Other Poached and Soft-cooked Egg Dishes

Eggs Argenteuil—*Oeufs argenteuil*

Poached eggs in tartlet shells filled with asparagus tips and covered with cream sauce.

Eggs Aurora Style—*Oeufs à l'aurore*

Poached or soft-cooked eggs on puff pastry shells covered with aurora sauce.

Figure 14-1. Eggs, grand duke style—*Oeufs à la grand duc.*

Eggs Belle Helene—*Oeufs belle Hélène*

Poached or soft-cooked eggs in pastry shells filled with asparagus tips and covered with suprême sauce.

Eggs, Florentine Style—*Oeufs florentine*

Eggs arranged on a base of leaf spinach covered with a Mornay sauce, sprinkled with cheese and melted butter, and gratinated under the broiler.

Eggs, Grand Duke Style—*Oeufs à la grand duc*

Poached eggs on fried bread croutons, coated with a Mornay sauce, sprinkled with cheese and melted butter, and gratinated in the oven. The eggs are arranged on a platter with bouquets of buttered asparagus spears placed between the eggs. Sautéed julienne of mushrooms and truffles sprinkled with Madeira sauce are placed in the center of the plate. (See figure 14-1.)

Eggs, Piedmont Style—*Oeufs à la piémontaise*

Soft-cooked or poached eggs on a base of braised white rice are sprinkled with a julienne of truffles; Madeira sauce is poured around the eggs.

Eggs, Swiss Style—*Oeufs suisse*

Soft-cooked or poached eggs are placed on tartlet shells filled with duxelles with chopped ham. Half of

Figure 14-2. Eggs in tartlet shells—*Oeufs en croustade.*

each egg is coated with tomato sauce; the other half with cream sauce.

Eggs in Tartlet Shells—*Oeufs en croustade*

Poached eggs are placed atop baked tartlet shells filled with duxelles. Sardine fillets are used as garnish. Madeira sauce is served separately. (See figure 14-2.)

14.4 Scrambled Eggs—*Oeufs brouillés*

Yield
U.S.—1 serving
Metric—1 serving

Ingredients	*U.S. Weight or Volume*	*Metric Weight or Volume*
Butter	1 tablespoon	15 grams
Eggs	3	3
Salt	¼ teaspoon	2 grams
Cream (optional)	1 tablespoon	15 milliliters

Procedure
1. Melt butter in a sauté pan.
2. Break eggs into a bowl and sprinkle with salt.
3. Put eggs in the butter and stir them into a thick mass, using a wooden spoon, over low heat.
4. If cream is to be used, it should be folded in after the eggs are cooked.

Other Scrambled Egg Dishes

Scrambled Eggs with Asparagus Tips—*Oeufs brouillés aux pointes d'asperges*

Scrambled eggs are garnished with asparagus tips.

Scrambled Eggs with Bread Croutons—*Oeufs brouillés aux croûtons*

Scrambled eggs are garnished with triangular or heart-shaped bread croutons.

Scrambled Eggs with Chicken Livers—*Oeufs brouillés aux foies de volaille*

Scrambled eggs are garnished with diced chicken livers in Madeira sauce.

Scrambled Eggs with Puff Pastry—*Oeufs broullés aux fleurons*

Scrambled eggs are garnished with puff pastry cut into diamond shapes.

Scrambled Eggs with Tomatoes—*Oeufs brouillés à la portugaise*

Scrambled eggs are garnished with diced tomatoes.

14.5 Fried Eggs—*Oeufs sur le plat*

Yield
U.S.—1 egg
Metric—1 egg

Ingredients	*U.S. Weight or Volume*	*Metric Weight or Volume*
Butter	½ teaspoon	5 grams
Eggs	1	1
Salt	to season	to season

Procedure

1. Melt butter in a skillet, add the egg, and season.
2. Baste the egg with hot butter over very low heat until it is done.
3. To get a firm white, cover the pan with a lid at once.
4. If a softer white is desired, pour a little water over the egg, cover, and cook for about 1 minute.

Other Fried Egg Dishes

Fried Eggs, American—*Oeufs sur le plat à l'amércaine*

Fried eggs served with grilled slices of bacon and grilled tomato halves.

Fried Eggs and Bacon—*Oeufs sur le plat au lard*

Fired eggs served on lean strips of grilled bacon.

Fried Eggs with Brown Butter—*Oeufs sur le plat au beurre*

Fried eggs covered with brown butter.

Fried Eggs with Chipolata Sausages—*Oeufs sur le plat chipolata*

Small chipolatas placed between fried eggs. The eggs are surrounded with glazed pearl onions or fried onion rings.

Fried Eggs with Ham—*Oeufs sur le plat au jambon*

Fried eggs served on slices of grilled ham.

Fried Eggs, Hunter's Style—*Oeufs sur le plat chasseur*

Fried eggs covered with sautéed chicken livers and mushrooms bound with Madeira sauce.

Fried Eggs, Meyerbeer—*Oeufs sur le plat Meyerbeer*

Fried eggs with slices of grilled lamb kidney, surrounded with a ring of truffle sauce.

Fried Eggs, Piedmont Style—*Oeufs sur le plat à la piémontaise*

Fried eggs with small mounds of braised rice surrounded with a ring of Madeira sauce.

Fried Eggs with Shrimp—*Oeufs sur le plat aux crevettes*

Fried eggs on a salpicon (a combination of small diced ingredients bound with a sauce) of shrimp. A shrimp sauce is poured around the eggs.

Fried Eggs with Tomatoes—*Oeufs sur le plat à la portugaise*

Fried eggs are served with small mounds of sautéed diced tomatoes.

Fried Eggs, Turkish Style—*Oeufs sur le plat à la turque*

Fried eggs with grilled chicken livers bound with a demi-glace.

14.6 Eggs in a Mold—*Oeufs moulés*

Yield
U.S.—1 egg
Metric—1 egg

Ingredients	U.S. Weight or Volume	Metric Weight or Volume
Eggs	1	1
Butter	½ teaspoon	5 grams

Procedure
1. Put the egg in a buttered mold.
2. Poach slowly in a water bath.
3. Serve the egg on a toasted slice of bread or an artichoke bottom.
4. Truffles, ham, tarragon, or chervil can be used as a garnish.

Note: This form of preparation is rarely used. A suitable sauce or butter can either be poured over or served separately.

14.7 Eggs in Cocotte—*Oeufs en cocotte*

Yield
U.S.—1 egg
Metric—1 egg

Ingredients	U.S. Weight or Volume	Metric Weight or Volume
Cream	1 tablespoon	15 milliliters
Eggs	1	1
Salt	½ teaspoon	3 grams
Butter	½ teaspoon	5 grams

Procedure
1. Put cream in a buttered cocotte.
2. Add the egg, season, and top with a piece of butter.
3. Poach in a water bath.

Note: A fried slice of lean bacon, a poached slice of sweetbread, or a salpicon of white meat may be placed on the bottom of the cocotte before adding the egg. The cream is often replaced with a spicy brown sauce.

14.8 Deep-fried Eggs—*Oeufs frits*

Yield
U.S.—1 egg
Metric—1 egg

Ingredients	U.S. Weight or Volume	Metric Weight or Volume
Fat	to cover eggs	to cover eggs
Eggs	1	1
Salt	½ teaspoon	3 grams

Procedure
1. Heat about 2 inches (5 centimeters) of fat to about 300°F (150°C).
2. Slide the egg into the fat, using two wooden spoons to shape the egg. The yolk should be enveloped by the white to keep it soft.
3. Remove excess fat by placing egg on absorbent paper.
4. Season.

Note: Deep-fried eggs are served on toast, croutons, or grilled tomato halves. Tomato sauce, Italian sauce, or deviled sauce may be served separately.

14.9 Omelets—*Omelettes*

Yield
U.S.—1 serving
Metric—1 serving

Ingredients	U.S. Weight or Volume	Metric Weight or Volume
Eggs	3	3
Salt	½ teaspoon	3 grams
Butter	1 tablespoon	15 grams

Procedure
1. Beat eggs and salt moderately until whites are blended with yolks.
2. Heat butter in an omelet pan and add beaten eggs.
3. Mixture should begin to cook immediately at the outer edges. Lift cooked portions at the edges so uncooked portions flow underneath. Slide pan rapidly back and forth over heat to keep mixture in motion and sliding freely to avoid sticking.
4. Mixture is set when egg no longer flows freely. Let it cook for 1 minute to brown slightly.
5. Fold into oval shape in front part of pan.
6. Turn omelet onto a warm plate.

Note: A properly prepared omelet should be moist and creamy inside, not cooked through. Garnishes and/or fillings can be served in various ways:

- The garnishes are sautéed and combined with the eggs before cooking the omelet.
- The filling is added to the partially cooked omelet with care taken to ensure that the filling remains on the inside when the omelet is folded.
- After the omelet has been prepared, it is cut lengthwise and filled.
- When the omelet is served, it is decorated with a garnish of vegetable bouquets, or a sauce may be served separately.

Other Omelets

Omelet with Asparagus Tips—*Omelette aux pointes d'asperges*

Asparagus tips, lightly sautéed in butter, are added to the beaten eggs before they are cooked. The omelet is garnished with a bouquet of asparagus tips when served.

Cheese Omelet—*Omelette au fromage*

Grated cheese is added to the omelet before folding.

Omelet, Country Style—*Omelette paysanne*

Chopped onions, diced ham, and precooked potato are sautéed in butter. Diced tomatoes and chopped parsley are added. The sautéed mixture is mixed in the beaten eggs and made into a pancake-shaped omelet.

Omelet, Emmentaler Style—*Omelette emmentaloise*

A prepared omelet is covered with Emmentaler cheese, quickly browned under a broiler, and served surrounded with a light cream sauce mixed with grated cheese.

Ham Omelet—*Omelet au jambon*

Finely diced ham is sautéed in butter and added to the omelet before folding.

Omelet with Herbs—*Omelette aux fines herbes*

Chopped herbs are mixed with the beaten eggs before cooking the omelet.

Omelet, Hunter's Style—*Omelette chasseur*

A prepared omelet is cut lengthwise and filled with sautéed chicken livers and mushrooms bound with a Madeira sauce.

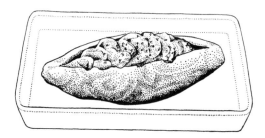

Figure 14-3. Omelet with kidneys—*Omelette aux rognons.*

Omelet with Kidneys—*Omelette aux rognons*

A prepared omelet is stuffed with sautéed kidneys bound with a Madeira sauce. (See figure 14-3.)

Mushroom Omelet—*Omelette aux champignons*

Sliced mushrooms, sautéed in butter, are added to the beaten eggs before cooking the omelet.

Omelet, Queen's Style—*Omelette à la reine*

A prepared omelet is filled with stuffing used in pastry shells, queen's style (*bouchées à la reine*).

Omelet Rossini—*Omelette Rossini*

Sautéed diced goose liver and truffles are mixed with the beaten eggs before the omelet is prepared. The omelet may be garnished with a border of goose liver and truffles. A small amount of demi-glace sauce is poured over the bottom of the plate.

Tomato Omelet—*Omelette portugaise*

A prepared omelet is filled with sautéed, diced tomatoes.

Chapter 15
Hot Fish Dishes—
Poissons chauds

Formerly, when the full menu was being served, the hot fish dishes always preceded the main course (grosse pièce). Today, they are used for hot hors d'oeuvre, hot snacks, main courses, and à la carte dishes. The cold fish dishes are mostly used as cold snacks, cold hors d'oeuvre, and for cold buffets.

The basic cooking methods for fish are these:

- Boiling—*Cuire*
    in court bouillon
    in white court bouillon
    in acidulated water (*au bleu*)
- Poaching—*Pocher*
    in white wine
    in red wine
- Braising—*Braiser*
- Sautéing—*Sauter*
    à la meunière
    in egg
    breaded
- Deep-frying—*Frire*
    plain
    breaded
    in egg
    in batter
- Grilling/broiling—*Griller*
- Gratinating—*gratiner*

To prepare fish for cooking:

- *Cleaning:* Clean fish and fillets under running water.

- *Killing eels:* Hold the eel wrapped in a towel and kill it with a heavy blow to the head. Sever the spine right behind the head, then open the eel and remove the heart and the intestines. Cut the skin around the neck fins, grab the skin between the dish towels, and pull it off.
- *General hints:* Immobilize fish with a blow on the head. Cut the opening from tail to head. Take care not to insert the knife too deeply, as this could injure the gallbladder and turn the meat bitter. Remove the heart and intestines and wash the remaining flesh thoroughly under running water.
- *Cooking* au bleu: Remove the fish from the tank after the order is taken. Kill it and wash it very carefully, making sure that the slime layer on the outside is undisturbed. After the fish is cleaned, push a needle through the spine to ensure that no reflexes cause the fish to move when it comes into contact with hot cooking liquids.
- *Marinating:* Use lemon juice, herbs, and pepper. With these, the fish will stay firmer, and there will be less odor.
- *Salt:* Add shortly before cooking.

15.1 Boiling—*Cuire*

The word used for this procedure is somewhat misleading, since the fish itself should never be exposed to actual boiling temperatures. Vegetables and spices are put on the bottom of the fish kettle. Large fish are placed on a rack and the rack of fish is placed over the vegetables. The kettle is filled with cold court bouillon, and the liquid is brought just to a boil. Once the boiling point has been reached, the heat is reduced, and the fish is covered and simmered slowly. Cooking time is 5 to 8 minutes per pound (15 minutes per kilogram). For cold fish dishes, the fish is allowed to cool in the liquid. Small fish and slices of fish are immersed in boiling court bouillon. Once the liquid returns to boiling, it is skimmed. The fish is then covered and simmered for a few minutes.

Lake trout, salmon trout, and salmon are prepared in court bouillon; cod, haddock, hake, skate, and turbot, in white court bouillon.

The following sauces and butter preparations are suitable for fish cooked in court bouillon: hollandaise sauce, mousseline sauce, melted butter, nut butter, or brown butter.

15.1.1 Court Bouillon—*Court-bouillon ordinaire*

Yield
U.S.—5 quarts
Metric—5 liters

Ingredients	U.S. Weight or Volume	Metric Weight or Volume
Water	4 quarts	4 liters
White wine	1 pint	5 deciliters
Vinegar	1 pint	5 deciliters
Salt	2 ounces	60 grams
White leeks, sliced thin	3½ ounces	100 grams
Carrots, sliced thin	14 ounces	400 grams
Onions, sliced thin	1 pound	500 grams
Parsley	few sprigs	few sprigs
Bay leaf	1	1
Thyme	¼ teaspoon	2 grams
Peppercorns, crushed	½ teaspoon	4 grams

Procedure
1. Combine all the ingredients and simmer for 30 minutes.

2. Strain.
3. Cook fish in the court bouillon according to the directions given above.

Note: This preparation can be used for poaching large freshwater fish that are suited neither for cooking *au bleu* nor for cold fish dishes. For a fish stew (*matelote*), the white wine and vinegar are replaced by 1 quart (1 liter) of strong red wine.

15.1.2 White Court Bouillon—*Court-bouillon blanc*

Yield
U.S.—5 quarts
Metric—5 liters

Ingredients	U.S. Weight or Volume	Metric Weight or Volume
Water	4½ quarts	4.5 liters
Milk	1 pint	5 deciliters
Lemon juice	of one lemon	of one lemon
Bay leaves	2	2
Dill	¼ teaspoon	2 grams
Salt	2 ounces	60 grams
Peppercorns, crushed	6	6

Procedure
1. Combine all the ingredients and place the fish in the mixture before heating.
2. Bring to a boil, skim the liquid, cover, and simmer slowly. Allow 5 to 8 minutes per pound (20 minutes per kilogram).

Note: White court bouillon is primarily for large, whole saltwater fish, such as cod, pike, ray, haddock, and turbot. If slices or pieces of fish are being cooked, they should not be added until the white court bouillon has simmered for about 30 minutes; however, they can also be prepared in basic court bouillon.

Cooking *au bleu*

Carp, rainbow trout, river trout, and golden trout can be prepared *au bleu*. Prepare 5 quarts (5 liters) of court bouillon, but do *not* add the vinegar. Bring the court bouillon to a boil. Just before serving, kill the fish with a sharp blow to the head. Dress the fish quickly. Pour the vinegar (1 pint/5 deciliters) over the dressed, fresh fish, and plunge into the boiling court bouillon. Skim, cover, and let stand in the kettle for a few minutes.

It is important to check that the slime on the skin of the fish is neither dried out nor rubbed off before cooking. Otherwise, the skin of the fish will not turn blue during cooking. Certain fish, distinguished by a high concentration of slime on the exterior when fresh, will turn a light blue when poached in an acid solution. This is the preferred way of serving fresh trout and carp in Europe.

15.2 Poaching—*Pocher*

Poaching is used for whole fish, such as sand dab and small turbot; for fillets or slices of all flatfish and of cod, grayling, haddock, hake, pike, pike perch, and trout.

15.2.1 Poaching in White Wine— *Pocher au vin blanc*

Yield
approximately 10 servings

Ingredients	U.S. Weight or Volume	Metric Weight or Volume
Shallots, sliced	2 ounces	50 grams
Butter	2 ounces	50 grams
Fish fillets *or*	3 pounds	1.5 kilograms
fish slices	5 pounds	2.5 kilograms
Salt	1 teaspoon	5 grams
Pepper	¼ teaspoon	2 grams
Lemon juice	from one lemon	from one lemon
White wine	¾ to 1¼ cups	2 to 3 deciliters
Fish stock	1 quart	1 liter

Procedure
1. Sprinkle sliced shallots into a buttered flat pan.
2. Place the seasoned fillets on top.
3. Pour lemon juice, white wine, and fish stock over the fish.

4. Heat, but do not boil. Then cover the fish with buttered parchment paper and poach in the oven at 325°F (163°C) until the fish flakes. Large pieces should be basted with the stock occasionally.
5. Pour the stock off the poached fish and reduce it to the desired consistency. Use it for finishing the sauce in which the fish is served. See white-wine sauce, chapter 11.

Note: If no fish velouté is available to make the sauce, the cooking liquid can be thickened with kneaded butter (*beurre manié*), reduced, and finished with cream and egg yolk. All poached fish should be accompanied with boiled potatoes or rice. The fish may be glazed with cream or hollandaise sauce. The sauce is poured over the fish, which is then broiled briefly in a salamander to develop a light crust.

15.2.2 Poaching in Red Wine—*Pocher au vin rouge*

Yield
approximately 10 servings

Ingredients	U.S. Weight or Volume	Metric Weight or Volume
Fish fillet *or*	3 pounds	1.5 kilograms
fish slices	5 pounds	2.5 kilograms
Salt	1 teaspoon	5 grams
Pepper	¼ teaspoon	2 grams
Shallots, sliced	2 ounces	50 grams
Butter	2 ounces	50 grams
Red wine	¾ to 1¼ cups	2 to 3 deciliters
Lemon juice	2 tablespoons	30 milliliters
Kneaded butter (*beurre manié*)	2 ounces	50 grams
Fish stock made with red wine	1 quart	1 liter

Procedure
1. Cut the fish into pieces or slices and season.
2. Sprinkle the sliced shallots in a buttered flat pan. Place the fish on top.
3. Pour the red wine and lemon juice over the fish. Heat.
4. Cover with buttered parchment paper and poach

slowly in the oven at 325°F (160°C) until the fish flakes. It may be flavored with brandy afterward. Remove the fish.

5. Reduce the poaching liquid, thicken with kneaded butter (*beurre manié*), and mix with a fish stock made with red wine. Reduce the sauce and strain.

Note: This form of preparation is particularly suitable for carp, eel, and burbot. Glazed pearl onions, sliced mushrooms, and a ring of heart-shaped bread croutons serve as garnishes.

Other Poached Fish Dishes

Fish with Asparagus Tips—*Poissons Argenteuil*

Poached fish are covered with a white-wine sauce and garnished with asparagus tips and puff pastry *fleurons*. (See figure 15-1.)

Fish, Bordeaux Style—*Poissons à la bordelaise*

The fish is poached with red wine and chopped shallots. Reduced stock is mixed with a bordelaise wine sauce and poured over the fish when it is served.

Fish Byron—*Poissons Byron*

The fish is poached in red wine, covered with the sauce, and garnished with mushrooms and truffles.

Fish with Chambertin Wine—*Poissons au Chambertin*

The fish is poached in Chambertin Burgundy, then glazed with the sauce. It is garnished on both sides with small strips of fish fried in butter.

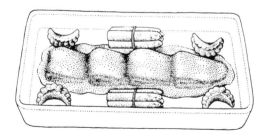

Figure 15-1. Fish with asparagus tips—*Poissons Argenteuil*.

Fish Choisy—*Poissons Choisy*

Poached fish is covered with a Mornay sauce made with reduced fish stock and sprinkled with a julienne of mushrooms and truffles.

Fish Dugléré—*Poissons Dugléré*

Fish, usually sole, is poached in fish stock with onions, diced tomatoes, and herbs. The reduced poaching liquid is mixed with a white-wine sauce, strained, and butter is added. When served, it is garnished with diced tomatoes.

Fish with Herbs—*Poissons aux fines herbes*

Poached fish is covered with white-wine sauce and sprinkled with finely chopped herbs.

Fish, Home Style— *Poissons à la bonne femme*

The fish is poached with chopped shallots, sliced mushrooms, and parsley. Reduced stock, unstrained, is added to the white sauce, and butter slivers are stirred in. After the sauce is poured over the fish, it is quickly browned. The dish is garnished with croutons, truffle slices, and mushroom caps.

Fish Indian Style—*Poissons à l'indienne*

Fish is poached in white wine. A little curry powder is mixed with the sauce and poured over the fish. Creole rice is served separately.

Fish Joinville—*Poissons Joinville*

Fish is covered with Joinville sauce and garnished with shrimps, truffle slices, and mushrooms.

Fish, Marguery Style—*Poissons Marguery*

Poached fillets are garnished with mussels and shrimps, covered with a white-wine sauce, and browned lightly under the broiler.

Fish, Marseille Style—*Poissons à la marseillaise*

Fish is served on slices of white bread lightly browned in butter, garnished with diced tomatoes, and covered with white-wine sauce flavored with saffron.

Fish, Normandy Style—*Poissons à la normande*

Poached fish is covered with a Normandy sauce made with oyster stock and garnished with oysters, small rolled fillets of fried fish, crayfish tails, and slices of truffles. It is surrounded with a ring of meat extract (*glace de viande*).

Fish, Old-fashioned Style—*Poissons à l'ancienne*

Fish are poached in white wine, covered with white-wine sauce, and garnished with small glazed pearl onions and mushroom caps.

Fish, Riche Style—*Poissons riche*

The fish is covered with riche sauce and garnished with crayfish tails and slices of truffles.

Fish, Sailor's Style—*Poissons en matelote*

Fish is poached in red wine, covered with sauce, and garnished with mushrooms, pearl onions, crayfish tails, and croutons.

Fish, Springtime Style—*Poissons à la printanière*

Fish is covered with a white-wine sauce and garnished with a printanière (carrots, turnips, celery root, and green beans cut in various shapes).

Fish with Tomatoes—*Poissons à la portugaise*

Fish is covered with a white-wine sauce and garnished with diced tomatoes.

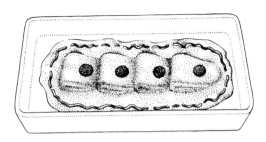

Figure 15-2. Fish with truffles—*Poissons demi-deuil.*

Fish with Truffles—*Poissons demi-deuil*

Fish is covered with white-wine sauce and sliced truffles, and decorated with a ring of meat extract (*glace de viande*). (See figure 15-2.)

Fish Valentino—*Poissons Valentino*

Mainly for fillets of sole. Poached fillets are arranged with a quantity of sliced mushrooms on braised rice, covered with Mornay sauce, and gratinated quickly in the oven or under the broiler.

Fish with White Wine—*Poissons au vin blanc*

Poached fillets are covered with a white-wine sauce and garnished with croutons or puff pastry cut in crescent shapes.

Salmon, Riche Style—*Tranche de saumon riche*

Fish is poached or boiled, covered with slices of rock lobster and truffles, and garnished with crayfish tails and boiled potatoes. Riche sauce is served separately. (See figure 15-3.)

Sole Rossini—*Sole Rossini*

Paupiettes of sole are cooked in white wine with chopped truffles and garnished with a salipicon of truffles. To make paupiettes, fillets of sole are spread with fish forcemeat and rolled.

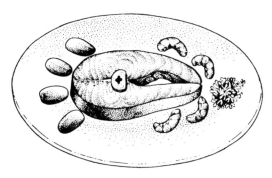

Figure 15-3. Salmon, riche style—*Tranche de saumon riche.*

15.3 Braising—*Braiser*

Large fish or fish pieces, such as carp, lake trout, salmon, sand dab, and turbot, may be braised. Butter an appropriate fish pan. Put a *matignon* beneath the rack where the fish is to be placed. Fill the pan to one-fourth the depth of the fish with red or white wine and fish stock. Cover and baste the fish from time to time with its own stock, while it braises. The stock should be well reduced by the time the fish is cooked so that it can be used to enrich the corresponding sauce.

15.4 Sautéing—*Sauter*

Sautéing is appropriate for whole fish, such as golden trout, grayling, river trout, Dover sole, and whitefish; and for fillets or slices of lake trout, pike perch, salmon, and whitefish.

Floured Fish Sautéed in Butter— Poissons à la meuniére

Marinate the fish (whole, sliced, or fillets) in a mixture of salt, pepper, and lemon juice. If a whole fish is used, slash it on both sides. Coat the marinated fish lightly with flour. Heat clarified butter over medium heat. Sauté the fish until golden brown on both sides. For larger fish, bake in the oven, basting from time to time. Drain the fat. Pour melted butter and lemon juice over the fish and garnish with a lemon wedge and a sprig of parsley.

If the fish are sautéed in clarified butter or fat and not garnished with hot butter, parsley, and lemon juice, they are described as *doré* on the menu. Slashing large fish along the sides permits the marinade and fats to permeate the flesh and increases the aroma and flavor.

Sautéing with Egg—Sauter à l'oeuf

Marinate the fish (whole, slices, or fillets) in lemon juice, salt, and pepper. Dredge the marinated fish with flour, dip into beaten eggs, and sauté slowly in oil and butter until the fish is golden brown. Pour the fats and juices over the fish and garnish with a lemon wedge and parsley.

Sautéing Breaded Fish—Pané sauté

Marinate fish fillets or thin slices of fish in lemon juice, salt, and a little pepper. Dredge the marinated fish in flour, dip into beaten eggs, coat with breadcrumbs, and sauté in oil and butter to a golden brown. Serve the fats and juices separately, mixed with a little lemon juice. Garnish with parsley.

Breaded fish are seldom cooked through. Always use this method for thin pieces. Fillets are the first choice; they will be done with brief cooking over heat that is not too high.

Other Sautéed Fish Dishes

with Bananas—*aux bananes*

The fish are prepared *à la meunière* or by boiling, garnished with bananas cut lengthwise, and sautéed in butter. The fish is sprinkled with chopped parsley and drenched with melted butter, together with a few drops of lemon juice. Lemons and halved tomatoes can be used as a garnish. (See figure 15-4.)

Colbert Style—*Colbert*

This is a variation for fish fillets. Fillets are breaded and sautéed. A Colbert sauce whipped with butter and lemon juice is served separately. (See also sole Colbert, in the section on deep-fried fish that follows.)

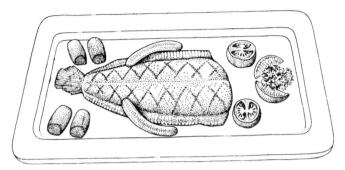

Figure 15-4. Fish with bananas—*Poissons aux bananes.*

English Style—*à l'anglaise*

Small fish (whiting, whitefish) are prepared as shown in figure 7-11. They are breaded and sautéed in butter, covered with melted herb butter, and garnished with a lemon wedge. Fish fillets can also be prepared in this way.

Garden Style—*à la belle jardinière*

Sautéed fish are covered with mushroom caps and garnished with beans, cauliflower, carrots, and straw potatoes. Hot herb butter is served separately.

Grenoble Style—*à la grenobloise*

Sautéed fish are served on a platter, topped with mushrooms. Small, peeled pieces of lemon, capers, and fine herbs are added to foaming melted butter and poured over the fish.

Italian Style—*à l'italienne*

An Italian sauce is prepared, adding reduced fish stock, whipped with butter and a little lemon juice. The sauce is served in a ring around the sautéed fish.

Lucerne Style—*à la lucernoise*

Sautéed fish are placed on a platter. Thin-sliced onion is sautéed in butter with cubes of tomatoes, capers, and herbs. Meat extract (*glace de viande*) is then added,

and the mixture is simmered for a short time and then poured over the fish.

Meunière Style—*à la belle meunière*

Sautéed fish are arranged on a platter. Drops of lemon juice, meat extract (*glace de viande*), and parsley are sprinkled over the fish; they are then covered with foaming melted butter and garnished with tiny sautéed potatoes, quartered mushrooms, and asparagus spears.

with Morels—*aux morilles*

Fish are prepared *à la meunière* and garnished with sautéed morels.

Murat Style—*Murat*

This variation is especially suited for fillets of sole. Fillets are cut into finger-size strips, mixed with seasoning, lemon juice, and chopped parsley, coated with flour, rolled, and sautéed in butter. Sautéed quartered tiny Parisian potatoes and sautéed artichoke quarters are mixed with the fish fillets. All the ingredients are covered with fresh butter or foaming melted herb butter. Slices of tomato are placed on top.

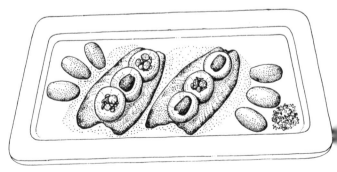

Figure 15-5. Whitefish fillets, Eva style—*Filets de féra Eva.*

Whitefish Fillets, Eva Style—*Filets de féra Eva*

Fillets, which have been prepared *à la meunière,* are arranged on a platter, sprinkled with lemon juice, and drenched with melted butter. Apple slices, poached in white wine, are filled with mushrooms (chanterelles) and sautéed tomatoes. These are placed on top of the fillets and served with potatoes. (See figure 15-5.)

15.5 Deep-frying—*Frire*

Small whole fish or fish fillets and slices—perch, pike, Dover sole, whitefish, and whiting—may all be deep-fried.

Deep-frying Plain Fish—Frire nature

Marinate the fish in a mixture of salt, a little pepper, lemon juice, and herbs. Coat it with flour, and fry in deep fat at 350° to 375°F (177° to 190°C). Place the fish on absorbent paper to drain excess fat, and season with salt. Arrange on a platter on top of a paper napkin, and serve with a lemon wedge and sprig of parsley. About 10 percent of the weight will be lost during deep-frying.

Sometimes beer or white wine and finely chopped herbs are used for the marinade. Larger quantities of fish should be prefried in deep fat at a lower temperature (blanched in oil), then completed at 350° to 375°F (177° to 190°C).

Deep-frying Breaded Fish—Pané frit

Marinate the fish in a mixture of salt, a little pepper, lemon juice, and herbs. Bread them, and fry in deep fat at 325° to 375°F (160° to 180°C). Place on absorbent paper to drain excess fat, season with salt, serve on a platter, and garnish with lemon and parsley.

Sole Colbert—*Sole Colbert*

On one side of a cleaned sole, make a cut along the line of the backbone to loosen the two fillets slightly. (See figure 7-6.) Bread the fish and fry in deep fat until it is golden yellow. Remove the backbone through the opening that has formed. Arrange the fish on a platter, and place either a few slices of herb butter in the opening, or pour melted herb butter in. Garnish with lemon and parsley.

Deep-frying in Egg—Frit à l'oeuf

Marinate the fish in a mixture of salt, a little pepper, lemon juice, and herbs. Coat with flour, dip into beaten egg, and fry in deep fat at 350° to 375°F (177° to 190°C). Place on absorbent paper to drain the fat, and season with salt. Serve on a paper napkin, garnished with lemon and parsley.

Larger quantities should be prefried at a lower temperature (blanched in oil), then completed at 350° to 375°F (177° to 190°C).

Deep-Frying in Plain Batter—Frite en pâte

Marinate the fish in a mixture of lemon juice and herbs. Prepare a batter made from 1 pound (500 grams) of flour, 2½ cups (650 milliliters) of water, salt, and a little pepper. Dust the marinated fish with flour, dip into the batter, and remove any surplus. Fry in deep fat, or prefry (blanch in oil) and then complete frying, at 350° to 375°F (177° to 190°C). Place on absorbent paper to drain excess fat and garnish with parsley.

Serve a mayonnaise sauce or one of its variations separately.

Deep-frying in Special Batter—Frit à l'Orly

Marinate the fish in a mixture of lemon juice and herbs. Prepare deep-frying batter (*pâte à frire*); see chapter 25. Dust the marinated fish with flour, dip into the deep-frying batter, and remove excess batter. Fry in deep fat, or prefry (blanch in oil) and fry, at 350° to 375°F (177° to 190°C). Place on absorbent paper to drain excess fat, and garnish with parsley. Serve a tomato sauce separately. The parsley can also be deep-fried.

15.6 Broiling/Grilling—*Griller*

Broiling is appropriate for whole fish, such as lemon sole, grayling, whitefish, and whiting; and for fillets or slices of pike perch, salmon, eel, and turbot. Thoroughly dry the fish before seasoning and coating with flour. Baste with oil and broil both sides of the fish. Usually a whipped butter-based sauce, herb butter, or an oil-based sauce is served with broiled fish.

15.7 Gratinating—*Gratiner*

Cod, grayling, haddock, hake, pike, pike perch, plaice, sand dab, Dover sole, and turbot can be gratinated. Remove the skin and bones from boiled or poached fish. Season the pieces of fish and add some lemon juice. Spread a little gratin sauce (see below) over the bottom of a buttered au gratin dish, place the fish in the dish, and cover with more gratin sauce. Sprinkle with grated cheese and drops of melted butter and gratinate in the oven.

Gratin Sauce—*Sauce au gratin*

Reduce fish stock, white wine, and chopped shallots. Add basic brown sauce and some duxelles. Then reduce the sauce slightly, beat in fresh butter, and add lemon juice and parsley.

Other Gratinated Fish Dishes

Mornay

Poached fish stock is reduced and mixed into Mornay sauce. A small part of this sauce is spread over the bottom of a buttered gratin dish. The poached fish is placed in the dish and covered with the remaining sauce. Cheese and melted butter droplets are sprinkled over the dish and browned either in the oven or under the broiler.

Sole au gratin

The fillets of a skinned and cleaned sole are loosened by cutting along the line of the backbone. A buttered au gratin dish is sprinkled with chopped shallots, and moistened with a little white wine. The sole is placed in the dish and seasoned with salt and lemon juice. The openings in the fish, created when the fillets were loosened, are filled with sautéed sliced mushrooms. A few mushroom caps are placed on top. The fish is covered with gratin sauce, sprinkled with white breadcrumbs and a few drops of melted butter, and gratinated in the oven until the fish is done.

15.7.1 Pike Dumplings, Old-fashioned Style—*Quenelles de brochet à l'ancienne*

Yield
8 to 10 servings

Ingredients	U.S. Weight or Volume	Metric Weight or Volume
Puree of raw boneless pike flesh	2 pounds	1 kilogram
Egg whites	5	5
Cream, chilled	1 pint	5 deciliters
Salt	1 teaspoon	5 grams
Pepper	¼ teaspoon	2 grams
Paprika	¼ teaspoon	2 grams
Anchovy fillets, chopped (optional)	4 to 6	4 to 6
Fish fumet	as needed	as needed
Mushrooms	2 pounds	1 kilogram
Cream	½ cup	1 deciliter
Mornay sauce	1 cup	2 deciliters
Cheese, grated	4 ounces	115 grams
Butter, melted	¼ cup	60 milliliters

Procedure
1. Thoroughly chill the pike puree. Gradually work in egg whites, using a wooden spatula. Add the cream very gradually and mix thoroughly.
2. Season the cold mixture with salt, pepper, and paprika. Anchovies can be added if desired.
3. Shape into nut-size dumplings with a spoon and poach in a well-seasoned fish fumet for 8 to 10 minutes.
4. Make a duxelles of sautéed minced mushrooms. Add a little cream and spread the mixture in a buttered au gratin dish dish to a depth of about ½ inch (1 centimeter).
5. Place the dumplings on the duxelles. Cover with Mornay sauce. Sprinkle with cheese and melted butter.
6. Gratinate in the oven or under the broiler.

Chapter 16
Shellfish and Other Seafood—
Coquillages

16.1 Crayfish—*Ecrevisses*

16.1.1 Boiled Crayfish—*Ecrevisses à la nage*

Yield
6 servings

Ingredients	U.S. Weight or Volume	Metric Weight or Volume
Fish fumet	1¾ cups	4 deciliters
White wine	1¼ cups	3 deciliters
Mirepoix	½ cup	115 grams
Salt	½ ounce	10 grams
Crayfish, eviscerated	20	20
Cayenne pepper	⅛ teaspoon	1 gram
Mayonnaise-based sauce	as needed	as needed

Procedure
1. Prepare a poaching liquid with the fish fumet, white wine, *mirepoix*, and salt.
2. Immerse the crayfish in the liquid. Heat to the boiling point and allow to stand for 10 minutes.
3. Add the cayenne pepper. Serve crayfish in a bowl with the *mirepoix*.
4. Serve mayonnaise-based sauce separately.

16.1.2 Crayfish Bordelaise—*Ecrevisses à la bordelaise*

Yield
10 servings

Ingredients	U.S. Weight or Volume	Metric Weight or Volume
Mirepoix	½ to ¾ cup	1 to 2 deciliters
Butter	4 ounces	120 grams
Salt	1 tablespoon	15 grams
Cayenne	⅛ teaspoon	1 gram
Crayfish, eviscerated	30	30
Brandy	½ cup	1 deciliter
White wine	1¼ cups	3 deciliters
Fish fumet	½ cup	1 deciliter
Fish velouté	¾ cup	2 deciliters
Meat extract	1 tablespoon	15 milliliters
Butter slivers	a few	a few
Parsley, chopped	2 tablespoons	30 grams

Procedure
1. Sauté the *mirepoix* in 2 ounces (60 grams) of butter.
2. Add 2 ounces (60 grams) of butter, the salt, cayenne, and the eviscerated crayfish. Continue sautéing until crayfish have turned completely red.
3. Flame crayfish with the brandy. Add the wine and reduce the liquids to one-third of the original volume.

continued

Procedure

4. Add the fish fumet and the fish velouté. Boil briefly.
5. Add the meat extract (*glace de viande*), a few slivers of butter, and the chopped parsley.
6. Pour the sauce over the crayfish and serve.

16.2 Scallops—*Coquilles Saint-Jacques*

16.2.1 Scallops au Gratin—*Coquilles Saint-Jacques au gratin*

Yield
10 servings

Ingredients	U.S. Weight or Volume	Metric Weight or Volume
Scallops	20	20
Shallots, sliced	1½ ounces	50 grams
Butter	3½ ounces	100 grams
White wine	¾ cup	2 deciliters
Duxelles	10.5 ounces	300 grams
Mushrooms, finely chopped	7 ounces	200 grams
White-wine sauce	2 cups	5 deciliters
Breadcrumbs	to gratinate	to gratinate

Procedure

1. Remove the scallops from their shells and clean. Scrub the shells and reserve.
2. Sauté the shallots and scallops in 1 ounce (30 grams) of butter. Add the white wine and poach for 5 minutes. Remove scallops and reserve poaching liquid.
3. Place a spoonful of duxelles in each scallop shell. Cover with chopped mushrooms, scallops, and shallots.
4. Reduce the poaching liquid and add to the white-wine sauce. Pour the sauce over the scallops.
5. Sprinkle each scallop with breadcrumbs. Melt the remaining butter and sprinkle over the breadcrumbs. Gratinate.

16.3 Lobster—*Homard*

16.3.1 Lobster, American Style—*Homard à l'américaine*

Yield
2 servings

Ingredients	U.S. Weight or Volume	Metric Weight or Volume
Lobsters	2 pounds total	1 kilogram total
Oil	3½ ounces	100 grams
Shallots, chopped	1 tablespoon	15 grams
Garlic, crushed	¼ clove	¼ clove
Thyme	⅛ teaspoon	1 gram
Parsley, chopped	1 tablespoon	15 grams
Brandy	¼ cup	50 milliliters
Tomatoes, diced	5 ounces	150 grams
White wine	¾ cup	2 deciliters
Fish fumet	½ cup	1 deciliter
Meat extract	1 tablespoon	15 milliliters
Salt	½ teaspoon	3 grams
Pepper	⅛ teaspoon	1 gram
Cayenne	⅛ teaspoon	1 gram
Butter	4 ounces	120 grams

Procedure

1. Kill the lobster quickly by splitting the front part of the body.
2. Cut up the lobster. Pry open the claws.
3. Remove the intestinal tract, the spongy gill tissues, and the sand sac (stomach) from the head. Reserve the coral (roe), if any, and the green tomalley (liver). Mash the remaining body portions with lobster juices and set aside.
4. Drop the cut lobster into the hot oil and sauté until shell turns completely red.
5. Drain off the oil.
6. Add the shallots, garlic, thyme, and parsley to the pan.
7. Heat and flame with brandy.
8. Add the tomatoes, white wine, fish fumet, meat extract (*glace de viande*), salt, pepper, and cayenne.

9. Cover and simmer slowly for 10 to 12 minutes.
10. Remove the lobster meat from the shells.
11. Combine the mashed body portions, coral, and tomalley, and add to the sauce. Reduce to the desired consistency.
12. Strain the reduced sauce and fluff in the butter, bit by bit, until the sauce is thick and smooth and expanded in bulk.
13. Place lobster pieces on a serving dish, spoon sauce over them, and decorate with the claw shells.

Note: Sometimes only the lobster tails and claws are used, and the body is reserved for making lobster butter.

16.3.2 Lobster Thermidor—*Homard Thermidor*

Yield
2 servings

Ingredients	U.S. Weight or Volume	Metric Weight or Volume
Lobster, freshly killed	2 (1 to 1¼ pounds each)	2 (500 to 750 grams each)
Oil	3½ ounces	100 grams
Basic white sauce	1½ cups	4 deciliters
Mustard, prepared, spicy	1 tablespoon	15 grams

Procedure
1. Split the raw lobster lengthwise down the middle.
2. Sauté slowly in oil.
3. Remove the tail meat from the shell and cut into slices.
4. Combine the basic white sauce and spicy mustard. Pour some of this sauce into the shell and arrange the slices of tail meat in the shell and in the claws.
5. Cover with sauce and brown or gratinate.

Note: Often the lobster halves are boiled in court bouillon before being mixed with the sauce.

16.3.3 Lobster Newburg

Yield
2 servings

Ingredients	U.S. Weight or Volume	Metric Weight or Volume
Butter, clarified	½ ounce	15 grams
Lobster tail, cooked, cut into ¼-inch slices or ¾-inch cubes	8 to 10 ounces	225 to 285 grams
Heavy cream	1½ cups	3 deciliters
Madeira	¼ cup	50 milliliters
Heavy cream	½ cup	1 deciliter
Egg yolk	1	1

Procedure
1. In a shallow pan (*sautoir*), heat clarified butter, add lobster, and sauté without coloring.
2. Add 1½ cups (3 deciliters) cream to cover lobster; simmer to reduce.
3. Add Madeira to taste.
4. Thicken with the remaining cream and egg yolk.

Note: This is the original recipe as it was prepared at Delmonico's Restaurant by Chef Ranhofer. Contemporary variations include sherry instead of Madeira, brandy, and the addition of coral or paprika to obtain a pinkish color.

Other Lobster Dishes

Boiled Lobster

Plunge live lobster head first into a large pot of boiling salted water or basic court bouillon. (True lobster lovers prefer theirs boiled in water only, as the flavor imparted from the court bouillon takes away from the natural taste.) When the water returns to boil, simmer for 6 to 8 minutes per pound of lobster. Serve lobster directly, accompanied by drawn butter and fresh lemon. The claws may be disjointed and cracked or portions of the shell removed for the convenience of the guest.

Broiled Lobster

Rinse live lobster (1 pound) thoroughly in cold water. Sever the vein at the base of the neck. Place lobster on chopping board with back down. Using a sharp knife and starting at the head, split the lobster into halves and open flat lengthwise; do not cut through the back shell. Remove the stomach, intestinal vein, coral (if any), and tomalley. (Tomalley and coral may be used in the stuffing.) Place lobster on grill rack, shell side up, and place under broiler. Broil for 3 or 4 minutes, or until shells are red. Remove from racks and fill body cavity (but not tail) with stuffing made from breadcrumbs, butter, chopped fresh parsley, and a little rubbed thyme. Tomalley and coral may be added. Place on a baking sheet or in a roast pan, shell side down, and broil at 400°F (205°C) in oven for 12 to 15 minutes. Crack claws after cooking, for the convenience of guests. Serve lobster on a platter with a claw on each side. Garnish with lemon and parsley. Serve with drawn butter.

Steamed Lobster

Place live lobster in steaming equipment; follow manufacturer's instructions for time. Serve as for boiled lobster.

Steamed Lobster in Seaweed

Place some seaweed in the bottom of a large pot and barely cover with water; place live lobster on top and cover with additional seaweed. Cover and steam, 6 to 8 minutes per pound. Serve as for boiled lobster. Lobsters are often delivered wrapped in seaweed to keep them moist. Ask your supplier.

16.4 Mussels—*Moules*

16.4.1 Mussels, Mariner's Style—*Moules à la marinière*

Yield
approximately 10 servings

Ingredients	U.S. Weight or Volume	Metric Weight or Volume
Mussels	7 to 9 pounds	3 to 4 kilograms
Salt	1 tablespoon	15 grams
Pepper	1 teaspoon	5 grams
White wine	¾ to 1¼ cups	2 to 3 deciliters
Shallots, chopped fine	3 ounces	80 grams
Chopped herbs: parsley, thyme, dill	2 tablespoons	30 grams
Butter	7 ounces	200 grams
Lemon juice	2 tablespoons	30 milliliters
Parsley, chopped	as needed for garnish	as needed for garnish

Procedure

1. Scrub the mussels well and remove beards.
2. Place them in a large kettle. Add the salt, pepper, white wine, and shallots. Simmer covered until the mussels open. Discard any that do not open.
3. Lift mussels out at once and strain the liquid through cloth. Return liquid to the kettle.
4. Add the herbs and reduce the liquid to two-thirds of its volume. Stir in the butter and adjust seasoning. Add lemon juice.
5. Remove the top shell of each mussel. Place the mussels in a flat container, cover with sauce, and sprinkle with parsley.

Note: For large quantities, the mussel liquid may be extended with a fish stock or fumet.

Other Mussel Dishes

Mussels, Oriental Style—*Moules à l'orientale*

Cooked mussels are removed from the shells and placed on rice. Curry powder is added to white-wine sauce. The sauce is poured over the mussels and rice before serving.

Mussels with White Sauce—*Moules à la poulette*

These are mussels, mariner's style, served with a white-wine sauce that has been mixed with the strained mussel liquid.

16.5 Snails—*Escargots*

16.5.1 Snails, Burgundy Style—*Escargots à la bourguignonne*

Yield

approximately 100 snails (6 to 12 per serving)

Ingredients	U.S. Weight or Volume	Metric Weight or Volume
Butter	10 ounces	300 grams
Garlic, crushed	¾ ounce	20 grams
Parsley, chopped	3½ ounces	100 grams
White wine	½ cup	1.5 deciliters

Ingredients	U.S. Weight or Volume	Metric Weight or Volume
Salt	1 teaspoon	4 grams
Shallots, chopped	2 ounces	50 grams
Lemon juice	2 tablespoons	30 milliliters
Snails, boiled	100	100

Procedure

1. Whip the butter until light.
2. Add all other ingredients except snails and mix well.
3. Force a little butter into each snail shell.
4. Place 1 boiled snail in each shell and fill completely with the snail butter.
5. Place the snails on a snail plate. Add some water and heat in the oven at 425°F (218°C) for 4 to 5 minutes.

Note: It is important to heat the snails in the oven until the butter is boiling. The snails may be marinated before being baked.

Chapter 17
Small Meat Dishes—*Entrées*

In the classical menu, the term *entrées* referred to the courses after the *grosse pièce,* or main dish. Today, however, the entrées are usually served as the main dish with suitable vegetable and salad garnishes. Both hot and cold entrées are frequently described as single dishes on the menu, where they appear in various categories, such as hot snacks, garnished main dishes, specialties of the day, or national dishes. The main difference between entrées and *grosses pièces* is that the entrées are cut up or jointed before being cooked and therefore do not require the same methods of preparation as the *grosses pièces,* which are prepared in single large pieces. It is, therefore, not possible to group the two types of dishes in the same category.

Entrées are divided into two main categories—cold entrées and hot entrées. This chapter covers the hot entrées; see chapter 24 for cold entrées. Figure 17-1 shows the different ways in which hot entrées can be prepared.

17.1 Sautéing—*Sauter à la minute*

As the term *à la minute* indicates, it is important that sautéed dishes be served directly out of the pan, since the quality will deteriorate (meat will toughen or become soggy) if they are held for any length of time after preparation.

The timing for such small pieces is difficult to determine. It depends upon the heat of the fat, the size of the sauté pan, the quantity of meat, its thickness, and quality. The degree of doneness may be tested by applying light pressure with the fingers to the center or largest portion of the meat. After quickly browning the meat, press with the finger from time to time. The more yielding or spongy the meat, the less the degree of doneness. The greater the resistance or the firmer the texture, the greater the degree of doneness. The degrees of doneness are described as follows:

- Rare—*bleu:* When pressed with a finger, the meat is very soft with a jellylike texture.
- Medium Rare—*saignant:* When pressed with a finger, the meat feels springy and resilient.
- Medium—*à point:* When pressed with a finger, the meat feels firm, and there is a definite resistance.
- Well done—*bien cuit:* When pressed with a finger, the meat feels hard, very firm.

Do not cut or pierce sautéed meat to check doneness, as valuable juices will be lost.

Sautéing Red Meat

To sauté red meat, heat oil or fat with a high smoking point. Sauté tournedos, châteaubriand, sirloin, or rump steak in oil; larger pieces of meat are basted with fat from time to time. Place on a plate after the required degree of doneness has been achieved. Drain the oil and deglaze the sauté pan with wine, stock, or demi-glace to make the sauce that will be served with the meat. This sauce is generally derived from demi-glace or basic brown sauce. In certain recipes the meat is served without sauce.

Sautéed beef tenderloin dishes, such as beef stroganoff, are prepared by the same method as the sliced white meat sautés. The tenderloin is cut into small cubes and sautéed to medium rare.

Sautéing White Meat

When sautéing white meat, a clear distinction must be made between thin-sliced meat and cutlets and chops, since each is prepared quite differently.

Preparation of Thin-sliced Meat

Heat peanut oil in a lyonnaise pan. Place seasoned and floured meat in the hot oil over high heat. Stir vigorously with a fork so that the pieces of meat are evenly sautéed; they are not browned, but done to a grayish color. This procedure requires only a few seconds. Sauté a small quantity at a time and remove the meat from the heat before any meat juices cook out. Then place the meat on a heated platter.

Drain any excess oil from the pan and replace it with butter. Add chopped shallots and sauté over low heat for a few seconds. Add white wine, reduce, and add demi-glace or stock, plus cream. Reduce once more and season to taste. Return the meat to the pan, but do not allow it to cook further. Arrange the meat slices on a warm platter and pour the sauces over the top.

Preparation of Chops and Cutlets

Heat peanut oil or butter or a mixture of the two in a sauté pan. Brown both sides of the meat carefully. As soon as the meat juice is visible on the surface of the meat, remove it from the pan. Deglaze the sauté pan and prepare a sauce with demi-glace, stock, or cream. Shallots or onion may be added. Arrange the meat on a heated platter and pour the sauce over the top.

Note: Breaded pieces of meat should not be covered with meat juices or sauce, as the liquid will soften the crust; merely garnish with *beurre noisette*. All sautéed white meats can be finished with butter alone.

Sautéed Dishes

Beef Goulash Stroganoff—*Filet goulache Stroganov*

This is a goulash made of small cubes of beef tenderloin tips that have been sautéed in melted butter and combined with chopped onions and strips of cucumber that have been dusted with paprika and added to sautéed diced potatoes. The pan is deglazed with a demi-glace containing a small amount of tomato puree, removed from the heat, and thickened with sour cream.

Beef Tenderloin Goulash—*Goulache à la minute*

Small cubes of beef tenderloin tip and chopped onions are sautéed over high heat until partially done, seasoned, and placed on a warm dish. Boiled diced potatoes are sautéed in butter. The pan drippings from the meat are deglazed with demi-glace, and the sauce is heated to the boiling point. Madeira is added. The meat and potatoes are reheated in the pan. Chopped parsley is scattered over the top.

Sliced Calf's Liver—*Foie de veau en tranches*

Thin slices of calf's liver are seasoned, coated with flour, and sautéed in butter. The liver is drenched with melted butter and sprinkled with lemon juice and parsley before serving.

Calf's Liver, English Style—*Foie de veau à l'anglaise*

Thin slices of calf's liver, coated with flour and sautéed in butter, are arranged on a platter alternatively with strips of bacon. Melted butter is drizzled over the top of the dish.

Calf's Liver, Italian Style—*Foie de veau à l'italienne*

This is a platter of thin slices of sautéed liver covered with an Italian sauce.

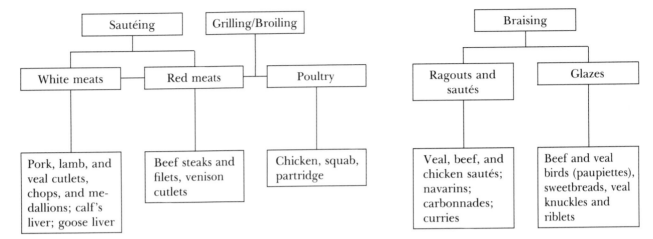

Figure 17-1. Types of hot entrées and methods of cooking.

Sautéed Calf's Liver with Madeira Sauce—*Foie de veau sauté au madère*

Thin slices of liver and chopped onion are sautéed in butter over high heat. The meat and onion are stirred constantly until lightly done. The meat and onion are then seasoned with salt and pepper and removed from the pan. The pan drippings are deglazed with demi-glace, and the sauce is heated to the boiling point. The liver is put back into the pan, and some Madeira is added. The liver is sprinkled with parsley and served immediately.

Sautéed Calf's Liver in a Rice Ring—*Foie de veau sauté en bordure*

This liver is prepared in the same way as sautéed calf's liver with Madeira sauce. The meat is arranged on a platter and surrounded by a ring of rice.

Calf's Liver on Skewers—*Foie de veau en brochette*

Small slices of liver that have been seasoned and lightly sautéed in butter are arranged on skewers, alternating liver, lean bacon slices, and mushrooms. They are coated with dry duxelles, breaded, and grilled or sautéed. A duxelles sauce is served separately.

Goose Liver, Strasbourg Style—*Foie gras à la strasbourgeoise*

A fresh goose liver, sliced, seasoned, and coated with flour, is sautéed quickly in butter. Thick slices of peeled apples are stewed in butter in the oven, until they are soft. Round bread croutons, sautéed in butter, are arranged on a platter and covered with the apple slices. The goose-liver slices are placed on top and coated with a demi-glace seasoned to taste with port wine.

Sweetbread Cutlets—*Escalopes de ris de veau*

Cutlets are sliced from blanched sweetbreads, seasoned, coated with flour, and sautéed in butter.

Veal Chop Nelson—*Côte de veau Nelson*

These veal chops are sautéed on one side and that side is spread with an onion puree. The chop is then breaded and sautéed. A tomato sauce is served separately.

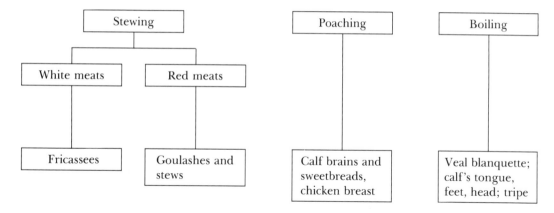

Figure 17-1. *continued*

Veal Chops Master Paul—*Côtes de veau "Maître Paul"*

Trimmed veal chops are seasoned, dusted with flour, and sautéed. Grated Sbrinz cheese and stewed diced tomatoes are bound with egg and seasoned. This mixture is spread on top of the chops and browned under the broiler. The chops are arranged on a plate and garnished with vegetables and potatoes Anna prepared in individual timbales.

Veal Chop Pojarski—*Côte de veau Pojarski*

Ground veal, sautéed onion, cream, and seasonings are mixed together and formed into chop-shaped pieces. The pieces are breaded with fine white breadcrumbs, sautéed in butter and garnished with young peas and asparagus spears.

Veal Chop en Papillote—*Côte de veau en papillote*

A piece of aluminum foil about three times as large as a veal chop is cut as indicated in figure 7-32. The inside of the foil is oiled and half the foil is covered with a sautéed slice of ham topped with a duxelles. A lightly sautéed veal chop is placed on top of the ham, then another layer of duxelles, and, finally, a second sautéed slice of ham. The foil is folded into an airtight bag, and the meat is baked in a hot oven. Basic brown sauce, served in a sauceboat, usually accompanies this dish.

Veal Cutlets in Cocottes—*Côtelettes de veau en cocotte*

This is a sautéed veal cutlet served in a cocotte with small onions, potato balls, and raw mushrooms.

Veal Cutlets, Holstein Style—*Escalopes de veau Holstein*

Unbreaded veal cutlets, sautéed in butter, are topped with fried eggs surrounded with anchovy fillets and capers. Veal stock is served separately.

Veal Cutlets, Home Style—*Côtelettes de veau bonne femme*

The cutlets are sautéed and then garnished with small onions and potato slices. The sauce and garnishes are poured over the finished cutlet.

Veal Cutlets with Paprika—*Escalopes de veau au paprika*

Sautéed veal cutlets are deglazed with cream and thickened stock, reduced slightly, and seasoned to taste with lemon juice and paprika. The sauce is poured over the cutlet.

Veal Cutlets, Viennese Style (*Wiener Schnitzel*) I—*Escalope de veau viennoise I*

These cutlets are breaded and sautéed. A slice of lemon with a ring of anchovy fillets is placed on top of each cutlet. An olive, stuffed with capers, is placed in the ring. Small heaps of chopped hard-cooked egg whites and yolks, and capers, are arranged around the cutlet. Hot butter is poured over the top.

Veal Cutlets, Viennese Style (*Wiener Schnitzel*) II—*Escalope de veau viennoise II*

Two connected slices of veal cutlet, from the rump, are pounded through a wet towel, breaded, and sautéed in a mixture of butter and oil. The cutlets are served on a paper napkin with a lemon wedge.

Grenadins of Veal—*Grenadins de veau*

These thick cutlets of veal top round are sautéed. Tomatoes are added to the juices, which are then thickened slightly.

Sautéed Veal Kidneys with Mushrooms—*Rognons de veau sautés aux champignons*

These veal kidneys are prepared in the same way as sautéed calf's liver with Madeira sauce, substituting thin-sliced calf's kidney for the liver. Mushrooms sautéed in butter are served over the top.

Sliced Veal Sauté—*Emincé de veau sauté*

This dish is prepared with the same method used for sautéed calf's liver with Madeira sauce. It is prepared with thin slices of fillet or top round of veal, cooked to the medium or well-done stage.

Veal Steak Zingara—*Steak de veau zingara*

This veal steak is seasoned with salt and paprika and sautéed in butter. The steak is cooked with a zingara sauce and topped with a sautéed slice of ham.

Veal Tenderloin Medallions Three Musketeers—*Medaillons de veau Trois Mousquetaires*

Fill 4 uniform artichoke bottoms with creamed morels. Sauté 4 tenderloin medallions and 4 slices of veal kidney in butter and place one on top of each artichoke bottom. Place a mushroom cap, a kidney slice, and a medallion on each of four sword-shaped skewers. Insert into artichokes, with skewer handle up. Garnish with stewed diced tomatoes.

Venison Cutlets, Baden-Baden Style—*Escalopes de chevreuil Baden-Baden*

These cutlets are seasoned, dusted with flour, and sautéed. The pan is deglazed with white wine, demiglace, and cream. The sauce is reduced, and the fat is skimmed off. It is seasoned with cayenne and lemon juice and strained. The cutlets are garnished with pear halves filled with cranberries. The sauce is served separately.

Venison Cutlets, Belle Forestière Style—*Côtelettes de chevreuil belle forestière*

Season trimmed venison cutlets and sauté until they are rose colored. Flame with gin. Sauté mushrooms with shallots, and season. At the last minute, add chopped parsley and a little meat extract (*glace de viande*) to the mushrooms. Arrange the mushrooms on a platter and place the venison chops on top.

Venison Cutlets, Hunter's Style—*Escalopes de chevreuil chasseur*

These cutlets are prepared like venison cutlets, Baden-Baden style. They are garnished with mushrooms, Brussels sprouts, turnips, and potatoes fondantes. Sauce and red currant jelly are served separately.

Venison Cutlets Mirza—*Escalopes de chevreuil Mirza*

These are prepared like venison cutlets, Baden-Baden style. Peeled apples are hollowed out and stewed in white wine with sugar. They are filled with red currant jelly and used as a garnish around the venison cutlets. The sauce is served separately.

Garnishes for Sautéed Red Meat

American Style—*à l'américaine*

For steaks. A fried egg with slices of sautéed lean bacon. The steak is topped with the egg and bacon and garnished with peas. A demi-glace blended with tomatoes is served separately.

Belle Hélène Style—*belle Hélène*

For tournedos. Tournedos on toasted rounds of bread garnished with asparagus tips and sliced truffles. A sauce is served separately.

Bordeaux Style—*à la bordelaise*

For tournedos. Tournedos on round slices of toasted bread, covered with slices of poached marrow. A bordelaise wine sauce is served separately.

Casino—*Casino*

For tournedos. Tournedos arranged on a base of spinach leaves, covered with mushroom caps dotted with truffles in the center, and surrounded with a ring of stuffed olives. Madeira sauce is served separately. (See figure 17-2.)

Choron—*Choron*

For tournedos. Artichoke bottoms filled with peas or asparagus tips, and potato balls placed beside the steak. Choron sauce is served separately. The tournedos are served on round slices of toasted bread.

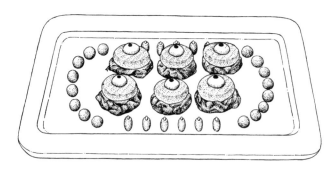

Figure 17-2. Tournedos casino

Dubarry—*Dubarry*

For sirloin steak. A bouquet of cauliflower and potato balls. A sauce is served separately.

with an Egg—*à cheval*

For steak or tournedos. A fried egg placed on top of the meat. A sauce may be served separately.

Florentine Style—*à la florentine*

A base of spinach with semolina gnocchi arranged on each side of the meat. A Madeira sauce is served separately.

Forestière Style—*à la forestière*

The meat is covered with a Madeira sauce and slices of bacon and garnished with cubed potatoes.

Helder Style—*Helder*

For tournedos. Sautéed tomato halves filled with béarnaise sauce. Potato balls, browned in butter, and the tomatoes are arranged on a platter with the meat. A Madeira sauce is served separately.

with Herb Butter—*à la maître d'hôtel*

For steak. Slices of herb butter, placed atop the meat. A sauce is served separately.

Hôtelier Style—*à la hôtelier*

For steak. Maître d'hôtel butter mixed with duxelles, served under a sirloin steak. The steak is covered with sauce.

Lyons Style—*à la lyonnaise*

For steak. Onions browned in butter, served with demi-glace sauce. The steak is covered with sautéed onions and coated with the demi-glace.

with Mushrooms—*aux champignons*

The meat is covered with a chasseur sauce and garnished with a ring of mushroom caps.

Provence Style—*à la provençale*

For tournedos. The tournedos are served on toasted rounds of bread and topped with tomatoes, provence style, and surrounded with mushrooms. A Madeira sauce is served separately.

Rossini—*Rossini*

For tournedos. Tournedos are served on toasted rounds of bread, topped with a garnish of thick slices of goose liver and slices of truffle. A Madeira sauce may surround the meat, or it may be served separately.

Tyrolian Style—*à la tyrolienne*

Sautéed onion rings and stewed diced tomatoes. The sauce is served separately.

Garnishes for Sautéed White Meat

Asparagus—*Argenteuil*

For veal, lamb, and mutton. Asparagus and potato balls or fried potatoes. A sauce is served separately.

Brussels Style—*à la bruxelloise*

For pork. Brussels sprouts and fried potatoes.

English Style—*à l'anglaise*

For veal. The meat is breaded in the English fashion, sautéed in butter, and covered with slices of sautéed ham.

Flemish Style—*à la flamande*

For pork. Braised endives and deep-fried potatoes. Sautéed cutlets or chops are topped with the garnish and coated with demi-glace.

Florentine Style—*à la florentine*

For lamb and mutton. Buttered spinach leaves and potatoes fondantes. A Madeira sauce is served separately.

with Goose Liver—*au foie gras*

For veal. Veal tenderloin medallions covered with slices of goose liver and truffles, served on toasted rounds of bread, and garnished with green beans, young carrots, straw potatoes, and small tomatoes. A sauce is served separately. (See figure 17-3.)

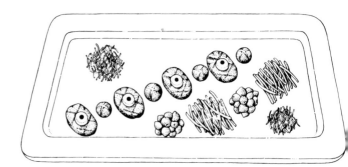

Figure 17-3. Veal tenderloin medallions with goose liver—*Noisettes de veau au foie gras.*

Gypsy Style—*Zingara*

For pork. The sautéed meat is covered with zingara sauce.

Home Style—*bonne femme*

For veal and pork. Small glazed onions, carrots, mushroom quarters, and sautéed slices of bacon. Chops or cutlets are covered with the garnish and served with fried potatoes. A sauce is served separately.

Italian Style—*à l'italienne*

For pork, lamb, and mutton. Artichoke hearts covered with Italian sauce surround the meat.

Lyons Style—*à la lyonnaise*

For lamb or mutton. Onions sautéed in butter cover the meat. A ring of demi-glace sauce is poured around the meat.

Marshall Style—*à la maréchal*

For lamb or mutton. Truffle slices and asparagus tips. Chops are breaded, sautéed, and covered with truffle slices and served with asparagus tips.

Milan Style—*milanaise*

For veal. The meat is breaded with white breadcrumbs mixed with grated cheese. It is garnished with buttered spaghetti, which is sprinkled with a julienne of ham, tongue, mushrooms, and truffles that have been sautéed in butter. Madeira sauce is served separately.

Naples Style—*napolitaine*

For veal. The sautéed meat is garnished with spaghetti napolitaine. A sauce is served separately.

Nelson—*Nelson*

For lamb or mutton. Sautéed chops are coated with an onion puree, sprinkled with breadcrumbs, and garnished with potato croquettes. A Madeira sauce is served separately.

Peasant Style—*paysanne*

For veal and pork. A strip of fried lean bacon, glazed pearl onions, and fried potatoes. The garnish is placed on top of the sautéed meat. It is covered with sauce and sprinkled with parsley.

Provençal Style—*à la provençale*

For lamb or mutton. Small, peeled baked tomatoes stuffed with a duxelles and with mushrooms. The chops are surrounded with the garnish.

Robert—*Robert*

For pork. The sautéed meat is covered with Robert sauce.

Shepherd's Style—*à la bèrgere*

For lamb or mutton. Sautéed slices of ham, morels, and small glazed onions.

17.2 Broiling/Grilling—*Griller*

Red and white meats used for sautéing are suitable for grilling, as is poultry. To sear the meat and seal its juices, the meat is placed close to the heat. As soon as the meat is seared, the meat is placed 3 to 4 inches (7.5 to 10 centimeters) away from the source of heat and is cooked to the desired degree of doneness.

Before grilling, clean the grill thoroughly and grease with oil or meat fat. Preheat the metal grill before placing the meat on it.

Garnishes for broiled or grilled meats are the same as those for sautéed meats.

Broiling/Grilling Red Meat

Baste the pieces of meat, tied where appropriate, with oil. Season and grill on both sides, so that the grill bars are branded onto the meat. Baste with oil frequently. The length of time on the grill depends on the size, cut, and quality of the piece of meat.

Grilled food is usually salted immediately after grilling. Larger pieces of meat should stand for a few minutes after grilling so that the heat is distributed evenly throughout the piece of meat and the juices are retained. Serve a seasoned butter sauce or herb butter with the meat.

Broiling/Grilling White Meat

Baste the pieces of meat with oil and grill over medium heat.

Breaded meat should not be grilled. Since there is much less juice in white meat than red meat, either a special sauce or a thickened strong veal stock may be served with it. Usually, however, white meat is served plain with a wedge of lemon.

Broiling/Grilling Poultry

Cut dressed fowl lengthwise along the back and remove about 1/3 to 1/2 inch (8 or 12 millimeters) of the backbone. Tuck the legs into the slits that have been pierced through the skin and press the pieces flat. Place the chicken on the grill, skin side down, baste, and grill until tender. Remove the breastbone and carve the bird. The bird should be basted frequently during broiling or grilling.

Broiled/Grilled Dishes

Grilled Chicken, American Style—*Poulet grillé à l'américaine*

Cut a chicken along the back, remove the backbone, flatten the chicken, and tuck the legs into slits in the skin. Season with salt and mustard powder mixed with a pinch of cayenne pepper. Baste with oil and grill until chicken is almost done. Turn and baste with butter frequently. Sprinkle with white breadcrumbs or bread lightly. Strips of lean bacon and seasoned, halved, seeded, tomatoes are grilled and used as a garnish with potato chips. A deviled sauce or a hot maître d'hôtel butter may be served separately.

Grilled Chicken with Deviled Sauce—*Poulet grille à la diable*

This chicken is prepared as described for grilled chicken, American style. The chicken is served on a platter garnished with a lemon wedge and watercress or parsley. A deviled sauce is served separately.

Mixed Grill, American Style—*Friture mixte à l'américaine*

A mixed grill—such as beef tournedos, veal medallions, lamb or mutton chops or cutlets, kidneys, sausage—is garnished with grilled tomatoes, mushrooms, and crisp bacon and covered with foaming hot butter. A demi-glace sauce, with a little black pepper, is served separately.

Porterhouse Steak

An English and American cut of meat, the steak is cut at the thickest part of the sirloin close to the loin, and includes both the loin and the tenderloin. The following are used as garnishes: potato chips, grilled tomatoes and bacon, sweet corn, or a black pepper sauce consisting of a demi-glace with a reduced stock of shallots, black peppercorns, and white wine. The steak may also be served as the main dish.

Rib of Beef—*Côte de boeuf*

Grill and garnish as for sautéed beef dishes. The grill is placed close to the source of heat to sear the meat and seal its juices. As soon as the meat is seared, the grill is placed within 3 inches (7.5 centimeters) of the source of heat, and the meat is cooked to the desired degree of doneness.

T-Bone Steak

This American cut of meat is similar to the porter-house steak, but cut from a piece close to the ribs. The garnishes suggested for porterhouse steak may be used.

Viennese Minute Steak—*Wiener Rostbraten*

This is a sirloin steak cut from the front part of the loin, cooked on a grill, garnished with sautéed onion rings, and surrounded with a rich sauce.

17.3 Braising—*Braiser*

Section 17.1 described those preparations involving fast sautéing with butter, oil, or fat. The term *braising* refers to preparations involving a rapid browning of the food, followed, however, by further cooking in a stock or sauce. The two main groups are ragouts (*sautés*) and glazed pieces of meat (*viandes glacées*).

These groups should not be confused with stewed meat (goulashes, stews, fricassees); the latter are never browned.

Ragouts (*Sautés*)

The following are the main ragout preparations:

- Veal Sauté—*Sauté de veau*
- Beef Sauté—*Sauté de boeuf*
- Chicken Sauté—*Poulet sauté*
- Sauté with Curry—*Sauté au curry*
- Mutton or Lamb Ragout—*Navarin de mouton ou agneau*
- Game Ragout—*Civet de gibier*
- Carbonnade—*Carbonnade*

In all these preparations, whether named a sauté or a ragout, the meat is first browned and then braised in a liquid.

17.3.1 Veal Sauté—*Sauté de veau*

Yield
approximately 10 servings

Ingredients	U.S. Weight or Volume	Metric Weight or Volume
Veal, breast or neck, cut in 1½-ounce (45-gram) cubes	3 to 4 pounds	1.5 to 2 kilograms
Oil	1¾ ounces	50 grams
Bouquet garni	1	1
Garlic	1 clove	1 clove
Salt	½ teaspoon	3 grams
Pepper	⅛ teaspoon	1 gram
White wine	¾ cup	2 deciliters
Tomato puree	2 tablespoons	30 milliliters
Basic stock	1 pint	5 deciliters
Demi-glace	1 pint	5 deciliters
Madeira	¼ cup	50 milliliters

Procedure

1. Brown the meat cubes, a small amount at a time, in the hot oil.
2. Add the *bouquet garni* and garlic and continue browning for a few minutes. Drain the excess oil.
3. Place the meat in a suitable container. Season.
4. Deglaze the pan drippings with the white wine, and reduce the liquid to a syruplike consistency. Add the tomato puree, the basic stock, and the demi-glace. Add the meat.
5. Cover and braise the meat for 1 hour or until it is tender. If excessive evaporation occurs, add more stock.
6. Remove the *bouquet garni*, strain the sauce, and add the Madeira. If necessary, the reduced stock can be thickened with a little cornstarch mixed with water.

Note: A *mirepoix* may be used instead of a *bouquet garni*. Because removing the *mirepoix* is time consuming, and because the demi-glace has already been flavored with a mirepoix, it is not necessary or recommended.

Other Veal Sauté Dishes

Veal Sauté, Marengo Style—*Sauté de veau Marengo*

The finished sauté is garnished with small glazed onions and sliced and buttered mushrooms, and surrounded with heart-shaped bread croutons.

Veal Sauté with Mushrooms—*Sauté de veau aux champignons*

Veal sauté is covered with sliced mushrooms that have been sautéed in butter.

Veal Sauté with Noodles—*Sauté de veau aux nouilles*

Veal sauté garnished with noodles.

Veal Sauté, Sailor's Style—*Matelote de veau*

This dish is prepared by deglazing veal sauté with red wine and flambéing it with brandy.

Veal Sauté with Spring Vegetables—*Sauté de veau printanière*

The finished veal sauté is garnished with glazed carrots, turnips, celery, pearl onions, and peas.

Beef Sauté—*Sauté de boeuf*

Meat from the rump of beef is recommended for this dish. It is prepared in the same way as veal sauté, although a longer cooking time is required.

17.3.2 Chicken Sauté—*Poulet sauté*

Yield
approximately 10 servings

Ingredients	U.S. Weight or Volume	Metric Weight or Volume
Chicken	6 to 7 pounds	3 kilograms
Flour	8 ounces	240 grams
Oil	¼ cup	50 milliliters
Shallots, chopped	1¾ ounces	50 grams
White wine	½ cup	1 deciliter
Demi-glace	1 pint	5 deciliters
Brandy	¼ cup	60 milliliters
Salt	2 teaspoons	12 grams
Pepper	½ teaspoon	3 grams

Procedure

1. Disjoint the chickens.
2. Season and dust the pieces lightly with flour.
3. Heat the oil in a sauté pan and brown the pieces of chicken on all sides. Add the shallots and sauté lightly.
4. Cover the pan and complete the cooking in the oven at 350°F (175°C).
5. Remove the wings and breast after about 8 minutes and the legs after 15 minutes. Place in a warm container.
6. Prepare the sauce in the sauté pan. Skim off the fat. Deglaze with white wine, reduce, add the demi-glace, and reduce before seasoning. Add the brandy. Add the pieces of chicken and let them simmer in the sauce for a few minutes.
7. Arrange the pieces in a serving dish and strain the sauce over them.

Note: If the chicken is entirely cooked in the sauce, then the dish is named differently: chicken curry, chicken fricassee, or coq au vin. The garnishes are then usually cooked in the sauté pan with the chicken, although they sometimes require longer cooking than the chicken. When large quantities are involved, the garnishes are cooked separately.

Variation of Chicken Sauté

Rabbit Sauté—*Sauté de lapin*

Use rabbit instead of chicken, following the same procedure.

Other Chicken Sauté Dishes

Chicken Sauté, Archduke Style—*Poulet sauté archiduc*

This chicken is sautéed without browning. The pan is deglazed with sherry, port, and whiskey. The sauce is reduced, strained, and whipped with fresh butter. Lemon juice is added and the chicken is coated with the sauce and garnished with a julienne of truffles.

Chicken Sauté Beaulieu—*Poulet sauté Beaulieu*

Sautéed and browned chicken pieces are added to small, slightly browned new potatoes and quartered artichoke hearts that have been fried in butter. The chicken and vegetables are placed in a cocotte with pitted olives. The sauté pan is deglazed with white wine and lemon juice. Reduced veal stock is added, and the sauce is boiled for 1 to 2 minutes and poured over the chicken. The cocotte is covered and heated in the oven at 325°F (160°C) for 15 minutes.

Chicken Sauté, Hunter's Style—*Poulet sauté chasseur*

This chicken is sautéed and browned and placed in a cocotte. Sliced raw mushrooms and chopped shallots are sautéed in butter and added to stewed diced tomatoes, white wine, and demi-glace. The sauce is simmered for a few minutes and seasoned to taste. Chervil, chopped parsley, and a few drops of lemon juice are added to the sauce before pouring it over the chicken.

Chicken Sauté, Piedmont Style—*Poulet sauté à la piémontaise*

Sliced white truffles, sautéed in butter, are added to the finished chicken, and it is served in a ring of rice.

Chicken Sauté, Stanley—*Poulet sauté Stanley*

Seasoned chicken pieces are floured lightly and sautéed in butter, without actually browning. Shallots and onions are added, and the mixture is covered and cooked for 10 minutes. White wine, curry powder, cayenne pepper, and chicken stock are then added. The meat is removed when it is done; the liquid is reduced and strained and cream is added. The chicken is garnished with sautéed mushrooms.

Chicken Sauté with Tarragon—*Poulet sauté à l'estragon*

A sauce flavored with tarragon is poured over the chicken and covered with blanched tarragon leaves.

Chicken Sauté with Tomatoes—*Poulet sauté à la portugaise*

The finished chicken is garnished with sautéed sliced mushrooms and surrounded with small tomatoes stuffed with rice.

Chicken Sauté with Truffles—*Poulet sauté aux truffes*

Sautéed chicken is garnished with sliced truffles that have been warmed in Madeira wine.

Sautéed Chicken Breasts—*Suprêmes de volaille sautés*

Breasts of chicken browned and sautéed with brown stock in the same way as chicken sauté. Chicken may be served on toasted white bread and garnished.

17.3.3 Lamb Ragout—*Navarin*

Yield
approximately 10 servings

Ingredients	U.S. Weight or Volume	Metric Weight or Volume
Lamb, neck or shoulder, cut into 1½-ounce (45-gram) cubes	4 pounds	2 kilograms
Oil	1¾ ounces	50 grams
Onion, chopped	3½ ounces	100 grams
Garlic cloves	1	1
Salt	1 teaspoon	6 grams
Pepper	¼ teaspoon	2 grams
Red wine	¾ cup	2 deciliters
Brown stock	1 pint	5 deciliters
Demi-glace	1 pint	5 deciliters
Tomatoes, fresh, peeled, diced *or*	1 pound	500 grams
Tomato puree	2 tablespoons	30 grams

continued

Ingredients	U.S. Weight or Volume	Metric Weight or Volume
Pearl onions	7½ ounces	200 grams
Potato balls, small blanched	10 ounces	300 grams

Procedure

1. Brown small portions of the meat in hot oil until all of it is browned. Add the onion and garlic. Brown all ingredients for a few more minutes. Season.
2. Drain off excess oil.
3. Place the meat in a baking dish.
4. Deglaze the pan with red wine. Reduce the liquid to a glaze.
5. Add the brown stock, the demi-glace, and the tomatoes. Pour over the meat.
6. Cover the baking dish and braise in the oven at 350°F (175°C) for 1 hour. Strain the sauce and pour back over the meat.
7. Add the pearl onions and potato balls. Continue braising until the meat is tender.
8. Serve with garnishes.

Other Lamb Ragouts

Lamb Ragout with Spring Vegetables— *Navarin à la printanière*

The ragout is prepared by the method used for lamb ragout. Carrots and turnips are added. The vegetables may be cooked or browned separately and served on the ragout.

17.3.4 Venison Ragout—*Civet de chevreuil*

Yield
approximately 10 servings

Ingredients	U.S. Weight or Volume	Metric Weight or Volume
Venison, boneless breast or shoulder, cut into 1½-ounce (45-gram) cubes	4 pounds	2 kilograms
Marinade:		
Red wine	1 quart	1 liter
Wine vinegar	¾ cup	2 deciliters
Mirepoix	8 ounces	240 grams
Juniper berries	4	4
Bay leaves	2	2
Peppercorns	6	6
Oil	3½ ounces	100 grams
Flour	3 ounces	80 grams
Salt	2 teaspoons	12 grams
Stock	1 quart	1 liter
Bacon, diced, browned	5 ounces	150 grams
Pearl onions, glazed	7 ounces	200 grams
Mushrooms, sautéed	10 ounces	300 grams
Bread, fried heart-shaped slices	10	10

Procedure

1. Place the meat in the marinade for 8 to 10 days. Drain thoroughly, retaining the marinade. Separate the meat from the *mirepoix*.
2. Brown the meat pieces quickly in hot oil. Add the *mirepoix* and continue sautéing.
3. Dust with flour, season, and sauté further until the flour is browned.
4. Bring the marinade to a boil. Strain and pour the marinade and the stock over the meat.
5. Season to taste and cook until the meat is tender.
6. If excessive evaporation occurs, add more stock.
7. Remove the meat from the sauce.
8. Strain the sauce and pour back over the meat.
9. Arrange the diced bacon, onions, mushrooms, and toast on top of the ragout as garnishes.

Note: In the original recipe ¾ cup (2 deciliters) of pork blood is added to the sauce before straining it. Because of inspection and sanitation codes, this ingredient has been omitted. If the sauce needs to be thickened, add 1 teaspoon of cornstarch, dissolved in water, and stir continuously.

Variations of Venison Ragout

Chamois Ragout—*Civet de chamois*

This dish is prepared like venison ragout, using chamois instead of venison.

Hare Ragout (*Hasenpfeffer*)—*Civet de lièvre*

This dish is prepared like venison ragout, using hare instead. The whole animal is cut into pieces of appropriate size and braised with the bones.

Red Deer Ragout—*Civet de cerf*

The method described for venison ragout is followed for this dish, using red deer instead of venison.

17.3.5 Flemish Carbonnades of Beef—*Carbonnades de boeuf flamande*

Yield
approximately 10 servings

Ingredients	U.S. Weight or Volume	Metric Weight or Volume
Round steak *or* boneless chuck	4 to 5 pounds	2 to 2.5 kilograms
Fat	3½ ounces	100 grams
Salt	2 teaspoons	12 grams
Pepper	½ teaspoon	3 grams
Onion rings	1 pound	500 grams
Flour, browned	1½ ounces	50 grams
Dark beer	1 pint	5 deciliters
Brown stock	1 pint	5 deciliters
Bouquet garni	1	1

Procedure
1. Cut the meat into 3- or 4-ounce (90- to 120-gram) pieces. Season and brown on both sides in the hot fat in a pan.
2. Brown the onions in the same hot fat.
3. In a braising pan, arrange alternate layers of meat and onion. Add the browned flour, the beer, the brown stock, and the *bouquet garni.*
4. Cover and braise for 1½ hours, adding liquid if necessary.
5. Drain the sauce, including the onions, off the meat. Boil the sauce. Skim the fat. Pour the strained sauce back over the meat.

Variations of Flemish Carbonnades of Beef

Carbonnades of Pork—*Carbonnades de porc*

Use the recipe for Flemish carbonnades of beef, substituting 3-ounce (90-gram) pieces of pork for the beef.

Curries—*Sautés au cari*

All curry dishes are ragouts in which the meat has been slightly browned. Chicken, mutton or lamb, and veal curries are described in chapter 23.

Glazed Meats—Viandes glacées

Cut the meat into serving portions and prefry all sides in either butter or fat. Place slices of bacon and onion, a few bay leaves, and the pieces of meat covered with butter in a greased sauté pan. Brown quickly over high heat. Pour a little veal stock over the meat, cover, and baste frequently. Reduce the stock to a glaze. Then pour on more stock until it reaches a level of one-sixth the height of the pieces of meat. Cover and braise in the oven until tender. Remove the pieces of meat, add a little stock and wine, bring to a boil, skim off the fat, strain, and season to taste, adding Madeira. For certain dishes, the sauce may be thickened with potato flour or brown sauce.

Tomato purée is often added to glazed veal, or sour cream is sometimes added to the thickened sauce. The meat pieces mentioned may be garnished by combining special garnishes or suitable flavorings with the sauce. For small quantities, the appropriate garnish is braised with the meat and served on top of the meat with the sauce. When this method is used, the slices of bacon and onion should not be placed in the sauté pan before the meat.

Small pieces of white meat, primarily veal and poultry, are glazed while the meat is braising. Glazing represents the braising of small pieces of white meat by stewing the meat in a small amount of stock under cover and subsequently glazing the meat in the reduced liquid without the cover.

The following are suitable garnishes for glazed meats:

- with cauliflower—*Dubarry*
- hunter's style—*chasseur*
- garden style—*à la jardinière*
- with mixed vegetables—*à la macédoine*
- with noodles—*aux nouilles*
- with spring peas—*aux petits pois*

Glazed Meat Dishes

Glazed Beef Birds—*Paupiettes de boeuf glacées*

These beef birds (slices from beef rump or shoulder) are prepared by the method described for glazed veal birds (see below), except a longer cooking time is required.

Glazed Calf Sweetbreads—*Ris de veau glacé*

Blanched sweetbreads are glazed for 20 minutes. The reduced sauce is strained and whipped with fresh butter.

Stuffed Chicken Legs—*Ballottines de volaille*

Boned chicken legs stuffed with a spicy mousseline forcemeat are browned lightly in butter with shallots. Veal stock is added to the pan, and the meat is braised in an oven at 325°F (160°C). The surface of the stuffed legs will be glazed by the reduced stock. When cooked, the chicken legs are removed, more stock is added to the pan, the fat is skimmed, the sauce is strained, and small quantities of Madeira and brandy are added. The sauce is thickened if necessary.

Stuffed Chicken Wings—*Ailerons de volaille farcis*

The wings (without the bones) of capons and roasters are used for this dish. It is prepared by the method described for stuffed chicken legs.

Breast of Veal, Mayor's Style—*Il piatto del sindaco*

This is an Italian veal dish. Trimmed slices of veal breast are folded, trussed, and glazed. The string is loosened, the slices are placed on a round serving platter, and they are sprinkled with a sautéed julienne of sweet peppers and topped with fluted mushroom caps.

Glazed Veal Birds—*Paupiettes de veau glacées*

Veal cutlets are stuffed with forcemeat (two parts veal, one part pork, one part lean bacon). The birds are glazed as described in the basic method. The juices are slightly bound and blended with tomato sauce.

Veal Birds with Mushrooms—*Paupiettes de veau aux champignons*

These veal birds are prepared like glazed veal birds. Sliced mushrooms are added to the strained sauce. A mushroom cap is placed on each veal bird.

Glazed Veal Knuckle Slices—*Rouelles de jarret de veau glacées*

Veal knuckles, including the bones, cut into slices 2½ inches (6 centimeters) thick, are glazed. Tomatoes are added to the brown stock. The sauce is simmered, strained, and bound.

Veal Knuckle Slices, Bourgeoise Style—*Rouelles de jarret de veau bourgeoise*

The knuckles are prepared like glazed veal knuckle slices. The meat is garnished with glazed carrots, turnips, and small onions.

Veal Riblets—*Tendrons de veau*

These individual portions of breast of veal are glazed. The glaze is blended with tomatoes and served with the veal riblets.

Glazed Veal Tenderloin—*Filet de veau glacé*

A trimmed and larded veal tenderloin is braised with a fine *mirepoix* and a veal stock or a demi-glace. The cooked tenderloin is glazed and removed from the stock. The stock is seasoned, strained, and thickened with cornstarch.

17.4 Stewing/Simmering—*Etuver*

The term *braising* refers to methods of preparation in which the meat is quickly browned, then cooked in a stock. *Stewing* refers to all methods of preparation for entrées in which the meat is not browned first, but only cooked in liquid. The two main categories are stewed white meats—*étuvées à blanc (fricassees)*; and stewed red meats—*étuvées à brun (goulaches et estoufades)*.

Stewed White Meats — *Etuvées à blanc*

These include all fricassees. The meat, onion, and vegetables are placed in the pan and stewed for a short time without browning. A white stock or broth is used for deglazing. This form of preparation is especially suitable for veal and poultry.

17.4.1 Veal Fricassee—*Fricassée de veau*

Yield
approximately 10 servings

Ingredients	U.S. Weight or Volume	Metric Weight or Volume
Butter	1¾ ounces	50 grams
Onion, chopped	5 ounces	150 grams
Veal, boneless shoulder, breast, or neck, cut into 1½-ounce (45-gram) pieces	4½ pounds	2 kilograms
Flour	2 ounces	60 grams
White wine	1¼ cups	3 deciliters
White stock	5 cups	1.2 liters
Bouquet garni	1	1
Salt	2 teaspoons	12 grams
Nutmeg	⅛ teaspoon	1 gram
Pepper	½ teaspoon	3 grams
Cream	½ cup	1 deciliter
Lemon juice	2 tablespoons	30 milliliters

Procedure
1. Melt the butter in a sauté pan. Add the onion and meat. Stew without browning.
2. Dust the meat and onion with flour.
3. Add the wine, stock, *bouquet garni*, and seasonings.
4. Cover and simmer for about 1½ hours or until tender. Add liquid during this time if needed.
5. Remove the meat. Strain the sauce and reduce. Gradually add the cream and the lemon juice.
6. Put the meat back into the sauce and heat.

Variations of Veal Fricassee

Chicken Fricassee—*Fricassée de volaille*

This dish is prepared with the method used for veal fricassee, using chicken instead of veal. The chicken is cut as described for chicken sauté.

Rabbit Fricassee—*Fricassée de lapin*

Use the same recipe as for veal fricassee, substituting rabbit for the veal.

Stewed Red Meats—*Etuvées à brun*

These include goulash dishes and simmered stews. The onion is simmered until the liquid has thickened to a glaze, then the brown stock or bouillon and red wine are added. Rump and round of beef are usually used for stews and goulashes.

17.4.2 Hungarian Goulash—*Goulache hungroise—Gulyás*

Yield
approximately 10 servings

Ingredients	U.S. Weight or Volume	Metric Weight or Volume
Fat	2 ounces	60 grams
Rump, shoulder, *or* round, boneless	4½ pounds	2 kilograms
Onion, chopped fine	14 ounces	400 grams
Paprika, sweet, mild	2 tablespoons	30 grams
Salt	2 teaspoons	12 grams
Tomatoes, peeled, seeded *or*	20 ounces	600 grams
Tomato puree	3½ ounces	100 grams
Brown stock	2½ cups	6 deciliters
Red wine	1¼ cups	3 deciliters
Potatoes, cut into large cubes	1½ pounds	700 grams

Procedure
1. Heat the fat in a heavy pan. Cut the meat into 2-ounce chunks. Add the meat and onion. Stew, stirring occasionally, until the juice released by the meat has been completely reduced and a light glaze is formed.
2. Add paprika, salt, and tomatoes or tomato puree.
3. Pour in the stock and the wine.
4. Cover and simmer for 1½ hours. Add the potato cubes and continue cooking until meat and pota-

toes are done. Ad liquid during the cooking period if too much evaporation occurs.

Note: In hotels and restaurants, the potatoes are usually cooked separately and added to the finished dish at service time.

Variation of Hungarian Goulash

Veal Paprika—*Paprikás Borjú*

The method is similar to that for Hungarian goulash, but the meat used is veal from the shoulder or breast, cut into cubes. Use Noble Rose paprika. Eliminate the stock completely and substitute white wine for red. Simmer for 3 minutes, covered. Then uncover and continue to cook until the liquid is evaporated. Watch carefully that the veal does not burn or dry out. Stir in ½ cup (1 deciliter) sour cream and gently mix over low heat until the cream is warmed and the meat coated with cream. More cream can be added if desired. The cooking time is about 1 hour. Eliminate potatoes from this stew and instead serve with noodles.

17.4.3 Beef Stew—*Estouffade de boeuf*

Yield
approximately 10 servings

Ingredients	U.S. Weight or Volume	Metric Weight or Volume
Fat	2 ounces	60 grams
Beef rump, boneless cut into 1½-ounce (45-gram) pieces	4½ pounds	2 kilograms
Bacon, large cubes	8 ounces	250 grams
Onion, chopped fine	10 ounces	300 grams
Garlic, crushed	1 clove	1 clove
Salt	2 teaspoons	12 grams
Pepper	½ teaspoon	3 grams
Flour	1 ounce	30 grams
Red wine	1¼ cups	3 deciliters
Brown stock	1¾ cups	4 deciliters
Bouquet garni	1	1

Procedure
1. Heat the fat. Add the beef, bacon, onion, and garlic.
2. Cook, stirring occasionally, until the meat juices have been reduced and a glaze has formed.
3. Season the meat. Mix in the flour. Pour in the wine and stock. Add the *bouquet garni.*
4. Cover tightly and simmer the meat for 1½ to 2 hours, until it is tender. Add more liquid during the cooking time if it is needed.
5. Remove the meat pieces from the sauce. Strain the sauce, season to taste, skim off the fat, and pour the sauce over the meat.

Variations of Beef Stew

Beef Stew with Mushrooms—*Estouffade de boeuf aux champignons*

The recipe for beef stew is used for this dish. Mushrooms are sautéed in butter and placed on top of the finished dish.

Beef Stew, Peasant Style—*Estouffade de boeuf à la paysanne*

The recipe for beef stew is used for this dish. The stew is garnished with glazed carrots, turnips, and pearl onions.

17.5 Poaching—*Pocher*

Calf sweetbreads, brains, and amourettes (spinal marrow) are suitable for this form of preparation. The taste of these variety meats is delicate, and therefore boiling is not recommended. Boil court bouillon for 15 minutes. Add skinned and rinsed calf brains or other variety meats, heat to the boiling point, and then poach at about 160°F (70°C).

Deep-Fried Calf's Brains—*Cervelles frites*

Poached brains, cut into slices, are breaded and deep-fried. Rémoulade sauce is served separately.

Calf's Brains in Batter—*Cervelles à l'Orly*

The brains are poached, cooled in court bouillon, and cut into four pieces. These pieces are dipped into frying batter and deep-fried at high temperature. Tomato or rémoulade sauce is served separately.

Calf's Brains in Brown Butter—*Cervelles au beurre noir*

Poached calf's brains are placed on a platter and sprinkled with capers, chopped parsley, and a few drops of vinegar. Brown butter is poured over the top.

Calf's Brains in Noisette Butter—*Cervelles au beurre noisette*

The skinned brains are poached in a seasoned court bouillon with a little vinegar. Capers, chopped parsley, and hot, foaming butter are poured over the brains.

Calf's Brains, Poulette Style—*Cervelles à la poulette*

Poached brains are covered with poulette sauce.

Calf's Sweetbreads, German Style—*Ris de veau à l'allemande*

The sweetbreads are blanched and then poached in white stock. An allemande sauce is made from the stock. The sweetbreads are covered with the sauce and garnished with diced mushrooms and cucumbers.

Poached Breast of Chicken—*Suprêmes de volaille pochés*

Breast of chicken is poached in a reduced chicken stock. A suprême sauce is made from the stock. Serve with truffles, rice, noodles, or with tarragon.

17.6 Boiling—*Bouillir*

The boiling process is used as the first step in preparing some cuts of meat, which are actually simmered, not cooked at a rolling boil. The meat may be in small or large pieces. The salted water or white stock is heated to the boiling point, and the meat is added. The heat is then reduced, and the meat is allowed to simmer until tender. The cooked meat can then be finished by various methods.

17.6.1 Veal Blanquette—*Blanquette de veau*

Yield
approximately 10 servings

Ingredients	U.S. Weight or Volume	Metric Weight or Volume
Veal, boneless shoulder, breast, or neck, cut into 1½-ounce (40-gram) cubes	4½ pounds	2 kilograms
White stock	1 quart	1.2 liters
White wine	1¼ cups	3 deciliters
Salt	2 teaspoons	12 grams
Pepper	½ teaspoon	3 grams
Bouquet garni:		
Onion, chopped	1	1
Carrot, chopped	1	1
Celery, chopped	1 stalk	1 stalk
Parsley	1 ounce	30 grams
Cloves	2	2
Bay leaf	½	½
Butter	2½ ounces	70 grams
Flour	2¾ ounces	80 grams
Egg yolks	3	3
Cream	½ cup	1 deciliter
Lemon juice	2 tablespoons	30 milliliters
Nutmeg	⅛ teaspoon	1 gram
Meat extract	as needed	as needed

Procedure
1. Blanch the veal and let it cool. Add the white stock until the meat is barely covered. Add the wine, salt, pepper, and *bouquet garni.*
2. Cover and simmer for approximately 1½ hours or until the meat is tender.
3. Transfer the meat to a warm platter and strain the broth through a cloth.
4. Make an allemande sauce from the broth, butter, flour, egg yolks, and cream.
5. Do not boil the sauce after you add the *liaison* of cream and egg yolks. Add the meat, lemon juice, and nutmeg.
6. Pour some heated meat extract (*glace de viande*) over the meat and garnish with assorted vegetables.

Variations of Blanquette of Veal

Veal Blanquette with Celery—*Blanquette de veau au céleri*

The recipe for veal blanquette is used but slightly reduced celery stock is added to the sauce and the meat is garnished with cooked celery.

Blanquette of Chicken—*Blanquette de volaille*

The recipe for veal blanquette is followed, using young chicken instead of veal.

Veal Blanquette with Noodles—*Blanquette de veau aux nouilles*

This is a veal blanquette garnished with noodles.

Veal Blanquette Old-fashioned Style—*Blanquette de veal à l'ancienne*

The recipe for veal blanquette is used. Sautéed mushrooms and pearl onions are placed on top of the meat and sauce.

Veal Blanquette in Puff Pastry—*Vol-au-vent de veau*

Veal blanquette is cut into small cubes and served in a vol-au-vent with mushrooms, chicken kidneys, and small onions. (See figure 17-4.)

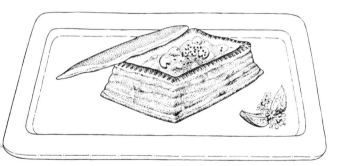

Figure 17-4. Veal blanquette in puff pastry—*Vol-au-vent de veau.*

Veal Blanquette with Rice—*Blanquette de veau au riz*

Veal blanquette is served on a base of white risotto or in a ring of rice.

Simmering Variety Meats

Breaded Calf's Feet—*Pieds de veau panés*

The calf's feet are simmered in water with white wine, seasoning, and a *bouquet garni* until tender. The feet are removed from the stock and allowed to dry. The joint bones are removed. The feet are dusted with flour, coated with egg and bread crumbs, and deep-fried. Tartar sauce is served separately.

Calf's Feet in Batter—*Pieds de veau en fritot*

The calf's feet are halved lengthwise, blanched, drained, and simmered in water with white wine, seasoning, and a *bouquet garni*. The feet are taken out of the stock and the joint bones are removed. The feet are coated with frying batter and deep-fried. Tomato sauce is served separately.

Calf's Head, Turtle Style—*Tête de veau tortue*

A boned calf's head is blanched and cut into large cubes. The meat is simmered in water with a little vinegar, lemon juice, an onion studded with bay leaf and cloves, carrots, *bouquet garni,* salt, and peppercorns. The drained meat is covered with tortue sauce and garnished with mushrooms, little dumplings, and pitted olives. Quartered hard-cooked eggs, pickles, and heart-shaped bread croutons are arranged on the platter around the meat.

Fried Calf's Head—*Tête de veau en fritot*

This dish is prepared by the method described for calf's head, turtle style, except the meat is dried after simmering, dipped into frying batter, and fried in deep fat. Tomato sauce is served separately.

Calf's Head, Poulette Style—*Tête de veau à la poulette*

The meat of the calf's head is simmered, covered with poulette sauce, and garnished with mushrooms and pearl onions. The meat is sprinkled with parsley and surrounded with bread croutons.

Calf's Head with Tomatoes—*Tête de veau aux tomates*

The calf's head is simmered as described for turtle style. It is arranged on a platter and surrounded with tomato slices and pickles. Tomato sauce is served separately.

Calf's Head Vinaigrette—*Tête de veau vinaigrete*

The calf's head is prepared by the method described for turtle style. It is garnished with quartered hard-cooked eggs and pickles. Vinaigrette sauce is served separately.

Calf's Tongue, German Style—*Langue de veau à l'allemande*

The calf's tongue is simmered in a well-seasoned stock. It is carved lengthwise and covered with allemande sauce.

Calf's Tongue with Madeira—*Langue de veau au madère*

The tongue is simmered in a well-seasoned white stock. Before serving, the tongue is peeled, carved lengthwise, and covered with Madeira sauce.

Tripe with Madeira—*Tripes au madère*

Slices of cooked tripe are sautéed with chopped onion, the pan is deglazed with demi-glace, and Madeira is added.

Tripe in Tomato Sauce—*Tripes napolitaine*

The method is the same as for tripe with Madeira, except the pan is deglazed with tomato sauce.

Tripe in White-wine Sauce—*Tripes au vin blanc*

Cooked and sliced tripe is sautéed with chopped onions, dusted with flour, and cooked in white wine and white stock for 30 minutes. Seasonings and caraway seed may be added before serving.

Chapter 18
Main Courses/Main Meat Dishes—*Grosses pièces*

In the classical menu, the term *grosse pièce* refers to the main course served before the entrée. This is a dish made from meat, poultry, or game. The *grosse pièces* differ from entrées in that they are always cooked in one large piece. Formerly, roasts were served as a separate course, following the sherbet. A *grosse pièce* frequently consisted of meat, meaning that the roast course was necessarily poultry or game. In the shortened menu, these two courses are combined, offering a much greater variety. Today, unless a classical menu is being served, the main course is usually carved in the kitchen, where it is also garnished and served on a platter. This course nowadays is very often the only meat dish; therefore, the preparation and presentation should be faultless. Main courses are frequently garnished with vegetables and potatoes and are described on the menu as the "dish of the day." Other than braised meat, these dishes should not be included under the à la carte items, since the quality both in terms of taste and of juiciness would suffer. Gravy or sauce should be served in a sauceboat, when possible, to keep it separate from the garnishes. Modern cookery emphasizes the importance of a variety of carefully prepared, nutritionally adequate dishes in portions of appropriate size. Figure 18-1 shows the different cooking methods for main courses.

18.1 Braising and Glazing—*Braiser et glacer*

Braising and glazing smaller pieces of meat was described in chapter 17. The same method of cooking may be used for cuts of meats up to 4 or 5 pounds (2 or 3 kilograms). Braising is a combination of dry- and moist-heat cookery. In general, this method is used for less tender cuts of meat.

Braising Red Meat

Gently heat fat in a braising pan of proper size. Brown the meat on all sides and remove it from the pan. Then brown a *mirepoix* with pork rinds and calf's feet, add tomato puree, and simmer for a few minutes. Return the meat to the pan and deglaze with wine or a marinade. Reduce the liquid to a syrupy consistency and baste the meat frequently to form a slight glaze. Deglaze with a strong brown stock until the meat pieces are one-quarter covered. Place a tight-fitting lid on the pan and braise in an oven at 300°F (150°C) until the meat is tender. If necessary, add more stock, strain the gravy, heat to the boiling point, skim off the fat, and reduce or thicken with cornstarch as needed. Madeira can also be added.

Note: Most meats in the United States have ade-

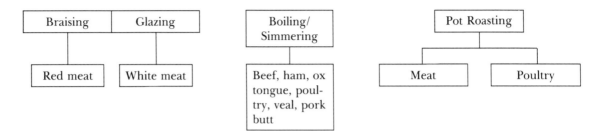

Figure 18-1. The basic cooking methods for hot main dishes.

quate marbling and do not require larding, but larding is suggested for game (venison), which is lean.

Glazing White Meat

Heat fat in a braising pan of the proper size. Add the meat and brown. Add a *mirepoix* and bacon trimmings quickly. Add tomatoes, and continue cooking for a few minutes. Deglaze with white wine, reduce, and add enough brown stock to reach one-sixth of the depth of the meat. Place a tight-fitting lid on the pan and braise the meat until tender, basting frequently. If necessary, add more stock. Remove the lid from the braising pan. Basting continuously, glaze the meat in the oven with the reduced stock. Remove the meat from the pan. Add a little white wine to the glaze and, if necessary, some appropriate stock. Strain the stock and heat to the boiling point. Skim off the fat, thicken slightly with cornstarch, and add Madeira.

All braised white meats should be glazed using a minimum of stock and utensils just large enough to hold the meat. An open braising pan is most suitable.

18.2 Boiling—*Bouillir*

Boiling is a moist-heat method of cookery. The term *boiling* is accepted terminology; however, meat should not be cooked in liquids at 212°F (100°C) for any extended period of time. The temperature of the liquid is lowered when the meat is added. When the temperature reaches the boiling point again, the heat should be reduced so that the meat will continue to simmer,

not boil, until it is tender. The following are examples of meat that may be boiled or simmered:

- Brisket of beef, corned
- Brisket of beef, fresh
- Ham, cured
- Ham hocks
- Ox tongue
- Poultry
- Shoulder or breast of beef or veal
- Smoked pork butt

The size of the pieces and the quality of the meat will determine the cooking time. Smaller or more tender pieces will cook faster, and these should be removed when done. The needle test is one method to check degree of doneness. Push the needle through the meat; if it pulls out easily, the meat is done.

Beef bones should always be placed in cold water. After the boiling point is reached, the heat should be reduced so that the liquid simmers. Stocks should not be covered. Mutton should be blanched before simmering.

Bouquet garni, a spice sachet, salt, or browned onions may be boiled along with the meat.

18.3 Pot Roasting or Casserole Roasting—*Poêlage*

This is a slow cooking method, particularly suitable for tender cuts of meat and poultry. The food is cooked in a container with a tight-fitting lid (casserole) in a generous amount of butter or oil with a small quantity of stock.

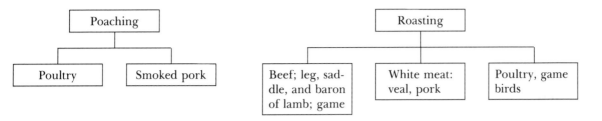

Figure 18-1. *continued.*

Pot-roasting Meat

Spread a *mirepoix* and bacon trimmings on the bottom of the braising pan. Place seasonings and the meat, larded when appropriate, on top. Add fat and lightly stew the meat in the oven. Then cover and place in the oven at 300°F (150°C), basting occasionally. Remove the lid and brown the meat in a hot oven. Then remove the meat, pour a little brown stock into the braising pan, and reduce with the *mirepoix* to the desired consistency or thicken slightly with cornstarch. Strain and heat the stock to the boiling point, skim the fat, and add Madeira.

Pot-roasting Poultry

Cover the bottom of a braising pan with *mirepoix* and diced lean bacon. Place the seasoned poultry, barded if necessary, on top. Pour clarified butter over the poultry, stew lightly, and then cover and finish the stewing in the oven, basting frequently. Remove the poultry. Deglaze with red or white wine, depending on the sauce that will accompany the dish. Add more stock and strain. Heat to the boiling point, skim the fat, and reduce before mixing in the demi-glace or Madeira sauce.

18.4 Poaching—*Pocher*

Poaching Poultry

Blanch the dressed and trussed poultry. Add a *bouquet garni*, spice sachet, stock, and white wine. Heat to the boiling point, reduce the heat, skim the stock, and poach at 160° to 175°F (70° to 80°C) until the meat is tender.

Some of the stock is used to prepare a suprême sauce, which is served with the poultry.

Poaching Smoked Pork

Place the pork in cold water and heat until the temperature reaches 160° to 175°F (70° to 80°C). Allow 20 minutes cooking time per pound (450 grams).

18.5 Roasting—*Rôtir*

The term *roasting* was originally applied to the cooking of large cuts of meat on a spit over an open fire. This method of cooking is now called barbecuing or spit-roasting. As used today, the term *roasting* refers to cooking in the oven in an uncovered container with little or no added liquid.

The fat content of the meat will determine whether additional fats or oils are required. Very lean cuts of meat are sometimes larded or barded before roasting. Since today there is a trend toward producing meat with less marbling or fat, the flavor and juiciness of very lean cuts of meat can be improved by larding or barding. *Larding* is the insertion of thin strips of fatback into the meat. *Barding* involves covering lean cuts of meat with slices of salt pork or unsalted fatback or bacon to prevent burning or drying out of the meat. Barding is most frequently used in the preparation of poultry and game birds.

Roasting Red Meat

Select a roasting pan of the appropriate size, possibly with a rack. Remove the roast from the refrigerator 2 hours before roasting. Season the roast. Preheat the oven to 500°F (260°C). Insert a meat thermometer into the thickest part of the muscle so that the tip does not touch fat or bone. Place the meat in the oven, fat side up, on a rack in a roasting pan. Reduce the temperature to 225° to 350°F (110° to 175°C)—the exact setting depends on the size and type of meat. Roast for 18 to 20 minutes per pound (450 grams) for medium rare. Baste frequently with the meat juices. When the meat is done, drain the fat carefully so that the drippings remain. Deglaze the pan with wine and stock, and heat the liquids to the boiling point. Skim the fat and strain before seasoning. Meat roasted English style (rare) should be accompanied by a natural gravy, served separately. The degree of doneness can be determined by applying pressure with the fingers, the needle test, a meat thermometer, or time-weight ratio.

Beef tenderloin, roast beef, rump, leg of lamb, and game (with the exception of wild boar) are the most suitable types of red meat for roasting English style (rare). Roast beef can also be roasted on the spit or in a convection oven. Meat should be at room temperature when placed in the oven. All roasts should stand for 20 to 30 minutes before carving. Always start carving on the thinner side.

Roasting White Meat

Remove the meat from the refrigerator 30 minutes before roasting. Season the pieces of meat. Preheat the oven to 450°F (225°C). Sear and brown the meat quickly. Reduce the heat to 300° to 350°F (150° to 180°C), depending on the size and type of meat, and continue roasting. Baste frequently with the pan drippings.

A *mirepoix,* consisting of fresh onion, celery, and carrots, is usually added to the meat during the roasting process. White meat loses more of its juices during cooking than other types of meat. Therefore, a good gravy that complements the flavor of the meat is necessary. When the meat is done, remove it from the pan, drain the fat, deglaze the pan with wine and then with stock. Cook the gravy with the *mirepoix.* Madeira can then be added. The degree of doneness can be determine by applying pressure with the fingers, the needle test, a meat thermometer, or time-weight ratio.

Veal, pork, and suckling pig are all considered white meat. All types of white meat should be sufficiently cooked. Pork must be cooked sufficiently to kill a parasite, found in the muscle of some pork, that may be transmitted to man, that causes a disease called trichinosis. The parasite is killed at 137°F (58°C). Pork will be soft when roasted to 170°F and yet will not be dried out. Fatty pieces of pork are often braised with a little hot water, instead of being roasted. The flavor of veal is improved if it is roasted in the bottom of a roasting pan so it may absorb the meat juice.

Roasting Poultry

Heat fat and place the seasoned bird in the pan on its side. Roast in the oven, basting frequently. Turn the bird so it rests for part of the time on back, breast, and each side, for even browning. Toward the end of cooking, set it breast up, especially if it is to be served whole, so the top is beautifully browned and glazed from the basting. Draining internal juices onto a plate shows when the bird is done. The juice should be absolutely clear. A *mirepoix* can be added at the last moment. Remove the bird from the pan, drain off the fat, deglaze the pan with wine and drippings, heat to the boiling point, and skim the fat. Strain the gravy and season to taste. Brown butter may be poured over the finished dish. Serve the gravy separately.

Young poultry is best suited for roasting. Pot roasting is preferred for such poultry as capon and large roasters. Roasting maybe done in an oven, on a spit, or in an automatic convection oven. The bird will retain more of its juices and it will be easier to carve if it stands for 15 to 20 minutes before serving.

Roasting Game Birds

Feathered game should be barded to prevent the breast from drying out. Roast the bird in an oven at

450° to 500°F (235° to 255°C) and baste throughout the roasting time. The smaller the bird, the shorter the roasting time. Doneness may be tested with a thermometer in large birds. If the drumstick bone twists easily on broilers, they are usually done. The plate test may also be used. The juice and the flesh will both be a pink color when the bird is done. Remove the slices of bacon from the bird and baste at regular intervals to brown the breast. Then remove the bird from the pan, drain off the fat, and deglaze the pan with wine and game stock. Heat the cooking liquid to the boiling point, skim the fat, thicken with cream or sour cream, strain, and season to taste. The slices of bacon may be cut into strips, lightly browned, and placed on top of the bird. Serve the sauce separately.

Binding the sauce with cream is not necessary; however, it does improve the flavor. Flaming with brandy when serving is recommended.

Older game birds are better when lightly braised and prepared as *salmis.*

Oven Baking

Oven baking is a dry-heat method of cooking, similar to roasting. Precooked (fried or poached) meat is wrapped in dough (puff pastry, pâté dough, or brioche dough) and baked. Fillets and roasts of beef, leg of lamb, ribs and fillets of pork, hams, fillets of veal, fillets of venison, and all types of poultry may be prepared in this way.

Wrap the dough around the meat; use trimmings from the dough to decorate. Brush with egg wash, and place on a baking sheet or in an appropriate mold. Choose baking time and temperature based on the cut of meat. After baking, allow the meat to rest for 15 to 30 minutes before cutting or serving. Serve a complementary sauce on the side.

18.6 Main Beef Dishes

18.6.1 Braised Beef—*Boeuf braisé*

Yield
approximately 10 servings

Ingredients	U.S. Weight or Volume	Metric Weight or Volume
Beef rump, round, shoulder, or short ribs	4½ pounds	2 kilograms
Larding bacon	5 ounces	150 grams
Fat *or* oil	1¾ ounces	50 grams
Mirepoix	7 ounces	200 grams
Bacon trimmings	2 ounces	60 grams
Tomato puree	1¾ ounces	50 grams
Salt	2 teaspoons	12 grams
Pepper	½ teaspoon	3 grams
Red wine *or* marinade	¾ cup	2 deciliters
Brown stock	1 quart	1 liter
Cornstarch (optional)	1 to 2 teaspoons	6 to 12 grams
Madeira	¼ cup	50 milliliters

Procedure
1. Lard the meat with strips of bacon.
2. Brown the meat in melted fat. Brown the *mirepoix* and bacon.
3. Add the tomato puree, salt, and pepper.
4. Deglaze the pan with the wine or marinade. Reduce the liquid until it has a syrupy consistency.
5. Add the brown stock.
6. Cover the pan and braise the meat until tender. Turn occasionally.
7. Remove the meat from the pan. Reduce the sauce to the desired consistency; if necessary, bind with cornstarch. Strain and skim the fat. Add Madeira to taste.
8. Pour a small quantity of sauce over the carved meat before serving.

Note: Most vegetables, pasta, polenta, and steamed or mashed potatoes are excellent garnishes.

Other Braised Beef Dishes

Braised Beef, Bourgeoise Style—*Boeuf à la bourgeoise*

Lard the rump and prepare initially like braised beef. After half the cooking time, add carrots, turnips, and pearl onions directly to the sauce; or cook the vegetables separately and add when the dish is ready to serve.

Braised Beef with Noodles—*Boeuf braisé aux nouilles*

Braise larded rump of beef and garnish with noodles.

Braised Beef, Piedmont Style—*Boeuf braisé à la piémontaise*

Follow the method for braising beef and serve the meat with a white risotto topped with a few sautéed mushrooms.

18.6.2 Braised Beef, Modern Style—*Boeuf à la mode*

Yield
approximately 10 servings

Ingredients	U.S. Weight or Volume	Metric Weight or Volume
Beef rump	4½ pounds	2 kilograms
Larding bacon	5 ounces	150 grams
Red wine	¾ cup	2 deciliters
Fat *or* oil	1¾ ounces	50 grams
Mirepoix	7 ounces	200 grams
Bacon	2 ounces	60 grams
Calf's feet, blanched	1 to 2	1 to 2
Brown stock	1 quart	1 liter
Tomato puree	1¾ ounces	50 grams
Salt	½ teaspoon	3 grams
Pepper	½ teaspoon	3 grams
Garnish:		
Carrots	7 ounces	200 grams
Celery	7 ounces	200 grams
Turnips	7 ounces	200 grams
Pearl onions	5 ounces	150 grams
Butter	1¾ ounces	50 grams

Procedure
1. Lard the beef rump with finger-thick strips of bacon.

2. Marinate in the wine for a few hours.
3. Brown the meat on all sides over medium heat. Brown the *mirepoix,* bacon, and calf's feet.
4. Deglaze the pan with the marinade. Reduce the liquid until it has a syrupy consistency.
5. Add the brown stock, tomato puree, and salt.
6. Cover the pan and braise until meat is three-quarters done.
7. Strain the stock. Add the garnish and the strained stock to the meat and finish braising together.
8. Reduce the stock to the desired consistency. Season to taste.
9. Cut the calf's feet into strips and return to the pan.
10. Cover the meat with the sauce and garnishes and serve.

Note: The vegetable garnishes may be cooked separately and added to the meat when it is served.

18.6.3 Boiled Beef—*Boeuf bouilli*

Yield
approximately 10 servings

Ingredients	U.S. Weight or Volume	Metric Weight or Volume
Beef short ribs, top round, or chuck	5½ pounds	2.5 kilograms
Beef bones	2 pounds	1 kilogram
Marrow bones	10 pieces	10 pieces
Bouquet garni	1 pound	500 grams
Salt, coarse	1 teaspoon	5 grams
Parsley, chopped	2 tablespoons	30 grams
Bouillon	to cover	to cover

Procedure
1. Cut the meat into two equal portions.
2. Blanch the beef bones. Place in cold water in a stockpot and bring to a boil.
3. Add the meat pieces. Skim and add the *bouquet garni.*
4. Simmer slowly and skim occasionally.
5. Cook for 2 to 2½ hours, or until meat is tender.

6. Combine the coarse salt and chopped parsley.
7. Before serving, cover the sliced beef with bouillon and sprinkle the salt and parsley mixture over the top.

Note: As garnishes the following items would be excellent: various vegetable salads, gherkins, radishes, pickled cucumbers, horseradish, and mustard.

Other Boiled Beef Dishes

Boiled Beef, Alsatian Style—*Boeuf bouilli à l'alsacienne*

Garnish boiled beef with sauerkraut and cover with slices of lean bacon. Serve boiled potatoes and horseradish sauce separately.

Boiled Beef, Flemish Style—*Boeuf bouilli à la flamande*

Garnish boiled beef with bouquets of carrots, turnips, and cabbage. Cover the cabbage with slices of lean bacon. Serve boiled potatoes and horseradish sauce separately.

Boiled Beef with Onion Sauce au Gratin—*Miroton de boeuf*

Coat the bottom of a gratin dish with Lyonnaise sauce. Place the slices of boiled beef in the dish in a symmetrical pattern and cover with onion sauce. Sprinkle with breadcrumbs and melted butter and gratinate in the oven.

18.6.4 Beef Tongue—*Langue de boeuf*

Yield
approximately 10 servings

Ingredients	U.S. Weight or Volume	Metric Weight or Volume
Beef tongue, salted or smoked	3 to 4 pounds	1½ to 2 kilograms

Procedure
1. Soak the tongue in lukewarm water overnight.
2. Blanch and then simmer for 3 hours, until tender.
3. Remove the tongue from the kettle and plunge into cold water. Skin. Return the tongue to the stock.

Note: Tongue loses less weight and is juicier when cooked in a pressure cooker. Serve Madeira or piquante sauce with the meat. Fresh beef tongue can also be cooked like boiled beef and served with caper or mushroom sauce.

Other Beef Tongue Dishes

Beef Tongue, Breton Style—*Langue de boeuf à la bretonne*

Cook a salted (pickled) beef tongue and serve with navy beans or lima beans. Sprinkle the beans with parsley and cover the tongue with Madeira sauce. Serve additional sauce separately.

Beef Tongue with Capers—*Langue de boeuf aux câpres*

Cook a fresh (unsalted) tongue, carve, cover with caper sauce, and garnish.

Beef Tongue, Florentine Style—*Langue de boeuf à la florentine*

Cook salted (pickled) tongue, carve, serve on a platter of spinach, covered with Madeira sauce. Serve additional Madeira sauce in a sauceboat.

Beef Tongue with Green Beans—*Langue de boeuf aux haricots verts*

Cook a salted (pickled) tongue, garnish with green beans, and cover with Madeira sauce. Serve more sauce separately.

Beef Tongue with Spinach—*Lange de boeuf aux épinards*

Cook a salted (pickled) tongue and serve garnished with creamed spinach. Glaze the tongue with a little Madeira sauce and serve more sauce separately in a sauceboat. A spicy brown sauce may be served instead of Madeira sauce.

18.6.5 Beef Wellington—*Filet de boeuf Wellington*

Yield
10 to 12 servings

Ingredients	U.S. Weight or Volume	Metric Weight or Volume
Beef tenderloin, whole, trimmed	5 pounds	2.5 kilograms
Larding bacon	10 ounces	300 grams
Oil	1¾ ounces	50 grams
Forcemeat:		
Duxelles	7 ounces	200 grams
Truffles, chopped	3	3
Goose liver, pureed	7 ounces	200 grams
Pork	10 ounces	300 grams
Eggs	2 to 3	2 to 3
Port wine	as needed	as needed
Salt	½ teaspoon	3 grams
Pepper	¼ teaspoon	1 gram
Puff pastry	1 pound	500 grams
Egg	1	1

Procedure
1. Use the tenderloin without the tip and without the head.
2. Lard the tenderloin with some of the bacon. Brown on all sides in an oven at 500°F (255°C) for about 20 minutes.
3. Allow the tenderloin to stand until cool enough to touch.
4. Prepare the forcemeat by grinding the duxelles, truffles, goose liver, and pork very finely. Mix with eggs, desired seasoning, and enough port wine to give the mixture a spreadable consistency.
5. Spread the forcemeat over the tenderloin to a thickness of ½ inch (1 centimeter).
6. Wrap the tenderloin in thin slices of larding bacon.
7. Roll the puff pastry into a rectangle about 1½ inches larger than the tenderloin in length and width. Place the tenderloin in the center of the dough and seal the dough around the tenderloin. Decorate with strips of puff pastry. Brush with slightly beaten egg. Let stand for a few minutes.
8. Finish baking in the oven at 400°F (200°C) for 30 to 40 minutes. The proper degree of doneness can best be determined by using a meat thermometer. When an internal temperature of 120°F (50°C) is reached, the fillet is rare.
9. Remove from oven and allow to stand for 15 to 20 minutes before serving. (See figure 18-2.)

Note: Pie pastry made without too much butter may be used instead of puff pastry. Serve truffle sauce separately with the beef Wellington.

Garnishes for Beef Tenderloin, Roast Beef, and Rump Roast

Beef tenderloin, roast beef, and rump roast are prepared by following roasting or pot-roasting procedures. Tenderloins and rump roasts should be larded.

Andalusian Style—*andalouse*

For roasts. Surround roast beef with stuffed eggplant, grilled tomatoes, and chipolata sausages. Serve meat juices separately.

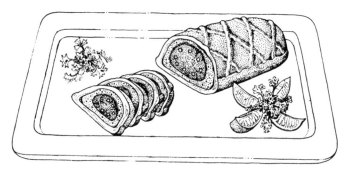

Figure 18-2. Beef Wellington—*Filet de boeuf Wellington.*

with Cauliflower—*Dubarry*

For roasts. Surround the roast with cauliflower bouquets. Serve meat juices separately.

Duchess Style—*duchesse*

For pot roasts. Surround the meat with duchess potatoes. Serve Madeira sauce separately.

Garden Style—*jardinière*

For roasts. Surround the roast with bouquets of various vegetables. Serve meat juices separately. (See figure 18-3.)

London House Style—*London House*

For tenderloin. Cut larded tenderloin lengthwise to its center and fill with strips of truffles and goose liver. Then close the slit at the top, bard with thin slices of larding bacon, tie with string, and pot-roast in the oven. Garnish with mushrooms and truffles. Serve truffle sauce separately. (See figure 18-4.)

Lorette—*Lorette*

For pot roasts. Garnish with potatoes Lorette and asparagus spears. Serve demi-glace separately.

with Mixed Vegetables—*macédoine*

For roasts. Garnish the roast with a macédoine of vegetables. Serve meat juices separately.

Figure 18-3. Roast beef, garden style—*jardinière*.

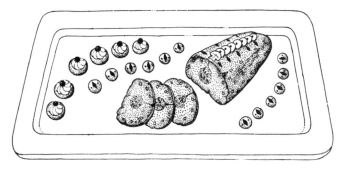

Figure 18-4. Beef tenderloin, London House style.

Nivernese Style—*nivernaise*

For roasts. Surround the roast with bouquets of glazed pearl onions, glazed carrots, and turnips. Serve meat juices separately.

Parisian Style—*parisienne*

For pot roasts. Garnish the meat with artichoke hearts and Parisian potatoes. Serve Madeira sauce separately.

with Potato Croquettes—*dauphine*

For pot roasts. Surround the meat with croquettes made from dauphine potato mixture. Serve Madeira sauce separately.

Provence Style—*provençale*

For pot roasts. Garnish with tomatoes, Provence style, and mushrooms. Serve demi-glace separately.

with Spring Vegetables—*printanière*

For roasts. Arrange glazed carrots, turnips, pearl onions, bouquets of asparagus spears, and peas around the roast. Serve meat juices separately.

Tivoli—*Tivoli*

For roasts. Garnish the meat with asparagus spears and mushrooms. Serve meat juices separately.

with Tomatoes—*portugaise*

For pot roasts. Garnish with tomatoes stuffed with duxelles and château potatoes. Serve Madeira sauce separately.

with Vegetable Bouquets—*bouquetière*

For roasts. Surround roast beef with bouquets of various vegetables. Serve meat juices separately.

Yorkshire

For roasts. Serve Yorkshire pudding with the roast (recipe follows).

Yorkshire Pudding

Yield
approximately 10 servings

Ingredients	U.S. Weight or Volume	Metric Weight or Volume
Beef kidney fat, chopped fine	8½ ounces	250 grams
Flour	14 ounces	400 grams
Milk	2½ to 3 cups	6 to 8 deciliters
Egg yolks	5	5
Salt	1 teaspoon	4 grams
Pepper	¼ teaspoon	1 gram
Egg whites	5	5
Drippings from roast beef (fat only)	8 ounces	240 grams

Procedure
1. Preheat the oven to 400°F (200°C).
2. Combine the finely chopped kidney fat with the flour.
3. Add the milk, egg yolks, salt, and pepper to the flour mixture. Stir until very thick.
4. When ready to bake, fold the stiffly beaten egg whites into the batter.
5. Heat a roasting pan containing the beef drippings.
6. Pour batter into the pan. Batter should be no more than 1 inch deep.

7. Bake pudding for 20 minutes. Reduce the heat to 350°F (175°C) and bake for 15 to 20 minutes longer, until golden brown.
8. Cut the Yorkshire pudding into diamond-shaped pieces and use to garnish the roast beef.

Note: Individual puddings may be made in tart pans or muffin tins.

18.7 Main Veal Dishes

18.7.1 Stuffed Breast of Veal—*Poitrine de veau farcie*

Yield
10 servings

Ingredients	U.S. Weight or Volume	Metric Weight or Volume
Breast of veal	5 to 6 pounds	2.5 to 3 kilograms
Forcemeat:		
Bread, white	1 pound	500 grams
Milk	¾ cup	2 deciliters
Onion, chopped fine	7 ounces	200 grams
Butter	1¾ ounces	50 grams
Parsley, chopped	2 tablespoons	30 grams
Raw veal *and/or* pork	1½ pounds	700 grams
Eggs	2	2
Salt	1 teaspoon	6 grams
Thyme	¼ teaspoon	1 gram
Pepper	½ teaspoon	2 grams
Butter	as needed	as needed
Shortening	3½ ounces	100 grams

Procedure
1. Bone the breast of veal and remove the cartilage. Cut an opening in the meat, starting on the thinner side, and cut through to the clod tip. (See figure 7-22.)
2. Soak the bread in the milk. Press to remove excess milk.
3. Sauté chopped onion in butter. Add the bread and parsley and stir until dry. Cool.

4. Grind the pork and/or veal. Add eggs, salt, thyme, and pepper. Add to the forcemeat and blend.
5. Stuff the forcemeat into the opening in the veal and sew up the pocket with a coarse needle and thread. Rub the meat with butter.
6. Brown the breast in the shortening. Glaze the meat in a covered pan with a very small amount of moisture. Add moisture only as needed. Cook until the internal temperature reaches 170°F (77°C).

Note: Different stuffings may be used such as a bread filling; a filling consisting of one-third panada and two-thirds forcemeat; or any special forcemeat. Garnishes include ham, strips or cubes of bacon, green peppers, blanched spinach, sautéed mushrooms, or hard-cooked eggs.

Other Breast of Veal Dishes

Breast of Veal, Home Style—*Poitrine de veau à la bourgeoise*

Bone and pound the breast, season, roll, tie with string, and glaze in the oven. Thicken the stock and pour it onto the carved breast; garnish with pearl onions, carrots, and turnips.

Glazed Breast of Veal—*Poitrine de veau glacée*

Bone the breast and glaze in the oven. Serve sauce separately.

18.7.2 Saddle of Veal Metternich—
Selle de veau Metternich

Yield
10 servings

Ingredients	U.S. Weight or Volume	Metric Weight or Volume
Saddle of veal	6 to 7 pounds	3 to 3.5 kilograms
Fat	3½ ounces	100 grams
Salt	1 teaspoon	6 grams
Pepper	¼ teaspoon	2 grams

Ingredients	U.S. Weight or Volume	Metric Weight or Volume
Mirepoix	as needed	as needed
Wine	as needed	as needed
Brown stock	as needed	as needed
Béchamel sauce	1¼ cups	3 deciliters
Truffles, sliced thin	30 slices	30 slices
Onion sauce	10 ounces	300 grams
Goose liver	3½ to 7 ounces	100 to 200 grams
Mornay sauce	1 quart	1 liter

Procedure
1. Remove the tendons of the saddle. Trim, tie, salt, and season the meat. Glaze in the oven, with *mirepoix*, wine, and brown stock. After the meat is fully cooked, cool it for 15 to 20 minutes.
2. Remove the fillets from the bone and slice. Coat the backbone with béchamel sauce. Arrange the slices along the backbone. Place a slice of truffle and some onion sauce mixed with goose liver on each slice.
3. Pour the Mornay sauce evenly over the saddle and gratinate in the oven for a few minutes.
4. Garnish with glazed vegetables.
5. Serve sauce separately.

Other Saddle of Veal Dishes

Saddle of Veal, Forester Style—*Selle de veau à la forestière*

Roast the saddle, remove the fillets, slice, and replace. Garnish with morels; diced, blanched, and browned bacon; and sautéed potato cubes. Serve duxelles sauce separately.

Saddle of Veal Orloff—*Selle de veau orlov*

This is prepared with the same recipe used for Metternich. Slices of truffles and some goose liver are placed between the fillets. Pureed onion is added to Mornay sauce, and it is served separately. The meat is garnished with asparagus tips and braised cucumbers.

Garnishes for Saddle, Loin, Fillet, and Tenderloin of Veal

with Asparagus—*Argenteuil*

Garnish with asparagus spears and noisette potatoes. Serve sauce separately.

with Cauliflower—*Dubarry*

Garnish with cauliflower. Serve sauce made with veal stock separately.

Flemish Style—*à la flamande*

Garnish with braised chicory (endive) and château potatoes. Serve sauce separately.

Garden Style—*à la jardinière*

Surround with bouquets of different vegetables. Prepare a sauce with veal stock and serve separately.

with Lettuce—*aux laitues*

Garnish with braised lettuce. Serve sauce separately.

Lorette—*Lorette*

Garnish with asparagus spears and Lorette potatoes. Serve sauce made from veal stock separately.

with Mixed Vegetables—*à la macédoine*

Garnish with mixed vegetables (carrots, turnips, peas, and beans). Serve sauce separately.

with Noodles—*aux nouilles*

Garnish with buttered noodles. Serve sauce separately.

Piedmont Style—*à la piémontaise*

Garnish with a white risotto and place sautéed mushrooms on top. Serve sauce separately.

Figure 18-5. Veal loin with spring vegetables—*à la printanière.*

Provence Style—*à la provençale*

Surround with tomatoes, Provence style. Serve sauce separately.

with Spinach—*à la florentine*

Serve on a base of cooked spinach and surround with sauce.

with Spring Vegetables—*à la printainière*

Surround with bouquets of various young vegetables. Serve sauce separately. (See figure 18-5.)

with Timbales—*en timbale*

Garnish with individual molds of rice, spinach, and carrot puree. Serve sauce separately.

18.8 Main Pork Dishes

18.8.1 Braised Smoked Ham—*Jambon braisé*

Yield
approximately 20 to 25 servings

Ingredients	*U.S. Weight or Volume*	*Metric Weight or Volume*
Smoked ham	10 to 12 pounds	5 to 6 kilograms
White wine	1 pint	5 deciliters
Madeira wine	1¼ cups	3 deciliters
Demi-glace	1 quart	1 liter

Procedure

1. Place ham in a large kettle and cover with cold water. Cover and simmer for 2½ to 3 hours. Drain. Remove rind and excess fat.
2. Braise ham in a suitable pan with the wine and Madeira for another hour, turning it from time to time.
3. Bring the stock in the pan to the boiling point and skim the fat. If necessary, reduce and then add the demi-glace.
4. Season the sauce as desired. Bring back to a boil and strain.

Other Smoked Ham Dishes

Boiled Ham with Sauerkraut—*Jambon à la choucroute*

Poach the ham. Garnish with sauerkraut and boiled potatoes. Serve Madeira sauce blended with white wine separately.

Braised Ham, Burgundy Style—*Jambon braisé à la bourguignonne*

Braise the ham and garnish with mushrooms. Serve Madeira sauce mixed with reduced braising stock separately.

Braised Ham with Lettuce—*Jambon braisé au laitue*

Braise the ham and surround with steamed lettuce. Serve demi-glace sauce blended with the reduced braising stock separately.

Braised Ham, Milanese Style—*Jambon braisé milanaise*

Braise the ham and garnish with spaghetti, Milanese style. Serve demi-glace sauce blended with tomato puree and the reduced braising stock separately.

Braised Ham with Spinach—*Jambon braisé aux épinards*

Braise the ham and garnish with buttered spinach or creamed spinach. Serve demi-glace sauce blended with the reduced braising pan stock separately.

18.8.2 Ham in Pastry—*Jambon en croûte*

Yield
approximately 20 servings

Ingredients	U.S. Weight or Volume	Metric Weight or Volume
Ham	15 to 20 pounds	7 to 9 kilograms
Water	1 quart	1 liter
Yeast	3½ ounces	100 grams
Salt	1 ounce	30 grams
Flour	5½ pounds	2.5 kilograms

Procedure

1. Soak the ham in water for 1 day.
2. To make the pastry, heat the water to 75°F (25°C). Add the yeast and salt and stir until dissolved.
3. Place the flour in a large bowl. Add the yeast and water mixture to flour. Stir until blended. Knead the dough vigorously for about 10 minutes.
4. Allow the dough to rise, covered, in a warm place for about 3 hours before using.
5. Rinse the ham with water and scrub with a brush.
6. Poach the ham until three-quarters done. Let it cool in the poaching liquid.
7. Dry the ham.
8. Roll out dough and place ham in the center. Enclose the ham with the dough. Seal the edges.
9. Bake in the oven at 450°F (225°C) for 25 minutes per pound of meat. Cover with aluminum foil for half of the baking time.
10. Allow the meat to rest for at least 30 minutes before cutting.

Note: The degree of doneness is best checked with a meat thermometer. Allow 1 hour of baking time for

continued

the first 2 pounds, 20 minutes for each additional pound. The following garnishes are suitable: a platter of different salads, pickles, mixed pickles, gherkins, or leaf spinach with grapes and roasted pine nuts. Serve Madeira sauce separately.

Garnishes for Loin, Fillet, Tenderloin, Shoulder, and Neck of Pork

Boulangère Style—*boulangère*

Serve on boulangère potatoes.

with Chestnuts—*aux marrons*

Garnish with glazed chestnuts.

Garden Style—*jardinière*

Surround the meat with bouquets of various vegetables.

German Style—*à l'allemande*

Serve with stewed apples or applesauce.

with Red Cabbage—*au chou rouge*

Serve with braised red cabbage.

Swedish Style—*à la suédoise*

Roast with presoaked prunes. Serve cranberry sauce separately.

with Braised White Cabbage—*au chou blanc braisé*

Serve with braised white cabbage.

18.9 Main Lamb or Mutton Dishes

18.9.1 Stuffed Shoulder of Lamb—*Ballottine d'agneau*

Yield
6 to 8 portions

Ingredients	*U.S. Weight or Volume*	*Metric Weight or Volume*
Lamb shoulder	6 pounds	3 kilograms
Stuffing:		
Veal	7 ounces	200 grams
Pork	7 ounces	200 grams
Bacon, lean diced	7 ounces	200 grams
Onions, chopped	1¾ ounces	50 grams
Garlic	½ clove	½ clove
Salt	1 teaspoon	6 grams
Seasonings	as needed	as needed
Parsley, chopped	8 sprigs	8 sprigs
Eggs	1 to 2	1 to 2
Oil	2 ounces	60 milliliters
Salt	2 teaspoons	12 grams
Pepper	½ teaspoon	2 grams
Rosemary	1 teaspoon	4 grams
Mirepoix:		
Onions, chopped	3 ounces	100 grams
Celery, chopped	2 ounces	50 grams
Carrots, chopped	2 ounces	50 grams
Wine	½ cup	1 deciliter
Brown stock	2½ cups	750 milliliters

Procedure
1. Flatten the boned shoulder. Spread with the prepared stuffing. Roll the shoulder and the stuffing. Tie securely with butcher's twine.
2. Rub the rolled lamb with oil, salt, pepper, and rosemary. Roast in oven at 325°F (165°C) for about 1 hour.
3. Turn roast and add *mirepoix*. Roast to an internal temperature of 180°F (80°C).
4. Remove the meat. Drain the fat into a saucepan and add flour to make a roux. Cook for 10 minutes, browning lightly.

5. Deglaze the roasting pan with wine and stock. Simmer until vegetables are tender. Strain.
6. Add strained stock to cooked *roux* and cook until thickened and smooth. Adjust seasoning.

18.9.2 Leg of Lamb, English Style—*Gigot d'agneau à l'anglaise*

Yield

approximately 8 servings

Ingredients	U.S. Weight or Volume	Metric Weight or Volume
Leg of lamb	1 leg, 5 pounds	1 leg, 2.5 kilograms
Bouquet garni	10 ounces	300 grams
Salt	1 teaspoon	4 grams
Peppercorns, crushed	6	6
Carrots, sliced	14 ounces	400 grams
Turnips, chopped	14 ounces	400 grams
Cabbage, chopped	14 ounces	400 grams
Green beans	14 ounces	400 grams
Stock	as needed	as needed
Caper sauce	as needed	as needed

Procedure
1. Blanch the lamb.
2. Simmer the lamb over low heat with the *bouquet garni,* the salt, and peppercorns until tender, for approximately 2½ hours.
3. Cook the vegetables in the stock. Arrange them in bouquets around the sliced lamb.
4. Pour a small amount of the stock over lamb and vegetables.
5. Serve caper sauce separately.

Note: The leg of lamb may also be served with a puree of turnips, celery, and potatoes, or beans. The vegetables may be cooked with the meat and then pureed.

18.9.3 Leg of Lamb, Boulangère Style—*Gigot d'agneau à la boulangère*

Yield

8 servings

Ingredients	U.S. Weight or Volume	Metric Weight or Volume
Leg of lamb	6 pounds	3 kilograms
Oil	2 ounces	60 milliliters
Marjoram	¼ teaspoon	1 gram
Thyme	¼ teaspoon	1 gram
Rosemary	¼ teaspoon	1 gram
Garlic	1 clove	1 clove
Potatoes, sliced	4 pounds	2 kilograms
Salt	1 teaspoon	6 grams
Pepper	½ teaspoon	3 grams
Onions, sliced	7 ounces	200 grams
Butter	1¾ ounces	50 grams

Procedure
1. Preheat the oven to 450°F (230°C).
2. Rub the lamb with oil, marjoram, thyme, rosemary, and garlic.
3. Insert a meat thermometer in center of meat. Place meat fat side up in a roasting pan. Reduce heat to 325°F (165°C) and roast for 1 hour.
4. Season sliced raw potatoes with salt and pepper and place in pan with lamb. Add onion.
5. Continue roasting until the meat reaches an internal temperature of 180°F (80°C).
6. Arrange the potatoes in a layer and place the carved meat on top. Coat with butter. Serve juices separately.

Saddle of Lamb—*Selle d'agneau*

Roast a saddle of lamb until rare (the English fashion). Young spring vegetables (mushroom caps with glazed pearl onions, tomatoes, leaf spinach) may be used as garnishes. A baron of lamb is the whole saddle with both legs attached. It is roasted in one piece, like a saddle.

Garnishes for Saddle, Baron, Loin,
and Leg of Lamb

Breton Style—*à la bretonne*

Prepare navy beans or lima beans and use as a garnish or an accompaniment for sliced lamb, roasted or braised. Serve meat juices separately.

with Green Beans—*aux haricots verts*

Sauté blanched green beans in butter and serve as a garnish or an accompaniment for roasted or braised meat. Serve meat juices in a sauceboat.

with Puréed Onions—*à la soubise*

For roasts. Serve with soubise sauce.

with Spinach—*aux épinards*

Use creamed spinach or spinach timbales as a garnish or an accompaniment for roasted meat. Serve meat juices separately.

18.10 Main Poultry Dishes

Chicken—Poulet

Chicken can be pot-roasted, poached, or roasted. The following are methods of serving chicken and capon.

Beaulieu—*beaulieu*

For roasts or pot roasts. Deglaze the pan with white wine, add demi-glace, boil, and strain. Garnishes include artichokes, olives, and quartered tomatoes. Serve sauce separately.

in a Cassserole—*en casserole*

Pot-roast without *mirepoix,* but with diced bacon. Just before serving, add preglazed carrots, turnips, and pearl onions. Deglaze casserole with Madeira and demi-glace. Serve the carved bird in a casserole covered with the sauce and vegetables. Sprinkle chopped parsley on top.

in Cocotte, Grandmother's Style—*en cocotte à la grand-mère*

Pot-roast with diced bacon. For the last few minutes, add preglazed onions and quartered mushrooms and cook with the chicken. Deglaze cocotte with Madeira and stock. Serve the carved chicken with the garnishes in a cocotte. Sprinkle bread croutons fried in butter and parsley over the top.

Demidoff—*Demidov*

For roasts or pot roasts. Deglaze casserole with Madeira or stock, reduce to the desired consistency, and strain. Garnishes or accompaniments include glazed celery, carrots, and turnips arranged in bouquets. Place slices of truffles on the top of the bird. Serve the sauce separately.

Farmer Style—*à la fermière*

For roasts or pot roasts. Deglaze the pan with white wine, add demi-glace, heat to the boiling point, and strain. Garnishes or accompaniments include carrots, peas, lettuce, and noisette potatoes. Serve the sauce separately.

Forester Style—*à la forestière*

For pot roasts. Deglaze the pan with white wine and stock. Reduce to the desired consistency and strain. Garnish with sautéed morels or cèpes over the bird, and noisette potatoes alongside. Coat lightly with sauce and serve additional sauce separately.

with Goose Liver Stuffing—*farci au foie gras*

Dress and wash spring chickens or smaller hens. Inject goose liver puree under the skin of the breast from the front, using a pastry bag. Truss the chicken, bind a thin slice of bacon onto the breast, and roast, basting frequently. Serve périgueux sauce separately.

Home Style—*bonne femme*

For roasts or pot roasts. Deglaze the pan with white wine and stock. Reduce to the desired consistency, and strain. Garnishes or accompaniments include fried slices of lean bacon, glazed pearl onions, and château potatoes. Serve sauce separately.

Mascot—*Mascotte*

For roasts or pot roasts. Deglaze the pan with white wine and stock. Reduce to the desired consistency, and strain. Garnishes or accompaniments include sautéed morels with slices of truffles placed on top of the bird. Serve the sauce separately.

with Noodles—*aux nouilles*

For pot roasts. Deglaze the pan with Madeira, add demi-glace, heat to the boiling point, and strain. Garnish with noodles and serve the sauce separately.

Poached—*poché*

Dress the bird and poach it. Prepare a suprême sauce from the stock and pour it over the carved bird when serving. Poached poultry should not be completely covered with the sauce. Additional sauce should be served in a sauceboat.

Poached with Rice—*poché au riz*

Poach the chicken and prepare a suprême sauce from the stock. Pour the sauce over the carved chicken. Garnish with white rice that has been cooked in bouillon.

Poached with Tarragon—*poché à l'estragon*

Poach in stock. Use the stock to prepare a suprême sauce flavored with tarragon. Pour the sauce over the carved chicken and garnish with blanched tarragon leaves.

Poached with Truffles—*demi-deuil*

Poach. Prepare a suprême sauce from the stock. Pour the sauce over the carved bird, and garnish with slices of truffles.

Richelieu—*Richelieu*

For roasts or pot roasts. Deglaze the pan with Madeira and stock. Reduce to the desired consistency and strain. Sauté julienne of carrots, celery, and onions in butter. Combine with a julienne of truffles and sprinkle over the chicken. Pour the sauce in a ring around the chicken and vegetables.

with Risotto—*au risotto*

For roasts or pot roasts. Deglaze the pan with white wine and stock. Reduce to the desired consistency and strain. Garnish with a risotto. Serve sauce separately.

with Spring Vegetables—*aux primeurs*

For roasts or pot roasts. Deglaze the pan with white wine and stock. Reduce to the desired consistency and strain. Garnish with bouquets of spring vegetables. Serve sauce separately.

Duck and Goose—Canards et oies

Roast, braise, or pot-roast duck and goose. Older birds should be braised.

Duck with Olives—*Canard aux olives*

For pot roasts. Add pitted olives to the sauce and pour the sauce over the carved bird. Surround with fried heart-shaped croutons. This dish is also served under the name salmi of duck.

Roast Duckling with Applesauce—*Caneton rôti avec compote de pommes*

Roast the duckling. Serve applesauce separately.

Duckling with Chestnuts—*Caneton aux marrons*

For roasts. Deglaze pan with Madeira and stock. Garnish with glazed chestnuts. Serve the sauce separately.

Duckling, Nivernese Style—*Caneton à la nivernaise*

For roasts. Surround with glazed pearl onions and carrots. Serve sauce separately.

Duckling with Orange Sauce—*Caneton bigarade*

For roasts. Drain the fat, then deglaze pan with stock. Reduce stock and add bigarade orange sauce. Cover the carved duck with slices of sautéed oranges. Pour sauce around the bird and serve the remainder of the sauce separately.

Braised Goose with Sauerkraut—*Oie braisée à la choucroute*

Braise the goose, then place it on the sauerkraut and steam for the last quarter of the cooking time. Prepare the sauerkraut using goose fat. Carve the goose, arrange on the sauerkraut, and surround with smoked sausage and lean bacon. Serve with the sauce and with boiled potatoes.

Goose with Applesauce—*Oie rôti avec compote de pommes*

Roast the goose. Serve applesauce separately.

Goose with Chestnuts—*Oie aux marrons*

Roast or braise. Garnish with glazed chestnuts. Serve sauce separately.

Goose with Chipolatas—*Oie aux chipolatas*

For roasts. Garnish with chipolata sausages.

Turkey—Dindonneau

Roast or pot-roast young birds; braise older birds.

Turkey with Chipolatas—*Dindonneau aux chipolatas*

Pot-roast the turkey. Deglaze the pan with white wine and stock. Reduce stock to the desired consistency and strain. Garnishes or accompaniments include glazed onions, carrots, chestnuts, quartered mushrooms, and chipolata sausages. Arrange the garnishes in bouquets around the carved bird. Pour a little gravy over the bird and serve the remainder separately. Capons, roasters, and goose may also be served this way.

Guinea Fowl—Pintades

Roast or pot-roast, barding the bird first.

Creamed Guinea Fowl—*Pintade à la crème*

For pot roasts. Deglaze the pan with white wine and a little demi-glace. Add sour cream, reduce to the desired consistency, and strain. Serve the sauce separately.

Guinea Fowl with Sauerkraut—*Pintade à la choucroute*

This dish is prepared by the method used for braised goose with sauerkraut.

Squab—Pigeons

Bard with slices of bacon and roast. Deglaze pan with Madeira. Garnishes or accompaniments include young vegetables and roasted or baked potatoes.

Stuffed Squab—*Pigeons farcis*

For the stuffing, finely chop the liver and heart of the squab and combine with chopped shallots and herbs. Add 7 ounces (200 grams) of minced raw veal and 2 ounces (60 grams) of bread that has been soaked in milk and pressed. Add 2 or 3 egg yolks, 1 teaspoon (6 grams) of salt, 1/4 teaspoon (2 grams) of pepper, and mix thoroughly. Stuff the birds with the stuffing, bard with slices of bacon, and roast in the oven, basting frequently. Deglaze the pan with Madeira and stock.

18.11 Main Dishes with Game Birds

Game birds should always be barded with slices of bacon before roasting. A hot oven, 450° to 500°F (220° to 250°C), is necessary, especially for small birds. Roast game birds are presented on correspondingly sized croutons or canapés. Canapés are flat toasts, the same size as the bird, spread with a gratin forcemeat. Older birds are not suitable for this preparation. Small game birds should be roasted. Carved woodcock, quail, and hazel grouse are served on canapés or croutons, with the sauce served separately.

For gratin forcemeat, lightly sauté chopped shallots in butter. Add diced bacon, game liver or chicken liver, and mushroom parings. Sauté a little longer, puree, and season.

Garnishes for game birds include glazed onions, chestnuts, mushrooms, truffles, and goose liver. Sauces include gravy, bread sauce, and cranberry sauce. Breadcrumbs may also be used.

Pheasant and Partridge—Faisan et perdreau

Bard with bacon slices or unsalted fatback and roast or pot-roast.

Creamed Pheasant—*Faisan à la crème*

Prepare as for creamed guinea fowl.

Pheasant on Canapé—*Faisan sur canapé*

Bard and roast the bird. Deglaze the pan with Madeira and stock. Place the pheasant on a canapé on a serving dish. Cut the bacon used for barding the bird into strips and place on top of the pheasant. Pour some sauce on the bottom of the serving dish and serve the remainder separately. Garnish with potato chips.

Pheasant in Cocotte—*Faisan en cocotte*

Bard the pheasant, pot-roast, carve, and place on a canapé in a cocotte. Garnish with mushroom caps, truffles, and noisette potatoes. Deglaze the pan with brandy and prepare a sauce. Pour the sauce over the pheasant, cover, and heat to the boiling point. Serve hot.

Pheasant with Sauerkraut—*Faisan à la choucroute*

Pot-roast the pheasant until it is medium-done and deglaze the pan with Madeira and stock. Place the carved bird on sauerkraut and heat to the boiling point. Surround with slices of lean bacon and smoked sausage. Serve the sauce and boiled potatoes separately.

Partridge with Cabbage—*Perdreau au chou*

Bard and roast a partridge until almost done. Deglaze the pan with Madeira and stock. Braise cabbage with lean bacon and smoked sausages and cook the roasted partridge with the cabbage for the last few minutes. Carve the bird and arrange on the cabbage. Garnish with the bacon and sausages. Serve sauce and boiled potatoes separately.

Partridge on Canapé—*Perdreau sur canapé*

Bard and roast, using a fairly high temperature, and finish in the same way as pheasant on canapé.

Partridge in Cocotte—*Perdreau en cocotte*

Prepare in the same way as pheasant in cocotte.

Poultry Salmis—*Salmis de volaille*

Sear the bird quickly, using a high temperature and leaving the meat underdone. Then remove the skin and cut the breast into slices, the legs into pieces. Chop the breastbone, trimmings, and skin and use them to make a salmi sauce. Cover the pieces of poultry, which have been kept warm in the meantime, with the sauce and garnish with slices of truffles and mushrooms. Game birds (wild ducks, partridge, pheasant, and snipe) are generally used for poultry salmis; however, duck, guinea fowl, and squab may be used.

18.12 Main Dishes with Game Animals

The main dishes prepared using game animals are saddle and leg of venison, of hare, and of young wild boar. For roasts taken from game animals, proper aging (hanging) is essential and more effective for tenderizing than marinading.

Baden-Baden—*Baden-Baden*

Roast with a *mirepoix*. Deglaze the pan with demi-glace, white wine, and cream. Reduce the sauce, skim the fat, add a pinch of cayenne and a few drops of lemon juice, and strain. Surround the carved roast with halved pears filled with cranberries. Serve the sauce separately.

German Style—*à l'allemande*

Roast the larded pieces of meat. Deglaze the pan with white wine, add demi-glace and sour cream or cream, together with a few juniper berries. Reduce the sauce to the desired consistency and strain. Skim the fat and season the sauce to taste with paprika. Coat the bottom of the serving dish with some of the sauce and serve the remainder separately. Spaetzle or noodles may be used as a garnish or an accompaniment.

Hunter's Style—*chasseur*

This dish is prepared by the method used for Baden-Baden. Garnish with mushrooms, Brussels sprouts, turnips, and potatoes fondantes. Serve red currant jelly and the sauce separately.

Master Hunter's Style—*grand veneur*

Marinate pieces of meat, fry, and flambé. Add pepper sauce, currant jelly, and cream to the drippings and prepare a sauce. Garnish with round potato croquettes and string beans.

Mirza—*Mirza*

Prepare with pepper sauce. Fill halved, stewed apples with red currant jelly and use as a garnish around the carved roast. Serve sauce separately.

with Pepper Sauce—*à la poivrade*

Roast the larded pieces of meat. Deglaze the pan with white wine. Add crushed peppercorns and demi-glace, heat to the boiling point, and strain. Add some lemon juice and butter. Accompaniments include spaetzle, noodles, glazed onions, carrots, chestnuts, mushrooms, and winter vegetables.

Chapter 19
Salads—*Salades*

Salads are usually divided into three categories: simple salads, tossed salads, and composed salads. Salads are generally further classified on the basis of their ingredients, their use, or whether they are hot or cold. A salad usually consists of fresh greens, vegetables, fruits, dairy products, meat, fish, or poultry, served simply or in combination with a dressing. The salad may be served as an hors d'oeuvre, an accompaniment, or a main course.

Salads usually consist of four parts: the base, the body, the dressing, and the garnish. The base is nearly always lettuce or some form of salad greens; the body is made up of the ingredients that constitute the main part of the salad; the salad dressing is used to blend the salad ingredients and to add flavor; the garnish is used to add color, texture, and flavor, and it should always complement the other ingredients of the salad.

Simple salads include green salads and those made with cooked vegetables. Simple salads, especially green salads, are served with the roast or the main course.

19.1 Salad Dressings—*Sauces à salade*

Simple Salad Dressing—*Sauce à salade simple*

Mix white-wine vinegar and oil thoroughly, in a ratio of about one to three, depending on the strength of the vinegar; season to taste with salt and pepper. A small amount of garlic powder, minced onion, and some Dijon mustard may be added. Sprinkle the prepared salad with chopped fresh parsley or snipped chives.

Italian Dressing—*Sauce à salade à l'italienne*

Mix red-wine vinegar and olive oil thoroughly in a ratio of about one to four, depending on the strength of the salad wine; season to taste with salt and pepper. Garlic put through a press may be added to the dressing. Sprinkle the prepared salad with chopped fresh parsley before serving.

19.1.1 American-style French Dressing—*Sauce à salade américaine*

Yield
U.S.—10 quarts
Metric—10 liters

Ingredients	U.S. Weight or Volume	Metric Weight or Volume
Mustard, dry	¾ ounce	20 grams
Water	¼ cup	50 milliliters
Egg yolks	20	20
Vinegar	2 quarts	2 liters
Paprika	¾ ounce	20 grams
Garlic powder	½ ounce	10 grams
Sugar	½ ounce	10 grams
Worcestershire sauce	¼ cup	50 milliliters
White pepper	½ ounce	10 grams

continued

401

Ingredients	U.S. Weight or Volume	Metric Weight or Volume
Salt	4 ounces	120 grams
Oil	7½ quarts	7 liters

Procedure
1. Dissolve the mustard in the water.
2. Combine the mustard, egg yolks, vinegar, paprika, garlic powder, sugar, Worcestershire sauce, pepper, and salt in a blender or mixer.
3. Add the oil slowly and whip until the dressing is smooth and thoroughly blended.

Note: This sauce can be prepared in advance. Crushed garlic and onion can be added.

19.1.2 Roquefort Dressing—*Sauce à salade au roquefort*

Yield
U.S.—1 quart
Metric—1 liter

Ingredients	U.S. Weight or Volume	Metric Weight or Volume
Roquefort cheese	3½ ounces	100 grams
French dressing, freshly prepared	1¾ pints	9 deciliters

Procedure
1. Crumble the cheese and add to the dressing.
2. Whip in a blender or mixer until smooth.

Note: Lemon juice may be substituted for the vinegar in the French dressing.

19.1.3 Cream Salad Dressing—*Sauce à salade à la crème*

Yield
U.S.—1 quart
Metric—1 liter

Ingredients	U.S. Weight or Volume	Metric Weight or Volume
Cream	3 cups	7 deciliters
Vinegar	¾ cup	3 deciliters

Ingredients	U.S. Weight or Volume	Metric Weight or Volume
Lemon juice	1 tablespoon	15 milliliters
Salt	1½ teaspoons	8 grams
Dry mustard	½ teaspoon	3 grams
Sugar	½ teaspoon	3 grams

Procedure
1. Whip all ingredients in a blender or mixer just before serving.

Note: The vinegar may be replaced with lemon juice.

19.1.4 Cream-Cheese Dressing—*Sauce à salade au séré*

Yield
U.S.—1 quart
Metric—1 liter

Ingredients	U.S. Weight or Volume	Metric Weight or Volume
Yogurt	2½ cups	6 deciliters
Cream cheese	10 ounces	300 grams
Salt	1 teaspoon	6 grams
Pepper	⅛ teaspoon	1 gram
Lemon juice	2 tablespoons	30 milliliters
Worcestershire sauce	1 tablespoon	15 milliliters
Chives, snipped	¼ cup	½ deciliter

Procedure
1. Beat the yogurt and cream cheese until creamy.
2. Add seasonings, lemon juice, Worcestershire sauce, and chives.

19.2 Simple Salads—*Salades simples*

Salad greens should be fresh and of good quality. They should be washed thoroughly in large quantities of water, separating the leaves to remove all the dirt and grit. The greens should be trimmed carefully, drained, and refrigerated in damp cloth bags or in a colander covered with a damp cloth. Salad greens should be torn, not cut, to avoid bruising.

Salads should be presented artistically and simply so that each ingredient can be identified. The ingredients should be fresh, with contrasts in color and texture, and they should be arranged attractively on the plate. Snipped chives or chopped parsley, a sprig of watercress, sliced truffles, or chopped or sliced hard-cooked eggs sprinkled over the salad will enhance the flavor and appearance.

Apple Salad—*Salade de pommes*

Cut peeled apples into quarters, remove the core, and slice very thin. Mix with salad dressing and sugar. Serve on crisp lettuce and sprinkle with chopped walnuts. This salad is excellent with roast poultry, game, pork, and with cold dishes.

Avocado Salad—*Salade aux avocats*

Serve slices of avocado on crisp lettuce with a cream or Roquefort dressing.

Beet Salad—*Salade de betteraves*

Wash whole beets and boil in water. Peel immediately and put back into the cooking water until cold. Heat equal quantities of wine vinegar and red wine to the boiling point with a studded onion (bay leaf and clove), a little salt, and sugar. Place the cooled beets in a bowl and cover with the hot vinegar and red wine mixture. A small amount of oil may be added if desired. Cover and refrigerate. These beets can be kept for long periods of time. Cut into slices or a rough julienne before serving. Sliced or julienne canned beets may be used.

Brittany Salad—*Salade bretonne*

Sauté chopped onion and diced bacon in oil, add soaked navy beans, cover with stock, and cook until tender. Mix with oil and vinegar and season to taste. This salad, a good accompaniment to sausages, should always be served lukewarm.

Cooked Carrot Salad—*Salade de carottes cuites*

Slice peeled and cooked carrots. Mix with salt, pepper, minced onion, and a spicy salad dressing. Sprinkle with parsley or chives before serving.

Raw Carrot Salad—*Salade de carottes crues*

Cut raw carrots into a fine julienne. Mix with cream-cheese salad dressing.

Cauliflower Salad—*Salade de chou-fleur*

Cut cooked cauliflower into florets. Arrange the florets in a single layer on the bottom of a salad bowl, cover lightly with thin mayonnaise, add a second layer of cauliflower and mayonnaise, and sprinkle with parsley.

Cooked Celery Salad—*Salade de céleri cuit*

Wash celery ribs, boil in salted water, cool, and drain. Cut the ribs into lengths of 1½ to 2½ inches (4 to 6 centimeters), and arrange in bowls. Cover with salad dressing and sprinkle with chopped parsley.

Raw Celery Salad—*Salade de céleri cru*

Wash celery roots, peel, and cut into julienne strips. Mix with a thin, spicy mayonnaise, and sprinkle with chopped parsley and lemon juice.

Coleslaw—*Salade de chou blanc*

Wash white cabbage and shred. Mix with vinegar and chopped onion. Sauté diced bacon and pour, together with the fat, over the salad. Then season with salt, pepper, and nutmeg. Add a little oil and marinate the salad for 1 to 2 hours. This salad may also be made with a spicy salad dressing. The shredded cabbage may be parboiled in hot water before the dressing is added.

Cucumber Salad—*Salade de concombre*

Cut peeled cucumbers lengthwise into halves and remove the seeds. Cut cucumber into thin slices, mix with some salt, place in a bowl, and press for at least 2 hours, using a plate with a suitable weight on top. Drain off the juice, add the salad dressing to the cucumbers, and sprinkle with parsley. Raw cucumber may be mixed with salad dressing without being pressed.

Elizabeth Salad—*Salade Elizabeth*

Pour lemon juice, seasoning, and fresh cream over Boston lettuce.

Endive Salad, Brussels Style—*Salade d'endives de Bruxelles*

Wash the endives, cut into strips or fine slices, wash again, and prepare with a thin mayonnaise sauce. Thin slices of apple or mandarin can be added to the endive. The salad may be garnished with walnuts. Whole leaves of endive may be served as a salad with a separate sauce.

Green Bean Salad—*Salade de haricots verts*

Blanch fresh green beans, cool, and drain. Cut the beans into 2-inch (5-centimeter) lengths and mix with salad dressing.

Lamb's Lettuce Salad—*Salade de mâches*

Dress lamb's lettuce (mâche) with salt, pepper, vinegar, and oil. Thick salad dressings are not suitable for this salad. Chopped hard-cooked eggs can be added, if desired.

Leek Salad—*Salade de poireau*

Cut the white part of leeks into 2½-inch (6-centimeter) pieces, wash, blanch, cool, and cook in the following marinade for approximately 10 minutes: ¼ cup (50 milliliters) of olive oil, juice of 1 lemon, ½ teaspoon (3 grams) of salt, 4 peppercorns, 1 bay leaf, 2 sprigs of parsley, ⅛ teaspoon (2 grams) minced tarragon, and water to cover the vegetables. Serve cold on crisp lettuce.

Mushroom Salad—*Salade de champignons*

Cut 1 pound (450 grams) of washed mushrooms into fine slices and immediately mix in lemon juice, salt, and pepper. Then add 1¾ ounces (50 grams) of chopped onion, a minced garlic clove, oil, and vinegar. Sprinkle with parsley and garnish with tomato slices.

Potato Salad—*Salade de pommes de terre*

Cook potatoes until slightly underdone. Peel the warm potatoes and cut into fine slices. Marinate the warm potatoes in a mixture of salt, pepper, chopped onion, and bouillon for several hours. Drain thoroughly and add a spicy salad dressing, adjust seasonings, and refrigerate until thoroughly chilled. Serve on crisp lettuce and sprinkle with parsley or chives.

Red Cabbage Salad—*Salade de chou rouge*

Prepare this salad by the same method used for coleslaw, using red cabbage instead of white.

Spinach Salad—*Salade d'épinards*

Clean and thoroughly wash 3 pounds (1.5 kilograms) of fresh spinach leaves. Arrange the leaves on a cloth, dry, and cut into strips. Just before serving, mix the spinach with a chopped onion, a chopped garlic clove, salt, pepper, oil, and vinegar. Salad dressing may be substituted for the oil and vinegar.

Sweet Corn Salad

Drain kernels of canned corn. Mix with a French dressing or well-seasoned mayonnaise. The salad may be garnished with pineapple wedges, sweet peppers, or chili sauce.

Tomato Salad—*Salade de tomates*

Plunge tomatoes into boiling water for a few seconds, peel, slice, and arrange attractively in a salad bowl. Pour salad dressings over the tomatoes and sprinkle with chopped parsley.

Watercress Salad—*Salade cressonière*

Combine clean watercress with salt, pepper, vinegar and oil, or with a suitable salad dressing.

19.3 Tossed Salads—*Salades mêlées*

There are many varieties of tossed salads. Some are made of mixed cooked vegetables and prepared like simple salads. Others include a variety of ingredients, such as mushrooms, truffles, and tongue in addition to the vegetables. Some of these more elaborate preparations may include chicken, meat, or fish. The latter are usually served as an accompaniment to cold main dishes, or they may be served as an hors d'oeuvre or a snack or as a cold entrée.

Andalusian Salad—*Salade andalouse*

Combine tomato wedges, julienne of sweet peppers, dry-cooked rice, and a few drops of garlic juice. Fold in a salad dressing, and sprinkle with parsley.

Avocado Salad, American Style—*Salade aux avocats à l'américaine*

Peel halved and pitted avocados and cut into slices. Add diced orange and grapefruit. Blend cream-cheese dressing into the salad, or serve the dressing over the top of the salad. Garnish with toasted pecans, sprigs of watercress, or pomegranate seeds.

Flemish Salad—*Salade flamande*

Combine a julienne of potatoes, diced anchovy fillets, chopped onion, and bite-size pieces of crisp chicory. Toss with a salad dressing and sprinkle with parsley.

Green Salad—*Salade verte*

Clean romaine lettuce carefully, break the large leaves, and remove any tough ribs. Break chicory and endive into strips. Wash the greens thoroughly, drain, and dry on a cloth. Toss the salad just before serving with oil, vinegar, and seasoning.

Iceberg Lettuce Salad

This salad is made by the method described for green salad, substituting iceberg lettuce for romaine.

Italian Meat Salad—*Salade italienne*

With the exception of game, all roasts and boiled meats are suitable for this recipe. Cut meat, pickles, apples, and a few potatoes into strips and mix with a spicy mayonnaise, chopped onions, and anchovies. Garnish with hard-cooked eggs, pickles, anchovies, capers, and olives.

Italian Vegetable Salad—*Salade italienne*

Mix finely diced carrots, turnips, potatoes, cut green beans, peas, a few capers, and anchovies with a spicy mayonnaise. Garnish with chopped hard-cooked eggs and parsley.

Russian Salad—*Salade russe*

Cube carrots, celery, and potatoes. Add peas and cut green beans. Mix with mayonnaise and garnish with caviar and smoked salmon. This salad may be bound with aspic and poured into coated and decorated molds. The molded salad should be inverted onto a serving plate and decorated with crisp lettuce or chicory.

Waldorf Salad—*Salade Waldorf*

Combine a julienne of crisp celery with diced apples and mayonnaise. Garnish with walnuts and cubes or wedges of chilled pineapple.

Windsor Salad—*Salade Windsor*

Mix a julienne of truffles, celery, chicken, tongue, and mushrooms with mayonnaise. Decorate with watercress or parsley.

19.4 Composed Salads—*Salades composées*

These salads include various ingredients, each one arranged in a separate group or a bouquet. The vegetables are arranged on the serving plate to emphasize the differences in shape, color, and texture. Some of these salads are combined and arranged in a serving bowl and decorated with bouquets or bundles of vegetables.

Belle Fermière Salad—*Salade belle fermière*

Prepare a julienne of cooked potatoes, beets, and celery, add dressing, arrange in bouquets, and sprinkle with parsley.

Emma Salad—*Salade Emma*

Arrange sliced tomatoes around cucumber salad and sprinkle with snipped chives.

Florida Salad—*Salade Florida*

Cut hearts of Boston lettuce in two, cover with salad dressing, and arrange chilled canned fruits (peaches, pears, red cherries) on the lettuce.

Jockey Club Salad—*Salade Jockey-club*

Arrange asparagus spears in layers on a platter and coat with a spicy light mayonnaise without covering the tips. Sprinkle with a julienne of truffles.

Lakme Salad—*Salade Lakme*

Combine dry-cooked rice with oil and lemon juice. Place the rice in a salad bowl and surround with slices of hard-cooked egg and sliced beets. Dust with paprika.

Lorette Salad—*Salade Lorette*

Prepare a julienne of romaine lettuce, celery, endives, and beets. Add salad dressing and arrange the vegetables in bouquets on a serving plate.

Salad Niçoise—*Salade niçoise*

Mix equal parts of sliced cooked potatoes and cooked green beans with a vinaigrette sauce. Chill thoroughly. Place in a salad bowl and garnish with anchovy fillets, olives, capers, and tomato wedges. Sprinkle with chopped tarragon or chervil.

Rachel Salad—*Salade Rachel*

Prepare a julienne of equal parts of celery, artichoke hearts, and cooked potatoes. Mix with mayonnaise. Arrange in bouquets and garnish with marinated asparagus.

Chapter 20
Vegetables—*Légumes*

For cutting and shaping vegetables, see chapter 7.

20.1 Blanching—*Blanchir*

Place clean vegetables in a wire basket and submerge in rapidly boiling water. Use ten parts water to one part vegetables. Cover and boil for the period of time specified in the recipe. If the vegetables are not to be used immediately, drain and plunge into ice water, and cool thoroughly.

Blanching is an essential part of the freezing process. All vegetables should be blanched before freezing to inhibit the enzyme action that continues after harvesting. Blanching will help preserve nutrients and color, firm the texture of vegetables, and remove bitter flavors. Blanching in oil is a preliminary stage of deep-frying used for large pieces or quantities of food.

20.2 Boiling—*Cuire*

Boiling Fresh Vegetables

Place the cleaned vegetables in simmering salted bouillon or stock, cover, and simmer until tender. It is important to choose the right size container for the amount of vegetables used.

Lemon juice, veal kidney fat, and a little flour dissolved in water may be added to black salsify, artichoke hearts, celeriac, and cardoons to prevent the vegetables from turning black.

Boiling Dried Vegetables

Place the dried vegetables (lentils, dried peas, dried beans) in cold water and bring to a boil. Skim, reduce heat, add a *bouquet garni,* and continue simmering until the vegetables are tender.

Dried vegetables, with the exception of dried beans, do not require soaking. These vegetables are often used for soups. When served as a side dish, the vegetables are usually bound with a sauce.

Vegetable purees are usually made of legumes such as peas, lentils, and dried beans. After boiling, they are put through a food mill or the attachment of the electric mixer. The purees are best seasoned with cream and butter. Béchamel sauce, butter, and cream will improve purees made from vegetables that have a high water content.

20.3 Steaming—*Cuire à vapeur*

Season and salt the vegetables and steam until tender. The time required for cooking will depend on the type and age of the vegetables and the equipment in which they are cooked. The variety of vegetable and the type of equipment will determine whether the vegetable should be covered during steaming. Information giving recommended steaming times and procedures for their own equipment is available from the various manufacturers of steaming equipment.

Pressure steaming requires less cooking time than the conventional boiling method. Nutrients, flavor, and shape of vegetables are conserved better by steaming than by boiling.

20.4 Braising—*Braiser*

Sauté a *mirepoix* and pork rind lightly in fat, place the blanched vegetables in the pan in layers, season with salt, and pour in stock up to one-third of the height of the vegetables. The higher the water content of the vegetables, the less stock needed. Cover with grease-proof paper, weight down. Bring to a boil, reduce heat, and braise in the oven. The stock should be reduced after the vegetables are cooked. Serve vegetables hot with a garnish or sauce.

Green beans and sugar peas are first fried with diced bacon, chopped onion, and some savory, and then braised until tender.

20.5 Stewing—*Etuver*

For vegetables with a high water content, such as tomatoes, zucchini, and mushrooms, place fat, salt, seasonings, lemon juice, shallots, and wine in a sauté pan and reduce. Add the washed mushrooms or the vegetables, cover, and simmer until cooked. The vegetables should be cooked at a low temperature to prevent evaporation of the liquid. When these delicately flavored vegetables are stewed carefully, a natural, strong stock is obtained.

20.6 Glazing—*Glacer*

Blanch peeled and cut vegetables if necessary. Drain and then place them in a wide, shallow pan. Add butter, sugar, seasoning, and a small amount of stock or water. Cover the pan and cook gently until the liquid is reduced to a light syrup. Remove the cover, and toss the vegetables in the syrup until they have a shiny, glazed appearance.

The vegetables may be boiled quickly in salted water and then carefully glazed *à la minute* in a sauté pan with butter, sugar, and seasoning. The best vegetables for glazing are those containing large amounts of sugar, such as carrots, chestnuts, turnips, and pearl onions.

20.7 Gratinating—*Gratiner*

Clean, then boil, steam, or braise the washed vegetables. Drain and place them in a buttered gratin pan, cover with the appropriate sauce, sprinkle the sauce with grated cheese and melted butter, and gratinate the vegetables in the oven or under the broiler. Asparagus, fennel, celery, and eggplant are especially suited for gratinating.

20.8 Deep-frying—*Frire*

Season the vegetables and coat with flour. Then either dip into beaten egg and then in breadcrumbs, or dip in frying batter. Deep-fry at 340°F (170°C). Drain off the fat, salt the vegetables lightly, and serve hot. Vegetables with a high water content, such as zucchini eggplants, and tomatoes, are deep-fried raw. Harder vegetables, such as celeriac, black salsify, artichoke hearts, and asparagus, should be boiled or steamed before deep-frying. Foods that have been blanched and that are not to be used immediately should be spread out on trays to prevent further cooking.

20.9 Sautéing—*Sauter*

Heat fat, add the vegetables, season, dust with flour if needed, toss carefully, brown lightly, and sauté until the vegetables are cooked.

This form of preparation is especially suitable for parboiled vegetables, if the cooking is to be completed *à la minute*. Tender vegetables, such as zucchini, peas, and eggplant, can be sautéed without parboiling.

20.10 Vegetable Preparations

Artichokes—Artichauts

Artichokes lend themselves to many different preparations. The young tender artichoke may be eaten raw; artichoke hearts may be cooked, chilled, and marinated; and whole boiled artichokes may be served hot with melted butter, hollandaise, or various hot sauces. They may be served cold with mayonnaise or other dressings. Large artichokes may be cooked and stuffed with goose liver or with a salipicon of chicken and truffles or with vegetables.

Artichokes Colbert—*Artichauts Colbert*

Boiled artichoke bottoms are filled with duxelles. Colbert sauce is served separately.

Artichokes with Young Peas—*Artichauts aux petits pois*

Boiled artichoke hearts are filled with peas and seasoned with melted butter.

Asparagus—Asperges

Boiled or steamed asparagus spears are served with hollandaise sauce, mayonnaise, or melted butter.

Creamed Asparagus Tips—*Pointes d'asperges à la crème*

Boiled or steamed asparagus tips are bound with a light cream sauce.

Gratinated Asparagus—*Asperges au gratin*

Boiled or steamed asparagus spears are arranged in layers on a gratin pan. The tips on each layer are covered with Mornay sauce, sprinkled with grated cheese and melted butter, and gratinated.

Asparagus, Milanese Style—*Asperges milanaise*

Boiled or steamed asparagus is arranged in layers in a gratin dish. The tips are sprinkled with cheese and melted butter and gratinated in the oven.

Asparagus, Polish Style—*Asperges polonaise*

Boiled or steamed asparagus tips are sprinkled with chopped hard-cooked egg and parsley, topped with white breadcrumbs that have been mixed with melted butter, and gratinated.

Brussels Sprouts—Choux de Bruxelles

Brussels Sprouts with Chestnuts—*Choux de Bruxelles aux marrons*

Brussels sprouts and chestnuts have become a traditional holiday dish. Served with turkey or goose, the Brussels sprouts are blanched, drained, and sautéed in butter. The chestnuts are washed, heated, and combined with the Brussels sprouts.

Creamed Brussels Sprouts—*Choux de Bruxelles à la crème*

These are tender, slightly crisp Brussels sprouts that have been blanched, sautéed in butter, covered with cream sauce, and heated in the oven.

Sautéed Brussels Sprouts—*Choux de Bruxelles sautés*

These Brussels sprouts are especially good with roast beef, roast pork, or lamb dishes. They are blanched and sautéed in butter until just tender.

Brussels Sprouts in White Sauce—*Choux de Bruxelles au velouté*

This dish is prepared with blanched, drained, and sautéed Brussels sprouts. They are placed in a serving dish, and covered with basic white sauce. They should be very hot when served.

Cabbage—Chou

Braised Kale—*Chou vert braisé*

Braised kale is used as a vegetable or as a part of many garnishes. It is trimmed, cut into large pieces, washed, blanched quickly in salt water, rinsed, and drained. Chopped onion is browned with small pieces of bacon and lard. The kale, salt, and a spice sachet are placed in a casserole with some stock. The vegetables are covered with buttered greaseproof paper and weighted. The dish is covered and heated to the boiling point. It is then braised in the oven for 1½ to 2 hours.

Braised Red Cabbage—*Chou rouge braisé*

For 10 servings, stew 7 ounces (200 grams) of diced lean bacon and 7 ounces (200 grams) of minced onion in 5 ounces (150 grams) of lard. Add 8 pounds (4 kilograms) finely sliced red cabbage. Continue stewing for a few minutes and deglaze with 1 pint (5 deciliters) of red wine and ¼ cup (50 milliliters) of vinegar. Season, add 2 teaspoons (12 grams) of sugar and 3 finely sliced, peeled apples. Cover the cabbage, heat to the boiling point, and braise in the oven at 350°F (175°C) for 1½ to 2 hours. Before serving, add ¼ cup (50 milliliters) of vinegar to give the cabbage a good red color.

Braised Red Cabbage with Bacon—*Chou rouge braisé au lard*

The method of preparation for braised red cabbage is followed, garnishing the cabbage with strips of bacon.

Braised Red Cabbage with Chestnuts—*Chou rouge braisé aux marrons*

The method of preparation for braised red cabbage is followed. The cabbage is garnished with chestnuts.

Braised Red Cabbage with Chipolata Sausages—*Chou rouge braisé aux chipolatas*

This braised red cabbage is garnished with chipolata sausages.

Braised White Cabbage—*Chou blanc braisé*

The method of preparation for braised kale is followed.

Braised White Cabbage with Bacon—*Chou blanc braisé au lard*

The method of preparation for braised kale is followed. Garnish the cabbage with strips of bacon.

Sauerkraut—*Choucroute*

Sauerkraut is made from shredded cabbage that has fermented in a brine with juniper berries. It is often cooked with brisket of beef, roast pork, frankfurters, sausages, spareribs, and poultry. A simple method of preparation is as follows: stew 10 ounces (300 grams) of diced lean bacon and 8 ounces (225 grams) of onion in 2 tablespoons (50 grams) of lard or poultry fat. Add 1 quart (1 liter) of fresh or canned sauerkraut, a spice sachet, 1 ounce (28 grams) of juniper berries, 1 peeled and grated potato, and ¼ cup (30 milliliters) of white wine. Cover the sauerkraut with stock and braise slowly, replacing the liquid as it evaporates. If salted or smoked meat is served with the sauerkraut, it is better to cook the meat separately without adding salt.

Stuffed Cabbage—*Chou farci*

These stuffed cabbage rolls may be made in various sizes. Separate the cabbage into individual leaves and blanch leaves in salted water for 10 minutes. Spread out two to four leaves for each roll; place an appropriate amount of stuffing on each roll and wrap the leaves around the stuffing. Tighten the cabbage rolls by rolling in a cloth; place them in a sauté pan with onion rings and bacon parings; add a little veal stock, cover, and cook in the oven. A raw mousseline forcemeat or a stuffing for simple hot dishes may be used for the stuffing.

Cardoons—Cardons

Cardoons, Bordeaux Style—*Cardons à la bordelaise*

These cardoons are boiled, arranged in a dish, and covered with bordelaise sauce.

Gratinated Cardoons—*Cardons Mornay*

These boiled cardoons are sliced and arranged in a gratin pan. The cardoons are covered with Mornay sauce, sprinkled with cheese and melted butter, and gratinated in the oven.

Cardoons with Stock—*Cardons au jus*

The cardoons for this dish are prepared in the same way as for Bordeaux style, except they are covered with a rich veal stock instead of bordelaise sauce.

Carrots—Carottes

Creamed Carrots—*Carottes à la crème*

Sliced or young whole carrots may be used. They are boiled and are served in a cream sauce.

Glazed Carrots—*Carottes glacées*

These carrots are glazed as described in section 20.6.

Carrots Vichy—*Carottes vichy*

Thin slices of peeled carrots are sautéed in a covered pan with salt, butter, a pinch of sugar, and a little stock or water, until the liquid is almost reduced. The carrots are tossed in the syrupy glaze and sprinkled with chopped parsley.

Cauliflower—Chou-fleur

Creamed Cauliflower—*Chou-fleur à la crème*

This is a dish of cauliflowerets that have been boiled, drained, and arranged in layers with a well-seasoned cream sauce over each layer.

Deep-fried Cauliflower—*Chou-fleur frit*

Cauliflower, prepared as described under cauliflower, English style, is cut into flowerets, dipped into batter, and deep-fried. It is served with a tomato sauce.

Cauliflower, English Style—*Chou-fleur à l'anglaise*

The cauliflower for this dish may be left whole or broken into flowerets. Boiled until just tender, the cauliflower is drained thoroughly, dried over very low heat, arranged in a warm serving dish, and covered with melted butter and minced parsley.

Gratinated Cauliflower—*Chou-fleur au gratin*

This dish is prepared by the method used for creamed cauliflower. The cauliflower is arranged in a gratin dish, covered with cheese and melted butter, and gratinated in the oven.

Cauliflower, Milanese Style—*Chou-fleur milanaise*

Cauliflower, prepared as described under English style, is served with grated cheese and brown butter.

Cauliflower, Polish Style—*Chou-fleur polonaise*

Cauliflower, prepared as described under English style, is garnished with sliced hard-cooked eggs, parsley, and a mixture of breadcrumbs and brown butter.

Celeriac—Céleri-rave

Celeriac, English Style—*Céleri-rave à l'anglaise*

Celeriac is boiled, sliced, and covered with melted butter and parsley.

Celeriac, Italian Style—*Céleri-rave à l'italienne*

Boiled and sliced celeriac is arranged on a warm dish and covered with an Italian sauce that has been mixed with reduced celery stock and garnished with parsley.

Celeriac with Stock—*Céleri-rave au jus*

This dish is prepared like celeriac, English style. A rich veal stock mixed with reduced celery stock is substituted for the melted butter.

Celery—Céleri

Celery with Brown Sauce—*Céleri en branches à la demi-glace*

Braised celery is arranged on a dish and covered with a demi-glace mixed with reduced vegetable stock.

Celery, English Style—*Céleri en branches à l'anglaise*

Braised celery, arranged on a dish, is covered with melted butter and sprinkled with chopped parsley.

Celery with Marrow—*Céleri en branches à la moelle*

Braised celery is covered with a bound veal stock mixed with reduced vegetable stock. It is decorated with poached slices of marrow and minced parsley.

Celery with Stock—*Céleri en branches au jus*

A rich veal stock mixed with a reduced vegetable stock is poured over the braised celery.

Corn

Sweet corn kernels are boiled in salted water and served with butter or with cream sauce. The kernels are also used in corn pancakes and croquettes. Sweet corn on the cob should be simmered in unsalted water.

Cucumbers—Concombres

Creamed Cucumbers—*Concombres à la crème*

The cucumbers in this dish are peeled and cut in the same shape as château potatoes. The cucumbers are then blanched, drained, and stewed in butter and a small amount of stock. They are bound with a thin cream sauce.

Cucumbers, Provence Style—*Concombres à la provençale*

These are thick slices of cucumber that have been blanched and glazed. Peeled, seeded, and quartered tomatoes, slightly browned shallots, and a piece of garlic are added to the glazed cucumbers. The vegetables are then stewed in the oven until tender.

Stuffed Cucumbers—*Concombres farcis*

This vegetable dish is prepared by hollowing the center of peeled cucumbers and cutting them into 2-inch (5-centimeter) lengths. They are stuffed with veal sausage mixed with duxelles and sprinkled with cheese. The stuffed pieces of cucumber are arranged in a buttered flat dish with some stock and butter and stewed in the oven until tender.

Eggplant—Aubergines

Deep-fried Eggplant—*Aubergines frites*

The eggplant is peeled and cut into ¼-inch (5-millimeter) slices. It is seasoned, coated with flour, dipped into beaten egg, and deep-fried at medium temperature. Tomato or Italian sauce is served separately.

Eggplant, Orly Style—*Aubergines à l'Orly*

Eggplant is sliced, dipped into a light batter, and deep-fried. A tomato sauce is served separately.

Endive—Endives

Braised Endive—*Endives braisées*

Braised endive may be finished in several ways: with butter, gratinated, Milanese style or Polish style. The basic method of preparing the endive is as follows: trim and wash the endive. Arrange it in layers in a well-buttered stainless-steel pan. Sprinkle with lemon juice. Add salt, cold water, and veal kidney fat. Cover with buttered greaseproof paper, weight with plates, and cover the pan. Heat to the boiling point and then place in the oven at medium temperature for 30 to 40 minutes.

Fennel—Fenouils

Fennel with Brown Sauce—*Fenouils à la demi-glace*

This dish is prepared by the method described for celery with brown sauce.

Fennel, English Style—*Fenouils à l'anglaise*

The method of preparation for this dish is the same as that used for celery, English style.

Fennel, Milanese Style—*Fenouils à la milanaise*

Braised fennel, arranged on a warm dish, is sprinkled with parsley. Hot, foaming butter is poured over the fennel before serving.

Green Beans—Haricots verts

Green Beans with Bacon—*Haricots verts au lard*

These beans are prepared as described for braised green beans, adding bacon to the beans before braising. Sliced bacon is arranged on the beans before serving.

Braised Green Beans—*Haricots verts braisés*

Wash the beans. Sauté diced lean bacon in butter, add a quantity of chopped onions, and sauté until they turn light yellow. Add the beans and a little stock, cover, and braise until beans are tender and the liquid is reduced to a small quantity. Drain the beans and mix the stock with a few pellets of kneaded butter. Add the beans to the stock and heat to the boiling point. Season and serve in a warm serving dish. A sprig of savory or a piece of lean bacon may be cooked with the beans.

Green Beans, English Style—*Haricots verts à l'anglaise*

These beans are blanched, drained, garnished with butter curls, and served piping hot.

Green Beans Sautéed in Butter—*Haricots verts sautés*

These are blanched green beans that have been sautéed in butter and seasoned.

Kohlrabi—Chou-rave

Creamed Kohlrabi—*Chou-rave à la crème*

Boil the kohlrabi, cut into bite-size pieces, and bind with cream or basic white sauce.

Leeks—Poireaux

Gratinated Leeks—*Poireau au gratin*

Boil and drain the leeks. Arrange in a gratin dish, sprinkle with cheese and melted butter, and gratinate. Béchamel or Mornay sauce may be used for gratinating.

Lettuce—Laitues

Braised Boston Lettuce with Bacon—*Laitues braisées au lard*

The recipe for braised Boston lettuce with brown sauce is followed. Crisp bacon strips are arranged on the lettuce, and veal stock is poured around the vegetable before serving.

Braised Boston Lettuce with Brown Sauce—*Laitues braisées à la demi-glace*

Braised lettuce may be served as a vegetable or as a garnish. Remove the tough and damaged leaves; wash and drain several times. Blanch the lettuce. Fold the leaves and arrange in a greased baking pan. Add some stock, cover, and keep warm in the oven. Pour demi-glace over the lettuce before serving.

Braised Boston Lettuce with Green Peas—*Laitues braisées aux petits pois*

The lettuce is prepared in the same way as braised Boston lettuce with brown sauce. The braised lettuce is arranged in a ring in a round dish, and the center is filled with green peas seasoned with melted butter. Reduced veal stock is poured over the lettuce before serving.

Braised Boston Lettuce with Stock—*Laitues braisées au jus*

This dish is prepared by the method used for braised Boston lettuce with brown sauce. A slightly bound veal stock is poured over it just before serving.

Stuffed Boston Lettuce—*Laitues farcies*

This classic French dish is served as a vegetable, and it is also used as a garnish. The lettuce leaves are washed, drained, and blanched. Each leaf is flattened, and a mousseline stuffing is placed in the center. The leaves are folded to enclose the stuffing. Each piece is placed in a saucepan with sliced onions, diced bacon, and some stock. The lettuce is covered and braised in the oven. The lettuce may be left whole or sliced. It is covered with a rich veal stock or allemande sauce.

Mushrooms—Champignons

Cèpes Bordeaux Style—*Cèpes à la bordelaise*

In Europe the cèpe is one of the favorite mushrooms. To prepare Bordeaux style, the cèpes are washed, sliced, sautéed quickly in hot oil, and seasoned with pepper and salt. Two tablespoons (30 grams) of chopped shallots and 2 tablespoons (30 grams) of breadcrumbs are sautéed and added to each pound (450 grams) of mushrooms. They are sprinkled with lemon juice and chopped parsley before serving.

Creamed Cèpes—*Cèpes à la crème*

These mushrooms are first sautéed in butter and then bound with a cream sauce and seasoned with lemon juice.

Cèpes, Provence Style—*Cèpes à la provençale*

The recipe is the same as the one for Bordeaux style, using onions and garlic instead of shallots.

Creamed Morels—*Morilles à la crème*

Prepare as for creamed mushrooms.

Morels Poulette—*Morilles à la poulette*

The morels for this dish are washed carefully, cut into halves or quarters, and sautéed in butter. For each pound (450 grams) of morels, 2 ounces (60 grams) of butter should be used. The stock is blended with poulette sauce. The morels are added to the sauce.

Sautéed Morels—*Morilles sautées*

This dish is prepared by the method described for sautéed mushrooms. The morels are sprinkled with lemon juice.

Creamed Mushrooms I—*Champignons à la crème I*

The recipe for stewed mushrooms is used for this dish. The stock is reduced and combined with a cream sauce. The mushrooms are folded into the sauce.

Creamed Mushrooms II—*Champignons à la crème II*

The mushrooms for this dish are also prepared as described in the recipe for stewed mushrooms. The reduced stock is mixed with a demi-glace and cream. The mushrooms are added to the sauce.

Sautéed Mushrooms—*Champignons sautés*

The mushrooms for this dish should be very fresh. They are sliced and sautéed in melted butter, seasoned with salt and pepper, and sprinkled with chopped parsley.

Stewed Mushrooms—*Champignons étuvés*

Many varieties of mushrooms may be used for stewing. They can be used whole, cut into quarters, or sliced. Cook chopped shallots in butter in a sauté pan. Deglaze with a little white wine, add the prepared mushrooms, some lemon juice, and cover. Season the mushrooms and continue cooking for approximately 10 minutes.

Stuffed Mushrooms—*Champignons farcis*

Large mushroom caps can be stewed as described under stewed mushrooms and stuffed with duxelles, sprinkled with cheese, and gratinated in the oven or under the broiler. They may be used as a garnish for fish or meat dishes, or served as a separate dish with Madeira sauce.

Peas—*Pois*

Green Peas in Butter—*Petits pois au beurre*

This dish is prepared by blanching, draining, and sautéeing the peas. They are seasoned with a small amount of sugar and fresh butter.

Green Peas, English Style—*Petits pois à l'anglaise*

These peas are blanched, drained, and arranged in a warm dish. They are garnished with butter curls.

Green Peas, French Style—*Petits pois à la française*

This is a casserole of fresh green peas, pearl onions, and a chiffonade of hearts of lettuce. The peas are seasoned and combined with a small amount of sugar and some stock. The vegetables are covered and simmered until tender. The peas are tossed in the remaining liquid and a few pellets of kneaded butter are added. For each pound (450 grams) of peas, use ½ ounce (15 grams) of kneaded butter.

Green Peas, Home Style—*Petits pois bonne femme*

Fresh garden peas are preferred for this dish. To prepare the dish, chopped onion and diced bacon are sautéed in butter. The peas, stock, a small amount of sugar, salt, and pepper are combined and braised in a covered saucepan until the peas are tender. Small amounts of kneaded butter are added, and the peas are heated to the boiling point.

Peppers—Poivrons

Stuffed Sweet Peppers—*Poivrons farcis*

The top part of the peppers is cut off, or the peppers are cut lengthwise into halves and the seeds are removed. The peppers are washed and filled with a mixture of minced meat mixed with rice. They are placed in a pan on a layer of sautéed sliced onion with some stock and tomato sauce and stewed in the oven.

Salsify—Salsifis

Creamed Black Salsify—*Salsifis à la crème*

This salsify is cut into 1½-inch (4-centimeter) pieces, boiled, and bound with a cream sauce.

Deep-fried Black Salsify—*Salsifis frits*

This salsify is boiled, drained, dipped into frying batter, and deep-fried. Tomato sauce is served separately.

Gratinated Black Salsify—*Salsifis au gratin*

This dish is prepared by boiling the salsify and binding it with a cream sauce. It is then arranged on a gratin dish, sprinkled with cheese and melted butter, and gratinated in the oven.

Black Salsify in White Sauce—*Salsifis au velouté*

The salsify is boiled and bound with a basic white sauce.

Spinach—Epinards

Spinach with Chipolata Sausages—*Epinards aux chipolatas*

This is creamed spinach garnished with chipolata sausages.

Creamed Spinach—*Epinards à la crème*

This dish is prepared with blanched, chopped spinach combined with a cream sauce in a ratio of one part sauce to five parts spinach. It may be garnished with sliced carrots that have been buttered and flavored with dill, or with sautéed mushroom slices or caps.

Spinach with Croutons—*Epinards aux croutons*

This is creamed spinach garnished with heart-shaped croutons.

Spinach with Eggs—*Epinards aux oeufs*

This is creamed spinach garnished with sliced hard-cooked eggs or fried or poached eggs.

Spinach, English Style—*Epinards à l'anglaise*

Spinach requires only brief cooking. For this dish blanched spinach is sautéed in butter and placed in a warm serving dish.

Spinach, Italian Style—*Epinards à l'italienne*

The spinach for this dish is blanched, drained, and sautéed in butter. Chopped, browned shallots and anchovy fillets are folded into the spinach. Use 2¾ ounces (80 grams) of shallots and 2¼ ounces (65 grams) of anchovy fillets per pound (450 grams) of spinach.

Spinach with White Sauce—*Epinards au velouté*

The spinach for this dish is blanched, drained, seasoned, and combined with basic white sauce. The ratio is one part sauce to five parts spinach. It may be garnished with tomato wedges and chopped parsley.

Tomatoes—Tomates

Deep-fried Tomatoes—*Tomates frites*

Deep-fried tomatoes are used as a garnish or with *fritto misto* (a mixed fry of meats, or variety meats, and vegetables). The tomatoes are cut into halves, seeded, seasoned, dipped into a frying batter, and deep-fried.

Tomatoes, Provence Style—*Tomates provençale*

Cut five tomatoes into halves. Seed, season, fill with the following stuffing, and gratinate in the oven. *Stuffing:* Lightly brown 3½ ounces (100 grams) of chopped onion and ½ garlic clove, crushed, in 3½ fluid ounces (100 milliliters) of oil. Mix in 7 ounces (200 grams) of grated white bread, 2 tablespoons (30 grams) of chopped parsley, 3 chopped anchovy fillets, and ¾ ounce (20 grams) of grated cheese. Continue sautéing for a few minutes and blend in ½ cup (1 deciliter) of veal stock or sauce from the braising pan.

Stewed Diced Tomatoes—*Tomates concassées*

These tomatoes may be flavored with various seasonings and herbs depending on the use. The tomatoes are washed, peeled, seeded, and cut into cubes. They are combined with chopped shallots that have been stewed in clarified butter. The mixture is covered and stewed slowly until the flavors are blended.

Stuffed Tomatoes—*Tomates farcies*

Wash the tomatoes and cut into halves, remove the seeds, and season with salt and pepper. Place the tomatoes in a buttered pan and stuff each with the prescribed filling (see stuffed cucumbers), sprinkle with cheese, and gratinate in the oven for about 10 minutes.

Zucchini—*Courgettes*

Zucchini may be stewed with a few shallots and tossed in butter.

Mixed Vegetables—Ratatouille

Sauté finely sliced onions in olive oil. Halve and seed green peppers, cube, and add to the onions. Wash and partially peel eggplants and zucchinis; cube and add. Sauté until vegetables are cooked but firm. Add salt, cover, and sprinkle with pepper, thyme, garlic, and basil. Add cubed tomatoes, bring to a boil, and garnish with parsley. This dish can also be spiced with vinegar and served cold.

Chapter 21
Potatoes—*Pommes de terre*

21.1 Blanching—*Blanchir*

Heat the water to the boiling point. Drop the potatoes into the water, bring back to the boil, and then drain. The ratio of potatoes to water should be at least one to five. When blanching, do not add salt to the water. Blanching can be done continuously by using the wire basket from the deep-fryer.

21.2 Boiling—*Cuire*

Peel the potatoes and cut into pieces of uniform size. Cover with salted water and bring to the boiling point in a tightly covered heavy saucepan. Reduce the heat and cook until tender. Drain and return the potatoes to the heat for a few minutes to dry out thoroughly.

Boiling in Stock—Cuire au bouillon

Cut the potatoes and blanch. Add other ingredients to the potatoes and treat according to the recipe. Add hot stock until the potatoes are just covered. Boil in a tightly covered saucepan until potatoes are tender and a small amount of liquid remains. Sprinkle the potatoes with chopped parsley.

21.3 Steaming—*Cuire à vapeur*

Steam the potatoes with some salt in a pressure steamer. If a pressure steamer is not available, use an ordinary saucepan in which a steamer basket 1½ to 2 inches (4 to 5 centimeters) high can be placed. The water should not be in contact with the potatoes. The saucepan should be covered with a heavy lid. This method of cooking reduces the loss of nutrients and is recommended for potatoes to be sautéed, mashed, or cooked in their jackets.

21.4 Baking—*Cuire au four*

Place washed, unpeeled potatoes on a tray that has been covered with a ½-inch (1 centimeter) layer of salt. Bake the potatoes in an oven at 400°F (205°C) for 40 to 60 minutes. Serve in a napkin placed on a platter, or in a special basket. Garnish with fresh butter, cream cheese, sour cream with chives, or with crisp strips of bacon.

Stuffed Potatoes

Bake the potatoes. Cut a pyramid-shaped piece off the flat side of the potatoes. Keep the cutout piece to use as a lid. Hollow out two-thirds of the potato pulp from the shell of the bottom and the top. Whip the pulp with milk, butter, and seasonings. Stuff the shells and serve with or without the lids. The potatoes may be gratinated.

21.5 Roasting—*Rôtir*

Blanch the uniformly cut potatoes. Heat some fat in a roasting pan, add the potatoes, and roast until golden brown, turning from time to time. Drain the excess fat; cover with melted butter and parsley before serving.

Roasting (baking) is also used for potato molds. Slice the blanched potatoes, toss in butter without browning, and arrange in overlapping layers in a mold. Bake in oven at 400°F (205°C) until tender. Invert on a serving dish.

21.6 Sautéing—*Sauter*

Cut the boiled or steamed peeled potatoes into thin slices. Heat the fat in a large omelet pan, add salted potatoes, brown lightly over low heat, and turn frequently. Form potatoes into cake shape, add butter, sauté both sides of the cake until golden brown, and carefully turn out on a round dish. Garnish with chopped parsley or chives. Onion, diced ham, bacon, or cheese may be added.

21.7 Deep-frying—*Frire*

Cut mature potatoes into uniform strips about 2 inches (5 centimeters) long and ⅜ inch (1 centimeter) thick. Soak in cold water until ready to cook. Drain and dry on a cloth. Place a few potatoes at a time in the wire basket of the deep-fryer. Blanch in oil at 275°F (130°C) for about 2 minutes. Remove potatoes, drain on paper towels, and cool. Just before serving, heat the oil to 350°F (185°C) and fry the potatoes until they are crisp. Drain the potatoes on absorbent paper. Keep warm in the oven, with the door open. Salt just before serving. Potato croquettes and potato fritters are deep-fried in oil at 375°F (190°C) until crisp.

21.8 Gratinating—*Gratiner*

Depending on the method of preparation, use raw potatoes or potatoes that have been blanched, boiled, steamed, or baked. Add stock, milk, salt, and seasoning as specified in the recipe. Sprinkle with cheese and melted butter, and gratinate. The potatoes may be covered with Mornay sauce and then gratinated.

21.9 Potato Preparations

Potatoes Anna—*Pommes Anna*

These potatoes are cut into thin, uniform-sized, round slices and mixed with seasoning and melted butter. A thick-bottomed mold is coated with clarified butter and filled with overlapping rows of sliced potatoes. Each layer is sprinkled with clarified butter. The potatoes are covered and baked in the oven at 400°F (205°C) for 30 to 40 minutes. The potatoes are inverted on a pan or plate to allow the excess butter to drain.

Potatoes with Bacon—*Pommes au lard*

These diced and blanched potatoes are combined with diced lean bacon and chopped onion that have been sautéed in butter. Stock is added and the potatoes are boiled until tender.

Bernese Potatoes—*Pommes à la bernoise*

Boiled potatoes are grated coarsely and sautéed in butter with diced bacon. The mixture is browned on one side and inverted onto a serving dish.

Berny Potatoes—*Pommes Berny*

A potato croquette dough is mixed with chopped truffles and shaped into small balls, dipped into beaten egg, and coated with chopped almonds. The potato balls are deep-fried. (See figure 21-1.)

Figure 21-1. Berny potatoes—*Pommes Berny.*

Potatoes, Berrichonne Style—*Pommes berrichonne*

These potatoes are cut into olive shapes and blanched. They are combined with lean bacon and chopped onion that have been sautéed in butter. The potatoes are then covered with stock and boiled until tender.

Boiled Potatoes—*Pommes nature*

These are potatoes that have been cut into oval shapes and boiled.

Boulangère Potatoes—*Pommes boulangère*

A potato dish made of equal parts of sliced, blanched potatoes and sliced onion, sprinkled with butter, and baked in the oven.

Byron Potatoes—*Pommes Byron*

The potatoes are cooked in salt water, allowed to dry in the pan, and mashed with butter. They are seasoned with parsley and nutmeg, and onions sautéed in butter are added. Shaped into balls with a ladle, they are covered with cream and cheese and baked in the oven.

Potato Cakes—*Pommes galettes*

Duchess potatoes are formed into sausage shapes, 1 to 2 inches (3 to 5 centimeters) in diameter and allowed to cool. The "sausages" are cut into ½-inch-thick (1-centimeter) slices and fried in butter.

Château Potatoes—*Pommes château*

Oval-shaped potatoes are blanched and roasted.

Potato Chips—*Pommes chips*

These chips may be served hot or cold. They are made from very thin slices of potatoes that have been cut with a potato slicer, soaked in cold water, drained, and fried in deep fat. Cold potato chips may be dusted with paprika. (See figure 21-2.)

Figure 21-2. Potato chips—*Pommes chips.*

Potatoes with Cream—*Pommes mousseline*

Mashed potatoes are prepared with cream instead of milk.

Potato Croquettes—*Pommes croquettes*

Croquettes are made from potatoes that have been mashed and mixed with seasoning, butter, and egg yolks. They are formed into either oblong or ball shapes, breaded, and deep-fried.

Potatoes Dauphine—*Pommes à la dauphinoise*

These are prepared by the same method as potatoes, Savoy style, using milk instead of stock.

Duchess Potatoes—*Pommes duchesse*

These potatoes are boiled, drained, peeled, mashed, and mixed with butter and seasoning. They are bound with egg yolk. The mixture is placed in a pastry bag and forced into shaped mounds on a buttered tray. The potatoes are brushed with egg yolk or melted butter and baked.

Emmentaler Potatoes—*Pommes emmentaloise*

These are duchess potatoes topped with a slice of Emmentaler cheese, basted with butter, and gratinated in the oven.

Potatoes, English Style—*Pommes à l'anglaise*

These potatoes are cut into oval shapes, boiled, and served in melted butter.

Potatoes, Farmer Style—*Pommes fermière*

The pulp of baked potato is removed from the shell and blended with two-thirds of its volume of chopped *pot-au-feu* vegetables, egg yolk, and butter. The shells are filled with the mixture, sprinkled with grated cheese, and melted butter, and gratinated.

Potatoes Fondantes—*Pommes fondantes*

These are potatoes that have been cut into small egg shapes and arranged in a flat pan. They are buttered, covered, and browned slowly on both sides. They are flattened slightly with a fork and topped with fresh butter.

French-fried Potatoes—*Pommes frites*

These are ½-inch-thick (1-centimeter) potato sticks that have been blanched and deep-fried just before serving.

Gratinated Potatoes—*Pommes Mont d'Or*

Pureed potatoes, in a buttered gratin dish, are sprinkled with cheese and melted butter and gratinated.

Potatoes with Herbs—*Pommes aux fines herbes*

These are boiled and steamed potatoes covered with chopped parsley.

Potatoes, Hungarian Style—*Pommes à lá hongroise*

These are diced and blanched potatoes that have been combined with sautéed, diced lean bacon and chopped onion. They are covered with stock and added to peeled, seeded, and finely chopped tomatoes and paprika, then boiled until tender.

Potatoes, Hunter's Style—*Pommes chasseur*

The pulp of a baked potato is combined with sautéed chicken liver and mushroom. The top of the potato is replaced. Hunter's sauce is served separately.

Potatoes with Leeks—*Pommes aux poireaux*

These are sliced and blanched potatoes. They are placed in a saucepan in alternate layers with blanched white leeks and then boiled in stock.

Lorette Potatoes—*Pommes Lorette*

These potatoes are made from a mixture of dauphine potatoes combined with grated Gruyère cheese, shaped into crescents, and baked.

Potatoes, Lyon Style—*Pommes lyonnaise*

These sliced potatoes are sautéed in butter with sliced onion.

Macaire Potatoes—*Pommes Macaire*

The pulp of baked potatoes is mashed with butter, seasoned, and placed in a buttered pan. The mixture is formed into a round cake and browned on both sides.

Maître d'Hôtel Potatoes—*Pommes maître d'hôtel*

These are made from steamed unpeeled potatoes. They are peeled while hot, sliced, and covered with cream sauce in a sauté pan. Salt, pepper, and nutmeg are added, and the potatoes are simmered. A small amount of cream and butter are added, and they are sprinkled with parsley before serving.

Mashed Potatoes—*Pommes purée*

Potatoes that have been boiled and drained are mashed to a creamy consistency. Hot milk, butter, and seasonings are added and the potatoes are beaten or whipped until light and thoroughly blended.

Minted Potatoes—*Pommes à la menthe*

These oval-shaped potato slices are boiled in stock with a bouquet of fresh mint. Sprigs of blanched mint leaves are served on the potatoes.

Mirette Potatoes—*Pommes Mirette*

These potatoes are blanched and sautéed. They are mixed with a julienne of truffles and some meat extract (*glace de viande*).

Nana Potatoes—*Pommes Nana*

Uniform-size potato sticks are mixed with seasonings and melted butter. The potatoes are arranged in baba molds and prepared by the method used for potatoes Anna.

Noisette Potatoes—*Pommes noisettes*

These potatoes are cut from pared raw potatoes with a melon baller to the size and shape of hazelnuts. They may be blanched, coated with butter, and roasted in the oven, or they may be sautéed in butter.

Potatoes, Old-Fashioned Style—*Pommes à l'ancienne*

These potato patties are made from a duchess potato mixture. The patties are dusted with flour and sautéed in butter.

Parisian Potatoes—*Pommes parisienne*

These are the same as noisette potatoes, but smaller in size. When potatoes are done, meat extract (*glace de viande*) is spooned over them until all pieces are coated. They are sprinkled with parsley.

Potatoes, Peasant Style—*Pommes paysanne*

These sliced and blanched potatoes are prepared by the same method used for preparing potatoes with bacon. Various vegetables can be sautéed with the onions and added.

Figure 21-3. Potatoes Saint Florence—*Pommes Saint-Florentin.*

Potatoes Saint-Florentine—*Pommes Saint-Florentin*

This is a potato croquette dough with chopped ham. It is shaped, breaded in crushed vermicelli, and deep-fried. (See figure 21-3.)

Sautéed Potatoes—*Pommes sautées*

These potatoes are boiled in their jackets, peeled, sliced, and sautéed in butter.

Potatoes, Savoy Style—*Pommes savoyarde*

Thinly sliced raw potatoes are arranged in a gratin dish and covered with boiling stock. When they are half done, they are covered with grated cheese and gratinated in the oven until cooked.

Figure 21-4. Waffle potatoes—*Pommes gaufrettes.*

Figure 21-5. Williams potatoes—*Pommes Williams.*

Shoestring Potatoes—*Pommes allumettes*

Potatoes are cut into ⅛-inch-thick (3-millimeter) sticks and deep-fried.

Soufflé or Puff Potatoes—*Pommes soufflés*

Soufflé potatoes require double cooking at different temperatures. Uniform-size mature potatoes are peeled, washed, and cut lengthwise into slices ⅛ inch (3 millimeters) thick, and dried on a cloth. The long, even slices may be cut into ovals or fancy shapes. The potatoes are precooked in fat at a temperature of 275° to 325°F (130° to 160°C). The basket is agitated throughout the cooking, and the potatoes cook until all the slices rise to the surface and small blisters have formed on them. The potatoes are drained and cooled in the frying basket. Just before serving, the potatoes are dropped into fat at a temperature of 375°F (190°C). Again, the basket is agitated throughout the cooking. The last cooking causes the potatoes to puff. The potatoes should be drained on paper towels, salted, and served immediately. Potatoes with too high a moisture content or those that are too mealy are not suitable for this recipe.

Potatoes with Spinach—*Pommes florentine*

These baked potatoes have had some of the pulp removed. They are stuffed with sautéed spinach, covered with Mornay sauce, sprinkled with grated cheese, and gratinated.

Steak Fries—*Pommes pont-neuf*

These potatoes are twice as thick as french-fried potatoes. They are first blanched and then deep-fried.

Straw Potatoes—*Pommes pailles*

These crisp potatoes are about ⅛ inch (3 millimeters) thick and 2½ inches (6 centimeters) long. They are fried in very hot deep fat.

Voisin Potatoes—*Pommes voisin*

These are prepared by the same method used for potatoes Anna, but with grated cheese between the layers.

Waffle Potatoes—*Pommes gaufrettes*

The potatoes are cut with a fluted slicer (mandoline) that cuts across the width of the potato to make round slices with a waffle pattern. The potatoes are deep-fried. (See figure 21-4.)

Williams Potatoes—*Pommes Williams*

These potato croquettes are pressed into pear shapes, breaded, and deep-fried. (See figure 21-5.)

Chapter 22
Pasta, Gnocchi, Rice, and Corn—*Farineux, gnocchi, riz, et maïs*

22.1 Pasta—*Farineux*

The term pasta refers to such products as spaghetti, noodles, and macaroni; they are stored when dried, usually industrially produced, and may or may not contain egg.

Hard-wheat flour (durum), strong in gluten content, is required for pasta products that will maintain their shape, texture, and form when cooked. The flour is kneaded into a dough with boiling water; it is then forced through special dies and comes out in various sizes and shapes. Egg noodles, an exception, must contain not less than 5.3 percent egg in the finished product, according to U.S. government standards.

Pasta must be cooked in rapidly boiling water in a ratio of 1 pound (450 grams) of pasta to 6 quarts (6 liters) of water. One tablespoon (15 milliliters) of oil and 1 ounce (28 grams) of salt should be added to the boiling water. Pasta should be cooked uncovered.

Pasta is cooked to the *al dente* stage, which literally means "to the tooth." This stage is reached when the pasta is still a bit resistant to the bite and is firm, slightly chewy, and has no taste of raw flour. When the *al dente* stage is reached, the pasta is drained, tossed with butter, and served in heated dishes. If the pasta is not to be served immediately, it may be reheated in hot water later, then tossed with butter. Grated cheese may be served on the side.

22.1.1 Ravioli

Yield
approximately 10 servings

Ingredients	U.S. Weight or Volume	Metric Weight or Volume
Stuffing:		
Shallots	1 ounce	30 grams
Garlic	1 clove	1 clove
Butter	3 ounces	85 grams
Ground beef, braised	10 ounces	300 grams
Spinach, cooked	10 ounces	300 grams
Egg yolks	3	3
Nutmeg	1/8 teaspoon	1 gram
Salt	1 teaspoon	5 grams
Pepper	1/4 teaspoon	2 grams
Dough:		
Flour	28 ounces	850 grams
Oil	1/4 cup	50 milliliters
Eggs	4	4

Ingredients	U.S. Weight or Volume	Metric Weight or Volume
Salt	½ ounce	15 grams
Water	½ to ¾ cup	100 to 150 milliliters

Procedure

1. Brown shallots and garlic in butter.
2. Add braised beef and cooked spinach.
3. Add egg yolks and seasonings, and blend thoroughly. If too thick, add a bit of demi-glace. If too thin, reduce over heat to desired consistency.
4. Sift flour. Make a well in the center of the flour.
5. Combine the oil, eggs, salt, and water. Mix slightly. Pour into the well.
6. Mix the flour in gradually and work into a smooth, firm dough. Let the dough stand for 1 to 2 hours.
7. Divide the dough into halves and roll into two very thin pieces. Put the stuffing into a pastry bag.
8. Place one piece of the dough on a ravioli board and pipe 2 to 3 teaspoons of stuffing in each hollow. (See figure 22-1.) Cover it with the other piece of the dough. Roll a rolling pin over the

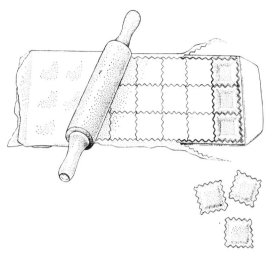

Figure 22-2. Using a rolling pin to cut the ravioli apart.

board to cut the ravioli squares apart. (See figure 22-2).

9. Heat 6 quarts (6 liters) of water, 1 tablespoon (15 grams) of salt, and 1 tablespoon (15 milliliters) of oil to the boiling point. Place five or six ravioli at a time in the water.
10. Remove with a skimmer to a buttered baking dish. Cover with a sauce or melted butter. Heat in oven at 350°F (175°C) for about 20 minutes. Serve immediately.

Other Ravioli Dishes

Ravioli Milanese Style—*Ravioli milanaise*

The ravioli are arranged in layers in a gratin dish and sprinkled with cheese. Melted butter is poured over the top, and the ravioli are heated in an oven at 350°F (175°C) for 15 minutes.

Ravioli, Naples Style—*Ravioli napolitaine*

The ravioli are arranged in layers and a tomato sauce is poured over each layer. The ravioli are covered with grated cheese and melted butter and heated in an oven at 350°F (175°C) for 15 minutes.

Figure 22-1. Piping the ravioli stuffing onto the dough on a ravioli board.

Ravioli, Nice Style—*Ravioli niçoise*

The ravioli are arranged in layers in a gratin dish. A demi-glace or a thickened veal stock whipped with butter is poured over the top. The ravioli are covered with cheese and melted butter and heated in an oven at 350°F (175°C) for 15 minutes.

22.1.2 Cannelloni

Yield
approximately 10 servings

Ingredients	U.S. Weight or Volume	Metric Weight or Volume
Ravioli dough	2 pounds	1 kilogram
Water	5 quarts	5 liters
Salt	1 tablespoon	15 grams
Oil	1 tablespoon	15 milliliters
Cheese, grated	7 ounces	200 grams
Stuffing (see ravioli)	20 to 28 ounces	600 to 800 grams
Mornay sauce	1 pint	5 deciliters
Butter	5 ounces	140 grams

Procedure
1. Roll the dough to ⅛-inch (3-millimeter) thickness. Cut into pieces 2½ by 3½ inches (6 by 9 centimeters). Dry thoroughly.
2. Pour salt, and oil into a large kettle. Heat to the boiling point.
3. Drop a few pieces of pasta at a time into the water and cook until *al dente*. Remove pasta with a skimmer. Cool and dry.
4. Sprinkle grated cheese over a cutting board. Arrange the cooked pasta on the board. Fill a pastry bag with the stuffing and position the stuffing lengthwise on the pasta.
5. Roll the pasta around the stuffing. Place in a buttered gratin dish, cover with Mornay sauce, sprinkle with cheese and butter, and bake in an oven at 400°F (205°C) for about 20 minutes, until thoroughly heated.

Note: A tomato sauce or demi-glace may be used instead of Mornay sauce. The term *al sugo* generally refers to a demi-glace with tomato. If the cannelloni are served without baking, they are served with browned butter and a few sage leaves.

22.1.3 Spaghetti with Meat Sauce—*Spaghetti au sauce bolognaise*

Yield
approximately 10 servings

Ingredients	U.S. Weight or Volume	Metric Weight or Volume
Spaghetti	28 to 32 ounces	800 to 1,000 grams
Water	8 quarts	7.5 liters
Salt	2 tablespoons	30 milliliters
Butter	¼ cup	50 milliliters
Oil	¼ cup	50 milliliters
Sauce:		
Oil	1¾ ounces	50 grams
Beef, lean, diced or ground	20 to 28 ounces	600 to 800 grams
Onion, chopped	5 ounces	150 grams
Garlic, grated	2 cloves	2 cloves
Vegetable brunoise	7 to 10 ounces	50 grams
Bouquet garni	1	1
Tomato puree	1¾ ounces	50 grams
Stewed diced tomatoes	7 ounces	200 grams
Red wine	¾ cup	2 deciliters
Brown stock	1 quart	1 liter
Salt	1 teaspoon	4 grams
Pepper	¼ teaspoon	1 gram
Paprika	¼ teaspoon	1 gram

Procedure
1. Boil the spaghetti in the salted water until *al dente*.
2. Drain.
3. Toss with the butter and oil.
4. Heat the oil in a pan.
5. Add the meat and brown.

6. Add the onion, garlic, vegetable brunoise, and *bouquet garni*. Cook for 5 minutes.
7. Add the tomato puree and sliced, diced tomatoes.
8. Deglaze the pan with red wine, and reduce the sauce.
9. Add brown stock and season with salt, pepper, and paprika.
10. Simmer very slowly for 2 hours.
11. The sauce can be mixed with the spaghetti, spooned over the spaghetti, or served separately, with grated cheese.

Other Spaghetti Dishes

Other noodles and macaroni may be used in place of spaghetti in any of these dishes.

Spaghetti au Gratin—*Spaghetti au gratin*

Spaghetti is tossed with butter and mixed with thin cream sauce. It is placed in a buttered gratin dish, sprinkled with cheese and butter, and gratinated.

Spaghetti with Cheese—*Spaghetti au fromage*

Spaghetti is tossed with butter and cheese and served with more cheese sprinkled on top.

Spaghetti, Milanese Style—*Spaghetti milanaise*

This is spaghetti au gratin served with a julienne of mushrooms, tongue, ham, and truffles that have been bound with a demi-glace. A depression is made in the center of the spaghetti. It is filled with the julienne and cheese is sprinkled over the top. If the spaghetti is being used as a side dish, the julienne is sautéed in butter and then dropped over the spaghetti.

Spaghetti with Tomatoes I—*Spaghetti napolitaine I*

This dish may be made with boiled spaghetti that has been tossed with butter and arranged in layers in a baking dish. Tomato sauce is poured between the layers of pasta. The dish is covered with cheese.

Spaghetti with Tomatoes II—*Spaghetti napolitaine II*

This is another Neapolitan pasta dish made with boiled spaghetti that has been tossed in butter. Chopped onion and sliced diced tomatoes are sautéed in butter, dusted with flour, deglazed with white wine and stock, and added to the tomato puree. The sauce is simmered slowly for 1 to 2 hours before it is mixed with the pasta and some cheese.

22.1.4 Homemade Egg Noodles I and II—*Nouilles maison I et II*

Yield
approximately 10 servings

Ingredients	U.S. Weight or Volume	Metric Weight or Volume
I		
Flour	14 ounces	400 grams
Semolina, hard-wheat	3½ ounces	100 grams
Oil	¼ cup	50 milliliters
Eggs	5	5
Salt	¼ ounce	7 grams
Water or milk	¼ cup	50 milliliters
II		
Flour	1 pound	500 grams
Eggs	3	3
Salt	¼ ounce	7 grams
Oil	¼ cup	50 milliliters
Milk	½ cup	1 deciliter

Procedure
1. Make a well in the flour and semolina (or flour only for *II*).
2. Mix the oil, eggs, salt, and water or milk in the well and gradually work in the flour until a smooth, thick dough is formed.
3. Wrap the dough in a damp towel and let it stand in a cool place for at least 2 hours.
4. Cut the dough into five pieces and roll and reroll each piece until it is paper thin and translucent.

continued

Procedure

5. Lay out the rolled pieces on a table or hang the pieces over a wooden rod to dry without allowing them to become brittle.
6. Fold the sheets of dough lengthwise into a scroll and cut into strips.
7. The noodles can be boiled while fresh and tossed with butter, or they can be dried by spreading out on a board in a well-ventilated area for at least 36 hours.

Variation on Egg Noodles

Green Egg Noodles—*Nouilles vertes*

Blanch spinach, squeeze out water, puree the leaves in a blender, and add to the noodle dough.

Egg Noodle Dishes

Buttered Noodles—*Nouilles au beurre*

These are noodles that have been boiled and tossed with butter.

Noodles with Cheese—*Nouilles au fromage*

These noodles are prepared in the same way as spaghetti with cheese. Commercial noodles may be used.

Noodles, Home Style—*Nouilles bonne femme*

This dish is made with boiled noodles that have been tossed with melted butter and covered with browned breadcrumbs.

Westphalian Noodles—*Nouilles westphalienne*

Thicken noodles with a light cream sauce, add julienned ham, and bake in a buttered platter covered with grated cheese.

22.1.5 Spaetzle—*Spätzli, frisettes*

Yield
approximately 10 servings

Ingredients	U.S. Weight or Volume	Metric Weight or Volume
Flour	1 pound	500 grams
Salt	½ ounce	15 grams
Nutmeg	⅛ teaspoon	1 gram
Milk and water mixture	1½ to 1¾ cups	350 to 400 milliliters
Eggs	4	4

Procedure

1. Sift the flour, salt, and nutmeg into a bowl. Make a well in the center.
2. Combine the lukewarm milk and water mixture with the eggs and pour into the well.
3. Gradually stir in the flour until the dough takes on a thick consistency, like molasses.
4. Beat the dough until bubbles start to form.
5. Force the dough through a spaetzle colander directly into boiling salted water.
6. When the spaetzle are all floating on the surface, remove them. Prepare like pasta, or sauté lightly in butter.

Note: If large quantities are made, the salted boiling water must be changed frequently.

Variation of Spaetzle

Spinach Spaetzle—*Spaetzli aux épinards*

Mix well-drained, finely chopped spinach into the finished dough.

22.2 Gnocchi—*Gnocchi*

Gnocchi are small dumplings, usually made from cream puff pastry (*pâte à choux*), semolina flour, or potato puree. They are poached and then baked, covered with cheese. They can also be used in soups.

22.2.1 Gnocchi, Parisian Style—*Gnocchi à la parisienne*

Yield

approximately 10 servings

Ingredients	U.S. Weight or Volume	Metric Weight or Volume
Cream puff pastry	2 pounds	1 kilogram
Cream sauce, thin	1¾ cups	4 deciliters
Cheese, grated	3½ ounces	100 grams
Butter	3½ ounces	100 grams

Procedure

1. Fill a pastry bag with cream puff pastry. Pipe out the paste into marble-size dumplings and drop into simmering, but not boiling, salted water.
2. When all the dumplings are floating on the surface, remove them from the water, place them in a buttered gratin dish, and cover with a thin cream sauce.
3. Sprinkle with the cheese and melted butter. Place the gnocchi in the oven at 425°F (220°C). After 8 to 10 minutes, reduce the heat to 375°F (190°C), and continue baking until a golden yellow crust has formed, about 25 minutes longer.
4. Serve gnocchi immediately after removing from the oven.

22.2.2 Gnocchi, Roman Style—*Gnocchi romaine*

Yield

approximately 10 servings

Ingredients	U.S. Weight or Volume	Metric Weight or Volume
Milk	1¼ quarts	1.2 liters
Butter	5 ounces	150 grams
Salt	½ teaspoon	2 grams
Nutmeg	¼ teaspoon	1 gram
Semolina	9 ounces	250 grams
Parmesan cheese, grated	5 ounces	150 grams
Egg yolks	2	2

Procedure

1. Combine the milk, 1¾ ounces (50 grams) of the butter, salt, and nutmeg in a saucepan. Heat to the boiling point.
2. Sprinkle the semolina into the milk and stir this mixture over a low heat for 15 minutes.
3. Add 1¾ ounces (50 grams) of the grated cheese and the egg yolks. Blend thoroughly.
4. Spread the mixture to a depth of ¾ to 1 inch (2 to 2.5 centimeters) on a buttered sheet pan. Cool.
5. Cut round slices 1¾ to 2 inches (4.5 to 5 centimeters) in diameter. Layer these in a buttered baking dish so that the edge of each slice lies on that of the last slice.
6. Sprinkle the remainder of the grated cheese and the butter over the gnocchi.
7. Bake in oven at 425°F (220°C) for 10 to 15 minutes, until a golden yellow crust is formed.

22.2.3 Gnocchi, Piedmont Style—*Gnocchi piémontaise*

Yield

10 servings

Ingredients	U.S. Weight or Volume	Metric Weight or Volume
Potatoes, simmered in hot water	2½ pounds	1,200 grams
Eggs	2 to 3	2 to 3
Salt, pepper, nutmeg	to taste	to taste
Flour	7 ounces	200 grams
Tomato sauce	2 cups	5 deciliters
Parmesan cheese	3½ ounces	100 grams
Butter	3½ ounces	100 grams

Procedure

1. Peel the potatoes while they are still hot and puree them.
2. Mix in the eggs, add the seasonings, and let cool.
3. When the mixture is almost cold, add flour until the mixture feels dry but is still elastic.

continued

Procedure

4. Form nut-size dumplings. Gently place them in boiling salt water and poach for 5 minutes.
5. Prepare a platter, butter it, and cover the bottom with tomato sauce. Drain the gnocchi and arrange them on the platter.
6. Dot with Parmesan cheese, freshly grated pepper, and hot butter, and gratinate.

Variations on Gnocchi

Gnocchi Natural Style

Add cheese, butter, sage, cream, or mushrooms before baking.

22.3 Rice—*Riz*

Every rice dish should be made with top-quality rice. Italian varieties of rice are especially suitable for risotto. Long-grain rices are preferred for main dishes, salads, and soups, where each grain should be separate, dry, and fluffy. Patna rice or converted rice is good for these purposes. Short- or medium-grain rice is best for puddings, croquettes, and rice rings.

The ratio of rice to water varies with the type and age of the rice.

22.3.1 Risotto

Yield
approximately 10 servings

Ingredients	*U.S. Weight or Volume*	*Metric Weight or Volume*
Butter	5 ounces	150 grams
Onion, chopped fine	7 ounces	200 grams
Rice	28 ounces	800 grams
Light stock with seasoning	2¼ quarts	2.3 liters
Parmesan cheese, grated	5 ounces	150 grams

Procedure

1. Sauté onion in one-third of the butter in a suitable pan.
2. Add rice and stir until the rice is covered with butter.
3. Pour in the boiling stock, cover, and cook the rice for about 15 minutes.
4. Remove from the heat. If necessary, add a little more stock. Stir until the rice absorbs all the liquid.
5. Add the remainder of the butter and the cheese.

Note: Risotto is best when served immediately. It should be *al dente*. If serving must be delayed, place the rice over very low heat and add a little cold stock.

Variations of Risotto

Risotto with Chipolata Sausages—*Risotto aux chipolatas*

This is a risotto surrounded with chipolata sausages and topped with sautéed mushrooms.

Risotto, Milanese style—*Risotto milanaise*

Risotto is prepared with rice that has been cooked in stock with saffron.

Risotto with Mushrooms—*Risotto aux champignons*

Risotto is garnished with a bouquet of sautéed mushrooms.

Risotto with Tomatoes—*Risotto tomate*

The rice for this dish is cooked in a broth with added tomato puree and diced tomatoes.

22.3.2 Rice, Creole Style—*Riz créole*

Yield
approximately 10 servings

Ingredients	U.S. Weight or Volume	Metric Weight or Volume
Rice	1 pound	500 grams
Water	1 quart	1 liter
Salt	½ teaspoon	3 grams
Butter	3½ ounces	100 grams

Procedure

1. Wash rice thoroughly to remove excess starch.
2. Add water to rice, cover, and heat to the boiling point.
3. Reduce heat to low and continue to cook for 20 minutes.
4. Separate rice grains with a fork and put rice into a buttered pan. Add salt and butter.
5. Cover rice with aluminum foil and heat in oven at 350°F (175°C) for 15 minutes.

Variations of Rice, Creole Style

White Rice—*Riz au blanc*

This is boiled rice that has been cooked in water or broth, drained, and sautéed in seasoned butter.

22.3.3 Rice Pilaf—*Riz pilav*

Yield
approximately 10 servings

Ingredients	U.S. Weight or Volume	Metric Weight or Volume
Oil	3½ ounces	100 grams
Onion, chopped fine	5 ounces	150 grams
Rice, long grain	1½ pounds	700 grams
Stock	1 to 1½ quarts	1 liter
Thyme	1 teaspoon	5 grams
Pepper, freshly ground	½ teaspoon	3 grams
Butter	5 ounces	150 grams
Salt	as needed	as needed

Procedure

1. Sauté the onion in the oil until translucent.
2. Add the rice and continue cooking for a few minutes.
3. Pour in the stock, thyme, and pepper.
4. Bring to a boil, cover, and simmer in the oven at 350°F (175°C) for 15 to 18 minutes.
5. Remove from oven. Add slivers of butter, loosen with a fork, and season to taste.

Variations of Rice Pilaf

Rice, Turkish Style—*Riz à la turque*

The rice used in this dish is cooked in a broth with saffron. It is then prepared like a rice pilaf. Peeled and chopped tomatoes, peas, and dried currants are added to the pilaf. Extra stock may be needed to finish the rice.

22.4 Corn—*Maïs*

Cornmeal is the basis for many traditional corn dishes.

22.4.1 Polenta

Yield
10 servings

Ingredients	U.S. Weight or Volume	Metric Weight or Volume
Onion	3½ ounces	100 grams
Garlic	2 cloves	2 cloves
Fat	1½ ounces	50 grams
Water	2½ cups	6 deciliters
Milk	2½ cups	6 deciliters
Salt	½ ounce	20 grams
Cornmeal, coarsely ground	8 ounces	250 grams
Parmesan cheese	3½ ounces	100 grams

continued

Procedure
1. Sauté onions and garlic in fat.
2. Add water and milk. Bring the mixture to a boil. Add salt.
3. Gradually add the cornmeal and boil rapidly for 5 minutes, stirring constantly.
4. Reduce heat and simmer for 90 minutes. Do not stir; a crust on the bottom of the pan is desirable.
5. Before serving, add grated Parmesan cheese, or serve it separately.

Other Corn Dishes

Corn Gnocchi—*Gnocchi de maïs*

Prepare like gnocchi, Roman style, but use cornmeal instead of semolina. The dough can be cut into different shapes, dipped in egg, and fried in butter.

Cornmeal Soufflé—*Soufflé de maïs*

Prepare polenta, but simmer for only 60 minutes. Let it cool and add 8 egg yolks. Beat 10 egg whites and fold them into the mixture. Pour into a buttered and floured soufflé mold; the mold should be three-quarters full. Cook for 30 minutes in a double boiler on the stove top. Transfer the double boiler to the oven, continue to cook for 1 hour at rising heat, or bake for 30 more minutes.

Chapter 23
National Dishes

23.1 Swiss National Dishes

23.1.1 Fondue

Yield
approximately 4 servings

Ingredients	U.S. Weight or Volume	Metric Weight or Volume
Garlic	1 clove	1 clove
White wine	1¾ cups	4 deciliters
Swiss cheese, grated	20 ounces	600 grams
Cornstarch	2 teaspoons	10 grams
Kirsch	2 ounces	60 milliliters
Pepper	⅛ teaspoon	1 gram
Nutmeg	⅛ teaspoon	1 gram

Procedure
1. Rub a garlic clove around the inside of the fondue dish.
2. Place the dish over the heat and pour in the wine.
3. Add the cheese gradually, stirring continuously in a figure-eight pattern. Continue stirring after the mixture boils.
4. Dissolve the cornstarch in the Kirsch and add to the mixture. Bring to a boil once more, stirring constantly.
5. Season to taste.
6. The fondue should continue to cook gently on the table. Place a small alcohol burner or hot plate under the fondue dish.

Note: If the fondue does not bind properly (the cheese may be too young or the wine too strong), add vinegar and continue stirring until it is smoothly bound.

Other Swiss Cheese Dishes

Ramequin—Cheese Gratin

This is made with 20 slices of white bread, 20 slices of Emmentaler cheese, 5 eggs, 1 quart (1 liter) of milk, 1 teaspoon (6 grams) of salt, and ¼ teaspoon (2 grams) of nutmeg. Place alternate slices of cheese and bread in a buttered gratin dish. Mix the eggs, milk, and seasoning together, and pour over the cheese and bread. Place the dish in a water bath, bake at 325°F (160°C), and gratinate. Sprinkle with paprika. Yield: approximately 10 servings.

Raclette

This specialty of the Swiss Valais canton requires a special oven called a "raclette" and the cheese from the Alpine region. The cheese is divided and its center is exposed to heat until just the surface begins to melt. This portion is scraped off and placed on a hot plate. The raclette is served with potatoes boiled in their jackets, dark bread, gherkins, and cocktail onions. The flavor is enhanced by freshly ground pepper.

Käseschnitten—Toasted Cheese

Slices of white bread are browned in butter, covered with slices of mature Emmentaler or Gruyère cheese, dusted with paprika, and baked until the cheese is melted and slightly brown.

In a second method grated cheese is mixed with a little cream or béchamel sauce, an egg yolk, nutmeg, and paprika. The cheese is spread on the slices of fried bread and gratinated in the oven or under the broiler.

Käseschnitte nach Oberlander Art—Toasted Cheese, Oberland Style

Slices of bread are sautéed in butter, spread with mustard, covered with sliced ham, topped with thick slices of mature Emmentaler cheese, dusted with paprika, and gratinated in a hot oven. Before serving, each piece is topped with a fried egg.

Champignonschnitten nach Emmentaler Style—Mushrooms on Toast, Emmentaler Style

Sliced fresh mushrooms, sautéed shallots, lemon juice, salt, pepper, nutmeg, and some white wine are covered and simmered for about 15 minutes, until most of the liquid is evaporated. Béchamel sauce and cream are added and heated to the boiling point. The mushrooms are placed on sautéed slices of bread and then covered with a slice of ham and a slice of Emmentaler cheese. These slices are gratinated in the oven and served with a fried egg on top of each.

23.1.2 *Quiche au Fromage*—Cheese Quiche

Yield
12 to 15 servings

Ingredients	U.S. Weight or Volume	Metric Weight or Volume
Milk	1 quart	1 liter
Cream	¾ cup	2 deciliters
Cornstarch	¾ to 1 ounce	20 to 30 grams

Ingredients	U.S. Weight or Volume	Metric Weight or Volume
Nutmeg	⅛ teaspoon	1 gram
Paprika	⅛ teaspoon	1 gram
Salt	½ teaspoon	3 grams
Eggs, well beaten	7	7
Emmentaler cheese, grated	10 to 14 ounces	300 to 400 grams
Short crust paste	as needed	as needed

Procedure
1. Bring the milk and cream to the boiling point.
2. Dissolve the cornstarch in a little cold water, add to the hot milk, and bring back to a boil, stirring constantly.
3. Allow this mixture to cool slightly. Then season with nutmeg, paprika, and salt.
4. Mix in the well-beaten eggs.
5. Mix in the cheese.
6. Line tart pans or pie pans with short crust paste. Pierce the bottom crust.
7. Pour the prepared cheese mixture into the crusts.
8. Place a few small slices of cheese on top.
9. Bake in the oven at 350°F (175°C), for 45 minutes if the pans are 8 inches (20 centimeters) in diameter, until nicely browned. Serve hot.

Other Swiss Cheese Pies

Käsekuchen nach Bauernart—Cheese Pie, Farmer's Style

The crust of this cheese pie is pierced and covered with diced ham or slices of bacon. It is then filled with the cheese mixture used for plain cheese quiche. Thin slices of ham or lean bacon are arranged on top. It is baked in the oven at 350°F (175°C) for approximately 40 minutes.

Käsekuchen mit Krautern—Cheese Pie with Herbs

This cheese pie is prepared using the cheese quiche recipe with the addition of 5 ounces (150 grams) of blanched spinach leaves, 1¾ ounces (50 grams) of chervil, 1 sprig of marjoram, and 1 ounce (28 grams) of parsley. The spinach and herbs are sautéed in butter and spread over the dough lining the bottom of the pan. The cheese mixture is poured into the dough, and the pie is baked in an oven at 350°F (175°C) for approximately 40 minutes.

23.1.3 Käsetörtchen—Cheese Tartlets

Yield
20 tartlets

Ingredients	U.S. Weight or Volume	Metric Weight or Volume
Puff pastry	10 ounces	300 grams
Milk	1¾ cups	4 deciliters
Emmentaler cheese and Gruyère cheese, grated	10 ounces	300 grams
Eggs	3	3
Pepper	⅛ teaspoon	1 gram
Nutmeg	⅛ teaspoon	1 gram

Procedure
1. Line the tart pans with puff pastry.
2. Mix the milk, cheese, eggs, and seasonings thoroughly.
3. Fill the molds half full.
4. Bake in oven at 350°F (175°C) for 25 to 30 minutes.
5. Serve piping hot.

Note: These tartlets are also known as *ramequins*.

23.1.4 Oberlander Käsetörtchen—Cheese Tartlets, Oberland Style

Yield
40 tartlets

Ingredients	U.S. Weight or Volume	Metric Weight or Volume
Milk	1 quart	1 liter
Cream	¾ cup	2 deciliters
Cornstarch	1 ounce	30 grams
Eggs, well beaten	7	7

Ingredients	U.S. Weight or Volume	Metric Weight or Volume
Emmentaler cheese	14 ounces	400 grams
Nutmeg	⅛ teaspoon	1 gram
Paprika	⅛ teaspoon	1 gram
Onion, chopped	3½ ounces	100 grams
Butter	1 teaspoon	5 grams
Ham, chopped fine	12 ounces	350 grams
Short crust paste	as needed	as needed

Procedure
1. Heat the milk and cream to the boiling point.
2. Dissolve the cornstarch in a little cold water and add to the hot milk. Bring back to the boiling point, stirring constantly.
3. Remove from heat and allow the mixture to cool slightly. Then mix in the well-beaten eggs, the cheese, and the seasonings.
4. Sauté the onion in the butter.
5. Add the ham and continue sautéing.
6. Line the tartlet pans with short crust paste.
7. On each crust, place a spoon of the onion and ham mixture.
8. Fill each tartlet with the warm cream mixture.
9. Bake in oven at 350°F (175°C) for 25 to 30 minutes.
10. Serve hot.

23.1.5 Rötel nach Genfer Art—Golden Trout, Geneva Style

Yield
approximately 10 servings

Ingredients	U.S. Weight or Volume	Metric Weight or Volume
Golden trout	4 pounds	2 kilograms
Lemon juice	¼ cup	50 milliliters
Salt	1 teaspoon	6 grams
Butter	4 ounces	100 grams
Shallots	1	1

continued

Ingredients	U.S. Weight or Volume	Metric Weight or Volume
Herbs, chopped: parsley, chives, thyme, rosemary, tarragon	1 tablespoon total	15 grams total
Water	¾ cup	2 deciliters
White wine	¾ cup	2 deciliters
Kneaded butter	3 tablespoons	45 grams
Egg yolks	2	2
Cream	¼ cup	50 milliliters

Procedure

1. Dress the fish and sprinkle the interiors with the lemon juice and salt.
2. Sauté the shallot and then the herbs in butter.
3. Add the wine and water, and bring to the boiling point.
4. Poach the fish in this court bouillon, then remove it and keep it hot.
5. Bind the liquid with the kneaded butter, and then add the egg yolks and cream.
6. Season to taste.
7. Pour the sauce over the golden trout, and serve hot with boiled potatoes.

Other Swiss Fish Dishes

Felchenfilets Schweizerhof—Fillets of Whitefish, Schweizerhof Style

Flatten and season 4 pounds (110 grams) of whitefish fillets. Spread onion sauce, containing chopped and sautéed fresh mushrooms, on every other fillet. Place the second fillet on top of the first one and press them together lightly. Coat the fish with flour and dip into the beaten eggs that have been flavored with herbs. Sauté the fish in butter. Before serving, cover the fish with melted butter and garnish with lemon and parsley. Serve Colbert sauce separately. Yield: 10 servings.

Barschfilets nach Berner Art—Fillets of Perch, Bernese Style

Season 4 pounds (110 grams) of perch fillets with salt, pepper, and lemon juice. Coat the fish with flour and sauté in butter. Meanwhile, prepare sautéed potatoes and place on a serving dish. Cover each fillet with Mornay sauce and arrange the fillets on the potatoes. Sprinkle with cheese and melted butter and gratinate in the oven. Yield: 10 servings.

23.1.6 Emmentaler Schafsvoressen—Mutton Stew, Emmentaler Style

Yield
10 servings

Ingredients	U.S. Weight or Volume	Metric Weight or Volume
Mutton breast and shoulder cut into 2½-ounce (70-gram) cubes	5 pounds	2.5 kilograms
Stock	3 cups	7 deciliters
White wine	¼ cup	40 milliliters
Pearl onions	1 pound	500 grams
Carrots, diced	8 ounces	250 grams
Celery, diced	3½ ounces	100 grams
Turnips, diced	3½ ounces	100 grams
Cornstarch	½ teaspoon	3 grams
Flour	1¾ ounces	50 grams
Saffron	¼ teaspoon	2 grams
Salt	½ teaspoon	3 grams

Procedure

1. Blanch meat and drain. Place in casserole.
2. Add stock and wine; cover and simmer for 45 minutes.
3. Add the vegetables and simmer until tender.
4. Mix the cornstarch, flour, and saffron in a small amount of water, and add to the meat.
5. Heat to the boiling point.
6. Serve with boiled potatoes.

Note: Lamb may be substituted for mutton.

23.1.7 *Zürcher Leberspiessli*—Liver Kebabs, Zurich Style

Yield
10 servings

Ingredients	U.S. Weight or Volume	Metric Weight or Volume
Calf's liver	2¼ pounds	1 kilogram
Sage sprigs	as needed	as needed
Bacon, lean, sliced	1 pound	500 grams
Salt, pepper	to taste	to taste
String beans	2½ pounds	1.2 kilograms

Procedure
1. Cut the liver in strips approximately 2 inches (4 centimeters) long and ½ inch (1 centimeter) thick. Put a leaf of sage on each strip and wrap in a slice of bacon. Season.
2. Arrange five kebabs on each wood or metal skewer and grill.
3. Serve on a bed of string beans.
4. Serve buttered potatoes separately.

23.1.8 *Kutteln nach Zürcher Art*—Tripe, Zurich Style

Yield
10 servings

Ingredients	U.S. Weight or Volume	Metric Weight or Volume
Tripe, precooked	4 pounds	1.8 kilograms
Fat	3½ ounces	100 grams
Onions	5 ounces	150 grams
Flour	2 ounces	50 grams
White wine	1 cup	2 deciliters
White stock	1 quart	1 liter
Caraway seeds	to taste	to taste
Cream	1 cup	2 deciliters

Procedure
1. Cut tripe into squares or strips.
2. Sauté onions in fat until translucent.
3. Add tripe to onions. Add the flour. Then add wine and enough white stock to cover the tripe.
4. Cook for 30 minutes and correct spices. Add caraway seeds as desired.
5. Add cream and heat until mixture is warm.
6. Serve with boiled potatoes.

23.1.9 *Pieds de porc braisés*—Braised Pigs' Feet

Yield
10 servings

Ingredients	U.S. Weight or Volume	Metric Weight or Volume
Pigs' feet	10	10
White wine	to cover	to cover
Celery, diced	1 cup	225 grams
Bay leaves	2	2
Thyme	½ teaspoon	3 grams
Parsley	¼ cup	65 grams
Fat	as needed	as needed
Onion, sliced	1 large	1 large
Garlic, crushed	2 cloves	2 cloves
Stock	1 cup	2 deciliters
Salt	2 teaspoons	12 grams
Peppercorns, crushed	8	8
Tomato puree	½ cup	1 deciliter
Madeira wine	¼ cup	50 milliliters
Mushrooms, sliced and sautéed	4 ounces	100 grams

Procedure
1. Wash the pigs' feet and split them lengthwise.
2. Combine white wine, celery, bay leaves, thyme, and parsley. Pour over the pigs' feet.
3. Marinate for 8 days.
4. Remove pigs' feet from marinade and sauté in fat until brown.
5. Sauté onion and garlic and add to the pigs' feet.

continued

Procedure

6. Add stock, salt, peppercorns, and tomato puree to the wine marinade.
7. Pour the marinade over the pigs' feet, cover, and braise in the oven at 325°F (160°C) until the meat is tender, about 3 hours.
8. Remove the feet and reduce the stock by one-third.
9. Strain and adjust seasonings.
10. Bone the feet and add Madeira wine to the gravy. Arrange the meat and gravy in individual cocottes topped with sautéed mushrooms. Serve pasta or rice separately.

23.1.10 *Schweizer Schnitzel*—Veal Steak, Swiss Style

Yield
2 servings

Ingredients	U.S. Weight or Volume	Metric Weight or Volume
Veal loin steaks (2)	2½ ounces each	150 grams each
Salt	½ teaspoon	3 grams
Egg, beaten	1	1
Breadcrumbs, dry, fine, white	as needed	as needed
Emmentaler cheese	1¾ ounces	50 grams
Cream *or* béchamel sauce	2 tablespoons	30 milliliters
Egg yolk	1	1
Paprika	⅛ teaspoon	1 gram
Ham slices	5 ounces	300 grams
Butter, melted	2 tablespoons	30 milliliters

Procedure

1. Pound the veal steaks slightly, not too thin.
2. Dip the meat into salted beaten egg and then bread with crumbs. Sauté until tender.
3. Mix the cheese, cream or béchamel sauce, egg yolk, and paprika. Spread the mixture on the slices of ham.
4. Gratinate the ham in the oven or under the broiler.
5. Place the ham on the veal steaks.

6. Pour foaming hot butter over the meat and serve at once. A thickened veal gravy may be served separately.

Note: This recipe was conceived to replace veal cordon bleu.

Other Swiss Meat Dishes

Berner Platte—Bernese Platter

This is prepared by boiling a piece of beef with lean bacon, smoked pork chop, cured pig's knuckle, and tongue sausage until tender. The meat is sliced and arranged on a platter of braised sauerkraut or green beans. Poached marrow bones are arranged around the edge of the dish. Broiled potatoes are served separately. Cranberry sauce is a good accompaniment.

Geschnetzeltes nach Zürcher Art—Sliced Veal, Zurich Style

This dish is prepared with equal parts of veal, veal kidney, and mushrooms that have been cut into very fine slices. The veal and kidneys are browned in butter and added to some sautéed onions. The meat and onions are placed on a dish and the pan is deglazed with a small amount of veal stock or demi-glace, white wine, and cream. The sauce is reduced and seasoned with lemon juice and paprika. The meat is seasoned, added to the sauce, and heated. The sautéed mushrooms are arranged over the top before serving.

23.2 French National Dishes

23.2.1 *Cassoulet de Mouton*—Mutton Cassoulet

Yield
approximately 10 servings

Ingredients	U.S. Weight or Volume	Metric Weight or Volume
Navy beans	10 ounces	300 grams
Water	1½ quarts	1.5 liters

Ingredients	U.S. Weight or Volume	Metric Weight or Volume
Bouquet garni	1	1
Salt	1 teaspoon	5 grams
Garlic cloves	2	2
Bacon ends or salt pork strips	10 ounces	300 grams
Lean bacon, chopped	10 ounces	300 grams
Garlic sausage or tongue sausage	1 pound	500 grams
Mutton, boneless shoulder or breast, cut into cubes	2 pounds	1 kilogram
Fat	as needed	as needed
Onion, chopped	1 pound	500 grams
Garlic clove, crushed	1	1
Salt	1 teaspoon	5 grams
Pepper	1/8 teaspoon	1 gram
Brown stock	1/2 cup	1 deciliter
Tomato puree	1 to 2 tablespoons	15 to 30 milliliters
Breadcrumbs, buttered and dry	4 ounces	120 grams

Procedure

1. Soak beans overnight, then boil them in water with the *bouquet garni,* salt, garlic cloves, and raw bacon ends or salt pork strips tied together.
2. After boiling for 1 hour, add the chopped lean bacon. Cook for a few minutes and add the sausage. Boil until the beans and sausage are cooked.
3. Meanwhile, brown the mutton in fat. Add the chopped onion and a crushed garlic clove and brown again. Add seasonings. Deglaze the pan with stock and tomato puree. Braise as for ragout until meat is fully cooked, about 2 hours.
4. Remove the bundle of bacon ends and the whole garlic cloves. Combine remaining mixture with the meat and cook together for 10 minutes.
5. Cut bacon ends into slices and line ovenproof terrines with the bacon slices.
6. Place alternate layers of the mutton and slices of the sausage in the terrines and sprinkle breadcrumbs on top.

7. Brown in the oven at 375°F (190°C) for about 15 minutes. Add more stock from the beans if necessary.

Note: Lamb may be substituted for mutton.

23.2.2 *Civet de lièvre bonne femme*—Hare Ragout (Hasenpfeffer), Home Style

Yield

approximately 10 servings

Ingredients	U.S. Weight or Volume	Metric Weight or Volume
Hare	6 to 7 pounds	3 to 3.5 kilograms
Fat	3½ ounces	100 grams
Onion, coarsely chopped	7 ounces	200 grams
Flour	1¾ to 2 ounces	50 to 60 grams
Spice sachet	1	1
Garlic cloves, crushed	2	2
Stock	1 pint	5 deciliters
Red Burgundy wine	3 cups	7 deciliters
Bacon, lean, diced	7 ounces	200 grams
Onions, small	7 ounces	200 grams
Cream	¾ cup	2 deciliters
Brandy	¼ cup	50 milliliters
Lemon juice	2 tablespoons	30 milliliters
Salt	1 teaspoon	5 grams

Procedure

1. Cut the hare into stew-size pieces, season, and brown in fat.
2. Add the chopped onion, dust with flour, and continue cooking until onion is brown.
3. Add the spice sachet and garlic.
4. Add enough of the stock and wine so that the meat is covered.
5. Cover the saucepan and braise in the oven at 300°F (150°C).

continued

Procedure

6. When the pieces of the hare are half cooked (after 1 hour) remove them from the saucepan, strain the gravy, reduce slightly, and then pour the gravy over the meat.
7. Sauté the diced bacon and small onions and add to the meat mixture. Continue braising until the meat is tender, about 1 hour longer.
8. Add the cream and mix thoroughly.
9. Bring the dish almost to the boiling point without allowing it to boil. Keep it hot.
10. Flame with the brandy. Add the lemon juice and salt.

Note: The original recipe calls for the blood from the hare to be mixed with the cream and added to the gravy. Due to inspection and sanitation codes, this ingredient has been omitted. If gravy requires further thickening, add 1 teaspoon of cornstarch, dissolved in water, along with the cream.

Other French Ragouts and Cassoulets

Cassoulet d'oie—Goose Cassoulet

This cassoulet is prepared by the method used for mutton cassoulet, substituting goose for the mutton. The legs of the goose are cut into pieces; the wings are removed from the breast and each cut into two pieces; and the boned breast meat is cut into pieces.

Gibelotte de lapin—Rabbit Ragout

Rabbit ragout is prepared by the same method used for hasenpfeffer. It is made with half red wine and half white stock or meat stock. To prepare rabbit ragout, home style (*bonne femme*), follow the same procedure and add quartered potatoes.

Haricot de mouton—Mutton with Navy Beans

This mutton dish is prepared by sautéing small onions and diced lean bacon. After these are browned, they are removed from the fat and set aside. Stew-sized pieces of mutton, crushed garlic, and some flour are browned in the fat. The drippings are deglazed

with water or stock, a spice sachet is added, and the braising is continued for 30 minutes. The meat is removed, the sauce is strained, and the onions, bacon, beans, and meat are added to the sauce. It is simmered gently and served in terrines. Lamb may be substituted for mutton.

Pilav de mouton—Mutton Pilaf

This pilaf is prepared using the recipe for lamb ragout. A ring of rice pilaf is arranged on a serving dish, and the center is filled with the meat and sauce. The sauce is prepared without onions and potatoes. Lamb may be substituted for mutton.

23.2.3 *Tripes à la mode de Caen*—Tripe, Caen Style

Yield
approximately 10 servings

Ingredients	U.S. Weight or Volume	Metric Weight or Volume
Tripe, raw	6 pounds	3 kilograms
Beef feet, split	2	2
Onions, chopped	9 ounces	250 grams
Carrots, sliced	7 ounces	200 grams
Garlic cloves	2	2
Celery, chopped	3½ ounces	100 grams
Pork rind *or* salt pork	7 ounces	200 grams
Parsley root	1	1
Apple cider	2 quarts	2 liters
Salt	1 tablespoon	15 grams
Pepper	¼ teaspoon	2 grams
Bay leaf	1	1
Whole cloves	3	3
Thyme	½ teaspoon	3 grams
Cayenne pepper	as needed	as needed
Calvados	½ cup	1 deciliter

Procedure
1. Blanch the tripe. Rinse with cold water.
2. Cut into rectangular pieces about 2 by 3 inches (5 by 7.5 centimeters).
3. Place the split beef feet in the bottom of a deep earthenware pot or a braising pan.
4. Add the onions, carrots, garlic, celery, pork rind

or salt pork, and parsley root. Place the tripe on top.

5. Add the cider, salt, pepper, bay leaf, cloves, and thyme.
6. Bring to a boil, cover, and seal the lid hermetically, using flour paste.
7. Braise in the oven at 250°F (120°C) for 8 to 10 hours.
8. Take the tripe and the feet out of the stock. Remove the meat from the feet and add it to the tripe.
9. Strain the stock. Reduce to the desired thickness. Return tripe to the stock. Bring to a boil again and season with cayenne pepper to taste.
10. Flame the dish with warmed Calvados.
11. Serve boiled potatoes or potatoes in their jackets separately.

Note: If a pressure cooker is used, the cooking time is 1½ hours instead of 8 to 10 hours at very low heat. Avoid reducing the stock too much during steaming. Tripe from young animals requires a shorter cooking time, about 7 hours.

23.3 German National Dishes

23.3.1 *Deutsches Hacksteak*—German Meat Patties

Yield
10 servings

Ingredients	U.S. Weight or Volume	Metric Weight or Volume
Beef and pork, ground	2½ pounds	1.2 kilograms
Bread, white	7 to 10 ounces	200 to 300 grams
Milk	½ cup	1 deciliter
Onion	7 ounces	200 grams
Eggs	2	2
Salt	1 tablespoon	15 grams
Pepper	¼ teaspoon	2 grams
Fat	2 tablespoons	20 grams

Procedure
1. Place the meat in a mixing bowl.
2. Soak the bread in the milk. Press out surplus milk.
3. Chop one-third of the onion and sauté until translucent.
4. Add the bread, cooked onion, eggs, and seasonings to the meat. Mix well and shape into ten individual patties.
5. Sauté in fat until well done.
6. Slice remaining onion and brown in fat.
7. When serving, top the meat with the browned onion and surround with some of the pan drippings.

Other German Meat Patties

Hamburger Steak

Combine 2½ pounds (1.2 kilograms) of ground beef, 7 ounces (200 grams) of sautéed chopped onion, 3 or 4 rolls that have soaked in ½ cup (1 deciliter) of milk, 1 teaspoon (5 grams) of salt, and ¼ teaspoon (2 grams) of pepper. The meat is shaped into patties and sautéed in fat. The hamburgers can be topped with fried onion.

23.3.2 *Gefülltes Spanferkel*—Stuffed Suckling Pig

Yield
Number of servings will depend on size of pig; dressed pig weighing 12 pounds yields 10 servings

Ingredients	U.S. Weight or Volume	Metric Weight or Volume
Liver	½ the liver of the pig	½ the liver of the pig
Shallots, chopped	1¾ ounces	50 grams
Butter	1 ounce	30 grams
Suckling pig	1	1
Forcemeat:		
Veal	9 ounces	250 grams
Bacon, lean, fresh	5 ounces	150 grams

continued

Ingredients	U.S. Weight or Volume	Metric Weight or Volume
Liver	½ the liver of the pig	½ the liver of the pig
Mushrooms, chopped	5 ounces	150 grams
Rolls	2	2
Milk	½ cup	1 deciliter
Cream	½ cup	1 deciliter
Eggs	4	4
Madeira	½ cup	1 deciliter
Brandy	¼ cup	50 milliliters
Salt	2 teaspoons	10 grams
Pepper	¼ teaspoon	2 grams
Breadcrumbs	as needed	as needed
Butter	as needed for basting	as needed for basting
Beer	as needed for basting	as needed for basting

Procedure
1. Dice half of the liver and quickly brown with the shallots in butter.
2. Prepare the forcemeat by grinding the veal, bacon, half of the liver, chopped mushrooms, and rolls. Stir in the milk, cream, eggs, Madeira, brandy, salt, and pepper. Add the browned diced liver and shallots.
3. Season the suckling pig inside and out.
4. Stuff with forcemeat and sew up.
5. Put front feet through parallel cuts made on each side of the neck.
6. Place the pig on a grill or on a layer of breadcrumbs in a roasting pan. Care must be taken that both hind legs are sitting correctly, that the rear feet are fixed together using a wooden peg, and that the head is placed a little higher than the rest of the body. Wrap the ears and tail in aluminum foil.
7. During the roasting, baste the pig alternately with butter and beer. Should blisters form on the skin during roasting, pierce them.
8. Roast in oven at 325° to 350°F (160°C to 175°C). Allow at least 30 minutes per pound.

Note: This form of preparation is used when the pig is to be presented whole to the guests. If it is not to be served whole, roast the pig without stuffing. Bake the stuffing separately in a buttered mold in a water bath in the oven. For garnishes, use julienne of potatoes, glazed chestnuts, and red cabbage. Serve the gravy separately.

23.3.3 *Kalbshaxe nach Bürgerlicher Art*—Veal Shank, Home Style

Yield
approximately 10 servings

Ingredients	U.S. Weight or Volume	Metric Weight or Volume
Fat	3½ ounces	100 grams
Veal shanks, large, whole	4	4
Salt	½ teaspoon	3 grams
Pepper	⅛ teaspoon	1 gram
Mirepoix	10 ounces	300 grams
Tomato puree	1 ounce	30 grams
White wine	¾ cup	2 deciliters
Basic stock *or* brown stock	1 quart	1 liter
Cornstarch	2 tablespoons	10 grams
Water	¼ cup	50 milliliters
Madeira	¼ cup	50 milliliters
Pearl onions	7 ounces	200 grams
Carrots, sliced	10 ounces	300 grams
Turnips, chopped	7 ounces	200 grams
Peas	3½ ounces	100 grams
Butter	3½ ounces	100 grams
Parsley, chopped	as needed to garnish	as needed to garnish

Procedure
1. Heat the fat in a braising pan that can be covered.
2. Place the seasoned shanks in the pan and brown on both sides over high heat.
3. Add the *mirepoix* and tomato puree, and sauté these ingredients together.

4. Deglaze the pan with wine and reduce the liquids. Add stock so that only the bottoms of the shanks are covered by the liquid.
5. Cover and braise for at least 1 hour. During the braising, turn the shanks from time to time and baste with the liquid.
6. When cooked, remove shanks from the pan. Thin the stock slightly if necessary or thicken with cornstarch dissolved in cold water. Bring to a boil. Add Madeira, strain, and season to taste.
7. Meanwhile, glaze the small onions, carrots, and turnips separately. Toss the peas quickly in butter and arrange with the glazed vegetables over the shanks.
8. Sprinkle with parsley. Serve the meat juices separately.

23.3.4 *Bayrische Leberknödel*— Bavarian Liver Dumplings

Yield
approximately 10 servings

Ingredients	U.S. Weight or Volume	Metric Weight or Volume
Onion, chopped	5 ounces	150 grams
Butter *or* vegetable oil	1¾ ounces	50 grams
White bread	10 ounces	300 grams
Milk	¾ to 1¼ cups	2 to 3 deciliters
Beef liver	1 pound	500 grams
Veal kidney fat	7 ounces	200 grams
Eggs	3 or 4	3 or 4
Salt	2 teaspoons	10 grams
Pepper	¼ teaspoon	2 grams
Parsley, chopped	2 tablespoons	30 grams
Breadcrumbs	as needed	as needed
Stock, boiling	as needed	as needed

Procedure
1. Sauté the onion in butter or oil.
2. Soak the bread in warm milk and press out the excess milk.

3. Skin the liver and grind it with the kidney fat and the bread.
4. Add the onion, eggs, salt, pepper, and parsley to the liver. Mix well. If necessary, add some breadcrumbs.
5. Shape the dumplings with a large spoon or ice-cream scoop and drop into the boiling stock. Cover and poach slowly in the simmering stock for 5 or 6 minutes.

23.3.5 *Kartoffelknödel*—Potato Dumplings

Yield
approximately 10 servings

Ingredients	U.S. Weight or Volume	Metric Weight or Volume
Potatoes	3 pounds	1.5 kilograms
Eggs	4 or 5	4 or 5
Flour	5 ounces	150 grams
Semolina, if needed	1¾ ounces	50 grams
Butter, warm	2¾ ounces	80 grams
Salt	1 tablespoon	15 grams
Pepper	¼ teaspoon	3 grams
Butter, browned	as needed	as needed
Onion, chopped	7 ounces	3 grams

Procedure
1. Boil the unpeeled potatoes until tender.
2. Peel and grate the potatoes.
3. Mix the potatoes with the eggs, flour, the semolina if necessary, warm butter, salt, and pepper.
4. Let stand for 10 minutes.
5. Form into dumplings and poach in gently boiling salted water.
6. Pour browned butter over the dumplings and top with browned onion.

Note: Small fried bread croutons may be added to the dumpling mixture. For this recipe, 3½ to 7 ounces (100 to 200 grams) of croutons would be adequate.

23.3.6 *Kartoffelpuffer*—Potato Pancakes

Yield
approximately 10 servings

Ingredients	U.S. Weight or Volume	Metric Weight or Volume
Potatoes	3 pounds	1.5 kilograms
Onion, chopped	3½ ounces	100 grams
Eggs	2	2
Flour	1¾ ounces	50 grams
Salt	1 tablespoon	2 grams
Pepper	¼ teaspoon	2 grams
Fat	7 ounces	200 grams

Procedure
1. Peel and grate the raw potatoes.
2. Add the onion, eggs, flour, salt, and pepper. Mix well.
3. Drop this mixture in uniform-size portions into hot fat. Fry until crisp on both sides and serve immediately.

Note: Chopped parsley or grated cheese may be added to the pancakes. When made without onion, the pancakes may be served with stewed fruits and with applesauce.

23.4 British and American National Dishes

23.4.1 Chicken Curry

Yield
approximately 10 servings

Ingredients	U.S. Weight or Volume	Metric Weight or Volume
Chicken fryers, cut up	6 pounds (2 at 3 pounds each)	3 kilograms (2 at 1.5 kilograms each)
Butter	3½ ounces	100 grams

Ingredients	U.S. Weight or Volume	Metric Weight or Volume
Salt	1 tablespoon	15 grams
Onions, chopped	10 ounces	300 grams
Apples, sliced	4	4
Curry powder	2 tablespoons	30 grams
Chicken stock	3½ cups	9 deciliters
Cornstarch	1½ tablespoons	20 grams
Cream	1¼ cups	3 deciliters
Lemon juice	2 tablespoons	30 milliliters
Rice, creole style	1 pound	500 grams

Procedure
1. Sauté the chicken pieces in butter. Sprinkle with salt.
2. Add the chopped onion and sliced apples and continue sautéing.
3. Dust with the curry powder and add enough stock so that the chicken is just covered by the liquid.
4. Braise for 10 to 20 minutes, until the chicken is tender.
5. Remove chicken pieces from the stock. Thicken the stock with cornstarch dissolved in water. Add the cream and lemon juice. Reduce the liquid to a smooth sauce. Strain. Return the chicken to the sauce and keep it warm.
6. Serve with rice, Creole style.

Note: Chicken curry was originally an Indian dish and was adapted by the British when they ruled India. Fresh coconut milk can replace some of the chicken stock as part of the cooking liquid. With variations such as chicken curry, Bombay style, separate garnishes must accompany the dish. In addition to the creole rice, the following are suitable:

- Bombay ducks
- Chopped pan-fried onion
- Chopped cooked egg whites
- Sweet peppers
- Diced pineapple
- Raisins
- Mango chutney
- Sautéed bananas

Variations of Chicken Curry

Lamb Curry

This curry is made from stew-size pieces of shoulder and breast of lamb. It is prepared like chicken curry and should cook for approximately 1 hour.

Veal Curry

This curry is made from shoulder and breast of veal cut into stew-size pieces. It is prepared like chicken curry and should cook for approximately 1 hour.

23.4.2 Irish Stew

Yield
approximately 10 servings

Ingredients	U.S. Weight or Volume	Metric Weight or Volume
Mutton, diced boneless breast and shoulder	3 to 4 pounds	1.5 to 2 kilograms
Onions, sliced	1 pound	500 grams
Leeks, sliced	7 ounces	200 grams
Carrots, sliced	10 ounces	300 grams
Turnips, sliced	3½ ounces	100 grams
Celery, sliced	7 ounces	200 grams
Potatoes, sliced	10 ounces	300 grams
Salt	1 tablespoon	15 grams
Spice sachet	1	1
Cabbage leaves, sliced	10 ounces	300 grams
Worcestershire sauce	1 tablespoon	15 milliliters

Procedure
1. Blanch the meat quickly and return to saucepan.
2. Add the sliced vegetables, salt, and spice sachet; cover with water. Place the sliced cabbage leaves on top and simmer for 1 hour. Thicken the liquid.

3. Serve in individual casseroles and garnish with additional boiled potatoes.
4. Sprinkle Worcestershire sauce on top.

Note: The carrots, celery, or turnips may be omitted. Sometimes the vegetables are cooked separately. When this is done, the quantity of onion and potatoes cooked with the meat is greatly increased. Lamb may be substituted for mutton.

23.4.3 Chicken Pie

Yield
approximately 10 servings

Ingredients	U.S. Weight or Volume	Metric Weight or Volume
Chicken fryer, cut up	3 to 4 pounds	1.5 to 2 kilograms
Salt	1 tablespoon	15 grams
Pepper	½ teaspoon	4 grams
Shallots	1¾ ounces	50 grams
Onions	1¾ ounces	50 grams
Mushrooms, quartered	5 ounces	150 grams
Butter	1¾ ounces	50 grams
Parsley, chopped	1 tablespoon	15 grams
Veal cutlets, thin	10 to 14 ounces	300 to 400 grams
Bacon slices, lean	7 ounces	200 grams
Eggs, hard-cooked	5	5
Brown poultry stock	1 pint	5 deciliters
Egg yolk	1	1
Puff pastry	10 to 14 ounces	300 to 400 grams
Egg, slightly beaten	1	1

Procedure
1. Season the chicken pieces with salt and pepper.
2. Sauté the shallots, onions, and mushrooms in but-

continued

Procedure

ter. Sprinkle this mixture and the parsley over the chicken.

3. Season the veal and arrange it and the bacon on the bottom of a deep-dish pie pan.
4. Cut the hard-cooked eggs into halves.
5. Add the chicken pieces and the eggs.
6. Pour in the stock until the pieces are just covered.
7. Moisten the edge of the pie dish with egg yolk and place a strip of puff pastry around the rim. Cover the dish with a lid made of the puff pastry, having first moistened the inside edge with egg. Press the lid and the strip around the edge together until sealed.
8. Garnish the pastry with shapes cut from the dough. Brush with beaten egg and bake the pie in the oven at 300°F (150°C) for approximately 40 minutes.
9. When the cooking time is up, make a small cut at the edge of the pastry and tilt the dish to see if any liquid remains. Add stock as required.

Other Meat Pies

Pigeon Pie

This is made in a cocotte, with the bottom lined with slices of uncooked bacon that have been sprinkled with chopped shallots and parsley. The halved pigeons are seasoned with salt and pepper and chopped parsley. They are placed on the bacon. Mushrooms that have been quartered and sautéed in butter, and partially cooked Parisian potatoes are added to the cocotte. The mixture is covered with stock. It is finished by the method used for chicken pie.

Steak Pie

This is a pie made from thin slices, ¼ inch (0.6 centimeters) thick, of beef tenderloin that have been seasoned, covered with chopped shallots and parsley,

and dusted with flour. The meat is arranged in a buttered cocotte in alternating layers with sautéed mushrooms. Rich stock is poured over the top. The pie is covered and finished as for chicken pie. The baking time is approximately 1 hour.

Steak and Kidney Pie

This pie is made with thin slices of beef tenderloin and slices of veal or sautéed sliced veal kidneys. It is prepared by the method used for chicken pie.

23.4.4 Deep-dish Apple Pie

Yield
10 servings

Ingredients	*U.S. Weight or Volume*	*Metric Weight or Volume*
Apples	10, large	10, large
Lemon juice	¼ cup	1 deciliter
Raisins	1½ ounces	50 grams
Sugar	9 ounces	250 grams
Butter	1½ ounces	50 grams
Cinnamon	¼ teaspoon	3 grams
Ginger	⅛ teaspoon	1 gram
Short crust paste	10 to 14 ounces	300 to 400 grams
Egg	1	1

Procedure

1. Peel, core, and slice the apples thinly.
2. Combine apples, lemon juice, raisins, and sugar. Place in deep-dish pie pan. Dot with butter and sprinkle with cinnamon and ginger.
3. Roll out the short crust paste and cover the pie with it. Cut vents in the top and flute the edges if desired.
4. Brush the crust with lightly beaten egg.
5. Bake for approximately 30 minutes in a 350°F (175°C) oven.

23.5 Italian National Dishes

23.5.1 *Piccata Milanese*—Veal Piccata, Milan Style

Yield
10 servings

Ingredients	U.S. Weight or Volume	Metric Weight or Volume
Veal cutlets	2 pounds	1 kilogram
Flour	3½ ounces	100 grams
Eggs	5	5
Parmesan cheese, grated	3½ ounces	100 grams
Oil	½ cup	1 deciliter
Butter	1½ ounces	50 grams
Tongue, julienne	3½ ounces	100 grams
Mushrooms, julienne	9 ounces	200 grams
Ham, julienne	3½ ounces	100 grams
Madeira sauce	1 pint	5 deciliters

Procedure
1. The cutlets should be sliced very thinly; there should be about thirty pieces altogether. Dredge them in the flour.
2. Lightly beat the eggs. Stir in the grated Parmesan cheese.
3. Dip the cutlets in the egg/cheese mixture.
4. Fry the cutlets in the oil.
5. Heat the butter and sauté the tongue, mushrooms, and ham.
6. Garnish the veal with the tongue, mushrooms, and ham. Serve the Madeira sauce separately. Spaghetti or risotto is a good accompiment.

Variations on Veal Piccata, Milan Style

Piccata

In addition to veal cutlets, veal liver cutlets and small cutlets of blanched sweetbreads may be prepared as piccata. Season the cutlets, dredge in flour, and sauté in butter. Combine grated lemon rind, minced garlic, and parsley, and sprinkle over the cutlets. Pour lemon juice and foaming hot butter over the top.

23.5.2 Saltimbocca

Yield
10 servings

Ingredients	U.S. Weight or Volume	Metric Weight or Volume
Veal cutlets	3 pounds	1.5 kilograms
Sage leaves	20	20
Prosciutto	2 ounces	60 grams
Flour	1½ ounces	50 grams
Salt	1 tablespoon	15 grams
Pepper	½ teaspoon	3 grams
Butter	5 ounces	150 grams
Marsala wine	½ cup	1 deciliter
Veal stock	1 cup	250 milliliters

Procedure
1. The cutlets should be sliced thinly; there should be twenty slices. Place a sage leaf and a slice of prosciutto on each cutlet, and secure with a toothpick.
2. Dredge the cutlets in flour, and season.
3. Sauté in butter until golden.
4. Deglaze the pan with the Marsala and veal stock and reduce. Pour a little of the sauce over the veal, and serve the rest separately.

23.5.3 *Osso Buco*—Braised Veal Shanks

Yield
10 servings

Ingredients	U.S. Weight or Volume	Metric Weight or Volume
Veal shanks, split	10 shanks (6 to 9 ounces each)	10 shanks (180 to 250 grams each)

continued

Ingredients	U.S. Weight or Volume	Metric Weight or Volume
Salt	2 teaspoons	10 grams
Seasoning	⅛ teaspoon	1 gram
Flour	as needed	as needed
Fat	1¾ ounces	50 grams
Onion, chopped	5 ounces	150 grams
Garlic	2 cloves	2 cloves
Vegetable brunoise	10 to 14 ounces	300 to 400 grams
Herbs, chopped	½ teaspoon	3 grams
Tomato puree	1¾ ounces	50 grams
Tomatoes, peeled, seeded, and crushed	7 ounces	200 grams
White wine	¾ to 1¼ cups	2 to 3 deciliters
Brown stock	1 to 2 quarts	1 to 2 liters

Procedure

1. Season the veal shanks. Coat with flour and brown on all sides in fat.
2. Add the onion, garlic, vegetables, and chopped herbs. Cook slightly.
3. Add the tomato puree, peeled, seeded, and crushed tomatoes, and the white wine.
4. Cook and reduce.
5. Add the stock and braise until meat is tender.
6. When serving, sprinkle with minced garlic, grated lemon peel, and parsley.

Other Italian Dishes

Trota al chianti—Trout with Chianti Wine

The browned fish is placed on a serving platter and the oil is drained from the pan. Some Chianti wine is poured into the pan and reduced by half. Tomato sauce, chopped parsley, and lemon peel are added to the wine. The sauce is heated to the boiling point, strained, and poured over the fish before serving.

Fritto di pollo—Fried Chicken

This chicken is cut into pieces, seasoned, coated with flour, and dipped into beaten eggs mixed with oil. The chicken is breaded with a mixture of white breadcrumbs and cheese, and deep-fried. It is garnished with deep-fried parsley. Tomato sauce is served separately.

Tagliatelle alla livornese

Tagliatelle are long thin flat strips of egg pasta. A sauce made of sautéed onion, peeled and diced tomatoes, tomato sauce, garlic, and sautéed diced beef tenderloin tips is poured over the pasta. Grated cheese is served separately.

Fritto misto—Deep-fried Sweetbreads, Veal, and Vegetables

This Italian dish is a mixed fry or a combination of deep-fried veal cutlets, sliced sweetbreads, veal liver, calf's brains, a boiled head of veal, and vegetables. The foods are coated with flour, dipped into a batter, and deep-fried. The vegetables are arranged in the center of a serving dish and surrounded with the variety meats. Tomato sauce may be served separately. A variety of fruits, vegetables, fish, and meat may be used for *fritto misto*. Lemon wedges are always served as a garnish.

Arrostino annegato milanese

The veal for this dish is a cut from the loin that includes a slice of loin, tenderloin, and kidney. (It corresponds to the porterhouse steak plus the kidney of beef.) A skewer is used to hold the steak together. The steak is seasoned, spiced with sage and rosemary, coated with flour, and sautéed in butter. It is placed on a warm plate and sprinkled with minced parsley and garlic and grated lemon rind. Foaming hot butter is poured over the steak. The pan is deglazed with white wine and veal stock. The sauce is heated to the boiling point and served with the steak. Pasta or risotto may be served as a garnish.

23.6 Austrian National Dishes

23.6.1 *Wiener Rindsgulasch*—Viennese Goulash

Yield

approximately 10 servings

Ingredients	U.S. Weight or Volume	Metric Weight or Volume
Fat	1¾ to 2 ounces	50 to 60 grams
Onion, sliced thin	16 to 20 ounces	500 to 600 grams
Beef cubes, shank and shoulder	3 to 4 pounds	1.5 to 2 kilograms
Salt	1 tablespoon	15 grams
Pepper	½ teaspoon	3 grams
Garlic cloves	2	2
Paprika, Hungarian	1½ ounces	45 grams
Thyme	1 small bunch	1 small bunch
Marjoram	1 small bunch	1 small bunch
Tomato puree	1¾ ounces	50 grams
Vinegar	½ cup	1 deciliter
Brown stock	1½ quarts	1.5 liters
Cumin seeds *or* caraway seeds	½ ounce	15 grams

Procedure

1. Sauté the onion in the fat. Add the seasoned meat and continue sautéing.
2. Add the garlic, paprika, herbs, and tomato puree.
3. Deglaze the pan with vinegar. Reduce the liquids. Add the stock. Cover and simmer until tender.
4. Add the cumin seeds or caraway seeds.
5. Adjust seasoning to taste.

23.6.2 *Wiener Schnitzel*—Breaded Veal Cutlets, Viennese Style

Yield

10 servings

Ingredients	U.S. Weight or Volume	Metric Weight or Volume
Veal cutlets	10	10
Salt	2 teaspoons	10 grams
Pepper	½ teaspoon	3 grams
Flour	1½ ounces	50 grams
Eggs	2	2
Breadcrumbs	14 ounces	400 grams
Fat	1 pound	500 grams
Butter	3½ ounces	100 grams
Lemon wedges	20	20
Parsley	20 sprigs	20 sprigs

Procedure

1. The veal cutlets should be thinly cut. Season them.
2. Dredge the cutlets in flour, dip in lightly beaten eggs, and coat with breadcrumbs.
3. Place the fat in a frying pan and heat to 350°F (180°C).
4. Sauté the cutlets quickly in the hot fat, shaking the pan as they cook. Sauté on both sides.
5. Heat the butter until it foams. Pour the hot foaming butter over the cutlets, garnish with lemon wedges and parsley, and serve immediately.

Other Austrian Meat Dishes

Rahmgulasch—Creamed Goulash

This goulash is prepared like Wiener Rindgulasch. It is bound with sour cream and braised for a few minutes before serving.

Zwiebelfleisch—Beef and Onions

This recipe can be made with top round or shoulder of beef. It is prepared by slicing and sautéing several onions in fat. The fat is drained, and the beef is added to the pan with some stock and seasonings. It is covered and simmered to the medium stage. The cover is then removed, and the meat is dusted with flour. More stock is added. The meat is covered and braised until tender.

Wiener Backhendl—Fried Chicken, Viennese Style

A corn-fed chicken or a Rock Cornish hen may be used for this Viennese specialty. The chicken is dressed and trussed without removing the head and neck. The chicken is seasoned inside and outside, rolled in flour, then in beaten eggs, and finally in breadcrumbs. It is deep-fried until the skin is crisp. The chicken is served whole on a paper napkin. It is garnished with deep-fried parsley and served with lemon wedges.

23.6.3 *Salzburger Nockerl*—Salzburg Dumplings

Yield
approximately 10 servings

Ingredients	U.S. Weight or Volume	Metric Weight or Volume
Milk	1¼ cups	3 deciliters
Sugar, granulated	2 ounces	60 grams
Vanilla extract	1 teaspoon	4 milliliters
Butter, melted	1¾ ounces	50 grams
Egg whites	8	8
Egg yolks	8	8
Flour	1¾ ounces	50 grams
Sugar, confectioners'	as needed	as needed

Procedure
1. Mix the milk, one-third of the granulated sugar, vanilla, and half of the butter in a saucepan. Heat.
2. In a suitable bowl, beat the egg whites until stiff, and carefully fold in 7 beaten egg yolks, half of the remaining sugar, the flour, and remaining butter.
3. With a spoon shape this mixture into large dumplings.
4. Place in the hot milk. Cover and poach.
5. When the dumplings begin to turn brown, turn them over and cook for a short while.
6. Remove the dumplings and beat the milk with the remaining egg yolk and remaining granulated sugar to a creamy consistency. Pour this over the dumplings.
7. Sprinkle with confectioners' sugar before serving.

23.6.4 *Apfelstrudel*—Apple Strudel

Yield
approximately 10 servings

Ingredients	U.S. Weight or Volume	Metric Weight or Volume
Dough:		
Flour	12 ounces	350 grams
Water, lukewarm	½ to ¾ cups	100 to 150 milliliters
Egg	1	1
Oil	1 tablespoon	15 milliliters
Salt	⅛ teaspoon	1 gram
Filling:		
Apples, peeled, cored, chopped	3½ pounds	1.5 kilograms
Sugar	5½ to 7 ounces	150 to 200 grams
Cinnamon	1 tablespoon	15 grams
Raisins	7 ounces	200 grams
Rum	2 ounces	60 milliliters
Breadcrumbs	9 ounces	250 grams
Butter	3½ ounces	100 grams
Pine nuts *or* hazelnuts	3½ ounces	100 grams
Cream	½ cup	1 deciliter
Butter, melted	3½ ounces	100 grams

Procedure
1. Make a well in the flour.
2. Place the water, egg, oil, and salt in the well and mix them together. Mix the flour in gradually until a firm smooth dough is formed.
3. Cover the dough with a prewarmed bowl and let it rest for 1 hour.
4. Macerate the apples with the sugar, cinnamon, raisins, and rum for a short time.
5. Brown the breadcrumbs in 3½ ounces (100 grams) of butter and mix with the pine nuts or hazelnuts.
6. Spread a cloth on a table and dust it with flour.
7. Roll out the dough on the cloth as thin as possible. (See figure 23-1.)
8. Place your hands between the dough and cloth, and draw out and stretch the dough with your

hands until it is paper thin. Trim the edges of the dough if thick or uneven.

9. Sprinkle the breadcrumb/nut mixture evenly over the dough. Distribute the apples evenly over the dough.
10. Hold the cloth on one side with both hands and lift it up little by little so that the dough rolls itself up around the filling.
11. Arrange on a baking pan.
12. Coat with cream and melted butter. Press dough together along the sides.
13. Bake the strudel in the oven at 375°F (185°C) for 30 minutes, basting frequently with butter. It should be brown and crisp when done.
14. When serving, cut the strudel into slices and sprinkle with confectioners' sugar. Vanilla sauce may be served separately.

Note: Strudels filled with plums are prepared in the same way.

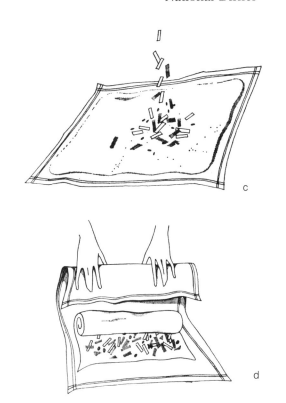

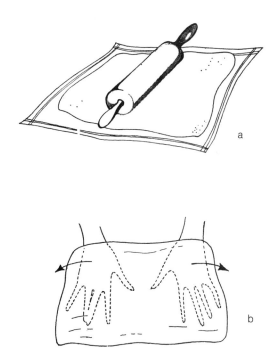

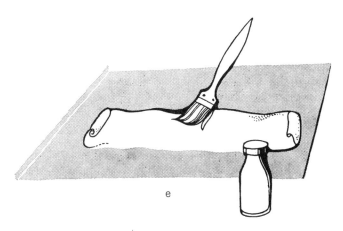

Figure 23-1. Preparation of dough for apple strudel: (a) on a cloth, roll the dough out very thinly; (b) with the hands between the dough and the cloth, palms down, stretch the dough carefully until it is as thin as possible; (c) distribute the filling evenly over the dough; (d) lift the cloth to roll the dough into a turnover shape; (e) brush with cream and melted butter.

Other Austrian Desserts

Palatschinken—Austrian Pancakes

Jam (apricot is most popular) is spread between two thin pancakes (crêpes). They are rolled and sprinkled with sugar.

Kaiserschmarren

Fold beaten egg whites into pancake batter. Coat the skillet with melted butter, pour the batter into the pan, and cook on one side. Sprinkle with raisins, turn the pancakes over, and allow to rise in the oven. Cut into small pieces, sprinkle with sugar, and serve immediately.

23.7 Other National Dishes

Hungarian National Dishes

Paprika Carp

This is a popular Hungarian dish. The carp is cut into slices and prepared *à la meunière.* A sauce is made by sautéing chopped onion in butter, dusting with flour and paprika, and deglazing with stock and sour cream. The fish slices are arranged in a baking dish, covered with the seasoned sauce, simmered until tender, and garnished with lemon wedges.

Esterházy Rostélyos—Braised Steaks

These are ½-inch (1-centimeter) sirloin or round steaks that are browned in butter and kept warm. Sliced carrots, parsnips, and celery are sautéed in the drippings and then coated with flour and paprika. Stock and capers are added to the vegetables. The steaks are added to the sauce and simmered until the meats and vegetables are tender. Sour cream is blended into the sauce just before serving.

23.7.1 *Szegedi Gulyás*—Goulash from Szeged

Yield
approximately 10 servings

Ingredients	U.S. Weight or Volume	Metric Weight or Volume
Fat	3½ ounces	100 grams
Onion, chopped fine	1 pound	500 grams
Lean pork, diced	3 to 4 pounds	1.5 to 2 kilograms
Paprika, sweet	1½ to 1¾ ounces	40 to 50 grams
Salt	1 tablespoon	15 grams
Pepper	½ teaspoon	3 grams
Garlic, minced	1 clove	1 clove
Tomato puree	1 ounce	30 grams
Sauerkraut, braised	28 ounces	800 grams
Stock	as needed	as needed
Sour cream	½ to ¾ cup	1 to 2 deciliters
Potatoes, peeled	1¾ pounds	800 grams

Procedure
1. Heat the fat. Add the onion and brown lightly.
2. Add the meat and seasonings and sauté until the meat is nearly tender.
3. Add the garlic, tomato puree, braised sauerkraut, and a little stock if it is needed.
4. Cover tightly and continue cooking for 1 to 1½ hours.
5. Add the sour cream. Season to taste and heat just to the boiling point.
6. Serve boiled potatoes separately.

Spanish National Dishes

23.7.2 *Paella Valenciana*—Valencia Paella

Yield
approximately 10 servings

Ingredients	U.S. Weight or Volume	Metric Weight or Volume
Olive oil	1¾ ounces	50 grams
Garlic cloves, crushed	2	2
Chicken meat, diced (mainly from legs and thighs)	28 ounces	800 grams
Pork, lean, diced, *or* chorizo sausage	7 ounces	200 grams
Onion, chopped	5 ounces	150 grams
Sweet peppers, all colors, diced	7 ounces	200 grams
Rice	1 pound	500 grams
White wine	1¼ cups	3 deciliters
Stock, boiling	1½ quarts	1.5 liters
Tomato puree	7 to 10 ounces	200 to 300 grams
Salt	2 teaspoons	10 grams
Saffron	⅛ teaspoon	1 gram
Large shrimps *or* lobsterettes	20	20
Octopus	5 ounces	150 grams
Sole *or* hake slices	10 ounces	300 grams
Peas	3½ ounces	100 grams
Mussels	20	20
Shrimps	3½ ounces	100 grams

Procedure

1. Heat the oil. Sauté the garlic, then remove it from the pan.
2. Brown the chicken and pork pieces or sausage on all sides.
3. Add onion and sweet peppers. Cover and cook for 10 minutes. Do not allow them to brown.
4. Add the rice. Heat and stir over high heat until rice becomes translucent.
5. Add the wine and boiling stock, the tomato puree, salt, saffron, large shrimps or lobsterettes, octopus, and sole or hake. Simmer, covered, for about 15 minutes.
6. Sprinkle in the peas.
7. Arrange mussels and shrimps on the top. Do not stir.
8. Serve in the pan.

Note: The rice must be cooked until just done, not dry. The dish should never be served dry. Add stock if necessary. Artichokes, mushrooms, julienne of beef tongue or ham, eel, and/or veal can be included in the dish; diced poultry, diced veal liver, or fried diced beef tenderloin can be used to garnish the top of the dish; however, these variations make a paella from another locality, not from Valencia.

Chapter 24
Cold Dishes—*Cuisine froide*

From a technical standpoint, cold dishes were formerly divided into cold entrées and cold buffets. Today, the term *cold dishes* refers to any dishes that are served cold, from cold hors d'oeuvre to the elaborately composed cold buffets.

On the menu, cold foods may be listed as cold dishes, cold snacks, cold specialties of the house, or specialties of the season.

When cold dishes form part of a complete menu, they are generally used as cold hors d'oeuvre or as cold main courses. Only on rare occasions do they appear as the *entrée froide,* a course that was formerly served between the *grosse pièce* (main course) and the *rôti* (roast).

All cold dishes, with the exception of cold hors d'oeuvre and salad dishes, are included in this chapter. A perfect *mise en place* and broad knowledge of foodstuffs are important. The skilled garde-manger will distinguish himself by his methods of preparation, cutting, trussing, and carving, as well as by his use of modern arrangements. Since the appearance of cold dishes is especially important, particular attention must be given to color combinations and attractive presentations. Cold dishes include the following categories:

- bases and ingredients (see chapter 10)
- methods of preparation, cutting, and dressing (see chapter 7)
- cold hors d'oeuvre (see chapter 13)
- cold egg dishes (see chapter 13)
- cold fish dishes
- cold shellfish
- cold entrées
- cold meat dishes
- cold buffets
- cold salads (see chapter 19)

24.1 Cold Fish Dishes—*Mets de poisson froids*

For cold dishes, fish are poached as described in chapter 15 and allowed to cool in the court bouillon. They can be presented in various ways, but, in general, simple and attractive presentations are preferred.

Fish Mayonnaise—*Mayonnaise de poisson*

Remove the skin and bones from cooked fish or canned salmon and marinate with seasoning and lemon juice. Place a few lettuce leaves on a dish, arrange the fish in a dome shape on the leaves, and coat with a spicy thick mayonnaise. Decorate the dome with anchovy fillets in a lattice pattern and place a caper in each square. Arrange slices of hard-cooked egg around the dome. Garnish with a few clusters of vegetable salad. Serve mayonnaise separately.

Lake Trout, Modern Style—*Truite de lac moderne*

Remove the head and tail of a dressed trout, and slice the middle section into uniform medallions. Poach the head and tail together with the slices of fish in a fish kettle. When cool, remove from the stock, skin the slices carefully, and arrange on a platter as shown

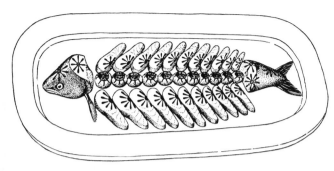

Figure 24-1. Lake trout, modern style—*Truite de lac moderne.*

in Figure 24-1. Decorate each slice. Serve with stuffed eggs, tomatoes, and asparagus spears. Coat the entire dish with aspic. Serve mayonnaise or rémoulade sauce separately.

Lake Trout with Tarragon—*Truite de lac à l'estragon*

Dress the trout and stuff with forcemeat. Place the fish in a fish kettle so that it need not be moved during cooking or cooling. Poach the trout. When cold, remove the trout very carefully from the fish kettle and skin from head to tail. Place on a platter and decorate with blanched tarragon leaves along both sides. Place slices of hard-cooked egg and truffles along the back. Surround the fish with stuffed eggs, slices of marinated cucumber with tomatoes on top, and Russian salad in timbales. Glaze the whole dish with fish aspic. Mix rémoulade sauce with chopped tarragon and serve in a sauceboat.

Salmon Medallions, Norwegian Style—*Médaillons de saumon norvégienne*

Cut the salmon into medallions, poach, and cool in the court bouillon. Place 2 shrimps on each medallion and coat with aspic. Coat a platter with aspic, place the medallions on the aspic in the original order, and surround with smoked salmon flakes, blanched and marinated cucumber slices, and peeled small tomatoes.

24.2 Cold Shellfish—*Crustacés et mollusques froids*

Place live, well-cleaned crustaceans in a simmering court bouillon, bring to a boil, remove from the heat, and let stand covered for 8 minutes per pound (500 grams). Cool completely in the court bouillon. The cooking time for crayfish is 4 minutes per pound (500 grams). Just before placing in the court bouillon, pull out the middle tail fin to remove the intestine.

Cold Crayfish—*Ecrevisses froides*

Remove the meat from the claws and tails of cooled, cooked crayfish; or the crayfish can be left whole and the claws opened. Crayfish arranged in this fashion can be used as a garnish for hors d'oeuvre and cold fish dishes.

If the crayfish are being served as a separate dish, break open the claws and arrange the whole crayfish on a paper napkin on a platter, garnish with lettuce leaves and parsley. Serve mayonnaise, radishes, and sweet pepper salad separately.

Cold Lobster—*Homard froid*

Cut a cooled, cooked, lobster lengthwise into halves (see figure 24-2). Remove the tail meat, slice, garnish each slice with truffles, and coat with aspic. Fill the two lobster shells with Russian salad, place on a platter, and arrange the halved slices of lobster on top.

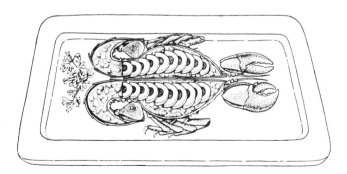

Figure 24-2. Cold lobster—*Homard froid.*

Place the opened claws in front of the lobster. Serve mayonnaise separately.

Lobster, Russian Style—*Homard à la russe*

Remove the tail meat from a cooled, cooked lobster. Slice, garnish with truffles, and coat with aspic. Arrange the slices on the lobster. Serve with eggs stuffed with caviar, tomatoes stuffed with Russian salad, and lobster mousse on small artichoke hearts. Serve mayonnaise separately. (See figure 24-3.)

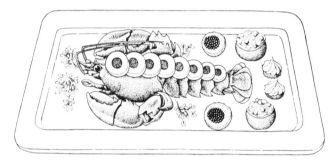

Figure 24-3. Lobster, Russian style—*Homard à la russe.*

Rock Lobster Mousse—*Mousse de langouste*

Grind the trimmings from cooled, boiled rock lobsters repeatedly and strain using a fine sieve; or pass through the meat grinder. Place a bowl in crushed ice. In the chilled bowl, mix ¾ cup (2 deciliters) of fish velouté and ½ cup (150 milliliters) of liquid aspic per 2 cups (500 milliliters) of the lobster puree. Immediately mix in ½ to ¾ cup (150 to 200 milliliters) of whipped cream.

Rock Lobster, Parisian Style—*Langouste à la parisienne*

Prepare the rock lobster as described in figure 7-19. Meanwhile, bind a Russian salad with a spicy mayonnaise and aspic. Remove the tail meat and cut into slices. Decorate the slices with truffles and coat with aspic. Arrange the rock lobster body with the tail shell on a base of Russian salad. Arrange the slices attractively on the tail. Serve with stuffed artichoke hearts, timbales, and stuffed eggs. Serve mayonnaise separately. (See figure 24-4.)

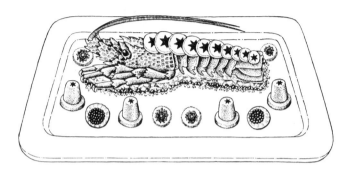

Figure 24-4. Rock lobster, Parisian style—*Langouste à la parisienne.*

Rock Lobster Timbale—*Timbale de langouste*

Coat the inside of a timbale mold with aspic. Place truffles on slices of rock lobster and arrange these in the mold (see figure 24-5). Fill the middle with rock lobster mousse. Allow to set in a cool place. Serve surrounded with diced aspic.

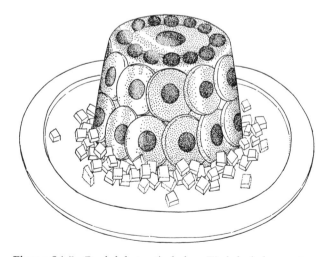

Figure 24-5. Rock lobster timbale—*Timbale de langouste.*

Oysters—*Huîtres*

These are generally served cold as an hors d'oeuvre. Open the oysters just before serving and remove the upper shell. Arrange the oysters on a bed of ice in a special oyster dish. Serve lemon wedges separately. A sauce made with wine vinegar, minced shallots, and pepper or Tabasco can also be served. Slices of black bread and butter are often served with this dish.

24.3 Cold Entrées—*Entrées froides*

24.3.1 *Aspic*

Line the appropriate molds with a thick layer of aspic, garnish with truffles and hard-cooked egg whites, and coat the garnish with aspic. Depending upon the name of the dish, arrange layers of goose liver slices, sliced paupiettes, or poultry fillets in the center of the mold. Coat each layer with aspic. Allow each layer to congeal before adding the next layer.

24.3.2 *Chaud-froid Dishes*—Chauds-froids

Chicken Chaud-froid—*Chaud-froid de volaille*

Poach a chicken, cool in the stock, and use the stock to prepare a chaud-froid sauce. Cut the chicken into attractive fillets or pieces. Arrange these in a lattice pattern and coat with lukewarm chaud-froid sauce. After the sauce has set, garnish with truffles, sweet peppers, tarragon, or blanched leeks, and coat with aspic that has cooled to the consistency of syrup. Depending upon the name of the dish, such pieces can either be arranged upon an aspic base, surrounded with a ring of aspic, or placed on a vegetable salad base. These cold specialties can also be ringed with diced aspic, marinated vegetables, or a vegetable salad. A smooth, shiny sauce and a clear aspic are necessary to make successful chaud-froid dishes.

Stuffed Poultry Chaud-froid—*Chaud-froid de volaille farci*

Poach the poultry and allow to cool in the stock. Remove the fillets, coat with chaud-froid sauce, garnish, and coat with aspic. Build up the trimmed carcass, including the legs, with a goose liver or ham mousse in the shape of the type of fowl. If the bird was poached after being stuffed, then cut the stuffing into cubes and add to the mousse before filling the trimmed carcass. Allow to cool and set. Coat with lukewarm chaud-froid sauce, garnish according to the description of the dish, and coat with aspic. Serve the stuffed poultry surrounded by the suprêmes (fillets).

24.3.3 *Galantines*—Galantines

A galantine is boned poultry (occasionally fish or meat is used) that is stuffed, rolled or shaped, poached, and served cold. Figure 24-6 shows how galantines are wrapped and a decorative way of serving them.

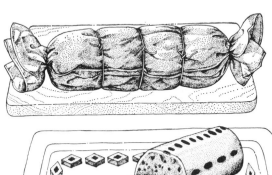

Figure 24-6. A rolled and wrapped galantine, and service of a galantine.

24.3.3.1 Chicken Galantine—*Galantine de volaille*

Yield
approximately 10 servings

Ingredients	U.S. Weight or Volume	Metric Weight or Volume
Chicken	3 to 3½ pounds	1.5 kilograms
Shallots	2 ounces	60 grams
Veal	10 ounces	300 grams
Pork	7 ounces	200 grams
Eggs, beaten	2	2
Cream	¾ cup	2 deciliters
Sausage seasoning	¼ teaspoon	2 grams
Tongue, diced	2 ounces	60 grams
Ham, diced	2 ounces	60 grams
Truffles, quartered	2¾ ounces	80 grams
Pistachios, blanched	1¾ ounces	50 grams
Brandy	1 ounce	30 grams
Madeira	1 ounce	30 grams
Poultry stock, rich	as needed	as needed

Procedure

1. Cut the skin open along the backbone of a dressed chicken. Carefully remove the skin from both sides of the bird so that the meat comes away with the skin, leaving the skeleton, including the leg and wing bones. Remove the leg meat and about 4 ounces (100 grams) of the breast meat, but leave a uniform layer of meat attached to the skin. (The leg meat is used in the forcemeat. The breast meat is diced for later use.)
2. Sauté the shallots and allow to cool.
3. Grind the veal, pork, chicken leg meat, and shallots *very finely*. Blend the mixture thoroughly in a bowl and set the bowl in a bed of crushed ice.
4. Add the eggs, cream, and seasoning gradually.
5. Add the diced meats, including the diced chicken breast, and pistachios, which have been marinating in the brandy and Madeira. Add the marinade.
6. Place the whole mixture on the chicken skin to which a layer of meat is still attached. Form into a slightly oval shape. Sew the skin together.
7. Wrap and tie the chicken in a cloth and poach in a rich poultry stock for 1 to 1½ hours. Do not remove from the stock until partially cooled.
8. Tighten the cloth once more around the galantine and keep it under pressure (tie to a board) until it has completely cooled. Coat the finished galantine with aspic or chaud-froid and garnish with truffles.
9. Use the stock to prepare chaud-froid sauce.

Other Galantines

Duck Galantine—*Galantine de canard*

The ingredients and method of preparation are the same as for chicken galantine, but use duck meat and skin instead of chicken.

24.3.4 *Mousses*—Mousses

Mousses are sweet or savory creams, sometimes lightened with beaten egg whites. They are often chilled in decorative molds (see figure 24-7).

Figure 24-7. An unmolded mousse, decoratively garnished.

24.3.4.1 Ham Mousse—*Mousse de jambon*

Yield
approximately 10 servings

Ingredients	U.S. Weight or Volume	Metric Weight or Volume
Liquid aspic	1¾ cups	4 deciliters
Ham, boiled, cold	2 pounds	1 kilogram

Ingredients	U.S. Weight or Volume	Metric Weight or Volume
Basic white sauce	1¼ cups	3 deciliters
Salt	½ teaspoon	3 grams
Pepper	¼ teaspoon	2 grams
Dry mustard	⅛ teaspoon	1 gram
Whipped cream	1¼ to 1¾ cups	3 to 4 deciliters
Brandy	½ ounce	15 grams
Madeira	½ ounce	15 grams

Procedure
1. Coat a mold with some of the liquid aspic.
2. Grind the ham very fine and cool on a bed of crushed ice.
3. Gradually mix in the basic white sauce, remaining liquid aspic, salt, pepper, and dry mustard.
4. Add the whipped cream, brandy, and Madeira.
5. Immediately spoon the mixture into the mold.
6. Chill until firm. Turn out onto a serving plate just before serving.

Other Mousses

Goose liver mousse, game mousse, chicken mousse, fish mousse, and tomato mousse are prepared in the same way as ham mousse. When using chicken, fish, and rock lobster, poach the meat and allow it to cool in the stock or court bouillon. Game meat should be roasted to the rare stage. Goose liver should be braised. Leftovers and trimmings of these meats may also be used. Vegetable mousse should be prepared with vegetables that have been blanched and thoroughly drained.

Stuffed Ham Horns with Chicken Mousse—
Cornets de jambon à la mousse de volaille

Roll sliced ham into horns. Stuff the ham horns with chicken mousse and place on a base of Russian salad. Arrange mushroom caps or rosettes of mousse between the cornets. Coat the dish with aspic. (See figure 24-8.)

Figure 24-8. Stuffed ham horns with chicken mousse—*Cornets de jambon à la mousse de volaille.*

24.3.5 *Mousselines*

Mousselines are made in the same fashion as mousses. Whereas mousses serve six, eight, or ten persons, a mousseline is served individually. They can be shaped in small molds or as quenelles, to be garnished and coated with aspic.

Goose Liver Mousselines—*Mousselines de foie gras à la gelée*

Coat a flat platter with a layer of aspic and allow to congeal. Place oval-shaped mousselines on the aspic, coat with a little aspic, and allow to set. Place a slice of truffle on each and coat again. Place the dish in a cool place. Cut out the mousselines so that each is coated with aspic. When serving, garnish with aspic and radishes. (See figure 24-9.)

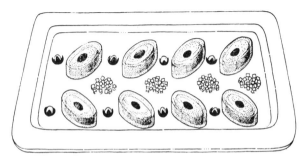

Figure 24-9. Goose liver mousselines—*Mousselines de foie gras à la gelée.*

24.3.6 *Cold Pâtés*—Pâtés froids

A pâté is a rich meat, poultry, game, seafood, or vegetable mixture; when baked in a pastry case (*pâtè en croûte*), the dish is referred to as a *pâté;* when baked in a mold without pastry (*pâté en terrine*), the dish is called a *terrine,* for the name of the original earthenware molds used.

To fill and finish a pâté, line a mold with rolled pastry dough and line the base and sides with thin slices of unsalted bacon or fatback. Fill the mold with a prepared stuffing containing diced meat and complete with another layer of thin slices of unsalted bacon or fatback. Close the pâté with a layer of pastry dough garnished with dough shapes, and brush the top with egg wash. Make a few holes, called chimneys, in the top layer of dough so the steam can escape. Depending on its size, the pâté is baked for 1 to 2 hours. Cool. When thoroughly chilled, fill the chimneys with the appropriate aspic jelly, which should be liquid though not hot. Refrigerate.

24.3.6.1 Pastry Dough for Pâtés—*Pâte à pâté*

Yield
U.S.—3 pounds
Metric—1.3 kilograms

Ingredients	U.S. Weight or Volume	Metric Weight or Volume
Flour	2 pounds	1 kilogram
Eggs	3	3
Butter	12 ounces	350 grams
Salt	¾ ounce	20 grams
Water, lukewarm	1¼ cups	3 deciliters

Procedure
1. Make a well in the flour.
2. Place the eggs, butter, salt, and water in the well. Mix these ingredients.
3. Gradually work the flour into the liquids and knead until a fairly firm dough is formed. Add a bit more water if necessary.
4. Cover and let the dough stand for 2 hours before using.

24.3.6.2 Pâté in Aspic—*Pâté à la gelée*

Yield
approximately 10 servings
(1-quart/1-liter pâté mold)

Ingredients	U.S. Weight or Volume	Metric Weight or Volume
Veal liver, diced	4½ ounces	125 grams
Shallots, chopped	1½ ounces	40 grams
Butter	¾ ounce	20 grams
Pork	9 ounces	250 grams
Veal	9 ounces	250 grams
Larding bacon, unsalted	7 ounces	200 grams
Apple	1	1
Cream	¾ cup	2 deciliters
Sausage seasoning	¼ teaspoon	2 grams
Ham, diced	2¾ ounces	80 grams
Tongue, diced	2¾ ounces	80 grams
Bacon, unsalted, diced	2¾ ounces	80 grams
Truffles, quartered	as desired	as desired
Madeira	1½ ounces	40 grams
Brandy	¾ ounces	20 grams
Pastry dough for pâtés	as needed	as needed
Bacon, unsalted, sliced thin	8 ounces	240 grams
Egg yolk	1	1
Meat aspic	1 pint	5 deciliters

Procedure
1. Quickly brown the diced liver and chopped shallots in the butter. Cool.
2. Grind the pork, veal, larding bacon, browned liver, and the apple. Then put through a very fine sieve.
3. Cool the mixture in a bowl on a bed of crushed ice.
4. Add the diced meats and truffles, which have been marinated in Madeira and brandy, to the mixture.
5. Line a pâté mold with rolled pastry dough and

line the base and sides with thin slices of unsalted bacon.

6. Place the prepared filling in the mold and cover with another layer of thin slices of unsalted bacon.
7. Close the pâté with a layer of pastry dough garnished with dough shapes.
8. Brush the top with egg yolk.
9. Make a few chimneys in the top so the steam can escape.
10. Bake in the oven at 350°F (175°C) for about 1½ hours.
11. Allow to cool, and then fill the chimneys with the meat aspic, which should be liquid but not hot.
12. Chill.

24.3.6.3 Game Pâté—*Pâté de gibier*

Yield

approximately 10 servings
(9-inch/20-cm loaf pan or 1-quart/1-liter pâté mold)

Ingredients	U.S. Weight or Volume	Metric Weight or Volume
Liver, from game or veal	5½ ounces	150 grams
Milk	as needed	as needed
Butter	¾ ounce	20 grams
Shallots, chopped	1 ounce	30 grams
Game meat, deer or hare	10 ounces	300 grams
Larding bacon, unsalted	7 ounces	200 grams
Pork	6½ ounces	180 grams
Veal	3½ ounces	100 grams
Apple	1	1
Juniper berries	2 or 3	2 or 3
Cream	¾ cup	2 deciliters
Sausage seasoning	¼ teaspoon	2 grams
Bacon, unsalted, diced	2¾ ounces	80 grams
Game meat, diced	2¾ ounces	80 grams
Truffles, quartered	as desired	as desired
Madeira	1 ounce	30 grams

Ingredients	U.S. Weight or Volume	Metric Weight or Volume
Brandy	1 ounce	30 grams
Pastry dough for pâtés	as needed	as needed
Bacon, unsalted, sliced thin	8 ounces	240 grams
Tenderloin of game, whole, browned, and wrapped in bacon	1	1
Egg yolk	1	1
Meat aspic	1 pint	5 deciliters

Procedure

1. Soak the liver in milk. Drain it, then dice and brown in butter with the shallots. Cool.
2. Grind the game meat, larding bacon, pork, veal, browned liver, apple, and juniper berries. Then put through a fine sieve.
3. Cool the mixture by placing it in a bowl on a bed of crushed ice. Gradually mix in the cream and the seasoning.
4. The diced meats and truffles are marinated in Madeira and brandy and added to the mixture.
5. Line a pâté mold with rolled pastry dough and line the base and sides with thin slices of unsalted bacon.
6. Place half of the filling in the mold. Lay the whole tenderloin on this and then add the rest of the filling. Cover with another layer of thin slices of unsalted bacon.
7. Close the pâté with a layer of pastry dough garnished with dough shapes.
8. Brush the top with egg yolk.
9. Make a few chimneys in the top so that the steam can escape.
10. Bake in the oven at 350°F (175°C) for about 1½ hours.
11. Allow to cool. Then fill the chimneys with meat aspic, which should be liquid but not hot.
12. Chill.

24.3.6.4 Chicken Pâté—*Pâté de volaille*

Yield
approximately 10 servings
(1-quart/1-liter pâté mold)

Ingredients	U.S. Weight or Volume	Metric Weight or Volume
Chicken liver	4 ounces	120 grams
Milk	as needed	as needed
Shallots, chopped	1½ ounces	40 grams
Butter	1 ounce	30 grams
Chicken	10 ounces	300 grams
Veal	5 ounces	150 grams
Pork	5 ounces	150 grams
Larding bacon, unsalted	8½ ounces	240 grams
Cream	¾ cup	100 grams
Sausage seasoning	¼ teaspoon	2 grams
Larding bacon, unsalted, diced	2¾ ounces	80 grams
Chicken breast, diced	2¾ ounces	80 grams
Ham, diced	2¾ ounces	80 grams
Truffles	1¾ ounces	50 grams
Pistachios	1¾ ounces	50 grams
Madeira	1 ounce	30 milliliters
Brandy	1 ounce	30 milliliters
Pastry dough for pâtés	as needed	as needed
Bacon, unsalted, sliced thin	8 ounces	24 grams
Egg yolk	1	1
Poultry aspic	as needed	as needed

Procedure
1. Soak the liver in milk. Drain. Then brown it with the chopped shallots in butter. Cool.
2. Grind the chicken, veal, pork, larding bacon, and braised liver. Then pass through a fine sieve.
3. Cool the mixture by placing it in a bowl on a bed of crushed ice. Gradually mix in the cream and the seasoning.
4. The diced meats, truffles, and pistachios are marinated in Madeira and brandy and added to the mixture.

5. Line a pâté mold with rolled pastry dough and line the base and sides with thin slices of unsalted bacon.
6. Place the prepared filling in the mold and cover with another layer of thin slices of unsalted bacon.
7. Close the pâté with a layer of pastry dough, garnished with dough shapes.
8. Brush the top with egg yolk.
9. Make a few chimneys in the top so that the steam can escape.
10. Bake in the oven at 350°F (175°C) for about 1½ hours.
11. Allow to cool and then fill the chimneys with aspic jelly, which should be liquid but not hot.
12. Chill.

Other Pâtés

Mushroom Pâté—*Pâté de champignons*

For stuffing, blend two-thirds of the forcemeat used for pâté in aspic with one-third pure mushroom duxelles. The pâté is garnished with diced beef tongue, pistachios, whole cooked mushrooms, and truffles.

24.3.6.5 Veal and Ham Pie

Yield
approximately 10 servings

Ingredients	U.S. Weight or Volume	Metric Weight or Volume
Veal cutlets	28 to 32 ounces	800 to 900 grams
Brandy	¼ cup	50 milliliters
Madeira	½ cup	1 deciliter
Salt	½ teaspoon	3 grams
Pepper	¼ teaspoon	2 grams
Ham, smoked, sliced	20 to 28 ounces	600 to 700 grams
Shallots	3½ ounces	100 grams
Salt	1 teaspoon	6 grams
Pastry dough for pâtés	10 ounces	300 grams

Ingredients	U.S. Weight or Volume	Metric Weight or Volume
Egg yolk	1	1
Meat aspic	1 pint	5 deciliters

Procedure

1. Marinate the veal cutlets in the brandy and Madeira with the salt and pepper.
2. Fill a baking dish with layers of smoked ham slices and veal cutlets, placing a few sautéed shallots between the layers.
3. Add the marinade and salt.
4. Cover the pie with rolled-out pastry dough. Decorate as desired.
5. Brush with egg yolk.
6. Place in the oven at 350°F (175°C). As soon as the dough cover puffs up a little and is slightly split, cut a vent into the center so that the steam can escape. Bake for about 40 minutes.
7. Allow to cool. Fill the vent with aspic jelly, which should be liquid, but not hot.
8. Chill.

24.3.7 Terrines

Terrines were originally earthenware containers used for poaching various meat and poultry forcemeats in a water bath. Today enamel containers and fireproof glass casseroles with covers are also used. The term *terrine* refers to any preparation put into a mold lined with strips of bacon and baked. Figure 24-10 shows how the mold is lined. Both the dish and the contents are called terrines. The finished terrines can either be kept in the containers, as is generally the case in France, or they can be turned out of the dish into a second container that has been coated with aspic and then decorated. The terrine in this container is then covered with more aspic. When cool, the terrine is turned out, sliced, and garnished with aspic cubes. Terrines are always served cold.

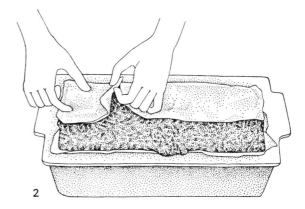

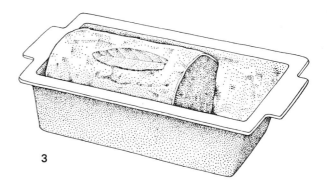

Figure 24-10. Lining a terrine: (1) line the terrine with thinly sliced bacon or fatback; (2) after adding the forcemeat, envelop it with the bacon or fatback; (3) serve the terrine, chilled, from the mold.

24.3.7.1 Terrine Chef's Style—*Terrine Maison*

Yield

approximately 10 servings

Ingredients	U.S. Weight or Volume	Metric Weight or Volume
Bacon, ground fine	9 ounces	250 grams
Pork, lean, ground fine	14 ounces	400 grams
Pork liver, ground fine	14 ounces	400 grams
Veal, ground fine	5 ounces	150 grams
Garlic, chopped fine	1 clove	1 clove
Shallots, chopped fine	1¾ ounces	50 grams
Butter	1 ounce	30 grams
Chicken livers	5 ounces	150 grams
Brandy	¼ cup	50 milliliters
Cream	¼ cup	50 milliliters
Lemon juice	from 1 lemon	from 1 lemon
Egg, beaten	1	1
Sausage seasoning	½ teaspoon	3 grams
Salt	1 teaspoon	5 grams
Pepper	½ teaspoon	3 grams
Tongue, boiled, diced	2 ounces	60 grams
Larding bacon, sliced thin	9 ounces	250 grams

Procedure

1. Mix the ground bacon, pork, pork liver, and veal together.
2. Lightly sauté the garlic and shallots in butter and add them to the meat.
3. Quickly sauté the chicken livers in the butter.
4. Remove the livers, deglaze the pan with brandy, and add it to the meat mixture.
5. Add the cream, lemon juice, egg, sausage seasoning, salt, and pepper to the meat. Blend it in a mixer so the ingredients combine to form a smooth and light forcemeat.
6. Add the diced tongue.
7. Adjust the seasoning, if necessary.
8. Line the terrine with the bacon slices.
9. Place half the mixture in the terrine. Press down. Smooth the surface.
10. Cut the chicken liver into small pieces and place them on the surface.
11. Cover with the remainder of the forcemeat mixture. Press it in firmly and smooth the surface.
12. Fold the slices of larding bacon over the top so the meat mixture is completely enveloped.
13. Place the bay leaf on top.
14. Cover with aluminum foil.
15. Poach in a water bath in the oven at 350°F (175°C) for about 2 hours, just until the fat on the surface is clear. Remove the bay leaf. Cover with a fresh sheet of aluminum foil, weight, cool, and store in the refrigerator.

24.4 Cold Meat Dishes—*Plats de viandes froides*

These are cold dishes made from meat, poultry, and game. Although they are often combined and prepared with aspic, pickles, and salads, they can also be served individually. The primary forms of preparation are roasting, braising, and pot roasting.

Beef—**Boeuf**

For filet, roast sirloin of beef, rib steak, rump pot roast, roast to desired degree of doneness. Use simple decorations for whole pieces, and coat with a thin layer of aspic. Accompaniments: spring vegetables, tomatoes, asparagus spears, pickles, mushrooms, fruits, aspic cubes, and parsley. Sauces: variations of mayonnaise, cold horseradish sauce, cream cheese with roquefort.

Tongue—*Langue*

Boil, trim, dress, and cool. Use simple decorations and coat with a thin layer of aspic. Accompaniment: same as beef, but without fruits. Sauces: horseradish sauce, cream cheese dressing with herbs.

Veal—*Veau*

For saddle, breast, fillet, filet mignon, loin, rump, round: whole pieces should be decorated simply and coated with a thin layer of aspic. Accompaniments: vegetables à la grecque, tomatoes, stuffed artichoke bottoms, asparagus spears, vegetable salad, mushrooms, fruit only as decoration. Sauces: variations of mayonnaise, cold horseradish sauce, and cream cheese dressing with herbs.

Pork—Porc

Roast or glaze a loin. Simmer or braise a ham, depending upon the type of dish. Use simple decorations for whole pieces, and coat with a thin layer of aspic. Accompaniments: sweet glazed vegetables, such as carrots, turnips; fruits, such as stewed apples and prunes. Sauces: applesauce, cold horseradish sauce, or cranberry sauce.

Lamb—Agneau

For baron, saddle, roast breast, and leg, roast the meat until rare. Use simple decorations for whole pieces, and coat with a thin layer of aspic. Accompaniments: mixed pickles, vegetables à la grecque, and those mentioned for veal. Sauces: mint sauce or cold horseradish sauce.

Poultry—Volaille

For chicken roasters, duck, goose, turkey, roast or pot-roast. Decorate according to the type of dish; coat with aspic or with chaud-froid sauce. Accompaniments for duck and turkey: stewed apples, oranges, sweet-and-sour fruits, glazed chestnuts, and spring vegetables. Accompaniments for chicken: spring vegetables coated with aspic, mushrooms, tomatoes, asparagus spears, and artichokes. Sauces for duck, goose, and turkey: cranberry, Cumberland, and cold horseradish sauce. Sauces for chicken: variations of mayonnaise or cream cheese dressing with herbs.

Game—Gibier

For woodcock, quail, grouse, pheasant, partridge, saddle and leg of roebuck, boar, and saddle of hare, roast the meat until rare. Depending on the dish, decorate, coat with aspic or with chaud-froid sauce. Accompaniments: stuffed apples and pears, pineapple, red cherries, oranges, mixed pickles, spring vegeta-

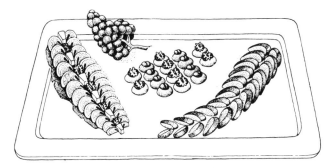

Figure 24-11. Saddle of deer with fruit—*Selle de chevreuil aux fruits.*

bles à la grecque, tomatoes, asparagus spears, and mushrooms. (See figure 24-11.) Sauces: Cumberland, cranberry, horseradish, and cream cheese dressing with ginger.

Special Variations

Cold Boiled Beef, Southern France Style— *Boeuf bouilli froid, mode du Midi*

Boil a beef rump and allow to cool. Slice, and garnish on one side with spring vegetables à la grecque and on the other side with stuffed tomatoes and cucumbers. Serve cold horseradish sauce and whipped cream cheese with herbs separately.

Cold Braised Beef—*Boeuf à la mode, froid*

This dish has been handed down from old French cuisine. Lard a beef rump roast, and braise with calf's feet and vegetables, but do not bind the gravy with flour. Coat an appropriate mold with aspic, garnish with the braised vegetables, and fix these with a second layer of aspic. Place the braised beef in the mold and fill it with the gravy. When cold, turn out and garnish.

Cold Beef Tenderloin with Asparagus Spears— *Filet de boeuf froid Argenteuil*

Roast the whole tenderloin and glaze. Arrange on a dish, carve a few slices, garnish with asparagus spears, and coat with aspic.

Cold Beef Tenderloin with Spring Vegetables—*Filet de boeuf froid à la printanière*

Roast the whole tenderloin and glaze. Arrange on a dish and surround with blanched and marinated spring vegetables that are coated with aspic.

Cold Roast Beef—*Roastbeef froid*

Roast the whole piece and glaze. Arrange on a dish, carve a few slices, and place them in front of the roast. Garnish the meat with vegetable salad and coat with aspic.

Duck with Tongue—*Caneton à l'écarlate*

Pot-roast a duck and cool in the stock. Remove the breast pieces and the skin, slice the breast meat, and rearrange on the breastbone with a half slice of orange between the slices of meat. Surround the bird with medallions of beef tongue, alternating with glazed orange slices. Serve cold horseradish sauce separately.

Ham Soufflé Marguerite—*Jambon soufflé Marguerite*

Simmer a smoked ham slowly and cool in the stock. Remove the top part horizontally along the bone. Prepare a mousse with this meat and arrange on the cut surface. Cover with slices of ham and cornets. Accompaniments: ham rolls, stuffed tomatoes, and stuffed green sweet peppers, all coated with a thin layer of aspic. Serve with horseradish sauce. (See figure 24-12.)

Breast of Chicken, Hawaiian Style—*Suprêmes de poularde Hawaii*

Slice the breasts of two roast chickens lengthwise. Place two pineapple halves, cut lengthwise and hollowed out, in the center of a platter, and garnish with celery salad and slices of pineapple and banana. Arrange a sliced breast half in a fan shape on each side of the two pineapple halves. Surround with small goose liver medallions garnished with truffle slices. Coat the whole dish with a thin layer of aspic. Serve Cumberland sauce separately. (See figure 24-13.)

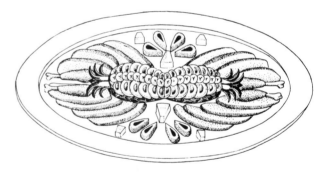

Figure 24-13. Breasts of chicken, Hawaiian style—*Suprêmes de poularde Hawaii.*

Breasts of Turkey with Ham Slices and Truffles—*Suprêmes de dinde au jambon saumoné et truffes*

Roast the turkey breasts, slice, and arrange in the original order with slices of truffles. Stuff a pineapple with celery salad and diced pineapple and surround

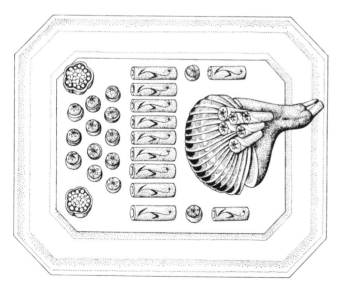

Figure 24-12. Ham soufflé Marguerite—*Jambon soufflé Marguerite.*

with ham rolls stuffed with celery salad and truffle coquettes. The truffles should be served in their natural shape.

Veal Cutlets with Ham Mousse—*Côtes de veau à la mousse de jambon*

Decorate the grilled cold cutlets and coat with aspic. Invert ham mousse in the center of a platter and surround with the cutlets. Garnish with aspic cubes. Serve horseradish sauce separately. (See figure 24-14.)

Figure 24-14. Veal cutlets with ham mousse—*Côtes de veau à la mousse de jambon.*

Saddle of Veal, Bohemian Style—*Selle de veau bohème*

Stuff a roasted, boned saddle of veal with a veal stuffing mixed with pistachios and sweet red peppers. Tie, coat with aspic, cool, slice, and arrange on a dish. Accompaniments: artichoke hearts stuffed with beans, tomatoes and mushrooms, and thin slices of hard-cooked eggs coated with aspic. An elegant decoration consists of round truffles on a skewer with garlands of raw carrots, cucumbers, radishes. (See figure 24-15.)

Cold Saddle of Venison Saint Hubert—*Selle de chevreuil froide Saint-Hubert*

Roast a saddle of venison and allow to cool. Remove the fillets and cut into uniform slices. Spread some

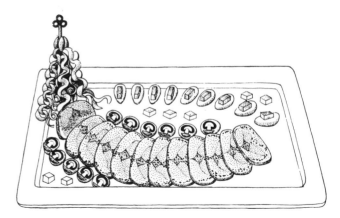

Figure 24-15. Saddle of veal, Bohemian style—*Selle de veau bohème.*

game mousse over the backbone, replace the slices in their original order, and coat with game mousse to give a smooth surface. Place thin, halved pineapple slices along the top of the backbone and decorate with cherries. Garnish both sides of the saddle with quartered pineapple slices. Arrange some game mousse on poached slices of apple and place a red cherry on top of each. Coat the whole dish with aspic. Serve Cumberland sauce and Waldorf salad separately. (See figure 24-16.)

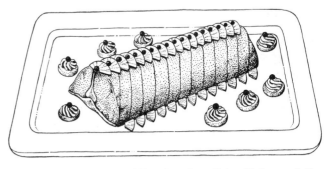

Figure 24-16. Cold saddle of venison Saint Hubert—*Selle de chevreuil froide Saint-Hubert.*

24.5 Buffets

This term is used for a choice of foods offered to the guests on various occasions, from simple to elaborate.

Melon—Grapefruit—Tomato juice	*Melon—Pamplemousse—Jus de tomate*
Terrine of caviar malossol	*Terrine de caviar malossol*
Consommé madrilène in a cup	*Consommé madrilène en tasse*
Poached eggs with tarragon	*Oeufs pochés à l'estragon*
Medallions of crawfish, Parisian style	*Mèdaillons de langouste parisienne*
Norwegian salmon	*Saumon norvégienne*
Fillets of sole Calypso	*Filets de sole Calypso*
Ham in aspic	*Jambon à la gelée*
Roast beef with spring vegetables	*Roastbeef printanière*
Veal tongue with asparagus	*Langue de veau Argenteuil*
Goose liver mousse with paprika	*Mousse de foie gras au paprika*
Pâté of venison, home style	*Pâté de chevreuil bonne femme*
Galantine of chicken with truffles	*Galantine volaille truffée*
Chicken Vendôme	*Poularde Vendôme*
Pheasant chaud-froid	*Faisan en chaud-froid*
Glazed quails	*Cailles glacées*
Russian salad—Hearts of lettuce	*Salade russe—Coeurs de laitue*
Fruit salad with Kirsch	*Macédoine de fruits au kirsch*
Frozen parfait	*Parfait glacé*
Pastries	*Pâtisserie*
Cake, Brittany style	*Gâteau à la bretonne*
Sweets	*Friandises*
Fruits	*Fruits*

Figure 24-17. A sample menu for a simple buffet.

The number of hot and cold dishes depends upon the type of occasion. A buffet can consist of a variety of sandwiches, a platter of cold meat cuts, fruitcakes, pies, and pastries, but can also involve the ultimate in luxury in terms of both choice of foods and the finesse of their preparation. When planning a buffet menu, one begins with the hors d'oeuvre dishes, continues with soup, then egg dishes, fish, and shellfish. Then come the various meat, poultry, and game dishes, accompanied by the appropriate salad, and the menu is completed with sweet dishes, pastries, fruit, and the dessert. Sample buffet menus are shown in figures 24-17 and 24-18.

Various shellfish	*Variations de fruits de mer*
Cold salmon	*Saumon froid moderne*
Avocados with shrimp	*Avocats aux crevettes*
Cold turbot Joinville	*Turbot froid Joinville*
Stuffed pike with lobster sauce	*Brochet farci cardinale*
Danish stuffed eel	*Anguille farcie danoise*
Swedish salmon	*Saumon suédoise*
Squid, Tuscan style	*Calamars à la toscane*
Rolls of sole Rosita	*Paupiettes de sole Rosita*
Double consommé with sherry	*Consommé double au Xérès*
Pâté, chef's style	*Pâté maison*
Roast beef in aspic	*Roastbeef à la gelée*
Beef Wellington	*Filet de boeuf Wellington*
Saddle of veal with garden vegetables	*Selle de veau jardinière*
Pheasant terrine with Calvados	*Terrine de faisan au Calvados*
Saddle of venison Diana	*Selle de chevreuil Diana*
Turkey, Mexican style	*Dinde mexique*
Veal and ham pie	*Pâtè de veau et de jambon*
Pheasant Bristol	*Faisan Bristol*
Beef tongue à l'écarlotte	*Langue de boeuf à l'écarlotte*
Variety of salads	*Salades diverses*
Boiled beef, cultivator style	*Boeuf bouilli cultivateur*
Country ham in pastry	*Jambon du pays en croûte*
Mixed boiled meats	*Bollito misto*
Potato salad	*Salade Parmentier*
Vacherin Mont d'Or	*Vacherin Mont d'Or*
Emmentaler cheese	*Fromage d'Emmental*
Seasonal fruits	*Fruits de la saison*
Charlotte russe	*Charlotte russe*
Frozen soufflé with Grand Marnier	*Soufflé glacé au Grand Marnier*
Champagne sherbet	*Sorbet au champagne*
Sugar Kirsch torte	*Tourte au kirsch de zoug*
Sweets	*Friandises*

Figure 24-18. A sample menu for a gala buffet.

Chapter 25
Basic Dessert
Preparations—*Entremets*

25.1 Fundamentals for Making Desserts—*Mise en place en pâtisserie*

There are two important rules in the bakery:

- Carefully weigh all ingredients
- Always sift the flour

Preparation of Baking Pans

Coat the pans with butter and dust them with flour, confectioners' sugar, or breadcrumbs, according to the recipe. Turn the pans upside down and knock out excess flour, sugar, or crumbs.

Baking Blind—Cuire à blanc

This means baking pastry without the filling. Line the forms or pans with raw pastry; to prevent it from rising or developing bubbles or shrinking, place parchment paper or foil on the pastry and cover it with dried beans, rice, cherry pits, or ceramic or aluminum pie pellets. Bake the pastry until half done or completely done, according to the needs of the recipe. Lift out the weights and paper and let the shell cool. Keep the beans, rice, or cherry pits in a special container to use again. The ceramic or aluminum pellets are more sanitary, as they can be washed (boiled, if necessary), drained, and dried after use, and they are never subject to attack from insects. This method of baking the pastry is used for any flan, tart, or quiche

with a filling that needs brief cooking only, or with a filling that would make the pastry soggy if cooked in the raw pastry.

Chilling and Resting Dough before Shaping or Rolling

Pat the dough into a block and wrap it tightly in plastic wrap or foil. Store in a cool place or in the refrigerator. Refrigerating between the turns is essential for puff pastry. For some other pastries, the dough must warm up a little before being rolled out, or it might crack.

Baking

Steam Vents

When baking puff pastry, bread, and cream puffs, éclairs, or other pâte à choux pastries, the oven's steam vents must be *closed*. The steam that develops in the oven during baking helps the dough or pastry to rise. When baking products that must become or remain smooth on top, the steam vents should be in the *open* position.

Temperature

Baking at too-high temperatures causes the dough or pastry to brown quickly on top but remain soggy and not fully cooked inside. Baking at too-low temperatures causes the dough or pastry to fail to rise enough and makes the products heavy in texture. Good baking results depend on correct baking temperatures.

Testing for Doneness

To test a baked dessert, use a long needle. Stick the needle into the middle of the thickest part of the food to be tested. If the needle comes out dry and warm, the food is cooked. If batter or dough sticks to the needle as it comes out of the mass, the food is not fully cooked.

Creaming Butter or Margarine

Place the butter or margarine in a bowl and set the bowl in a container of warm water so that the butter or margarine warms up to room temperature, 68°F (20°C). Make sure the butter or margarine does not melt; it should only become soft and malleable.

Whipping Egg Whites

No particle of egg yolk may be left in the whites to be beaten. The mixing bowl and whisk or beater must be perfectly clean and free of any grease. Whip the egg whites slowly at first, then gradually speed up. Sugar is added little by little, and beating is continued until the mixture of egg white and sugar is stiff, but not dry. The sugar must be beaten into the egg whites until no graininess remains.

Folding Beaten Egg Whites into a Batter

If the batter or mixture is rather heavy, it pays to *stir* a small part of the egg whites into the batter first, to lighten the texture of the mixture. After that, the rest of the egg whites is folded in, gently, so as not to break the air bubbles.

Folding in Flour

Always fold in flour with a wooden spatula. Do not fold it in too vigorously, or you will burst air bubbles, which will cause the mixture to collapse.

Working with Ingredients
Leaf Gelatin

Leaf gelatin is always first soaked in cold water until the leaves become flexible. After soaking, the leaves must be wrung out. The leaves are then added to the liquid to be jellied; the liquid should be warm enough for the gelatin to dissolve.

Powdered Gelatin

This is much easier to use than leaf gelatin. First stir the gelatin into cold water, allowing four times as much water as gelatin by volume. The gelatin absorbs the water and becomes soft. It is then added to hot liquid to be dissolved before mixing it into the rest of the ingredients to be jellied.

Hazelnuts—*Noisettes*

To remove skins spread shelled hazelnuts in a single layer on a baking sheet and bake in a 350°F (175°C) oven for 10 to 15 minutes, until the skins crack and the nuts turn brown. As soon as the nuts are cool enough to handle, rub them in a cloth to remove the skins.

Almonds—*Amandes*

To remove skins place shelled almonds in a heavy bowl and cover with boiling water. Let them stand for 2 to 3 minutes, then drain and drop into cold water. Drain again. Pull off the skins and let almonds dry. Once dry, almonds can be chopped, slivered, sliced, grated, ground; or they can be toasted, salted, sugared, or glazed.

Raisins and Currants—*Raisins sec et groseille à grappe*

Most recipes call for macerated raisins and currants. To do this, wash the fruits and drain, then soak them in rum, brandy, Kirsch, or whatever the recipe calls for. Before adding the macerated fruit to the batter or dough, drain and dry them. If you roll the raisins or currants in flour before adding them to a batter, the fruit will not sink to the bottom during baking.

Candied Fruits—*Fruits confits*

These are fruits that have been preserved in sugar. They are used in cakes and as garnishes for desserts and pastries. Candied lemon peel and candied orange peel are used in cakes and pastries.

Marzipan—*Pâte d'amandes fondante*

This is a paste made from ground almonds or almond paste, sugar, and egg whites. It is used for confections and to coat cakes and pastries and can be molded into many shapes for decorative purposes. Persipan is a mock marzipan, made from various kernels instead of almonds.

Nougat

This is a confection made from roasted almonds or hazelnuts, honey, sugar, and beaten egg whites. There are many distinctive flavored nougats, the specific flavor resulting from the honey used. There are hard, soft, white, and colored nougats. White nougat is usually made commercially. Nougats from Montélimar, France, are known throughout the world.

To make nougat, dry 30 ounces (850 grams) of shelled almonds or hazelnuts in the oven. Rub off any skins and crush the nuts into small pieces. Cook 10 ounces (300 grams) of sugar plus 7 ounces (200 grams) of corn syrup and ¼ cup (100 milliliters) of water to 310°F (155°C). Cook 17.5 ounces (500 grams) of honey to 239°F (115°C). While the sugar and honey are cooking, beat 4 egg whites until peaks are almost firm. Pour the cooked honey in a fine stream into the beaten egg whites and beat for 4 or 5 minutes. Pour the cooked sugar into the mixture and beat over a hot water bath until a bit of the mixture, cooled in cold water, does not stick to the fingers. Add the nuts, beating just to blend. Press the warm mixture into molds or roll into a thin sheet and cut to the desired shape.

Nougatine is not the same as nougat. It is a mixture of cooked sugar and chopped almonds that is shaped decoratively. It can also be ground and used like pralines to flavor sauces, glazes, fillings, and soufflés.

Chocolate—*Chocolat*

True chocolate is a mixture made from the nibs of cocoa beans; it contains about 50 percent cocoa butter. Without added ingredients, this is called unsweetened chocolate, bitter chocolate, or baking chocolate. Sugar, flavorings, nuts, milk, and other ingredients may be added, depending on the variety of the chocolate. The ingredients and additives determine the taste, character, and name of the product. Although half of the cocoa mass is cocoa butter, more may be added to improve the taste and melting qualities.

Coating Chocolate—*Couverture*

This usually contains a maximum of 50 percent sugar and a minimum of 33 percent cocoa mass. Cocoa butter is added to bring its content to a minimum of 35 percent. Coating chocolate is used to coat chocolate-covered candies and on pastries and cakes.

Vanilla Beans

To derive full flavor from a vanilla bean, split it before adding it to the liquid to be flavored. The small black particles in the split pod are the seeds. Both seeds and pod are used for flavoring. Lacking the beans, use an alcoholic extract made from the natural bean. Do not use imitation vanilla.

Liqueurs and Other Alcoholic Beverages

When cooking a sauce or beating a butter cream, the alcohol used for flavoring must be added toward the end of the boiling or beating process. Alcohol evaporates quickly, especially in a warm mass. With the evaporating alcohol goes much of the taste as well.

25.2 Doughs—*Pâtes*

Flour must be sifted before measuring. Sifting removes lumps, separates granules, and incorporates air. Flour that is measured by weighing does not require sifting. For storing or resting periods, doughs are wrapped in aluminum foil, plastic wrap, or airtight containers to prevent drying or the formation of a crust.

25.2.1 Puff Pastry—*Feuilletage*

Yield

30 medium-size pastries

Ingredients	U.S. Weight or Volume	Metric Weight or Volume
Flour, sifted	2 pounds	1 kilogram
Water	1 pint	5 deciliters
Butter	24 to 28 ounces	700 to 900 grams
Salt	¾ ounce	20 grams
Lemon juice (optional)	1 teaspoon	5 milliliters

Procedure

1. Place the flour on a table. Make a well in the center.
2. Pour the water, 3½ ounces (100 grams) of butter, the salt, and the lemon juice (if used) into the well. Work into a ball of dough as quickly as possible.
3. Allow to rest for 1 hour.
4. Cut a cross in the top of the ball of dough and roll it out into a cross shape, leaving the center four times as thick as the four ends. (See figure 25-1.)
5. Knead the remaining butter until it has exactly the same consistency as the dough, and form into a block. Place the block on the middle of the cross and fold the four ends over it. Roll out to an oblong shape. Fold the ends to the center and then fold in half. This procedure is called giving the dough one double turn. Rest the dough in the refrigerator for at least 20 minutes. Repeat this rolling out and folding four times, wrapping the dough and allowing it to rest in the refrigerator for 20 minutes before each double turn.
6. Bake medium-size pastries made from this dough in an oven preheated to 475°F (245°C) for 5 minutes. Reduce the temperature to 400°F (200°C) and continue baking for about 25 minutes longer.

Note: It is important to roll the dough on a marble or other smooth surface previously dusted with flour. Any sticking should be avoided. The flour used for dusting should always be brushed off the dough before it is folded. The dough must be rolled right into the corners without flattening the edges.

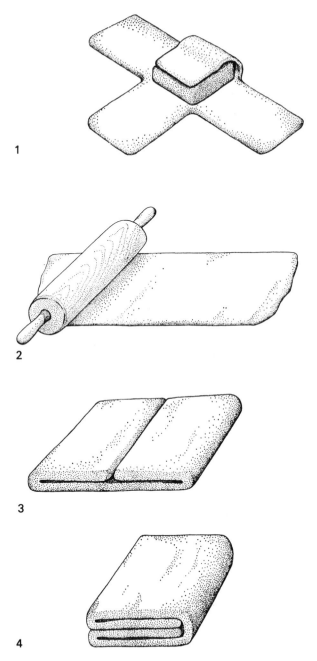

Figure 25-1. Making puff pastry turns: (1) roll the dough into a cross shape, place the square of butter in the center, and cover it with the flaps; (2) roll the dough into a rectangle; (3) fold each end toward the center; (4) fold the piece in half.

25.2.2 Short Crust Paste (Tart and Pie Dough)—*Pâte brisée*

Yield
6 10-inch crusts

Ingredients	U.S. Weight or Volume	Metric Weight or Volume
Butter	21 ounces	600 grams
Flour, sifted	2 pounds	1 kilogram
Water	1¾ to 2 cups	4 to 5 deciliters
Salt	¾ ounce	20 grams

Procedure
1. With the fingers, press chunks of the butter into the flour, as if crushing the two, until the mixture resembles fine breadcrumbs. Form a well in the center.
2. Pour the water into the well. Add the salt. Work into a ball of dough as quickly as possible. Chill for 1 hour before using.

Note: When using tart pans measuring 10 inches (26 centimeters) across, about 10 ounces (280 grams) of this dough will be required per pan.

25.2.3 Cream Puff Pastry—*Pâte à choux*

Yield
Beignets—50 servings
Gnocchi—25 servings
Eclairs—200 servings

Ingredients	U.S. Weight or Volume	Metric Weight or Volume
For puffed beignets:		
Water or milk	1 quart	1 liter
Butter	7 ounces	200 grams
Salt	½ ounce	10 grams
Sugar	1 ounce	30 grams
Lemon rind, grated	as desired	as desired
Flour, sifted	1 pound	500 grams
Eggs	18	18

Ingredients	U.S. Weight or Volume	Metric Weight or Volume
For gnocchi parisienne and pommes dauphine:		
Water	1 quart	1 liter
Butter	7 ounces	200 grams
Salt	½ ounce	10 grams
Nutmeg	as desired	as desired
Flour, sifted	20 ounces	600 grams
Eggs	18	18
For éclairs and cream puffs:		
Milk	1 quart	1 liter
Butter	10 ounces	280 grams
Salt	½ ounce	10 grams
Sugar	1 ounce	30 grams
Lemon rind, grated	as desired	as desired
Flour, sifted	20 ounces	600 grams
Eggs	20	20

Procedure
1. Place the water or milk, butter, salt, sugar, and lemon rind or nutmeg in a pan. Bring to a boil.
2. Add the flour and mix with a wooden spoon until the mixture no longer clings to the pan or spoon.
3. Remove from the heat and beat in the eggs, one after another, beating thoroughly after each addition.

25.2.4 Frying Batter—*Pâte à frire*

Yield
U.S.—2 quarts
Metric—2 liters

Ingredients	U.S. Weight or Volume	Metric Weight or Volume
Flour, sifted	2 pounds	1 kilogram
Beer	3 cups	8 deciliters
Water	2½ cups	6 deciliters
Oil	¾ cup	2 deciliters
Egg yolks	4	4

Ingredients	U.S. Weight or Volume	Metric Weight or Volume
Salt	½ ounce	15 grams
Sugar	½ ounce	15 grams
Nutmeg	optional	optional
Egg whites	8	8

Procedure

1. Place the flour in a bowl. Make a well in the center of the flour. Add the beer, water, oil, egg yolks, salt, sugar, and nutmeg. Blend into the flour.
2. Beat the egg whites until stiff, but not dry. Fold into the flour mixture.

25.2.5 Brioche—*Pâte à brioches*

Yield
40 to 50

Ingredients	U.S. Weight or Volume	Metric Weight or Volume
Yeast	1 ounce	30 grams
Water, lukewarm	¾ cup	2 deciliters
Flour, sifted	2 pounds (4 ounces + 28 ounces)	1 kilogram (110 + 890 grams)
Butter	20 ounces	600 grams
Sugar	1½ ounces	40 grams
Salt	¾ ounce	20 grams
Eggs	10 to 12	10 to 12

Procedure

1. To prepare the starter dough, dissolve the yeast in lukewarm water and add to 4 ounces (110 grams) of the sifted flour. Mix until a thin dough forms. Allow to rise in a warm place for 1 to 1½ hours.
2. Meanwhile, knead the butter until soft and mix with the sugar until smooth. Add remaining flour, salt, and eggs. Work into a firm dough. If necessary, add a small quantity of lukewarm water. The dough should be dry and firm, not soft. Knead the dough vigorously by hand until bubbles form.

3. Mix in the starter dough quickly and knead vigorously once more. Allow the dough to rise twice more, for about 1 hour each time, until doubled in volume. Knead between each rising.
4. Fill the molds one-third full and allow the dough to rise at a moderate temperature until the dough reaches the top of the molds.
5. Bake at 450°F (230°C) for 10 minutes, or until golden brown.

25.2.6 Sweet Tart Pastry—*Pâte sucrée*

Yield
50 to 60 individual tart shells or 7 to 8 9-inch shells

Ingredients	U.S. Weight or Volume	Metric Weight or Volume
Flour	2 pounds	1 kilogram
Butter	1 pound	500 grams
Sugar	14 ounces	400 grams
Egg yolks	8	8
Water	2 tablespoons	25 milliliters
Lemon rind, grated	½ teaspoon	3 grams

Procedure

1. Make a well in the center of the flour.
2. Place the butter, sugar, egg yolks, water, and lemon rind in the well, and mix these ingredients together before working the flour into the mixture.
3. Gradually work in the flour to give a smooth dough.

Note: Prepare this dough as quickly and with as little handling as possible. Otherwise, it will become tough. It is used primarily as a base for fruit tarts.

25.3 *Basic Mixtures*—Appareils

25.3.1 Génoise—*Pâte à génoise*

Yield
2 10-inch round layers

continued

Ingredients	U.S. Weight or Volume	Metric Weight or Volume
Eggs	10	10
Sugar	10 ounces	300 grams
Flour	5 ounces	150 grams
Cornstarch	5 ounces	150 grams
Butter, melted	3½ ounces	100 grams
Lemon rind, grated	½ teaspoon	3 grams

Procedure

1. Whip the eggs and sugar, either in a pan over very low heat on the stove or over a warm (not boiling) water bath, to a soft foam that forms a ribbon when a spoonful of it is spilled into the mixture.
2. Remove from the heat and continue whipping the mixture until it is almost cold.
3. Carefully fold in the flour and cornstarch, and finally fold in the melted butter and lemon rind.
4. Divide the batter between two 10-inch layer-cake pans.
5. Bake in oven at 425°F (220°C), with open steam vents, for 25 to 30 minutes.

Note: Careful distinctions must be made among whipping, mixing, and folding in. The amount of butter to be added depends on the requirements of the batter; light batters require only 2¾ ounces (80 grams), while 7 ounces (200 grams) can be necessary for heavier ones. Usually, about 3½ ounces (100 grams) should be added. This batter may be used for little cakes, or it may be baked in ring molds or timbales. The batter may be flavored with vanilla instead of lemon rind.

25.3.2 Cold Sponge Cake Batter—*Biscuit Fouétte à Fro;d*

Yield
2 10-inch round layers

Ingredients	U.S. Weight or Volume	Metric Weight or Volume
Eggs	8	8
Water	½ cup	1 deciliter
Sugar	10 ounces	300 grams

Ingredients	U.S. Weight or Volume	Metric Weight or Volume
Whipping agent	1½ ounces	40 grams
Flour	11 ounces	320 grams
Baking powder	½ ounce	14 grams
Lemon rind, grated	½ teaspoon	3 grams

Procedure

1. Place the eggs and water in a mixing bowl.
2. Add the sugar and the whipping agent and mix at medium speed for 4 to 5 minutes.
3. Reduce the speed and add the sifted flour, baking powder, and lemon rind. Mix at high speed for 4 to 5 minutes. Prepare and bake as for génoise.

Note: Since the excellent modern whipping agents give a sponge cake similar in quality to a génoise, the latter is seldom used. This batter may also be used for jelly rolls and small cakes.

25.3.3 Horns or Cornets—*Masse à cornets*

Yield
60 cornets

Ingredients	U.S. Weight or Volume	Metric Weight or Volume
Sugar	1 pound	500 grams
Hazelnuts *or* almonds	9 ounces	250 grams
Egg whites	12	12
Flour	6½ ounces	180 grams

Procedure

1. Mix the sugar and hazelnuts or almonds with 2 egg whites and put through the milling machine.
2. Place the milled nut mixture in a bowl. Add the remainder of the egg whites and work in the flour. Stir vigorously until the mixture is smooth and thick. Add more flour if required.
3. Use an appropriate template or form, and arrange the dough on a buttered baking pan. Bake in oven at 375°F (200°C) for 12 to 15 minutes.
4. While still hot, wrap around a dummy cornet made of wood, or shape as desired.

Note: If a milling machine is not available, the nuts must be grated. This mixture can also be used for rolls, leaves, and little tubs.

25.3.4 Pralines—*Masse praliné*

Yield
U.S.—2½ pounds
Metric—1 kilogram

Ingredients	*U.S. Weight or Volume*	*Metric Weight or Volume*
Sugar	1¼ pounds	600 grams
Hazelnuts	10 ounces	300 grams
Almonds	10 ounces	300 grams

Procedure
1. Place the sugar in a heavy pan. Stir continuously over low heat until the mixture is golden brown.
2. Brown the hazelnuts and almonds slightly. Add immediately to the sugar, and pour the mixture onto an oiled marble surface.
3. When cold, crush the praline mixture in the milling machine and sift.

Note: This mixture is used to flavor ice cream, puddings, soufflés, creams, icings, and fillings.

25.3.5 Meringue—*Pâte à meringue*

Yield
50 to 60 meringue shells

Ingredients	*U.S. Weight or Volume*	*Metric Weight or Volume*
Egg whites	10	10
Sugar	1 pound	500 grams

Procedure
1. Beat egg whites until stiff, but not dry.
2. Add 1¾ ounces (50 grams) of sugar and beat until sugar is thoroughly blended.

3. Add the remaining sugar gradually, folding it in with a wooden spoon.
4. Fill a pastry bag with the meringue mixture. Pipe out the meringue into shell forms on a baking sheet covered with parchment paper.
5. Preheat the oven to 225°F (105°C). Bake the meringue shells for 1 hour or longer.
6. If shells are not used immediately, let them cool and store them in an airtight container.

25.3.6 Japanese Meringue—*Pâte à meringue à la japonaise*

Yield
6 tart shells

Ingredients	*U.S. Weight or Volume*	*Metric Weight or Volume*
Egg whites	10	10
Sugar	1 pound	500 grams
Flour	2¼ ounces	65 grams
Hazelnuts, grated fine	7 ounces	200 grams

Procedure
1. Beat the egg whites until stiff but not dry. Add 3½ ounces (100 grams) of the sugar and continue beating until the sugar is thoroughly blended.
2. Combine the flour, hazelnuts, and the remainder of the sugar. Fold this mixture into the beaten egg whites and sugar.
3. Place the mixture in a pastry bag with a flat nozzle. Pipe the mixture into a spiral form on buttered baking sheets.
4. Bake in oven at 360°F (200°C) for 15 to 20 minutes.

Note: This mixture may also be used for Japanese pastries and tarts. Replace one-fourth of the hazelnuts with almonds. Spread the mixture on a buttered baking tray to a depth of 1/10 inch (2.5 millimeters).

25.3.7 Italian Meringue—*Pâte à meringue italienne*

Yield
approximately 50 shells
or topping for 4 9-inch pies

Ingredients	U.S. Weight or Volume	Metric Weight or Volume
Sugar	1 pound	500 grams
Water	1 cup	250 milliliters
Egg whites	10	10
Sugar, confectioners'	3½ ounces	100 grams

Procedure
1. Heat the sugar and water in a heavy pan and stir until the sugar is dissolved.
2. Cook until the syrup reaches the soft ball stage, 234° to 240°F (110° to 115°C).
3. Meanwhile, beat the egg whites until stiff and fold in the confectioners' sugar
4. Add the cooked syrup slowly (in threads) to the beaten egg whites. Continue beating until the mixture is cool.

Note: This meringue may be used for shells or as a pie topping. It may be used for a topping without further preparation, or it may be placed in the oven to brown lightly.

25.3.8 Crêpes—*Pâte à crêpes*

Yield
U.S.—1 quart (40 crêpes)
Metric—1 liter

Ingredients	U.S. Weight or Volume	Metric Weight or Volume
Flour	7 ounces	200 grams
Sugar	1¾ ounces	50 grams
Salt	¼ ounce	5 grams
Milk	1 pint	5 deciliters
Eggs	6	6
Oil	¼ cup	50 milliliters

Procedure
1. Combine the flour, sugar, and salt.
2. Add the milk gradually and stir until the mixture is free of lumps.
3. Add the beaten eggs and the oil. Blend well.
4. Butter crêpe pans lightly and sauté the crêpes until golden on both sides.

Note: If the crêpes are to be served sweet, grated orange rind, vanilla, or other flavoring may be added.

25.4 Creams—*Crèmes*

Creams are light sweet dishes. They are also used as bases for many desserts. Whipped cream, fruits, chocolate, liqueurs, and/or nutmeats may be added to increase the richness and variety of flavors. Creams served with a colorful garnish in crystal coupes, bowls, or stemware are simple but attractive desserts.

25.4.1 Vanilla Cream I—*Crème à la vanille I*

Yield
U.S.—1½ quarts
Metric—1.5 liters

Ingredients	U.S. Weight or Volume	Metric Weight or Volume
Egg yolks	10	10
Sugar	9 ounces	250 grams
Milk	1 quart	1 liter
Vanilla extract	2 teaspoons	10 milliliters
Cream	1¼ cups	3 deciliters

Procedure
1. Beat the egg yolks and the sugar until slightly foamy.
2. Scald the milk and add it gradually to the beaten eggs and sugar.
3. Pour the mixture into a saucepan and heat the

cream just to the boiling point. Continue to cook slowly until it coats a wooden spoon. At this point, remove the cream from the heat.

4. Add the vanilla extract.
5. Strain.
6. Stir until cool.
7. Add the cream before serving.

Note: Never allow the cream to boil. This cream may be flavored with chocolate, ground hazelnuts, coffee granules, ground pistachios, or pralines.

25.4.2 Vanilla Cream II—*Crème à la vanille II*

Yield

U.S.—1¼ quarts
Metric—1.25 liters

Ingredients	U.S. Weight or Volume	Metric Weight or Volume
Vanilla cream (flan) powder	1½ to 2 ounces	50 to 60 grams
Sugar	8 ounces	220 grams
Egg yolks	4	4
Milk	1 quart	1 liter

Procedure

1. Blend the vanilla cream powder, the sugar, and the egg
2. Scald the milk and add gradually to the mixture.
3. Pour the mixture into a saucepan and bring to the boiling point, stirring constantly for a few moments.
4. Immediately transfer to a cool container and stir until cool.
5. Strain.

Note: Cream may be added if desired.

25.4.3 English Custard Cream—*Crème anglaise*

Yield

U.S.—1¼ quarts
Metric—1.25 liters

Ingredients	U.S. Weight or Volume	Metric Weight or Volume
Egg yolks	10	10
Sugar	9 ounces	250 grams
Milk	1 quart	1 liter
Vanilla bean	1	1

Procedure

1. Beat the egg yolks with half the sugar until the mixture forms a ribbon.
2. Scald the milk with the remaining sugar and the split vanilla bean and add gradually to the egg yolk/sugar mixture.
3. Return the mixture to the saucepan and briefly bring to a boil, stirring constantly.
4. Remove from the heat. Stir while cooling, until the mixture coats a spoon.
5. Strain.

25.4.4 Mousseline Cream—*Crème mousseline*

Yield

U.S.—approximately 2 quarts
Metric—2 liters

Ingredients	U.S. Weight or Volume	Metric Weight or Volume
Milk	1 quart	1 liter
Vanilla cream (flan) powder	1½ ounces	40 grams
Sugar	9 ounces	250 grams
Egg yolks	5	5
Gelatin, unflavored	½ ounce	14 grams
Water, cold	½ cup	1 deciliter
Heavy cream, whipped	3 cups	750 milliliters

Procedure

1. Heat the milk to the boiling point.
2. Beat the vanilla cream powder, sugar, and egg yolks until the mixture forms a ribbon.
3. Gradually add the hot milk to the egg mixture.

continued

Procedure

4. Pour the mixture into a saucepan and heat, stirring constantly.
5. Add the gelatin, which has been soaked in the cold water. Stir until gelatin is dissolved.
6. Remove from heat and cool the mixture.
7. Strain.
8. As soon as the custard begins to thicken, fold in the whipped cream.

Note: Mousseline cream can be flavored with liqueur, coffee, or chocolate as desired.

25.4.5 Pastry Cream—*Crème pâtissière*

Yield
U.S.—1¼ quarts
Metric—1.25 liters

Ingredients	U.S. Weight or Volume	Metric Weight or Volume
Milk	1 quart	1 liter
Vanilla cream (flan) powder	2½ ounces	70 grams
Sugar	8 ounces	200 grams
Egg yolks	8	8
Vanilla extract	2 teaspoons	10 milliliters

Procedure

1. Heat the milk to the boiling point.
2. Beat the vanilla cream powder, sugar, and egg yolks until the mixture forms a ribbon.
3. Gradually pour the hot milk into the sugar and egg mixture.
4. Heat the mixture to the boiling point.
5. Stir quickly and cook only until the cream is thick and smooth.
6. Add the vanilla extract.

25.4.6 Saint Honoré Cream—*Crème Saint-Honoré*

Yield
U.S.—approximately 2 quarts
Metric—2 liters

Ingredients	U.S. Weight or Volume	Metric Weight or Volume
Vanilla cream (flan) powder	2½ ounces	70 grams
Sugar	8 ounces	200 grams
Egg yolks	8	8
Milk	1 quart	1 liter
Gelatin, unflavored	½ ounce	14 grams
Water, cold	½ cup	1 deciliter
Vanilla extract	2 teaspoons	10 milliliters
Egg whites, beaten	6	6
Whipping cream	¾ cup (more if desired)	2 deciliters (more if desired)

Procedure

1. Beat the vanilla cream powder, sugar, and egg yolks until the mixture forms a ribbon.
2. Heat the milk to the boiling point. Add the milk gradually to the sugar and egg mixture. Stir constantly.
3. Heat the mixture to the boiling point. Stir quickly and cook only until the cream is thick and smooth.
4. Add the gelatin, which has been soaked in the cold water, and stir until it is completely dissolved.
5. Add the vanilla.
6. Fold the beaten egg whites gently into the cream.
7. Cool until the cream begins to thicken.
8. Whip the cream and fold it in.

Note: This cream is used to fill the Saint-Honoré cake (*gâteau Saint-Honoré*).

25.4.7 Butter Cream I—*Crème au beurre I*

Yield
U.S.—approximately 1 quart
Metric—1 liter

Ingredients	U.S. Weight or Volume	Metric Weight or Volume
Eggs	8	8
Sugar	14 ounces	400 grams
Butter	1 pound	500 grams
Flavoring	as desired	as desired

Procedure
1. Beat the eggs and sugar in a double boiler over low heat or in a water bath until foamy (like a génoise batter).
2. Remove from heat and beat the mixture until it is cool.
3. Whip the butter and then gradually add it to the egg and sugar mixture, beating constantly.
4. Flavor as desired.

25.4.8 Butter Cream II—*Crème au beurre II*

Yield
U.S.—approximately 1 quart
Metric—1 liter

Ingredients	U.S. Weight or Volume	Metric Weight or Volume
Sugar syrup 28° Baumé	1¾ cups	4 deciliters
Egg yolks	5	5
Butter	1 pound	500 grams
Flavoring	as desired	as desired

Procedure
1. Combine the sugar syrup and the egg yolks in a saucepan. Heat to the boiling point.
2. Remove from the heat and beat the mixture continuously until it is cooled.
3. Whip the butter and add it gradually to the cooked and cooled mixture.
4. Flavor as desired.

Note: A 28° syrup is prepared by combining 2 pounds 6 ounces (1.07 kilograms) of sugar with enough water to produce 1 quart (1 liter).

25.5 Sauces—*Sauces*

The individual portion size for sauces will vary between ¼ and ½ cup (50 and 100 milliliters) depending on the use and the consistency of the sauce. Cream sauces should be thinned with milk. The appropriate fruit juice should be used to thin fruit sauces.

25.5.1 Apricot Sauce—*Sauce aux abricots*

Yield
U.S.—approximately 1 quart
Metric—1 liter

Ingredients	U.S. Weight or Volume	Metric Weight or Volume
Apricot jam	1¼ pounds	600 grams
Sugar	3½ ounces	100 grams
Water	1¼ cups	3 deciliters
Kirsch	2 tablespoons	25 milliliters
Lemon juice	1 teaspoon	5 milliliters

Procedure
1. Combine the jam, sugar, and water in a saucepan. Bring to the boiling point.
2. Remove from heat and strain or blend.
3. Add Kirsch and lemon juice.

Variations of Apricot Sauce

Fruit Sauce—*Sauce aux fruits*

Prepare as for apricot sauce. Use fruit, jam, or purée as desired.

Strawberry Sauce—*Sauce aux fraises*

Prepare as for apricot sauce. Use strawberry jam or purée.

25.5.2 Chocolate Sauce—*Sauce chocolat*

Yield
U.S.—approximately 1 quart
Metric—1 liter

Ingredients	U.S. Weight or Volume	Metric Weight or Volume
Chocolate, semisweet or coating (couverture)	1 pound	500 grams

continued

Ingredients	U.S. Weight or Volume	Metric Weight or Volume
Sugar syrup	¾ cup	2 deciliters
Cream	1¼ cups	3 deciliters

Procedure

1. Melt the chocolate with the sugar syrup in a hot water bath.
2. Gradually add chocolate mixture to the cream and blend thoroughly.

25.5.3 Raspberry Sauce—*Sauce Melba*

Yield

U.S.—approximately 1 quart
Metric—1 liter

Ingredients	U.S. Weight or Volume	Metric Weight or Volume
Raspberries, fresh or frozen, *or* raspberry puree	1¾ pounds	900 grams
Sugar, confectioners'	7 to 10 ounces	200 to 300 grams
Lemon juice	2 tablespoons	25 milliliters

Procedure

1. Rub fresh raspberries through a sieve.
2. Add confectioners' sugar and lemon juice.

Note: If raspberry puree is used, boil the puree and sugar quickly and add the lemon juice. If frozen raspberries are used, rub them through a sieve and boil quickly with the sugar. Cool and add the lemon juice.

25.5.4 Red-wine Sauce—*Sauce Bischof*

Yield

U.S.—approximately 1 quart
Metric—1 liter

Ingredients	U.S. Weight or Volume	Metric Weight or Volume
Red wine	1 pint	5 deciliters
Water	1¼ cups	3 deciliters

Ingredients	U.S. Weight or Volume	Metric Weight or Volume
Sugar	7 ounces	200 grams
Clove, whole	1	1
Cinnamon stick	1	1
Cornstarch	¼ to ½ ounce (as needed to dissolve cornstarch)	5 to 10 grams (as needed to dissolve cornstarch)
Currants, dried	1¾ ounces	50 grams
Almonds, sliced thin	1¾ ounces	50 grams
Kirsch	2 tablespoons	25 milliliters

Procedure

1. Combine the wine, water, sugar, clove, and cinnamon stick in a saucepan. Heat to the boiling point. Strain.
2. Dissolve cornstarch in the cold water and add to the liquid. Bring to a boil, stirring constantly.
3. Add the dried currants and sliced almonds.
4. Flavor with Kirsch.

25.5.5 Sabayon—*Sabayon*

Yield

U.S.—approximately 1 quart (10 servings)
Metric—1 liter

Ingredients	U.S. Weight or Volume	Metric Weight or Volume
White wine	1¼ cups	3 deciliters
Lemon	1	1
Marsala wine	½ cup	1 deciliter
Sugar	7 ounces	200 grams
Egg yolks	5	5
Eggs	3	3
Curaçao, rum, Kirsch, *or* Maraschino	¼ cup	40 milliliters

Procedure

1. Combine all ingredients and place over a water bath on medium heat. Whip mixture continuously until the foam is stiff.
2. Serve at once.

Note: The brief period of beating will not coagulate the eggs, as might be expected, since the alcoholic content of the mixture lowers the boiling point. When made without the liqueurs, this mixture can also be called by its commonly known Italian name, *zabaglione.*

25.5.6 Cold Sabayon—*Sabayon frappé*

Yield
10 to 12 servings

Ingredients	U.S. Weight or Volume	Metric Weight or Volume
Sabayon	1 quart	1 liter
Gelatin	½ ounce	14 grams
Water, cold	½ cup	1 deciliter
Whipping cream	1¼ cups	3 deciliters

Procedure
1. Prepare the sabayon.
2. While the mixture is hot, add the gelatin, which has been softened in the cold water. Stir until thoroughly blended.
3. Whip the mixture until very thick. Place over cracked ice and continue beating until the sauce is cold.
4. Whip the cream and fold into the sauce.
5. Pour into dessert dishes or serve over fruit.

25.6 Cooking Sugar—*Cuisson de sucre*

Cooking sugar is divided into two phases, the preparations and the stages of sugar cooking.

A solution is composed of two parts, the solute, or the dissolved substance; and the solvent, or the liquid in which the solute is dissolved. In sugar solution, the sugar is the solute, and water, unless otherwise stated, is the solvent. The degree of solubility in a sugar solution will vary with the amount and kind of sugar, the amount and kind of solvent, and the temperature. Sugars are usually more soluble at higher temperatures.

An unsaturated sugar solution, or a *syrup,* is one in which more sugar can be dissolved in the solvent at a given temperature. These solutions remain liquid when cooled. They are measured with the Baumé sugar scales and can be measured when cold. An unsaturated sugar solution is 1° to 28° Baumé. In theory, hot supersaturated solutions can be measured this way; however, the sugar scale does not function properly with thick liquids. The addition of 3 to 5 percent glucose will prevent crystallization.

The following are examples of commonly used sugar syrups:

- 13 ounces (400 grams) of sugar in 1 quart (1 liter) of boiling water will produce a syrup of about 12° to 15° Baumé, used in fruit compotes
- 19 ounces (600 grams) of sugar in 1 quart (1 liter) of boiling water will produce a sugar syrup of about 15° Baumé, used to moisten sponge cake
- 24 ounces (750 grams) of sugar in 1 quart (1 liter) of boiling water will produce a sugar syrup of about 20° Baumé, used in fruit icings and glazes
- 32 ounces (1 kilogram) of sugar in 1 quart (1 liter) of boiling water will produce a sugar syrup of about 25° Baumé, used to glaze fruits

Cold solutions register about 2° to 5° Baumé higher.

A saturated sugar solution (clarified sugar syrup), at 29° Baumé, refers to a solution that, after cooling, crystallizes slowly if no glucose is added. It is one in which the solvent can absorb no more sugar at the given temperature. Five percent glucose should be added to prevent crystallization. Saturated syrup can be stored and used when diluted with liquids, such as water or liquors. The saturated sugar solution is also the basis from which supersaturated sugar solutions are made. A saturated sugar solution is made when 48 ounces (1.5 kilograms) of water is added to 1 quart (1 liter) of boiling water.

A supersaturated sugar solution (cooked sugar) is one that contains more sugar than solution would normally hold at a given temperature. After cooling, this solution will solidify into a firm, crystalline form. The excess sugar is capable of crystallizing out of the solution. Depending on the use, an addition of 5 to 20 percent glucose is necessary to prevent crystallization. These solutions are too thick to be measured by a Baumé sugar scales. A Réaumur or Fahrenheit sugar thermometer should be used. The solution may be

84° to 130° Réaumur or 221°F to 324°F (105°C to 162.5°C). Cooked sugar may also be judged by touch. Figure 25-2 shows the temperatures and stages of cooked sugar.

The following equipment is needed to prepare sugar syrups: Baumé sugar scales, sugar thermometer, saucepan, a brush, and a container for storing the sugar solution (saturated syrups should not be hermetically sealed). Combine the water and sugar in a saucepan and, if necessary, add glucose. Stir frequently to dissolve the sugar crystals. Measure with

the sugar scales or the thermometer to test the degree of doneness. Dip the brush into water and moisten the sides of the pan to wash down and dissolve any sugar crystals. The solution should be clear and colorless. A saturated syrup made from 3 pounds (1.5 kilograms) of sugar and 1 quart (1 liter) of water is required for making supersaturated sugar solutions. Further boiling reduces the moisture and increases the concentration of sugar in the solution. The degree of doneness can be measured most accurately with a thermometer.

Density Designation	Temperature		Judging Density
Weak thread	84°R	221°F/105°C	Dip the thumb and index finger into cold water, then into the sugar solution. Take a drop of the sugar solution between the two fingers; when pulled apart, a very fine thread forms.
Strong thread	86°R	225.5°F/107.5°C	Dip the thumb and index finger into cold water, then into the sugar solution. Take a drop of the sugar solution between the two fingers; when pulled apart, a strong thread forms.
Weak puff	89°R	232.5°F/111.5°C	Dip a metal ring into the sugar solution; a skin will form, which cannot be broken by lightly blowing on it.
Strong puff	90°R	234.5°F/112.5°C	Dip a metal ring into the sugar solution; a skin will form, which cannot be broken by blowing hard on it.
Soft ball	92°R	239°F/115°C	Drop half a teaspoon of the sugar solution into cold water; it will form a small lump, and a soft ball can be formed with the fingers.
Medium ball	94°R	243.5°F/117°C	Drop half a teaspoon of the sugar solution into cold water; a firm but malleable ball can be formed with the fingers.
Firm ball	97°R	250°F/121°C	Drop half a teaspoon of the sugar solution into cold water; a hard ball can be formed with the fingers.
Soft crack	100°R	257°F/125°C	A spoonful of sugar solution dropped into water breaks into threads that can be bent; it sticks to the teeth when bitten.
Medium crack	113°R	286°F/141°C	The sugar solution spins threads as it flows from a spoon; there is a very sharp cracking when bitten.
Hard crack	115°R	291°F/144°C	A spoonful of sugar solution dropped into water breaks into brittle threads that crack like glass.
Caramel	122°R	306.5°F/152.5°C	The sugar solution turns golden yellow.
Burned sugar	130°R	324.5°F/162.5°C	The sugar solution is bitter tasting and very dark brown or black.

Figure 25-2. Densities of cooked sugar.

25.7 Sugar Icings and Glazes— *Glaces au sucre*

25.7.1 Fondant—*Pâte à fondant*

Yield
U.S.—approximately 15 pounds
Metric—6.8 kilograms

Ingredients	U.S. Weight or Volume	Metric Weight or Volume
Sugar	12 pounds	6 kilograms
Glucose	1¼ pounds	600 grams
Water	2 quarts	2 liters

Procedure
1. Boil the sugar, glucose, and water. Cool slightly by adding a little cold water. Skim and strain. Bring to a boil again, cool with a little water, skim, and strain again. Repeat the procedure six times.
2. Place the syrup back over high heat and continue boiling. Wipe the sides of the pan frequently with a wet brush to remove any sugar crystals that have formed.
3. When the sugar solution reaches 250°F (121°C) or 97° Réaumur, pour it onto a wet marble slab.
4. Cool. Work the fondant with a spatula by lifting and folding it from the edges to the center until it turns milky and then white.
5. Work it even more vigorously as it begins to thicken until it is very smooth and creamy.
6. Cover with a damp cloth and store in an airtight container.
7. When using, heat the necessary quantity in a water bath.

Note: Fondant is used to make fine pralines, candies, and icing. Flavor as desired.

25.7.2 Confectioners' Sugar Icing—*Glace au sucre en poudre*

Yield
U.S.—⅔ cup
Metric—160 milliliters

Ingredients	U.S. Weight or Volume	Metric Weight or Volume
Egg whites	2	2
Sugar, confectioners'	½ cup	120 grams
Flavoring	as desired	as desired

Procedure
1. Mix egg whites, confectioners' sugar, and flavoring until the mixture becomes glossy and can be drawn into a ribbon.

25.7.3 Royal Icing—*Glace royale*

Yield
U.S.—⅔ cup
Metric—160 milliliters

Ingredients	U.S. Weight or Volume	Metric Weight or Volume
Egg whites	2	2
Sugar, confectioners'	10 ounces	300 grams
Lemon juice	few drops	few drops
Acetic acid (vinegar essence)	1 to 2 drops	1 to 2 drops

Procedure
1. Combine the egg whites and confectioners' sugar.
2. Add lemon juice and 1 to 2 drops of acetic acid.

Note: The finished icing should always be white, glossy, smooth, and stiff. Keep covered until used.

25.7.4 Water Glaze—*Glace à l'eau*

Yield
U.S.—approximately ⅔ cup
Metric—160 milliliters

Ingredients	U.S. Weight or Volume	Metric Weight or Volume
Sugar, confectioners'	7 ounces	200 grams
Thin sugar syrup at 15° Baumé	2 tablespoons	30 milliliters

Procedure
1. Blend confectioners' sugar and syrup until a thick, glossy mixture forms.

Chapter 26
Hot Desserts—*Entremets chauds*

26.1 Soufflés

Soufflés are especially susceptible to dropping temperature and are, therefore, served in the cocottes (straight-sided ovenproof soufflé dishes) in which they were baked. Accurate baking temperatures and proper beating of the egg whites to the stiff but not dry stage are essential for delicate, tender soufflés.

26.1.1 Vanilla Soufflé—*Soufflé à la vanille*

Yield
approximately 10 servings

Ingredients	U.S. Weight or Volume	Metric Weight or Volume
Milk	1 pint	5 deciliters
Sugar	4½ ounces	125 grams
Butter	3½ ounces	100 grams
Flour	3½ ounces	100 grams
Egg yolks	8	8
Vanilla extract	2 teaspoons	10 milliliters
Egg whites	8 to 10	8 to 10
Butter and flour for soufflé dishes	as needed	as needed
Sugar, confectioners'	as needed to dust tops	as needed to dust tops

Procedure
1. Place the milk and sugar in a saucepan and heat to the boiling point.
2. In a second pan, melt the butter and stir in the flour. Mix until smooth.
3. Pour the boiling milk over the butter and flour mixture and stir constantly. Remove from the heat. Cool slightly.
4. Beat the egg yolks until light. Stir them into the cooled mixture. Add vanilla extract.
5. Just before baking, carefully fold in the stiffly beaten egg whites.
6. Butter the soufflé dish carefully and dust with flour. Spoon the soufflé mixture into the soufflé dish.
7. Place the baking dish in a water bath and heat on the stove for a few minutes to warm the mixture.
8. Place the baking dish in the oven at 325°F (160°C). Halfway through the baking time, increase the temperature to 350°F (175°C). The approximate baking times are: 10 individual soufflés, 8 to 10 minutes; two 7- to 8-inch (17.5- to 20-centimeter) soufflés, 20 to 30 minutes; one 10- to 12-inch (25- to 30-centimeter) soufflé, 35 to 45 minutes. After the soufflé has risen, test for doneness by inserting a long needle. It should come out clean.
9. When done, dust with confectioners' sugar and serve at once. A cream or fruit sauce may be served with the soufflé.

Other Soufflés

Almond Soufflé—*Soufflé aux amandes*

Combine 3½ ounces (100 grams) of almonds that have been peeled, chopped fine, and lightly browned with 3½ ounces (100 grams) of ground almonds. Fold the almond mixture into 1 quart (1 liter) of uncooked vanilla soufflé batter. Finish as described in the recipe for vanilla soufflé.

Cherry Soufflé—*Soufflé aux cerises*

Flavor 1 quart (1 liter) of vanilla soufflé batter with Kirsch and lemon juice and add 9 ounces (250 grams) of pitted cherries. Finish as described in the recipe for vanilla soufflé.

Chocolate Soufflé—*Soufflé au chocolat*

Add 9 ounces (250 grams) of melted baking chocolate or 1½ ounces (50 grams) cocoa powder to vanilla soufflé batter. Follow procedure described in the recipe for vanilla soufflé.

Hazelnut Soufflé—*Soufflé aux avelines*

Mix 1 quart (1 liter) of vanilla soufflé batter with 7 ounces (200 grams) of hazelnut pralines. Finish as described in the recipe for vanilla soufflé.

Lemon Soufflé—*Soufflé au citron*

Flavor vanilla soufflé batter with lemon juice and grated lemon rind. Finish as described in the recipe for vanilla soufflé.

Mocha Soufflé—*Soufflé au moka*

Flavor vanilla soufflé batter with mocha extract or instant coffee granules. Finish as described in the recipe for vanilla soufflé.

Soufflé Rothschild—*Soufflé Rothschild*

Add pitted cherries and strawberries to lemon soufflé batter. Proceed as for vanilla soufflé except, halfway through the baking time, arrange a ring of pitted cherries and strawberries on top.

Strawberry Soufflé—*Soufflé aux fraises*

Flavor vanilla soufflé batter with lemon juice and pureed strawberries. Finish as described in the recipe for vanilla soufflé. After half the baking time, arrange a circle of strawberries on the top.

26.2 Hot Puddings—*Poudings chauds*

Molded puddings are turned out and served on a dish covered with a paper napkin. These puddings are baked and served as described in the recipes for soufflés. Puddings in large cocottes should be baked for about 30 minutes and those in individual cocottes for about 10 minutes.

English puddings are served in the special pudding dishes in which they are baked. Puddings are popular in England and are usually served with fruit syrup or stewed fruit.

Saxon Soufflé Pudding—*Pouding Saxon*

Yield
approximately 10 servings

Ingredients	U.S. Weight or Volume	Metric Weight or Volume
Milk	1 pint	5 deciliters
Sugar	4½ ounces	125 grams
Vanilla bean	1	1
Butter	3½ ounces	100 grams
Flour	4½ ounces	125 grams
Egg yolks	8	8
Lemon rind, grated	1 teaspoon	6 grams
Lemon juice	2 tablespoons	25 milliliters
Raisins	1¾ ounces	50 grams
Egg whites	8	8
Butter and flour for mold	as needed	as needed

Procedure
1. Place the milk, sugar, and vanilla bean in a saucepan and heat to the boiling point. Remove from

continued

Procedure

heat, cover, and steep for 20 minutes. Remove vanilla bean.

2. In a second pan, melt the butter and stir in the flour. Mix until smooth.
3. Pour the milk over the butter and flour mixture and stir well while it is still over the heat. Remove from the heat and cool slightly.
4. Add the egg yolks, one at a time, beating well after each addition. Stir the grated lemon rind, lemon juice, and the raisins into the cooled mixture.
5. Just before baking, carefully fold in the stiffly beaten egg whites.
6. Butter a smooth-walled pudding mold and coat with flour. Pour the pudding mixture into the mold.
7. Set the mold in a water bath and heat slowly on the stove until the mixture is thoroughly warmed.
8. Place the pudding, still in its water bath, in the oven at 350°F (175°C) and bake until done, 35 to 45 minutes.
9. Invert the pudding onto a dish covered with a paper doily.
10. Serve a rich fruit sauce separately, or serve a cream sauce over the pudding.

Other Soufflé Puddings

Almond Soufflé Pudding—*Pouding soufflé aux amandes*

Blend almonds into the pudding mixture as specified under almond soufflé. Finish as described in the basic soufflé pudding recipe. Serve a praline sauce separately.

Cherry Soufflé Pudding—*Pouding soufflé aux cerises*

Add 4 ounces (60 milliliters) of Kirsch and 9 ounces (25 grams) of pitted cherries to the pudding mixture. Serve a fruit sauce separately.

Hazelnut Soufflé Pudding—*Pouding soufflé aux avelines*

Blend hazelnuts into the Saxon pudding. Serve praline sauce separately.

Regency Pudding—*Pouding soufflé régence*

Coat the molds with caramel, fill with the pudding mixture, and finish as described in the basic recipe. Serve caramel sauce separately.

Royal Pudding—*Pouding soufflé royale*

Line the buttered molds with thin slices of jelly roll. Fill with Saxon pudding mixture and bake. Serve apricot sauce separately.

Sans-Souci Pudding—*Pouding soufflé Sans-Souci*

Sauté diced apples in butter and add to the pudding mixture. Pour pudding into molds and bake. Serve vanilla cream II as a sauce separately.

Strawberry Soufflé Pudding—*Pouding soufflé aux fraises*

Add some pureed strawberries and a few sliced strawberries to the pudding mixture. Serve a strawberry sauce separately.

26.2.2 Pudding, Diplomat Style—*Pouding diplomate*

Yield
approximately 10 servings

Ingredients	U.S. Weight or Volume	Metric Weight or Volume
Milk	3 cups	8 deciliters
Sugar	4¼ ounces	120 grams
Vanilla bean	1	1
Eggs	5	5
Raisins	1¾ ounces	50 grams
Sponge cake, diced	7 ounces	200 grams

Ingredients	U.S. Weight or Volume	Metric Weight or Volume
Candied orange peel *or* candied lemon peel	1¾ ounces	50 grams
Rum	¾ ounce	20 grams

Procedure

1. Heat the milk, sugar, and split vanilla bean to the boiling point. Cover and steep for 20 minutes. Remove vanilla bean.
2. Beat the eggs slightly and add the hot milk gradually.
3. In a separate bowl, mix the raisins, sponge cake, and candied peel. Pour in the rum. Then add the milk and egg mixture.
4. Butter the molds. Line the bottoms with buttered, greaseproof paper. Carefully pour in the sponge cake mixture.
5. Set the molds in a water bath and poach the pudding in the oven at 350°F (175°C) for 35 to 45 minutes (if it is one large mold), or until a knife or long needle inserted into the center of the pudding comes out clean.
6. When done, turn out of mold.
7. Serve a fruit sauce separately.

Note: The cake can be replaced by cubes of plain dinner rolls. If dinner rolls are used, add 7 ounces (200 grams) of sugar.

26.2.3 Frankfurt Pudding—*Frankfurter Pudding*

Yield

approximately 10 servings

Ingredients	U.S. Weight or Volume	Metric Weight or Volume
Butter	7 ounces	200 grams
Sugar	9 ounces	250 grams
Egg yolks	12	12
Sponge cake crumbs, dried and sifted	7 ounces	200 grams

Ingredients	U.S. Weight or Volume	Metric Weight or Volume
Almonds, unpeeled, grated fine	7 ounces	200 grams
Cinnamon, ground	½ teaspoon	3 grams
Raisins (optional)	3 to 4 ounces	100 grams
Egg whites	12	12
Butter for mold	as needed	as needed
Breadcrumbs	as needed	as needed

Procedure

1. Whip the butter and sugar until creamy.
2. Add egg yolks gradually.
3. Add sponge cake crumbs, almonds, and cinnamon. Add raisins if desired.
4. Beat the egg whites until stiff, but not dry, and carefully fold them into the mixture.
5. Butter the pudding mold and sprinkle the mold with breadcrumbs. Turn the mixture into the mold.
6. Place the mold in a water bath. Poach in the oven at 350°F (175°C) for about 30 to 35 minutes.
7. Invert pudding onto plate. Serve red-wine sauce on the side.

Note: Crumbs of ladyfingers may be used instead of the sponge cake.

26.2.4 Rice Soufflé Pudding—*Pouding soufflé au riz*

Yield

approximately 10 servings

Ingredients	U.S. Weight or Volume	Metric Weight or Volume
Rice	3½ ounces	100 grams
Milk	1 pint (more if needed)	5 deciliters (more if needed)
Vanilla bean	1	1
Sugar	3½ ounces	100 grams
Butter	1½ ounces	40 grams

continued

Ingredients	U.S. Weight or Volume	Metric Weight or Volume
Raisins	1¾ ounces	50 grams
Lemon rind, grated	1 teaspoon	6 grams
Egg yolks, beaten	8	8
Butter	as needed for molds	as needed for molds
Sponge cake crumbs	7 ounces	200 grams
Egg whites	8 to 10	8 to 10

Procedure

1. Wash the rice thoroughly. Drain.
2. Combine the milk and vanilla bean and heat to the boiling point. Cover and steep for 20 minutes. Remove vanilla bean.
3. Combine the rice and milk and cook for approximately 30 minutes.
4. Add the sugar.
5. If the mixture becomes too thick, add a little more milk. Cool slightly.
6. Add the butter, raisins, lemon rind, and beaten egg yolks.
7. Butter the molds and coat with dried sponge cake crumbs.
8. Beat the egg whites until stiff, but not dry. Carefully fold them into the pudding mixture.
9. Pour the pudding into the molds. Set them in a hot water bath.
10. Poach in oven at 350°F (175°C) for 35 to 45 minutes (if it is one large mold), or until a long needle inserted into the center of the pudding comes out clean.
11. Remove from oven and turn out of mold.
12. Serve as quickly as possible.
13. Serve a fruit sauce separately.

Variations of Rice Soufflé Pudding

Rice Pudding with Caramel—*Pouding de riz au caramel*

Coat the molds with caramel and finish the pudding as described in the recipe for rice pudding.

26.2.5 English Bread and Butter Pudding

Yield
approximately 10 servings

Ingredients	U.S. Weight or Volume	Metric Weight or Volume
Bread, sliced thin	7 ounces	200 grams
Butter	3½ ounces	100 grams
Milk	1½ pints	8 deciliters
Vanilla bean	1	1
Eggs	4 to 5	4 to 5
Sugar, granulated	4 ounces	120 grams
Raisins	1½ ounces	50 grams
Butter	1½ ounces	50 grams
Sugar, confectioners'	1 tablespoon	20 grams

Procedure

1. Brush thin slices of bread with melted butter and place them overlapping in a buttered pudding dish.
2. Combine the milk and vanilla bean and heat to the boiling point. Remove the vanilla bean.
3. Beat the eggs with the sugar until a ribbon forms. Add the milk slowly to the eggs and sugar.
4. Sprinkle the raisins over the bread.
5. Slowly pour the milk mixture over the bread.
6. Top with a few slivers of butter.
7. Set the pudding dish in a water bath and poach in an oven at 350°F (175°C) for about 45 minutes, until a light crust forms.
8. Sprinkle with confectioners' sugar before serving.

26.2.6 Rice Pudding, English Style—*Pouding de riz à l'anglaise*

Yield
approximately 10 servings

Ingredients	U.S. Weight or Volume	Metric Weight or Volume
Rice	5 ounces	150 grams
Milk	1 quart	1 liter

Ingredients	U.S. Weight or Volume	Metric Weight or Volume
Vanilla bean *or* lemon rind, grated	1 1 teaspoon	1 6 grams
Sugar	4 ounces	120 grams
Eggs	2	2
Butter	1¾ ounces	50 grams
Sugar, confectioners'	1 tablespoon	20 grams

Procedure

1. Wash the rice thoroughly. Drain.
2. Heat the milk and vanilla bean to the boiling point. (Lemon rind may be substituted.) Add the rice to the milk and boil for about 35 minutes. If necessary, add a little more milk.
3. Beat the sugar and eggs until a ribbon forms. Add to the milk and rice mixture.
4. Pour the mixture into a buttered baking dish. Top with a few slivers of butter.
5. Set the baking dish in a water bath. Bake at 350°F (175°C) for 35 to 40 minutes, until the pudding is golden yellow.
6. Dust with confectioners' sugar.
7. Serve a stewed fruit or a fruit sauce with this pudding if desired.

Other English Puddings

Semolina Pudding, English Style—*Pouding de semoule à l'anglaise*

Combine 1 quart (1 liter) of milk with 1 vanilla bean and heat to the boiling point. Cover and steep for 20 minutes. Remove vanilla bean. Add 5 ounces (150 grams) of semolina to the hot milk. Cook for 10 minutes and finish as described for rice pudding.

Tapioca Pudding, English Style—*Pouding au tapioca à l'anglaise*

Combine 1 quart (1 liter) of milk and 1 vanilla bean and heat to the boiling point. Cover and steep for 20 minutes. Remove vanilla bean. Add 5 ounces (150 grams) of tapioca to the hot milk. Cook for 10 minutes and finish as described for rice pudding.

26.3 Desserts Made with Leavened Dough—*Entremets à la pâte levée*

26.3.1 Rum Savarins—*Savarin au rhum*

Yield
approximately 10 servings

Ingredients	U.S. Weight or Volume	Metric Weight or Volume
Dough:		
Yeast	¾ ounce	20 grams
Milk, lukewarm	½ cup	1 deciliter
Flour	12 ounces	350 grams
Kneaded butter	5 ounces	150 grams
Sugar	½ ounce	15 grams
Eggs	4	4
Salt	¼ ounce	5 grams
Lemon rind, grated	½ teaspoon	3 grams
Butter and flour	as needed for mold	as needed for mold
Syrup:		
Black tea	¾ cup	2 deciliters
Water	¾ cup	2 deciliters
Sugar	9 ounces	250 grams
Lemon peel	from 1 lemon	from 1 lemon
Orange peel	from 1 orange	from 1 orange
Clove, whole	1	1
Cinnamon, stick	¼ stick	¼ stick
Rum	¾ cup	2 deciliters
Apricot jam	4 ounces	120 grams

Procedure

1. Dissolve the yeast in the lukewarm milk and mix in a little flour until a soft dough is formed. Cover and allow this starter dough to rise in a warm place until double in bulk.
2. Combine the kneaded butter and sugar and blend. Add the other dough ingredients and work into a dough. This must then be kneaded by hand until

continued

Procedure

bubbles form. Mix in the starter dough and once more knead the mixture hard for several minutes.

3. Butter a ring-shaped mold and dust with flour. Fill one-third full with dough. Cover and let rise in a warm place until dough reaches the top of the mold.
4. Bake in oven at 375°F (190°C) for 30 minutes, until savarin is golden yellow.
5. Turn out and allow to cool.
6. To make the syrup, place all ingredients except the rum in a saucepan and bring to a boil.
7. Remove from heat. Strain. Add the rum.
8. When the savarin is to be served, soak it in this hot syrup, then place on a platter and coat with apricot jam.
9. Serve a fruit sauce separately.

Other Savarins and Babas

Savarin Chantilly (Cold)—*Savarin Chantilly*

Prepare the savarin as described. After soaking in hot syrup, cool the savarin on a serving plate. Just before serving, fill with sweetened, vanilla-flavored whipped cream (*crème Chantilly*).

Savarin with Chocolate Pears (Cold)—*Savarin aux poires Suchard*

Finish the savarin as described. After soaking in hot syrup, cool the savarin on a serving platter. Fill with stewed pears and coat with a mouseline cream mixed with chocolate.

Savarin with Fruit (Hot)—*Savarin aux fruits*

Finish the savarin as described. Soak in hot syrup, arrange on a serving plate, and fill with stewed apricots, peaches, or cherries. Coat with apricot jam. Serve a fruit sauce separately.

Rum Baba—*Baba au Rhum*

Make the dough for rum savarins; add 3½ ounces (100 grams) of dried currants to the dough. Butter and flour baba molds. Turn the dough into a pastry bag and pipe the dough into the molds. Cover and let the dough rise to two-thirds of the height of the molds. Bake in the oven at 375°F (190°C) for 15 to 20 minutes, until babas are golden. Make the rum syrup used for the savarin and soak the babas in the syrup. Coat with apricot jam and serve apricot sauce separately.

Baba Chantilly (Cold)—*Baba Chantilly*

Prepare rum baba, soak in syrup, cool, place on a serving platter, and garnish with sweetened, vanilla-flavored whipped cream (*crème Chantilly*).

Baba with Sabayon (Hot)—*Baba au sabayon*

Prepare rum baba, soak in syrup, and serve hot, coated with sabayon. Serve additional sabayon separately.

26.3.2 Jelly Doughnuts—*Boules de Berlin*

Yield
30 to 35 doughnuts

Ingredients	U.S. Weight or Volume	Metric Weight or Volume
Yeast	2 ounces	60 grams
Milk, lukewarm	1¼ cups	3 deciliters
Flour	2¼ pounds	1 kilogram
Sugar	2 ounces	60 grams
Salt	¾ ounce	20 grams
Lemon rind, grated	1 teaspoon	6 grams
Eggs	10	10
Butter	7 ounces	200 grams
Jelly *or* jam	17.5 ounces	500 grams
Cinnamon sugar	as needed	as needed

Procedure

1. Dissolve the yeast in half of the lukewarm milk.
2. Place the flour in a bowl and make a well in the center. Pour the milk containing the yeast into this well and mix in some of the flour until a soft dough is formed. Dust this starter dough with a

little flour and allow it to rise in a warm place until about double in bulk.

3. Mix the sugar, salt, lemon rind, eggs, the remainder of the lukewarm milk, and the flour with the starter dough. Beat it vigorously by hand until bubbles form.
4. Work in the slightly melted butter and beat the mixture a second time until it no longer sticks to the hands. Should the dough be too firm, it may be necessary to add more milk. Should the dough be too soft, more flour can be added.
5. Place the dough in a floured bowl, cover, and allow to rise slightly in a warm place.
6. Dust a pastry board with flour. Place the dough on it and roll to ½-inch (1 centimeter) thick. Cut out rounds about 2 inches (5 centimeters) in diameter, about 1½ ounces (50 grams) each.
7. Place these balls upside down on a floured cloth. Cover with another floured cloth and allow to rise in a warm place until doubled in size.
8. Deep-fry in fat heated to 375°F (190°C). When properly prepared, the doughnuts should have a light-colored ring around the center. Let them cool completely.
9. Fill the doughnuts with jelly, using a pastry bag or jelly pump.
10. Before serving, roll the doughnuts in cinnamon sugar.

26.3.3 Raised Dumplings—*Dampfnudeln*

Yield
approximately 30 servings

Ingredients	U.S. Weight or Volume	Metric Weight or Volume
Yeast	2 ounces	60 grams
Milk, lukewarm	1 pint	5 deciliters
Flour	2 pounds	1 kilogram
Sugar	2½ ounces	70 grams
Salt	¾ ounce	20 grams
Lemon rind, grated	1 teaspoon	6 grams
Eggs	4	4
Egg yolks	4	4
Butter	6 ounces	170 grams

Ingredients	U.S. Weight or Volume	Metric Weight or Volume
Cream, lukewarm	3 cups	750 milliliters
Sugar for sprinkling	as needed	as needed

Procedure
1. Dissolve the yeast in half of the lukewarm milk.
2. Place the flour in a bowl and make a well in the center. Pour the milk containing the yeast into this well and mix in some of the flour until a soft dough is formed. Dust this starter dough with a little flour and allow it to rise in a warm place until about double in bulk.
3. Mix the sugar, salt, lemon rind, eggs, egg yolks, the remainder of the lukewarm milk, and the flour with the starter dough. Beat vigorously by hand until bubbles form.
4. Work in the slightly melted butter and beat the mixture a second time until it no longer sticks to the hands.
5. Form the dough into egg-size pieces and round them slightly on a floured board. Place them in a buttered flat pan leaving 1/16 inch (1.5 millimeters) of space between them. Brush each dumpling with butter. Cover the pan and allow dumplings to rise in a warm place.
6. When dumplings are doubled in size, pour on the warm cream and sprinkle with sugar.
7. Bake at 275°F (135°C) for 1 hour or more until they are golden in color.
8. Separate the dumplings before placing on a serving dish. Sprinkle with sugar.

26.4 Omelets—*Omelettes*

26.4.1 Baked Alaska—*Omelette norvégienne*

Yield
approximately 10 servings

Ingredients	U.S. Weight or Volume	Metric Weight or Volume
Sponge cake	7 ounces	200 grams
Liqueur	¼ cup	50 milliliters

continued

Ingredients	U.S. Weight or Volume	Metric Weight or Volume
Fruit salad mixture	10 to 14 ounces	300 to 400 grams
Ice cream	1 pint	½ liter
Candied fruits	1¾ ounces	50 grams
Omelet soufflé (recipe follows)	1 recipe	1 recipe
Sugar, confectioners'	as needed	as needed

Procedure
1. Using about half of the sponge cake, place a ½-inch-thick (1-centimeter) layer on an ovenproof platter.
2. Cut the remainder of the cake into thin slices.
3. Sprinkle liqueur over all the cake.
4. Combine the fruit salad with the ice cream. Arrange the mixture on top of the cake.
5. Surround and cover the ice cream with the thin slices of cake.
6. Spread the omelet mixture over the sponge cake and decorate with some of the same mixture and with the candied fruits.
7. Sprinkle with confectioners' sugar and lightly glaze in the oven at 500°F (240°C). Watch carefully. Sprinkle with confectioners' sugar again and serve immediately. (See figure 26-1.)

Note: A meringue mixture may be used instead of the omelet soufflé.

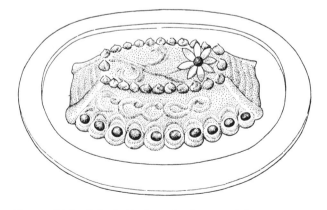

Figure 26-1. Baked Alaska—*Omelette norvégienne.*

26.4.2 Omelet with Jam—*Omelette à la confiture*

Yield
1 serving

Ingredients	U.S. Weight or Volume	Metric Weight or Volume
Eggs	2 to 3	2 to 3
Salt	¼ teaspoon	2 grams
Sugar	1 teaspoon	6 grams
Butter	as needed	as needed
Jam	2 tablespoons	30 grams
Sugar	½ teaspoon	3 grams

Procedure
1. Combine the eggs, salt, and 1 teaspoon (6 grams) sugar and beat until light.
2. Heat some butter in a pan. Add the egg mixture and stir. While still liquid, form the eggs into a long oval. Shape and continue frying for a few moments. Then fill with jam and fold over.
3. Turn the omelet out onto a platter and sprinkle with sugar. Caramelize the sugar on the omelet in a lattice pattern, using a red-hot iron.

26.4.3 Omelet Soufflé—*Omelette soufflé*

Yield
2 servings

Ingredients	U.S. Weight or Volume	Metric Weight or Volume
Egg yolks	6	6
Sugar	5 ounces	150 grams
Egg whites	8	8
Vanilla extract	½ teaspoon	3 milliliters
Lemon rind, grated	¼ teaspoon	2 grams
Butter and flour	as needed for baking pan	as needed for baking pan
Sugar, confectioners'	as needed	as needed

Procedure
1. Whip the egg yolks and sugar until they form a ribbon.
2. Add the stiffly beaten egg whites, vanilla extract, and lemon rind.

3. Place about two-thirds of the mixture in a long oval baking platter that has been buttered and lightly floured. Form a well in the center.
4. Place the remaining third of the mixture in a pastry bag and pipe it around the well in a decorative pattern.
5. Dust the soufflé with confectioners' sugar and bake in the oven at 350°F (175°C) for 10 minutes.
6. Dust once more with confectioners' sugar and serve immediately.

26.4.4 Omelet Stephanie—*Omelette Stéphanie*

Yield
2 servings

Ingredients	U.S. Weight or Volume	Metric Weight or Volume
Egg yolks	4	4
Sugar	2¾ ounces	80 grams
Egg whites	6	6
Flour	1½ ounces	40 grams
Cream	1 tablespoon	10 milliliters
Butter, melted	¾ ounce	20 grams
Lemon rind, grated	¼ teaspoon	2 grams
Vanilla extract	½ teaspoon	3 milliliters
Butter	as needed, for omelet pan	as needed, for omelet pan
Strawberry jam	1½ ounces	50 grams
Orange liqueur (Grand Marnier, Curaçao, Cointreau)	3 tablespoons	50 milliliters
Sugar for sprinkling	as needed	as needed

Procedure
1. Whip the egg yolks and sugar until they form a ribbon.
2. Fold in the stiffly beaten egg whites and flour alternately.
3. Add cream, melted butter, lemon rind, and vanilla extract.
4. Heat the butter in an omelet pan. Pour the omelet mixture into the pan and bake in the oven at 325°F (160°C) for 25 minutes, or until firm.
5. Combine the strawberry jam and liqueur.
6. Cover the omelet with the strawberry mixture, fold the omelet, sprinkle with sugar, and serve immediately.

Note: The omelet can be filled with fresh strawberries that have been macerated in sugar and liqueur.

Other Omelets

Rum Omelet—*Omelette au rhum*

Prepare the omelet as described in the recipe for omelet with jam without adding the jam. Invert the omelet onto a platter, sprinkle with sugar, and caramelize. Pour rum over the top, ignite it, and flame the omelet.

26.5 Crêpes—*Crêpes*

26.5.1 Crêpes Suzette I—*Crêpes Suzette I*

Yield
2 servings—3 crêpes each

Ingredients	U.S. Weight or Volume	Metric Weight or Volume
Sugar cubes	2	2
Orange peel	from 1 orange	from 1 orange
Sugar	1½ ounces	50 grams
Butter	1½ ounces	50 grams
Orange juice	¾ cup	2 deciliters
Lemon juice	1 teaspoon	5 milliliters
Grand Marnier	3 tablespoons	50 milliliters
Crêpes	6	6
Brandy	1 teaspoon	5 milliliters

Procedure
1. Rub the sugar cubes over orange peel.
2. Slightly caramelize the sugar and sugar cubes in a flambé pan.
3. Add the butter (do not brown) and deglaze the pan

continued

Procedure

with the orange and lemon juice. Continue stirring until the sugar is completely dissolved.

4. Add the Grand Marnier. Dip each side of the crêpes into the sauce.
5. Fold each crêpe into fourths and arrange in the pan. Pour the brandy over the crêpes, ignite it, and flambé them.
6. Moisten crêpes once more with the liquid. Serve on plates with remaining liquid.

26.5.2 Crêpes Suzette II—*Crêpes Suzette II*

Yield

10 servings—2 crêpes each

Ingredients	U.S. Weight or Volume	Metric Weight or Volume
Butter	10 ounces	300 grams
Sugar	10 ounces	300 grams
Orange juice	1¼ cups	3 deciliters
Orange rind, grated	from 4 oranges	from 4 oranges
Lemon juice	3 tablespoons	50 milliliters
Grand Marnier	5 fluid ounces	150 milliliters
Crêpes	20	20
Sugar	2 tablespoons	30 grams
Brandy	2¾ fluid ounces	75 grams

Procedure

1. Whip the butter and sugar until a ribbon forms.
2. Add the orange juice, orange rind, lemon juice, and Grand Marnier, and mix well.
3. Spread a thick layer of this cream over the crêpes. Fold each crêpe twice and arrange side by side on a warmed silver platter.
4. Sprinkle with sugar. Glaze quickly in a hot oven.
5. Flambé with the heated brandy.

Other Crêpe Desserts

German Pancakes—*Pannequets*

These pancakes are generally larger and thicker than crêpes, although the same batter is used. German pancakes are baked in the oven and then filled with applesauce, jam, or poached strawberries.

Pancakes, Normandy Style—*Crêpes normande*

Stew sliced apples in butter, add white wine, sugar, a few drops of lemon juice, a pinch of cinnamon, a few drops of Kirsch, and some raisins. Roll the mixture into thin hot crêpes, sprinkle with sugar, and glaze. Serve apricot sauce separately.

Pancakes, Parisian Style I—*Crêpes parisienne I*

Flavor apricot jam with Kirsch and spread on crêpes. Roll the crêpes, arrange on a platter, dust with sugar, and glaze under the broiler.

Pancakes, Parisian Style II—*Crêpes parisienne II*

Fill the crêpes with a rich fruit salad bound with a thick vanilla sauce. Sprinkle with sugar and rum. Brown slightly.

26.6 Fritters—*Beignets*

26.6.1 Apple Fritters—*Beignets de pommes*

Yield

approximately 10 servings

Ingredients	U.S. Weight or Volume	Metric Weight or Volume
Apples, sour	2½ to 3 pounds	1.2 to 1.5 kilograms
Kirsch	¼ cup	50 milliliters
Sugar	5 ounces	150 grams
Cinnamon, ground	1 teaspoon	6 grams
Frying batter	as needed	as needed
Fat	as needed	as needed
Cinnamon sugar	as needed	as needed
Fruit sauce	1 pint	5 deciliters

Procedure

1. Peel and core the apples.
2. Cut the apples into thin crosswise rings.

3. Combine the Kirsch, sugar, and cinnamon. Add the apple rings and macerate them for several hours, turning frequently.
4. Meanwhile, prepare the frying batter.
5. Drain the apple rings, dip into the batter, and fry in fat heated to 320°F (160°C).
6. Drain well.
7. Coat with cinnamon sugar and serve immediately.
8. The fruit sauce should be served separately.

Note: Moisture or juice accumulates on the cut surface of fresh fruit that has been macerated in sugar. The fruit should be dipped into the batter a bit at a time, otherwise, the batter becomes too thin.

Other Fritters

Apricot Fritters—*Beignets d'abricots*

Cut fresh apricots into halves, coat with sugar, and sprinkle with Kirsch. Dip the apricots into frying batter and deep-fry in hot oil. Coat with cinnamon sugar before serving.

Pineapple Fritters—*Beignets d'ananas*

Macerate slices of pineapple in sugar and liqueur. Dip into frying batter and deep-fry. Coat with cinnamon sugar and serve a fruit sauce separately.

26.6.2 Puffed Fritters—*Beignets soufflés*

Yield
10 servings

Ingredients	U.S. Weight or Volume	Metric Weight or Volume
Cream puff pastry	2 to 3 pounds	1 to 1.5 kilograms
Fat	as needed	as needed
Cinnamon sugar	3½ ounces	100 grams
Fruit sauce	1 to 2 pints	5 to 10 deciliters

Procedure
1. Use a pastry bag to form 1-ounce (30-gram) dumplings of the pastry on buttered parchment paper.
2. Carefully place the dumplings in the deep-fryer and fry slowly at 325°F (160°C).
3. Drain excess fat on absorbent cloth or paper.
4. Coat the fritters with cinnamon sugar.
5. Serve at once. (See figure 26-2.)
6. Serve the fruit sauce separately.

Figure 26-2. Puffed fritters—*Beignets soufflés.*

26.7 Fried Turnovers—*Rissoles*

26.7.1 Jam Turnovers—*Rissoles à la confiture*

Yield
10 servings—2 per serving

Ingredients	U.S. Weight or Volume	Metric Weight or Volume
Puff pastry	16 to 20 ounces	500 to 600 grams
Jam	7 ounces	200 grams
Egg, beaten	1	1
Egg yolk	1	1
Sugar, confectioners'	as needed	as needed

continued

Procedure
1. Prepare the puff pastry.
2. Roll the pastry out on a marble slab dusted with flour.
3. Using a round pastry cutter, cut the dough into 3-inch (7.5-centimeter) circles.
4. Place a teaspoon (4 grams) of rich jam in the center of each disc, brush the edges with beaten egg, and fold one half over the other to form semicircular turnovers.
5. Seal the edges of each turnover.
6. Brush with egg yolk.
7. Place on a dampened baking sheet and allow to stand for 1 hour.
8. Deep-fry at 365°F (185°C), or bake at 400°F (205°C).
9. When serving, sprinkle with confectioners' sugar.

Other Turnovers

Apple Turnovers, Normandy Style—
Rissoles normande

Stew thin-sliced apples in butter with sugar, a little white wine, a few drops of Kirsch, lemon juice, and some raisins. Fill the turnovers as described under jam turnovers.

Fruit Turnovers—*Rissoles aux fruits*

Prepare a salpicon of fresh or canned fruits. Bind with sugar, a few drops of Kirsch, and some jam. Prepare the turnovers as described under jam turnovers and fill them with the salpicon. Serve a fruit sauce separately.

Strawberry Turnovers—*Rissoles aux fraises*

Mix fresh strawberries with some sugar, Kirsch, and a small quantity of strawberry jam. Prepare the turnovers as described for jam turnovers, using this strawberry filling instead of the jam. Serve strawberry sauce separately.

26.8 Fruit Toasts—*Croûtes aux fruits*

26.8.1 Pineapple Toasts—*Croûtes à l'ananas*

Yield
10 servings

Ingredients	U.S. Weight or Volume	Metric Weight or Volume
Bread, white	10 slices	10 slices
Butter	4 ounces	100 grams
Pineapple slices, canned	15 slices	15 slices
Apricot sauce	1 pint	5 deciliters
Cherries or strawberries	10	10

Procedure
1. Sauté the bread in butter until golden.
2. Heat the pineapple in its juice.
3. Arrange 3 half-slices of pineapple on a piece of bread.
4. Coat the pineapple with hot apricot sauce.
5. Garnish with red cherries or strawberries and serve.

Other Fruit Toasts

Apple Toasts, Normandy Style—*Croûtes normande*

Prepare the slices of bread as described in the recipe for pineapple toasts. Stew peeled and sliced apples. Add white wine, a few drops of Kirsch and lemon juice, sugar, and raisins. Pour hot fruit onto the toasts, arrange the toasts in a mound on a platter, cover with more hot apple mixture, and coat with apricot sauce.

Strawberry Toasts—*Croûtes aux fraises*

Prepare the slices of bread as described for pineapple toasts. Decorate with strawberries that have been poached in sugar syrup, and coat with a strawberry sauce.

26.9 Hot Fruit Desserts—*Entremets chauds aux fruits*

26.9.1 Apple Charlotte—*Charlotte aux pommes*

Yield
approximately 10 servings

Ingredients	U.S. Weight or Volume	Metric Weight or Volume
Bread, toasting	10 slices	10 slices
Butter, melted	4 ounces	100 grams
Butter	1½ ounces	50 grams
Apples	3 pounds	1.5 kilograms
White wine	½ cup	1 deciliter
Sugar	10 ounces	300 grams
Raisins	1½ ounces	50 grams
Lemon rind, grated	½ teaspoon	3 grams
Cinnamon, ground	⅛ teaspoon	1 gram
Cloves, ground	⅛ teaspoon	1 gram
Rum	¼ cup	50 milliliters
Apricot sauce	1 pint	5 deciliters

Procedure
1. Line the bottom of a timbale with bread that has been cut into wedges, forming a circle (like a pie), dipped into melted butter.
2. Cut ½-inch-wide (1-centimeter) strips of bread the same length as the height of the timbale. Dip them into melted butter to line the timbale, overlapping them as they are put in place.
3. Heat 1½ ounces (50 grams) of butter in a saucepan.
4. Place peeled and thin-sliced apples in the saucepan with the wine, sugar, raisins, lemon rind, cinnamon, and cloves. Cook until slightly thickened, stirring constantly. Place the thick part of the mixture in the lined timbale and press down lightly.
5. Reduce the remaining liquid from the apple mixture to a syruplike consistency, flavor with rum, and pour into the mold.
6. Place a buttered slice of bread on top. Bake in an oven at 375°F (190°C) for 30 to 40 minutes.
7. Remove from oven and let the charlotte rest a few minutes.
8. Turn out carefully just before serving.
9. Serve apricot sauce separately.

26.9.2 Apple Roll—*Roulade de pommes*

Yield
approximately 10 servings

Ingredients	U.S. Weight or Volume	Metric Weight or Volume
Apples	3 pounds	1.5 kilograms
Sugar	3 to 5 ounces	100 to 150 grams
Lemon juice	few drops	few drops
Cinnamon, ground	1 teaspoon	6 grams
Butter	1½ ounces	50 grams
White wine	½ cup	150 milliliters
Currants, dried	4 ounces	100 grams
Sweet tart pastry	20 to 28 ounces	600 to 800 grams
Egg yolks	1 to 2	1 to 2
Sugar, confectioners'	as needed	as needed
Apricot sauce	1 pint	5 deciliters

Procedure
1. Peel and slice the apples and stew in a flat pan with the sugar, lemon juice, cinnamon, butter, white wine, and soaked dried currants. When apples are tender, remove the mixture from the heat and cool.
2. Roll out the pastry into a long strip about 11 inches (27.5 centimeters) wide.
3. Place the apple mixture in the center down the full length of the strip. Fold the sides of the pastry over the mixture, moistening the edges with egg yolk and pressing them together to form a straight seam.
4. Place the roll on a baking tray with the seam side down. Brush with egg yolk. Garnish with pastry cutouts as desired.

continued

Procedure

5. Bake in the oven at 375°F (190°C) for about 45 minutes, until the crust is golden brown.
6. To serve, cut into slices and sprinkle with confectioners' sugar.
7. Serve apricot sauce separately.

26.9.3 Apples, Basel Style—*Pommes à la bâloise*

Yield
10 servings

Ingredients	U.S. Weight or Volume	Metric Weight or Volume
Apple, medium size	10	10
White wine	¾ to 1¼ cups	2 to 3 deciliters
Sugar	3 to 5 ounces	100 to 150 grams
Butter	3½ ounces	100 grams
Jam	7 ounces	200 grams
Kirsch	¼ cup	50 milliliters
Sugar, confectioners'	as needed	as needed
Almonds, sliced and roasted	1½ ounces	50 grams

Procedure

1. Peel the apples.
2. Using a melon baller, remove the cores without completely cutting through the apples.
3. Place the apples in a buttered flat dish. Add the white wine.
4. Fill the holes in the apples with sugar and top with a sliver of butter.
5. Bake in the oven at 375°F (190°C) for 40 to 60 minutes, until apples are tender.
6. When serving, fill the apples with jam mixed with the Kirsch. In each serving dish, place some of the syrup from the baking dish.
7. Sprinkle the apples with confectioners' sugar and roasted almond slices.

26.9.4 Apricots with Meringue—*Abricots meringués*

Yield
approximately 10 servings

Ingredients	U.S. Weight or Volume	Metric Weight or Volume
Milk	1 quart	1 liter
Salt	¼ teaspoon	2 grams
Rice, blanched	5 ounces	150 grams
Sugar	4 ounces	120 grams
Cinnamon, ground	½ teaspoon	3 grams
Vanilla extract	1 teaspoon	5 milliliters
Apricots, cooked	2 to 3 pounds	1 to 1.5 kilograms
Meringue	1 recipe	1 recipe
Sugar, for sprinkling	as needed	as needed
Apricot sauce	1 pint	5 deciliters

Procedure

1. Heat the milk and salt to the boiling point.
2. Add the blanched rice and cook by the method described for rice pudding.
3. Add the sugar, cinnamon, and vanilla.
4. Spread the rice mixture on a buttered platter.
5. Arrange the apricots on top and cover with meringue. More meringue may be used to decorate the dish if desired.
6. Sprinkle with sugar and bake at 350°F (175°C) until the meringue is slightly browned.
7. Serve the apricot sauce separately.

Other Fruit Meringues

Apples with Meringue—*Pommes meringuées*

Prepare the rice as for apricots with meringue. Spread the rice on a buttered platter, top with stewed apples, and cover with the meringue mixture. Sprinkle with sugar and bake at a low temperature. Serve apricot sauce separately.

26.9.5 Baked Apples, Home Style—*Pommes bonne femme*

Yield
10 servings

Ingredients	U.S. Weight or Volume	Metric Weight or Volume
Apples, large	10	10
Sugar	3½ to 5 ounces	100 to 150 grams

Ingredients	U.S. Weight or Volume	Metric Weight or Volume
Raisins	3½ ounces	100 grams
Cinnamon, ground	½ teaspoon	3 grams
Butter	5 ounces	150 grams
Wine, white	¾ to 1¼ cups	2 to 3 deciliters

Procedure

1. Wash the apples.
2. Pare a ¼-inch-wide (5-millimeter) strip of apple skin in a spiral pattern from top to bottom.
3. Core the apples.
4. Fill the centers with a mixture of sugar, raisins, and cinnamon.
5. Place in a buttered flat baking dish. Top each apple with a sliver of butter.
6. Add the wine.
7. Bake in the oven at 375°F (190°C) for 40 to 60 minutes, until the apples are tender but not mushy.

26.9.6 Baked Apples in Pastry—*Pommes en cage*

Yield

approximately 10 servings

Ingredients	U.S. Weight or Volume	Metric Weight or Volume
Apples, medium size	10	10
Sugar	2¾ to 3½ ounces	80 to 100 grams
Raisins	1½ to 2 ounces	50 to 60 grams
Puff pastry	20 to 24 ounces	600 to 700 grams
Pastry cream	1 cup	250 milliliters
Egg yolks	1 to 2	1 to 2

Procedure

1. Peel and core the apples. Fill them with a mixture of sugar and raisins.
2. Roll out the puff pastry very thin and cut out 5½-inch (14-centimeter) squares.

3. Place some pastry cream on each square and place an apple on it.
4. Wrap each apple in a puff pastry square, moisten the edges with water, and seal, covering each apple completely (see figure 26-3).
5. Brush the puff pastry with egg yolk, put a round leaf of puff pastry on top of each apple, and brush again with the egg yolk.
6. Bake in the oven at 350°F (175°C) for about 45 minutes. Use a needle to test for doneness.

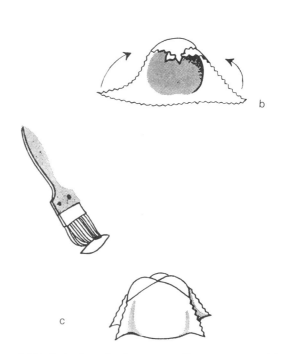

Figure 26-3. Baked apples in pastry—*Pommes en cage:* (a) cut puff pastry into squares; (b) wrap cream and apples in pastry; (c) decorate with additional puff pastry.

Other Hot Fruit Desserts

Pineapple Rice Pudding—*Ananas Condé*

For approximately 10 servings: 1 quart (1 liter) of milk, 5 ounces (150 grams) of rice, 4 ounces (120 grams) of sugar, 1½ ounces (50 grams) of butter, 1 vanilla bean, pinch of salt, a little ground cinnamon, 20 small pineapple slices, 10 ounces (300 grams) of apricot jam, and approximately 1 pint (5 deciliters) of fruit sauce. Prepare the rice as described for rice pudding. Spread on a buttered platter, place the pineapple slices on top, and coat with hot apricot jam. Serve fruit sauce separately.

Plums au Gratin—*Gratin aux prunes*

Place a round sponge cake or pudding mixture (semolina pudding, English style) in a gratin dish. Cut plums into halves and arrange over the cake or pudding. Decorate with meringue or a soft marzipan, and gratinate in the oven. Stew plums in red wine and serve separately.

Stewed Fruit Rice Pudding—*Fruits Condé*

Decorate a bed of rice pudding with hot stewed fruits and coat with hot apricot jam. Serve fruit sauce separately.

Stewed Pears Rice Pudding—*Poires Condé*

Decorate a bed of rice pudding with hot stewed pears and cover with melted pear jelly. Serve fruit sauce separately.

Chapter 27
Cold Desserts—*Entremets froids*

These cold desserts include custards, jellies, puddings, mousses, tarts, cakes, and cookies. The puddings, custards, and tarts may be made in large serving dishes, molds, or pie pans. Many of these desserts may also be made in individual cups, cases, molds, or tart shells. They can be garnished with fruits, chocolate, toasted nuts, whipped cream, or sauces.

27.1 Custards—*Crèmes renversées*

27.1.1 Blancmange—*Blanc-manger*

Yield
approximately 10 servings

Ingredients	*U.S. Weight or Volume*	*Metric Weight or Volume*
Milk	2½ cups	6 deciliters
Salt	¼ teaspoon	2 grams
Gelatin, unflavored	¾ ounce	20 grams
Water, cold	½ cup	1 deciliter
Almond paste	9 ounces	250 grams
Vanilla extract	2 teaspoons	10 milliliters
Whipping cream	1¼ cups	3 deciliters

Procedure
1. Heat the milk and salt to the boiling point.
2. Soak the gelatin in the cold water. Press out the excess water, and add the gelatin and the almond paste to the hot milk. Stir well until the gelatin is dissolved.
3. Strain through a cheesecloth.
4. Add vanilla extract.
5. Set the saucepan in cold running water. Stir the mixture frequently until cold. Whip the cream.
6. As soon as the mixture begins to congeal, fold in the whipped cream and immediately pour into the mold.
7. Chill until thoroughly set. Unmold to serve.

Note: The almond paste can be replaced by almond essence and sugar. A little Kirsch may be added if desired.

Variations of Blancmange

Apricots, Favorite Style—*Abricots favorite*

Stewed apricots are arranged around the bottom of a ring mold. The mold is filled with blancmange, cooled, and inverted onto a plate. Apricot sauce is served on the side.

Surprise Eggs—*Oeufs en surprise*

A blancmange mixture is poured into a casserole and allowed to set. Stewed apricot halves are arranged, round side up, on the blancmange. A few drops of clear syrup are poured over each apricot. Fruit sauce is served separately.

27.1.2 Caramel Custard—*Crème caramel*

Yield
approximately 10 servings

Ingredients	U.S. Weight or Volume	Metric Weight or Volume
Milk	1 quart	1 liter
Eggs	8	8
Salt	¼ teaspoon	2 grams
Sugar	14 ounces	400 grams
Vanilla extract	2 teaspoons	10 milliliters
Water	¼ cup	100 milliliters

Procedure
1. Heat the milk to the boiling point.
2. Beat the eggs. Add salt and 7 ounces (200 grams) sugar and mix thoroughly.
3. Add the hot milk, stirring constantly.
4. Add the vanilla extract. Strain.
5. Coat the insides of the custard cups with caramelized sugar. (See note.)
6. Pour the custard into the coated custard cups.
7. Set the cups or molds on a rack in a pan of hot, but not boiling, water. Poach in the oven at 325°F (160°C) for approximately 30 minutes.
8. To test for doneness, insert the tip of a knife into the custard near the edge of the cup. If the blade comes out clean, the custard should be removed from the oven and the water bath. There is sufficient heat stored in the custard and the cup to complete the cooking process after removal from the oven. The custard will be firm in the center by the time it has cooled.
9. Invert the custard cup onto a platter or individual dessert dishes. (See figure 27-1.) The liquid caramel will flow down the sides of the custard. If the custard is thoroughly chilled, it may be necessary to dip the cups, to the depth of the caramel syrup, quickly into hot water so that all the syrup will be released.

Note: To caramelize sugar, heat in a heavy pan over low heat 7 ounces (200 grams) of sugar. Stir constantly with a wooden spoon until sugar is melted. Remove pan from heat and add ¼ cup (115 millili-

ters) water very slowly and carefully. (Adding water quickly can be very dangerous and may cause an explosive action.) Return the pan to low heat and cook until the mixture is golden brown.

Figure 27-1. Caramel custard—*Crème caramel.*

Variations of Caramel Custard

Custard with Whipped Cream—*Crème Beau-Rivage*

This is a caramel custard baked in a ring-shaped mold. The center is filled with flavored whipped cream. The ring is surrounded with small cream-filled pastry horns. (See figure 27-2.)

Figure 27-2. Custard with whipped cream—*Crème Beau-Rivage.*

Custard, Florence Style—*Crème florentine*

Custard is poured into a mold that has been coated with caramel. It is poached in the oven, cooled, and inverted onto a serving plate. The center is filled with whipped cream flavored with Kirsch.

Royal Custard—*Crème royale*

This is a custard that has been poured into a buttered ring-shaped mold without caramel coating. The custard is poached, cooled, and inverted onto a serving dish. The center is filled with whipped cream.

Figure 27-3. Custard, French style—*Crème à la française.*

27.1.3 Custard, French Style—*Crème à la française*

Yield
approximately 10 servings

Ingredients	U.S. Weight or Volume	Metric Weight or Volume
Milk	1 quart	1 liter
Eggs	6	6
Sugar	5 ounces	150 grams
Salt	¼ teaspoon	2 grams
Vanilla extract	2 teaspoons	10 milliliters
Nutmeg	few grains	few grains
Whipped cream	as needed	as needed

Procedure
1. Heat the milk to the boiling point.
2. Beat the eggs. Add sugar and salt and mix thoroughly.
3. Add the hot milk, stirring constantly.
4. Add the vanilla extract. Strain.
5. Pour into a baking dish or into individual custard cups.
6. Dust the tops with grated nutmeg.
7. Set the molds on a rack in a pan of hot, but not boiling, water. Poach in the oven at 325°F (160°C).
8. To test for doneness, insert the tip of a knife into the custard near the edge of the cup. If the blade comes out clean, the custard should be removed from the oven and water bath. There is sufficient heat stored in the cups to complete the cooking process after removal from the oven. The custard will be firm in the center by the time it has cooled.
9. Garnish with a rosette of whipped cream. (See figure 27-3.)

Variations of Custard, French Style

Apricot Custard in Cocottes—*Petits pots de crème aux abricots*

This is custard, French style, topped with stewed apricot halves, covered with thick apricot sauce, and sprinkled with chopped and browned hazelnuts. Surround the apricots with whipped cream.

Fruit Custard in Cocottes—*Petits pots de crème jardinière*

This custard, French style, is garnished with diced fruits, covered with a thick apricot sauce, and decorated with whipped cream.

27.2 Bavarian Creams—*Crèmes bavaroises*

27.2 Bavarian Cream—*Bavarois à la crème*

Yield
approximately 10 servings

Ingredients	U.S. Weight or Volume	Metric Weight or Volume
Gelatin, un-flavored	½ ounce	15 grams
Water, cold	½ cup	1 deciliter

continued

Ingredients	U.S. Weight or Volume	Metric Weight or Volume
Milk	2¼ cups	6 deciliters
Vanilla bean	1, split	1, split
Egg yolks	5	5
Sugar	4 ounces	120 grams
Heavy cream	1¼ cups	3 deciliters

Procedure
1. Soak the gelatin in the cold water until dissolved.
2. Boil the milk and the split vanilla bean together for 5 minutes. Remove the vanilla bean.
3. Beat the egg yolks with the sugar until they form a ribbon.
4. Beat the milk into the egg yolk/sugar mixture. Place in a saucepan.
5. Stir with a wooden spoon in a hot water bath, about 175°F (85°C).
6. Stir in the gelatin.
7. Strain through a china cap. Place in a cold water bath.
8. As soon as the cream begins to congeal, stir in the whipped cream.
9. Place the cream in a chilled mold. Refrigerate until firm.
10. Dip the mold quickly into hot water and invert the mold on a chilled plate. Garnish with whipped cream and candied fruits if desired.

Variations of Bavarian Cream

Bavarian Cream with Apple—*Bavarois á la normande*

This is bavarian cream combined with apples that have been stewed with sugar, rum, white wine, and lemon juice. The cream is served with a ring of stewed apple quarters. Apricot sauce is served separately.

Chocolate Bavarian Cream—*Bavarois au chocolat*

Crushed chocolate is added and blended into the basic recipe for bavarian cream while it is still hot. Chocolate sauce is served separately.

Bavarian Cream, Diplomat Style—*Bavarois diplomate*

This is a bavarian cream combined with sponge cake and fruits that have been drizzled with rum and maraschino. It is inverted onto a serving plate and decorated with whipped cream.

Bavarian Cream with Hazelnuts—*Bavarois aux avelines*

This is a bavarian cream mixed with a finely ground pralines.

Bavarian Cream with Maraschino—*Bavarois au marasquin*

This bavarian cream is flavored with maraschino and a few drops of Kirsch.

Mocha Bavarian Cream—*Bavarois au moka*

This is a bavarian cream flavored with mocha extract. Mocha sauce may be served separately.

Neopolitan Bavarian Cream—*Bavarois rubané*

The bavarian cream is divided into equal amounts in three containers. Each is tinted with a different color. One is flavored with vanilla, one with chocolate, and the other with mocha. After each layer is set, the next is poured on. Vanilla cream II may be served separately.

Charlotte Russe—*Charlotte russe*

The base and sides of a mold are lined with ladyfingers. Bavarian cream flavored with Kirsch and maraschino is poured into the mold. After the cream is set, it is inverted onto a serving plate and garnished with whipped cream. (See figure 27-4.)

Eugenia Cake with Raspberry Sauce—*Eugénie Melba*

A round génoise is sliced into two layers and filled with basic bavarian cream. The upper side is coated

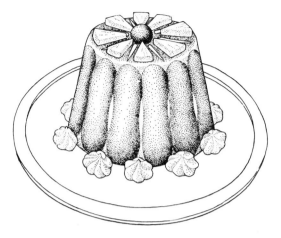

Figure 27-4. Charlotte russe.

with the same cream and covered with sliced peaches and whipped cream. The cake should be cool before cutting. Raspberry sauce is served separately.

Charlotte Royale—*Charlotte royale*

Thin slices from a 1½-inch (4-centimeter) jelly roll are used to line the base and sides of a charlotte mold. The mold is filled with bavarian cream flavored with Kirsch. After the mold is firm, it is inverted onto a serving plate and garnished with whipped cream. (See figure 27-5.)

Figure 27-5. Charlotte royale.

27.3 Desserts Made with Cream Puff Pastry—*Entremets à la pâte à choux*

Cream Puffs with Whipped Cream—*Choux Chantilly*

These puffs are prepared from cream puff pastry that is forced through a pastry tube into walnut-size balls onto a buttered sheet pan. They are brushed with beaten egg yolk and baked in an oven at 400°F (205°C) for 15 minutes. When cool, they are slit and filled with sweetened, vanilla-flavored whipped cream and sprinkled with sugar. Two pounds (1 kilogram) of cream puff pastry yields about 50 cream puffs. About 2 tablespoons (30 milliliters) of whipped cream is allowed per puff.

Cream Puffs with Pastry Cream—*Choux à la crème*

These puffs are filled with pastry cream or Saint-Honoré cream and sprinkled with sugar.

Chocolate Eclairs—*Eclairs Suchard*

These are éclairs filled with chocolate cream and coated with chocolate fondant or coating chocolate.

Chocolate Profiteroles—*Profiteroles au Chocolat*

These are tiny cream puffs filled with whipped cream. The puffs are arranged in a serving dish, coated with chocolate sauce, and sprinkled with toasted almonds.

Eclairs with Kirsch—*Eclairs au Kirsch*

These éclairs are made from cream puff pastry shaped into finger-length strips and placed on a buttered sheet pan. The éclairs are brushed with beaten egg yolk and baked in an oven at 400°F (205°C) for 10 minutes. When cool, the éclairs are slit on one side and filled with pastry cream or Saint-Honoré cream flavored with Kirsch. The éclairs are coated with Kirsch-flavored icing. Two pounds (1 kilogram) of cream puff pastry yield about 60 eclairs or 120 profiteroles.

Mocha Eclairs—*Eclairs au moka*

These are éclairs filled with mocha cream and coated with mocha icing.

Saint-Honoré Cake—*Gâteau Saint-Honoré*

This cake is made with short crust pastry and cream puff pastry. The short crust pastry is shaped into circles 8 inches (20 centimeters) in diameter. These are placed on a sheet pan. Cream puff pastry is piped around the rims of the bases. The bases are pierced and baked. On a separate sheet pan, cream puff pastry is formed into about 2 dozen hazelnut-size balls. These are baked in an oven at 375°F (190°C). Saint-Honoré cream is spread on the bases. The small puffs are dipped into a sugar solution boiled to 84°R., thread stage, and immediately placed around the outer ring of the cake. The cake is often garnished with whipped cream and fruits.

27.4 Desserts with Chantilly Cream—
Entremets à la crème Chantilly

Chantilly cream (*crème Chantilly*) is heavy cream whipped with sugar and vanilla extract to taste. It is the classic whipped cream.

27.4.1 Meringues Chantilly—*Meringues Chantilly*

Yield
approximately 40 shells
(20 servings)

Ingredients	U.S. Weight or Volume	Metric Weight or Volume
Egg whites	10	10
Vanilla extract	1 teaspoon	5 milliliters
Cream of tartar	⅛ teaspoon	0.5 grams
Sugar	1 pound	500 grams
Whipping cream	2 cups, or as needed	500 milliliters, or as needed
Sugar and vanilla for cream	as needed	as needed

Procedure
1. Whip the egg whites until foamy. Add the vanilla extract and cream of tartar.
2. While continuing to whip, add 1 tablespoon (15 milliliters) of the sugar at a time. Whip until mixture forms very stiff peaks.
3. Cover sheet pans with parchment paper. Form meringues with a spoon or put mixture in a pastry bag and pipe onto the sheet pan. Dust meringues lightly with granulated sugar.
4. Bake in the oven at 250°F (120°C) for 2 to 4 hours, depending on the size. The meringues should dry out, rather than bake, and they should not brown.
5. After half the baking time has elapsed, dent the bottom of the meringue.
6. When done, cool. Remove meringues from baking sheet and store in a warm dry place.
7. To serve, fill 2 shells with Chantilly cream, using about 1¾ ounces (55 milliliters) of whipped cream per portion. Press the shells together and garnish with more whipped cream.

27.4.2 Vacherin with Chantilly Cream—
Vacherin Chantilly

Yield
30 to 40 portions

Ingredients	U.S. Weight or Volume	Metric Weight or Volume
Egg whites	10	10
Vanilla extract	1 teaspoon	5 milliliters
Cream of tartar	⅛ teaspoon	0.5 grams
Sugar	1 pound	500 grams
Whipped cream	as needed	as needed
Sugar and vanilla for cream	as needed	as needed

Procedure
1. Whip the egg whites until foamy. Add the vanilla extract and cream of tartar.
2. While continuing to whip, add 1 tablespoon (15 milliliters) of the sugar at a time. Whip until mixture forms very stiff peaks.

3. Cover baking sheets with parchment paper. Fill a pastry bag with the meringue mixture. Pipe onto the baking sheets in lattice pattern to form cake bases. It should make 6 or 8 bases.
4. Bake in the oven at 175° to 200°F (80° to 90°C) for 2 to 4 hours, depending on the size. The vacherins should dry out, rather than bake, and they should not brown.
5. When done, cool. Remove from baking sheet and store in a warm dry place.
6. To serve, fill 2 shells with sweetened and flavored whipped cream. Press the shells together and garnish with more whipped cream.

Other Desserts with Chantilly Cream

Chestnuts with Chantilly Cream—*Mont Blanc*

Chestnuts are shelled, peeled, and simmered in milk with a vanilla bean. Then they are grated and worked into a smooth puree. Sugar syrup, a few drops of Kirsch, and milk are added to the puree. It is put into a pastry bag and piped into a circle on a platter. The center is filled with Chantilly cream.

Pastry Horns with Chantilly Cream— *Cornets Chantilly*

These horns are made from an almond batter and then filled with Chantilly cream.

27.5 Jellies—*Gelées*

27.5.1 Port Jelly—*Gelée au porto*

Yield
approximately 2 quarts

Ingredients	U.S. Weight or Volume	Metric Weight or Volume
Water	1 pint	5 deciliters
Sugar	1 pound	500 grams
Lemon juice	1 pint	5 deciliters
Lemon rind	from 1 lemon	from 1 lemon

Ingredients	U.S. Weight or Volume	Metric Weight or Volume
Gelatin, unflavored granular	1½ ounces	50 grams
Water, cold	1½ cups	300 milliliters
White wine	1¼ cups	3 deciliters
White port	¾ cup	2 deciliters

Procedure
1. Place the water, sugar, lemon juice, and lemon rind in a saucepan and mix well.
2. Stir continuously and cook to the boiling point.
3. Cover pan, lower the heat, and simmer gently for 10 minutes.
4. Soak the gelatin in the cold water.
5. Add the soaked gelatin to the saucepan and stir until completely dissolved.
6. Strain the jelly through a cloth.
7. When the jelly is almost cool, add the white wine and the port.

Note: This jelly can be used for lining and coating molds and for jellied fruits. It may be tinted if desired.

Other Jellies

White-wine Jelly—*Gelée au vin blanc*

This jelly is prepared by the method for port jelly, except 1 pint (5 deciliters) of white wine is used and the port wine is omitted.

Kirsch Jelly—*Gelée au kirsch*

This is a white-wine jelly flavored with Kirsch.

27.6 Cold Puddings—*Poudings froids*

27.6.1 Rice Pudding, Empress Style— *Riz à l'impératrice*

Yield
approximately 10 servings

continued

Ingredients	U.S. Weight or Volume	Metric Weight or Volume
Rice	3½ ounces	100 grams
Milk	1 pint	5 deciliters
Gelatin, unflavored	½ ounce	14 grams
Water, cold	½ cup	1 deciliter
Sugar	5 ounces	150 grams
Vanilla extract	1 teaspoon	5 milliliters
Kirsch	2 tablespoons	30 milliliters
Candied fruits	3½ ounces	100 grams
Heavy cream, whipped	1 pint	5 deciliters
White-wine jelly	¾ cup	2 deciliters
Raspberry syrup	as needed	as needed

Procedure
1. Wash the rice thoroughly.
2. Scald the milk. Add the rice to the milk and cook to a thin, smooth consistency.
3. Soak the gelatin in cold water. Add gelatin, sugar, and vanilla extract to the hot rice mixture. Stir until gelatin is dissolved.
4. Cool. When the mixture begins to congeal, quickly add the Kirsch, fruits, and whipped cream.
5. Place white-wine jelly in individual molds to a depth of ¼ inch (5 millimeters). Fill with the rice mixture and refrigerate until firm.
6. Dip the molds into hot water for a moment, then invert on a serving dish.
7. Thin the raspberry syrup slightly. Serve the syrup separately.

Note: This rice pudding can be served in cups rather than molds. It is then topped with macerated fruits and whipped cream. Raspberry syrup is served separately.

Variations of Rice Pudding, Empress Style

Apricots Sybilla—*Abricots Sybille*

A thin sponge cake base is covered with a layer of rice pudding, empress style, that has been mixed with minced apricots. It is topped with thin slices of nougatine and apricots. An apricot sauce with cherries and almond chips is served separately. This is an elegant and impressive dessert.

Pineapples, Empress Style—*Ananas à l'impératrice*

This is rice pudding, empress style, that has been poured into ring molds lined with thin slices of pineapple. It is unmolded when cool and served with apricot sauce.

Semolina Victoria—*Semoule Victoria*

This pudding is prepared like rice pudding, empress style, except 5 ounces (140 grams) of semolina are substituted for the rice and 1 quart (1 liter) of milk is used. The pudding is poured into molds that have been lined with jelly. A slightly thinned raspberry sauce is served separately.

Apricots, Florence Style—*Abricots florentine*

This is a semolina Victoria mixture that has been poured into ring molds. When set, it is turned onto a serving plate and filled with apricot halves, covered with apricot sauce, and sprinkled with chopped and toasted almonds. It may be decorated with whipped cream.

27.6.2 Strawberry Flummery—*Flamri aux fraises*

Yield
approximately 10 servings

Ingredients	U.S. Weight or Volume	Metric Weight or Volume
Water	1¼ cups	3 deciliters
White wine	1¼ cups	3 deciliters
Semolina	4 ounces	100 to 120 grams
Egg yolks, beaten	4	4
Sugar	4 ounces	120 grams
Salt	¼ teaspoon	2 grams
Lemon juice	2 tablespoons	30 milliliters

Ingredients	U.S. Weight or Volume	Metric Weight or Volume
Lemon rind, grated	½ teaspoon	4 grams
Egg whites	6	6
Strawberries, fresh	20 to 24 ounces	600 to 700 grams
Sugar	8 ounces	225 grams
Liqueur	2 tablespoons	30 milliliters
Strawberries, fresh whole	to garnish	to garnish
Liqueur	as needed	as needed

Procedure

1. Combine the water and wine, and heat to the boiling point. Add the semolina slowly and stir constantly. Simmer until the mixture is thick and smooth.
2. Remove from the heat. Add the egg yolks, sugar, salt, lemon juice, and grated lemon rind. If mixture is very thick, it may be necessary to thin with water. Finally fold in the beaten egg whites.
3. Fill buttered molds and poach in a water bath in the oven at 325°F (160°C) for 40 to 60 minutes, until puddings test done.
4. Cool. Turn out of molds. Puree the strawberries, and combine with sugar and liqueur. Pour the puree over the molds.
5. Macerate the whole strawberries in liqueur and use to decorate molds as desired.

27.7 Fancy Cookies—*Petits fours sec*

27.7.1 Almond Macaroons—*Macarons aux amandes*

Yield

approximately 60 macaroons

Ingredients	U.S. Weight or Volume	Metric Weight or Volume
Almond powder	9 ounces	250 grams
Sugar, confectioners'	1 pound	500 grams
Lemon rind, grated	½ teaspoon	3 grams
Egg whites	3 to 4	3 to 4
Sugar, coarse	1¾ ounces	50 grams

Procedure

1. Combine the almonds, confectioners' sugar, and lemon rind.
2. Add the unbeaten egg whites and blend well.
3. Whip slowly until foamy so the mixture can be put through a pastry bag.
4. Line a sheet pan with parchment paper.
5. Pipe out batter in small mounds.
6. Moisten the mounds with a drop of water and sprinkle with coarse sugar.
7. Bake in the oven at 250°F (120°C) for 15 minutes. Increase the heat to 300°F (150°C) and continue baking for about 15 minutes longer, until macaroons are golden brown.

Note: Dried nuts other than almonds, ground fine, may be used. The amount should always be 1 part nuts to 2 parts of confectioners' sugar.

27.7.2 Almond Cookies—*Biscuit aux amandes*

Yield

about 50 cookies

Ingredients	U.S. Weight or Volume	Metric Weight or Volume
Butter cookie dough	2 pounds	1 kilogram
Almonds, sliced and lightly toasted	3½ ounces	100 grams

Procedure

1. Mix the almonds with the dough.
2. Form into a roll about 1½ inches (4 centimeters) in diameter. Chill.
3. Cut the roll into ¼-inch thick (5-millimeter) slices and place on a baking sheet.
4. Bake in oven at 400°F (200°C) for approximately 8 minutes.

27.7.3 Butter Cookies—*Petit beurre*

Yield

50 to 60 cookies

continued

Ingredients	U.S. Weight or Volume	Metric Weight or Volume
Flour	1 pound	500 grams
Butter	14 ounces	400 grams
Sugar, confectioners'	5 ounces	150 grams
Salt	1/2 teaspoon	3 grams
Vanilla extract	2 teaspoons	10 milliliters

Procedure
1. Make a well in the flour.
2. Place the butter, confectioners' sugar, salt, and vanilla extract in the well and mix thoroughly.
3. Work in the flour gradually and knead to a smooth dough.
4. Refrigerate the dough for 1 hour.
5. Roll the dough to 1/4-inch (5-millimeter) thickness on a marble slab dusted with flour. Cut into circles and pierce with a fork.
6. Bake in oven at 375°F (190°C) for approximately 8 minutes, or until lightly colored.

Note: The following combination of ingredients can be used instead, following the same procedure: 1 pound (500 grams) flour, 10 ounces (300 grams) butter, 7 ounces (200 grams) confectioners' sugar, 2 to 3 egg yolks, 1/2 teaspoon (3 grams) salt, and 2 teaspoons (10 milliliters) vanilla extract.

27.7.4 Cuisses de Dames

Yield
180 to 200 thin cookies

Ingredients	U.S. Weight or Volume	Metric Weight or Volume
Eggs	15	15
Sugar	2 pounds	1 kilogram
Butter	14 ounces	400 grams
Flour	3 pounds	1.5 kilograms
Almonds, peeled and ground fine	9 ounces	250 grams
Lemon rind, grated	from 2 lemons	from 2 lemons

Ingredients	U.S. Weight or Volume	Metric Weight or Volume
Kirsch	1 3/4 ounces	50 grams
Baking soda	1/8 teaspoon	1 gram

Procedure
1. Combine the eggs and sugar and blend.
2. Cream the butter until it is soft. Add the butter, flour, almonds, lemon rind, Kirsch, and baking soda to the egg and sugar mixture.
3. Mix well, and knead the dough on a marble slab dusted with flour, until firm.
4. Shape into finger-shaped pieces, 4 to 5 inches (8 to 10 centimeters) long.
5. Deep-fry in fat heated to 375°F (190°C).

27.7.5 Ladyfingers—*Pèlerines; Biscuits à la cuillère*

Yield
100 to 120 ladyfingers

Ingredients	U.S. Weight or Volume	Metric Weight or Volume
Egg yolks	12	12
Egg whites	15	15
Sugar	9 ounces	250 grams
Flour	7 ounces	200 grams
Salt	1/2 teaspoon	3 grams
Cornstarch	3 1/2 ounces	100 grams
Lemon rind, grated	1 tablespoon	15 grams
Sugar for baking sheet and ladyfinger tops	as needed	as needed

Procedure
1. Beat the egg yolks until thick and lemon colored.
2. Whip the egg whites until stiff, but not dry. Fold the sugar into the egg whites gradually. Whip until thick.
3. Fold in the egg yolks.
4. Sift the flour, salt, and cornstarch together. Fold the dry ingredients into the egg mixture. Add lemon rind.

5. With a pastry tube, pipe the mixture into finger-size strips on a greased baking sheet sprinkled with sugar. (See figure 27-6.)
6. Sprinkle the ladyfingers with sugar and bake in an oven at 375°F (190°C) for about 12 minutes.

Figure 27-6. Piping out ladyfingers—*pèlerines; biscuits à la cuillère.*

27.7.6 Madeleines—*Madeleines*

Yield
40 to 50 madeleines

Ingredients	U.S. Weight or Volume	Metric Weight or Volume
Eggs	5	5
Sugar	9 ounces	250 grams
Cake flour, sifted	9 ounces	250 grams
Butter, melted	9 ounces	250 grams
Lemon rind, grated	2 teaspoons	12 grams

Procedure
1. Combine eggs and sugar in a double boiler and heat *over* boiling water. Stir constantly. Remove from heat and beat until cool and very thick.
2. Fold the flour into the egg mixture.
3. Add the melted butter and lemon rind. Stir until blended.
4. Fill madeleine pans or small muffin tins with the mixture.

5. Bake madeleine forms for about 8 minutes, muffin tins for 12 to 15 minutes, in an oven at 350°F (175°C).

27.7.7 Milanese Cookies—*Petits milanais*

Yield
about 50 to 60 cookies

Ingredients	U.S. Weight or Volume	Metric Weight or Volume
Flour	1 pound	500 grams
Sugar	9 ounces	250 grams
Butter	9 ounces	250 grams
Egg yolks	4 to 5	4 to 5
Lemon rind, grated	from 1 lemon	from 1 lemon
Salt	¼ teaspoon	2 grams
Baking soda	⅛ teaspoon	1 gram
Egg yolk for glazing	as needed	as needed

Procedure
1. Make a well in the flour.
2. Combine the sugar, butter, egg yolks, lemon rind, salt, and baking soda in the well.
3. Work in the flour gradually and knead to a smooth dough.
4. Refrigerate the dough.
5. Roll out the dough on a marble slab dusted with flour. Cut shapes as desired. Brush with egg yolk.
6. Bake in the oven at 375°F (190°C) for 8 minutes, or until cookies are golden in color.

27.7.8 Prussian Cookies—*Prussiens*

Yield
25 to 30 cookies

Ingredients	U.S. Weight or Volume	Metric Weight or Volume
Puff pastry trimmings	10 ounces	300 grams
Sugar, granulated	3 to 4 ounces	80 to 120 grams
Sugar, confectioners'	1½ ounces	50 grams

continued

Procedure

1. Roll out the puff pastry on a board coated with sugar instead of flour, and complete one turn as for regular puff pastry.
2. Roll to a strip 15 inches (27.5 centimeters) long and 8 inches (20 centimeters) wide. Roll each long side of the dough toward the center. Place one roll on top of the other and flatten slightly.
3. Cut this double roll into slices. Place each slice on a baking tray and sprinkle lightly with confectioners' sugar.
4. Bake in oven at 375°F (190°C) for 8 to 10 minutes. Then turn the cookies over and sprinkle with a little more confectioners' sugar. Continue baking for 8 to 10 minutes longer, or until firm and golden in color.

27.7.9 Vanilla Waffles—*Bricelets à la vanille*

Yield

approximately 80 to 120 waffles

Ingredients	U.S. Weight or Volume	Metric Weight or Volume
Flour	2 pounds	1 kilogram
Butter	14 ounces	400 grams
Sugar	1 pound	500 grams
Eggs	8	8
Salt	½ teaspoon	2 grams
Vanilla extract	1 tablespoon	15 milliliters
Lemon rind, grated	½ teaspoon	2 grams

Procedure

1. Make a well in the flour.
2. Combine all other ingredients and place in the well.
3. Work the flour into the mixture little by little until a smooth dough is formed.
4. Shape the dough into walnut-size balls and bake in a French waffle iron until golden in color.

27.8 Cakes—*Gâteaux*

27.8.1 Black Forest Cake—*Tourte Forêt-Noire*

Yield

1 cake (12 to 16 servings)

Ingredients	U.S. Weight or Volume	Metric Weight or Volume
Cocoa powder	1 ounce	30 grams
Flour	2½ ounces	75 grams
Eggs	5	5
Sugar	5 ounces	150 grams
Cornstarch	2½ ounces	75 grams
Butter	1½ ounces	50 grams
Sugar syrup	1 pint	5 deciliters
Kirsch	2 teaspoons	10 milliliters
Heavy cream, whipped	1 pint	5 deciliters
Chocolate shavings	9 ounces	250 grams

Procedure

1. Combine the cocoa powder and flour.
2. Prepare the cake batter as described for sponge cake.
3. Bake in a cake pan 1¼ inches (3 centimeters) deep, in an oven at 350°F (175°C) for 20 to 25 minutes.
4. When cool, cut the cake into three layers.
5. Combine the sugar syrup and Kirsch.
6. Moisten the bottom layer and the top layer with the Kirsch-flavored sugar syrup.
7. Spread whipped cream over the bottom layer of the cake to a thickness of ¼ inch (5 millimeters). Place the second layer on top, and spread it with whipped cream. Place remaining layer on top.
8. Spread whipped cream over the top and sides of the entire cake.
9. Sprinkle with shaved chocolate. (See figure 27-7.)

Note: Pitted and macerated red cherries may be placed between the layers.

Figure 27-7. Black Forest cake—*Tourte Forêt-Noire.*

27.8.2 Gugelhupf—*Kouglof*

Yield

approximately 10 portions

Ingredients	U.S. Weight or Volume	Metric Weight or Volume
Butter	9 ounces	250 grams
Sugar	10 ounces	300 grams
Eggs	6	6
Flour	20 ounces	600 grams
Milk	¾ cup	2 deciliters
Baking powder	¾ ounce	25 grams
Lemon rind, grated	from 1 lemon	from 1 lemon
Almonds, sliced	as needed	as needed

Procedure

1. Cream the butter and sugar together.
2. Add the eggs and about one-third of the flour. Mix well.
3. Add the milk, the remainder of the flour, the baking powder, and the lemon rind. Mix again.
4. Butter and flour a gugelhupf mold and line with sliced almonds.
5. Pour the batter over the almonds.
6. Bake in the oven at 350°F (175°C) for 45 to 50 minutes, until cake is golden yellow and tests done.

Note: Raisins may be added to the mixture.

27.8.3 Jelly Roll—*Biscuit roulé*

Yield

40 to 50 slices

Ingredients	U.S. Weight or Volume	Metric Weight or Volume
Sponge cake batter	1 recipe	1 recipe
Sugar, confectioners'	as needed	as needed
Jam, warm	as needed	as needed

Procedure

1. Spread the sponge cake batter about ½ inch (1 centimeter) thick in a sheet pan lined with parchment paper.
2. Bake in the oven at 375°F (190°C) for about 15 minutes.
3. Remove the cake from the oven and loosen the edges. Reverse onto a clean cloth sprinkled with confectioners' sugar.
4. Spread the sponge cake with warm jam.
5. Roll the cake and place on a serving plate with the seam side down. Cool before serving. (See figure 27-8).

Note: Fruit sauce may be served separately. Butter cream may be used instead of jelly.

Figure 27-8. Jelly roll—*Biscuit roulé.*

27.8.4 Fruit Loaf Cake, Home Style—
Gâteau ménagère

Yield
about 20 slices

Ingredients	U.S. Weight or Volume	Metric Weight or Volume
Flour	14 ounces	400 grams
Raisins	4 ounces	100 grams
Currants, dried	4 ounces	100 grams
Butter	9 ounces	250 grams
Sugar	9 ounces	250 grams
Eggs	4	4
Milk	¼ cup	50 milliliters
Baking powder	1½ teaspoons	6 grams
Ginger, ground	½ teaspoon	3 grams
Candied fruits	4 ounces	100 grams
Rum	¼ cup	50 milliliters

Procedure
1. Sift the flour.
2. Dust the raisins and currants with some of the flour.
3. Cream the butter and sugar together until fluffy.
4. Add the eggs and flour alternately.
5. Add the milk gradually.
6. Add raisins and currants, baking powder, ginger, candied fruits, and rum.
7. Mix until thoroughly blended.
8. Line two loaf pans with parchment paper. Fill with cake mixture.
9. Bake in oven at 350°F (175°C) for 50 to 60 minutes, or until the needle test shows the cake is done.

27.8.5 Raisin Pound Cake—*Gâteau aux raisins*

Yield
about 50 slices

Ingredients	U.S. Weight or Volume	Metric Weight or Volume
Flour	1½ pounds	750 grams
Raisins	20 ounces	600 grams

Ingredients	U.S. Weight or Volume	Metric Weight or Volume
Butter	1½ pounds	750 grams
Sugar	1½ pounds	750 grams
Eggs	16 to 18	16 to 18
Baking powder	1½ teaspoons	6 grams
Candied fruits	1½ pounds	750 grams
Lemon rind, grated	from 1 lemon	from 1 lemon
Rum	½ cup	1 deciliter

Procedure
1. Sift the flour.
2. Dust the raisins with some of the flour.
3. Cream the butter and sugar until fluffy.
4. Add the eggs and flour alternately to the butter and sugar. Blend.
5. Add raisins, baking powder, candied fruits, lemon rind, and rum.
6. Line four loaf pans with parchment paper. Fill the pans with the cake mixture.
7. Bake in the oven at 350°F (175°C) for 50 to 60 minutes, or until the needle test shows the cake is done.

Note: Instead of using baking powder, the eggs can be separated, whipped until stiff, and then folded into the mixture after all the other ingredients have been added.

27.8.6 Napoleons—*Tranches et tourtes mille-feuilles*

Yield
20 slices or 1 large pastry

Ingredients	U.S. Weight or Volume	Metric Weight or Volume
Puff pastry trimmings	1¾ pounds	900 grams
Sugar, confectioners'	3½ ounces	100 grams
Pastry cream *or* mousseline cream	1½ pounds	700 grams
Fondant	7 ounces	200 grams
Kirsch	1 ounce	30 grams

Procedure

1. Roll out the puff pastry to an oblong 16 by 24 inches (40 by 60 centimeters). Allow to rest for 30 minutes.
2. Prick with a roller docker.
3. Bake in oven at 350°F (175°C). After 10 minutes, dust lightly with confectioners' sugar. Continue baking for 15 to 20 minutes longer.
4. Cut into 3 strips about 5 inches (12.5 centimeters) wide.
5. Spread cream filling on two of the strips and place one on top of the other.
6. Blend the Kirsch into the fondant.
7. Place the third layer on top and frost it with a thin coating of the fondant mixture.
8. Cut into 1-inch (2.5-centimeter) slices.

Note: Individual pastries may be prepared if desired. Roll the dough into three 10-inch (25-centimeter) circles. Cut each into six pie-shaped wedges. Roll into cone shapes and bake. Various creams and fruits may be used for fillings.

27.8.7 Pound Cake—*Gâteau quatre-quarts*

Yield
2 cakes

Ingredients	U.S. Weight or Volume	Metric Weight or Volume
Butter	1 pound	500 grams
Sugar	1 pound	500 grams
Eggs, whole	2	2
Egg yolks	8	8
Flour	1 pound	500 grams
Egg whites	8	8
Lemon rind, grated	from 1 lemon	from 1 lemon

Procedure

1. Cream the butter and sugar thoroughly.
2. Add the whole eggs, the yolks, and 3½ ounces (100 grams) of the flour. Mix well.
3. Beat the egg whites until stiff. Add the remaining flour and the lemon rind to the creamed mixture.
4. Fold in the beaten egg whites.

5. Grease and flour two loaf or layer-cake pans. If loaf pans are used, line them with parchment paper before filling. Pour the batter into the pans.
6. Bake loaves in the oven at 325°F (163°C) for 1 hour. If layer-cake pans are used, the baking time will be 20 to 25 minutes.

Other Cakes

Mocha Cake—*Gâteau au moka*

This is a sponge cake with a mocha-flavored butter cream filling. The sides and top of the cake are iced with mocha fondant and sprinkled with chopped toasted almonds.

Pineapple Cake—*Gâteau à l'ananas*

This is made with sponge cake and filled with butter cream to which chopped pineapple has been added. The cake is iced with pineapple-flavored fondant and decorated with pineapple slices.

27.9 Tortes—*Tourtes*

27.9.1 Almond Torte—*Gâteau aux amandes*

Yield
2 tortes (12 to 16 servings each)

Ingredients	U.S. Weight or Volume	Metric Weight or Volume
Egg yolks	16	16
Sugar, granulated	14 ounces	400 grams
Egg whites	16	16
Flour	9 ounces	250 grams
Almond powder	14 ounces	400 grams
Lemon rind, grated	½ teaspoon	3 grams
Sugar, confectioners'	1½ ounces	50 grams

Procedure

1. Beat the egg yolks and granulated sugar until they form a ribbon.

continued

Procedure

2. Beat the egg whites until stiff and fold them into the egg yolk mixture alternately with the flour, almonds, and lemon rind.
3. Pour the mixture into pans buttered and dusted with flour.
4. Bake in the oven at 350°F (175°C) for 40 to 50 minutes.
5. Sprinkle confectioners' sugar over the torte.

Variation of Almond Torte

Hazelnut Torte—*Gâteau aux noisettes*

The recipe for almond torte is used, but hazelnuts are substituted for almonds.

27.9.2 Linzertorte—*Gâteau de Linz*

Yield
3 tortes

Ingredients	U.S. Weight or Volume	Metric Weight or Volume
Flour	1 pound	500 grams
Sugar	12 ounces	350 grams
Butter	10 ounces	300 grams
Eggs	3	3
Hazelnuts, ground fine	9 ounces	250 grams
Cinnamon, ground	⅛ teaspoon	1 gram
Salt	½ ounce	5 grams
Rum	1 tablespoon	15 milliliters
Milk	as needed	as needed
Raspberry jam	as needed	as needed
Egg wash	as needed	as needed
Sugar, confectioners'	as needed	as needed

Procedure

1. Put flour on a board or marble slab and make a well in the center of the flour.
2. Place sugar, butter, and eggs in the well and blend thoroughly. Add the hazelnuts, cinnamon, salt, and rum.
3. Gradually mix in the flour.
4. Milk is added as needed until the ingredients form a stiff dough.
5. Allow the dough to rest in a cool place.
6. Roll the dough to ¼-inch (5-millimeter) thickness. Line the bottoms of springform pans with the dough. Moisten the edges and place a ½-inch-thick (1-centimeter) strip of dough all around the sides of the rim.
7. Fill the center with raspberry jam. Arrange thin strips of dough in a lattice pattern over the jam. Brush the dough with egg yolk.
8. Bake in the oven at 400°F (205°C) for 20 to 25 minutes.
9. When the torte has cooled, remove it from the form and fill the squares with more jam. Sprinkle with confectioners' sugar. (See figure 27.9.)

Figure 27-9. Linzertorte—*Gâteau de Linz.*

27.9.3 Sachertorte—*Tourte Sacher*

Yield
2 tortes

Ingredients	U.S. Weight or Volume	Metric Weight or Volume
Butter	9¾ ounces	280 grams
Chocolate, semisweet, melted	9¾ ounces	280 grams
Egg yolks	14	14
Sugar	8½ ounces	240 grams

Ingredients	U.S. Weight or Volume	Metric Weight or Volume
Egg whites	18	18
Flour	9¾ ounces	280 grams
Apricot preserves	1 pint	5 deciliters
Chocolate glaze	2 pints	1 liter

Procedure

1. Cream the butter.
2. Mix in the cooled, melted chocolate.
3. Gradually add the egg yolks and sugar alternately to the butter and chocolate mixture.
4. Fold in the stiffly beaten egg whites alternately with the flour.
5. Bake in two springform pans in an oven preheated to 325°F (160°C), for 50 to 60 minutes.
6. Slice the tortes horizontally through the middle. Reverse the layers so the top of the cake will be flat.
7. Spread 1 cup of apricot preserves between the layers of each torte.
8. Cover the tortes with chocolate glaze and decorate. (See figure 27-10.)

Figure 27-10. Sachertorte—*Tourte Sacher.*

27.9.4 Zugar Kirschtorte—*Tourte au Kirsch*

Yield

1 cake (12 to 16 servings)

Ingredients	U.S. Weight or Volume	Metric Weight or Volume
Sugar syrup at 29° Baumé	7 ounces	200 grams
Cherries, red	7 ounces	200 grams
Butter cream, pink, Kirsch	10 ounces	300 grams
Japanese meringue	2 layers	2 layers
Sponge cake	1 layer	1 layer
Almonds, slivered	3½ ounces	100 grams
Sugar, confectioners'	as needed	as needed

Procedure

1. Combine sugar syrup and cherries.
2. Spread a very thin layer of thick, pink butter cream over a layer of Japanese meringue.
3. Remove the upper crust from the sponge cake and dip both sides into the sugar-cherry mixture. Place this cake on the Japanese meringue that has been covered with butter cream.
4. Press the layers lightly with a flat plate.
5. Place the second Japanese layer on top and then cover the sides and the top of the cake with butter cream.
6. Press almond slivers into the sides of the cake.
7. Dust the top with confectioners' sugar and decorate in a diamond pattern.

27.10 Fruit Tarts—*Tartes aux fruits*

27.10.1 Apple Tart—*Tarte aux pommes*

Yield

1 tart (6 to 8 servings)

Ingredients	U.S. Weight or Volume	Metric Weight or Volume
Short crust paste	10 ounces	300 grams
Apples, peeled, and cut into wedges	28 ounces	800 grams
Sugar	2¾ to 3½ ounces	80 to 100 grams
Apricot jam	as needed	as needed

continued

Procedure

1. Line a tart pan with the short crust paste.
2. Arrange the apple wedges over the pastry in a ring-shaped pattern.
3. Sprinkle with the sugar and bake in the oven at 425°F (220°C) for about 25 minutes.
4. Glaze with apricot jam before serving.

27.10.2 Apple Tart with Custard—*Tarte aux pommes à la crème*

Yield

1 tart

Ingredients	U.S. Weight or Volume	Metric Weight or Volume
Short crust pastry	10 ounces	300 grams
Apples, peeled and cut into wedges	28 ounces	800 grams
Sugar	2¾ to 3½ ounces	80 to 100 grams
Custard:		
Milk	¾ cup	2 deciliters
Cream	¼ cup	50 milliliters
Egg	1	1
Sugar	1½ ounces	50 grams
Cinnamon, ground	⅛ teaspoon	1 gram
Vanilla extract	1 teaspoon	5 milliliters

Procedure

1. Line the tart pan with pastry. Prick it.
2. Arrange the apple wedges on the pastry and sprinkle with sugar.
3. Bake at 375°F (190°C) for about 20 minutes, or until almost done.
4. Combine and mix well the milk, cream, egg, sugar, cinnamon, and vanilla extract. Strain.
5. Pour the custard mixture over the apples in the tart shell.
6. Return to oven and bake for approximately 20 minutes longer. (See figure 27-11.)

Note: Sweet tart pastry may be used instead of the short crust paste.

Figure 27-11. Apple tart with custard—*Tarte aux pommes à la crème.*

27.10.3 Strawberry Tart—*Tarte aux fraises*

Yield

1 tart (8 to 10 servings)

Ingredients	U.S. Weight or Volume	Metric Weight or Volume
Puff pastry	10 ounces	300 grams
Strawberries, fresh	16 to 20 ounces	450 to 600 grams
Sugar	9 ounces	250 grams
Kirsch	¼ cup	50 milliliters
Jelly, strawberry *or* red currant	½ cup	1 deciliter

Procedure

1. Line the tart pans with puff pastry.
2. Fill the tart with uncooked rice or dried beans and bake it in the oven at 450°F (230°C) for 20 to 25 minutes. When baked, remove the rice or beans. Cool the shell.
3. Macerate the strawberries in sugar and Kirsch.
4. Arrange the strawberries in the baked tart shell and coat them with the jelly. (See figure 27-12.)

Figure 27-12. Strawberry tart—*Tartes aux fraises.*

27.10.4 Strawberry Tart with Meringue Topping—*Tarte aux fraises meringuée*

Yield
1 tart (8 to 10 servings)

Ingredients	U.S. Weight or Volume	Metric Weight or Volume
Puff pastry	10 ounces	300 grams
Egg whites	6	6
Sugar	9 ounces	250 grams
Strawberries, fresh, small, or halved large	8 ounces	200 grams

Procedure
1. Line the tart pan with puff pastry.
2. Fill with uncooked rice or dried beans and bake in the oven at 450°F (230°C) for 20 to 25 minutes. When done, remove the rice or beans and cool the shell.
3. Beat the egg whites to the soft-peak stage. Add sugar gradually and continue beating until stiff peaks form.
4. Divide the meringue into two equal portions.
5. Add the strawberries to one part of the meringue and pour into the tart shell.
6. Decorate with the remaining meringue and sprinkle with sugar.
7. Bake in the oven at 450°F (230°C) until lightly browned.

Other Fruit Tarts

Plum Tart—*Tarte aux prunes*

Tart pans are lined with short crust paste. The pastry is pierced with a fork, sprinkled with cracker crumbs, covered with halved plums, sprinkled with a little sugar, and baked. Additional sugar is sprinkled over the top before serving.

Apricot Tart—*Tarte aux abricots*

These tarts are prepared the same as plum tart, using apricots instead of plums.

27.11 Cold Fruit Desserts—*Entremets froids aux fruits*

27.11.1 Birchermüesli

Yield
approximately 10 servings

Ingredients	U.S. Weight or Volume	Metric Weight or Volume
Oatmeal	4 to 5 ounces	120 to 150 grams
Milk	¾ cup	150 milliliters
Almonds, grated fine	4½ ounces	130 grams
Sugar	4 ounces	120 grams
Apples, grated	2 to 3 pounds	1 to 1.5 kilograms
Lemon juice	½ cup	1 deciliter
Cream or yogurt	½ cup	1 deciliter
Honey	as desired	as desired
Fruits of the season	as desired	as desired
Heavy cream, whipped	to garnish	to garnish
Pecans or almonds	to garnish	to garnish

continued

Procedure

1. Soak the oatmeal in the milk for about 15 minutes.
2. Add the almonds and sugar.
3. Combine the apples, lemon juice, and cream, and add to the oatmeal mixture.
4. Add a little honey and some fresh fruit if desired.
5. Garnish with whipped cream and pecans or almonds.

Other Cold Fruit Desserts

Apricots, Royal Style—*Abricots royale*

Tartlet molds are coated with cherry jelly and filled with alternate layers of well-formed stewed apricots and cherry jelly, and refrigerated. A génoise base flavored with Kirsch and filled with red currant jelly is placed on a serving plate. The molds are arranged on the génoise base. A coating of warm red currant jelly is poured over the top. Chopped pistachios are sprinkled over the top.

Fruits in Jelly—*Fruits à la gelée*

Pour some white-wine jelly or port wine jelly into attractive wine glasses. Place in the refrigerator and allow to set. Fill the glasses with alternate layers of jelly and fruits or stewed fruits of different colors. Allow to set. The fruits should always be dry when put in place.

Fruit Salad—*Fruits rafraîchis (Madédoine de fruits)*

Pineapple, apples, pears, bananas, peaches, and oranges are cut into uniform-size pieces. Strawberries or peeled grapes may be added. The fruits are combined with sugar or thick sugar syrup, Kirsch, maraschino, and a few drops of lemon juice, and then chilled in the refrigerator. The fruits are arranged in a glass bowl and topped with various colored fruit slices. Whipped cream may be served on the side.

Strawberries, Marquess Style—*Fraises à la marquise*

This is a strawberry puree combined with Chantilly cream and arranged in glass bowls. Strawberries that have been macerated in sugar and Kirsch and coated with sugar are placed on top of the cream. This is served very cold.

Strawberries Romanoff—*Fraises Romanov*

These strawberries are macerated in liqueur and sugar. They are combined with Chantilly cream and garnished with additional strawberries.

Chapter 28
Frozen Desserts—
Entremets glacés

Frozen desserts are popular and add variety to a menu at reasonable cost. Frozen desserts are classified in this section on the basis of the method of preparation. These classifications are plain ice creams and sherbets and fancy still-frozen specialties. The ice creams, sherbets, and ices are frozen in a mechanical freezer that churns or stirs the mixtures and incorporates air into them as they freeze. Fancy specialties, such as bombes, frozen puddings, mousses, parfaits, and soufflés, are frozen without agitation.

Ice creams are prepared by freezing a pasteurized and homogenized mixture. The milk fat content of plain ice cream must reach 10 percent. When ice cream is mixed with fruits, chocolate, nuts, or other products, the milk fat content must be at least 8 percent. All ice cream manufacturers are required to abide by the laws within the state where ice cream is produced. Manufacturers who ship ice cream across state lines must also follow federal regulations.

The facilities, equipment, and utensils used for processing, freezing, and storing frozen desserts must meet sanitation and safety regulations. All areas must be ventilated to remove moisture. Equipment that comes in contact with the ice cream mixture must be constructed of stainless steel or noncorrosive material. Equipment and utensils must be steam-cleaned or sanitized. Usually equipment is rinsed, dismantled, washed with steam or hot water, sanitized, and air-dried. Mechanical equipment should be rinsed, sterilized, and rinsed again just before it is used.

28.1 Ice Creams and Sherbets— *Glaces simples*

28.1.1 Plain Ice Cream—*Glaces à la crème*

Yield
approximately 20 servings

Ingredients	U.S. Weight or Volume	Metric Weight or Volume
Egg yolks	10	10
Sugar	9 ounces	250 grams
Milk	1 quart	1 liter
Cream	1¼ cups	3 deciliters

Procedure
1. Combine the egg yolks and the sugar. Beat until slightly foamy.
2. Scald the milk. Add gradually to the eggs and sugar.
3. Pour the combined mixture into a saucepan and simmer until the mixture coats a spoon.
4. Remove from heat and stir vigorously until cool. Strain.
5. Add the cream and stir until blended.
6. Freeze.

Flavored Ice Creams

Chocolate Ice Cream—*Glace au chocolat*

Semisweet grated chocolate—5 ounces (140 grams) semisweet chocolate per quart (1 liter) of ice cream— is added to the ice cream mixture before freezing.

Mocha Ice Cream—*Glace au moka*

Mocha extract is added to the ice cream mixture before freezing.

Praline Ice Cream—*Glace au praliné*

Crushed praline—4 ounces (115 grams) praline to 1 quart (1 liter) of ice cream—is added to the ice cream mixture before freezing.

Tea Ice Cream—*Glace au thé*

This ice cream is prepared with a mixture of 1 quart (7½ deciliters) sugar syrup at 18° to 19° Baumé, 1½ cups (3 deciliters) of strained strong tea, ½ cup (120 milliliters) rum, and 1¾ cups (415 milliliters) cream. The mixture is then frozen.

Vanilla Ice Cream—*Glace à la vanille*

This is ice cream made with vanilla beans. One vanilla bean is heated with the milk for each quart (liter) of ice cream mixture. The vanilla bean is removed before the mixture is put in the freezer.

28.1.2 Fruit Sherbet—*Glace aux fruits*

Yield
20 to 30 servings

Ingredients	U.S. Weight or Volume	Metric Weight or Volume
Water	1 quart	1 liter
Sugar	3 pounds	1.5 kilograms
Fruit puree	1 to 1½ quarts	1 to 1.5 liters
Lemon juice	¼ cup	60 milliliters

Ingredients	U.S. Weight or Volume	Metric Weight or Volume
Optional:		
Egg whites, beaten	4 to 5	4 to 5
or		
Cream	1 quart	1 liter

Procedure
1. Combine water and sugar and cook to the boiling point, 29° Baumé. Cool.
2. Add pureed fruit and lemon juice.
3. Freeze.
4. If egg whites or cream are used, they should be added after the mixture is slightly frozen.

28.1.3 Pineapple Sherbet—*Glace à l'ananas*

Yield
20 to 30 servings

Ingredients	U.S. Weight or Volume	Metric Weight or Volume
Sugar syrup at 22° Baumé	1 quart	1 liter
Crushed pineapple and juice	1 cup	2 deciliters
Lemon juice	1 lemon	1 lemon
Egg white	1	1

Procedure
1. Combine sugar syrup, pineapple, and lemon juice. Strain.
2. Beat egg white until stiff, but not dry, and fold into the mixture.
3. Check syrup and when it reaches 19° Baumé, freeze the mixture.

Other Sherbets

Apricot Sherbet—*Glace aux abricots*

This sherbet is made with pureed apricots. It is prepared like fruit sherbet.

Lemon Sherbet—*Glace au citron*

This sherbet is prepared with 1 quart (1 liter) of sugar syrup at 20° Baumé, the juice of 3 to 4 lemons, and thin slices of the peel of 2 lemons. The mixture should stand for 1 to 2 hours. When ready to freeze, a well-beaten egg white is added. The freezing process should be continued until the sherbet turns a brilliant white color.

Orange Sherbet—*Glace à l'orange*

This sherbet is prepared with a mixture of 1 quart (1 liter) of sugar syrup at 23° Baumé, the juice of 12 to 14 oranges, the grated peel of 2 oranges, and the juice of 1 lemon. The mixture should register 19° Baumé. About 1¾ cups (415 milliliters) of cream is added to the chilled mixture. It is then strained and frozen.

Peach Sherbet—*Glace aux pêches*

This sherbet is made with pureed fresh or frozen peaches. It is prepared by the method used for fruit sherbet.

Raspberry Sherbet—*Glace aux framboises*

This sherbet is made with pureed fresh or frozen raspberries. It is prepared by the same method used for fruit sherbet.

Strawberry Sherbet—*Glace aux fraises*

Pureed fresh or frozen strawberries are used in this sherbet. It is prepared by the method used for fruit sherbet.

Wine Sherbet—*Sorbet au vin*

The mixture for wine sherbets is made by combining 1 quart (1 liter) of sugar syrup at 28° Baumé with 1 quart (1 liter) of sparkling wine or white wine. The mixture should register 15° Baumé. Lemon or orange juice is usually added; ½ cup (1 deciliter) may be substituted for the wine. The sherbet is made in an ice cream freezer. After the mixture starts to freeze, the sides of the container should be scraped down and 2 beaten egg whites should be added. The consistency of the sherbet should be similar to that of slush. These sherbets are served in Champagne glasses.

28.1.4 Curaçao Sherbet—*Glace au curaçao*

Yield
U.S.—1 quart
Metric—1 liter

Ingredients	U.S. Weight or Volume	Metric Weight or Volume
Sugar syrup at 18° to 19° Baumé	1 quart	1 liter
Curaçao	½ cup	120 milliliters
Orange juice	of 2 oranges	of 2 oranges
Orange rind	from 2 oranges	from 2 oranges
Lemon juice	of 1 lemon	of 1 lemon
Egg white	1	1

Procedure
1. Combine the syrup, the Curaçao, the orange juice and rind, and the lemon juice.
2. Blend thoroughly.
3. Fold beaten egg white into the syrup mixture.
4. Pour into a mold and freeze.

28.1.5 Kirsch Sherbet—*Glace au Kirsch*

Yield
U.S.—approximately 1 quart
Metric—approximately 1 liter

Ingredients	U.S. Weight or Volume	Metric Weight or Volume
Sugar syrup at 18° to 19° Baumé	1 quart	1 liter
Kirsch	½ cup	120 milliliters
Maraschino	½ cup	120 milliliters

continued

Ingredients	U.S. Weight or Volume	Metric Weight or Volume
Lemon juice	of 1 lemon	of 1 lemon
Lemon rind, grated	from 1 lemon	from 1 lemon

Procedure
1. Combine the syrup, Kirsch, maraschino, lemon juice, and rind.
2. Strain and freeze.

28.2 Sundaes—*Coupes*

Ice cream served in frosted silver or glass cups or Champagne glasses is an attractive dessert. Plain ice cream may be served in various ways. All varieties of plain ice cream may be served either individually or combined. The ice cream may be topped with poached fruits, fresh fruits, syrups, nuts, coconut, or a combination of any of these. The sundaes are often garnished with whipped cream.

Denise Sundae—*Coupe Denise*

Mocha ice cream decorated with liqueur-filled chocolates and whipped cream.

Helene Sundae—*Coupe Hélène*

Vanilla ice cream topped with half a stewed or canned pear and covered with a light-colored fruit sauce. Whipped cream is piped around the rim of the dish. Hot chocolate sauce is served separately.

Jacques Sundae—*Coupe Jacques*

Lemon sherbet and strawberry ice cream garnished with a pyramid of fruit salad and covered with fruit sauce. Whipped cream is piped around the rim of the cup.

Melba Sundae—*Coupe Melba*

Peach Melba served in a cup.

Mexican Sundae—*Coupe mexicaine*

Mandarin or orange ice cream topped with diced pineapple that has been macerated in Kirsch and sugar. Whipped cream is piped around the rim of the cup.

Mikado Sundae—*Coupe Mikado*

Vanilla ice cream sprinkled with fine-chopped ginger-root and garnished with a small cluster of pitted cherries. Whipped cream is piped around the rim of the cup.

Romanoff Sundae—*Coupe Romanov*

A layer of vanilla ice cream covered with a pyramid of strawberries that have been macerated in sugar, Kirsch, and maraschino. Flavored strawberry puree is poured over the top, and the rim of the cup or glass is piped with whipped cream.

Singapore Sundae·—*Coupe Singapour*

Pineapple ice cream garnished with diced pineapple and sliced bananas that have been macerated in Kirsch and sugar. Whipped cream is piped around the rim of the cup.

Valais Sundae—*Coupe valaisanne*

Vanilla ice cream flavored with Kirsch and maraschino is topped with 2 stewed apricot halves and covered with apricot marmalade. Whipped cream is piped around the rim of the cup.

White Lady Sundae—*Coupe dame blanche*

Vanilla ice cream covered with a thin slice of pineapple, then with a poached or canned peach half and a light-colored fruit sauce. Whipped cream is piped around the rim of the glass.

28.3 Fancy Ice Creams—*Glace fantaisie*

Ice cream lends itself to elaborate forms of presentation. It can be molded in intricate forms and shapes; it can be combined with other foods to give variety of texture, color, or shape; it can be served in fruit shells, coconut shells, or attractive glassware; it can serve as a foundation for other foods, such as layers of meringue, pastries, and fruit combinations; it is used as a filling for tart shells, cream puffs, and meringue shells.

Frozen Mandarins—*Mandarines givrées*

The top of each piece of fruit is removed near the stem end. The juice is extracted and the pulp removed. A sherbet is made using the mandarin juice (follow recipe for orange sherbet, substituting mandarins for oranges). The sherbet is served in chilled mandarin shells covered with the mandarin tops which have been dusted with confectioners' sugar.

Ice Cream Charlotte—*Charlotte glacée*

Vanilla ice cream flavored with Kirsch and maraschino and poured into a mold lined with ladyfingers. After the mold is firm, it is turned onto a serving plate and garnished with whipped cream.

Meringues glacées

A dipper of ice cream is placed between 2 meringue shells. The meringues are arranged on a dish and garnished with whipped cream.

Ice Cream, Garden Style—*Seille jardinière*

Small buckets are made of pastry horn batter and filled with vanilla ice cream flavored with Kirsch and maraschino. The buckets are decorated with fruit and whipped cream.

Ice Cream Vacherin—*Vacherin glace*

Vanilla ice cream is spread between 2 vacherin layers. These are placed on a dish and decorated with whipped cream.

Peach Melba—*Pêche Melba*

(See figure 28-1.) Ripe, soft peaches with white flesh are blanched in boiling water for a few seconds and then immediately plunged into ice-cold water. The peaches are then peeled and arranged on a dish that has been dusted with sugar. Peaches that are not quite ripe should be poached in a light syrup for a few minutes, and then cooled in the syrup. The peaches are arranged on a layer of good-quality vanilla ice cream and covered with sweetened raspberry puree and a few sliced fresh almonds.

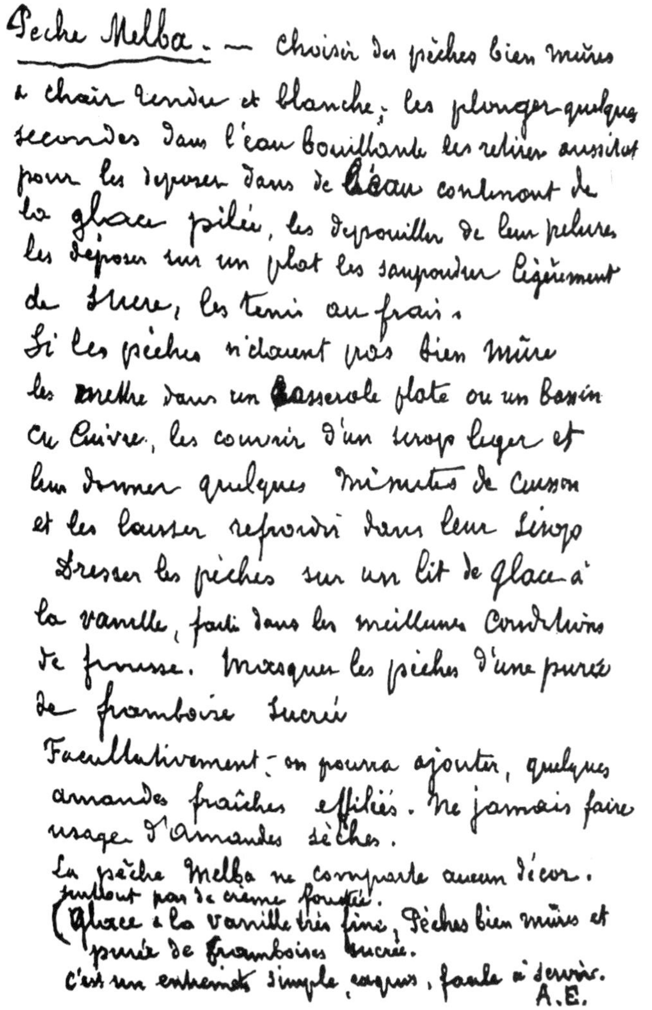
Pêche Melba. — Choisir des pêches bien mûres à chair tendre et blanche; les plonger quelques secondes dans l'eau bouillante les retirer aussitôt pour les déposer dans de l'eau contenant de la glace pilée, les dépouiller de leur pelures les déposer sur un plat les saupoudrer légèrement de sucre, les tenir au frais.
Si les pêches n'étaient pas bien mûre les mettre dans un casserole plate ou un bassin en cuivre, les couvrir d'un sirop léger et leur donner quelques minutes de cuisson et les laisser refroidir dans leur sirop.
Dresser les pêches sur un lit de glace à la vanille, faite dans les meilleures conditions de finesse. Masquer les pêches d'une purée de framboise sucrée.
Facultativement: on pourra ajouter, quelques amandes fraîches effilées. Ne jamais faire usage d'amandes sèches.
La pêche Melba ne comporte aucun décor. surtout pas de crème fouettée.
(Glace à la vanille très fine, pêches bien mûres et purée de framboises sucrée.
C'est un entremets simple, exquis, facile à servir.
A.E.

Figure 28-1. The original recipe for peach Melba, *pêche Melba,* written by Auguste Escoffier. This famous dessert was named for the Australian soprano Nellie Melba.

Pear Melba—*Poires Melba*

Poached pears arranged on a layer of vanilla ice cream and covered with raspberry puree.

Pears Helene—*Poires Hélène*

Halved, stewed, or canned pears arranged on a layer of vanilla ice cream in a glass bowl are coated with a clear white-wine jelly or a fruit jelly and decorated with whipped cream. Hot chocolate sauce is served on the side.

28.4 Other Frozen Mixtures

Granita—*Granités*

This is a sherbet made of two-thirds sugar syrup and one-third raspberry, strawberry, or red currant juice or puree. Lemon juice and Kirsch are added, and the mixture is adjusted to register 17° to 18° Baumé. This mixture is frozen by the method used to freeze sherbet; egg whites, however, are not used in granita sherbets. The texture has a granular appearance.

Soft-serve Frozen Products

Soft-frozen dairy desserts have less total milk solids than ice cream does. The product is frozen in a machine that injects up to 120 percent air into the mixture. The finished product is light and creamy. Since the mixture is usually frozen plain, the soft ice is often served with toppings such as strawberry, pineapple, and chocolate.

28.5 Fancy Still-frozen Specialties— *Glaces légères*

28.5.1 Molded Ice Cream—*Biscuits glacés*

Yield
15 to 20 servings

Ingredients	U.S. Weight or Volume	Metric Weight or Volume
Egg yolks	10	10
Sugar	12 ounces	350 grams
Egg whites	6	6
Whipped cream	1 quart	1 liter
Liqueur	1 ounce	30 milliliters
Whipped cream	as needed to decorate	as needed to decorate

Procedure
1. Beat the egg yolks and combine with sugar. Place in a warm water bath and continue beating until creamy.
2. Remove from water bath and beat until the mixture is cool.
3. Whip the egg whites until stiff, but not dry.
4. Fold the egg whites, whipped cream, and liqueur into the egg and sugar mixture.
5. Pour the mixture into chilled molds. Place cover on mold and freeze.
6. Cut into slices and serve garnished with whipped cream. (See figure 28-2.)

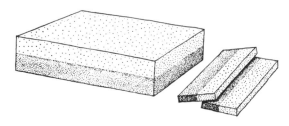

Figure 28-2. Molded ice cream—*Biscuits glacés.*

28.5.2 Ice Cream Bombes—*Bombes glacées*

Yield
approximately 30 servings

Ingredients	U.S. Weight or Volume	Metric Weight or Volume
Vanilla ice cream *or* fruit sherbet	1 quart	1 liter
Egg yolks	18	18

Ingredients	U.S. Weight or Volume	Metric Weight or Volume
Sugar syrup at 28° Baumé	1 pint	5 deciliters
Heavy cream, whipped	3 cups	750 milliliters
Liqueur	1 ounce	30 milliliters

Procedure

1. Chill the molds and line with the ice cream or sherbet.
2. Beat the egg yolks. Add the syrup. Place in a warm water bath and continue beating until light and creamy.
3. Fold the whipped cream and liqueur into the egg and syrup mixture.
4. Pour mixture into the sherbet- or ice-cream-lined molds. (See figure 28-3.)
5. Freeze.

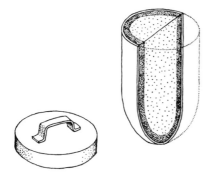

Figure 28-3. Ice cream bombe—*Bombe glacée.*

Variations on Ice Cream Bombes

Ice Puddings—*Poudings glacés*

Timbale forms are lined with ice cream and filled with alternate layers of bombe mixture and thin layers of sponge cake that have been soaked in a liqueur. Wax paper is placed over the mixture and the timbale is sealed and placed in a freezer.

28.5.3 Cassata

Yield
8 servings

Ingredients	U.S. Weight or Volume	Metric Weight or Volume
Ice cream, 3 flavors	1 pint, each flavor	5 deciliters, each flavor
Egg whites	6	6
Sugar	12.5 ounces	350 grams
Heavy cream	1 quart	1 liter
Candied fruits	7 ounces	200 grams
Kirsch *or* maraschino	½ cup	1 deciliter
Almonds, slivered	7 ounces	200 grams

Procedure

1. Line a half-sphere mold with the three layers of ice cream, one on top of another. Each layer should be about ½ inch (1 centimeter) thick.
2. Prepare Italian meringue from the egg whites and sugar.
3. Whip the cream.
4. Macerate the candied fruits in the Kirsch or maraschino.
5. Lightly roast the slivered almonds.
6. Fold the fruits and almonds into the whipped cream. Fold this mixture into the Italian meringue.
7. Fill the ice-cream-lined molds with the cream/meringue mixture. Freeze for at least 5 hours before serving. (See figure 28-4.)

Note: Chopped nougatine or chopped chocolate may also be used in the filling.

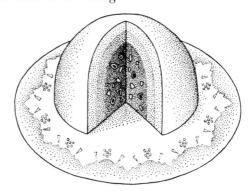

Figure 28-4. Cassata.

Variations on Cassata

Cassata, Naples Style—*Cassata napoletana*

This cassata is prepared like a regular cassata, but the 3 ice creams used to line the molds must be vanilla, chocolate, and strawberry.

28.5.4 Frozen Mousse I—*Mousse glacée I*

Yield
approximately 15 servings

Ingredients	U.S. Weight or Volume	Metric Weight or Volume
Sugar syrup at 29° Baumé	1 pint	5 deciliters
Fruit puree, unsweetened, thick	1 pint	5 deciliters
Liqueur	1 ounce	30 milliliters
Whipping cream	1 quart	1 liter

Procedure
1. Combine the sugar syrup, fruit puree, and liqueur.
2. Whip the cream and fold into syrup mixture.
3. Pour the mixture into chilled molds.
4. Freeze.

28.5.5 Frozen Mousse II—*Mousse glacée II*

Yield
approximately 15 servings

Ingredients	U.S. Weight or Volume	Metric Weight or Volume
Sugar	12 ounces	350 grams
Water	¾ cup	180 milliliters
Egg whites	5	5
Fruit puree	1 pound	500 grams
Lemon juice	2 tablespoons	30 grams
Heavy cream, whipped	1 pint	5 deciliters

Procedure
1. Combine the sugar and water. Cook to the soft ball stage, 234° to 240°F (112° to 116°C) or 29° Baumé.
2. Beat the egg whites until stiff. Continue beating while adding the hot sugar syrup very gradually. Beat until cold.
3. Add the fruit puree and lemon juice to the meringue mixture.
4. Fold in the whipped cream.
5. Pour into molds and freeze.

Note: This mixture may also be used for filling ice cream bombes. If it is being used as a mousse, it should be named in accordance with the variety of fruit puree used.

28.5.6 Frozen Parfaits—*Parfaits glacés*

Yield
approximately 15 servings

Ingredients	U.S. Weight or Volume	Metric Weight or Volume
Egg yolks	15	15
Sugar syrup at 36° Baumé	1 pint	5 deciliters
Flavoring	as desired	as desired
Whipped cream	1 quart	1 liter

Procedure
1. Mix the egg yolks with a dash of cold water.
2. Add the hot sugar syrup, and beat the mixture in a hot water bath.
3. Remove from the heat and continue whipping until cool.
4. Add desired flavoring.
5. Fold in the whipped cream.
6. Pour into bombe molds and freeze.

Note: Choose from a variety of flavorings, such as vanilla, chocolate, mocha, or liqueur.

28.5.7 Frozen Soufflé I—*Soufflé glacés I*

Yield
15 to 20 servings

Ingredients	U.S. Weight or Volume	Metric Weight or Volume
Sugar	1 pound	450 grams
Water	1 cup	250 milliliters
Egg whites	10	10
Heavy cream, whipped	3 cups	750 milliliters
Liqueur	2 tablespoons	30 milliliters
Fruit puree	2½ cups	600 milliliters
Cocoa powder	as needed	as needed

Procedure

1. Boil the sugar and water until they form a syrup at 92° Réaumur or 238°F (115°C).
2. Beat the egg whites until stiff and slowly add the boiling syrup, beating constantly until mixture is cool.
3. Carefully fold in the whipped cream, liqueur, and the fruit puree.
4. Take cocottes or suitable paper molds and attach paper strips to the upper edge of the inside walls so that the strips project 1 inch (2.5 centimeters) above the rims.
5. Pour the mixture into the molds to the top of the paper strips (see figure 28-5) and freeze.
6. When serving, remove the paper strips and dust the soufflé with cocoa powder.

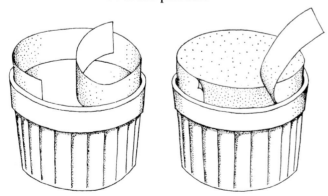

Figure 28-5. Frozen soufflé—*Soufflé glacés.*

28.5.8 Frozen Soufflé II—*Soufflé glacés II*

Yield
15 to 20 servings

Ingredients	U.S. Weight or Volume	Metric Weight or Volume
Egg whites	10	10
Sugar	7 ounces	200 grams
Heavy cream, whipped	3½ cups	825 milliliters
Liqueur	2 tablespoons	30 milliliters
Egg yolks, beaten	3	3

Procedure

1. Beat the egg whites, adding 1½ tablespoons (20 grams) of sugar when they are slightly foamy. Beat until stiff. Add the remainder of the sugar gradually.
2. Fold in whipped cream combined with liqueur and egg yolks.
3. Freeze.

Variations of Frozen Soufflés

Frozen Grand Marnier Soufflé—*Soufflé glacé Grand Marnier*

This is frozen soufflé I or II made with Grand Marnier. It is dusted with cocoa powder and garnished with strawberries or cherries.

Glossary

ABATS: (Fr.) Variety meats of animals—brains, heart, kidney, liver, sweetbreads, tongue, tripe.

ABATTIS: (Fr.) Variety meats of poultry, or giblets—heart, gizzard, liver, usually also including the neck and wing tips.

AGAR-AGAR: A gelatinous extraction of various red algae used as a jelling and stabilizing agent in foods because of its ability to swell in cold water.

AGING: The ripening process of meat; the action of enzymes on the connective tissue increases tenderness in meat.

AGNEAU: (Fr.) Lamb.

AIGUILLETTES: (Fr.) Fine slices of meat or poultry; also a special cut of the beef sirloin.

A L': (Fr.) According to a style; used before words beginning with a vowel, as *à l'andalouse*.

A LA: (Fr.) According to a style, as *à la française*.

A LA CARTE: (Fr.) A list of menu selections with each item priced separately.

A LA KING: Food prepared in a white cream sauce containing pimientos, mushrooms, and green peppers.

A LA MODE: (Fr.) Literally, "in the fashion"; in the United States pie à la mode is topped with ice cream; in France, *boeuf à la mode* is pot-roasted beef with vegetables.

AL DENTE: (It.) Literally, "to the tooth"; pasta or grain cooked to a slightly underdone stage; there should be texture to chew.

ALMOND PASTE: Mixture of ground blanched almonds with granulated and confectioners' sugar.

AMANDINE: (Fr.) Prepared with or garnished with almonds.

AMONTILLADO: (Sp.) Medium-dry sherry with a nutty taste.

ANCIENNE, A L': (Fr.) Old-fashioned.

ANDALOUSE, A L': (Fr.) Andalusian style; used for dishes prepared with tomato puree and sweet peppers.

ANGLAISE, A L': (Fr.) English style. An *anglaise* is also a mixture of egg, oil, water, and seasoning used to coat foods before breading them.

ANTIPASTO: (It.) The course served before the pasta; often includes anchovies, olives, sardines, and carefully prepared vegetables.

APPAREIL: (Fr.) A mixture that is complete but has not yet been cooked or baked, such as a cake batter.

ARGENTEUIL: City near Paris, known for its excellent asparagus; therefore used for a dish served with or garnished with asparagus.

AROMATES: (Fr.) Herbs (such as thyme, bay leaf, chervil) and vegetables (carrots, onions, celery, leeks) used as flavoring for braised dishes and many others.

ARROSER: (Fr.) To baste a roast.

ARROWROOT: Starch obtained from the rootstock of the arrowroot plant; used in the preparation of delicate soups, puddings, and custards.

ARTICHAUT: (Fr.) Artichoke.

ASIAGO: Italian hard cheese made from cows' milk in the province of Vicenza.

ASPIC: Jellied meat, poultry, or fish stock used to coat hors d'oeuvre and galantines, as an ingredient in salads, and to coat and garnish dishes for the cold buffet.

AS PURCHASED (A.P.): Food as purchased on the market before the inedible portions, such as husks, outer leaves, peels, or skins, have been removed.

ASSAISONNER: (Fr.) To season food.

AUBERGINE: (Fr.) Eggplant; also used in Great Britain.

AU GRATIN: (Fr.) Food covered with grated breadcrumbs and/or cheese and browned under the broiler or in the oven.

AU JUS: (Fr.) With natural juice instead of gravy or sauce.

AU LAIT: (Fr.) With milk, as *café au lait*.

AU NATUREL: (Fr.). Plainly cooked or served in natural state.

BABA: (Fr.) A cake made with yeast-raised savarin dough and soaked in rum.

BAIN-MARIE: (Fr.) A water bath, a double boiler insert, or a steam table with openings to hold food at controlled temperatures for serving.

BANNOCK: A large, round unleavened scone or oatcake.

BARD, BARDING: To wrap poultry, meat, game, or fish with thin slices of unsalted fat or salt pork to prevent drying during roasting.

BAR-LE-DUC: Jam made of red currants, from which the seeds have been removed; Bar-le-Duc, a town in Lorraine, France, is famous for this jam.

BARON: A single roast consisting of the leg and loin of lamb or mutton; or a double baron of both legs and loins.

BARQUETTES: Small boat-shaped molds and the pastries baked in them.

BASTE: To moisten food while cooking in order to add flavor and to prevent drying. Meat drippings, melted fats, and sauces are used for basting.

BATTER: A mixture of flour, liquid, and other ingredients that is thin enough to pour; used for cakes, pancakes, and as a coating for foods.

BAUME: A scale used in hydrometers for liquids lighter or heavier than water that indicates specific gravity in degrees. Named after Antoine Baumé.

BEAT: To incorporate air into ingredients or a food mixture by turning the ingredients in an up-and-over motion, using a spoon, rotary beater, or electric mixer.

BEEF TEA: Essence of beef, extracted by long, slow simmering.

BEIGNETS: (Fr.) Fritters.

BEL PASSE: Italian soft-textured cheese made of cows' milk.

BEURRE: (Fr.) Butter.

BEURRE MANIE: (Fr.) Kneaded butter and flour used as a thickening agent for sauces.

BEURRE NOIR: (Fr.) Butter cooked until it is almost black; used for brains; often combined with parsley, vinegar, and seasonings.

BIFTEK: (Fr.) Beefsteak.

BISCOTTE: (Fr.) Crisp toast; zwieback.

BISCUIT: (Fr.) Sponge cake.

BISQUE: Thick cream soup or puree made from shellfish or bivalves.

BLANC: (Fr.) White. A culinary term used to describe a court bouillon or white stock.

BLANCHIR: (Fr.) To blanch; (1) to dip into boiling water to remove skins (almonds, tomatoes); (2) to parboil, to end enzyme action and set the color of vegetables.

BLANCMANGE: (Fr.) Pudding made of milk, sugar, cornstarch, and flavoring.

BLANQUETTE: (Fr.) Ragout made of lamb, veal, or chicken and a rich velouté sauce, always pale in color.

BLEND: To combine two or more ingredients and mix to a smooth consistency.

BLINI: Russian buckwheat-flour pancakes.

BOMBAY DUCK: Fast Indian dried fish; a delicacy served with curries.

BOMBE: (Fr.) A dessert of ice cream, or several kinds of ice cream or sherbet, frozen in a bomb-shaped mold.

BONNE FEMME: (Fr.) Used to describe dishes prepared according to simple home style or family style.

BORDURE: (Fr.) Decorative ring of aspic, rice, vegetables, duchess potatoes; an edible garnish.

BOUQUET GARNI: (Fr.) Fresh parsley, thyme, and bay leaf tied together and used to flavor stews, soups, braised meats, and vegetables.

BOURGEOISE, A LA: (Fr.) Plain family style, such as meats served with vegetables.

BRAISER: (Fr.) To braise, stew.

BRAZIER: Heavy-duty stewing pan with two handles and a tight-fitting lid.

BRIDER: (Fr.) To truss: tying up poultry, meat, or game before cooking.

BRIE: French soft cheese in large rounds from northern France.

BRINE: Solution of water and salt.

BRIOCHE: A rich raised dough made of yeast, milk, butter, eggs, sugar, and flour. Dough is often formed into small rolls but can be baked in larger sizes to use as cases for other foods.

BROCHETTE: (Fr.) A skewer, and the cubes or strips of meat broiled and served on it. Vegetables and fruits are sometimes combined with the meat.

BRUNOISE: (Fr.) Vegetable cubes, 1/8 inch, used for aromatics.

BUNUELOS: (Sp.) Fritters.

CALORIE: Large calorie or kilocalorie; the unit used to express food energy; the amount of heat required to raise the temperature of 1 kilogram of water 1°C.

CAMEMBERT: French soft, creamy cheese with an edible crust; made in Normandy.

CANAPES: Small pieces of toast or other edible base, spread with butter and meat, fish, or cheese; finger food.

CANARD: (Fr.) Duck.

CANDIED: When applied to fruit, the fruit or fruit rind is cooked in a heavy syrup until translucent, then drained and dried. When applied to yams, sweet potatoes, or carrots, the vegetables are boiled, then cooked in a heavy syrup.

CANNELE: (Fr.) Fluted, grooved; for example, a fluted mushroom for garnish.

CANNELLONI: (It.) Squares of pasta stuffed with meat, fish, cheese, or vegetables, rolled, baked with a sauce, and usually topped with cheese.

CAPERS: The unopened flower buds of a plant grown in Greece, northern Africa, and southern Europe. The buds are pickled in salt and vinegar and used as flavoring and garnish.

CAPON: Castrated male chicken weighing between 5 to 7 pounds.

CARAMEL: Sugar cooked to 350° to 355°F (176° to 178°C). To caramelize means to coat a food with caramel or to cook it with the sugar as it is reduced to caramel.

CARCASSE: (Fr.) Skeleton of poultry.

CARDOON: Vegetable of the thistle family; the tender ribs are used in soups and as a vegetable.

CARRE: (Fr.) Rack, as rack of lamb, rack of mutton; the rib portion of either animal.

CASSATA: (It.) Ice cream mixed with candied fruits.

CASSOLETTE: (Fr.) Small fireproof bowl for individual portions; also a small porcelain bowl.

CASSONADE: (Fr.) Moist brown sugar.

CAUL: Web fat or membrane surrounding the paunch and intestines of animals; used as a casing for sausages, minced meats, and salpicon.

CAVIAR: Roe (eggs) of salmon, sturgeon, or other fish. Black caviar from sturgeon, imported from Russia, is the most select.

CELESTINE: (Fr.) A garnish made of shredded unsweetened pancakes, usually for consommé.

CEPES: A type of mushroom.

CERISES: (Fr.) Cherries

CERVELAT: A sausage similar to salami, but more mildly seasoned.

CERVELLES: (Fr.) Brains.

CHAMPIGNON: (Fr.) Mushroom, especially the cultivated mushroom.

CHANTERELLE: Species of wild mushroom.

CHANTILLY CREAM: Sweetened whipped cream, flavored with vanilla; dishes named Chantilly are always garnished with whipped cream.

CHAPELURE: (Fr.) Dried breadcrumbs.

CHARCUTERIE: (Fr.) Pork butcher's meat, or the pork butcher's shop.

CHATEAUBRIAND: A thick steak cut from the center of the beef tenderloin.

CHAUD: (Fr.) Hot.

CHAUD-FROID: (Fr.) Literally, hot, cold; an opaque sauce stabilized with aspic, used to coat cooked meat,

game, poultry, and fish, especially for buffet service.

CHEF DE CUISINE: (Fr.) Executive chef, or chef in charge.

CHEF DE PARTIE: (Fr.) The chef in charge of a department, such as the fry station.

CHEMISER: (Fr.) To coat the inside of a mold.

CHESHIRE: English hard yellow cheese made of cows' milk.

CHEVREUIL: (Fr.) Venison.

CHIANTI: (It.) A light semidry wine, red or white, from Tuscany.

CHICORY: A salad green, also called endive and succory. The mature roots are roasted and ground and used as an additive for coffee.

CHIFFONADE: Shredded vegetables used for soups, salads, salad dressing, or garnish.

CHILES: (Sp.) Hot peppers, used whole fresh or dried, and ground. Various chiles are used to make cayenne pepper, Tabasco, chili powder; also used for sauces, pickles, and meat dishes.

CHINOIS: (Fr.) China cap, a conical strainer.

CHIQUETER: (Fr.) To make small indentations around the edges of tarts and other pastries; to flute.

CHORIZO: (Sp.) Spiced sausage made from pork, or pork and beef.

CHOUX PASTE: Pâte à choux, cream puff and éclair batter.

CHUTNEY: Indian condiment made from mangoes or other fruits, sugar, vinegar, and spices; usually served with curries.

CILANTRO: (Sp.) Fresh green coriander; also called Chinese parsley.

CISELER: (Fr.) To make small cuts in the skin and top fillet of whole fish, to speed the cooking.

CITRON: A yellow citrus fruit with thick, rough skin, larger than a lemon, but not as acid. The peel is

candied and used in fruitcakes, breads, and confections.

CIVET: (Fr.) A ragout made of the meat of furred game, traditionally, with the blood of the animal used in the sauce.

CLARIFIER: (Fr.) To clarify a liquid: consommé, butter.

COCOTTE: (Fr.) Deep round or oval cooking pot, with handles on both sides; food cooked in a cocotte is often served in it. Also a small ramequin for individual service.

COGNAC: Brandy from the Charente district of France; the name may be used only for brandy produced there.

COINTREAU: An orange-flavored liqueur used to flavor desserts as well as for after-dinner drinks.

COLLER: (Fr.) To stick; to become firm with the addition of flour or gelatin. *Mayonnaise collée* is mayonnaise stiffened with gelatin.

COLORER: (Fr.) To color, tint, or mix in color.

CONCASSER: (Fr.) To chop with a knife or pound in a mortar; to crush. *Tomatoes concassées* are tomatoes peeled and diced, then stewed in clarified butter.

CONDE: Dessert of creamed rice combined with fruit (especially pears), with a sauce of red preserves or jam.

CONDIMENT: A prepared sauce used for flavoring foods, such as Worcestershire, mustard, ketchup.

CONSOMME: A clear soup made from concentrated clarified stock; may be served plain or garnished, hot, chilled, or jellied.

CONVENIENCE FOOD: Food available in varying degrees of preparation, to spare the cook the problems of paring, chopping, blanching, etc.

COQ AU VIN: (Fr.) Chicken cooked with wine; originally a young cockerel with red wine.

COQUILLE: (Fr.) A shell or a shell-shaped dish; a scallop.

CORAL: The roe of various shellfish, as lobster, rock lobster, scallops, sea urchins.

CORNET: A conical-shaped, thin, crisp pastry used to hold a rich cream or ice cream; also thin slices of ham or other cold meat rolled into a horn shape and filled.

CORSER: (Fr.) To make a liquid stronger by boiling it down quickly.

COULIS: (Fr.) Liquid, but thick, purees of meat, fish, or vegetables made without flour, as tomato coulis, the base for sauces.

COUPE: (Fr.) A shallow stemmed glass; also ice cream with fruit and Chantilly cream served in such a glass.

COURT BOUILLON: Aromatic liquid (not a stock) in which various foods are cooked, but especially fish and delicate variety meats (brains, sweetbreads); when prepared for fish, court bouillon usually contains an acid—wine, vinegar, or lemon juice.

CREAM: To beat a fat (butter, shortening) to a creamy consistency; also to blend shortening and sugar until light, with the sugar thoroughly dissolved in the fat.

CREPE: (Fr.) A thin pancake.

CREPINETTE: (Fr.) A sausage meat or forcemeat mixture wrapped in a layer of *crêpine* (caul fat), brushed with butter, covered with breadcrumbs, and sautéed or baked.

CROISSANT: (Fr.) Crescent-shaped French roll made of leavened puff pastry.

CROQUANT: (Fr.) Crisp, crusty, crunchy.

CROUSTADE: (Fr.) A container made of shaped and fried or toasted bread or baked pastry, filled with various mixture for hors d'oeuvre, or with a roasted quail or other meat entrée.

CROUSTADINE: (Fr.) Puff pastry baked into various shapes.

CROUTONS: Cubes or small slices of bread fried in butter and/or oil, added to salads or soups, or used as garnish.

CRUSTACEANS: Shellfish with jointed shells: crab, lobster, shrimp.

CUISINE: Style of cookery, as Chinese, French, Italian.

CURAÇAO: Liqueur made from the zest of the bitter orange; used for flavoring in creams, icings, jellies; also as an after-dinner drink.

CUT IN: To cut fat into dry ingredients with a pastry blender, so that the fat remains in small particles, rather than being melted.

DAL: (Indian) Dried beans, peas, or lentils, or a mash made of them used as a side dish, or as a thickening in curries.

DARIOLE: A small cylindrical mold used for making individual sweets or savories.

DARNE: (Fr.) A slice; center section of large fish (salmon, sturgeon, etc.).

DAUPHINE-MASSE: (Fr.) Mixture of potatoes and *pâte à choux;* it is shaped into croquettes and deep-fried.

DECANTER: (Fr.) To decant; to transfer a liquid, especially wine, from one bottle to another to separate the sediment from the liquid.

DECORER: (Fr.) To decorate a cake, ham, or aspic or chaud-froid dish.

DECORTIQUER: (Fr.) To remove the rind from fruits, the husk from grains, or the shell from a crustacean.

DEGLACER: (Fr.) Deglaze; to dissolve or dilute the concentrated juices in the pan in which meat, poultry, fish, or game has been roasted or braised; the liquid may be stock, wine, cream, or fruit or vegetable juice.

DEGORGER: (Fr.) To clean parts of fish such as the brain, roe, etc., in fresh running water.

DEGRAISSER: (Fr.) To remove excess fat from boiling stock, or to cut the fat from pieces of meat.

DEJEUNER: (Fr.) Lunch or midday meal.

DEMI: (Fr.) Half.

DEMI-GLACE: Reduced brown sauce.

DEMOULER: (Fr.) To remove from a mold.

DEPLUMER: (Fr.) To pluck a fowl.

DESOSSER: (Fr.) To remove the bones from meat, poultry, or game.

DESSECHER: (Fr.) To dry out.

DICE: To cut food into small cubes.

DIET: Daily allowance of food and drink.

DIETITIAN: One who has completed a prescribed academic program and earned a baccalaureate degree from an accredited college or university and has completed an approved dietetic internship; plans and directs foodservice programs in hospitals, colleges, and commercial establishments.

DINDE: (Fr.) Turkey hen.

DINDON: (Fr.) Tom turkey.

DINDONNEAU: (Fr.) Young turkey.

DRAWN BUTTER: Melted butter.

DREDGE: To sprinkle food with flour, sugar, or other fine-ground ingredient.

DRESSER: (Fr.) To dress; to dish up food.

DRUPE: A single-stoned fruit, such as a peach, cherry, almond.

DUCHESSE: (Fr.) Potatoes pureed, mixed with egg yolk, and piped out in decorative mounds or shapes; dishes decorated with these potatoes are also called *duchesse.*

DU JOUR: (Fr.) Literally, "of the day"; describes food that is ready to serve on that day.

DUSTING: Sprinkling lightly with fine sugar or flour.

DUXELLES: (Fr.) Mushroom hash made

of minced mushrooms sautéed with shallots and seasonings; used for filling and as a sauce base.

EAU: (Fr.) Water.

ECLAIR: Finger-shaped pastry made of *pâte à choux,* usually filled with whipped cream or vanilla pastry cream and iced with chocolate.

EDAM: Dutch low-fat yellow cheese, rather dry, with a red wax outer casing.

EDIBLE PORTION (E. P.): The portion of the food that is eaten after all the waste or trimmings, such as parings or rind, are removed. Compare with *As Purchased.*

EGOUTTER: (Fr.) To drain, to drip.

EMINCER: (Fr.) To cut into small slices or to mince.

EMMENTALER: Swiss hard cheese with large holes, with a sweet delicate flavor, made from whole or semifat milk.

ENTRECOTE: (Fr.) Literally, "between the ribs"; a rib steak (Delmonico or club steak) in the United States.

ENTREE: In France the third course; in the United States the main course.

ENTREMETIER: (Fr.) The cook who prepares the vegetables.

ENTREMETS: (Fr.) Desserts.

EPINARDS: (Fr.) Spinach.

ESCALOPE: (Fr.) Thin round slices of meat or fish; a scallop; in Italian, *scaloppina.*

ESCARGOTS: (Fr.) Snails.

ESCOFFIER: A famous French chef who is considered the master of modern classical cuisine.

ESPAGNOLE: (Fr.) Literally, "Spanish"; brown sauce made with *mirepoix* and tomatoes; a long slow-cooking process; now considered out of date.

ESSENCE: Extract from a food substance.

ETAMINE: (Fr.) Sieve, strainer, or cloth used for straining.

ETUVER: (Fr.) To cook food in a covered pan without added liquid.

EXTRACT: A concentrate used for flavoring (almond, anise, vanilla).

FAISAN: (Fr.) Pheasant.

FAISANDE: (Fr.) The term for high or gamy taste, when referring to game.

FARCE: (Fr.) Forcemeat or stuffing.

FARCIR: (Fr.) To stuff meat, poultry, and vegetables.

FARINER: (Fr.) To coat, dust, or sprinkle with flour.

FERMIERE, A LA: (Fr.) Farmer's wife style; chicken or meat pot-roasted and garnished with vegetables.

FEUILLETAGE: (Fr.) Puff pastry.

FICELER: (Fr.) To dress using string; to bind or tie with string.

FILET: (Fr.) Fillet; in beef, the whole tenderloin.

FILETER: (Fr.) To fillet, that is to remove the flesh from the side of a fish, lengthwise, removing it from the spine.

FILET MIGNON: A slice from the tenderloin of beef; fine textured and tender.

FILLET: Inside piece of the loin of beef, pork, lamb, veal, and furred game; boned fish; boned breast of poultry.

FINES HERBES: (Fr.) Mixture of minced herbs (parsley, tarragon chervil, and chives) used for flavoring sauces, steaks, omelets, and salads.

FLAMBER: (Fr.) To singe, to hold over the flame, to pass through the flame, to blaze.

FLANQUER: (Fr.) To garnish.

FLEURONS: Crescents of puff pastry, used for garnish.

FLORENTINE, A LA: (Fr.) As prepared in Florence; usually a dish served with or garnished with spinach.

FOIE: (Fr.) Liver.

FOIE GRAS: (Fr.) Fat goose liver.

FOLD: A method of combining fragile ingredients, such as beaten egg whites, into a mixture without mashing or breaking or losing air.

FONCER: (Fr.) To line a pan or mold with vegetables or with dough. The dough is called *pâte à foncer.*

FOND: (Fr.) 1. Stock for soups or sauces. 2. Bottom, as *fond d'artichaut,* artichoke bottom.

FOND BLANC: (Fr.) White stock; the basis for white sauces.

FOND BRUN: (Fr.) Brown stock; the basis for brown sauces and thickened gravies.

FONDS DE BRAISE: (Fr.) The aromatics (herbs and vegetables) plus the pork rind used in the bottom of the braising pot; the meat to be braised is placed on this bed.

FONDUE: (Fr.) Melted cheese with Kirsch and or wine into which pieces of French bread are dipped; also special sauces into which cooked cubes of meat are dipped. Cheese fondue is a Swiss specialty.

FORCEMEAT: Chopped meats and seasonings used for stuffing; or the mixture rolled into balls and sautéed.

FORESTIERE, A LA: (Fr.) Forester style; method of preparing small pieces of meat or poultry; the dish is garnished with mushrooms or morels.

FOUETTER: (Fr.) To beat with a wire whip; to stir.

FRAISER: (Fr.) To flatten or crush pastry dough with the fingertips, to give homogeneity to the mixture without developing a lot of gluten. Compare with *Knead.*

FRAISES: (Fr.) Strawberries.

FRAMBOISES: (Fr.) Raspberries.

FRAPPER: (Fr.) To freeze to a soft mush, or to mix with crushed ice (especially drinks, liqueurs, etc.).

FRICASSEE: A stew made of poultry, veal, or lamb; the meat is seared without browning, and the stew remains pale in color.

FRIRE: (Fr.) To fry, meaning to deep-fry.

FRITTO MISTO: (It.) Mixture of various meats, poultry, fish, vegetables, all deep-fried.

FRIVOLITES: (Fr.) Hors d'oeuvre, consisting of little tarts, barquettes, and creams.

FROID: (Fr.) Cold.

FROMAGE: (Fr.) Cheese.

FROTTER: (Fr.) To rub, rub out, rub in.

FRUITS DE MER: (Fr.) All kinds of sea-food—crustaceans, mollusks, salt-water fish.

FUMER: (Fr.) To smoke, as salmon (*saumon fumé*).

FUMET: (Fr.) Strong concentrated stock or essence of poultry, game, or fish; most often used for fish.

FUMET BLANC DE POISSON: (Fr.) White fish stock.

GALANTINE: Boned, stuffed, rolled fish or meat or poultry, poached, pressed, glazed with aspic, and served cold.

GALETTE: (Fr.) A broad thin cake. There are many types, such as galette of potatoes, sea biscuits, or *galette des rois* (Twelfth-Night cake).

GAME: Edible wild animals, such as deer, bear, hare, squirrel, and buffalo.

GAME FOWL: Edible wild birds, such as pheasant, partridge, pigeon, duck, goose, grouse, quail, woodcock.

GARDE-MANGER: (Fr.) Pantry, larder, cold meat department, or the person in charge of this department.

GARNISH: A food used to enhance or decorate a dish, such as watercress or parsley sprigs; radishes, carrots, and other vegetables cut into shapes; turned mushrooms; lemon rind, croutons, nutmeats, or chocolate curls.

GARNITURE: (Fr.) The vegetables and starch served with meat, fish, or poultry; the solid foods in soups or sauces; garnishes.

GAUFRES: (Fr.) Thin sweet wafers or waffles.

GENOISE: (Fr.) Literally, of Genoa; a sponge cake containing butter; the only leavening is the air beaten into the eggs.

GHEE: (Indian) Clarified butter made from buffalo milk.

GIBIER: (Fr.) Game.

GIGOT D'AGNEAU: (Fr.) Leg of lamb. Gigot alone is sometimes used.

GJETOST: Norwegian national cheese, made from the whey of goats' milk; it has a sweet caramel flavor and brown color.

GLACE DE VIANDE: (Fr.) Meat extract or glaze; strong flavorful stock reduced to the texture of a thick jelly; used for flavoring sauces.

GLACER: (Fr.) To glaze; to coat cakes with a sweet glaze; to freeze a liquid until it turns to ice; to steam vegetables until the cooked juices glaze the vegetables; to glaze roasted meats with reduced meat stock.

GNOCCHI: (It.) Small dumplings made of potatoes, semolina, or puff pastry.

GORGONZOLA: Italian semisoft blue-veined cheese.

GOUDA: Dutch full-fat cheese, round and yellow.

GOUTER: (Fr.) To taste.

GRAND MARNIER: Orange-flavored liqueur based on Cognac.

GRANITE: (Fr.) A water ice; in Italian, *granita*.

GRATINER: (Fr.) To prepare foods with a crust on top, usually bread-crumbs.

GRENADIN: (Fr.) A thick slice cut from the round of the veal leg, thicker than a veal scallop; usually braised to keep the meat from drying.

GRENADINE: Syrup made from the juice of the pomegranite and sugar.

GRILLER: (Fr.) To grill; to broil.

GROATS: Hulled and coarsely crushed grains used for making porridge (oats), grits (corn), and kasha (buckwheat).

GROSSE PIECE: (Fr.) A large joint of meat or poultry, usually served as the main dish of a meal.

GRUYERE: A hard, light-yellow, cooked cheese with small holes, made in Switzerland, France, Finland, and Argentina; originally Swiss.

GUGELHUPF: German cake made of yeast dough, with almonds and raisins; usually baked in a fluted pan.

HAGGIS: (Scot.) A dish made from hearts, lungs, and livers of calves or sheep; highly seasoned, combined with oatmeal, and cooked in a sheep's stomach.

HARICOTS: (Fr.) Beans.

HARICOTS VERTS: (Fr.) Green snap beans.

HASENPFEFFER: (Ger.) Rabbit stew with peppercorns.

HELVELLA: A conical-shaped fungus similar to the conical morel.

HERB BOUQUET: See *Bouquet garni*.

HORS D'OEUVRE: (Fr.) Hot or cold dish served as a first course; also used for canapés and other finger food for cocktail parties.

HUILE: (Fr.) Oil.

HUITRES: (Fr.) Oysters.

INFUSER: (Fr.) To steep herbs, tea, coffee, or other ingredients in boiling liquid until the liquid absorbs the aroma and flavor.

ISINGLASS: Very pure gelatin prepared from the air bladders of fishes, especially sturgeon; used as a replacement for gelatin in jellies and puddings, and as a clarifying agent.

JAMBON: (Fr.) Ham.

JARDINIERE: (Fr.) Literally, "garden style"; fresh vegetables cut into thin strips or diced, cooked, and arranged as a garnish around meat.

JULIENNE: Small sticks, 1/8 to 1/6 inch wide, cut from vegetables and other foods; used as a garnish; poached in butter or served raw.

JUS: (Fr.) Juice; the natural juice of broiled or roasted meats.

KEBOB: Pieces of marinated meat, poultry, fish, vegetables, and fruits cooked on a skewer. Compare with *Brochette*.

KIRSCH, KIRSCHWASSER: (Ger.) Cherry brandy.

KNEAD: To fold, stretch, and press dough to incorporate air, to develop gluten, and to improve its texture.

KONVECTOMAT: (Ger.) Convectomat, a convection oven.

KÜMMEL: (Ger.) Caraway seed. Also a liqueur flavored with caraway seeds.

LAIT: (Fr.) Milk.

LANGOUSTE: (Fr.) Spiny lobster with no large claws such as the American lobster has.

LAPIN: (Fr.) Rabbit.

LARD: The fat of hogs that has been melted, clarified, and hardened; used for frying or as a shortening.

LARDING: To insert thin strips of salt pork, bacon, or unsalted fat into uncooked meat or poultry to keep it moist while cooking.

LARDOON: Thin strips of salt pork, bacon, or unsalted fatback, often rolled in herbs and/or brandy, inserted into meat for larding.

LEGUMES: (Fr.) Fruits or seeds of leguminous plants: peas, beans, lentils; used fresh or dried; also vegetables generally.

LENTILS: Small flat seeds of leguminous plants; they may be red, yellow, or dark green; usually sold dried; used especially in soups.

LIAISON: (Fr.) A binding agent, such as eggs, most often egg yolk and cream, used to thicken sauces and soups.

LIER: (Fr.) To thicken soups and sauces.

LIMBURGER: Belgian soft cheese with a strong flavor and odor.

LIQUEUR: Alcoholic beverage, often sweet, usually served as an after-dinner drink, but also used for flavoring desserts.

LYONNAISE: (Fr.) Food served with or garnished with fried shredded onions.

MACEDOINE: (Fr.) A mixture of vegetables or fruit; large specimens are diced; served plain, or mixed with a liqueur, or molded in a jellied dessert.

MACERATE: To steep foods in liquid to soften them and flavor them; usually used of fruits; the liquid usually contains wine and/or liqueur. Compare with *Marinate*.

MADEIRA: A full-bodied wine originating in the Portuguese island of Madeira; it may be sweet or dry.

MADELEINE: A small cake baked in a scallop-shaped mold; the batter is similar to pound cake.

MADRILENE: (Fr.) Literally "one from Madrid"; a double-strength consommé that may be served jellied or hot, flavored with tomatoes.

MAITRE D'HOTEL: (Fr.) The person in charge of a dining room.

MAITRE D'HOTEL BUTTER: Butter mixed with lemon juice, parsley, salt, and pepper; served on broiled or grilled meats.

MARASCHINO: A liqueur made from Marasca cherries grown in Dalmatia.

MARINADE: A combination of an acid (lemon juice, vinegar, wine), oil, and seasonings used to flavor and tenderize foods, usually meat or game.

MARINATE: To soak foods in liquid to flavor and tenderize them; usually used of meats; the liquid contains an acid, seasoning, aromatics, oil. Also to soak foods in brine. Compare with *Macerate*.

MARMITE: (Fr.) Stockpot for meat or soup.

MARRON: (Fr.) Chestnut.

MARSALA: (It.) Wine made in Marsala, Sicily; it may be fortified, dry, or sweet.

MARZIPAN: A mixture of almond paste, sugar, and egg whites; used for confections and to garnish desserts.

MASK: To cover a food completely, usually with a sauce such as mayonnaise, or aspic.

MATELOTE: (Fr.) A fish stew of freshwater fish, usually including eels, made with red or white wine. Matelotes made in coastal areas may include saltwater fish and shellfish.

MATIGNON: (Fr.) Minced raw or cooked vegetables used for garnishing meats.

MEAT EXTRACT: A preparation made by reducing stock to a gelatinous consistency. See *Glace de viande*.

MEDALLIONS: Small rounds of tenderloin or *foie gras* or lobster tail.

MELBA SAUCE: Pureed raspberries mixed with currant jelly (optional), sugar, and cornstarch; usually served over ice cream.

MELBA TOAST: Very thin slices of white bread toasted in the oven until crisp.

MELER: (Fr.) To mix different foods.

MERINGUE: Egg whites stiffly beaten with sugar and browned or dried in the oven. Used as a topping for pies and puddings, and baked Alaska; also formed into shells, baked, and used as a base for ice cream, whipped cream, and other fillings.

METABOLISM: A term used to designate the sum of all chemical and physical changes that affect substances within the body after absorption.

MEUNIERE, A LA: (Fr.), Literally, "miller's wife style"; lightly floured fish sautéed in butter and flavored with lemon juice and parsley.

MIGNONNETTE: (Fr.) Peppercorns, white or black, crushed to coarse pieces, not ground. Also foods cut into small shapes (rounds, ovals).

MIJOTER: (Fr.) To cook slowly, simmer.

MILANAISE, A LA: (Fr.) Milan style; used of foods dipped into egg and breadcrumbs mixed with grated Parmesan cheese and sautéed; also used for the Milan style of cooking rice—a risotto made with saffron and wine.

MIREPOIX: (Fr.) Vegetables cut into ⅙-inch cubes to use as a garnish or flavoring; a *mirepoix* of carrots and onions, with added herbs, is used as a *fonds de braise.*

MISE EN PLACE: (Fr.) Literally, "put in place." Interpreted as organizing and completing, in advance, all the preliminary tasks involved in the preparation of a meal.

MIX: To combine two or more ingredients and stir until blended.

MIXED GRILL: Assorted grilled meats, such as chop, kidney, and sausage, garnished with tomatoes and mushrooms.

MOCHA: Strong coffee mainly used in blended coffee; also a mixture of coffee and chocolate flavors used in ice cream, frosting, cakes, and pies.

MOHN: (Ger.) Poppy seed.

MONTER: (Fr.) To whip up, as a sauce or egg whites.

MORTADELLA: A large pork sausage of Italian origin, also made in France; often served as an hors d'oeuvre.

MOUILLER: (Fr.) To steep, to moisten, to soak.

MOUSSE: (Fr.) A savory or sweet preparation made from whipped cream and a pureed food; it may also contain eggs or egg whites. A mousse may be baked, or it may be chilled and molded; cold or frozen mousses usually contain gelatin.

MOUSSELINE: (Fr.) A fine muslin. Also a dish or sauce containing whipped cream. Also used of brioche and sponge cake, made very light in texture.

MOUTON: (Fr.) Mutton.

MOZZARELLA: Italian soft cheese that can be sliced or shredded, used in pizza and other cooked foods.

MUNSTER: French semisoft, mild-flavored cheese, the specialty of Alsace and Lorraine; often has caraway seeds added.

MYSOST: Norwegian caramel-flavored whey cheese, similar to Gjetost, but Mysost is made entirely from cows' milk.

NAPPER: (Fr.) To coat.

NEUFCHATEL: French soft cream cheese.

NOIR: (Fr.) Black.

NOISETTE: (Fr.) Hazelnut. The word is also used for small round pieces of beef tenderloin or the boneless center portions of chops, especially lamb. Noisette potatoes are shaped with a melon-ball cutter to hazelnut shapes and sautéed in butter until brown. Noisette butter is clarified butter cooked until golden brown.

NOUILLE: (Fr.) Noodle.

NUTRIENTS: Nutritive substances such as proteins, carbohydrates, fats, vitamins, and minerals.

NUTRITION: The sum of the processes by which the living organism receives and utilizes food substances necessary for maintenance of its

functions and to promote growth, replace loss, and provide energy.

OEUF: (Fr.) Egg.

OFFAL: Variety meats: brains, heart, kidney, liver, sweetbreads, tongue, tripe.

ORGEAT: (Fr.) A nonalcoholic almond-flavored syrup used in mixed drinks or as a food flavoring.

OSHA: Occupational Safety and Health Administration.

OSSO BUCO: (It.) Veal shanks, sautéed, then cooked with tomato, onion, wine, garlic; served with rice.

OVERRUN: The increase in volume of a frozen dessert resulting from the incorporation of air into the mixture during freezing.

PAELLA: (Sp.) Dish of rice flavored with saffron and cooked with tomatoes, peas, wine, chicken, shellfish, and other ingredients.

PAIN: (Fr.) Bread.

PAMPLEMOUSSE: (Fr.) Grapefruit.

PANADE: (Fr.) Preparation made of flour or bread cooked in water, milk, or stock; used to bind forcemeats or stuffings.

PANER: (Fr.) To coat a food with breadcrumbs.

PAN-FRY: To cook in a small amount of fat in an uncovered skillet.

PAPILLOTE: (1) A heart-shaped piece of kitchen parchment paper in which fish or other delicate foods are placed, with the ingredients for dressing or sauce; the paper is folded over and crimped on the edges; the packets are baked or deep-fried. Today aluminum foil is more often used. The packet is opened at table. (2) A paper frill used to cover a chop bone or the shoulder bone of a chicken suprême.

PARER: (Fr.) To trim meat or fish.

PARFAIT: Frozen dessert made of alternate layers of ice cream and fruits or flavored syrups, topped with whipped cream. In France, a parfait is a mousselike frozen dessert mixture, different from ice cream.

PARFUMER: (Fr.) To flavor a dish; to add an aroma.

PARMENTIER: An eighteenth-century chemist who introduced the potato to the French court. All dishes characterized by potatoes are called Parmentier.

PARURES: (Fr.) The trimmings of meat and fish.

PASSER: (Fr.) To strain, to puree.

PASTA: (It.) Products made from hard-wheat flour dough and forced through dies of various sizes and shapes. Pasta types are known by different names according to their shape and size.

PASTY: A half-moon pastry case containing chopped meat, potatoes, and seasonings; baked; a specialty of Cornwall.

PÂTE: (Fr.) A dough or batter; do not confuse with pâté.

PÂTÉ: (Fr.) A rich pastelike forcemeat that may contain chunks of meat, fish, game, or vegetables; often baked in pastry (*en croûte*).

PATE A CHOUX: (Fr.) Cream puff or éclair pastry.

PATISSERIE: (Fr.) French pastry; also a pastry shop.

PAUPIETTE: (Fr.) A slice of meat or poultry, flattened, stuffed, rolled, and usually braised (veal bird).

PAYSANNE, A LA: (Fr.) Peasant or country style; a soup or meat dish served with buttered vegetables.

PESTO: (It.) A sauce made from fresh basil, garlic, pine nuts, and olive oil; a specialty of Genoa.

PETIT DEJEUNER: (Fr.) Breakfast.

PETITE MARMITE: (Fr.) A rich soup made of meat, poultry, and vegetables served in individual covered pots with cheese-covered toast floating on top of the soup.

PETITS FOURS: (Fr.) Small rich cakes dipped into fondant and decorated.

PETITS FOURS SEC: Fancy cookies, such as macaroons, shortbread, butter cookies; different from the first in not being filled or iced, therefore *sec* or "dry."

PETITS POIS: (Fr.) Fresh small garden peas.

PICCATA: (It.) Literally, larded; in general use meaning "piquant," especially dishes flavored with lemon juice, as veal piccata.

PIE: A baked pastry with sweet or savory filling. In Britain a pie has a top crust and no bottom crust; in America a pie may have either top or bottom crust or both.

PIGNOLI: (It.) Pine nuts; the seeds in the cones of the stone pine.

PILER: (Fr.) To pound, to crush.

PIQUANT: Pungent, highly seasoned.

PIQUER: (Fr.) To insert short strips of fat into lean meats, with the ends of the strips sticking up like tufts, to add richness and flavor. Compare with *Larding*.

PLATS DU JOUR: (Fr.) The specialties of the day in a restaurant.

POCHER: (Fr.) To poach.

POELER: (Fr.) To pot-roast a meat or poultry in a covered pan only large enough to hold the meat; the meat is not first browned as for braising; French casserole roasting.

POISSON: (Fr.) Fish.

POIVRADE: (Fr.) Brown sauce flavored with peppercorns, traditional for venison, but used as the base for other game sauces; usually includes some of the strained marinade used for the game.

POLENTA: (It.) Yellow cornmeal mush.

POMME: (Fr.) Apple.

POMME DE TERRE: (Fr.) Potato.

PORT DU SALUT: French semisoft creamy cheese with mellow to robust flavor.

POTAGE: (Fr.) Soup.

POT-AU-FEU: (Fr.) Soup and meat course cooked in one pot; beef, stock, and vegetables are the chief ingredients; in some parts of France other meats and poultry are used.

PRALINE: A confection made from almonds or hazelnuts mixed with caramel. This mixture, when hardened, is crushed or reduced to powder to be used to flavor desserts and cake fillings and icings.

PREPARER: (Fr.) To prepare.

PRINTANIERE: (Fr.) Used of a dish garnished with spring vegetables.

PROFITEROLES: Small puffs made of *pâte à choux* and filled with sweet or savory fillings, most often whipped cream.

PROSCIUTTO: Italian dry-cured raw Parma ham, dried in air-swept caves.

PROVENÇALE: (Fr.) Used of dishes containing olive oil, tomatoes, and garlic; the cookery of sunny Provence.

PSI: Pounds per square inch.

PULPE: (Fr.) A moist paste or pulp of fruits or vegetables.

PUREE: Foodstuffs reduced to a smooth consistency by mashing, blending, or straining. Also a thick soup.

QUARTIERS: Quarters of vegetables, fruits, or meat.

QUENELLE: Dumpling of meat, fish, poultry, or game.

QUICHE: An open custard tart, usually with cheese.

RACLETTE: Swiss dish: scraped melted cheese served with boiled potatoes and gherkins.

RAGOUT: (Fr.), A stew of browned

meat, fish, or poultry with vegetables.

RAMEKIN or RAMEQUIN: Individual shallow earthenware or china dish in which food can be baked and served.

RECHAUFFER: (Fr.) To warm up; to reheat.

RECONSTITUTE: To restore to the original form or condition by adding water.

REDUCTION: A process used to increase the flavor and richness of liquids and sauces. The liquids thicken during very slow simmering by the evaporation process until reduced to about half of their original volume, with the flavors greatly concentrated.

REDUIRE: (Fr.) To reduce a liquid; to boil down.

RELEVE: (Fr.) The main dish in a formal dinner.

RELEVER: (Fr.) To improve the taste by adding spices.

REMOULADE: A cold sauce made of mayonnaise, sour pickles, caper, mustard, chervil, parsley, and tarragon; used for cold fish and shellfish.

REMOUILLAGE: (Fr.) Stockpot gravy.

REVENIR: (Fr.) (*faire revenir*) To brown ingredients lightly in butter or fat.

RICE FLOUR: Flour milled from rice.

RISOTTO: (It.) Rice dish.

RISSOLE: (Fr.) Turnover made with very thin puff pastry filled with forcemeat and deep-fried.

RISSOLER: (Fr.) To brown in butter or fat.

ROE: Mass of fish eggs. Beluga caviar is the best of the hard roes. Herring and salmon roe are soft roes, used as a substitute for caviar and for garnishes.

ROQUEFORT: French semisoft cheese with veins of blue-green mold and a sharp piquant flavor; matured in limestone caves in the Aveyron district.

ROSE HIPS: Red fruit of the dog rose used for making jellies, sauces, and beverages.

ROSEWATER: Liquid distilled from rose petals.

ROUX: Mixture of melted butter or other fat and flour, cooked and used to thicken soups and sauces; may be white, blond, or brown, depending on the length of cooking.

ROYALE: Molded custard cut into shapes for soup garnish.

SABAYON: (Fr.) A sauce or dessert composed of whipped eggs, sugar, white wine, and flavoring. See *Zabaglione.*

SACCHARIN: Ortho-benzosulfimide; 300 times sweeter than sucrose. It has no food value and is used as a calorie-free sweetener.

SAGO: Starch made from the sago palm tree, used as a thickening agent.

SAISIR: (Fr.) (*faire saisir*) To sear meat over brisk heat at the start of cooking, to seal in the juices.

SAIGNANT: (Fr.) Bloody; underdone meat.

SALAMANDER: A small broiler with the heat source at the top and a shelf below.

SALMIS: (Fr.) A stew made from previously roasted game.

SALPICON: A mixture of diced meat and vegetables bound with a sauce and used for canapés, croquettes, and timbales. Also aromatic vegetables cut into 1/3-inch cubes.

SAUCER: (Fr.) To sauce.

SAUMURE: (Fr.) Brine, pickle.

SAUPOUDRER: (Fr.) To dust with flour, pepper, or salt.

SAUTER: (Fr.) To cook food quickly in a shallow pan (*sauteuse* or *sautoir*) over brisk heat, using only enough fat to keep the food from sticking. Compare with *Frire* and *Pan-fry.*

SAUTOIR: (Fr.) Large, round, shallow, heavy pan with straight sides and a long handle; used for sautéing.

SAVORIES: Light dishes, such as cheese straws, tartlets, and cheese biscuits, served at the end of the meal, especially in Great Britain.

SCAMPI: (It.) Lobsterettes or *langoustines* (not shrimps).

SCORE: (1) Nomenclature used in the U.S. standards for grades of butter. The score designates the grade, for example: U.S. Grade AA or U.S. 93 Score is the highest quality. The score or grade is determined on the basis of classifying the characteristics of the flavor, body, color, and salt content. (2) To cut gashes on the fat surrounding a steak or on the layer of fat covering a ham or on the crust of a pie.

SEAR: To brown the surface of meat at a high temperature to seal in the juices.

SEC: (Fr.) Dry, as in wine.

SEMOLINA: Fine particles of the gluten of durum wheat (middlings) used for making pasta. Also coarse particles used for puddings and breakfast cereal.

SHALLOT: A mild-flavored onion that grows in clusters of lateral bulbs; each bulb has a reddish or purple skin.

SHELLFISH: *Crustaceans*, which include crab, lobster, shrimp; *mollusks*, which include abalone, clam, oyster, scallop. Also oddities such as squid and sea urchin.

SIMPLE SYRUP: Equal portions of sugar and water boiled until the sugar is dissolved; used as a sweetener for drinks and as a basis for dessert sauces and cake icings.

SKEWER: Thin pointed wooden or metal pin to hold small pieces of meat and/or vegetables in place for broiling. See also *Brochette* and *Kebob*.

SORBET: (Fr.) Frozen mixture of fruit juice and sugar; gelatin and Italian meringue are sometimes added.

SORBETIERE: (Fr.) Container in which ice cream, sherbet, and ice are frozen.

SOUBISE: (Fr.) Pureed onion mixed with butter or cream; onion sauce.

SOUFFLE: Literally, "puff"; a sweet or savory dish puffed up by air beaten into eggs; true soufflés are baked and served as soon as ready.

SOUFFLE GLACE: A dish, usually for dessert, that looks like a baked soufflé but is actually a frozen rich mousse.

SOUFFLER: (Fr.) To puff up.

SOUPER: (Fr.) Supper.

SOUS CHEF: (Fr.) Assistant to the head chef who supervises the kitchen and the personnel responsible for certain units of the kitchen.

SOYBEAN: Legume often used as a meat substitute. The beans are used as a vegetable, for an edible oil and flour, and for soy sauce, served with Oriental foods.

SPÄTZLE: (Ger.) Small dumplings made of noodle batter cooked in stock and served in soups, as garnishes, or with meats; in German, Austrian, and Hungarian cookery.

SPICE SACHET: A mixture of spices and herbs tied in cheesecloth; used to flavor soups, sauces, and other dishes.

SPIT: A pointed rod on which meat is held while roasting or barbecuing above or in front of open heat.

SPRINGFORM PAN: Baking pan with removable rim; a hinged clamp holds the rim and bottom together.

STEAMER: Vesicle, pressure cooker, in which food is cooked in steam.

STEEP: To soak something, as an herb or a vanilla bean, in hot liquid to extract flavor.

STILTON: English semisoft cheese with veins of mold; it has a spicy flavor; made in Leicestershire and adjacent counties.

STOCK: A liquid in which bones and trimmings of meat, fish, game, or vegetables have been cooked, to give a flavorful and nutritious cooking liquid.

SUET: Hard fat around the kidneys of beef, mutton, veal, and lamb; used in steamed puddings, mincemeat, and suet-crust pastry.

SUPREME: (Fr.) (1) A mushroom-flavored chicken velouté sauce enriched with cream. (2) One side of a chicken breast with a small piece of the wing bone attached and rib bones, skin, and tendons removed.

SWEDE: Yellow rutabaga.

SWEETBREAD: The thymus gland of the calf and lamb. Veal sweetbreads are used as a garnish or with other foods. The taste and texture are delicate.

SYLLABUB: A traditional English drink made with stiffly beaten cream, sugar, and wine; similar to eggnog.

TABASCO: Brand name of a hot, spicy condiment sauce made of vinegar and hot peppers.

TABLE D'HOTE: (Fr.) A complete meal at a fixed price, as opposed to *à la carte*, in which each item is priced separately.

TAGLIATELLE: (It.) Flat noodles, ¾ inch wide.

TAHINA: (Greek *Tahini*) A paste made from crushed sesame seeds.

TARRAGON VINEGAR: A white or white-wine vinegar flavored with tarragon.

TARTAR STEAK: Raw beef, chopped, highly seasoned and garnished, usually served as a first course.

TART: A baked pastry with sweet or savory filling, with a bottom crust and no top crust; in America also used for a small pie.

TARTLET: A small tart, usually for individual serving.

TERRAPIN: A North American turtle, living in fresh or brackish waters.

TERRINE: An earthenware casserole. The term is also used for foods, usually pâté mixtures, prepared and baked in such a dish, as terrine of chicken.

THICKEN: To give body to a sauce, broth, or other liquid food by adding flour, starch, arrowroot, eggs, butter, or roux.

TIMBALE: A crisp pastry shell filled with a sauced mixture and carefully garnished. Also a straight-sided mold in which the pastry is baked. Small molds may be used to bake rice or other food, which is then turned out for serving.

TIMBALE SHELLS or ROSETTES: Crisp shells or cases made by dipping a hot timbale iron into a light batter and then into deep fat. The shells are pushed off the iron and filled.

TORRONE: (It.) Nougat.

TORTUE: (Fr.) Turtle.

TOURNEDOS: Small steaks cut from the beef tenderloin, half or less as thick as a châteaubriand, and smaller around since cut from the thinner part of the tenderloin.

TOURNER: (Fr.) To "turn" potatoes, vegetables, mushrooms, etc.; to carve or flute them.

TRANCHER: (Fr.) To cleave; to carve; to cut into slices.

TREACLE: Chiefly British: a heavy dark syrup, a by-product of the sugar refining process; similar to molasses.

TREMPER: (Fr.) To soak, to steep.

TRIFLE: An English dessert made of sponge cake sprinkled with wine and covered with jam, a rich custard sauce, and whipped cream.

TRIPE: First and second stomachs (rumen and reticulum) of bovines, cleaned and scalded.

TRUFFLES: Round, pungent black fungi found in Périgord, France, and in Umbria, Italy; used in sauces, pâtés, stuffings, and for decoration; a necessity for *poularde demi-deuil*. White truffles are found in Piedmont, Italy.

TRUSS: To tie or skewer the legs and wings of poultry and game so as to retain the shape during cooking.

VEAU: (Fr.) Veal.

VERMICELLI: (It.) Long, very thin pasta strands, sold as straight rods or in rolled clusters.

VERT: (Fr.) Green.

VESIGA: Spinal marrow of sturgeon, especially the beluga sturgeon.

VIANDE: (Fr.) Meat.

VICHY, A LA: (Fr.) Vegetables cooked in water with butter and a small amount of sugar; usually refers to carrots. The water of the Vichy Springs gave the vegetables a unique delicate flavor.

VICHYSSOISE: Soup made of pureed potatoes and leeks, chicken stock, and cream; served chilled and garnished with snipped chives.

VIN: (Fr.) Wine.

VINAIGRETTE: (Fr.) a mixture of oil, wine vinegar, and herbs.

VITAMIN: An organic substance found in animal and plant tissues that is essential in the regulation of metabolic functions.

VOLAILLE: (Fr.) Poultry.

VOL-AU-VENT: (Fr.) A puff pastry shell in which meat, poultry, or fish bound with a sauce is served.

WHIP: To beat ingredients, such as eggs, into a froth in order to increase volume by incorporating air.

WORCESTERSHIRE SAUCE: A dark spicy condiment sauce, used to flavor meats and other foods.

ZABAGLIONE: (It.) A dessert or sweet sauce made with beaten egg yolks, Marsala wine, and honey or sugar. Beaten egg whites are folded in when it is used as a dessert. See *Sabayon*.

ZAMPONI: (It.) The skin of pigs' feet stuffed with a sausage mixture.

ZEST: The rind, the outer bright-colored portion containing essential oil, of a citrus fruit.

ZITI: (It.) Thick tubular pasta.

ZWIEBACK: Hard, crisp, toasted biscuits.

Index

Conversion Scales

Weights and Liquid Measures

Weights

½	oz	=	14 grams	9	oz	=	254 grams
¾	oz	=	21 g	10	oz	=	283 g
1	oz	=	28 g	11	oz	=	311 g
1½	oz	=	43 g	12	oz	=	340 g
1¾	oz	=	50 g	13	oz	=	368 g
2	oz	=	57 g	14	oz	=	396 g
2½	oz	=	71 g	15	oz	=	425 g
2¾	oz	=	78 g				
3	oz	=	85 g	1	lb	=	453 g
3½	oz	=	99 g	1¼	lb	=	566 g
4	oz	=	114 g	1½	lb	=	679 g
5	oz	=	142 g	1¾	lb	=	792 g
6	oz	=	170 g	2	lb	=	905 g
7	oz	=	199 g	2¼	lb	=	1018 g
8	oz	=	226 g				

Liquid Measures

1	teaspoon	=	0.005 liters	1½	cups	=	0.36 liters
1	tablespoon	=	0.015 l	1¾	cups	=	0.42 l
2	tablespoons	=	0.03 l				
				1	US pint	=	0.47 l
¼	cup	=	0.06 l	1¼	US pt	=	0.60 l
½	cup	=	0.12 l	1½	US pt	=	0.72 l
¾	cup	=	0.18 l	1¾	US pt	=	0.83 l
1	cup	=	0.24 l	1	US quart	=	0.94 l
1¼	cups	=	0.30 l				

Note: Throughout this volume, quantities quoted in pints and quarts refer to the US measures.